B. Joyce
1014 St. Peter St.

7.95

# principles of CRIMINOLOGY

# principles of

# CRIMINOL

## seventh edition

J. B. LIPPINCOTT COMPANY

by the late
EDWIN H. SUTHERLAND

and DONALD R. CRESSEY
University of California, Santa Barbara

PHILADELPHIA AND NEW YORK

This is a revised and completely reset edition of E. H. Sutherland's and Donald R. Cressey's work of the same title, copyright, 1960, by J. B. Lippincott Company. Original copyright, 1924, by J. B. Lippincott Company under the title Criminology. Rewritten and reset in 1934 under the title Principles of Criminology. Rewritten and reset in 1939, in 1947, and 1955.

# PREFACE

Like the Fifth and Sixth Editions, the Seventh Edition of *Principles of Criminology* is a direct extension of the work done by Professor Edwin H. Sutherland in the earlier editions. Since this textbook first appeared, in 1924, it has always been more than a mere set of lesson plans or lectures for students. In his Preface to the Fourth Edition, Professor Sutherland said: "Much factual information regarding crime has been accumulated over several generations. In spite of this, criminology lacks full scientific standing. The defects of criminology consist principally of the failure to integrate this factual information into consistent and valid general propositions." Like the earlier editions, the Seventh attempts to correct some of these defects. *Principles of Criminology* has always been designed to place emphasis upon the organization and systematization of knowledge, and this edition adheres to that tradition. In fact, it was the task of writing earlier editions of this book that led Professor Sutherland to formulate his differential association theory, a principle which a number of social scientists have found useful for putting order into a wide range of data on delinquency and crime causation. When preparing the Fifth Edition, I found this principle to be useful, also, for organizing the research materials on the effectiveness of various systems and techniques for rehabilitating criminals—probation, parole, group therapy, vocational training, and so forth—and this system of organization has continued into the Seventh Edition.

Part One examines facts of crime and delinquency and relates them to the differential association and differential social organization theories. The factual data examined include variations of crime and delinquency rates with age, sex, race, poverty, educational status, urbanization, and other variables, as well as the incidence among criminals and delinquents of various biological, psychological and social traits, characteristics, and processes. The differential association theory and alternative theories of crime causation are evaluated in the light of their comparative capacity to "make sense" of the facts.

In Part Two factual materials pertaining to control of crime are related to sociological and psychological theories of punishment and treatment, as well as to the differential association and differential social organization theories. Imprisonment, probation, parole, corporal punishment, group therapy, and psychoanalysis, for example, are identified as societal reactions to crime, variations in these societal reactions are observed, and theories to account for the variations are presented. The contemporary conflict between punishment and treatment of criminals is documented, and the consequences of this conflict for practices and organization of police, courts, probation departments, parole departments, and prisons are examined. The implications of the differential association and differential social organization theories for correctional administration and for reform and rehabilitation of criminals are explored.

Substantial portions of all chapters have been rewritten. Statistics have been brought up to date wherever possible, and the results of latest research have been included. Research reports on delinquency, crime, and corrections have been produced at an accelerated rate in recent years, and this increased activity among researchers has made it impossible to cite *all* the recent research findings. However, extensive revision of our materials on delinquent and criminal subcultures, on delinquent gangs, and on prison life have been made in this Edition, for it is in these three areas that researchers have recently been concentrating their attention.

The data on which the book is based come principally from the United States, for two reasons. The authors, as Americans, are more familiar with American research than with research in other nations, and most of the money and energy devoted to criminological research is expended in the United States. Nevertheless, the general framework of the book permits incorporation of research findings of other nations, as these appear and become known. The legal procedures for dealing with delinquents and criminals vary from nation to nation, but the basic principles pertaining to delinquency and crime causation, and to the effectiveness of correctional techniques, should be the same in all nations, just as the "laws" of physics are the same in all nations. As the questions asked by criminologists become more basic in character, and as communications improve among the criminologists of the world, generalizations about delinquent and criminal conduct will necessarily be the subject of closer scrutiny than has been the case in the past.

After considerable deliberation, and after consultation with a wide range of colleagues, it was decided that the formal statement of the theory of differential association (Chapter 4) should not be modified at this time. The theory has been found defective by some criminologists and sociologists, and suggestions for its modification have been made. It seems highly probable that it will have to undergo revision, just as the formal statement in the Third Edition underwent revision. However, it also is significant that the theory of differential association is currently in the period of its greatest popularity, if one can judge by the number of journal articles reporting on how it is being tested, analyzed, and extended. It would be inappropriate to modify the theory in such a way that research work now in progress would be undermined. Moreover, the "great debates" about the present statement of the theory probably are of more value to undergraduates than would be a revised formal statement that would take some of the criticisms into account. Finally, the theory in its present form has become rather basic to the thinking of American researchers, who are beginning to refer to "the theory of differential association," or just "differential association," without citing Sutherland or anyone else, apparently on the assumption that readers are familiar with the theory and its origins. It would not be wise to revise the statement in such a way that these references became meaningless.

For these reasons, then, I have left Sutherland's statement of the theory intact. However, I have appended to the formal statement a detailed discussion of the extensive literature which has grown up around it. This discussion identifies both the strengths and the weaknesses of the principle.

*Santa Barbara, California*
March 1, 1966

DONALD R. CRESSEY

# CONTENTS

# part 1 THE STUDY OF CRIME

# 1. CRIMINOLOGY AND CRIMINAL LAW

CRIMINOLOGY IS THE BODY of knowledge regarding crime as a social phenomenon. It includes within its scope the processes of making laws, of breaking laws, and of reacting toward the breaking of laws. These processes are three aspects of a somewhat unified sequence of interactions. Certain acts which are regarded as undesirable are defined by the political society as crimes. In spite of this definition some people persist in the behavior and thus commit crimes; the political society reacts by punishment, treatment, or prevention. This sequence of interactions is the object-matter of criminology.

Criminology consists of three principal divisions, as follows: (a) the sociology of law, which is an attempt at scientific analysis of the conditions under which criminal laws develop and which is seldom included in general books on criminology; (b) criminal etiology, which is an attempt at scientific analysis of the causes of crime; and (c) penology, which is concerned with the control of crime. The term "penology" is unsatisfactory because this division includes many methods of control which are not penal in character.

The objective of criminology is the development of a body of general and verified principles and of other types of knowledge regarding this process of law, crime, and treatment or prevention. This knowledge will contribute to the development of other sciences and through these other social sciences it will contribute to efficiency in general social control. In addition, criminology is concerned with the immediate application of knowledge to programs of social control of crime. This concern with practical programs is justified, in part, as experimentation which may be valuable because of its immediate results but at any rate will be valuable in the long run because of the increased knowledge which results from it. If practical programs wait until theoretical knowledge is complete, they will wait for eternity, for theoretical knowledge is increased most significantly in the efforts at social control. John Dewey described the relationship between knowledge and control thus:

It is a complete error to suppose that efforts at social control depend upon the prior existence of a social science. The reverse is the case. The building up of a social science, that is, of a body of knowledge in which facts are ascertained in their significant relations, is dependent upon putting social planning into effect. . . . Physical science did not develop because inquirers had piled up a mass of facts about observed phenomena. It came into being when men intentionally experimented, on the basis of ideas and hypotheses, with observed phenomena to modify them and disclose new observations. This process is self-corrective and self-developing. Imperfect and even wrong hypotheses, when acted upon, brought to light significant phenomena which made improved ideas and improved experimentations possible. The change from a passive and accumulative attitude into an active and productive one is the secret revealed by the progress of physical inquiry. Men obtained knowledge of natural energies by trying deliberately to control the conditions of their operation. The result was knowledge, and then control on a larger scale by the application of what was learned.[1]

While experimentation may increase theoretical knowledge and thereby contribute to ultimate improvements in policies, it is unnecessarily wasteful unless it is directed by the best organized and critical thought available. The average citizen is confronted by a confusing and conflicting complex of popular beliefs and programs in regard to crime. Some of these are traditions from eighteenth-century philosophy; some are promulgations of special-interest groups; and some are blind emotional reactions. Organized and critical thinking in this field is therefore peculiarly difficult and also peculiarly necessary.

CONVENTIONAL DEFINITION OF CRIME AND THE CRIMINAL LAW. Criminal behavior is behavior in violation of the criminal law. No matter what the degree of immorality, reprehensibility, or indecency of an act, it is not a crime unless it is prohibited by the criminal law. The criminal law, in turn, is defined conventionally as a body of specific rules regarding human conduct which have been promulgated by political authority, which apply uniformly to all members of the classes to which the rules refer, and which are enforced by punishment administered by the state. The characteristics which distinguish this body of rules regarding human conduct from other rules are, therefore, politicality, specificity, uniformity, and penal sanction.

---

[1] John Dewey, "Social Science and Social Control," New Republic, 67:276–277; July 29, 1931. Reprinted by permission.

However, these are characteristics of an ideal, completely rational system of criminal law; in practice the differences between the criminal law and other bodies of rules for human conduct are not clear cut. Also, the ideal characteristics of the criminal law are not always features of the criminal law in action.

CHARACTERISTICS OF THE CRIMINAL LAW.   The vast majority of the rules which define certain behavior as crime are found in constitutions, treaties, common law, enactments by the legislatures of the state and its sub-divisions, and in judicial and administrative regulations. However, the criminal law is not merely a collection of written proscriptions. The agency of enforcement of law is the court, and thus it is the court rather than the legislature which determines what the law is. According to one school of thought, courts merely "apply" the law in an even-handed manner to all persons who come before them. However, both the techniques used by the court in interpreting and applying the statutes and the body of ideals held by the court are a part of the law in action, as truly as are the written statutes. The court decision in one controversy becomes a part of the body of rules used in making decisions in other controversies. Consequently, law students must read court decisions in order to learn law. Further evidence supporting this view that the courts as well as the legislatures make law is found whenever the nation is confronted with the problem of selecting a justice of the Supreme Court. At such times it is explicitly recognized that the nature of the federal law itself, not merely its administration, is determined to a considerable extent by the proportion of liberals and conservatives on the supreme bench. Thus behind the behavior of courts is public opinion. Also, between the courts and the legislature are intermediate agencies, such as the police, which affect the enforcement and administration of the law. Many statutes are never enforced; some are enforced only on rare occasions; others are enforced with a striking disregard for uniformity. These enforcement and administrative agencies, also, are affected by public opinion, and a leader in the field of jurisprudence concluded that law in action is determined chiefly by public opinion.[2] Consequently, the law does not consist in the statutes alone and may change while the statutes remain constant.

Politicality is regarded almost universally as a necessary element in criminal law. The rules of the trade union, the church, or the family are not regarded as criminal law, nor are violations of these rules regarded as crimes. Only violations of rules made by the state are crimes. This distinction between the state and other groups is not only arbitrary but also is

---

[2] Roscoe Pound, *Criminal Justice in America* (New York: Holt, 1930), p. 120.

difficult to maintain when attention is turned to societies where patriarchal power, private self-help, popular justice, and other forerunners of legislative justice are found. This may be illustrated by the gypsies, who have no territorial organization and no written law, but who do have customs, taboos, and a semi-judicial council which makes definite decisions regarding the propriety of behavior of members of the group and often imposes penalties. These councils have no political authority in the territory in which they happen to be operating, but they perform the same function within the gypsy group that courts perform in the political order. Similarly, early Chinese immigrants in Chicago established an unofficial court which had no political authority but which in practice exercised the functions of an authorized court in controversies among the Chinese people, just as did the guild and the family council in their home country.[3] Thus, the element of politicality is arbitrary and is not sharply defined. The earlier systems of law, together with the present relation between public opinion and legal precepts, raise the question, When should the rules of a group be regarded as the law and violations of these rules as crimes?[4]

Specificity is included as an element in the definition of criminal law because of the contrast in this respect between criminal law and civil law. The civil law may be general. One German civil code, for instance, provided that whoever intentionally injured another in a manner contrary to the common standards of right conduct was bound to indemnify him. The criminal law, on the other hand, generally gives a strict definition of a specific act, and when there is doubt as to whether a definition describes the behavior of a defendant the judge is obligated to decide in favor of the defendant. In one famous case, for example, the behavior of a person who had taken an airplane was held to be exempt from the consequences of violating a statute regarding the taking of "self-propelled vehicles," on the ground that at the time the law was enacted "vehicles" did not include airplanes.[5] Some laws, to be sure, are quite general, as the laws in regard to nuisances, conspiracy, disorderly conduct, use of the mails to defraud, and official misfeasance. The criminal law, however, contains no general provision that any act which, when done with culpable intent, injures the public can be prosecuted as a punishable offense.[6] Consequently it fre-

[3] Chu Chai, "Administration of Law among the Chinese in Chicago," Journal of Criminal Law and Criminology, 22:806–818, March–April, 1932.

[4] See E. Adamson Hoebel, The Law of Primitive Man: A Study in Comparative Legal Dynamics (Cambridge: Harvard University Press, 1954).

[5] McBoyle vs. United States, 283 U. S. 25 (1931).

[6] A German law of June 28, 1935, seems to be an exception to this generalization. It provided: "Whoever commits an action which the law declares to be punishable or which is deserving of punishment according to the fundamental idea of a penal law and the sound perception of the people, shall be punished. If no determinate penal

quently happens that one act is prohibited by law while another act which is very similar in nature and effects is not prohibited and is not illegal.

Uniformity or regularity is included in the conventional definition of criminal law because law attempts to provide even-handed justice without respect to persons. This means that no exceptions are made to criminal liability because of a person's social status; an act described as a crime is crime, no matter who perpetrates it. Also, uniformity means that the law-enforcement process shall be administered without regard for the status of the persons who have committed crimes or are accused of committing crimes. This ideal, however, has varied widely in practice. Rigid rule and judicial discretion have alternated in importance. Rigid rule treats all persons in the class to which the law refers exactly alike, while judicial discretion takes cognizance of varying elements in the situations of the members of the class and thus approaches closer to individualization. Equity, also, developed as a method of doing justice in particular situations where iron regularity would not do justice. As precedents in equity have accumulated, the decisions tend to become uniform, and thus similar to law. In line with the present tendency toward judicial discretion, authority has been conferred by legislative assemblies upon many administrative bodies to make regulations applicable to particular situations.

Penal sanction, as one of the elements in the orthodox definition of law, refers to the notion that violators will be punished or, at least, threatened with punishment by the state. Punishment under the law differs from that imposed by a mob in that it is applied dispassionately by representatives of the state in such a manner that it may win the approval of the cool judgment of impartial observers. A law which does not provide a penalty that will cause suffering is regarded as quite impotent and in fact no criminal law at all. However, the punishment provided may be very slight; in the Courts of Honor a verdict was reached, a party was declared guilty, and the disgrace of the declaration of guilt was the only punishment. In view of the difficulty of identifying the criminal law of primitive societies, where the institution of "the state" is not obvious, the suggestion has been made that the penal sanction is the only essential element in the definition of criminal law, and that wherever proscriptions are enforced by a penal sanction, there criminal law exists. This is in contrast to the tort law, where the court orders the defendant to reimburse the plaintiff, but does

---

law is directly applicable to the action, it shall be punished according to the law, the basic idea of which fits it best." Lawrence Preuss, "Punishment by Analogy in Nationalist Socialist Penal Law," *Journal of Criminal Law and Criminology*, 26:847, March–April, 1936. See also Frederick Hoefer, "The Nazi Penal System," *Journal of Criminal Law and Criminology*, 35:385–393, March–April, 1945, and 36:30–38, May–June, 1945.

not punish him for damaging the plaintiff. It is evident, however, that the punitive aspect of criminal law is on the wane at present. In the juvenile court and to a smaller extent in the criminal courts, the tendency is to use methods which have been found to be effective in forestalling crime, regardless of whether they are coercive and punitive or not. By using juvenile court procedures we have attempted to avoid applying the "stigma of crime" to the acts of children. In theory, the juvenile court does not determine the guilt or innocence of a criminal; it merely acts in behalf of a child who is in need of help. The court's objective is treatment, not the meting out of penalties. However, except for children who are called delinquent because they have been neglected, most juvenile delinquencies are in fact defined as acts which would be crimes if committed by an adult. Consequently, juvenile delinquencies continue to be acts which are punishable by law, even if the punishment is kept in the background.[7] Similarly, the states and the federal government for a generation or two have been enacting laws for the regulation of manufacturing, commerce, agriculture, and other occupations. The persons affected by such laws are ordinarily respectable and powerful, and the legislatures have adapted the procedures to the status of these persons. Violations of these laws are crimes, but they are not always tried in the criminal courts. Instead, they are handled in civil and equity courts or in administrative commissions; the conventional penalties of fine and imprisonment are kept in the background to be used only as a last resort, and coercion in the first instance consists of injunctions and cease-and-desist orders. Thus these persons of social importance avoid the "stigma of crime," just as, to a lesser degree, juvenile delinquents do. The acts remain as crimes, however, for they are punishable by law.[8]

The conventional view is that a crime is an offense against the state, while in contrast a tort in violation of civil law is an offense against an individual. A particular act may be considered as an offense against an individual and also against the state, and is either a tort or a crime or both according to the way it is handled. A person who has committed an act of assault, for example, may be ordered by the civil court to pay the victim a sum of $500 for the damages to his interests, and he may also be ordered by the criminal court to pay a fine of $500 to the state. The payment of the first $500 is not punishment, but payment of the second $500 is punishment. This distinction between individual damage and social harm

---

[7] See the discussion in Chapter Twenty, pp. 456–467.

[8] Edwin H. Sutherland, "Is 'White Collar Crime' Crime?" *American Sociological Review*, 10:132–139, April, 1945; Edwin H. Sutherland, *White Collar Crime* (New York: Dryden, 1949), pp. 29–55.

is extremely difficult to make in the legal systems of nonliterate societies, where court procedures are relatively informal. Even in modern society, the distinction is dubious, for it rests upon the assumption that "individual" and "group" or "state" are mutually exclusive. For practical purposes, the individual is treated as if he were autonomous, but in fact an act which harms an individual also harms the group in which he has membership. Also, in modern society the indefiniteness of the distinction between torts and crimes is apparent when the victim of an act which is both a tort and a crime uses the criminal law as a method of forcing restitution which could not be secured with equal facility in the civil courts. Prosecutors frequently complain about the use of the criminal law as a collecting agency, especially because the victim who is reimbursed by the offender prior to trial then refuses to act as a witness.

For many centuries, the philosophers of jurisprudence have attempted by deductive reasoning to determine the principle justifying the use of specific laws. Divine will, the will of the sovereign, nature, reason, history, public opinion, and other principles have been presented.[9] Jerome Frank has attempted to explain by a quasi-psychoanalytic method the effort to secure exactness, certainty, and predictability in the law as due to the persisting childish need for an authoritative father, and he suggests that the solution of the conflict between the wish for certainty and the impossibility of securing certainty is to get rid of the need for the father authority.[10] Pound stated that a final answer to the question, "What is law?", is impossible because law is a living, changing thing, which may at one time be based on sovereign will and at another time on juristic science, which may at one time be uniform and at another time give much room for judicial discretion, which may at one time be very specific in its proscriptions and at another time much more general.[11]

NATURE OF CRIMINAL LAW FROM THE GENETIC POINT OF VIEW. Many theories of the origin of the criminal law as an agency of social control have been developed. First, in the classical theory the criminal law was regarded as originating in torts, or wrongs to individuals. According to this theory, all wrongs produced efforts at self-redress in the injured parties and were therefore treated as injuries to particular individuals; and later, by a series of transitions, the group took charge of the treatment, and the

---

[9] John W. Burgess, *The Sanctity of Law* (Boston: Ginn, 1927); Roscoe Pound, *Interpretations of Legal History* (New York: Macmillan, 1923); Roscoe Pound, *Law and Morals* (Chapel Hill, North Carolina: University of North Carolina Press, 1926); Morris R. Cohen, *Reason and Law* (Glencoe, Illinois: The Free Press, 1950).

[10] Jerome Frank, *Law and the Modern Mind* (New York: Brentano's, 1930).

[11] Pound, *Interpretations of Legal History, op. cit.,* Chapter 3.

wrongs came to be regarded as injuries to the group or to the state. These transitions included a requirement that the avenger announce his intention of seeking revenge; a requirement that the avenger secure the consent of the group before taking vengeance; the regulation of the amount of injury that could be done to the wrongdoer by the injured party; the limitation of time and place in which vengeance could be secured; public investigation of the merits of the case in connection with the requirements mentioned previously or independently of these; and participation of some members of the group in the efforts of the injured party to secure self-redress. There can be no doubt that some crimes did originate in torts and became crimes through one or more of the steps described. The theory is inadequate, however. It assumes the priority of the individual to the group and this is not justified, for it is certain that in early societies some wrongs were regarded as wrongs against the group. Such wrongs were regarded as dangerous to the group directly, as in treason and in violations of the hunting rules, or indirectly, as in sacrilege and witchcraft which might bring down the wrath of the gods upon the group.[12] Furthermore, for those crimes which originated from torts, the process is not adequately described. It is at this point, in part, that some of the other theories are concentrated.

2      A second theory is that the criminal law originated in the rational processes of a unified society. When wrongs occurred, the society took action and made a regulation to prevent a repetition of such wrongs. An alternative interpretation is that the enactment of a statute is an expression of emotion. Something occurs which upsets a group, and it rushes to the legislature to secure a prohibition of such acts. One of the founders of American sociology, Professor Robert Park said in one of his lectures, "We are always passing laws in America. We might as well get up and dance. The laws are largely to relieve emotion, and the legislatures are quite aware of that fact." It is obvious that some criminal laws are made in this manner, but the theory is inadequate as a general description of how the criminal law has developed.

3      A third theory is that the criminal law originated in and is a crystallization of the mores. Customs developed with little or no rational analysis, but after persisting for a time they achieved an ethical foundation. Infraction of such customs produced antagonistic reactions of the group, which were expressed in the form of criminal law with penal sanctions. This statement is a fairly accurate description of primitive law and of

[12] S. R. Steinmetz, *Ethnologische Studien zur ersten Entwicklung der Strafe* (Leiden: Harrassowitz, 1894), Vol. II, pp. 327–348; H. Oppenheimer, *The Rationale of Punishment* (London: University of London Press, 1913), pp. 66–91.

modern common law, but is not an accurate description of many of the modern statutes which deal with railways, factories, automobiles, television, and taxes.[13] It should be noted, however, that even in the laws dealing with these modern inventions the general values are, for the most part, taken over from the mores of the time, although the specific practices had not previously become customary.

4    A fourth theory is that criminal law originated in conflict of interests of different groups. When an interest group secures the enactment of a law, it secures the assistance of the state in a conflict with a rival interest group; the opposition of the rival group thus becomes criminal. According to this theory, wrongful acts are characteristic of all classes in present-day society; the upper classes are subtle in their wrongdoing, the underprivileged classes are direct. The upper classes are politically important and they prohibit the wrongful acts of the underprivileged classes, but the laws are defined and implemented in such manner that many of the wrongful acts of the upper classes do not come within their scope. In this theory, the criminal law originates in the conflict of groups and in the inconsistency of the mores. Like the other theories, it correctly describes a part of the process of law-making but fails in accuracy regarding other aspects of the law.

For one or more of the reasons described, laws are being utilized in America with increasing frequency. The number of statutes in a selected group of states increased approximately 40 percent from 1900 to 1930, and the same trend appears in regard to football rules, bridge rules, trade union rules, and probably almost all other rules.[14] At least one-half million new state laws have been enacted in the last fifty years. Laws have accumulated because the mores have been weak and inconsistent; and because the laws have not had the support of the mores, they have been relatively ineffective as a means of control. When the mores are adequate, laws are unnecessary; when the mores are inadequate, the laws are ineffective.

No positive conclusion can be reached about the comparative efficiency of the various theories concerning the origin of criminal law. Research on social aspects of criminal law is greatly needed. While the medical profession is constantly engaged in research work as to the origin of

[13] See R. C. Fuller, "Morals and the Criminal Law," *Journal of Criminal Law and Criminology*, 32:624–630, March–April, 1942; and Clarence Ray Jeffery, "Crime, Law and Social Structure," *Journal of Criminal Law and Criminology*, 47:423–435, November–December, 1956.

[14] President's Research Committee on Social Trends, *Recent Social Trends in the United States* (New York: McGraw-Hill, 1933), Vol. II, pp. 1115–1123. For an analysis of the long-time trend in criminal laws, see P. Sorokin, *Social and Cultural Dynamics*, New York: American Book, 1937), Vol. II, pp. 566–575.

diseases and the effects of treatment, the legal profession engages in practically no research work of an analogous kind; it confines its research work almost entirely to a study of what the law *is*. Three of the small number of exceptions to this approach are the analysis by Jerome Hall of the development of the law of theft in modern society, the analysis by a group of Norwegian scholars of the changes in the laws relevant to domestic servants, and the more general analysis by Leon Radzinowicz of the development of criminal law in England.[15]

THE DIFFERENTIAE OF CRIME. The rules of criminal law contain only definitions of specific crimes, such as burglary, robbery, and rape, but legal scholars have been able to abstract certain general principles from such definitions. These general principles apply ideally to all crimes and are the criteria actually used in determination of whether any particular behavior is or is not criminal. They are consistent with the ideal characteristics of the whole body of the criminal law—politicality, specificity, uniformity, and penal sanction—and, in fact, they may be viewed as translations of the ideal characteristics of the criminal law into statements of the ideal characteristics of all crimes. The concern is shifted from determination of the characteristics of a body of rules to determination of the general characteristics of the many specific acts described in those rules. Thus, for example, penal sanction is a general characteristic of the criminal law, and liability to legally prescribed punishment is a characteristic of all acts or omissions properly called crime. Obviously, a set of criteria used for deciding whether or not any specific act is a crime must be more precise than statements of the general characteristics of a body of rules.

One extensive and thorough analysis of crimes has resulted in a description of seven interrelated and overlapping differentiae of crime.[16] Ideally, behavior would not be called crime unless all seven differentiae were present. The following brief description of the differentiae is greatly simplified.

*First,* before behavior can be called crime there must be certain external consequences or "harm." A crime has a harmful impact on social interests; a "mental" or emotional state is not enough. Even if one decides

*harm*

---

[15] Jerome Hall, *Theft, Law, and Society,* Second Edition (Indianapolis: Bobbs-Merrill, 1952); Vilhelm Aubert, Torstein Eckhoff, and Knut Sveri, *En Lov i Sökelyset: Sosialpsykologisk undersökelse ave den Norske Hushjeplov* (Oslo: Akademisk Forlag, 1952); Leon Radzinowicz, *A History of English Criminal Law and Its Administration from 1750* (New York: Macmillan, 1948, 1957).

[16] Jerome Hall, *General Principles of Criminal Law,* Second Edition (Indianapolis: Bobbs-Merrill, 1960). See especially pp. 14–26.

to commit a crime but changes his mind before he does anything about it, he has committed no crime. The intention is not taken for the deed.

Second, the harm must be legally forbidden, must have been proscribed in penal law. Anti-social behavior is not crime unless it is prohibited by law. As indicated previously, the law must have specifically prohibited the harm which occurs. Penal law does not have a retroactive effect; there is a long-standing tradition against the enactment of *ex post facto* legislation.

Third, there must be "conduct"; that is, there must be an intentional or reckless action or inaction which brings the harmful consequences about. One who is physically forced to pull the trigger of a gun does not commit murder, even if someone dies from the bullet.

Fourth, "criminal intent" or *mens rea* must be present. Hall suggests that legal scholars have often confused intentionality (deliberate functioning to reach a goal) and motivation (the reasons or grounds for the end-seeking).[17] *Mens rea* is identified with the former, not with the latter. The "motives" for a crime might be "good," but the intention itself might be an intention to effect a harm forbidden by the criminal law, a criminal intent. Thus if a man decides to kill his starving children because he feels that they will pass on to a better world, his motive is good, but his intention is wrong. Persons who are "insane" at the time they perpetrate legally forbidden harms do not commit crimes, for the necessary *mens rea* is not present.

Fifth, there must be a fusion or concurrence of *mens rea* and conduct. This means, for example, that a policeman who goes into a house to make an arrest and who then commits a crime after making the arrest while still in the house, cannot be considered a trespasser from the beginning. The criminal intent and the conduct do not fuse or concur.

Sixth, there must be a "causal" relation between the legally forbidden harm and the voluntary misconduct. The "conduct" of one who fails to file an income tax return is his failure to take pen and ink, fill out the form, *etc.*; the "harm" is the absence of a return in the collector's office. In this case, the "causal" relation between the two obviously is present. But if, for example, one shot a person (conduct) and the victim suffocated while in a hospital recovering from the wound, the relationship between conduct and harm (death) is not so clear-cut.

Seventh, there must be legally prescribed punishment. Not only must the harm be proscribed by law but, as indicated above, the proscription must carry a threat of punishment to violators. The voluntary conduct must be punishable by law.

17 *Ibid.*, pp. 84–93.

These differentiae of crime are all concerned with the nature of the behavior which can properly be called crime, but in making decisions about most cases each criterion need not be considered separately and individually. If the *mens rea*, conduct, and legally proscribed harm are obviously present, for example, the "causal" relation between harm and misconduct almost certainly will be present. In sum, the differentiae represent the kinds of subject matter with which both criminal lawyers and criminal law theorists must deal.

There are, of course, many exceptions to the generalization that these are the elements of all crimes. Criminal law theory is not a body of precise principles, and consequently there are deviations from that which is logical and ideal. For purposes of illustration, we may cite two major exceptions to the above differentiae. *First*, criminal intent, in the ordinary meaning of the concept, need not be present for some crimes. In some cases, the so-called "strict liability" cases, the offender's intent is not considered. Instead, the person is held responsible for the results of his conduct, regardless of his intention. The handling of "statutory rape" is a case in point—no matter how elaborate the calculations, inquiries, or research which a male utilizes in reaching the conclusion that his female companion is above the age of consent, if he has sexual relations with her and it is subsequently shown that she was below the age of consent, he has committed statutory rape. Certain "public welfare" offenses, such as selling adulterated food and traffic offenses, are handled under the same rule. Similarly, under the "felony-murder—misdemeanor-manslaughter doctrine" defendants are held criminally liable for much more serious offenses than they intended to commit. If one sets fire to a building and a fireman dies trying to extinguish the flames, the offender is liable for murder; if the offense had been a misdemeanor rather than arson, he would have been liable for manslaughter. Hall has severely criticized this doctrine and the general conception of strict liability in the criminal law, and he contends that it is "bad law," stating that "there is no avoiding the conclusion that strict liability cannot be brought within the scope of penal law."[18] A behavioristic school in jurisprudence, however, insists that the intent can be determined only by the circumstances of the act and that a translation of these circumstances into mental terms confuses rather than clarifies the procedure. It contends that the doctrine of *mens rea* should be greatly modified or even abandoned.[19] In criminology, the inclusion in the concept "crime" of

[18] *Ibid.*, p. 336.
[19] Albert Levitt, "The Origin of the Doctrine of *Mens Rea*," *Illinois Law Review*, 17:117–137, June, 1922; Albert Levitt, "Extent and Function of the Doctrine of *Mens Rea*," *Illinois Law Review*, 17:578–595, April, 1923; O. W. Holmes, *The Common*

behavior which was not intended by the actor makes general theoretical explanation of all crime extremely difficult. No current theoretical expla-nation of criminal behavior can account for the strict liability offenses.

Second, "motive" and "intention" are confused in many court decisions. In the crime of libel, for instance, motive is explicitly considered. In many states, one cannot publish truthful, albeit damaging, statements about another unless his motive is good. Criminal conspiracy also fre-quently involves consideration and evaluation of a defendant's motives as well as his intention. In most instances, however, motivation is taken into account only in the administration of the criminal law, i.e., in making a decision as to the severity of the punishment which should be accorded a criminal.

NATURE OF CRIME FROM THE SOCIAL POINT OF VIEW. The statement that we would have no crime if we had no criminal laws and that we could eliminate all crime merely by abolishing all criminal laws is logomachy. It is true that if the laws against stealing were repealed, stealing would not be a crime, but it would still be offensive and the public would react to it by lynch law and public disgrace. The name of the behavior would be changed but the behavior and the societal reaction to the behavior would remain essentially the same, for the "social interests" damaged by the behavior would remain essentially unchanged. Because of this, efforts have been made to include within the definition of crime a description of the nature of the acts which the law prohibits and thus to define crime in social rather than legal terms. Garofalo developed a concept of the natural crime and defined it as a violation of the prevalent senti-ments of pity and probity.[20] The anthropologist Radcliffe-Brown defined crime as a violation of usage which gives rise to the exercise of the penal sanction, and the sociologist Thomas defined crime as an action which is antagonistic to the solidarity of that group which the individual considers as his own.[21] Crime may be considered, in the light of the discussion in the preceding sections, to involve three elements: a value which is appreciated by a group or a part of a group which is politically important; isolation of or cultural conflict in another part of this group so that its members do not appreciate the value or appreciate it less highly and consequently tend to endanger it; and a pugnacious resort to coercion decently applied by

Law (Boston: Little, Brown, 1881), ch. 2; F. B. Sayre, "Mens Rea," Harvard Law Review, 45:974–1026, April, 1932. See also Colin Howard, Strict Responsibility (Lon-don: Sweet and Maxwell, 1963).

[20] R. Garofalo, Criminology (Boston: Little, Brown, 1914), p. 59.

[21] W. I. Thomas and F. Znaniecki, The Polish Peasant in Europe and America (New York: Knopf, 1927), Vol. II, pp. 1753–1755.

those who appreciate the value to those who disregard the value. When
a crime is committed, these relationships are involved. Crime is this set
of relationships when viewed from the point of view of the group rather
than of the individual. This conception of the social nature of crime,
as well as the preceding definitions, is suggestive and may be developed
into a fundamental definition, but at present certainly lacks precision.

THE RELATIVITY OF CRIME.    Crime is relative from the legal point of view
and also from the social point of view. The criminal law has had a constantly changing content. Many of the early crimes were primarily
religious offenses, and these remained important until recent times; now
few religious offenses are included in the penal codes. It was a crime
in Iceland in the viking age for a person to write verses about another,
even if the sentiment was complimentary, if the verses exceeded four
strophes in length. A Prussian law of 1784 prohibited mothers and nurses
from taking children under two years of age into their beds. The English
villein in the fourteenth century was not allowed to send his son to
school, and no one lower than a freeholder was permitted by law to
keep a dog. The following have at different times been crimes: printing
a book, professing the medical doctrine of circulation of the blood,
driving with reins, sale of coin to foreigners, having gold in the house,
buying goods on the way to market or in the market for the purpose
of selling them at a higher price, writing a check for less than $1.00.
On the other hand, many of our present laws were not known to earlier
generations—quarantine laws, traffic laws, sanitation laws, factory laws.

Laws differ, also, from one jurisdiction to another at a particular time.
The laws of some states require automobile owners to paste certificates
of ownership or inspection certificates on the windshield, while adjoining
states prohibit the pasting of anything on the windshield. Georgia has
a $1,000 fine or six months' incarceration as the maximum penalty for
adultery, while in Louisiana adultery is not a crime at all.[22]

In a particular jurisdiction at a particular time there are wide variations
in the interpretation and implementation of the law. These variations are
related to the specific characteristics of the crimes and to the status of
the offenders. For example, gross forms of fraud are easily detected by
the regular police, but expert investigators must deal with the subtler
forms of fraud which flourish in many areas of business and of the
professions. As such experts are provided, what has been mere chicanery
has sometimes been interpreted and dealt with as crime. In this sense,

[22] Robert C. Bensing, "A Comparative Study of American Sex Statutes," *Journal of
Criminal Law and Criminology*, 42:57–72, May–June, 1951.

also, crime is relative to the status of the criminals and the situations in which they violate law.

CLASSIFICATION OF CRIMES.  Since crime is not a homogeneous type of behavior, efforts have been made to classify crimes. They are frequently classified in respect to atrocity as felonies and misdemeanors. The more serious are called felonies and are usually punishable by death or by confinement in a state prison; the less serious are called misdemeanors and are usually punishable by confinement in a local prison or by fines. As a classification of crimes this is not very useful, as was pointed out long ago by Sir James Stephen, and it is difficult to make a clear-cut distinction between the classes. Though one may agree that murders, as a class, are more serious offenses than permitting weeds to grow on a vacant lot in violation of a municipal ordinance, the effects of permitting the weeds to grow, in a particular case, may be more serious because of the hay fever produced by the pollen and the resulting incapacity of many people. The fact that many things which are classed as felonies in one state are classed as misdemeanors in near-by states shows how difficult it is to make a real distinction between them. Even within a single state the distinction is often vague.

The greatest objection to the classification of crimes as felonies and misdemeanors is that it is used also as a classification of criminals. The individual who commits a felony is a felon; the individual who commits a misdemeanor is a misdemeanant. It is assumed that misdemeanants are less dangerous and more susceptible to rehabilitative measures than felons. But it is quite fallacious to judge the danger to the group or the probability of reformation from one act, for an individual may commit a misdemeanor one week, a felony the second week, and a misdemeanor the third. The acts do not represent changes in his character or changes in the danger to the group. In an older study, Queen found that there were few respects in which the criminals judged to be felons were different from those judged to be misdemeanants and many respects in which the two groups overlapped.[23] It is evident, for instance, that some misdemeanants are more dangerous and more costly than some felons. Of the persons sentenced to the state farm in Massachusetts in 1950, for offenses ordinarily classed as misdemeanors, 88 percent had served terms previously in penal institutions, as contrasted with 70 percent of those in the state prison; and their average number of previous commitments was seventeen, as contrasted with three in the case of those in the state

[23] S. A. Queen, *The Passing of the County Jail* (Menasha, Wisconsin: Banta, 1920), pp. 87–94.

prison. Moreover, the definition is influenced by various other considerations. Since 1852, when a felony was first defined in Massachusetts as a crime punishable by confinement in the state prison, at least four changes have been made in the laws of that state, determining the conditions under which a sentence is served in state prison rather than in a jail or house of correction. These changes, which also changed crimes from felonies to misdemeanors or the reverse, were not made because of alterations in views regarding the atrocity of crimes but for purely administrative reasons, generally to relieve the congestion of the state prison. Consequently there seems to be good reason to abandon this classification.

Bonger, the Dutch criminologist, classified crimes by the motives of the offenders as economic crimes, sexual crimes, political crimes, and miscellaneous crimes (with vengeance as the principal motive).[24] But no crime can be reduced to one motive. A desire for excitement or vengeance may be very important in such crimes as burglary, which Bonger classified as economic crime. The classification is clearly inadequate.

Crimes are frequently classified for statistical purposes as crimes against the person, crimes against property, and crimes against public decency, public order, and public justice. Most recorded crimes are crimes against public order or public morality, such as disorderly conduct and drunkenness; next in frequency come the crimes of dishonesty without violence. Of the persons arrested by the police in 1964, 45 percent were arrested for drunkenness or disorderly conduct or vagrancy. The crimes which are regarded as most serious are relatively few, according to this criterion. Homicide constituted 0.2 percent, rape 0.2 percent, burglary 4 percent, and robbery 0.8 percent, a total for these serious offenses of 5.2 percent of all arrests.[25] It is probable that if all cases of fraud could be recorded, fraud would rank close to drunkenness and disorderly conduct in frequency.

An attempt was made by police officials to obtain a uniform classification of crimes for statistical purposes,[26] and some effort has been made to classify crimes for purposes of codification of criminal laws.[27] Each

[24] W. A. Bonger, *Criminality and Economic Conditions* (Boston: Little, Brown, 1916), pp. 536–537.

[25] Federal Bureau of Investigation, United States Department of Justice, *Uniform Crime Reports for the United States, 1964* (Washington: Government Printing Office, 1965), p. 106.

[26] International Association of Chiefs of Police, *Uniform Crime Reporting: A Complete Manual for Police* (New York: Author, 1929).

[27] John W. MacDonald, "The Classification of Crimes," *Cornell Law Quarterly*, 19:524–563, June, 1933.

of these classifications has value for its own purposes, but neither of them serves adequately for theoretical analysis.

In a classification of crimes for theoretical purposes each class should be a sociological entity, differentiated from the other classes by variations in causal processes. Professional crime, for instance, would be a class, or more likely a combination of classes, differentiated from other crimes by the regularity of this behavior, the development of techniques, and the association among offenders and the consequent development of a group culture. Within this class might be included some cases of murder, arson, burglary, robbery, and theft, but not all of the cases in any of those legal categories.[28] Similarly, specific criteria for describing cases as "criminal violation of financial trust" have been developed, with the result that some, but not all, cases of embezzlement, confidence game, forgery, larceny by bailee, and other crimes are included.[29] The new classification avoided the error of extending a legal concept beyond its legal meaning, e.g., calling all the behavior "embezzlement," and at the same time it provided a rigorous definition of the behavior being studied. Jerome Hall has made an excellent analysis of theft from this point of view.[30] It is not worth while at present to attempt a complete classification of crimes from this point of view. Such a classification should grow out of research work rather than of *a priori* speculation.[31]

THE CRIMINAL. Who is a criminal? An answer consistent with the previous discussion is: A person who commits a crime. However, in the democratic legal tradition even one who admits to having committed a crime is not designated a criminal until his criminality has been proven by means of the accepted court procedures. Consequently, a prison warden would not be justified in receiving as a prisoner a person who had not been officially convicted and sentenced, and public officials could not rightfully deny civil rights to persons who had not been convicted of some crime. Similarly, criminologists cannot rightfully designate as "criminals" persons who have behaved in an antisocial

[28] Don C. Gibbons and Donald L. Garrity, "Some Suggestions for the Development of Etiological and Treatment Theory in Criminology," *Social Forces*, 38:51–58, October, 1959; and Jack P. Gibbs, "Needed: Analytical Typologies in Criminology," *Southwestern Social Science Quarterly*, 12:321–329, March, 1960.

[29] Donald R. Cressey, *Other People's Money* (Glencoe, Ill.: The Free Press, 1953), pp. 19–22; Donald R. Cressey, "Criminological Research and the Definition of Crimes," *American Journal of Sociology*, 56:546–551, May, 1951.

[30] Jerome Hall, *Theft, Law, and Society, op. cit.*

[31] Cf. Jerome Hall, "Some Basic Questions Regarding Legal Classifications for Professional and Scientific Purposes," *Journal of Legal Education*, 5:329–343, 1953.

manner but who have not violated a criminal law.[32] However, for scientific purposes it is not necessary that every decision be made in court; the criminologist must only know that a certain class of acts is defined as crime and that a particular person has committed an act of this class. Just as there is justification for writing of "crimes known to the police" and "unsolved crimes," there is justification for writing of "unapprehended criminals" and "criminals at large."[33]

This answer, that a criminal is one who commits a crime, however, raises other questions, for even the criminal law does not specify the length of time a person remains a criminal after he has committed a crime. Is one a criminal only during the time he is committing the crime, until he has "paid the penalty," or during the remainder of his life? The question is perhaps unimportant and is difficult to answer only because we use the word "criminal" to stigmatize the one who violates the law. In public thought the word "criminal" is generally applied only to those who are ostracized by society. It is in this sense that Tarde stated that criminals are "social excrement."[34]

Some criminologists are inclined to restrict the term "criminal" to those persons who conform to a social type, which is defined by those persons and by society generally as criminal.[35] The term then refers to the violator of law who has a body of skills, attitudes, and social relationships which signify maturity in criminal culture. This usage is analogous to the practice of reserving the terms "plumber," "electrician," or "preacher" for those who engage regularly and expertly in certain occupations. If the term is restricted in this manner, it is not applied to many occasional violators of law, even those who commit murder. The "criminal" then becomes "the real criminal." Most of the inmates of state prisons would not be "criminals" by this criterion. The use of the word "criminal" in this manner does not direct attention to most of the pertinent problems of criminology.

**POSSIBILITY OF A SCIENCE OF CRIMINOLOGY.** Criminology at present is not a science, but it has hopes of becoming a science. The argument has

---

[32] Cf. Paul W. Tappan, "Who is the Criminal?" *American Sociological Review*, 12:96–102, February, 1947; Frank E. Hartung, "White-collar Offenses in the Wholesale Meat Industry in Detroit," *American Journal of Sociology*, 56:25–34, July, 1950; and Robert G. Caldwell, "A Reexamination of the Concept of White Collar Crime," *Federal Probation*, 22:30–36, March, 1958.

[33] See Donald R. Cressey, "Foreword" to Edwin H. Sutherland, *White Collar Crime*, New edition (New York: Holt, Rinehart and Winston, 1961), pp. 4–8.

[34] G. Tarde, *Penal Philosophy* (Boston: Little, Brown, 1912, p. 222).

[35] See, for example, E. W. Burgess, "Discussion" of Frank E. Hartung, "White-Collar Offenses in the Wholesale Meat Industry in Detroit," *American Journal of Sociology*, 56:32–34, July, 1950.

been made, however, that criminology cannot possibly become a science. According to this argument, general propositions of universal validity are the essence of science; such propositions can be made only regarding stable and homogeneous units; crime is not a stable and homogeneous unit but varies from one time or place to another; therefore universal propositions cannot be made regarding crime, and scientific studies of criminal behavior are impossible.[36]

The emphasis on universal propositions might be regarded by some students as exaggerated, but all will agree on the value of such universal propositions when they can be obtained and the desirability of organizing a study so that such propositions may be reached. Furthermore, this criticism neglects the possibility of selecting areas and types of crimes in which definitions are essentially uniform, or at least of taking into account variations in definitions. As indicated above, it is possible to some extent for the criminologist by selection of criminal cases to redefine crime for his own purposes. But in general the difficulties arising from the legal definition of crime should be recognized.

Sellin implicitly acknowledges the validity of the criticism described above and proceeds to redefine crime as a violation of any conduct norm whatever. He argues that a solid basis for a science of criminology cannot be found unless the arbitrary definitions of the legislatures are replaced by definitions drawn up by scientists and for scientific purposes.[37] Even if this is done, it is not possible to escape the evaluations of behavior which are made by groups. Courage, for instance, cannot be defined as a fixed aspect of behavior, for behavior which is called courageous in one situation is called cowardly in another, and the difference in the names applied to the behavior makes the behavior different. Physiologically, acts can be defined apart from group evaluations, sociologically they cannot be. In this respect crime is like all other social phenomena, and the possibility of a science of criminal behavior is similar to the possibility of a science of any other behavior. Social science has no stable unit, for all social sciences are dealing with phenomena which involve group evaluations. Consequently the methodological problems are by no means solved when crime is redefined as a violation of any conduct norm.

A universal explanation of crime must necessarily be extremely broad and may not be especially enlightening or valuable for purposes of control. In medicine, progress is being made principally by defining and explaining particular diseases. Similarly, in criminology the significant

[36] See George L. Wilber, "The Scientific Adequacy of Criminological Concepts," *Social Forces*, 28:165–174, December, 1949.

[37] Thorsten Sellin, *Culture Conflict and Crime* (New York: Social Science Research Council, 1938).

explanations will probably relate not to crime as a whole, but to particular types or classes of crimes, each class being defined in terms of universal elements. Obviously, the legal definitions should not confine the work of the criminologist, and he should be completely free to push across the barriers of legal definitions whenever he sees non-criminal behavior which resembles criminal behavior.

Some students, admitting the criticisms outlined above, have abandoned the effort to make criminology a science and place their emphasis on the study of social control. A study of the sequence of lawmaking, lawbreaking, and reactions to lawbreaking from the point of view of the efficiency of the law as a method of control is a useful objective in a criminology of this nature.

THE PROBLEM OF CRIME. The seriousness of the social problem of crime hardly needs to be described. The general public is, by definition, always the victim of crime. The general public suffers losses from crime either directly (as in treason or theft and destruction of public property), or indirectly (in the form of the expense of maintaining the police and the courts and in the form of uneasiness or even terror because of the prevalence of crime). In this sense every individual in the state is a victim of crime. In addition, some individuals are victims of crime in a more specific sense. The victims of crime may lose anything that has value. Personal safety, money, and property are perhaps basic values, because they contribute to the satisfaction of many wishes. Approximately ten thousand persons a year are victims of homicides, of which perhaps one-third are felonious homicides not due to negligence. The financial losses from fraudulent stock and bond issues and from fraudulent business transactions of other types are probably many times as great as the financial losses from burglary, robbery, and ordinary larceny. One chain of stores has about five hundred burglaries and robberies a year, with a total of about $100,000 a year. The same chain had one embezzlement which caused a loss of more than $600,000. A management consulting firm recently found dishonesty in 50 percent of the assignments it undertook in one year, when there was no prior hint of dishonesty. That is, the firm makes surveys of employee morale, performance in connection with plant layout, efficiency, and other matters which are essentially engineering in nature. In these cases they found dishonesty in 50 percent. The same firm unearthed in 1959 $60 million worth of dishonesty with more than 60 percent attributable to supervisory and executive personnel.[38]

38 Norman Jaspan with Hillel Black, The Thief in the White Collar (Philadelphia: J. B. Lippincott, 1960), p. 10.

The loss of status in the community is frequently a result of crime. The victim of rape, especially, suffers this loss, and the loss is immensely magnified by the continued publicity given to it in the newspapers. Also the loss of status may be suffered by persons not ordinarily considered to be the victims, as the relatives of the prostitute or of the murderer or embezzler. The victim is sometimes immediately aware of the loss he suffers, but the realization is frequently delayed. The child who is employed in violation of the child-labor law, for instance, may not have an immediate realization of the loss he suffers by this crime and, in fact, may never realize the relation of his childhood labor to his subsequent career.

In crimes of personal violence, the victims and the offenders are generally of the same social group, and have residences not far apart. Negroes murder Negroes, Italians murder Italians, and Chinese murder Chinese. These crimes of personal violence are generally committed against persons with whom the offenders have personal dealings.[39] Crimes against property, however, are generally committed against strangers. They may be either direct and personal attacks, as in robbery or burglary, or may be much more general and public, as in fraudulent stock and bond sales or fraudulent advertisements. In modern society these general and impersonal crimes have become much more serious in their effects than have the direct and personal attacks; although the impersonal crimes generally represent no antagonism toward the victims, they do represent a ruthless and reckless pursuit of interests at variance with the interests of the victim.

Estimates have been made that the total financial cost of crime, both direct and indirect, is twenty or twenty-five billion dollars a year. These estimates are completely worthless. In the first place, they are principally guesses; and in the second place, they are based on unwarranted assumptions. They start with the question, How much would be saved if no crimes were committed and no precautions had to be taken against future crimes? But in order to bring about a crimeless state of society, it is possible that the annual expenditure would need to be greater than the expenditure for crime at present.[40]

It is urged by some persons that crime makes certain contributions

[39] Harold Garfinkel, "Research Note on Inter- and Intra-Racial Homicides," *Social Forces*, 27:369–381, May, 1949; Henry A. Bullock, "Urban Homicide in Theory and Fact," *Journal of Criminal Law and Criminology*, 45:565–575, January, 1955; Marvin E. Wolfgang, *Patterns in Criminal Homicide* (Philadelphia: University of Pennsylvania Press, 1957).

[40] Frederick A. Conrad, "Statistics in the Analysis of Social Problems," *Sociology and Social Research*, 26:538–549, July, 1942; E. R. Hawkins and Willard Waller, "The Cost of Crime," *Journal of Criminal Law and Criminology*, 26:679–694, January–February, 1936.

to society which offset this loss to some extent. One suggested contribution is that it promotes the solidarity of the group, just as does war.[41] While it is true that the group is welded together by certain spectacular crimes of murder or rape, it is probable that many other crimes promote dissension, suspicions, and divisions in society. Moreover, the solidarity which is aroused in this manner is generally rather futile, for it is an emotional expression which drives criminals into organized groups. In this respect crime, like war, may have some effect in producing group solidarity, but the values can be produced more effectively in other ways.

Again, it is urged that we must have crime in order to prevent morality from going to an extreme. If under an existing régime all criminals were eliminated, the standards would be set a little higher. If those at the bottom who violated the new standards were eliminated, the standards would be set still higher. Thus the group would become more and more strict in its morality until the situation became impossible. This argument, also, is not entirely convincing. At least, many primitive groups retained essentially the same standards with practically no violations for long periods of time.[42]

The social function of crime is to act as a notification of maladjustments. Just as pain is a notification to an organism that something is wrong, so crime is a notification of a social maladjustment, especially when crime becomes prevalent. Crime is a symptom of social disorganization and probably can be reduced appreciably only by changes in social organization.

## SUGGESTED READINGS

Aubert, Vilhelm, "Researches in the Sociology of Law," *American Behavioral Scientist*, 7:16–20, December, 1963.

Bloch, Herbert A., "Legal, Sociological, and Psychiatric Variations in the Interpretation of the Criminal Act," Chapter V in Richard Nice, Editor, *Crime and Insanity*, New York: Philosophical Library, 1958, pp. 65–103.

Christie, Nils, "Scandinavian Criminology," *Sociological Inquiry*, 31:93–104, Winter, 1961.

Cohen, Morris R., *Reason and Law*. Glencoe: The Free Press, 1950.

Conrad, F. A., "Statistics in the Analysis of Social Problems," *Sociology and Social Research*, 26:538–549, July, 1942.

[41] G. H. Mead, "The Psychology of Punitive Justice," *American Journal of Sociology*, 23:577–602, March, 1918; A. C. Hall, *Crime in Its Relation to Social Progress* (New York: Columbia University Press, 1902), pp. 1–10.

[42] Emile Durkheim, *The Rules of Sociological Method* (Chicago: University of Chicago Press, 1938), pp. 67–73.

Evan, William M., Editor, *Law and Society*. New York: The Free Press of Glencoe, 1962.

Frank, Jerome, *Law and the Modern Mind*. New York: Brentanos, 1930.

Fuller, R. C., "Morals and the Criminal Law," *Journal of Criminal Law and Criminology*, 32:624–630, March–April, 1942.

Geis, Gilbert, "Sociology and Sociological Jurisprudence: Admixture of Lore and Law," *Kentucky Law Journal*, 52:267–293, Winter, 1964.

Gurvitch, Georges, *Sociology of Law*, New York: Philosophical Library, 1941.

Guttmacher, M. S., and H. Weihofen, *Psychiatry and the Law*. New York: Norton, 1952.

Hall, Jerome, "Interrelations of Criminal Law and Torts," *Columbia Law Review*, 43:735–779, 967–1001, September–November, 1943.

Hall, Jerome, *General Principles of Criminal Law*, Second Edition. Indianapolis: Bobbs-Merrill, 1960.

Hall, Jerome, *Theft, Law, and Society*, Second Edition. Indianapolis: Bobbs-Merrill, 1952.

Hall, Jerome, "Legal Sanctions," *Natural Law Forum*, 6:119–126, 1961.

Harno, A. J., "Some Significant Developments in Criminal Law and Procedure in the Last Century," *Journal of Criminal Law, Criminology, and Police Science*, 42:427–467, November–December, 1951.

Hart, Henry M. Jr., "The Aims of the Criminal Law," *Law and Contemporary Problems*, 23:401–441, Summer, 1958.

Hartung, Frank E., "White-Collar Offenses in the Wholesale Meat Industry in Detroit," *American Journal of Sociology*, 56:25–34, July, 1950.

Hawkins, E. R., and W. Waller, "The Cost of Crime," *Journal of Criminal Law and Criminology*, 26:679–694, January–February, 1936.

Michael, J., and M. J. Adler, *Crime, Law, and Social Science*. New York: Harcourt, Brace, 1933.

Nettler, Gwynn, "Antisocial Sentiment and Criminality," *American Sociological Review*, 24:202–208, April, 1959.

Pound, Roscoe, *Criminal Justice in America*. New York: Holt, 1930.

Quinney, Richard, "Crime in Political Perspective," *The American Behavioral Scientist*, 8, 19–22, December, 1964.

Radzinowicz, Leon, *A History of English Criminal Law and Its Administration from 1750*, Vols. 1–3, New York: Macmillan, 1948 and 1957.

Sellin, Thorsten, *Culture Conflict and Crime*. New York: Social Science Research Council, 1938.

Sellin, Thorsten, "The Challenge of Criminality," *Excerpta Criminologica*, 1:1–2, January, 1961.

Skolnick, Jerome H., "The Sociology of Law in America: Overview and Trends," pp. 1–39 in *Law and Society*, a supplement to *Social Problems*, Summer, 1965.

Sutherland, E. H., "Is 'White Collar Crime' Crime?" *American Sociological Review*, 10:132–139, April, 1945.
Sutherland, E. H., *White Collar Crime*. New York: Dryden, 1949.
Tappan, P. W., "Who is the Criminal?" *American Sociological Review*, 12:96–102, February, 1947.
Timasheff, N. S. *An Introduction to the Sociology of Law*, Cambridge: Harvard University Committee on Research in the Social Sciences, 1939.
Vold, George B., "Some Basic Problems in Criminological Research," *Federal Probation*, 17:37–42, March, 1953.

Specific references to the standard textbooks in criminology are not included in the suggested readings because of their ready accessibility. The following textbooks should be consulted on each chapter.

Barnes, Harry Elmer, and Negley K. Teeters, *New Horizons in Criminology*, Third Edition. New York: Prentice-Hall, 1959.
Bloch, Herbert A., and Gilbert Geis, *Man, Crime, and Society*. New York: Random House, 1962.
Caldwell, Robert G., *Criminology*, New York: Ronald Press, 1956.
Cavan, Ruth S., *Criminology*, Second Edition. New York: Crowell, 1955.
Elliott, Mabel A., *Crime and Modern Society*. New York: Harper, 1952.
Hartung, Frank E., *Crime, Law, and Society*, Detroit: Wayne State University, 1965.
Johnson, Elmer H., *Crime, Correction, and Society*, Homewood, Illinois: Dorsey, 1964.
Korn, Richard R., and Lloyd W. McCorkle, *Criminology and Penology*. New York: Holt-Dryden, 1959.
Reckless, Walter C., *The Crime Problem*, Second Edition. New York: Appleton-Century-Crofts, 1955.
Taft, Donald R., and Ralph W. England, Jr., *Criminology*, Fourth Edition. New York: Macmillan, 1964.
Tappan, Paul W., *Crime, Justice, and Correction*, New York: McGraw-Hill, 1960.
Vold, George B., *Theoretical Criminology*, New York: Oxford University Press, 1958.

# 2. INDEXES OF CRIME

THE GENERAL STATISTICS of crime and criminals are probably the most unreliable and most difficult of all social statistics. It is impossible to determine with accuracy the amount of crime in any given jurisdiction at any particular time. Obviously a large proportion of the crimes committed go undetected, others are detected but not reported, others are reported but not officially recorded. Consequently any record of crimes, such as crimes known to the police, arrests, convictions, or commitments to prison, can be considered only as an "index" of the crimes committed. But these "indexes" of crime do not maintain a constant ratio with the true rate, whatever it may be. (We measure the extent of crime with elastic rulers whose units of measurement are not defined.) Ordinarily, a statistical index, such as a "cost of living index," is a compilation of fluctuations in a sample of items taken from the whole; the relationship to the whole is known, and the index serves as a convenient short cut to a sufficient approximation of variation in the whole. But in crime statistics the rate as indicated by any set of figures cannot be a sample, for the whole cannot be specified. Both the true rate and the relationship between the true rate and any "index" of this rate are capricious "dark figures" which vary with changes in police policies, court policies, and public opinion.[1] In most nations, the variations in this "dark figure" in crime statistics make it almost foolhardy to attempt a comparison of crime rates of various cities, and it even is hazardous to compare national rates or the rates of a given city or state in a given year with the rates of the same jurisdiction in a different year. International comparisons are even more difficult.

CRIMES KNOWN TO THE POLICE. The crimes which are reported to the police and recorded by the police are designated "crimes known to the police." These statistics are an inadequate index of the true crime rate.

---

[1] Donald R. Cressey, "The State of Criminal Statistics," *National Probation and Parole Association Journal*, 3:230–241, July, 1957; M. Grünhut, "Statistics in Criminology," *Journal of the Royal Statistical Society*, 114:139–157, Part II, 1951.

Yet the decision to use this rate is probably the best way out of a bad situation, for as Professor Sellin has repeatedly pointed out, "The value of criminal statistics as a basis for measurement of criminality in geographic areas decreases as the procedures take us farther away from the offense itself."[2] That is, these police records are a more reliable index than arrest statistics, arrest statistics are more reliable than court statistics, and court statistics are more reliable than prison statistics.

Even within a single police department, many crimes are "lost" between recording and arrest, the exact number varying with the honesty and efficiency of the police department and with the policy regarding handling cases informally, without actual arrest. Van Vechten has shown that in selected cities in the United States arrests are made in only 25 percent of the serious offense cases known to the police.[3] In 1964, the police of 2,680 cities who reported crimes to the Federal Bureau of Investigation "cleared by arrest" 90 percent of the murders, 67 percent of the rapes, 74 percent of the aggravated assaults, 37 percent of the robberies, 25 percent of the burglaries, 19 percent of the larcenies, and 26 percent of the automobile thefts known to them.[4] For the whole of England, the percentage of serious offenses "cleared up" by the police was 50 in 1938, 43 in 1947 and 1948, and 47 in 1949. In the last-mentioned year the Metropolitan Police in England cleared up 31 percent of all known serious offenses, the highest proportion ever attained since crime records have been available, but there were wide variations in the proportions of specific crimes which were cleared up.[5] For example, three-fourths of the cases of "larceny by servant" and fraud were cleared up, but only one-tenth of the cases of larceny from vehicles were cleared up.

Similarly, many crimes are "lost" between arrest and prosecution. The English reports on criminal statistics have since 1857 included as indexes of crime both the number of crimes known to the police and the number of prosecutions; these two indexes were fairly consistent until about the end of World War I, but they have been diverging since that time. Just as some types of crime are cleared by arrest more frequently than others, some types of crime are more frequently prosecuted than others. In 1,658 cities in the United States in 1964, persons were held for prosecution in 73

[2] Thorsten Sellin, "The Significance of Records of Crime," *The Law Quarterly Review*, 67:496–504, October, 1951; *Research Memorandum on Crime in the Depression* (New York: Social Science Research Council, 1937), Chapter 4; "The Basis of a Crime Index," *Journal of Criminal Law and Criminology*, 22:335–356, September–October, 1931.

[3] C. C. Van Vechten, "Differential Criminal Case Mortality in Selected Jurisdictions," *American Sociological Review*, 7:833–839, December, 1942.

[4] Federal Bureau of Investigation, United States Department of Justice, *Uniform Crime Reports for the United States, 1964* (Washington: Government Printing Office, 1965), p. 95.

[5] Grünhut, *op. cit.*

percent of the murder cases, 57 percent of the rape cases, 52 percent of the aggravated assault cases, 40 percent of the robbery cases, 18 percent of the burglary cases, 15 percent of the larceny cases, and 22 percent of the automobile theft cases known to the police.[6]

In addition, many crimes are "lost" between prosecution and conviction; this process, too, is selective—some types of crime are "lost" more frequently than are others. In 1,751 cities in 1964, 46 percent of the persons charged with murder were found guilty, as compared to 31 percent of those charged with rape, 34 percent of those charged with aggravated assault, 39 percent of those charged with robbery, 28 percent of those charged with burglary, 40 percent of those charged with larceny, and 21 percent of those charged with automobile theft.[7] It is obvious that prison statistics are not in constant ratio to the crimes committed, for there are wide variations in the use of fines, probation, and other alternatives to imprisonment. These variations indicate that if crimes known to the police are a good index of crimes committed, then arrests, prosecutions, convictions, and commitments to prison are not—at least for purposes of comparing types of crime.

However, even the number of crimes known to the police is not an adequate index of crime.[8] There are five examples of evidence for this assertion.

First, the number of crimes known to the police is certainly much smaller than the number actually committed. Sellin reports that the number of cases of shoplifting known to three Philadelphia department stores was greater than the total number of thefts of all kinds in the entire city which were known to the police.[9] In 1944 and 1945, the detectives of one Chicago department store arrested two-thirds as many adult women for shoplifting as were formally charged with petty larceny of all forms (including shoplifting) by the police in the entire city of Chicago.[10] Undoubtedly, this is due principally to the failure of victims to complain to the police. In one six-month period, only 8.7 percent of the discovered cases of shoplifting in four Chicago department stores were reported to the police department either as to the offense or the person caught in the offense.[11] Victims may consider the crime insignificant and not worth

---

[6] Federal Bureau of Investigation, op. cit., p. 101.

[7] Ibid., pp. 101.

[8] See S. B. Warner, "Report on Criminal Statistics," in National Commission on Law Observance and Enforcement, Report No. 3 (Washington: Government Printing Office, 1931); S. B. Warner, "Crimes Known to the Police—An Index of Crime," Harvard Law Review, 45:307–334, December, 1931; Audrey M. Davies, "Criminal Statistics and the National Commission's Report," Journal of Criminal Law and Criminology, 22:357–374, September–October, 1931.

[9] Sellin, Research Memorandum on Crime in the Depression, op. cit., p. 69.

[10] Loren E. Edwards, Shoplifting and Shrinkage Protection for Stores, Springfield, Ill.: Charles C Thomas, 1958, p. 130.

[11] Virgil W. Peterson, cited by Donald R. Taft, Criminology, Second Edition (New York: Macmillan, 1956), p. 63.

reporting, they may wish to avoid the publicity which might result if the crime were reported, they may wish to avoid the inconvenience of calling the police, appearing as a witness, etc., they may be opposed to the punitive policies of our legal system, or they may feel that the police are so inefficient that they will be unable to catch the offender even if the offense is reported.

Second, the number of crimes known to the police is a reasonably efficient index of crime only if the police are honest and efficient in making their reports. Police have an obligation to protect the reputation of their cities, and when this cannot be done efficiently under existing administrative machinery, it is sometimes accomplished statistically. Politicians up for reelection are likely to be accused of neglect of duty if the crime rate has gone up during their administration, and they are likely to be praised if the crime rate has declined. Consequently, political administrations often try to show statistically that during their term in office the crime rate declined. In Chicago, the number of known robberies increased from 1,263 to 14,544 between 1928 and 1931, and burglaries increased from 879 to 18,689 in the same period. This change was due almost completely to a change in the recording practices of the police following an investigation by the Chicago Crime Commission.[12] Similarly, in the 1952 annual report of the New York City police department, a revised system of recording crimes was cited as a major factor in the 254 percent rise in the city's crime rate between 1950 and 1951.[13] Bloch recently found a community in which the delinquency rate had apparently been cut in half by establishment of a youth bureau attached to the police department, but investigation indicated that the rate actually increased and that the reported drop was the result of a change in the reporting system.[14] Variations in crime rates among cities or among other jurisdictions must be interpreted with extreme caution, for the differences may be due merely to differential recording practices in the various police departments.

Third, the value of crimes known to the police as an index of crime is sharply limited by the fact that the ratio of crimes committed to crimes reported and recorded varies according to offense. As Sellin has said:

We cannot use the total recorded criminality. We must extract from the total the data for only those offenses in which the recorded sample is large enough to permit the assumption that a reasonably constant relationship exists between the recorded and the total criminality of these types. We may make that assumption when the offense seriously injures a strongly

[12] Virgil Peterson, "An Examination of Chicago's Law Enforcement Agencies," *Criminal Justice*, January, 1950, pp. 3–6.

[13] *The New York Times*, October 18, 1952, p. 32.

[14] Herbert A. Bloch, "Juvenile Delinquency: Myth or Threat," *Journal of Criminal Law and Criminology*, 49:303–309, November–December, 1958.

embraced social value, is of a public nature in the sense that it is likely to come to the attention of someone besides the victim, and induces the victim or those who are close to him to cooperate with the authorities in bringing the offender to justice.[15]

Fourth, variations in the criminal law may affect the volume of crimes known to the police, reducing the value of the index for comparative purposes. Behavior which is crime in one place or time may not be crime in another place or time; the difference reduces the value of the index for long-range comparative purposes. Further, categorization of an offense in one of the classifications used for recording may be unsystematized and irregular, so that variation in a particular offense is created when none exists in fact.[16] Philadelphia magistrates pay little attention to the charges against the bums who come before them; in 1950, as a consequence, there were 1,430 commitments of vagrants to the House of Correction, but only 1,241 arrests for that offense.[17] Similarly, comparisons of the crime rates of various countries are seriously limited by wide variations in the national legal systems. Such comparisons should be of decided value in securing an understanding of criminality, because these statistics show the wider variations which may not be apparent within a particular country. In Europe, considerable interest has developed in a program for the international codification of criminal laws and for the development of international statistics of crime and criminals. The essential problem is to develop units that can be used for international comparisons. Several interesting studies have been made on the basis of international statistics of crime.[18]

Fifth, the number of crimes known to the police must, for purposes of comparison, be stated in proportion to the population or to some other base, and the determination of this base is often difficult. United States census figures on the general population collected in the first year of a decade often must be used throughout the decade as the base for computing crime rates. Since the increasing United States population is not taken into account, the number of crimes per 100,000 population appears to increase each year throughout the decade. If 1960 population figures

[15] "The Significance of Records of Crime," *op. cit.*

[16] Cf. Samuel A. Stouffer, "Indices of Psychological Illness," in Paul F. Lazarsfeld and Morris Rosenberg, Editors, *The Language of Social Research* (Glencoe, Illinois: The Free Press, 1955), pp. 63–65.

[17] Caleb Foote, "Vagrancy-Type Law and Its Administration," *University of Pennsylvania Law Review*, 104:603–650, March, 1956, at p. 612.

[18] See especially Veli K. Verkko, *Verbrechen wider das Leben und Körperverletzungsverbrechen über die Bestimmung ihrer Entwicklungsrichtung und Stufe* (translated from the Finnish, 1931, Helsinki: Valtioneuvoston kirjapaino, 1937); Veli K. Verkko, *Väkivaltarikollisuuden Riippuvaisuus Kansanluonteesta ja Muista Etnillisistä* (Helsinki, 1936); E. Hacker, *Kriminalstatistiche und Kriminalaetiologische Berichte* (Miskolc: Ludwing, 1941); Mabel A. Elliott, "Perspectives on the American Crime Problem," *Social Problems*, 5:184–193, Winter, 1957.

are used to compute the crime rates for both 1960 and 1969, for example, the latter year shows a higher rate, not because of an increase in crime, but because the population increase between 1960 and 1969 is not included in the base for the 1969 rate. Similarly, 1969 crime rates based on 1960 population figures will be higher than 1970 rates based on the 1970 population figures, for the 1970 rates take into account the increases which took place between 1960 and 1970. Also, the population figures must be corrected for variations in age, sex, racial composition, and urban-rural composition, and much of this information is available only in the years in which decennial enumerations of the population are made. Moreover, in many cases it is necessary to have other information. For instance, in 1941 a total of 8,605 automobile thefts were reported to the Los Angeles police, in comparison to 8,424 in 1940. This is a raw, uncorrected, increase of 2.15 percent. When the number of thefts is stated in proportion to the size of the population in the two years, however, the theft rate in 1941 is only .49 percent higher than the rate in 1940. But when the number of vehicles in Los Angeles in the two years is taken into account, it may be seen that the automobile theft rate actually *decreased* between 1940 and 1941. In 1940 there were 154.4 automobiles stolen for every 10,000 motor vehicle registrations; in 1941 the rate was 138.6, or a decrease of 10.2 percent. A further refinement could be made, for not all the "motor vehicles" registered were automobiles. The difficulty of securing an adequate base for computing a rate is evident.

SOURCES OF STATISTICS ON CRIME IN THE UNITED STATES.   Police, court, and prison statistics may be published by the agency which collects them, or they may be reported to a central state or federal agency which organizes, combines, and publishes the statistics from many agencies. Only rarely do the local or central agencies do more than catalog the incidence of various crimes; computation of rates, analyses of interrelationships between various statistical facts, and the making of inferences about the statistics are left to outside research workers. The various agencies, in other words, merely take censuses of various dimensions of the criminal population, just as the Department of Commerce takes censuses of the total United States population. Some of the agencies explicitly state the limitations of the statistics which they publish, but most of them do not.

*Federal Reports.*   Since 1930, the United States Department of Justice has published a periodical bulletin on crime statistics, *Uniform Crime Reports.* The number of known crimes reported to the F.B.I. by the police of about 3,000 cities and towns is used as an index of "major" crimes (murder, rape, aggravated assault, burglary, robbery, larceny, and automobile theft), and the "arrests" (fingerprint records sent to the F.B.I.) are used as an index of other crimes. The bulletin was first published monthly, became a quarterly in 1932, was converted into a semi-annual publication during World War II, and became an annual publication in 1959. Local police departments are supplied with a manual on reporting, but participation by police departments is on a voluntary basis. Consequently not all communities are covered and the large metropolitan centers are over-represented. In 1964 the total population represented in one set of statistics on arrests numbered 132 million, while the total population of the United States was about 191 million.[19] Although the *Uniform Crime Reports* have many limitations and the F.B.I. will not vouch for their accuracy, they comprise the best available indexes of crime in the United States. Table I shows the estimated number of serious crimes known to the police in 1964, and Table II shows the number of police department arrests recorded in 1964 by the F.B.I. on the basis of the fingerprint cards sent to it. In the latter table it should be noted that only 16.7 percent of the arrests were for the seven "major" crimes and that there is a great discrepancy between the estimated number of major crimes committed and the number of arrests for those crimes.

The Department of Justice also publishes, through the Federal Bureau

## TABLE I

ESTIMATED NUMBER OF MAJOR CRIMES IN THE UNITED STATES, 1964[20]

| Crime Index Classification | Estimated Crime, 1964 | | Percent Change Over 1963 | |
|---|---|---|---|---|
| | Number | Rate Per 100,000 Inhabitants | Number | Rate |
| Total | 2,604,400 | 1,361.2 | +13 | +11 |
| Murder | 9,250 | 4.8 | +8 | +7 |
| Forcible rape | 20,550 | 10.7 | +21 | +20 |
| Robbery | 111,750 | 58.4 | +12 | +10 |
| Aggravated assault | 184,900 | 96.6 | +17 | +15 |
| Burglary | 1,110,500 | 580.4 | +12 | +11 |
| Larceny $50 and over | 704,500 | 368.2 | +13 | +11 |
| Auto theft | 463,000 | 242.0 | +16 | +14 |

[19] Federal Bureau of Investigation, United States Department of Justice, *Uniform Crime Reports for the United States, 1964* (Washington: Government Printing Office, 1965), p. 106.

For a history of this bulletin and a critique of the statistics reported in it, see Marvin E. Wolfgang, "Uniform Crime Reports: A Critical Appraisal," *University of Pennsylvania Law Review*, 111:708–738, April, 1963.

[20] *Ibid.*, p. 3. The estimated crime totals for the United States appearing in this table are not comparable to such totals published in *Uniform Crime Reports* in the years prior to 1959. "Negligent manslaughter" has been omitted. "Larceny" no longer includes petty offenses, and "rape" no longer includes "statutory rape."

of Prisons, statistics on commitments to state and federal penal institutions in the United States. This series, *National Prisoner Statistics*, was published until 1948 by the Bureau of the Census, with the title *Prisoners in State and Federal Prisons and Reformatories*. Included are data on the number of commitments to the various institutions, the number of prisoners present at the end of each year, and the number of prisoners discharged under each of the various systems of release. When the series was

## TABLE II

TOTAL ARRESTS, DISTRIBUTION BY SEX, 1964[21]

| Offense Charged | Number | | | Percent | | |
|---|---|---|---|---|---|---|
| | Total | Male | Female | Total | Male | Female |
| Total | 4,685,030 | 4,138,099 | 546,981 | 100.0 | 100.0 | 100.0 |
| Criminal homicide | 9,097 | 7,686 | 1,411 | .2 | .2 | .2 |
| Forcible rape | 9,450 | 9,450 | — | .2 | .2 | — |
| Robbery | 39,134 | 37,062 | 2,072 | .8 | .9 | .4 |
| Aggravated assault | 79,895 | 69,018 | 10,877 | 1.7 | 1.7 | 2.0 |
| Burglary—breaking or entering | 187,000 | 180,153 | 6,847 | 4.0 | 4.4 | 1.3 |
| Larceny—theft | 358,569 | 285,705 | 72,864 | 7.7 | 6.9 | 13.3 |
| Auto theft | 97,356 | 93,241 | 4,115 | 2.1 | 2.3 | .8 |
| Other assaults | 191,455 | 171,906 | 19,549 | 4.1 | 4.2 | 3.6 |
| Arson | 5,220 | 4,765 | 455 | .1 | .1 | .1 |
| Forgery and counterfeiting | 30,637 | 25,064 | 5,573 | .7 | .6 | 1.0 |
| Fraud | 45,998 | 37,238 | 8,760 | 1.0 | .9 | 1.6 |
| Embezzlement | 8,610 | 7,124 | 1,486 | .2 | .2 | .3 |
| Stolen property; buying, receiving, possessing | 18,152 | 16,374 | 1,778 | .4 | .4 | .3 |
| Vandalism | 76,814 | 72,173 | 4,641 | 1.6 | 1.7 | .8 |
| Weapons; carrying, possessing, etc. | 47,287 | 44,172 | 3,115 | 1.0 | 1.1 | .6 |
| Prostitution and commercialized vice | 28,190 | 6,191 | 21,999 | .6 | .1 | 4.0 |
| Sex offenses (except forcible rape and prostitution) | 58,082 | 49,041 | 9,041 | 1.2 | 1.2 | 1.7 |
| Narcotic drug laws | 37,802 | 32,492 | 5,310 | .8 | .8 | 1.0 |
| Gambling | 103,814 | 95,264 | 8,550 | 2.2 | 2.3 | 1.6 |
| Offenses against family and children | 57,454 | 52,118 | 5,336 | 1.2 | 1.3 | 1.0 |
| Driving under the influence | 225,672 | 210,871 | 14,801 | 4.8 | 5.1 | 2.7 |
| Liquor laws | 153,829 | 135,001 | 18,828 | 3.3 | 3.3 | 3.4 |
| Drunkenness | 1,458,821 | 1,342,494 | 116,327 | 31.1 | 32.4 | 21.3 |
| Disorderly conduct | 475,756 | 412,080 | 63,676 | 10.2 | 10.0 | 11.6 |
| Vagrancy | 132,955 | 120,876 | 12,079 | 2.8 | 2.9 | 2.2 |
| All other offenses (except traffic) | 510,624 | 437,501 | 73,123 | 10.9 | 10.6 | 13.4 |
| Suspicion | 102,106 | 91,147 | 10,959 | 2.2 | 2.2 | 2.0 |
| Curfew and loitering law violations | 64,784 | 52,484 | 12,300 | 1.4 | 1.3 | 2.2 |
| Runaways | 70,517 | 39,408 | 31,109 | 1.5 | 1.0 | 5.7 |

[21] *Ibid.*, p .112.

published by the Bureau of the Census, information about the type of crime, age, race, and sex of prisoners also was included. The annual report of the Federal Bureau of Prisons, *Federal Prisons* (formerly named *Federal Offender*), gives statistical data on persons convicted of violations of federal laws. Table III presents *National Prisoner Statistics* data on the recent trends in rates of commitment to both state and federal institutions.

Local coroners keep records of known homicides and the National Office of Vital Statistics summarizes annually in *Vital Statistics in the United States* the homicide rates for all states and cities in the "registration area." Until 1946, these statistics were published by the Bureau of the Census. The registration area is the area covered by the coroner's statistics; since 1933 this area has contained the entire population of the United States. Table IV shows the number of deaths by homicide per hundred thousand population in the entire registration area and in those states which were in the registration areas in 1900. The original registration area was composed almost entirely of New England states, to which have been added many southern and western states to compose the present registration area. The states that have been added have distinctly higher homicide rates than the original states. The only figures that are significant for the purpose of determining the trend before 1933, therefore, are those in the original registration area. Moreover, the reports for the period 1900–1904 were declared by the Director of the Census to be "incorrect and absolutely misleading." These inaccuracies were not completely corrected until shortly before 1910. Consequently, the trend in the original area during the period 1910–1934, for which the figures are accurate, is from 4.1 to 4.7, with a decrease in 1935–1939 to 3.2 and a continued decrease during the period of 1940–1963. Even if homicides had increased, it would not necessarily follow that murder and felonious manslaughter, as ordinarily understood, had increased. These homicides include justifiable and excusable homicides, such as killing in self-defense, killing a prisoner who is trying to escape, and similar acts. Also, the principal increase in homicides has probably been due to homicides by negligence, especially in the form of automobile killings. The number of homicides by negligence is at present about equal to the number of other criminal homicides. Since the total number of homicides has decreased and since the portion of all homicides which are due to negligence has increased, it necessarily follows that murder, as popularly understood, has decreased very significantly.

The homicide rate in the United States is, however, much higher than in many European countries. In 1931, the average rate in thirty-one American cities was 10.8 per 100,000 population, while it was 0.3 in Amsterdam, 0.6 in Liverpool, 1.8 in Berlin, 1.9 in Prague, 2.7 in Vienna, 3.3 in Brussels,

## TABLE III

PRISONERS IN INSTITUTIONS AND RECEIVED FROM COURT, 1939–1963,
RATES PER 100,000 OF THE ESTIMATED CIVILIAN POPULATION[22]

| Year | Present at End of Year | | | Received from Court | | | |
| | All Institutions | Federal Institutions | State Institutions | All Institutions | Federal Institutions | State Institutions | |
| --- | --- | --- | --- | --- | --- | --- | --- |
| 1939 | 137.1 | 15.0 | 122.0 | * | * | * | |
| 1940 | 131.7 | 14.6 | 117.1 | 55.4 | 11.5 | 44.0 | |
| 1941 | 125.3 | 14.0 | 111.3 | 52.0 | 11.6 | 40.4 | |
| 1942 | 116.8 | 12.9 | 103.8 | 45.7 | 10.7 | 35.0 | |
| 1943 | 107.9 | 12.7 | 95.2 | 39.4 | 9.6 | 29.8 | |
| 1944 | 104.1 | 14.3 | 89.9 | 39.4 | 11.0 | 28.4 | |
| 1945 | 99.9 | 13.9 | 86.0 | 39.8 | 10.6 | 29.2 | |
| 1946 | 99.4 | 12.5 | 86.9 | 43.5 | 10.6 | 32.9 | |
| 1947 | 105.0 | 11.9 | 93.1 | 45.0 | 9.0 | 36.0 | |
| 1948 | 106.6 | 11.2 | 95.4 | 43.6 | 8.5 | 35.1 | |
| 1949 | 109.9 | 11.3 | 98.6 | 46.3 | 8.8 | 37.5 | |
| 1950 | 110.3 | 11.4 | 98.9 | 46.1 | 9.5 | 36.7 | |
| 1951 | 108.9 | 11.4 | 97.4 | 44.1 | 9.3 | 34.9 | |
| 1952 | 108.8 | 11.6 | 97.1 | 45.8 | 9.9 | 35.9 | |
| 1953 | 110.2 | 12.3 | 97.9 | 47.1 | 10.4 | 36.7 | |
| 1954 | 113.8 | 12.4 | 101.3 | 50.3 | 10.4 | 40.0 | |
| 1955 | 113.4 | 12.3 | 101.1 | 47.9 | 9.3 | 38.5 | |
| 1956 | 113.5 | 12.1 | 101.4 | 46.7 | 8.1 | 38.6 | |
| 1957 | 114.9 | 12.0 | 102.9 | 47.4 | 7.8 | 39.5 | |
| 1958 | 118.8 | 12.5 | 106.3 | 51.2 | 8.0 | 43.3 | |
| 1959 | 117.5 | 12.7 | 104.8 | 49.4 | 7.9 | 41.5 | |
| 1960 | 118.6 | 12.9 | 105.7 | 49.4 | 7.6 | 41.7 | |
| 1961 | 120.8 | 13.0 | 107.8 | 51.3 | 7.4 | 43.9 | |
| 1962 | 118.3 | 12.9 | 105.3 | 48.2 | 7.3 | 40.8 | |
| 1963 | 115.7 | 12.3 | 103.4 | 46.8 | 6.9 | 39.9 | |

* Comparable data not available.

and 4.4 in Rome.[23] Such comparisons should not be accepted uncritically because the definitions of homicide vary in the several nations, and especially many deaths which are classified as homicides in the United States are not so classified in some European countries. Even if the comparison is regarded as valid, a considerable part of the difference, here also, is probably due to the greater frequency of excusable and justifiable homicides and of homicides due to automobiles in the United States. Wide differences within the United States are found. In 1964, Dallas had the

[22] Federal Bureau of Prisons, "Prisoners in State and Federal Institutions, 1963," National Prisoner Statistics, No. 36, December, 1964, Table 1, p. 12.

[23] Frederick Hoffman, "The Homicide Record for 1931," Spectator, 128:4–5, 12–13, March 31, 1932.

TABLE IV

AVERAGE ANNUAL NUMBER OF HOMICIDES PER 100,000
POPULATION, UNITED STATES[24]

| Years | Entire Registration Area | Registration Area of 1900 |
|---|---|---|
| 1900–04 | 2.4 | 1.2 |
| 1905–09 | 5.6 | 3.1 |
| 1910–14 | 6.7 | 4.1 |
| 1915–19 | 7.2 | 4.0 |
| 1920–24 | 8.1 | 4.4 |
| 1925–29 | 8.7 | 4.9 |
| 1930–34 | 9.1 | 4.7 |
| 1935–39 | 7.4 | 3.2 |
| 1940–44 | 5.7 | — |
| 1945–49 | 5.7 | — |
| 1950–54 | 5.0 | — |
| 1955–59 | 4.5 | — |
| 1960–63 | 4.8 | — |

highest rate of any American city with more than a million population, having nearly twice as high a rate as New York or Cleveland, and more than four times the rate of Pittsburgh and Boston.

Statistics on juvenile delinquency are also published by the federal government, through the Children's Bureau of the Social Security Administration. Until 1939, the reports were issued as bulletins called *Children in the Courts*; from 1939 to 1945 they appeared occasionally as supplements to the Children's Bureau publication, *The Child*; since 1945 they have been published irregularly in mimeographed form and in a special *Children's Bureau Statistical Series*. Until 1955, only about 400 courts, out of approximately 3,000 courts that deal with children's cases, made reports to the Bureau. In 1955, the Bureau revised its statistical reporting plan to include a national sample representative of all juvenile courts. The earlier Children's Bureau statistics have been criticized on the ground that a very small proportion of the population is represented, that the standards for reporting are not uniform, that definitions of delinquency vary from jurisdiction to jurisdiction, that the ages of children over whom the courts have jurisdiction varies, and that there are variations in the proportions of juvenile delinquents who are referred to the courts.[25] Table V shows the recent

[24] United States Department of Health, Education and Welfare, National Center for Health Statistics, *Vital Statistics of the United States, 1963* (Washington: 1964), Vol. 2, Part A, p. 1–8.

[25] See James F. Short, Jr. and F. Ivan Nye, "Extent of Unrecorded Juvenile Delinquency: Tentative Conclusions," *Journal of Criminal Law and Criminology*, 49:296–302, November–December, 1958.

# TABLE V

TREND IN DELINQUENCY CASES DISPOSED OF BY JUVENILE COURTS,
UNITED STATES, 1940–1963[26]

| Year | Delinquency Cases[a] | | Child Population of U.S. (10–17 Years of Age)[b] |
|---|---|---|---|
| | Including Traffic | Excluding Traffic | |
| 1940 | 200,000 | | 19,138,000 |
| 1941 | 224,000 | | 18,916,000 |
| 1942 | 250,000 | | 18,648,000 |
| 1943 | 344,000 | | 18,309,000 |
| 1944 | 330,000 | | 17,738,000 |
| 1945 | 344,000 | | 17,512,000 |
| 1946 | 295,000 | | 17,419,000 |
| 1947 | 262,000 | | 17,344,000 |
| 1948 | 254,000 | | 17,314,000 |
| 1949 | 272,000 | | 17,365,000 |
| 1950 | 280,000 | | 17,398,000 |
| 1951 | 298,000 | | 17,705,000 |
| 1952 | 332,000 | | 18,201,000 |
| 1953 | 374,000 | | 18,980,000 |
| 1954 | 395,000 | | 19,551,000 |
| 1955 | 431,000 | | 20,112,000 |
| 1956 | 520,000 | | 20,623,000 |
| 1957 | 603,000 | 440,000 | 22,173,000 |
| 1958 | 703,000[c] | 473,000 | 23,443,000 |
| 1959 | 773,000[c] | 483,000 | 24,607,000 |
| 1960 | 813,000 | 510,000 | 25,364,000 |
| 1961 | 801,000 | 503,000 | 26,023,000 |
| 1962 | 867,000 | 555,000 | 26,936,000 |
| 1963 | 967,000 | 601,000 | 27,983,000 |

[a] Data for 1955–1963 estimated from the national sample of juvenile courts. Data prior to 1955 estimated by the Children's Bureau, based on reports from a comparable group of courts. Inclusion of data for Alaska and Hawaii beginning in 1960 does not materially affect the trend.

[b] Data based on estimates from Bureau of Census, U.S. Department of Commerce (Current Population Reports, Series P-25).

[c] Much of the increase is accounted for in one State by an administrative change in the method of handling juvenile traffic cases.

[26] U. S. Department of Health, Education and Welfare, *Juvenile Court Statistics, 1963* (Washington: Children's Bureau, Statistical Series No. 79, 1964), p. 15. See Figure I, p. 255, below.

trends in juvenile delinquency, as measured by the representative national sample for 1955–63 and by reports from another group of courts for 1940–55.

*State Reports.*   Generally, the states are less efficient than the federal government in making reliable crime statistics available. In most states, one or more state departments obtain reports from a particular type of county or municipal official, and no attempt is made to use a uniform system of reporting, so that the resulting summaries would be comparable. The Attorney General may receive information from county attorneys, the Department of Correction may receive information from sheriffs, the Department of Public Welfare from juvenile courts and welfare agencies dealing with delinquency, etc. In a few states, the only criminal statistics are those published by individual institutions or agencies. Only eleven states—California, Hawaii, Louisiana, Massachusetts, Michigan, Minnesota, New York, Pennsylvania, Rhode Island, South Dakota, and Texas—have central statistical bureaus which collect and publish statistical information drawn from reports made by a variety of local, county, or state agencies. Some of these bureaus have very comprehensive programs, but others are greatly limited in their activities.[27] For some states, crimes known to the police, arrests, and convictions are summarized, but in most states the statistics are restricted to the number of persons admitted to probation, prison, and parole. The data in Table VI are from the Bureau of Statistics, California Department of Justice; this Bureau acts as a statistical agency for the Department of Corrections.

*Other Reports.*   Statistics on specific crimes are published regularly by some federal and state agencies, and certain private organizations maintain running accounts of the offenses committed against them. The Federal Deposit Insurance Corporation, the Treasury Department, and the Attorney General's Department, for example, all publish annual indexes of the number of violations of certain federal laws. Similarly, the American Bankers Association keeps records of offenses against banks; fidelity bonding companies keep records of crimes against bonded business firms, and large corporations record their annual losses to various kinds of crime. Ordinarily, the statistics reported by a single agency or private organization are not comparable with the statistics compiled and published for the entire nation or for an entire state.

Government agencies and private foundations also have promoted and conducted a number of crime surveys, one general aim of which has been

[27] Thorsten Sellin, "The Uniform Criminal Statistics Act," *Journal of Criminal Law and Criminology*, 40:679–700, March–April, 1950.

## TABLE VI

MALE PRISONERS NEWLY RECEIVED FROM COURT
CALIFORNIA, 1959 AND 1960[28]

| Offense | 1959 | | 1960 | | Percent Change in Rate— 1960 Over 1959 |
|---|---|---|---|---|---|
| | Number | Rate per 100,000 Population* | Number | Rate per 100,000 Population* | |
| Total | 5,426 | 35.5 | 5,701 | 35.9 | 1.2 |
| Homicide | 197 | 1.3 | 218 | 1.4 | 6.2 |
| Robbery | 747 | 4.9 | 781 | 4.9 | 0.6 |
| Assault | 183 | 1.2 | 187 | 1.2 | —1.7 |
| Burglary | 1,070 | 7.0 | 1,143 | 7.2 | 3.0 |
| Theft except auto | 339 | 2.2 | 313 | 2.0 | —10.9 |
| Auto theft | 226 | 1.5 | 280 | 1.8 | 19.6 |
| Forgery and checks | 1,022 | 6.7 | 1,147 | 7.2 | 8.2 |
| Sex offenses | 344 | 2.3 | 296 | 1.9 | —16.9 |
| Rape | 129 | — | 109 | — | — |
| Other sex offenses | 215 | — | 187 | — | — |
| Narcotics | 920 | 6.0 | 940 | 5.9 | —1.5 |
| Other offenses | 378 | 2.5 | 396 | 2.5 | 0.4 |

* California population estimates from State Department of Finance publication, "California's Population," August 1959, and special report December 16, 1960.

the discovery of the proportions of crimes not reported in the usual statistics of crime. Among the more famous surveys are the Cleveland survey, the Missouri survey, the Illinois survey, the study by the "Wickersham Commission," the Oregon survey, and the Attorney General's survey.[29]

Occasionally, a comprehensive first-hand investigation by an independent research worker produces new statistical indexes. Short and Nye have demonstrated that statistics compiled from reports of delinquencies by offenders are acceptable and desirable in scientific analyses.[30] Gehlke and Sutherland organized the principal available statistics for the purpose of determining what they show regarding the trend in crime rates from 1900 to 1930. The general conclusion is that, when traffic offenses and drunkenness are excluded, these statistics show a slight upward trend during this

28 *California Prisoners, 1960* (Sacramento: Department of Corrections, 1961), p. 12.
29 Roscoe Pound and Felix Frankfurter, Editors, *Criminal Justice in Cleveland* (Cleveland: The Cleveland Foundation, 1922); Missouri Association for Criminal Justice, Survey Committee, *The Missouri Crime Survey* (New York: Macmillan, 1926); Illinois Association for Criminal Justice, *The Illinois Crime Survey* (Chicago: Author, 1929); National Commission on Law Observance and Enforcement, *Reports* (Washington: Government Printing Office, 1931); Wayne L. Morse and Ronald H. Beattie, *Survey of the Administration of Justice in Oregon* (Eugene: University of Oregon Press, 1932); *Attorney General's Survey of Release Procedures*, 5 volumes (Washington: Government Printing Office, 1939–40).
30 James F. Short, Jr., and F. Ivan Nye, "Reported Behavior as a Criterion of Deviant Behavior," *Social Problems*, 5:207–213, Winter, 1957.

period, with no sudden surge that could be called a crime wave.[31] An analysis of Canadian criminal statistics for the same period indicated that the crime rate increased, but that if urbanization had remained constant the crime rate would have remained constant, also.[32]

THE PERVASIVENESS OF CRIME IN THE UNITED STATES. Crime is much more general and pervasive than the ordinary statistics indicate, and an entirely incorrect impression regarding criminality is formed if conclusions are limited to these statistics. Opposition to law has been a tradition in the United States. Popular rebellions against laws constitute an almost continuous series from the early colonial period to the prohibition controversy, and the violations of many of the early laws were quite as general as were the violations of the national prohibition law. The manufacture of nails and of other commodities in violation of English law, the sale of firearms and of liquor to Indians, smuggling and other violations of laws regulating commerce, Shay's Rebellion in 1787, the whiskey insurrection in 1794, trading with the enemy during the War of 1812, riots against the Catholics, the Irish, and the Mormons, the Dorr Rebellion in 1841–1842, trading in slaves, harboring fugitive slaves, Negro disfranchisement, violation of antitrust laws, violation of banking laws, and violation of prohibition laws are some of these popular rebellions.[33] These violations of law cannot be measured statistically, and it is not possible to determine from the descriptions whether the number of violations in such cases has increased.

The criminal tradition is also reflected in the fact that certain occasions are defined as holidays from morality. Halloween, New Year's Eve, election nights, spring celebrations, and important football victories are occasions of this nature. Crimes are committed on these occasions by persons who would ordinarily not commit such crimes, and may take the form of destruction of property and of assaults. Individual crimes are committed primarily in a spirit of exuberance, and they coincide with institutionalized collective behavior involving many persons. There is much evidence that the delinquency of boys in the deteriorated areas is an extension of this attitude through the entire year. Strikes are in certain respects like these moral holidays. There is a gathering of persons with a common interest,

[31] C. E. Gehlke and E. H. Sutherland, "Crime and Punishment," in President's Research Committee on Social Trends, *Recent Social Trends in the United States* (New York: McGraw-Hill, 1933), Volume XX, pp. 1123–1135.

[32] R. E. Watts, "The Influence of Population Density on Crime," *Journal of the American Statistical Association*, 26:11–20, March, 1931.

[33] See Mabel A. Elliott, "Crime and the Frontier Mores," *American Sociological Review*, 9:185–192, April, 1944.

an attitude during the early period of the strike which is much like that of a picnic, and an exuberance which is like that of the spring celebration. Assaults and destruction of property occur on these occasions, just as on other holidays from morality. The violation of law, however, is much more purposive in the strike than in these other outbursts. Factory workers, skilled tradesmen, and farmers, without much differentiation, violate the laws on such occasions. These holidays from morality are so generally recognized that penalties for lawlessness seldom result.

The fact that almost all persons have at some time deliberately committed crimes, often of a serious nature, is further evidence of our criminal tradition. In a questionnaire study, 1,020 men and 678 women were asked to check which of 49 offenses they had committed.[34] In the distribution of the questionnaire an effort was made to obtain a balanced religious and racial cross-section of the population, but the group of subjects contained an excess of persons from upper social classes. Ninety-one percent of the subjects admitted that they had committed one or more offenses, excluding juvenile delinquencies, for which they could have received a jail or prison sentence. Men had an average of 18 and women an average of 11 adult offenses. Thirteen percent of the men admitted to grand larceny, 26 percent to auto theft, 17 percent to burglary, and 11 percent to robbery. The corresponding figures for women were 11, 8, 11, and 1. Sixty-four percent of the men and 27 percent of the women admitted to committing at least one felony. Such percentages can be accepted only with many reservations. However, the study certainly reveals that the number of crimes committed is far greater than the number reported in crime statistics, as do studies of students at the University of Oslo and the University of Uppsala.[35] In a similar study of juvenile delinquencies Short found that a group of 65 college boys reported that they had committed an average of 9.9 offenses against property, 12.3 behavior problem offenses, 9.6 offenses against persons, 16.5 sex offenses, 20.8 "casual offenses," and 12.6 miscellaneous offenses. A group of 94 training school boys reported that they had committed an average of 13.4 offenses against property and 19.1 behavior problem offenses; their average number of other offenses was about the same as that of the college boys. In comparison with the training school boys, the college men had only very rarely been arrested for

[34] James S. Wallerstein and Clement J. Wyle, "Our Law-Abiding Law-Breakers," *Probation*, 25:107–112, March–April, 1947.

[35] Johs. Andenaes, Knut Sveri, and Ragnar Hauge, "Kriminalitetshyppigheten hos Ustraffede," *Nordisk Tidsskrift for Kriminalvidenskab*, 48:97–112, 1960; Ola Nyquist and Ivar Strahl, "Kriminalitetshyppigheten hos Ustraffede," *Ibid.*, 48:113–117, 1960.

their offenses.[36] One explanation for this differential lies in the fact that many of the complaints to juvenile authorities are made by parents against their own children—parents of college students do not file complaints as frequently as do the parents of noncollege students.[37]

3    White-collar crimes—crimes committed by persons of respectability and high social status in the course of their occupations—also are extremely widespread, but an index of their frequency is not found in police reports. Prosecution for this kind of crime frequently is avoided because of the political or financial importance of the parties concerned, because of the apparent triviality of the crimes, or because of the difficulty of securing evidence sufficient for prosecution, particularly in the cases of crimes by corporations.[38] Even more important, methods other than prosecution in the criminal courts are frequently used to protect society against white-collar crime—action may be taken in the civil courts or in hearings before boards and commissions. Consequently, a precise statement regarding the extent of white-collar crime is impossible. Differences in administrative procedures, however, do not justify the designation of this behavior as something other than crime.[39] In general, underlying these failures to prosecute is the lack of a developed social feeling and ethical code in the groups concerned and, to some extent, in the general public. The danger from robbery or kidnaping is clearly realized, for they involve direct sensory processes and are based on social relations which have existed for many centuries. Theft by fraudulent advertisements and prospectuses is a recent development, and affects persons who may be thousands of miles away from the thief. Codes of behavior have not been developed in regard to this behavior. These white-collar criminals, however, are by far the most dangerous to society of any type of criminal from the point of view of effects on private property and social institutions.[40]

---

[36] James F. Short, Jr., "A Report on the Incidence of Criminal Behavior, Arrests, and Convictions in Selected Groups," *Research Studies of the State College of Washington*, 22:110–118, June, 1954.

[37] See Austin L. Porterfield, "Delinquency and Its Outcome in Court and College," *American Journal of Sociology*, 49:199–208, November, 1943.

[38] See Edwin H. Sutherland, "White Collar Criminality," *American Sociological Review*, 5:1–12, February, 1940.

[39] *Cf.* Edwin H. Sutherland, "Is 'White Collar Crime' Crime?" *American Sociological Review*, 10:132–137, April, 1945. See also Vilhelm Aubert, "White Collar Crime and Social Structure," *American Journal of Sociology*, 58:263–271, November, 1952.

[40] See Edwin H. Sutherland, "Crime and Business," *The Annals of the American Academy of Political and Social Science*, 217:112–118, September, 1941.

An analysis has been made of the number of instances in which 70 of the largest United States mining, manufacturing, and mercantile corporations violated, over a period of about 40 years, the laws outlawing the following practices: restraint of trade; misrepresentation in advertising; infringements of patents, trademarks, and copyrights; "unfair labor practices" as defined by the National Labor Relations Law and other laws; rebates; financial fraud and violation of trust; violations of war regulations; and some miscellaneous activities.[41] The records reveal that every one of the seventy corporations had violated one or more of the laws, with an average of about 13 adverse decisions per corporation and a range of from one to fifty adverse decisions per corporation. The corporations had a total of 307 adverse decisions on charges of restraint of trade, 222 adverse decisions on charges of infringements, 158 adverse decisions under the National Labor Relations Law, 97 adverse decisions under the laws regulating advertising, and 196 adverse decisions on charges of violating other laws. Thus, generally, the official records reveal that these corporations violated the trade regulations with great frequency. The "habitual criminal" laws of some states impose severe penalties on criminals convicted the third or fourth time. If this criterion were used here, about 90 percent of the large corporations studied are habitual white-collar criminals. Moreover, this enumeration of official decisions is far from complete and it is concerned with violations of only a few laws. Even a complete enumeration of all adverse decisions against all corporations would represent only a crude index of the total amount of crime perpetrated by those corporations.

Financial corporations and institutions also have a high incidence of hidden criminality. The Comptroller of the Currency reported that approximately three-fourths of the national banks examined in a particular quarter were found to be violating the national banking laws. Dishonesty was found in 50.4 percent of the national bank failures during the period 1865–1899, and in 61.4 percent during the period 1900–1919. The highest rate of dishonesty in bank failures was found in the New England banks in the period before 1900, where it was 76.5 percent, but after 1900 this decreased to 58.3 percent, which was slightly less than the average in the United States.[42] Lie detector tests of the employees of certain Chicago banks showed that 20 percent of them had taken

41 Edwin H. Sutherland, White Collar Crime (New York: Dryden Press, 1949).
42 These statistics were included in the annual reports of the Comptroller of the Currency and of the Department of the Treasury until 1923, when they were discontinued. See, also, Thomas P. Kane, The Romance and Tragedy of Banking (New York: The Bankers' Publishing Company, 1922), pp. 320–321 and 368.

money or property from the bank, and in almost all cases these tests were supported by subsequent confessions.[43]

Fraud, also, is frequently a white-collar crime. The statistics on crime in European countries show a general trend toward a decrease in crimes of violence and an increase in crimes involving fraud. It is probable that the trend is even more pronounced in America, but neither the trend nor the present extent of fraud can be determined by available statistics. It is probable, also, that fraud is the most prevalent crime in America. Insull, after his flight from America to escape prosecution for fraud and embezzlement, is quoted as saying that he could not understand why people in the United States hated him so much, for he had done only what all other businessmen had been doing. Misleading balance sheets which public accountants have been able to invent and develop; wash sales by which the value of a security is fraudulently determined; concessions in rent by real estate dealers for the purpose of fraudulently increasing the sales price of property; excessive and misleading claims made by the manufacturers, vendors, and advertisers of patent medicines, toothpaste, cosmetics, and many other articles; transfer of deteriorated securities from the banker's own possession to the trust funds under his direction; and a considerable part of present-day salesmanship and of advertising—all these examples illustrate this kind of criminality. These things represent either active fraud with the intent to deceive the prospective purchaser or else misrepresentation by silence. Expert techniques of concealment have developed in many occupations for the purpose of preventing the purchaser from learning the defects of the commodity. Not many farmers would sell hogs with the knowledge that the hogs were infected with cholera and would die within a few days, and those farmers who did this would be regarded as dishonest, even if the misrepresentation consisted merely in silence regarding the danger. On the other hand, not many brokers or bankers would hesitate to sell securities which, by advance information, they had learned would soon be worthless, and the few who did refrain from immediate sale would be regarded as foolish. The physical disease of the hogs is more readily appreciated than the financial disease of the securities, and the effects are likely to be more definitely recognized. Defects in commodities are frequently concealed and labels often misrepresent. Shirting of inferior quality may be filled with clay in order that the defects may be con-

[43] F. P. McEvoy, "The Lie Detector Goes Into Business," *Reader's Digest*, 38:69–72, February, 1941; F. E. Inbau, "Scientific Investigation in Criminal Cases," *Journal of Criminal Law and Criminology*, 24:1140–1148, March–April, 1934.

cealed until the sale is consummated. This is essentially the same principle that was used by the old horse-trader in concealing the blemishes in the horses. Manufacturers offer merchants a wide variety of "list prices" for the same item, so that the merchants can advertise that they sell at a very small percentage of "list price." These cases of misrepresentation and fraud have not been subject to prosecution in most cases, for the courts have operated on the principle *caveat emptor*, which has meant that the purchaser must protect himself against ordinary dishonesty and could appeal to the courts for protection only against extraordinary dishonesty. President Roosevelt in 1933 insisted that the principle be reversed and *caveat vendor* be substituted, especially with regard to securities.

An immense amount of fraud is involved in insurance, both on the part of the insured and the insurers. Murders are committed, houses burned, automobiles destroyed, and sickness or injury feigned in order that insurance may be collected. Fraud in personal injury cases is unusually extensive, and was once an important source of income for unscrupulous lawyers, known as "ambulance chasers," who generally worked on contingent fees. Fraud in these cases seldom results in prosecution, although murder and arson may be occasion for prosecution of those crimes as such. The insurance company is seldom free to prosecute for fraud, for it seldom has clean hands. The insurance company adopts the usual policy that "business is business" and that sentiment must be eliminated; it makes a settlement at the lowest possible figure rather than at the figure which the nature of the loss justifies. For this purpose, claim agents, lawyers, and physicians for the insurance company frequently practice misrepresentation. Physicians for the company for instance, frequently minimize the extent of injuries, in the expectation that the physician on the other side will magnify them. Also, in many cases the claim agent collects an additional sum for settlement and divides this with the attorney for the injured party.

Fraud is also present in the legal profession. Popular feeling inclines to the belief that a lawyer cannot be successful if completely honest and that almost any law firm will take any case within its field of specialization no matter how extreme the dishonesty required for representing the interests of the client. Though absence of official statistics makes it impossible to determine the truth or falsity of this popular opinion, it probably exaggerates the extent of dishonesty in the profession. While fraud is still common, flagrant practices seem to have decreased in the past generation, due to increased "professionalization" of legal occupations. Bar associations have been organized to promote codes of ethics and to prosecute unethical and openly-criminal practices. Nevertheless, the "spirit of combat" in legal trials continues to make it necessary for some lawyers to practice fraud and misrepresentation by misstatement and concealment of whole truth if they are to win cases. Such practices generally are not grounds for disbarment proceedings by bar associations but, again, they illustrate our criminalistic traditions.

Fraudulent reports of property and income for tax purposes are general. The person who reported his personal property honestly would generally be regarded as a freak, for the only method by which a person can avoid paying more than his share of the taxes is by accepting the common level of dishonesty. Most citizens would probably prefer to make honest reports, if they were assured that others would do the same. Dishonesty in reporting incomes has become more dangerous, but the general methods of concealing a part of the income or making fraudulent claims for exemptions are extremely widespread.

Many churches and denominational colleges have misapplied funds, under the direction of boards of trustees composed of clergy, lawyers, and businessmen. Gifts for endowment have been used for current expenses, gifts for missions have been used for pastors' salaries, and in other ways funds have been misapplied.

These white-collar frauds are sometimes committed under the drive of "necessity," but frequently are an expression of a desire to beat a competitor for the sake of the game. This gaming interest is very general and is found in all types of cultures, but has been immensely developed in modern life and has been accompanied by an efflorescence of bizarre forms, such as flagpole-sitting, gum-chewing contests, hog-calling contests, and marathon dancing. The extraordinary development of fraud in modern life has been an aspect of the drive for profits, which in itself has been regarded as one of the primary virtues and which for that reason has appeared to remove somewhat the taint from illegal practices. Persons practicing fraud have ordinarily felt no pangs of conscience, for the effects of fraudulent behavior have not become apparent in individual victims known to the defrauders but have been impersonal and diffuse. If the effects were discernible in particular persons known to the defrauders and if the practices were not purified by attachment to the virtuous search for profits, many business and commercial practices would be clearly recognized as crimes.

Although bribery is not always white-collar crime, it is another extremely prevalent crime for which arrests are seldom made. Bribery of public officials is a crime both for the bribe-taker and the bribe-giver. Influencing of private persons by giving them gifts, money, or services is not crime, but it is closely akin to bribery in effects and attitudes. Both public and private "influence peddling" may be in the form of a direct exchange of money, but it is much more frequently a concealed and indirect method of putting a person under obligation to return a service.

In many cities and states an immense amount of white-collar bribery of public officials occurs in connection with the purchase of supplies, the making of contracts, the enforcement of regulations, and the enactment of legislation. It is involved when coal is purchased, when school books are purchased, when roads or buildings are constructed, when land is bought for public purposes, when franchises are granted to railroads, bus companies, steamship companies, and other public utility companies, and on hundreds of other occasions. Agents of book-publishing companies have testified regarding their methods of bribing school boards, and many public investigations have shown the wide prevalence of bribery of public officials. In some cities, any purchase of commodities which is strictly honest is an oversight. Much of the wealth of some public officials was secured from these bribes, and it came from the most important of the financial and commercial concerns as well as from the agencies of the underworld. Enforcement of regulations regarding insurance, banking, factories, housing, building construction, streets, garbage, public utilities, weights and measures, and most other important functions is often a matter of bargaining between the agents of the state and the agencies subject to the law. The process, once started, grows and involves firms which were previously honest. The honest firm is forced to bribe the inspector in order to protect itself against arbitrary and persecutory enforcement of laws, but the inspector's expectation of securing bribes has grown out of bribes given previously by other concerns. Campaign contributions may protect a firm against demands for petty graft and may be effective in protecting agencies and interests against laws which may decrease profits. Bribery is not the only method used to prevent the enactment of legislation which might change quasi-criminal acts into definite criminal acts. Dishonest propaganda is a method frequently used. During 1933 and 1934 the investment bankers engaged in much propaganda of this nature for this purpose of emasculating the national securities bill of 1933. This law made a person or firm selling securities financially responsible for the honesty of the statements made in connection with the sale, thus destroying a privilege which investment bankers had previously enjoyed. Consequently, they made every possible effort, including much misrepresentation regarding the true situation, in order to maintain this special privilege which had proved to be highly injurious to the investing public.[44] In 1939, one of the judges in a high court of the federal government resigned under charges that he had accepted more than a half million dollars in thinly concealed bribes from important national business concerns which had cases in court before him.

Corruption is extremely prevalent, also, in private business. Buyers for department stores, hotels, factories, railways, and almost all other concerns which make purchases on a large scale accept and sometimes demand gifts or money payments. In doing so, they violate the trust their employer has placed in them, although not necessarily in a criminal way. The cost of the gifts is added to the price of the merchandise being sold, so that the employer and, eventually, the consumer actually are forced to subsidize the employee. Agents of general credit bureaus and of credit bureaus of special trade associations have reported that they are frequently approached by businessmen who offer bribes if information which tends to lower their credit rating is concealed or if their credit rating is raised. Persons who have had experience in both business and politics claim that the honesty standards among politicians are higher than they are among businessmen.

Aiding and abetting criminals is itself a crime. Although, for obvious reasons, this crime is seldom reported to the police, the number of persons who, in the course of their business, aid and abet criminals is very great. Cigar stores and night clubs are sometimes the arsenals of gunmen, though the proprietors may not themselves engage in crimes of violence. Some lawyers are regularly retained to advise professional criminals and to protect the professional criminals in case of arrest, and are an essential part of any criminal organization. Certainly some part of the perjury by witnesses in trials grows out of the suggestions and instructions of lawyers. Reputable business concerns frequently purchase the proceeds of thefts with a clear realization of the source of the commodities. The manufacturers and distributors of guns, especially machine-guns, of silencers, and of material for bombs are important assistants of gangsters. All large cities and most of the smaller cities have persons who make a business of "fixing" cases for professional thieves. The police, bailiffs, clerks, prosecutors, and judges frequently cooperate with these "fixers," either for direct money payments or under orders from political leaders who control appointments and elections.

The police constantly break the laws. The laws of arrest are rigidly limited, but the police exercise their authority with little reference to these limitations and in violation of law. Hopkins refers to illegal arrests

[44] Bernard Flexner, "The Fight on the Securities Act," *Atlantic Monthly*, 153:232–250, February, 1934.

as kidnapings, and in this sense, the number of kidnapings by the police is thousands of times as great as the number of kidnapings by burglars and robbers.[45] The courts, similarly, are not immune from criminal contagion, and this is true especially of the lower courts.

Thus crime is found in most occupations and is very prevalent. The people of the business world are probably more criminalistic in this sense than are the people of the slums. The crimes of the slums are direct physical actions—a blow, a physical grasping and carrying away of the property of others. The victim identifies the criminal definitely or indefinitely as a particular individual or group of individuals. The crimes of the business world, on the other hand, are indirect, devious, anonymous, and impersonal. A vague resentment against the entire system may be felt, but when particular individuals cannot be identified, the antagonism is futile. The perpetrators thus do not feel the resentment of their victims and the criminal practices continue and spread.

## SUGGESTED READINGS

Adams, J. T., "Our Lawless Heritage," *Atlantic Monthly*, 142:732–740, December, 1928.

Antilla, Inkeri, "The Criminological Significance of Unregistered Criminality," *Excerpta Criminologica*, 4:411–414, 1964.

Atiyah, E. S., *The Thin Line*. New York: Harpers, 1952.

Aubert, Vilhelm, "White Collar Crime and Social Structure," *American Journal of Sociology*, 58:263–271, November, 1952.

Ball, John C., Alan Ross, and Alice Simpson, "Incidence and Estimated Prevalence of Recorded Delinquency in a Metropolitan Area," *American Sociological Review*, 29:90–93, February, 1964.

Beattie, Ronald H., "Sources of Statistics on Crime and Correction," *Journal of the American Statistical Association*, 54:582–592, September, 1959.

Beattie, Ronald H., "Criminal Statistics in the United States—1960," *Journal of Criminal Law and Criminology*, 51:49–65, June, 1960.

Bell, Daniel, "Crime as an American Way of Life," *Antioch Review*, 13:131–154, June, 1953.

Cressey, Donald R., "The State of Criminal Statistics," *National Probation and Parole Association Journal*, 3:230–241, July, 1957.

Dodd, W. E., "Our Ingrowing Habit of Lawlessness," *Century Magazine*, 116:691–698, October, 1928.

Eaton, Joseph W., and Kenneth Polk, *Measuring Delinquency*. Pittsburgh: University of Pittsburgh Press, 1961.

45 Ernest J. Hopkins, *Our Lawless Police* (New York: Viking Press, 1931).

Elliott, Mabel A., "Crime and the Frontier Mores," *American Sociological Review*, 9:185–192, April, 1944.

Gehlke, C. E., "Development of Criminal Statistics in the Past Century," *Proceedings of the American Prison Association*, 1931, pp. 176–190.

Geis, Gilbert, "Toward a Delineation of White-Collar Offenses," *Sociological Inquiry*, 32:160–171, Spring, 1962.

Gibney, Frank, *The Operators*. New York: Harpers, 1960.

Hartung, Frank E., "White Collar Crime: Its Significance for Theory and Practice," *Federal Probation*, 17:31–36, June, 1953.

Keniston, Kenneth, "Entangling Juvenile Delinquency," *Commentary*, 29:486–491, June, 1960.

Lane, Robert E., "Why Businessmen Violate the Law," *Journal of Criminal Law, Criminology, and Police Science*, 44:151–165, July–August, 1953.

Murphy, F. J., M. M. Shirley, and H. L. Witmer, "The Incidence of Hidden Delinquency," *American Journal of Orthopsychiatry*, 16:686–696, October, 1946.

Neale, A. D., *The Antitrust Laws of the United States of America* (Cambridge: Cambridge University Press, 1960).

Nettler, Gwyn, "Antisocial Sentiment and Criminality," *American Sociological Review*, 24:202–208, April, 1959.

Peterson, Virgil, "An Examination of Chicago's Law Enforcement Agencies," *Criminal Justice*, January, 1950, pp. 3–6.

Quinney, Earl R., "Occupational Structure and Criminal Behavior: Prescription Violation by Retail Pharmacists," *Social Problems*, 11:179–185, Fall, 1963.

Quinney, Earl R., "The Study of White Collar Crime: Toward a Reorientation in Theory and Research," *Journal of Criminal Law, Criminology, and Police Science*, 55:208–214, June, 1964.

Robinson, L. N., "History of Criminal Statistics, 1908–1933," *Journal of Criminal Law and Criminology*, 24:125–139, May–June, 1933.

Schwartz, Edward E., "Statistics of Juvenile Delinquency in the United States," *Annals of the American Academy of Political and Social Science*, 261:9–20, January, 1949.

Sellin, Thorsten, "The Basis of a Crime Index," *Journal of Criminal Law and Criminology*, 22:335–356, September–October, 1931.

Sellin, Thorsten, "The Measurement of Criminality in Geographic Areas," *Proceedings of the American Philosophical Society*, 97:163–167, April, 1953.

Shannon, Lyle W., "Types and Patterns of Delinquency Referral in a Middle-Sized City," *British Journal of Criminology*, 14:24–36, July, 1963.

Short, James, F. Jr., and F. Ivan Nye, "Reported Behavior as a Criterion of Deviant Behavior," *Social Problems*, 5:207–213, Winter, 1957.

Simon, M. J., *The Law for Advertising and Marketing.* New York: Norton, 1956.

Smigel, Erwin O., "Public Attitudes Toward Stealing as Related to the Size of the Victim Organization," *American Sociological Review,* 21:320–327, June, 1956.

Smith, Richard A., "The Incredible Electrical Conspiracy," *Fortune,* April, 1961, pp. 132–180; and May, 1961, pp. 161–224.

Sutherland, E. H., *White Collar Crime.* New York: Dryden, 1949.

Van Vechten, C. C., "Differential Criminal Case Mortality in Selected Jurisdictions," *American Sociological Review,* 7:833–839, December, 1942.

Wolfgang, Marvin E., "Uniform Crime Reports: A Critical Appraisal," *University of Pennsylvania Law Review,* 111:708–738, April, 1963.

# 3. PERSPECTIVES AND METHODS IN CRIMINOLOGY

SYSTEMATIC STUDY of crime causation is of rather recent origin. During the medieval and early modern periods many unorganized and ephemeral explanations of crimes were stated and accepted. Probably the principal explanation during this time was that crime was due to innate depravity and the instigation of the devil. The English indictment used as late as the nineteenth century not only accused the defendant of violating the law, but also of "being prompted and instigated by the devil and not having the fear of God before his eyes." And the Supreme Court of North Carolina as late as 1862 declared: "To know the right and still pursue the wrong proceeds from a perverse will brought about by the seductions of the evil one."[1]

During the period when this explanation was used most frequently the conception of natural causation was not developed even with reference to such things as disease, and of course, was not developed with reference to crime. Little interest was manifested in motives, intentions, circumstances, or other immediate conditions in the causation of crime. Punishments were arbitrary and unequal, with the general principle of heaping tortures on criminals in accordance with the divine example and of relying on divine interposition as the method of control.

OUTLINE OF SCHOOLS OF CRIMINOLOGY. Schools of criminology have developed during the last two centuries. A "school of criminology" is a system of thought, together with the proponents of that system of thought. The system of thought consists of an integrated theory of the causation of crime and of policies of control implied in the theory of causation. Obviously, many popular "explanations" of crime are not included in this definition. The principal schools of criminology are listed

[1] Quoted by H. Shepard, *Journal of Criminal Law and Criminology*, 13:486, January–February, 1923.

in Table VII. These schools can be distinguished from each other only in the writings of the more extreme adherents, who were customarily the early writers in the school. Each of the schools, with the possible exception of the last, has been broken down as a complete explanation of criminal behavior and has then merged with the other explanations. Furthermore, the outline below cannot do justice to the many variations in each school of thought or to the inter-relations among the schools. The dates of origin are approximations. Each of these schools will be described briefly, and in later chapters the more pertinent research pertaining to each school will be discussed.

## TABLE VII

### SCHOOLS OF CRIMINOLOGY

| School | Date of Origin | Content of Explanation | Methods |
|---|---|---|---|
| Classical | 1775 | Hedonism | Arm-chair |
| Cartographic | 1830 | Ecology, culture, composition of population | Maps, statistics |
| Socialist | 1850 | Economic determinism | Statistics |
| Typological | | | |
|   1. Lombrosian | 1875 | Morphological type, born criminal | Clinical, statistics |
|   2. Mental testers | 1905 | Feeble-mindedness | Clinical, tests, statistics |
|   3. Psychiatric | 1905 | Psychopathy | Clinical, statistics |
| Sociological | 1915 | Groups and social processes | Clinical, statistics |

THE CLASSICAL SCHOOL.   The classical school of criminology and of criminal law developed in England during the last half of the nineteenth century and spread to other European countries and to America. It was based on hedonistic psychology. According to this psychology, man governs his behavior by considerations of pleasures and pains; the pleasures anticipated from a particular act may be balanced against the pains anticipated from the same act, or the algebraic sum of pleasures and pains from one act may be balanced against the algebraic sum of pleasures and pains from another act. The actor was assumed to have a free will and to make his choice with reference to the hedonistic calculation alone. This was regarded as the final and complete explanation of the causes of crime and no need for further investigation of causation could be imagined.

Beccaria in 1764 made the principal application of this doctrine to penology.[2] His objective was to make punishment less arbitrary and severe than it had been. He contended that all persons who violated a specific law should receive identical punishments regardless of age, sanity, position, or circumstance. This was justified on the ground that the rights of individuals could be preserved only by treating all individuals alike, and also on the ground that the punishment must be definitely determined in advance in order that it might be taken into account in the calculation of pains and pleasures that would result from violation of the law. According to this school the penalty should be just severe enough so that the pains would exceed the pleasures derived from violation of the law. This extreme idea of equality was soon modified at two points: children and "lunatics" were exempted from punishment on the ground that they were unable to calculate pleasures and pains intelligently, and the penalties were fixed within narrow limits rather than absolutely so that a small amount of judicial discretion was possible. With these modifications this classical doctrine became the backbone of the body of the criminal law and has persisted in popular thought and judicial decisions to the present day.

The psychology underlying this theory is now generally questioned. It is individualistic, intellectualistic, and voluntaristic. It assumes freedom of the will in a manner which gives little or no possibility of further investigation of the causes of crime or of efforts to prevent crime. All of the schools which developed subsequent to this accepted the hypothesis of natural causation and for that reason they are sometimes called positivistic.

THE CARTOGRAPHIC SCHOOL.    The second school of criminology was called the cartographic or geographic school and was similar to the school which in recent years has been called the ecological. The leaders of this school were concerned primarily with the distribution of crimes in certain areas, both geographical and social. They were interested in crime as a necessary expression of the social conditions. Quetelet and A. M. Guerry were the leaders of this approach in France, and they had a large number of followers in that country and in England and Germany. The school flourished from about 1830 to 1880. Not only did the adherents of this method analyze the distribution of general crime rates, but they made special studies of juvenile delinquency and of professional crime which

---

[2] Cesare Beccaria, *An Essay on Crimes and Punishments* (London: Almon, 1767); see also Marcello T. Maestro, *Voltaire and Beccaria as Reformers of the Criminal Law* (New York: Columbia University Press, 1942). Bentham applied the hedonistic psychology to legislation: Jeremy Bentham, *An Introduction to the Principles of Morals and Legislation* (London: Pickering, 1823).

are comparable with those of the present century and superior to almost anything published in the interval between 1880 and the present. This period in the history of criminological theory was practically unknown to the present generation of criminologists until it was "re-discovered" by Lindesmith and Levin. They have listed a very large number of factual studies by this method.[3]

THE SOCIALIST SCHOOL. The socialist school of criminology, based on writings of Marx and Engels, began about 1850 and emphasized economic determinism. This school was concerned with crime only as a by-product, but it conducted many factual studies, principally by the statistical methods, and provided much material regarding the variations in crime rates in association with variations in economic conditions. The conclusions which were derived from these factual studies were generally in agreement with the preconceptions of the students who were using this approach and were regarded as supporting the socialist program. Nevertheless, this school may properly be called scientific, for it began with a general hypothesis and collected factual data in a manner which enabled others to repeat the work and test their conclusions.

TYPOLOGICAL SCHOOLS. Three schools of criminology which have been called "typological" or "bio-typological" have developed. They are similar in their general logic and methodology; all of them are based on a postulate that criminals differ from non-criminals in certain traits of personality, which promote unusual tendencies to commit crimes in situations in which others do not commit crimes; these tendencies to commit crimes may be inherited or may be the necessary expression of unique personal traits. The three typological schools differ from each other as to the specific traits which differentiate criminals from non-criminals.

The Lombrosians. Lombroso was the leader of a school which was known as the "Italian School." The first statement of his theory was in the form of a pamphlet, published in 1876; it grew to a three-volume book in subsequent editions.[4] In its earlier and more clear-cut form this theory consisted of the following propositions: (a) Criminals are by birth a distinct type. (b) This type can be recognized by stigmata or anomalies, such as asymmetrical cranium, long lower jaw, flattened nose, scanty

---

[3] Alfred Lindesmith and Yale Levin, "The Lombrosian Myth in Criminology," *American Journal of Sociology*, 42:653–671, March, 1937; Yale Levin and Alfred Lindesmith, "English Ecology and Criminology of the Past Century," *Journal of Criminal Law and Criminology*, 27:801–816, March–April, 1937.

[4] C. Lombroso, *L'uomo delinquente*. (Torino: Bocca, 1896–97). See Marvin E. Wolfgang, "Pioneers in Criminology: Cesare Lombroso (1835–1909)," *Journal of Criminal Law and Criminology*, 52:361–391, December, 1961.

beard, and low sensitivity to pain.[5] The criminal type is clearly represented in a person with more than five such stigmata, incompletely represented by three to five, and not necessarily indicated by less than three. (c) These physical anomalies do not in themselves cause crime; rather they identify the personality which is predisposed to criminal behavior and this personality is either a reversion to the savage type—an atavism—or else degeneration, especially akin to epilepsy. (d) Because of their personal natures, such persons cannot refrain from crime unless the circumstances of life are unusually favorable. (e) Some of Lombroso's followers concluded that the several classes of criminals, such as thieves, murderers, or sex offenders are differentiated from each other by physical stigmata. This Lombrosian school was directed at first against the classical school, and was concentrated on the question of determinism versus free will; later it was directed against Tarde's theory of imitation[6] and was concentrated on the question of biological versus social determinism. As a result of these controversies, Lombroso gradually modified his conclusions, especially as to the "born criminal," and reduced the proportion of criminals who were "born criminals" from approximately 100 percent to about 40 percent. Garofalo, Ferri, and other followers of Lombroso made other modifications, so that the school lost its clear-cut characteristics. The conception that criminals constitute a distinct physical type was disproved to the satisfaction of most scholars when Goring, an English physician, made a comparison of several thousand criminals and several thousand non-criminals and found no significant difference between them.[7] Lombroso and his followers had never made a careful comparison of criminals and non-criminals and had little knowledge of the "savage" whom the criminals were supposed to resemble. The morphological emphasis has continued in modified form in the southern European countries and in South America. It was in vogue in the United States until about 1915, and it still maintains a certain popularity among laymen.

*The Mental Testers.* When the Lombrosian school fell into disrepute, its logic and methodology were retained, with feeble-mindedness substituted for physical type as the characteristic which differentiated criminals from non-criminals. This school was represented most clearly by Goddard's theory that feeble-mindedness, inherited as a Mendelian unit, causes crime for the reason that the feeble-minded person is unable to appreciate the

---

[5] The belief that criminals have unique physical characteristics appeared long before Lombroso. See C. Bernaldo de Quiros, *Modern Theories of Criminality* (Boston: Little, Brown, 1911), pp. 4–5.

[6] G. Tarde, *Penal Philosophy* (Boston: Little, Brown, 1912).

[7] Charles Goring, *The English Convict* (London: His Majesty's Stationery Office, 1913). See pp. 99–100.

consequences of his behavior or appreciate the meaning of law.[8] Goddard's tests showed that almost all criminals were feeble-minded and he asserted, also, that almost all feeble-minded persons were criminals. As mental tests became standardized and were applied to a larger number of criminal and non-criminal persons, the importance attributed to feeble-mindedness in the causation of crime decreased greatly and this school of thought tended to disappear.

*The Psychiatric School.* The psychiatric school is a continuation of the Lombrosian school without the latter's emphasis on morphological traits. In the earlier years it emphasized, as did Lombroso, psychoses, epilepsy, and "moral insanity," but it has attributed increasing importance to emotional disturbances and other minor psychopathies as the school of mental testers fell into disrepute. Also, in the later history of this school, it has held that these emotional disturbances are acquired in social interaction rather than by biological inheritance. Many variations are found within this school but the major influence has been the Freudian theory, especially in its earlier form, which placed great emphasis on frustration and "the unconscious." The central thesis of the psychiatric school at present is that a certain organization of the personality, developed entirely apart from criminal culture, will result in criminal behavior regardless of social situations. Criminal patterns are said to be omnipresent for selection by a person with this organization of the personality and if they were not present would be invented. The most extreme writers hold that all or almost all criminals develop by this process; the less extreme writers attempt to isolate a smaller fraction of the criminals for explanation in this manner. The less extreme writers tend to merge with the sociologists.

THE SOCIOLOGICAL SCHOOL. Of the schools of criminology, the sociological is the most varied and diverse. Analysis of the causes of crime in a sociological manner actually began with the cartographic and socialist schools. Also, many nineteenth-century European scholars belonging to neither of these schools interpreted crime as a function of social environment. Among these were Von Liszt (Germany), Prins (Belgium), Van Hamel (Holland), and Fointsky (Russia). Tarde, a French social psychologist and a contemporary of Lombroso, refuted the prevailing biological notions and developed a theory emphasizing the importance of "imitation" in crime causation. His basic notion was that one behaves according to the customs of his society; if a man steals or murders he is merely imitating someone else.

[8] H. H. Goddard, *Feeblemindedness* (New York: Macmillan, 1914).

The greatest development of the sociological school has taken place in the United States. Late in the nineteenth century, criminology was accepted as a field of study by the growing university departments of sociology, and in the United States since that time systematic studies of crime and criminals have been made primarily by sociologists. A survey made in 1901 indicated that criminology and penology were among the first courses offered under the general title "sociology" in United States colleges and universities,[9] and the *American Journal of Sociology* included articles and book reviews on criminology when it was first published in 1895. However, American sociologists, like most European scholars, were deeply impressed by many of the Lombrosian arguments,[10] and it was not until about 1915, after the publication of Goring's work, that a strong environmentalist position was cultivated. It was probably this trend which prompted a sociologist to write in 1914:

The longer the study of crime has continued in this country, the greater has grown the number of causes of crime which may be described as social. This is the aspect in the development of American criminology which has given to that study in this country the title of "The American School."[11]

The central thesis of the sociological school is that criminal behavior results from the same processes as other social behavior. Analyses of these processes as they pertain to criminality have taken two principal forms. First, sociologists have attempted to relate variations in crime rates to variations in social organization, including the variations in larger institutional systems. The following are some of the social conditions which have been discussed in relation to variations in the crime rates of societies and sub-societies: the processes of mobility, culture conflict, competition, and stratification; political, religious, and economic ideologies; population density and composition; and the distribution of wealth, income, and employment. This kind of analysis fell into disfavor in the years between about 1940 and 1955, principally because criminologists have become

[9] Frank L. Tolman, "Study of Sociology in Institutions of Learning in the United States," *The American Journal of Sociology*, 7:797–838, May, 1902; 8:85–121, July, 1902; 8:251–272, September, 1902; 8:531–558, January, 1903.

[10] See, for example, Carroll D. Wright, *Outline of Practical Sociology* (New York: Longmans Green, 1899); Maurice F. Parmelee, *The Principles of Anthropology and Sociology in Their Relations to Criminal Procedure* (New York: Macmillan, 1908); Phillip Parsons, *Responsibility for Crime* (New York: Columbia University Press, 1909).

[11] John L. Gillin, "Social Factors Affecting the Volume of Crime," in *Physical Basis of Crime: A Symposium* (Easton, Pa.: American Academy of Medicine, 1914, pp. 53–67).

extremely cautious about basing generalizations on the available crime statistics. Because variations in crime rates may represent mere differences in statistical procedures, rather than real variations in the frequency of crime, sociological analysis of the variations is extremely hazardous. Nevertheless, the trend in criminology since about 1955 has been toward analysis of the relationships between aspects of the social structure and variations in crime rates, especially variations by social class.

Second, sociologists have attempted to define the processes by which a person becomes a criminal. These analyses are related to general theories of social learning and have utilized such concepts as imitation, attitude-value, compensation, frustration-aggression, and differential association. The principal orientation at the present is generally taken from the social psychological theories of John Dewey, George Mead, Charles Cooley, and W. I. Thomas, and the development of criminal behavior is considered as involving the same learning processes as does the development of the behavior of a banker, waitress, or doctor. The content of learning, not the process itself, is considered as the significant element determining whether one becomes a criminal or a non-criminal.

EPIDEMIOLOGY AND INDIVIDUAL CONDUCT.  The basic controversy in criminology in the United States at present is that between the psychiatric school and the sociological school. Members of the sociological school recognize that psychogenic traits must be taken into account in the explanation of criminal behavior, and members of the psychiatric school have recognized the importance of social and cultural conditions. But there is disagreement over the extent to which "personality" and "culture" should be emphasized in criminological theories, largely because there is no consensus as to the specific manner in which personality and culture interact to produce specific forms of non-criminal behavior. Some writers in both schools have made classifications of criminals, with the conception that one class is due to personality and another to culture.[12] Lindesmith and Dunham have suggested that criminals constitute a continuum, with personality and culture as two variables; personality as a cause is zero at one extreme and 100 percent at the other, with culture ranging between the same extremes in reverse order. Thus, at one extreme would be the individualized type, represented by the psychotic, whose "crime" is an expression of individual values and not supported by a culture; at the other extreme is the "social criminal," represented by the professional thief,

[12] See Guy Houchon, "Contribution a la Methode Differentielle en Criminologie," *Revue Internationale de Criminologie et de Police Technique*, 18:19–32, March, 1964.

whose objectives are approved by the general society and whose methods are approved only within his smaller variant culture.[13]

This conception of the relation between personality and culture seems to form a basis for merging the psychiatric and sociological approaches to an explanation of criminal behavior, but it is unduly simplified. The problem of how, or whether, basic personality traits and culture combine in the less extreme cases remains as a point of controversy. Perhaps a new school of criminology will soon develop. Ideally, the theory forming the basis of this school will have two distinct but consistent aspects.[14] First, there will be a statement that explains the statistical distribution of criminal behavior in time and space (epidemiology), and from which predictive statements about unknown statistical distributions can be derived. Second, there will be a statement that identifies, at least by implication, the process by which persons come to exhibit criminal behavior, and from which can be derived predictive statements about the behavior of individuals. Concentration on either the epidemiological segment or the individual conduct segment of a theoretical problem is sometimes necessary, but it is erroneous and inefficient to ignore the second segment or to turn it over to another academic discipline. This means that as time goes on the psychiatric school, which now concentrates on individual criminality, will attempt to explain crime rates with a consistent set of theory, and that those sociologists who concentrate only on explaining the distribution of crime will develop a consistent set of theory of explanation of individual criminal conduct.

*indiv cases*

THE MULTIPLE-FACTOR APPROACH.  In contrast with the preceding schools of criminology which attempt to formulate theoretical explanations of criminal behavior, many scholars have insisted that crime is a product of a large number and great variety of factors and that these factors cannot now and perhaps cannot ever be organized into general propositions which have no exceptions; that is, they insist that no scientific theory of criminal behavior is possible. The multiple-factor approach, which is not a theory, is used primarily in discussions of individual cases of crime, but one form of this approach is also used in analyses of variations in crime rates.

Persons who study individual cases by means of this approach are convinced that one crime is caused by one combination of circumstances or "factors," another crime is caused by another combination of circum-

---

[13] A. R. Lindesmith and H. W. Dunham, "Some Principles of Criminal Typology," *Social Forces*, 19:307–14. March, 1941. See also Walter C. Reckless, "A New Theory of Delinquency and Crime," *Federal Probation*, 25:42–46, December, 1961.

[14] See Donald R. Cressey, "Epidemiology and Individual Conduct: A Case From Criminology," *Pacific Sociological Review*, 3:47–58, Fall, 1960.

stances or "factors." This eclecticism is often considered more rigorously "empirical" than explanations stated in terms of an integrated theory. William Healy's emphasis upon "multiple causation" in the cases of individual delinquents, at a time when many persons were seeking arguments for discounting the biological and physical explanations of crime, played an important role in the rise of this assumption.[15] Healy was determined that no theoretical orientation or preconception would influence his findings and that he would simply observe any "causal factor" present. The inevitable consequence of such crass empiricism was the discovery, in a now-famous study, of no less than 170 distinct conditions, every one of which was considered as conducive to delinquency.[16] The following is an example of multiple-factor thinking about individual cases:

Elaborate investigations of delinquents give us conclusive evidence that there is no single predisposing factor leading inevitably to delinquent behavior. On the other hand, the delinquent child is generally a child handicapped not by one or two, but usually by seven or eight counts. We are safe in concluding that almost any child can overcome one or two handicaps, such as the death of one parent or poverty and poor health. However, if the child has a drunken unemployed father and an immoral mother, is mentally deficient, is taken out of school at an early age and put to work in a factory, and lives in a crowded home in a bad neighborhood, nearly every factor in his environment may seem to militate against him.[17]

Although this statement seems to be based on an assumption that each "factor" is of equal importance, adherents of the multiple-factor notion ordinarily argue that either the presence of one or two "important" factors or seven or eight "minor" factors will cause delinquency.

When variations in crime rates are the object of consideration, conditions found to be statistically associated with high crime rates are taken as the units of study. Thus, in the United States males have a higher crime rate than females, Negroes than whites, young adults than middle-aged, and city residents than rural residents. The advocates of the multiple-factor approach to the study of crime rates make little or no attempt to discover the crime-producing processes that are common to males, Negroes, young adults, and city residents. However, they do not impute causal power to

---

[15] William Healy, *The Individual Delinquent* (Boston: Little, Brown, 1915).

[16] Cyril Burt, *The Young Delinquent,* Fourth Edition (London: University of London Press, 1944), p. 600.

[17] Mabel A. Elliott and Francis E. Merrill, *Social Disorganization* (New York: Harper, 1941), p. 111. Reprinted by permission of the publishers. A similar statement appears in Martin H. Neumeyer, *Juvenile Delinquency and Modern Society,* Second Edition (New York: Van Nostrand, 1955), pp. 80–81. The quoted statement is modified in the 1950 edition of *Social Disorganization.*

the "factors" either; this is in contrast to the persons who use the multiple-factor approach in studying individual cases. Ogburn has used this procedure in comparison of crime rates of American cities,[18] and Reckless has advocated its use under the name "actuarial method":

The actuarial approach assumes that individuals have a greater or lesser liability to be caught and reported as violators [of the criminal law] by virtue of the position they occupy in society as determined by their age, sex, race, nativity, occupational level, and type of residence. The behavior which is studied is only that which is reported in contrast to that which is not recorded. The liability is strictly that of becoming the sort of violator who is reported.[19]

The adherents of the multiple-factor "theory" sometimes take pride in their position, pointing to the narrow particularistic explanations of other schools and to their own broadmindedness in including all types of factors.[20] However, the position seems to be based upon a confusion of single-factor explanations and single theories of criminality. Sometimes the adherents of the multiple-factor notion agree on the desirability of a generalized and integrated theory and on the possibility of developing such a theory in the long run, but they point to the breakdown of all such explanations and insist that the most economical procedure for the present generation is to accumulate factual knowledge rather than add to the futile attempts at new generalizations. Often the contribution of multiple-factor studies to criminal law administration, rather than to the development of a body of scientific principles, is emphasized. The popularity of the multiple-factor approach probably reflects the great prestige of statisticians in current social research.

Albert Cohen has made one of the best critiques of the multiple-factor approach in criminology and some of the comments above are from his work.[21] There are three major points in the critique, which is directed at the approach as it is used in the study of individual cases. He points out,

[18] William F. Ogburn, "Factors in the Variation of Crimes Among Cities," *Journal of the American Statistical Association*, 30:12–34, March, 1935.

[19] Walter C. Reckless, *The Etiology of Delinquent and Criminal Behavior* (New York: Social Science Research Council, 1943), p. 74. Reprinted by permission of the publishers. See also Walter C. Reckless, *The Crime Problem*, Second Edition (New York: Appleton-Century-Crofts, 1950), pp. 26–42. See also Gunnar Dahlberg, "Risken att Dommas for Svaare Brott," (The Risk of Being Sentenced for Serious Crime) *Nordisk Tidskrift for Kriminalvidenskap*, 31:145–201, 1943.

[20] See Sheldon Glueck, "Theory and Fact in Criminology," *British Journal of Delinquency*, 7:92–109, October, 1956.

[21] Albert K. Cohen, *Juvenile Delinquency and the Social Structure* (Unpublished Ph.D. Dissertation, Harvard University, 1951), pp. 5–13. See also his *Delinquent Boys: The Culture of the Gang*, Glencoe, Illinois: The Free Press, 1955.

first, that there has been a confusion of explanations by means of a *single* factor and explanation by a *single theory* or system of theory applicable to all cases. A single theory does not explain crime in terms of a single factor, and it is often concerned with a number of variables. A variable is a characteristic or aspect—such as "velocity" or "income"—with respect to which something may vary. We make statements of fact in terms of the *values* of these variables, e.g., "The crime rate is high among persons with incomes of less than $2,000 per year." The pertinent variable here is "income," and its value is "2,000." But neither a statement of one fact ("single factor") nor a series of such statements ("multiple factors") about crime is a theoretical explanation of crime. A theoretical explanation, a single *theory*, organizes and relates the variables; it is an abstract statement of how the known variations in the values of one variable are related to known variations in the values of other variables. A test of the theory is how well it accounts for all of the variations in the values of the variables.

Second, "factors" are not only confused with "causes," but each factor also is assumed to contain *within itself* a capacity to produce crime, a fixed amount of crime-producing power. Thus, one factor is not always considered powerful enough to produce crime in individual cases—several factors must conspire to do so. As Burt has said, "It takes many coats of pitch to paint a thing thoroughly black." Sometimes the basis for imputing causal power to a factor in an individual case is statistical association between high crimes rates and that factor. Thus, if a study of various areas of a city has revealed that crime rates and "poor housing" are usually found together, an investigator studying a juvenile delinquent who lives in a poor house may assign causal power to the condition of the house. Or if the delinquency rate among "only children" is high, causal power may be assigned to the fact that a particular child is an "only child." Statisticians have pointed out that this practice is fallacious, and it is not an intrinsic part of the "actuarial approach."[22] Sometimes, also, the basis for imputing causal power to a factor cannot be determined at all, for it is based upon rather subjective, intuitive, judgments of the investigators. Furthermore, each factor is assumed to be independent of all other factors and to operate independently of the actor's definition of the situation. However, the factor "only child," for example, has been shown to have no intrinsic qualities which produce delinquency or non-delinquency; instead, the meaning of

---

[22] William S. Robinson, "Ecological Correlations and the Behavior of Individuals," *American Sociological Review*, 15:351–357, June, 1950; Leo A. Goodman, "Some Alternatives to Ecological Correlation," *American Journal of Sociology*, 64–610–625, May, 1959.

being an only child varies with differences in local customs, national or ethnic mores, and various other social conditions.[23]

Third, Cohen points out, the "evil-causes-evil fallacy" usually characterizes multiple-factor studies, although it is neither a necessary part of the approach nor peculiar to it. This fallacy is that "evil" results (crime) must have "evil" precedents (broken home, psychopathic personality, etc.) and that "evil" precedents can produce only "evil" results. Thus, when we "explain" crime or almost any other "social problem" we tend merely to catalog a series of sordid and ugly circumstances which any "decent citizen" would deplore, and attribute causal power to those circumstances. In criminology, this fallacious procedure might stem from a desire to eradicate crime without changing other existing conditions which we cherish and esteem; that is, criminologists tend to identify with the existing social order and seek "causes" of crime in "factors" which might be eliminated without changing social conditions which they hold dear, or which may be safely deplored without hurting anyone's feelings.

METHODS OF STUDYING CRIME. The explanations of crime have been derived from two general types of methodology. The first is the common-sense methodology by which people become acquainted with a community, a business, politics, or religion. This methodology is used by the historian and by all social scientists. It consists of the collection and arrangement of all data that are believed to be significant. It is not the methodology of science outlined in the textbooks on logic. It is impressionistic and deals with general tendencies rather than with specific interpretations. Because of this it is possible to take into account a great variety of conditions which are eliminated in the more specific studies. One of the most important of these omissions in criminology is the immense amount of fraud in modern social life which cannot be presented statistically and which seldom results in arrest or imprisonment, but which, nevertheless, is either vaguely or clearly in violation of law and is similar to the other crimes in its social effects and in the attitudes with which it is perpetrated.

The second general methodology is the systematic study of persons who are arrested or convicted of crimes or of the statistics of such arrests and convictions. This methodology is more precise and "scientific" than the first; it deals with specific variables and, usually, specific types of criminal behavior. The more popular techniques or "methods" included within the scope of this methodology are discussed below. In later chapters, many

[23] William W. Wattenberg, "Delinquency and Only Children: A Study of a 'Category,'" *Journal of Abnormal and Social Psychology*, 44:356–366, July, 1949.

examples of research studies utilizing the various methods will be given.

*Statistics of crimes.* One common criminological method is the determination of the correlation between arrests or convictions and certain specific physical or social variables. Bonger used this method and presented a mass of materials purporting to show a close correlation between crime rates and economic conditions.[24] Others have used the same method in an effort to determine the statistical significance of seasons, of unemployment, of congestion of population. Thus, the correlations may be between crime rates and certain conditions over a period of time, or they may be between crime rates and certain conditions in space. One of the difficulties of this method has been the lack of reliable crime statistics. Another difficulty is that it at most merely identifies general relationships. It may determine, for instance, that more crimes are committed against the person in hot weather than in cold weather, but it does not tell whether this is due to the direct effect of temperature upon temper, or to a greater frequency of contacts between people in hot weather than in cold weather, or to a greater frequency of intoxication in hot weather, or to something else. Consequently this method is of value in collecting facts but does not necessarily lead to theoretical statements about the facts.

*Statistics of traits and conditions of criminals.* A second statistical method is comparison of the frequency with which one or more traits or conditions appears among criminals with the frequency with which it occurs among non-criminals. Thus, personality tests have been used to determine the relative frequency of emotional disturbances among criminals and non-criminals. An enumeration is also made of the criminals who come from homes broken by death, divorce, and desertion of one or both parents in comparison with the number of law-abiding persons who come from such homes. Similarly, race, sex, age, nativity, alcoholism of self or of parents, education, and other conditions are studied. In the course of such studies many traits and conditions are compared, but in general each one is abstracted from the others. Often, as indicated above, each trait showing a relatively high incidence among criminals is considered one of many "factors" in crime. No pretense is made of studying any criminal as a unit, and no effort is made to determine the cause of the criminality of a particular person by this method. Goring stated the rationale of this method in the following paragraph:

Our science, recognizing the protean nature of any one human soul, the mutability and interchangeableness of all human influences, does not attempt to "reckon with" the individual. Its methods sketch the broader

24 W. A. Bonger, *Criminality and Economic Conditions* (Boston: Little, Brown, 1916), pp. 1–246.

outline, the cruder features of a portrait of human beings *in the mass*. In more technical language, we seek to estimate the final resultant value and direction of certain universal influences and tendencies which, invisible and intangible in their action upon individuals, by the study of individuals can never be measured or appraised; but which, by their operation and interaction over a wide field and in the hearts of all people, lead in the long run to inevitable results; and become not only tangible and visible but capable of the finest definition and measurement.[25]

Valuable information, preliminary to the formulation of a theory, may be secured in this way; the ideal study of this kind would reveal that certain traits or conditions were present among all criminals, or all criminals of a certain type, and that these traits or conditions were absent among all non-criminals. But there are several difficulties and inadequacies in this method:

(a) There is practically no information accessible in regard to criminals, as such. The only information generally available concerns prisoners. Prisoners are a selected group of criminals and an enumeration of traits or conditions of prisoners would, presumably, yield results different from an enumeration of the same traits or conditions of all criminals. This is a difficulty that confronts any method of studying criminals, but it is more distinctly a limitation of this method than of some of the others because this method depends on mass information. Apparently, the best than can be done at present is to recognize the apparent biases in the statistics and make allowances for them, or attempt to secure other statistics regarding the classes of criminals not adequately represented in prisons.

(b) The data regarding prisoners are doubtful in many respects.[26] Such evident conditions as race, sex, and age can be determined with a fair degree of accuracy, but it is impossible to secure other data, such as nativity, home conditions, or the character of parents, without intensive investigations in the communities in which the prisoners lived prior to confinement. Beyond these rather formal items, reliable information can be secured from prisoners themselves if the relationship between the offender and the interviewer is friendly and congenial, although an element of unreliability may enter because of errors of memory and interpretation.

(c) When this method is used it is necessary to make comparisons with the general population and also with specialized occupational, racial, sex, age, and other groups from which the prisoners come. It is often necessary to assume, therefore, that the sample of the general population contains

---

[25] *Op. cit.*, p. 364, note.
[26] Edwin H. Sutherland and C. C. Van Vechten, Jr., "The Reliability of Criminal Statistics," *Proceedings of the American Prison Association*, 1933, pp. 315–322.

only non-criminals, that it does not contain persons who have violated the criminal law without detection or apprehension. This assumption is unwarranted. Standards for the entire population and especially for particular groups are also lacking. It has been customary for those who use this method to enumerate their cases and then, without knowing how prevalent the same traits are in the general population, assert that the enumerated traits are important "causes of" or "factors in" crime. For instance, it is frequently reported that a specified part of the criminal population is found, on examination, to be psychopathic, and that this trait is therefore extremely important in the causation of crime. But no one knows how large a percentage of the general population would also be found, by the same standards, to be psychopathic.[27] In addition, many of the standards that we have for the general population are unreliable. It was once frequently asserted that feeblemindedness was much more common among criminals than among non-criminals, but the general administration of army tests during World War I revealed that the proportion of the population estimated to be feebleminded had been far too small.

(d) It is possible to secure measurements of only a few traits or conditions and therefore this method cannot by itself locate the cause or causes of crime. It does not explain the mechanisms by which criminality is produced. We may find, for instance, that the male is ten times as criminalistic, judged by commitments to prison, as the female. But males are also five times as likely to be killed by lightning. Is this a sex difference, or a result of differences in occupations, or the general mode of life, or something else? If we find that there is a close correlation between the criminality of juveniles and the alcoholism of their parents, we want to know whether this connection is due to a constitutional defect that is responsible both for the alcoholism of the parent and the delinquency of the child, or whether the child is delinquent because the parent spends money for alcohol that ought to be used to obtain necessities for the child, or because the discipline of the home is irregular or brutal, or because the child becomes emotionally disturbed, or because alcoholism of parents creates a condition whereby the child comes into contact with an excess of delinquent behavior patterns. Goring's total positive conclusion from his statistical study was that the criminal is mentally inferior. Even if this is true, it does not explain why the inferior person is more likely to commit crime. His correlations are, therefore, merely the beginning of an explanation, locating the field in which to look for an explanation rather than furnishing the explanation. As Thomas stated, "Taken in themselves,

27 See Michael Hakeem, "A Critique of the Psychiatric Approach to Crime and Correction," *Law and Contemporary Problems*, 23:650–682, Autumn, 1958.

statistics are nothing more than symptoms of unknown causal processes."[28]

(e) Sometimes the traits and conditions which are compared are so loosely defined that their frequency distribution in the two populations can only be asserted, not demonstrated. The incidence of "constitutional inferiority," "bad home environment," and "psychological tensions," for example, cannot be determined with accuracy simply because the concepts are so vague that investigators cannot agree on their presence or absence in individual cases.

(f) The statistical enumeration of traits and conditions tells us that certain of these are important and perhaps measures the importance in mathematical terms. It may tell us how much more frequently children become delinquent from homes broken by divorce, desertion, or death than children from homes not so broken. But we need to know more than that: why some children from broken homes do not become delinquent. We need to know not only why feeble-minded persons become criminals more frequently than normal persons (if they do), but also why some feeble-minded persons do not become delinquent and why some normal persons do become delinquent. That is, we should have information that will enable us to state that a person with such and such a nature or such and such attitudes in such and such a situation will always become delinquent. Perhaps it will never be possible to construct precise laws of this kind, but it is certain that the statistics of traits of criminals will not be sufficient in themselves. The differential association theory, presented in Chapter 4, represents an attempt to organize, integrate, and give meaning to the statistics of crimes and criminals.

*Individual case study.* In the individual case-study method, the criminal rather than the trait or condition is regarded as the unit. The traits and conditions of one criminal are all studied together. It is not necessary to abstain from statistics in this method, and it differs from the method just described largely in that the individual, rather than any abstracted trait or condition, is the unit of study. The same traits may be studied by each method. If the importance of the home environment to crime is determined by a comparison of the grades or indices of the homes of criminals and of non-criminals, it is not the individual case method. If the importance of the home environment is determined by a consideration of the home in relation to the rest of the life situation of a criminal, it is the individual case method. The differences in the methods are further emphasized by recalling that the purpose of the comparison of the home-indices of criminals and non-criminals is to determine the relative fre-

---

[28] W. I. Thomas, *The Unadjusted Girl* (Boston: Little, Brown, 1923), p. 244. Reprinted by permission of the publishers.

quency of home conditions of specified kinds among the two groups. The purpose of the individual case study is to determine how and why certain types of homes produce delinquency—how they produce delinquency, rather than how frequently delinquency is found in them.

The study of individual cases can be made on a multiple-factor level or it can be used to discover meaningful hypotheses to be tested by other methods or by analyses of other cases. The first use of the method, the enumeration of multiple factors, has already been discussed. The assertion that a certain combination of factors caused the delinquency in an individual case often rests on an implicit, "hidden," theory which the person making the study has in mind. It is important, in scientific work, that these implicit theories be made explicit.[29] In his pioneer study of delinquents, Healy listed factors located by means of reviewing the child's family and "developmental" histories, by examining his environment (including home and neighborhood), by taking physical and psychological measurements, and by making medical and psychiatric examinations.[30] The list of specific items under these heads covers nine pages in his book. But Healy emphasized the importance of studying psychological factors, e.g., mental dissatisfaction, irritative mental reactions to environmental conditions, obsessional imagery, adolescent mental instabilities and impulsions, emotional disturbances, worries and repressions, antisocial grudges, mental peculiarities or aberrations, and mental defects.[31] This would indicate that the "causal factors" considered as "significant" to the delinquency of each case actually were those which supported a hidden, implicit, psychiatric hypothesis about delinquency. In later books, Healy explicitly stated this hypothesis and reported on specific efforts to test it by the method of examining the traits of delinquents and nondelinquents.[32] An alternative interpretation is that the earlier case studies were conducted on an exploratory basis and that the psychiatric theory was suggested by them. While this hypothesis is doubtful in this particular instance, exploratory examination of case histories, including life histories and autobiographies of criminals and delinquents,[33] can provide significant hypotheses about the etiology of criminal behavior.

[29] See the discussion in Cohen, *Juvenile Delinquency and the Social Structure*, op. cit., p. 8.
[30] Healy, op. cit., pp. 53–63.
[31] *Ibid.*, pp. 28 and 32.
[32] William Healy and Augusta F. Bronner, *New Light on Delinquency and Its Treatment* (New Haven: Yale University Press), 1936.
[33] See Clifford R. Shaw, *The Jack-Roller* (Chicago: University of Chicago Press, 1930); Clifford R. Shaw, *The Natural History of a Delinquent Career* (Chicago: University of Chicago Press, 1931); Clifford R. Shaw, *Brothers in Crime* (Chicago: University of Chicago Press, 1938).

The individual case study method is subject to two general criticisms: (a) Explanations of the specific delinquencies are too much subject to the individual whim or prejudice of the investigator. Consequently, there is danger of making much of factors which are really insignificant and neglecting factors that are very significant. This means that one sees in the materials of an individual case those things which fit into his own pre-existing scheme for explaining delinquency, even if that scheme is not stated. The check on this explanation is the judgment of other investigators who examine the same case and carefully state their causal hypotheses. (b) Most of the persons making case studies are employed by agencies dealing with delinquents, and their studies must result in advice regarding procedure. Consequently, there is a probability that the studies will be directly oriented toward temporary modification of delinquency rather than toward understanding delinquency causation. The items which can be readily modified may be selected as causes, or considerations of practicability in dealing with the offender may determine the explanation which is given. In addition, there is a tendency to be concerned with any physical or other defect that may need to be corrected, even if it is not considered relevant to the causation of the individual's criminality.

*Limited case study.* In an attempt to explain drug addiction, Lindesmith used a method which is aimed at the production of universal generalizations rather than a multiple-factor "theory." This system also has been used in a study of embezzlement.[34] The method involves case studies, directed by explicit hypotheses, of rigorously defined categories of behavior. The procedure has essentially the following steps. First, a rough definition of the behavior to be explained is formulated. Second, a hypothetical explanation of the behavior is formulated. Third, one case is studied in the light of the hypothesis with the object of determining whether the hypothesis fits the facts in that case. Fourth, if the hypothesis does not fit the facts, either the hypothesis is reformulated or the behavior to be explained is redefined, so that the case is excluded. This definition must be more precise than the first one, and it may not be formulated solely to exclude a negative case. The negative case is viewed as a sign that something is wrong with the hypothesis, and redefinition takes place so that the cases of behavior being explained will be homogeneous. Fifth, practical certainty may be attained after a small number of cases have been examined in this way, but the location by the investigator, or anyone else, of a negative case disproves the explanation and requires a reformula-

[34] Alfred R. Lindesmith, *Opiate Addiction* (Bloomington: Principia Press, 1947); Donald R. Cressey, *Other People's Money: A Study of the Social Psychology of Embezzlement* (Glencoe: The Free Press, 1953). See also Howard S. Becker, *Outsiders: Studies in the Sociology of Deviance,* New York: Free Press, 1963.

tion. Sixth, this procedure of examining cases, redefining the behavior and reformulating the hypothesis, is continued until a universal relationship is established, each negative case calling for a redefinition or a reformulation. The negative case—that is, the one which does not fit the hypothesis—is the important point in the procedure for it calls for redefinition or reformulation. Seventh, for purposes of proof, cases outside the area circumscribed by the definition are examined to make certain that the final hypothesis does not apply to them. This step is in keeping with the observation that scientific generalizations consist of descriptions of conditions which are always present when the phenomenon being explained is present but which are never present when the phenomenon is absent.

This method is not statistical in the ordinary sense, nor is it the case-study method in the ordinary sense. It combines the individual case-study method and the method of statistical examination of traits of criminals, for it examines individual cases of criminality in the light of a hypothesis and then, for purposes of proof, attempts to determine whether or not that hypothesis also pertains to cases of non-criminality. At the same time, however, it differs from either of these methods: it does not attempt to secure a general picture of the person but only such facts as bear on the hypothesis, and it attempts to go beyond statistical tendencies to a theoretical explanation. The method has been criticized on the ground that it merely produces precise definitions of various types of behavior, rather than causal explanations of that behavior.[35]

*Study of the criminal "in the open."* Another method of studying crime is by association with criminals "in the open." It is asserted by those who have had intimate contacts with criminals "in the open" that criminals are not "natural" in police stations, courts, and prisons and that they must be studied in their everyday life outside of institutions if they are to be understood. By this is meant that the investigator must associate with them as one of them, seeing their lives and conditions as the criminals themselves see them. In this way, he can make observations on attitudes, traits, and processes which can hardly be made in any other way. Also, his observations are of unapprehended criminals, not the criminals selected by the processes of arrest and imprisonment.

There is no doubt of the desirability of securing information in this way, but it is clearly limited by considerations of practicability. Few individuals can acquire the technique to pass as criminals; it sometimes is necessary to engage in crime in order to retain a position once secured. One individual cannot build upon the work of another to a very great

[35] Ralph H. Turner, "The Quest for Universals in Sociological Research," *American Sociological Review*, 18:604–611, December, 1953.

extent, for precise, controlled, techniques of observation can scarcely be employed. It is extremely difficult to secure information regarding the origin of most of the attitudes of the criminals, for few of them will permit interrogations regarding their earlier lives or will volunteer information regarding the processes by which they became criminals. Nevertheless the more information we can secure in this way, the less likely we are to be led astray by the other methods. So far as it can contribute, it is very valuable.

*Experimental method.* It is possible to test hypotheses regarding the causes of delinquency by changing the behavior of individuals or of groups, under controlled conditions. This is somewhat like the experimental method in the physical and biological sciences, although the control is necessarily much less complete in social situations. The Chicago Area Projects were undertaken primarily to test the hypothesis that community disorganization causes high crime rates.[36] Hypotheses regarding the processes by which persons become criminals can also be tested by application to criminals of therapeutic methods based upon the hypotheses. The Cambridge-Somerville Youth Study was an experiment of this kind.[37] However, the results of such experiments must be interpreted with extreme caution: evidence that a person's behavior changes in the expected direction when therapy based upon a theory is applied to him cannot, by itself, be taken as evidence that the theory correctly describes the process by which the behavior was originally acquired. His change might have been produced by things rather extraneous to the therapy, or the therapy might have been based on several theories, rather than on a single theory. The careful observation and elimination of such extraneous things is the essence of a *controlled* experiment.

CONCLUSION. All of the methods which have been described have a proper place in the program for developing an understanding of criminal behavior. Much futile argument has been devoted to controversies between methods and especially to the controversy between the statistical and the non-statistical methods. The value of any method is determined by its relation to the problem which is stated, the statement of a problem is justified by the position of that problem in the total body of knowledge. At a particular stage in the development of knowledge some problems are more important than others and consequently some methods are more useful than others.

The "exploratory method" is needed continuously. This is a congeries

---

[36] See the discussion in Chapter Twenty-nine, pp. 685–687.
[37] See the discussion below, pp. 692–693.

of methods, including statistical descriptions and comparisons in the form of averages, percentages, and correlations, and casual "armchair" observations. This exploratory method is justified in new areas of study because it may pave the way for later definitive studies, based on general theory. Both in the total field of criminal behavior and in smaller areas within this field, the exploratory method is the only method available for developing hypotheses and theories. Several generalizations have been made by different schools of thought regarding criminal behavior as a whole. None of these generalizations is completely satisfactory, and revision of them calls for new hypotheses which may be tested. Similarly, if a particular area of criminal behavior, such as kleptomania, is selected for study, the student must become acquainted with the available statistical data and use other exploratory methods before he is prepared to formulate definite hypotheses regarding it.

The principal argument which has been presented in this chapter is that the multiple-factor approach, defined as a mere enumeration of the series of factors related in some manner or other to criminal behavior, is not adequate. The pride which some criminologists take in this multiple-factor approach is entirely misplaced. This "theory" should be recognized as an admission of defeat, for it means that criminological studies must always be "exploratory." The criminologist can carry his conclusions beyond multiple factors and reduce the series of factors to simplicity by the method of logical abstraction.

For purposes of understanding and controlling criminal behavior, definitive generalizations are needed regarding criminal behavior as a whole, with specifications of the general theory applied to particular criminal behaviors. The relation between the general theory and the particular criminal behaviors is analogous to the relation between a germ theory of disease and the particular germs which cause particular diseases.

Work along both of these lines is desirable. Continued efforts should be made to state valid generalizations regarding criminal behavior as a whole, and continued efforts should be made to explain particular criminal behaviors. Research work of the former type should guide the efforts of those who are attempting to explain particular criminal behaviors, and conclusions from the studies of particular areas of criminal behaviors should lead to revisions of the generalizations regarding criminal behavior as a whole. Just as the germ theory of disease does not explain all diseases, so it is possible that no one theory of criminal behavior will explain all criminal behavior. In that case, it will be desirable to define the areas to which any theory applies, so that the several theories are coordinate and, when taken together, explain all criminal behavior.[38]

## SUGGESTED READINGS

Becker, Howard S., *Outsiders: Studies in the Sociology of Deviance*. New York: Free Press, 1963.

Bernaldo de Quiros, C., *Modern Theories of Criminality*. Translated by Alfonso de Salvio. Boston: Little, Brown, 1911.

Burgess, E. W., "The Study of the Delinquent as a Person," *American Journal of Sociology*, 28:657–680, May, 1923.

Cantor, Nathaniel, "The Search for Causes of Crime," *Journal of Criminal Law and Criminology*, 22:854–863, March–April, 1932.

Clinard, Marshall B., "Contributions of Sociology to Understanding Deviant Behaviour," *British Journal of Delinquency*, 13:110–129, October, 1962.

Cloward, Richard A., and Lloyd E. Ohlin, *Delinquency and Opportunity: A Theory of Delinquent Gangs*. Glencoe: Free Press, 1961.

Cohen, Albert K., *Delinquent Boys: The Culture of the Gang*. Glencoe: Free Press, 1955.

Cohen, Albert K., "Sociological Research in Juvenile Delinquency," *American Journal of Ortho-Psychiatry*, 27:781–788, October, 1957.

Cressey, D. R., *Other People's Money: A Study in the Social Psychology of Embezzlement*. Glencoe: The Free Press, 1953.

Geis, Gilbert, "Sociology and Crime," in Joseph S. Roucek, Editor, *Sociology of Crime*. New York: Philosophical Library, 1961.

Hartung, Frank E., "Methodological Assumption in a Social Psychological Theory of Criminality," *Journal of Criminal Law and Criminology*, 45:652–661, April, 1955.

Hartung, Frank E., "A Critique of the Sociological Approach to Crime and Correction," *Law and Contemporary Problems*, 23:703–734, Autumn, 1958.

Healy, William, *The Individual Delinquent*. Boston: Little, Brown, 1915.

Hentig, Hans von, "A Statistical Test of Causal Significance," *American Sociological Review*, 5:930–936, December, 1940.

Jeffery, Clarence R., "Pioneers in Criminology: The Historical Development of Criminology," *Journal of Criminal Law and Criminology*, 50:3–19, June, 1959.

Levin, Yale, and A. R. Lindesmith, "English Ecology and Criminology of the Past Century," *Journal of Criminal Law and Criminology*, 27:801–816, March–April, 1937.

---

[38] *Cf.* Marshall B. Clinard and Andrew L. Wade, "Toward the Delineation of Vandalism as a Sub-Type in Juvenile Delinquency," *Journal of Criminal Law and Criminology*, 48:493–499, January–February, 1958; and Don C. Gibbons and Donald L. Garrity, "Some Suggestions for the Development of Etiological and Treatment Theory in Criminology," *Social Forces*, 38:51–58, October, 1959.

Lindesmith, A. R., *Opiate Addiction*. Bloomington: Principia Press, 1947.

Lindesmith, A. R., and Yale Levin, "The Lombrosian Myth in Criminology," *American Journal of Sociology*, 42:653–671, March, 1937.

Mannheim, Hermann, *Group Problems in Crime and Punishment*. London: Routledge and Kegan Paul, 1955.

Mannheim, Hermann, Editor, *Pioneers in Criminology*. Chicago: Quadrangle Books, 1960.

Martin, John P., *Juvenile Vandalism: A Study of Its Nature and Prevention*, Springfield, Illinois: Charles C. Thomas, 1961.

Mayhew, Henry, *London Labour and the London Poor*. London: Charles Griffin, 1861.

Morris, Albert, "Crime Causation," *Federal Probation*, 7:17–20, July, 1943.

Radzinowicz, Leon, *In Search of Criminology*, London: Heinemann, 1961.

Reckless, Walter C., *The Etiology of Delinquent and Criminal Behavior*. New York: Social Science Research Council, 1943.

Riemer, Svend, "Theory and Quantitative Analysis in Criminological Research," *American Journal of Sociology*, 48:188–201, September, 1942.

Sewell, William H., "Some Observations on Theory Testing," *Rural Sociology*, 21:1–2, March, 1956.

Shaloo, J. P., "Trends in Criminological Research," *Federal Probation*, 6:21–24, October, 1942.

Wheeler, Stanton, "The Social Sources of Criminology," *Sociological Inquiry*, 32:139–159, Spring, 1962.

Witmer, Helen L., and Ruth Kotinsky, Editors, *New Perspectives for Research on Juvenile Delinquency*. Washington: Government Printing Office, 1956.

Wolfgang, Marvin E., "Criminology and the Criminologist," *Journal of Criminal Law, Criminology and Police Science*, 54:155–162, June, 1963.

# 4. A SOCIOLOGICAL THEORY
# OF CRIMINAL BEHAVIOR

THE PRECEDING discussion has indicated that a scientific explanation consists of a description of the conditions which are always present when a phenomenon occurs and which are never present when the phenomenon does not occur. Although a multitude of conditions may be associated in greater or less degree with the phenomenon in question, this information is relatively useless for understanding or for control if the data are left as a hodgepodge of unorganized factors. Scientists strive to organize their knowledge in interrelated general propositions, to which no exceptions can be found.

THE PROBLEM FOR CRIMINOLOGICAL THEORY. If criminology is to be scientific, the heterogeneous collection of "multiple factors" known to be associated with crime and criminality should be organized and integrated by means of an explanatory theory which has the same characteristics as the scientific explanations in other fields of study. That is, the conditions which are said to cause crime should always be present when crime is present, and they should always be absent when crime is absent. Such a theory would stimulate, simplify, and give direction to criminological research, and it would provide a framework for understanding the significance of much of the knowledge acquired about crime and criminality in the past. Furthermore, it would be useful in control of crime, providing it could be "applied" in much the same way that the engineer "applies" the scientific theories of the physicist.

There are two complementary procedures which may be used to put order into criminological knowledge, to develop a causal theory of criminal behavior. The first is logical abstraction. Negroes, urban-dwellers, and young adults all have comparatively high crime rates. What do they have in common that results in these high crime rates? Research studies have shown that criminal behavior is associated in greater or less degree with the social and personal pathologies, such as poverty, bad housing, slum-residence, lack of recreational facilities, inadequate and demoralized families, feeble-mindedness, emotional instability, and other traits and conditions. What do these conditions have in common which apparently produces excessive criminality? Research studies have also demonstrated that many persons with those pathological traits and conditions do not commit crimes and that persons in the upper socio-economic class frequently violate the law, although they are not in poverty, do not lack recreational facilities, and are not feeble-minded or emotionally unstable. Obviously, it is not the conditions or traits themselves which cause crime, for the conditions are sometimes present when criminality does not occur, and they also are sometimes absent when criminality does occur. A causal explanation of criminal behavior can be reached by abstracting, logically, the mechanisms and processes which are common to the rich and the poor, Negroes and whites, urban- and the rural-dwellers, young adults and old adults, and the emotionally stable and the emotionally unstable who commit crimes.

In arriving at these abstract mechanisms and processes, criminal behavior must be precisely defined and carefully distinguished from non-criminal behavior. The problem in criminology is to explain the criminality of behavior, not behavior, as such. The abstract mechanisms and processes common to the classes of criminals indicated above should not also be common to non-criminals. Criminal behavior is human behavior, has much in common with non-criminal behavior, and must be explained within the same general framework used to explain other human behavior. However, an explanation of criminal behavior should be a specific part of a general theory of behavior. Its specific task should be to differentiate criminal from non-criminal behavior. Many things which are necessary for behavior are not for that reason important to the criminality of behavior. Respiration, for instance, is necessary for any behavior, but the respiratory process cannot be used in an explanation of criminal behavior, for it does not differentiate criminal behavior from non-criminal behavior.

The second procedure for putting order into criminological knowledge is differentiation of levels of analysis. This means that the problem is limited to a particular part of the whole situation, largely in terms of chronology. The causal analysis must be held at a particular level. For example, when physicists stated the law of falling bodies they were not concerned with the reasons why a body began to fall except as this might affect the initial momentum. It made no difference to the physicist whether a body began to fall because it was dropped from the hand of an experimental physicist or rolled off the edge of a bridge because of vibration caused by a passing vehicle. Also, a round object would have rolled off the bridge more readily than a square object, but this fact was not significant for the law of falling bodies. Such facts were considered as existing on a different level of explanation and were irrelevant to the problem with which the physicists were concerned. Much of the confusion regarding criminal behavior is due to a failure to define and hold constant the level of explanation. By analogy, many criminologists would attribute some degree of causal power to the "roundness" of the object in the illustration above. However, consideration of time sequences among the factors associated with crime and criminality may lead to simplicity of statement. In the heterogeneous collection of factors associated with criminal behavior, one factor often occurs prior to another factor (in much the way that "roundness" occurs prior to "vibration," and "vibration" occurs prior to "rolling off a bridge"), but a theoretical statement about criminal behavior can be made without referring to those early factors. By holding the analysis at one level, the early factors are combined with or differentiated from later factors or conditions, thus reducing the number of variables which must be considered in a theory.

A motion picture several years ago showed two boys engaged in a minor theft; they ran when they were discovered; one boy had longer legs, escaped, and became a priest; the other had shorter legs, was caught, committed to a reformatory, and became a gangster. In this comparison, the boy who became a criminal was differentiated from the one who did not become a criminal by the length of his legs. But "length of legs" need not be considered in a criminological theory for, in general, no significant relationship has been found between criminality and length of legs and certainly many persons with short legs are law-abiding and many persons with long legs are criminals. The length of the legs does not determine criminality and has no necessary relation to criminality. In the illustration, the differential in the length of the boys' legs may be observed to be significant to subsequent criminality or non-criminality only to the degree that it determined the subsequent experiences and associations of the two boys. It is in these experiences and associations, then, that the mechanisms and processes which are important to criminality or non-criminality are to be found. A "one-level" theoretical explanation of crime would be concerned solely with these mechanisms and processes, not with the earlier factor "length of legs."

**Two Types of Explanations of Criminal Behavior.**  Scientific explanations of criminal behavior may be stated either in terms of the processes which are operating at the moment of the occurrence of crime or in

1) at time or crime - situational
2) earlier - historic

terms of the processes operating in the earlier history of the criminal. In the first case, the explanation may be called "mechanistic," "situational," or "dynamic"; in the second, "historical" or "genetic." Both types of explanation are desirable. The mechanistic type of explanation has been favored by physical and biological scientists, and it probably could be the more efficient type of explanation of criminal behavior. However, criminological explanations of the mechanistic type have thus far been notably unsuccessful, perhaps largely because they have been formulated in connection with the attempt to isolate personal and social pathologies among criminals. Work from this point of view has, at least, resulted in the conclusion that the immediate determinants of criminal behavior lie in the person-situation complex.

The objective situation is important to criminality largely to the extent that it provides an opportunity for a criminal act. A thief may steal from a fruit stand when the owner is not in sight but refrain when the owner is in sight; a bank burglar may attack a bank which is poorly protected but refrain from attacking a bank protected by watchmen and burglar alarms. A corporation which manufactures automobiles seldom or never violates the Pure Food and Drug Law, but a meat-packing corporation might violate this law with great frequency. But in another sense, a psychological or sociological sense, the situation is not exclusive of the person, for the situation which is important is the situation as defined by the person who is involved. That is, some persons define a situation in which a fruit-stand owner is out of sight as a "crime-committing" situation, while others do not so define it. Furthermore, the events in the person-situation complex at the time a crime occurs cannot be separated from the prior life experiences of the criminal. This means that the situation is defined by the person in terms of the inclinations and abilities which the person has acquired up to date. For example, while a person could define a situation in such a manner that criminal behavior would be the inevitable result, his past experiences would for the most part determine the way in which he defined the situation. An explanation of criminal behavior made in terms of these past experiences is an historical or genetic explanation.

The following paragraphs state such a genetic theory of criminal behavior on the assumption that a criminal act occurs when a situation appropriate for it, as defined by the person, is present. The theory should be regarded as tentative, and it should be tested by the factual information presented in the later chapters and by all other factual information and theories which are applicable.

GENETIC EXPLANATION OF CRIMINAL BEHAVIOR.   The following statement refers to the process by which a particular person comes to engage in criminal behavior.

1. *Criminal behavior is learned.*   Negatively, this means that criminal behavior is not inherited, as such; also, the person who is not already trained in crime does not invent criminal behavior, just as a person does not make mechanical inventions unless he has had training in mechanics.

2. *Criminal behavior is learned in interaction with other persons in a process of communication.*   This communication is verbal in many respects but includes also "the communication of gestures."

3. *The principal part of the learning of criminal behavior occurs within intimate personal groups.*   Negatively, this means that the impersonal agencies of communication, such as movies and newspapers, play a relatively unimportant part in the genesis of criminal behavior.

4. *When criminal behavior is learned, the learning includes (a) techniques of committing the crime, which are sometimes very complicated, sometimes very simple; (b) the specific direction of motives, drives, rationalizations, and attitudes.*

5. *The specific direction of motives and drives is learned from definitions of the legal codes as favorable or unfavorable.*   In some societies an individual is surrounded by persons who invariably define the legal codes as rules to be observed, while in others he is surrounded by persons whose definitions are favorable to the violation of the legal codes. In our American society these definitions are almost always mixed, with the consequence that we have culture conflict in relation to the legal codes.

6. *A person becomes delinquent because of an excess of definitions favorable to violation of law over definitions unfavorable to violation of law.*   This is the principle of differential association. It refers to both criminal and anti-criminal associations and has to do with counteracting forces. When persons become criminal, they do so because of contacts with criminal patterns and also because of isolation from anti-criminal patterns. Any person inevitably assimilates the surrounding culture unless other patterns are in conflict; a Southerner does not pronounce "r" because other Southerners do not pronounce "r." Negatively, this proposition of differential association means that associations which are neutral so far as crime is concerned have little or no effect on the genesis of criminal behavior. Much of the experience of a person is neutral in this sense, e.g., learning to brush one's teeth. This behavior has no negative or positive effect on criminal behavior except as it may be related to associations which are concerned with the legal codes. This neutral behavior is important especially as an occupier of the time of a child so

that he is not in contact with criminal behavior during the time he is so engaged in the neutral behavior.

7. *Differential associations may vary in frequency, duration, priority, and intensity.* This means that associations with criminal behavior and also associations with anti-criminal behavior vary in those respects. "Frequency" and "duration" as modalities of associations are obvious and need no explanation. "Priority" is assumed to be important in the sense that lawful behavior developed in early childhood may persist throughout life, and also that delinquent behavior developed in early childhood may persist throughout life. This tendency, however, has not been adequately demonstrated, and priority seems to be important principally through its selective influence. "Intensity" is not precisely defined but it has to do with such things as the prestige of the source of a criminal or anti-criminal pattern and with emotional reactions related to the associations. In a precise description of the criminal behavior of a person these modalities would be stated in quantitative form and a mathematical ratio be reached. A formula in this sense has not been developed, and the development of such a formula would be extremely difficult.

8. *The process of learning criminal behavior by association with criminal and anti-criminal patterns involves all of the mechanisms that are involved in any other learning.* Negatively, this means that the learning of criminal behavior is not restricted to the process of imitation. A person who is seduced, for instance, learns criminal behavior by association, but this process would not ordinarily be described as imitation.

9. *While criminal behavior is an expression of general needs and values, it is not explained by those general needs and values since non-criminal behavior is an expression of the same needs and values.* Thieves generally steal in order to secure money, but likewise honest laborers work in order to secure money. The attempts by many scholars to explain criminal behavior by general drives and values, such as the happiness principle, striving for social status, the money motive, or frustration, have been and must continue to be futile since they explain lawful behavior as completely as they explain criminal behavior. They are similar to respiration, which is necessary for any behavior but which does not differentiate criminal from non-criminal behavior.

It is not necessary, at this level of explanation, to explain why a person has the associations which he has; this certainly involves a complex of many things. In an area where the delinquency rate is high, a boy who is sociable, gregarious, active, and athletic is very likely to come in contact with the other boys in the neighborhood, learn delinquent behavior from them, and become a gangster; in the same neighborhood the psychopathic boy who is isolated, introverted, and inert may remain at home, not become acquainted with the other boys in the neighborhood, and not become delinquent. In another situation, the sociable, athletic, agressive boy may become a member of a scout troop and not become involved in delinquent behavior. The person's associations are determined in a general context of social organization. A child is ordinarily reared in a family; the place of residence of the family is determined largely by family income; and the delinquency rate is in many respects related to the rental value of the houses. Many other aspects of social organization affect the kinds of associations a person has.

The preceding explanation of criminal behavior purports to explain the criminal and non-criminal behavior of individual persons. As indicated earlier, it is possible to state sociological theories of criminal behavior which explain the criminality of a community, nation, or other group. The problem, when thus stated, is to account for variations in crime rates and involves a comparison of the crime rates of various groups or the crime rates of a particular group at different times. The explanation of a crime rate must be consistent with the explanation of the criminal behavior of the person, since the crime rate is a summary statement of the number of persons in the group who commit crimes and the frequency with which they commit crimes. One of the best explanations of crime rates from this point of view is that a high crime rate is due to social disorganization. The term "social disorganization" is not entirely satisfactory and it seems preferable to substitute for it the term "differential social organization." The postulate on which this theory is based, regardless of the name, is that crime is rooted in the social organization and is an expression of that social organization. A group may be organized for criminal behavior or organized against criminal behavior. Most communities are organized both for criminal and anti-criminal behavior and in that sense the crime rate is an expression of the differential group organization. Differential group organization as an explanation of variations in crime rates is consistent with the differential association theory of the processes by which persons become criminals.

DIFFERENTIAL ASSOCIATION AND INDIVIDUAL CRIMINALITY. Professor Sutherland introduced the theory of differential association in the 1939 edition of *Principles of Criminology*. He modified the theory in the 1947 edition, but this version was not changed in the 1955 or 1960 editions. Neither has it been changed in the current edition. The theory is presently in its period of greatest popularity, judging by the number of journal articles reporting on how it is being tested, analyzed, and extended.

It would be inappropriate to modify the statement in such a way that research work now in progress would be undermined. Accordingly we shall merely elaborate on the basic statement by describing some of the principal interpretive errors apparently made by readers and some of the principal criticisms advanced by criminologists and others.[1]

*Some Literary Errors.* The basic statement of the theory of differential association is not clear. In two pages, we present nine propositions, with little elaboration, that purport to explain both the epidemiology of crime and delinquency and the presence of criminality and delinquency in individual cases. It therefore is not surprising that Sutherland's words do not always convey the meaning he seemed to intend. Most significantly, as we shall see later, the statement gives the impression that there is little concern for explaining variations in crime and delinquency rates. This is a serious error in communication. In reference to the delinquent and criminal behavior of individuals, however, the difficulty in communication seems to arise as much from readers' failure to study the words presented as from the words themselves. Five principal errors, and a number of minor ones, have arisen because readers do not always understand what Sutherland seemed to be trying to say.

First, it is common to believe, or (perhaps necessarily) to assume momentarily, if only for purposes of research and discussion, that the theory is concerned only with contacts or associations with criminal and delinquent behavior patterns.[2] Vold, for example, says, "One of the

---

[1] The remainder of this chapter is taken, with modifications, from Donald R. Cressey, "Epidemiology and Individual Conduct; A Case from Criminology," *Pacific Sociological Review,* 3:47–58, Fall, 1960.

[2] Robert G. Caldwell, *Criminology* (New York: Ronald Press, 1956), p. 182; Ruth S. Cavan, *Criminology,* 2nd edition (New York: Crowell, 1955), p. 701; Marshall B. Clinard, "The Process of Urbanization and Criminal Behavior," *American Journal of Sociology,* 48:202–213, September, 1942; "Rural Criminal Offenders," *American Journal of Sociology,* 50:38–45, July, 1944; "Criminological Theories of Violations of Wartime Regulations," *American Sociological Review,* 11:258–270, June, 1946; "The Sociology of Delinquency and Crime," in Joseph Gittler, editor, *Review of Sociology* (New York: Wiley, 1957), p. 477; and *Sociology of Deviant Behavior* (New York: Rinehart, 1957), p. 240; H. Warren Dunham and Mary Knauer, "The Juvenile Court in Its Relationship to Adult Criminality," *Social Forces,* 32:290–296, March, 1954; Mabel A. Elliott, *Crime in Modern Society* (New York: Harper & Bros., 1952), pp. 347–348; Sheldon Glueck, "Theory and Fact in Criminology," *British Journal of Delinquency,* 7:92–109, October, 1956; Robert E. Lane, "Why Businessmen Violate the Law," *Journal of Criminal Law and Criminology,* 44:151–165, July–August, 1953; Walter C. Reckless, *The Etiology of Delinquent and Criminal Behavior* (New York: Social Science Council, 1943) p. 60; James F. Short, Jr., "Differential Association and Delinquency," *Social Problems,* 4:233–239, January, 1957; and "Differential Association with Delinquent Friends and Delinquent Behavior," *Pacific Sociological Review,* 1:20–25, Spring, 1958; Harrison M. Trice, "Sociological Factors in Association with A.A.," *Journal of Criminal Law and Criminology,* 48:374–386, November–December, 1957; George B. Vold, *Theoretical Criminology* (New York: Oxford University Press, 1958), pp. 194–195.

persistent problems that always has bedeviled the theory of differential association is the obvious fact that not everyone in contact with criminality adopts or follows the criminal pattern."[3] At first glance, at least, such statements seem to overlook or ignore the words "differential" and "excess" in the theory, which states that a person becomes delinquent because of an excess of definitions favorable to violation of law over definitions unfavorable to violation of law. "This is the principle of differential association. It refers to both criminal and anti-criminal associations and has to do with counter-acting forces." Thus, the theory does not say that persons become criminals because of associations with criminal behavior patterns; it says that they become criminals because of an overabundance of such associations, in comparison with associations with anti-criminal behavior patterns. Accordingly, it is erroneous to state or imply that the theory is invalid because a category of persons— such as policemen, prison workers, or criminologists—have had extensive association with criminal behavior patterns but yet are not criminals.

Second, it is commonly believed that the theory says persons become criminals because of an excess of associations with *criminals*.[4] Because of the manner in which the theory is stated, and because of the popularity of the "bad companions" theory of criminality in our society, this error is easy to make. The theory of differential association is concerned with ratios of associations with patterns of behavior, no matter what the character of the person presenting them. Terms such as "definitions of legal codes as favorable or unfavorable," "definitions favorable to violation of law over definitions unfavorable to violation of law," and "association with criminal and anti-criminal patterns" are used throughout the formal statement. Thus, if a mother teaches her son that "Honesty is the best policy" but also teaches him, perhaps inadvertently, that "It is all right to steal a loaf of bread when you are starving," she is presenting him with an anti-criminal behavior pattern and a criminal behavior pattern, even if she herself is honest, noncriminal, and even anti-criminal. One can learn criminal behavior patterns from persons who are not criminals,

---

[3] *Op. cit.*, p. 194. But see footnote 41 below.

[4] Harry Elmer Barnes and Negley K. Teeters, *New Horizons in Criminology*, 3rd edition (Englewood Cliffs, New Jersey: Prentice-Hall, 1959), p. 159; Caldwell, *op. cit.*, pp. 182–183; Cavan, *op. cit.*, p. 701; Clinard, "The Process of Urbanization and Criminal Behavior," *op. cit.*; "Rural Criminal Offenders," *op. cit.*, and "Criminological Theories of Violations of Wartime Regulations," *op. cit.*, Elliott, *op. cit.*, p. 274; Daniel Glaser, "The Sociological Approach to Crime and Correction," *Law and Contemporary Problems*, 23:683–702, Autumn, 1958; and "Differential Association and Criminological Prediction," *Social Problems*, 8:6–14, Summer, 1960; Glueck, *op. cit.*; Lane, *op. cit.*, Reckless, *op. cit.*, p. 60; Harry M. Schulman, "The Family and Juvenile Delinquency," *Annals of the American Academy of Political and Social Science*, 261:21–31, January, 1949; Donald R. Taft, *Criminology* (New York: Macmillan, 1956), p. 338.

and one can learn anti-criminal behavior patterns from hoods, professional crooks, habitual offenders, and gangsters.

Third, in periods of time ranging from five to twelve years after the first publication of the above statement (1947), at least five authors have erroneously believed that the theory consists of the version published in 1939.[5] This error is not important to the substance of the current statement of the theory, but discussing it does tell something about the nature of the theory. The 1939 statement was qualified so that it pertained only to "systematic" criminal behavior, rather than to the more general category "criminal behavior."[6] The word "systematic" was then deleted, and Sutherland explained that it was his belief that all but "the very trivial criminal acts" were "systematic," but he deleted the word because some research workers were unable to identify "systematic criminals," and other workers considered only an insignificant proportion of prisoners to be "systematic criminals."[7] The theory now refers to all criminal behavior. Limitation to "systematic" criminality was made for what seemed to be practical rather than logical reasons, and it was abandoned when it did not seem to have practical utility.

Fourth, it is commonplace to say that the theory is defective because it does not explain why persons have the associations they have.[8] Although such expressions are valuable statements of what is needed in criminological research, they are erroneous when applied to differential association. Determining why persons have the associations they have is a desirable problem for research, and we shall later see that when the

---

[5] Caldwell, op. cit., pp. 182–184; Cavan, op. cit., p. 701; Elliott, op. cit., p. 274; Richard R. Korn and Lloyd W. McCorkle, Criminology and Penology (New York: Holt, 1959), pp. 297–298; Vold, op. cit., pp. 197–198.

[6] See Edwin H. Sutherland, Principles of Criminology, 3rd edition (New York: Lippincott), 1939, pp. 5–9. This statement proposed generally that systematic criminality is learned in a process of differential association but then went on to use "consistency" as one of the modes of affecting the impact of the various patterns presented in the process of association. Thus, "consistency" of the behavior patterns presented was used as a general explanation of criminality, but "consistency" also was used to describe the process by which differential association takes place. Like the word "systematic," "consistency" was deleted from the next version of the theory.

[7] Edwin H. Sutherland, "Development of the Theory," in Albert K. Cohen, Alfred R. Lindesmith, and Karl F. Schuessler, editors, The Sutherland Papers (Bloomington: Indiana University Press, 1956), p. 21. See also Arthur L. Leader, "A Differential Theory of Criminality," Sociology and Social Research, 26:45–53, September, 1941.

[8] Glueck, op. cit.; Clarence R. Jeffery, "An Integrated Theory of Crime and Criminal Behavior," Journal of Criminal Law and Criminology, 49:533–552, March–April, 1959; Leader, op. cit.; Martin H. Neumeyer, Juvenile Delinquency in Modern Society, 2nd edition (New York: Van Nostrand, 1955), p. 152; James F. Short, Jr., "Differential Association as a Hypothesis: Problems of Empirical Testing," Social Problems, 8:14–25, Summer, 1960; Trice, op. cit.; S. Kirson Weinberg, "Theories of Criminality and Problems of Prediction," Journal of Criminal Law and Criminology, 45:412–429, November–December, 1954.

differential association theory is viewed as a principle that attempts to account for variations in crime rates it does deal in a general way with differential opportunities for association with an excess of criminal behavior patterns. Nevertheless, the fact that the "individual conduct" part of the theory does not pretend to account for a person's associations cannot be considered a defect in it.

Fifth, other authors have erroneously taken "theory" to be synonymous with "bias" or "prejudice," and have condemned the statement on this ground. For example, in connection with criticizing Sutherland for deleting "systematic" from the earlier version of his theory, Caldwell has written that by 1947 "we had not acquired enough additional facts to enable [Sutherland] to explain all criminal behavior."[9] This statement does not clearly recognize that facts themselves do not explain anything, and that theory tries to account for the relationships between known facts, among other things. Confusion about the role of theory also is apparent in Clinard's statement that the theory is "arbitrary," Glueck's statement that "social processes are dogmatically shaped to fit into the prejudices of the pre-existing theory of 'differential association'," and Jeffery's statement that "the theory does not differentiate between criminal and non-criminal behavior, since both types of behavior can be learned."[10]

Additional errors stemming from the form of the formal statement, from lack of careful reading of the statement, or from assumptions necessary to conducting research, have been made, but not with the frequency of the five listed above. Among these are (a) confusion of the concept "definition of the situation" with the word "situation,"[11] (b) confusion of the notion that persons associate with criminal and anti-criminal behavior patterns with the notion that it is groups that associate on a differential basis,[12] (c) belief that the theory is concerned principally with learning the *techniques* for committing crimes,[13] (d) belief that the theory refers to learning of behavior patterns that are neither criminal nor anti-criminal in nature,[14] (e) belief that "differential association," when used in reference to professional thieves, means maintaining "a certain necessary

[9] *Op. cit.*, p. 182.
[10] Clinard, *Sociology of Deviant Behavior*, op. cit., p. 204; Glueck, op. cit., p. 99; Jeffery, op. cit., p. 537.
[11] Milton L. Barron, *The Juvenile in Delinquent Society* (New York: Knopf, 1954), p. 101.
[12] Elliott, op. cit., p. 274.
[13] Clinard, "Criminological Theories of Violations of Wartime Regulations," op. cit.
[14] Taft writes of differential association "with others who have become relative failures or criminals," but Sutherland's theory has nothing to say about association with "failures," unless "failures" and "persons presenting criminal behavior patterns" are used synonymously. *Op. cit.*; p. 338.

aloofness from ordinary people,"[15] (f) failure to recognize that the short-hand phrase "differential association" is equivalent to "differential association with criminal and anti-criminal behavior patterns," with the consequent assumption that the theory attempts to explain all behavior, not just criminal behavior,[16] and (g) belief that the theory is concerned only with a raw ratio of associations between the two kinds of behavior patterns and does not contain the statement, explicitly made, that "differential association may vary in frequency, duration, priority, and intensity."[17]

*Some Popular Criticisms.* Identification of some of the defects that various critics have found in the theory also should make the theory clearer. Five principal types of criticism have been advanced in the literature. It would be incorrect to assume that a criticism advanced by many readers is more valid or important than one advanced by a single reader, but commenting on every criticism would take us too far afield. We can only mention, without elaboration, some of the criticisms advanced by only one or two authors. It has been stated or implied that the theory of differential association (a) is defective because it omits consideration of free will,[18] (b) is based on a psychology assuming rational deliberation,[19] (c) ignores the role of the victim,[20] (d) does not explain the origin of crime,[21] (e) does not define terms such as "systematic" and "excess,"[22] (f) does not take "biological factors" into account,[23] (g) is of

15 Walter C. Reckless, *The Crime Problem*, 2nd edition (New York: Appleton-Century-Crofts, 1955), p. 169. This kind of error may stem from Sutherland himself, for in his work on the professional thief he used the term "differential association" to characterize the members of the behavior system, rather than to describe the process presented in the first statement of his theory, two years later. See Edwin H. Sutherland, *The Professional Thief* (Chicago: University of Chicago Press, 1937), pp. 206–207.

16 Howard B. Gill, "An Operational View of Criminology," *Archives of Criminal Psychodynamics*, October, 1957, p. 284; Jeffery, *op. cit.*

17 Clinard, "Criminological Theories of Violations of Wartime Regulations," *op. cit.* If these "modalities," as Sutherland called them, are ignored, then the theory would equate the impact of a behavior pattern presented once in a radio show with the impact of a pattern presented numerous times to a child who deeply loved and respected the donor. It does not so equate the patterns.

18 Caldwell, *op. cit.*, p. 182.

19 Weinberg, *op. cit.*

20 Clinard, "The Sociology of Delinquency and Crime, *op. cit.*, p. 479.

21 Jeffery, *op. cit.*, p. 537.

22 Leader, *op. cit.*; Caldwell, *op. cit*; Marshall B. Clinard, "Criminological Research," in Robert K. Merton, Leonard Broom, and Leonard Cottrell, editors, *Sociology Today* (New York: Basic Books, 1959), pp. 510–513; Short, "Differential Association and Delinquency," *op. cit.*

23 Barnes and Teeters, *op. cit.*, p. 159; Caldwell, *op. cit.*, p. 182; Gill, *op. cit.*, pp. 289–291; Glueck, *op. cit.*, pp. 98–99. Olof Kinberg, "Kritiska reflexioner över den differentiella associationhypotesen," Chapter 24 in Ivar Agge, Gunnar Boalt, Bo Gerle, Maths Heuman, Carl-Gunnar Janson, Olof Kinberg, Sven Rengby, Torgny Segerstedt, and Thorsten Sellin, *Kriminologi* (Stockholm: Wahlström and Widstrand, 1955), pp. 415–429.

little or no value to "practical men,"[24] (h) is not comprehensive enough because it is not interdisciplinary,[25] (i) is not allied closely enough with more general sociological theory and research,[26] (j) is too comprehensive because it applies to non-criminals,[27] (k) and assumes that all persons have equal access to criminal and anti-criminal behavior patterns.[28] Some of these comments represent pairs of opposites, one criticism contradicting another, and others seem to be based on one or more of the errors described above. Still others are closely allied with the five principal types of criticism, and we shall return to them.

One popular form of "criticism" of differential association is not, strictly speaking, criticism at all. At least ten scholars have speculated that some kinds of criminal behavior are exceptional to the theory. Thus, it has been said that the theory does not apply to rural offenders, to landlords who violated OPA regulations, to criminal violators of financial trust, to "naive check forgers," to white-collar criminals, to perpetrators of "individual" and "personal" crimes, to irrational and impulsive criminals, to "adventitious" and/or "accidental" criminals, to "occasional," "incidental," and "situational" offenders, to murderers, non-professional shoplifters and non-career type of criminals, to persons who commit crimes of passion, and to men whose crimes were perpetrated under emotional stress.[29] It is important to note that only the first five comments—those referring to rural offenders, landlords, trust violators, check forgers, and some white-collar criminals—are based on research. At least two authors have simply stated that the theory is subject to criticism because there are exceptions to it; the kind of behavior thought to be exceptional is not specified.[30]

---

[24] Barnes and Teeters, *op. cit.*, p. 210.

[25] *Ibid.*, p. 162; Caldwell, *op. cit.*, p. 182; Gill, *op. cit.*, p. 284; Glueck, *op. cit.*, pp. 105, 108; Howard Jones, *Crime and the Penal System* (London: University Tutorial Press, 1956), p 95.

[26] Clarence Schrag, "Review of Principles of Criminology," *American Sociological Review*, 20:500–501, August, 1955.

[27] Gill, *op. cit.*, p. 284; Jeffery, *op. cit.*, p. 537.

[28] Cloward, *op. cit.*; Short, "Differential Association as a Hypothesis," *op. cit.*, p. 3.

[29] Clinard, "The Process of Urbanization and Criminal Behavior," "Rural Criminal Offenders," *op. cit.*; and "Criminological Theories of Violations of Wartime Regulations," *op. cit.*; Donald R. Cressey, "Application and Verification of the Differential Association Theory," *Journal of Criminal Law and Criminology*, 43:43–52, May–June, 1952; Edwin M. Lemert, "Isolation and Closure Theory of Naïve Check Forgery," *Journal of Criminal Law and Criminology*, 44:293–307, September–October, 1953; Clinard, *Sociology of Deviant Behavior*, *op. cit.*, p. 240; Korn and McCorkle, *op. cit.*, pp. 299–300; Marshall B. Clinard, "Criminal Behavior is Human Behavior," *Federal Probation*, 13:21–27, March, 1949; "Research Frontiers in Criminology," *British Journal of Delinquency*, 7:110–122, October, 1956; *Sociology of Deviant Behavior*, *op. cit.*, p. 229; and "Criminological Research," *op. cit.*, p. 512; Elliott, *op. cit.*, pp. 347–348, 402; Vold, *op. cit.*, pp. 197–198; Jeffery, *op. cit.*; Daniel Glaser, "Criminality Theories and Behavioral Images," *American Journal of Sociology*, 61:441, March, 1956.

[30] Barnes and Teeters, *op. cit.*, p. 159; Taft, *op. cit.*, p. 340.

The fact that most of the comments are not based on research means that the "criticisms" actually are proposals for research. Should a person conduct research on a particular type of offender and find that the theory does not hold, a revision is called for, providing the research actually tested the theory, or part of it. As indicated, this procedure has been used in five instances, and these instances need to be given careful attention. But in most cases, there is no evidence that the kind of behavior said to be exceptional is exceptional. For example, we do not know that "accidental" or "incidental" or "occasional" criminals have not gone through the process specified in the theory. Perhaps it is sometimes assumed that some types of criminal behavior are "obviously exceptional." However, one theoretical analysis indicated that a type of behavior that appears to be obviously exceptional—"compulsive criminality"—is not necessarily exceptional at all.[31]

A second principal kind of criticism attacks the theory because it does not adequately take into account the "personality traits," "personality factors," or "psychological variables" in criminal behavior. This is real criticism, for it suggests that the statement neglects an important determinant of criminality. Occasionally, the criticism is linked with the apparent assumption that some kinds of criminality are "obviously" exceptional. However, at least a dozen authors have proposed that the statement is defective because it omits or overlooks the general role of personality traits in determining criminality.[32]

In an early period Sutherland stated that his theory probably would have to be revised to take account of personality traits.[33] Later he pointed out what he believed to be the fundamental weakness in his critics' argument: "Personality traits," and "personality" are words that merely specify a condition, like feeblemindedness, without showing the relationship between that condition and criminality. He posed three questions for advocates of "personality traits" as supplements to differential association: (1) What are the personality traits that should be regarded as significant? (2) Are there personal traits, to be used as supplements to differential

---

[31] Donald R. Cressey, "The Differential Association Theory and Compulsive Crimes," Journal of Criminal Law and Criminology, 45:49–64, May–June, 1954.

[32] Barnes and Teeters, op. cit., p. 159; Barron, op. cit., p. 147; Caldwell, op. cit., pp. 179, 182, 184; Clinard, "Criminological Theories of Violations of Wartime Regulations, op. cit.; "Sociologists and American Criminology," Journal of Criminal Law and Criminology, 41:549–577, January-February, 1951; "The Sociology of Delinquency and Crime," op. cit.; Sociology of Deviant Behavior, op. cit., pp. 204–205, 229, 240–241; Gill, op. cit., p. 286; Glueck, op. cit., p. 97; Kinberg, op. cit.; Lane, op. cit.; Leader, op. cit.; S. F. Lottier, "Tension Theory of Criminal Behavior," American Sociological Review, 7:840–848, December, 1942; Neumeyer, op. cit., pp. 152–153; Short, "Differential Association as a Hypothesis," op. cit., p. 4; Vold, op. cit., p. 197.

[33] Sutherland, "Development of the Theory" (1942), op. cit., pp. 25–27.

association, which are not already included in the concept of differential association? (3) Can differential association, which is essentially a *process* of learning, be combined with personal traits, which are essentially the *product* of learning?[34]

Sutherland did not attempt to answer these questions, but the context of his discussion indicates his belief that differential association does explain why some persons with a trait like "aggressiveness" commit crimes, while other persons possessing the same trait do not. It also reveals his conviction that terms like "personality traits," "personality," and "psychogenic trait components" are (when used, with no further elaboration, to explain why a person becomes a criminal) synonyms for "unknown conditions."[35]

Closely allied with the "personality trait" criticism is the assertion that the theory does not adequately take into account the "response" patterns, "acceptance" patterns, and "receptivity" patterns of various individuals.[36] The essential notion here is that differential association emphasizes the social process of transmission but minimizes the individual process of reception. Stated in another way, the idea is that the theory deals only with external variables and does not take into account the meaning to the recipient of the various patterns of behavior presented to him in situations which are objectively quite similar but nevertheless variable, according to the recipient's perception of them. One variety of this type of criticism takes the form of asserting that criminals and non-criminals are sometimes reared in the "same environment"—criminal behavior patterns are presented in two persons, but only one of them becomes a criminal.

Sutherland was acutely aware of the social psychological problem posed by such concepts as "differential response patterns." Significantly, his proposed solution to the problem was his statement of the theory of differential association.[37] One of the principal objectives of the theory is to account for differences in individual responses to opportunities for crime

---

[34] Edwin H. Sutherland, *White Collar Crime* (New York: Dryden, 1949), p. 272.

[35] See the discussion in Chapter 7, below.

[36] John C. Ball, "Delinquent and Non-Delinquent Attitudes Toward the Prevalence of Stealing," *Journal of Criminal Law and Criminology*, 48:259–274, September–October, 1957; Caldwell, *op. cit.*, p. 182; Clinard, "The Process of Urbanization and Criminal Behavior," *op. cit.*; "Sociologists and American Criminology," *op. cit.*; *Sociology of Deviant Behavior*, *op. cit.*, pp. 240–241; and "Criminological Research," *op. cit.*; Glueck, *op. cit.*; Jeffery, *op. cit.*; Korn and McCorkle, *op. cit.*, p. 298; Leader, *op. cit.*; Neumeyer, *op. cit.*, p. 152; Reckless, *The Crime Problem, op. cit.*, p. 109; and *The Etiology of Delinquent and Criminal Behavior, op. cit.*, p. 62; Trice, *op. cit.*; Vold, *op. cit.*, p. 196; Weinberg, *op. cit.*

[37] See Edwin H. Sutherland, "Susceptibility and Differential Association," in Cohen, Lindesmith, and Schuessler, *op. cit.*, pp. 42–43. See also Solomon Kobrin, "The Conflict of Values in Delinquency Areas," *American Sociological Review*, 16:653–661, October, 1951.

and in individual responses to criminal behavior patterns presented. To illustrate, one person who walks by an unguarded and open cash register, or who is informed of the presence of such a condition in a nearby store, may perceive the situation as a "crime committing" one, while another person in the identical circumstances may perceive the situation as one in which the owner should be warned against carelessness. The difference in these two perceptions, the theory holds, is due to differences in the prior associations with the two types of definition of situation, so that the alternatives in behavior are accounted for in terms of differential association. The differential in "response pattern," or the difference in "receptivity" to the criminal behavior pattern presented, then, is accounted for by differential association itself.[38] Elsewhere, we have pointed out that one of the greatest defects in the theory is its implication that receptivity to any behavior pattern presented is determined by the patterns presented earlier, that receptivity to those early presentations was determined by even earlier presentations, and so on back to birth.[39] But this is an assertion that the theory is difficult to test, not an assertion that it does not take into account the "differential response patterns" of individuals.

If "receptivity" is viewed in a different way, however, the critics appear to be on firm ground.[40] The theory does not identify what constitutes a definition "favorable to" or "unfavorable to" the violation of law. The same objective definition might be "favorable" or "unfavorable," depending on the relationship between the donor and the recipient. Consequently, the theory indicates that differential associations may vary in "intensity," which is not precisely defined but "has to do with such things as the prestige of the source of a criminal or anti-criminal pattern and with emotional reactions to the associations." This statement tells us that some associations are to be given added *weight*, but it does not tell us how, or whether, early associations affect the *meaning* of later associations. If earlier associations determine whether a person will later identify specific behavior patterns as "favorable" or "unfavorable" to law violation, then these earlier associations determine the very meaning of the later ones, and do not merely give added weight to them. In other words, whether a person is prestigeful or not prestigeful to another may be determined by

[38] *Cf.* Ralph L. Beals, "Acculturation," in A. L. Kroeber, editor, *Anthropology Today* (Chicago: University of Chicago Press, 1953), pp. 621–641; and Richard Thurnwald, "The Psychology of Acculturation," *American Anthropologist*, 34:557–569, October–December, 1932.

[39] Cressey, "Application and Verification of the Differential Association Theory," *op. cit.*

[40] I am indebted to Albert K. Cohen for assistance with this paragraph and with other points.

experiences that have nothing to do with criminality and anti-criminality. Nevertheless, these experiences affect the meaning (whether "favorable" or "unfavorable") of patterns later presented to the person and, thus, they affect his "receptivity" to the behavior patterns.[41]

_A fourth kind of criticism_ is more damaging than the first three, for it insists that the ratio of learned behavior patterns used to explain criminality cannot be determined with accuracy in specific cases.[42] Short, for example, has pointed out the extreme difficulty of operationalizing terms such as "favorable to" and "unfavorable to"; nevertheless, he has devised various measures of differential association and has used them in a series of significant studies. Glaser has argued that "the phrase 'excess of definitions' itself lacks clear denotation in human experience," and Glueck has asked, "Has anybody actually counted the number of definitions favorable to violation of law and definitions unfavorable to violation of law, and demonstrated that in the pre-delinquency experience of the vast majority of delinquents and criminals, the former exceeds the latter?" In a study of trust violators, Cressey found that embezzlers could not identify specific persons or agencies from whom they learned behavior patterns favorable to trust violation. The general conclusion was, "It is doubtful that it can be shown empirically that the differential association theory applies or does not apply to crimes of financial trust violation or even to other kinds of criminal behavior."[43] It should be noted that these damaging criticisms of the theory of differential association as a precise statement of the mechanism by which persons become criminals do not affect the value of the theory as a general principle which organizes and makes good sense of the data on crime rates. As we shall see below, a principle accounting for the distribution of crime, delinquency, or any other phenomenon, can be valid even if a presumably coordinate theory specifying the process by which deviancy occurs in individual cases is *incorrect*, let alone untestable.

_The fifth kind of criticism_ states in more general terms than the first four that the theory of differential association oversimplifies the process

---

[41] This actually is the important point Vold was making in the quotation cited at footnote 3 above.

[42] Ball, *op. cit.*; Clinard, "Criminological Research," *op. cit.*; Cressey, "Application and Verification of the Differential Association Theory," *op. cit.*; Glaser, "Criminality Theories and Behavioral Images," *op. cit.*; Glueck, *op. cit.*, p. 96; Lane, *op. cit.*; Reckless, *The Etiology of Delinquent and Criminal Behavior*, *op. cit.*, p. 63; Schrag, *op. cit.*; Short, "Differential Association and Delinquency," *op. cit.*; "Differential Association as a Hypothesis," *op. cit.*; and Albert J. Reiss, Jr. and Lewis Rhodes, "An Empirical Test of Differential Association Theory," *Journal of Research in Crime and Delinquency*, 1:5–18, January, 1964.

[43] Cressey, "Application and Verification of the Differential Association Theory," *op. cit.*, p. 52.

by which criminal behavior is learned.[44] Such criticism ranges from simple assertions that the learning process is more complex than the theory states or implies, to the idea that the theory does not adequately take into account some specific type of learning process, such as differential identification.[45] Between these two extremes are assertions that the theory is inadequate because it does not allow for a process in which criminality seems to be "independently invented" by the actor. But it is one thing to criticize the theory for failure to specify the learning process accurately and another to specify which aspects of the learning process should be included and in what way.[46] Clinard's and Glaser's attempts to utilize the process of identification, and Weinberg's, Sykes and Matza's, and Cressey's efforts to utilize more general social psychological theory, seem to be the only published attempts that specifically substitute alternative learning processes for the mechanistic process specified in the theory. Even these attempts are, like the differential association statement itself, more in the nature of general indications of the kind of framework or orientation one should use in formulating a theory of criminality than they are statements of theory.

**DIFFERENTIAL ASSOCIATION AND CRIME RATES.** Students should carefully note that the theory of differential association is concerned with making sense of the gross facts about crime, rather than concentrating exclusively on individual criminality.[47] Examination of Sutherland's writings clearly

[44] Caldwell, op. cit., p. 183; Clinard, "The Sociology of Delinquency and Crime," op. cit.; and "Criminological Research," op. cit.; Cressey, "Application and Verification of the Differential Association Theory, op. cit.; and "The Differential Association Theory and Compulsive Crime," op. cit.; Daniel Glaser, "Review of Principles of Criminology," Federal Probation, 20:66–67, December, 1956; "The Sociological Approach to Crime and Correction," op. cit.; and "Differential Association and Criminological Prediction," op. cit.; Glueck, op. cit., pp. 93, 97; Korn and McCorkle, op. cit., p. 299; Leader, op. cit.; Short, "Differential Association as a Hypothesis," op. cit.; Gresham Sykes and David Matza, "Techniques of Neutralization: A Theory of Delinquency," American Sociological Review, 22:664–670, December, 1957; Weinberg, op. cit.

[45] See, for example, Clinard, "The Process of Urbanization and Criminal Behavior," op. cit.; Glaser, "Criminality Theories and Behavior Images, op. cit.; and Richard Jessor, "A Social Learning Approach to Culture and Behavior," in T. Gladwin and W. C. Sturtevant, Editors, Anthropology and Human Behavior, Washington: Anthropological Society of Washington, 1962, pp. 94–114.

[46] Despite the fact that Sutherland described a learning process, it should be noted that he protected himself by saying, "The process of learning criminal and anti-criminal patterns involves all the mechanisms that are involved in any other learning."

[47] One of Sutherland's own students, colleagues, and editors has said, "Much that travels under the name of sociology of deviant behavior or of social disorganization is psychology—some of it very good psychology, but psychology. For example, Sutherland's theory of differential association, which is widely regarded as pre-eminently sociological, is not the less psychological because it makes much of the cultural milieu. It is psychological because it addresses itself to the question: How do people become the kind of individuals who commit criminal acts? A sociological question would be: What is it about the structure of social systems that determines the kinds of criminal acts that occur in

indicates that when he formulated the theory he was greatly, if not primarily, concerned with organizing and integrating the factual information about crime rates. In his account of how the theory of differential association developed, he made the following three relevant points:

More significant for the development of the theory were certain questions which I raised in class discussions. One of these questions was, Negroes, young-adult males, and city dwellers all have relatively high crime rates: What do these three groups have in common that places them in this position? Another question was, Even if feeble-minded persons have a high crime rate, why do they commit crimes? It is not feeble-mindedness as such, for some feeble-minded persons do not commit crimes. Later I raised another question which became even more important in my search for generalizations. Crime rates have a high correlation with poverty if considered by areas of a city but a low correlation if considered chronologically in relation to the business cycle; this obviously means that poverty as such is not an important cause of crime. How are the varying associations between crime and poverty explained?[48]

It was my conception that a general theory should take account of all the factual information regarding crime causation. It does this either by organizing the multiple factors in relation to each other or by abstracting them from certain common elements. It does not, or should not, neglect or eliminate any factors that are included in the multiple-factor theory.[49]

The hypothesis of differential association seemed to me to be consistent with the principal gross findings in criminology. It explained why the Mollaccan children became progressively delinquent with length of residence in the deteriorated area of Los Angeles, why the city crime rate is higher than the rural crime rate, why males are more delinquent than females, why the crime rate remains consistently higher in deteriorated areas of cities, why the juvenile delinquency rate in a foreign nativity is high while the group lives in a deteriorated area and drops when the group moves out of the area, why second-generation Italians do not have the high murder rate their fathers had, why Japanese children in a deteriorated area of Seattle had a low delinquency rate even though in poverty, why crimes do not increase greatly in a period of depression. All of the general statistical facts seem to fit this hypothesis.[50]

The formal statement of the theory indicates, for example, that a high

---

these systems and the way in which such acts are distributed within these systems?" Albert K. Cohen, "The Study of Social Disorganization and Deviant Behavior," Chapter 21 in Robert K. Merton, Leonard Broom, and Leonard S. Cottrell, Jr., editors, *Sociology Today* (New York: Basic Books, 1959), p. 462.

[48] Sutherland, "Development of the Theory," *op. cit.*, p. 15.

[49] *Ibid.*, p. 18.

[50] *Ibid.*, pp. 19–20.

Λi crime rate in urban areas can be considered the end product of social conditions that lead to a situation in which relatively large proportions of persons are presented with an excess of criminal behavior patterns. Similarly, the fact that the rate for all crimes is not higher in some urban areas than it is in some rural areas can be attributed to differences in conditions which affect the probabilities of exposure to criminal behavior patterns.[51] The important general point is that in a multi-group type of social organization, alternative and inconsistent standards of conduct are possessed by various groups, so that an individual who is a member of one group has a high probability of learning to use legal means for achieving success, or learning to deny the importance of success, while an individual in another group learns to accept the importance of success and to achieve it by illegal means. Stated in another way, there are alternative educational processes in operation, varying with groups, so that a person may be educated in either conventional or criminal means of achieving success. As indicated above, this situation may be called "differential social organization" or "differential group organization." "Differential group organization" should explain the crime rate, while differential association should explain the criminal behavior of a person. The two explanations must be consistent with each other.[52]

It should be noted that, in the quotations above, Sutherland referred to the differential association statement as both a "theory" and a "hypothesis," and did not indicate any special concern for distinguishing between differential association as it applies to the epidemiology of crime and differential association as it applies to individual conduct. In order to avoid controversy about the essential characteristics of theories and hypotheses, it is preferable to call differential association, as it is used in reference to crime rates, a "principle." Many "theories" in sociology are in fact principles that order facts about rates—now called epidemiology—in some way. Durkheim, for example, invented what may be termed a "principle of group integration" to account for, organize logically, and integrate systematically the data on variations in suicide rates. He did not invent a theory of suicide, derive hypotheses from it, and then collect data to determine whether the hypotheses were correct or incorrect. He tried to "make sense" of known facts about rates, and the principle he suggested remains the most valuable idea available to persons who would understand the differences in the rates of suicide between Protestants and Jews, urban dwellers and rural dwellers, etc.

[51] Cf. Henry D. McKay, "Differential Association and Crime Prevention: Problems of Utilization," Social Problems, 8:25–37, Summer, 1960.
[52] Sutherland, "Development of the Theory," op. cit., p. 21.

The differential association statement, similarly, is a "principle of normative conflict" which proposes that high crime rates occur in societies and groups characterized by conditions that lead to the development of extensive criminalistic subcultures. The principle makes sense of variations in crime rates by observing that modern societies are organized for crime as well as against it, and then observing further that crime rates are unequally distributed because of differences in the degree to which various categories of persons participate in this normative conflict. Sutherland invented the principle of normative conflict to account for the distribution of high and low crime rates; he then tried to specify the mechanism by which this principle works to produce individual cases of criminality. The mechanism proposed is differential association:

The second concept, differential association, is a statement of [normative] conflict from the point of view of the person who commits the crime. The two kinds of culture impinge on him or he has association with the two kinds of cultures and this is differential association.[53]

THE VALUE OF DIFFERENTIAL ASSOCIATION. As an organizing principle, normative conflict makes understandable most of the variations in crime rates discovered by various researchers and observers, and it also focuses attention on crucial research areas.[54] In Chapter 2 and in chapters to follow we have listed numerous facts about the statistical distribution of crime rates. The principle of normative conflict does not make good sense out of all the facts, but it seems to make better sense out of more of the facts than do any of the alternative theories.

On the other hand, it also seems safe to conclude that differential association is not a precise statement of the process by which one becomes a criminal. The idea that criminality is a consequence of an excess of intimate associations with criminal behavior patterns is valuable because, for example, it negates assertions that deviation from norms is simply a product of being emotionally insecure or living in a broken home, and then indicates in a general way why only some emotionally insecure persons and only some persons from broken homes commit crimes. Also, it directs attention to the idea that an efficient explanation of individual conduct is consistent with explanations of epidemiology. Yet the state-

[53] Sutherland, "Development of the Theory," op. cit., pp. 20–21.
[54] Cf. Llewellyn Gross, "Theory Construction in Sociology: A Methodological Inquiry," Chapter 17 in Llewellyn Gross, editor, Symposium on Sociological Theory (Evanston: Row, Peterson, 1959), pp. 548–555. See also Donald R. Cressey, "Crime," Chapter 1 in Robert A. Nisbet, editor, Social Problems and Social Disorganization (New York: Harcourt, Brace, 1961), pp. 30–44; and Donald R. Cressey, "The State of Criminal Statistics," National Probation and Parole Association Journal, 3:230–241, July, 1957.

ment of the differential association process is not precise enough to stimulate rigorous empirical test, and it therefore has not been proved or disproved. This defect is shared with broader social psychological theory.
Although critics agree, as we have indicated, that the differential association statement oversimplifies the process by which normative conflict "gets
into" persons and produces criminality, an acceptable substitute that is
consistent with the principle of normative conflict has not appeared.

It is important to observe, however, that the "individual conduct" part
of the theoretical statement does order data on individual criminality in a
general way and, consequently, might be considered a principle itself.
Thus, "differential association" may be viewed as a restatement of the
principle of normative conflict, so that this one principle is used to account for the distribution of criminal and non-criminal behavior in both
the life of the individual and in the statistics on collectivities. In this case,
both individual behavior data and epidemiological rate data may be
employed as indices of the variables in the principle, thus providing two
types of hypotheses for testing it.[55] Glaser has recently shown that differential association makes sense of both the predictive efficiency of some
parole prediction items and the lack of predictive efficiency of other
items.[56] In effect, he tested the principle by determining whether parole
prediction procedures which could have proven it false actually failed to
prove it false. First, he shows that a majority of the most accurate predictors in criminology prediction research are deducible from differential
association theory while the least accurate predictors are not deducible at
all. Second, he shows that this degree of accuracy does not characterize
alternative theories. Finally, he notes that two successful predictors of
parole violation—type of offense and non-criminal employment opportunities—are not necessarily deducible from the theory, and he suggests a
modification that would take this fact into account.

## SUGGESTED READINGS

Becker, Howard S., and Blanche Geer, "Latent Culture: A Note on the
Theory of Latent Social Roles," *Administrative Science Quarterly*, 5:
304–313, September, 1960.

Bordua, David J., "Some Comments on Theories of Group Delinquency,"
*Sociological Inquiry*, 32:245–260, Spring, 1962.

[55] I am indebted to Daniel Glaser for calling this point to my attention.

[56] "Differential Association and Criminological Prediction," *op. cit.* See also Daniel
Glaser, "A Reconsideration of Some Parole Prediction Factors," *American Sociological
Review*, 19:335–341, June, 1954; and "The Efficiency of Alternative Approaches to
Parole Prediction," *American Sociological Review*, 20:283–287, June, 1955; and Daniel
Glaser and Richard R. Hangren, "Predicting the Adjustment of Federal Probationers,"
*National Probation and Parole Association Journal*, 4:258–267, July, 1958.

Cohen, Albert K., Alfred R. Lindesmith, and Karl F. Schuessler, Editors, *The Sutherland Papers*. Bloomington: Indiana University Press, 1956.

Cressey, Donald R., "Application and Verification of the Differential Association Theory," *Journal of Criminal Law, Criminology, and Police Science*, 43:43–52, May–June, 1952.

Cressey, Donald R., "Epidemiology and Individual Conduct: A Case From Criminology," *Pacific Sociological Review*, 3:47–58, Fall, 1960.

Cressey, Donald R., *Delinquency, Crime and Differential Association*. The Hague: Martinus Nijhoff, 1964.

Eynon, Thomas G., and Walter C. Reckless, "Companionship at Delinquency Onset," *British Journal of Criminology*, 13:162–170, October, 1961.

Glaser, Daniel, "Criminological Theories and Behavioral Images," *American Journal of Sociology*, 61:433–444, March, 1956.

Glaser, Daniel, "Differential Association and Criminological Prediction," *Social Problems*, 8:6–14, Summer, 1960.

Glaser, Daniel, "The Differential Association Theory of Crime," Chapter in Arnold Rose, Editor, *Human Behavior and Social Processes*. Boston: Houghton-Mifflin, 1962, pp. 425–443.

Glueck, Sheldon, "Theory and Fact in Criminology," *British Journal of Delinquency*, 7:92–109, October, 1956.

Gross, Llewellyn, "Theory Construction in Sociology: A Methodological Inquiry," Chapter 17 in Llewellyn Gross, Editor, *Symposium on Sociological Theory*. Evanston: Row, Peterson, 1959, pp. 531–564.

Haller, A. O., and C. E. Butterworth, "Peer Influences on Levels of Occupational and Educational Aspiration," *Social Forces*, 38:289–295, May, 1960.

Hyman, Herbert H., "Reflections on the Relation Between Theory and Research," *Centennial Review* (Michigan State University), 7:431–453, Fall, 1963.

Jeffery, Clarence R., "An Integrated Theory of Crime and Criminal Behavior," *Journal of Criminal Law, Criminology, and Police Science*, 49:533–552, March–April, 1959.

Jessor, Richard, "A Social Learning Approach to Culture and Behavior," in T. Gladwin and W. C. Sturtevant, Editors, *Anthropology and Human Behavior*. Washington: The Anthropological Society of Washington, 1962.

Lane, Robert E., "Why Businessmen Violate the Law," *Journal of Criminal Law, Criminology, and Police Science*, 44:151–165, July–August, 1953.

Leader, Arthur L., "A Differential Theory of Criminality," *Sociology and Social Research*, 26:45–53, September, 1941.

Lottier, S. F., "Tension Theory of Criminal Behavior," *American Sociological Review*, 7:840–848, December, 1942.

McKay, Henry D., "Differential Association and Crime Prevention: Problems of Utilization," *Social Problems*, 8:25–37, Summer, 1960.

Mechanic, David, "The Influence of Mothers on Their Children's Health Attitudes and Behavior," *Pediatrics*, 33:444–453, March, 1964.

Merton, Robert K., "Social Structure and Anomie," Chapter 4 in *Social Theory and Social Structure*. Glencoe, Illinois: The Free Press, 1957.

Orzack, Louis H., "Occupational Impressions, Occupational Preferences, and Residence," *Personnel and Guidance Journal*, 20:358–363, January, 1960.

Reckless, Walter C., *The Etiology of Delinquent and Criminal Behavior*. New York: Social Science Research Council, 1943.

Reckless, Walter C., S. Dinitz, and Barbara Kay, "The Self Component in Potential Delinquency and Potential Non-delinquency," *American Sociological Review*, 22:566–570, October, 1957.

Reiss, Albert J., Jr., and Lewis Rhodes, "An Empirical Test of Differential Association Theory," *Journal of Research in Crime and Delinquency*, 1:5–18, January, 1964.

Scheff, Thomas J., "Social Support for Stereotypes of Mental Disorder," *Mental Hygiene*, 47:461–469, July, 1963.

Sewell, William H., "Some Recent Developments in Socialization Theory and Research," *Annals of the American Academy of Political and Social Science*, 349:163–181, September, 1963.

Short, James F., Jr., "Differential Association as a Hypothesis: Problems of Empirical Testing," *Social Problems*, 8:14–25, Summer, 1960.

Slocum, Walter L., *Family Culture Patterns and Adolescent Behavior*. Washington Agricultural Experiment Stations, Institute of Agricultural Sciences, Washington State University, Bulletin No. 648, October, 1963.

Sutherland, Edwin H., "The Development of the Concept of Differential Association," *Ohio Valley Sociologist*, 15:3–4, May, 1942.

Sutherland, Edwin H., *White Collar Crime*. New York: Dryden, 1949.

Sykes, Gresham, and David Matza, "Techniques of Neutralization: A Theory of Delinquency," *American Sociological Review*, 22:664–670, December, 1957.

Toby, Jackson, "Criminal Motivation," *British Journal of Criminology*, 14:317–336, April, 1962.

Weinberg, S. Kirson, "Theories of Criminality and Problems of Prediction," *Journal of Criminal Law, Criminology, and Police Science*, 45:412–429, November–December, 1954.

# 5. CRIME, DELINQUENCY, AND SOCIAL STRUCTURE

THE PURPOSE of this chapter is to present the general historical background of present-day crime and delinquency in terms of the social processes by which they developed. This is, for the most part, in the nature of hypothesis rather than demonstrated fact. Further, the assumption is made that the actual incidence of crime is much greater than is indicated by the various statistics.

DIFFERENTIAL SOCIAL ORGANIZATION.   In nonliterate and peasant societies the influences surrounding a person were relatively steady, uniform, harmonious, and consistent. Until recently, China exemplified this situation perfectly except in a few of the coastal cities. The individual was surrounded by all of his relatives, and this larger family determined his career and his ambitions. His principal satisfactions were found in cooperation with that group, which was considered as extending beyond his own life into the distant future. Within this group he had perfect individual security, for the group cared for him in case of sickness, accident, old age, insanity, or any other emergency. Such charity involved no stigma or disgrace whatsoever. This large family, moreover, was supported by the surrounding community, which also was harmonious in its traditional culture. In such a situation the behavior of the individual was almost completely predictable, for he had few alternative patterns to follow. The social organization provided few opportunities for "individualism" in behavior. The local group had little contact with outsiders, since the community was a self-supporting and self-contained society, and this isolation also was conducive to consistency in the behavior patterns presented to persons in the socialization process. Within this group, few crimes were committed; the occasional offenses were chiefly committed by non-residents upon members of the group, or by members of the group upon non-members.[1] This social isolation is illustrated by certain Labrador Indians, who have been characterized as follows:

They are primary in pattern since, through the intimate association of individuals forming them, the social fusion of kin results in producing a community whole within which there is a tendency toward harmony and the most thoroughgoing cooperation. Strife is scarcely present, violence strenuously avoided; competition even courteously disdained. These, they think, lead to ridicule. In their place are met subjection of self, generosity in respect to property, service, and opinion, the qualities which we often speak of as being found in "good sports" and which seem to develop as social habits. And these are the qualities that to them represent honor and a welcome place in the thoughts of their associates.[2]

At present no such consistency and uniformity is evident in Western civilization, although certain isolated rural settlements are the closest approach to it. In contemporary urban society, a child is confronted with various ways of behaving even within his own home, for no parent can act consistently in modern life; the parent himself is the recipient of many alternative roles and behavior patterns. Similarly, groups outside the home have standards of conduct which often are extremely different from those within the home. A great deal of behavior is in the nature of the role-playing, and when roles are conflicting or ambiguous the behavior is inconsistent. Sellin has described the normative conflicts within contemporary communities thus:

Every person is identified with a number of social groups, each meeting some biologically conditioned or socially created need. Each of these groups is normative in the sense that within it there grow up norms of conduct applicable to situations created by that group's specific activities. As a member of a given group, a person is not only supposed to conform to the rules which it shares with other groups, but also to those which are peculiarly its own. A person who as a member of a family group—in turn the transmitting agency for the norms which governed the groups from which the parents come—possesses all its norms pertaining to conduct in routine life situations, may also as a member of a play group, a work group, a political group, a religious group, etc., acquire norms which regulate specialized life situations and which sustain, weaken, or even contradict the

[1] Ching Yueh-yen, "Crime in Relation to Social Change in China," *American Journal of Sociology*, 40:298–308, November, 1934.

[2] Frank G. Speck, "Ethical Attributes of Labrador Indians," *American Anthropologist*, 35:559–594, October–December, 1933. Reprinted by permission of the publishers. See also Louis Wirth, "Urbanism as a Way of Life," *American Journal of Sociology*, 44:1–24, July, 1938; Robert Redfield, "The Folk Society," *American Journal of Sociology*, 52:293–309, May, 1947; G. Devereux and E. M. Loeb, "Some Notes on Apache Criminality," *Journal of Criminal Psychopathology*, 4:424–430, January, 1943.

norms earlier incorporated in his personality. The more complex a culture becomes, the more likely it is that the number of normative groups which affect a person will be large, and the greater is the chance that the norms of these groups will fail to agree, no matter how much they may overlap as a result of common acceptance of certain norms. A conflict of norms is said to exist when more or less divergent rules of conduct govern the specific life situation in which a person may find himself. The conduct norm of one group of which he is a part may permit one response to this situation, the norm of another group may permit perhaps the very opposite response.[3]

This condition of normative conflict is ordinarily considered as social "disorganization" or "unorganization," for the social pressures for conformity on the part of the person are not uniform and harmonious. In this condition, the society does not possess consensus with respect to societal goals or else does not possess consensus regarding means of achieving agreed-upon societal goals. Consequently, the individual is confronted with alternative goals or means, or he exists under conditions in which the norms of many members of the society are unknown to other members. He finds that behavior which is "right" or "correct" in one group is "wrong" or "improper" from the point of view of other groups in which he has membership; or, in the condition of *anomie*, he literally does not know how to behave, for he does not know what is expected of him. The presence of this heterogeneous set of conflicting norms is considered social disorganization largely on the ground that an earlier form of social organization has disappeared or is disappearing. Actually, the social conditions in which the influences on the person are relatively inharmonious and inconsistent are themselves a kind of social organization.[4] Such social organization is characteristic of all except the earliest societies and the most isolated contemporary societies, although there are wide variations in the degree of heterogeneity and in the pervasiveness of the cultural inconsistencies.

So far as delinquency and crime are concerned, a heterogeneity of norms in a society means that both a delinquent or criminal subculture and an anti-delinquent or anti-criminal subculture has developed. Society has become organized in such a way that a premium has been placed both on refraining from crime and on perpetrating crime. A person may now be

[3] Thorsten Sellin, *Culture Conflict and Crime* (New York: Social Science Research Council, 1938), pp. 29–30. Reprinted by permission of the publishers. See also John Dewey, *Human Nature and Conduct* (New York: Henry Holt and Company, 1930), p. 130.

[4] See Edwin H. Sutherland, *White Collar Crime* (New York: Dryden, 1949), pp. 253–256.

a member of a group organized against crime while, at the same time, he is a member of a group organized for criminal behavior. For example, a person who accumulates large sums of money through white-collar crimes may be an ardent advocate of community recreational facilities which, he feels, will prevent juvenile delinquency. Under such conditions of differential group organization one would expect the crime rates to be relatively high, for there are "rules for crime" as well as "rules against crime." The person participates in delinquent subcultures as well as in non-delinquent and anti-delinquent subcultures. A sociological problem of first-rate importance is discovery of the conditions under which "rules for crime" and "rules for delinquency" have developed. The task here is not to identify the processes by which criminal behavior patterns are adopted by an individual or a group; it is to identify the processes which brought the behavior patterns into existence in the first place.

**DEVELOPMENT OF NORMATIVE CONFLICT.** One recent impetus to development of delinquent and criminal subcultures was the colonization of America, which threw the Old World out of economic balance. This was followed by the final breakup of the feudal system, in which the ownership of the land had been limited and in which the fixed social classes had mutual duties to each other. Experimental science developed, resulting in the rise of modern technology. With the development of machinery, the production of wealth passed from the control of the consumer to the control of the capitalist, the laborer followed his work from the home to the factory, and thus the city developed around the factory and the market place. The traditional restrictions on economic activity were irksome as world commerce began to develop, and rebellion against these restrictions resulted in a system of relatively free competition, with an accompanying individualistic ideology according to which social welfare is best attained if every person works only for his own selfish interests. Thus, the new system placed great emphasis upon individual enterprise, and it became shameful for an individual to withdraw from economic competition. Each person was expected to pursue his private ends in the most efficient manner possible, and the expected result was increased economic wealth for all.

The democratic revolutions, with accompanying ideologies of natural and inalienable rights, cannot be clearly separated from this economic revolution. The participants in the relatively new economic system resisted any measures which would inhibit free competition, and the slogan "the least government the best" was given homage.[5] Each participant rebelled

[5] See Joseph S. Himes, "Value Analysis in the Theory of Social Problems," *Social Forces*, 33:259–262, March, 1955.

against restrictions on his own behavior and therefore attempted to keep government weak. However, as competition developed it became apparent that competitive advantages could be secured through governmental manipulation. Individuals and industries secured tariffs, franchises, patents, and other special privileges. Both by emphasis on a "hands-off" policy and by emphasis on special privileges, government was made less effective as a control of behavior.

The attitudes and ideology which developed with the industrial and democratic revolutions were opposed to the authoritarian principle in government and in other institutions. Economic and political individualism was useful at the time of revolt against the fixed status and restrictions of the feudal system and against the absolutism of the political system. But individualism is not a positive principle of social organization, and when the revolutions were ended, the usefulness of the negative principle was ended. Since that time, the ideology of individualism has encouraged the individual to disregard social welfare in the interest of his selfish satisfactions. Under such conditions of normative conflict the significance of laws becomes relative: some are obeyed and others are not, depending on whether one "believes in" them.[6] Public welfare need not be considered, for it will be best realized if each person works for his own selfish interest.[7] The gangster and the grafter believe that social welfare need not be an object of consideration and that they may get what they can by whatever methods they can. The gangster is a man who acquires by personal merit and a gun that which is denied him by the complex orderings of a stratified society.[8] As Veblen said:

> The ideal pecuniary man is like the ideal delinquent in his unscrupulous conversion of goods and persons to his own ends, and in a callous disregard of the feelings and wishes of others and of the remoter effects of his actions, but he is unlike him in possessing a keener sense of status and in working more farsightedly to a remoter end.[9]

Similarly, with the industrial and democratic revolutions the ambition for luxurious standards of life became effective for all social classes, since the values which previously restricted these standards to the nobility had

[6] Marshall B. Clinard, *The Black Market: A Study of White Collar Crime* (New York: Rinehart, 1952), pp. 331, 334.

[7] *Cf.* Edward A. Duddy, "The Moral Implications of Business as a Profession," *Journal of Business*, 15:70–71, April, 1945.

[8] Daniel Bell, "Crime as an American Way of Life," *Antioch Review*, 13:131–154, June, 1953.

[9] Thorstein Veblen, *Theory of the Leisure Class* (New York: Macmillan, 1912), p. 237. Reprinted by permission of the publisher. See also David Matza and Gresham M. Sykes, "Juvenile Delinquency and Subterranean Values," *American Sociological Review*, 26:712–719 October, 1961.

been altered. The noted French sociologist, Emile Durkheim, made the following observation about stable societies:

The economic ideal assigned each class of citizens is itself confined to certain limits, within which the desires have free range. But it is not infinite. This relative limitation and the moderation it involves make men contented with their lot while stimulating them moderately to improve it; and this average contentment causes the feeling of calm, active happiness, the pleasure in existing and living which characterizes health for societies as well as for individuals. Each person is then at least, generally speaking, in harmony with his condition, and desires only what he may legitimately hope for as the normal reward of his activity. Besides, this does not condemn man to a sort of immobility. He may seek to give beauty to his life; but his attempts in this direction may fail without causing him to despair.[10]

But rapid technological advancements and discovery of vast unexploited markets raised the level of aspirations by presenting what appeared to be unlimited possibilities for accumulation of wealth. After the disappearance of the nobility, businessmen constituted the élite, and wealth became respected above all other attainments; necessarily, poverty became a disgrace. Wealth was therefore identified with worth, and worth was made known to the public by conspicuous consumption. The desire for symbols of luxury, ease, and success, developed by competitive consumption and by competitive salesmanship, spread to all classes and the simple life was no longer satisfying. Now, "it is everlastingly repeated that it is man's nature to be eternally dissatisfied, constantly to advance, without relief or rest, toward an indefinite goal. The longing for infinity is daily represented as a mark of moral distinction. . . . The doctrine of the most ruthless and swift progress has become an article of faith."[11] Planned acquisition through hard work and careful saving became a virtue, and failure to acquire became evidence of poor character. The doctrine of equality meant that each man was to compete against "all comers," even if his social and economic status put him at great disadvantage in doing so. As Durkheim said:

Overweening ambition always exceeds the results obtained, great as they may be, since there is no warning to pause here. Nothing gives satisfaction and all this agitation is uninterruptedly maintained without appeasement. Above all, since this race of an unattainable goal can give no other

[10] Emile Durkheim, *Suicide: A Study in Sociology*, translated by John A. Spaulding and George Simpson (Glencoe, The Free Press, 1951), p. 250. This book was first published in Paris in 1897.

[11] *Ibid.*, p. 257.

pleasure but that of the race itself, if it is one, once it is interrupted the participants are left empty-handed. At the same time the struggle grows more violent and painful, both from being less controlled and because competition is greater. All classes contend among themselves because no established classification any longer exists. Effort grows, just when it becomes less productive.[12]

In sum, this analysis maintains that in the attempt to locate and train the most talented persons to occupy technical roles, industrial societies maintain that goals of personal, material success are available to all, regardless of social origins. By maintaining that great rewards are available to all, and by maintaining that achievement of the rewards is a sign of moral worth,[13] an optimum number of persons can be motivated to compete for the rewards. But the social structure of industrialized societies is not necessarily consistent with this set of values, this culture. The social structure is the patterned sets of relationships among people and, as Merton has pointed out, in industrial society this structure effectively blocks access to success goals for some parts of the population.[14] One result is invention of a set of values which makes it "all right," even if illegal, to achieve success by routes other than the standard ones provided in the social structure. A set of values of this kind is "deviant," or "delinquent," or "criminal," in the sense that it inspires persons to achieve success by means which are not sanctioned by the legal institutions of society. Normative conflict is present, and both individuals and groups now have the opportunity to learn both the illegitimate means and the legitimate means for achieving personal success. In this kind of social arrangement, the generally approved "rules of the game" may be known to those who evade them, but the emotional supports which accompany conformity to these rules are offset by the stress on the success goal and by the "rules for violating rules" which develop in these circumstances. As Merton has said, "It is only when a system of cultural values extols, virtually above all else, certain *common* success-goals for the population at large while the social structure rigorously restricts or completely closes access to approved modes of reaching these goals *for a considerable part of the same population*, that deviant behavior ensues on a large scale."[15]

[12] *Ibid.,* p. 253.

[13] See Max Weber, *The Protestant Ethic and The Spirit of Capitalism,* translated by Talcott Parsons (London: Allen and Unwin, 1930).

[14] Robert K. Merton, *Social Theory and Social Structure,* Revised and Enlarged Edition (Glencoe: The Free Press, 1957), Chapters 4 and 5.

[15] *Ibid.,* p. 146. It should be noted that in this statement Professor Merton slips into a theory of deviant behavior, rather than limiting himself to a theory of the origin of deviant subcultures. "Deviant behavior on a large scale" can arise only after invention of deviant subcultures.

Cloward and Ohlin have summarized the general observations on the origins of delinquent and criminal subcultures and, thus, the observations on the origins of normative conflict, in the following terms:

Interaction among those sharing the same problem [discrepancies between aspiration and opportunity] may provide encouragement for the withdrawal of sentiments in support of the established system of norms. Once freed of allegiance to the existing set of rules, such persons may devise . . . delinquent means of achieving success. A collective delinquent solution to an adjustment problem is more likely to evolve by this process in a society in which the legitimacy of social rules can be questioned apart from their moral validity. . . . What seems expedient, rational, and efficient often becomes separable from what is traditional, sacred, and moral as a basis for the imputation of legitimacy. Under such conditions it is difficult for persons at different social positions to agree about the forms of conduct that are both expedient and morally right. Once this separation takes place, the supporting structure of the existing system of norms becomes highly vulnerable.[16]

Many types of delinquent, criminal, and deviant subcultures exist in contemporary society, with the result that normative conflict is present on a large scale. Accordingly, no juvenile gang, neighborhood group, ethnic group, or social class needs to invent a criminal subculture in order to take on a high rate of criminality. Although new sets of values which make delinquency and criminality "all right" even if illegal are invented from time to time, most apparent inventions are merely variations on old themes, invented long ago. As Bordua has observed, "Each generation does not meet and solve anew the problems of class structure barriers to opportunity but begins with the solution of its forbears. This is why reform efforts can be so slow to succeed."[17] However, it appears that various types of delinquent subcultures have arisen, and thrive, at different locations in the social structure.[18] The evidence is fragmentary, impressionistic, and uncoordinated, but it seems to indicate that some types of delinquent and criminal subcultures have arisen in large metropolitan centers and particularly in those areas of cities that are characterized by poverty, while other types have arisen among middle-class persons or, as indicated by values conducive to the commission of white-collar crimes, among upperclass persons. Because the sets of delinquent and criminal values are located in different parts of the social structure, they are not equally avail-

[16] Richard A. Cloward and Lloyd E. Ohlin, *Delinquency and Opportunity: A Theory of Delinquent Gangs* (Glencoe: The Free Press, 1960), pp. 108–109.

[17] David J. Bordua, "Delinquent Subcultures: Sociological Interpretations of Gang Delinquency," *Annals of the American Academy of Political and Social Science*, 338: 119–136, November, 1961.

[18] Cloward and Ohlin, *op. cit.*, pp. 26–27.

able for adoption by all segments of the society. Working-class persons living in areas inhabited by certain racial and ethnic groups in large American cities have available to them for adoption a different kind of criminal subculture than do upper-class persons. High delinquency and crime rates of various kinds become, from this perspective, "location data" which direct the attention of researchers to the study of the origin and continuation of various kinds of delinquent and criminal subcultures in various parts of the society.[19]

In one of the best studies using "location data" as a stimulus to exploration of the origin of a type of delinquent subculture, Cohen examined "non-utilitarian" delinquency.[20] Statistical data indicated that a destructive kind of "hell-raising" vandalism was more prevalent among working-class boys than among middle-class boys. Traditionally, criminologists have assumed that such data indicated the existence of a delinquent subculture and, thus, a high incidence of normative conflict among working-class boys, and then they have gone on to try to explain how the delinquent subculture is taken over by individual boys. Cohen, on the other hand, followed the leads provided by Durkheim and Merton and asked why such a subculture is "there" to be "taken over." The theory he developed in response to this question maintains that the non-utilitarian delinquent subculture has arisen in response to a conflict between the aspirations inspired by middle-class values and the ability and opportunity that working-class boys have for fulfilling these aspirations. Middle-class values have been incorporated into the law and into other general codes of legitimate and moral conduct, codes which prescribe proper conduct for everyone. At the same time, however, society is organized in such a way that all working-class persons cannot achieve the goals implied in these values— goals such as personal "success" and achievement of the kind requiring rational, honest labor, careful long-range planning, and deferral of gratifications. For example, while all boys might be inspired with the notion that "anyone" who works honestly and soberly can graduate from college, and with the idea that it is a "good thing" to graduate from college, the fact is that some boys entering this competition will be defeated, for they are not adequately equipped for the competition. In response to this conflict between values and social structure, rules have been developed for achieving personal success by turning the middle class rules "upside down." Once this subculture had been invented, boys could achieve a symbol of status, for example, either by doing well in school or by vandalizing

---

[19] *Ibid.*, pp. 33–34.
[20] Albert K. Cohen, *Delinquent Boys: The Culture of the Gang* (Glencoe: The Free Press, 1955), esp. pp. 121–137.

the school at night. Or, more generally, they could achieve a symbol of status either by getting a good education, working hard, and saving their money until they were able to join the country club, or by doing none of these things and, instead, ripping up the country club's golf greens late at night.

It should be noted that Cohen's theory does not attempt to account for the delinquency or non-delinquency of any particular boy. It is a theory that explains why certain values are more readily available for learning by some boys than by others. Since the rules for non-utilitarian delinquency are carried, by and large, by working-class persons, they are more readily available for learning by working-class persons than by middle-class persons. Further, since the rules for delinquency arise in connection with differences between culturally defined aspirations regarding "success" on the one hand, and opportunities for achieving this success on the other, they are more readily available for learning by boys than by girls.

Walter B. Miller's work on working-class delinquency indicates more concern for diffusion of delinquency values within the working class than for the origin of these rules for delinquency among working-class people. Unlike Cohen, he has not developed a specific theory which attempts to account for the development of certain of the rules for delinquency. Instead, he develops the notion that working-class values include a delinquent subculture.[21] Accordingly, he finds the origin of the delinquent subculture in the values of the working class, but he does not report in detail on the structural conditions leading to the invention of these values. Essentially, Miller sees working-class values emerging from the shaking-down process of immigration, internal migration, and vertical mobility.[22] Normative conflict has developed on a class basis, and, accordingly, rules for delinquency are present for learning by lower-class boys. For example, Miller observes an intense concern for "toughness" and "masculinity" in lower-class culture, a concern which is expressed in a set of rules demanding that boys "act tough" in certain circumstances. Since "acting tough" and "being tough" often are defined as delinquency by the agencies of law enforcement, the stress on toughness amounts to a delinquent subculture. Miller emphasizes the importance of the structure of the family relationships in the working class to development of this delinquent subculture in that class:

21 Walter B. Miller, "Lower Class Culture as a Generating Milieu of Gang Delinquency," *Journal of Social Issues*, 14:5–19, No. 3, 1958.
22 See David J. Bordua, "Delinquent Subcultures: Sociological Interpretations of Gang Delinquency," *Annals of the American Academy of Political and Social Science*, 338: 119–136, November, 1961; and Walter B. Miller, "Implications of Urban Lower Class Culture for Social Work," *The Social Service Review*, 33:219–236, September, 1959.

A significant proportion of lower-class males are reared in a predominantly female household and lack a consistently present male figure with whom to identify and from whom to learn essential components of a "male" role. Since women serve as a primary object of identification during the pre-adolescent years, the almost obsessive lower-class concern with "masculinity" probably resembles a type of compulsive reaction-formation.[23]

According to Miller's theory, delinquent subcultures develop, then, because of problems of adjustment confronting lower-class males and because of conflicts between (a) values which, on a class basis, stress achievement and (b) social structure which, on a class basis, restricts that achievement. His thesis has been reduced by Cloward and Ohlin to three main propositions: (1) The lower class is characterized by distinctive values. (2) These values vary markedly from the middle-class values which undergird the legal code. (3) The result is that conformity with certain lower-class values may automatically result in violation of the law.[24] As Miller says, "Engaging in certain cultural practices which comprise essential elements of the total life pattern of lower-class culture automatically violates certain legal norms."[25] This observation is consistent with one made earlier by two astute observers of American social life:

Activities [such as] gregarious theft and gang warfare by the boys and gregarious sex by the girls appear to be channels for the playful, sociable and conformist impulses of the lower-class youth. If, in many urban areas, we find a lower-class boy or girl who is not delinquent in this sense, we can be fairly sure that he or she is either headed up the class ladder or is psychologically deviant or both, being unwilling or unable to join in the group activities sanctioned by his peers.[26]

Cloward and Ohlin have recently attempted to account for the invention of delinquent subcultures in terms which closely resemble those used by Cohen. Their concern, like that of Miller, is more for the question of why delinquent subcultures persist and diffuse once they are invented, than for the question of how they get invented in the first place. Nevertheless, they follow the writings of Durkheim and Merton to the conclu-

23 "Lower Class Culture as a Generating Milieu of Gang Delinquency," *op. cit.,* p. 9.
24 *Op. cit.,* p. 65.
25 W. C. Kvaraceus and W. B. Miller, *Delinquent Behavior: Culture and the Individual* (Washington: National Education Association, 1959), pp. 68–69.
26 Reuel Denney and David Riesman, "Leisure in Urbanized America," in Paul K. Hatt, Editor, *Reader in Urban Sociology* (Glencoe: The Free Press, 1951), p. 471. See also David M. Downes, *Aspects of An Enquiry into Delinquent Subcultures in East London,* Research Report, London School of Economics and Political Science, 1964 (mimeographed), pp. 27–37.

sion that at least three different types of delinquent subcultures have been invented as a response to a clash between values which promote unlimited aspirations and a social structure which restricts accomplishment of the aspirations. They then go on to observe that among some segments of the population even the possibilities of legitimately achieving limited success goals are also restricted, and they find three delinquent subcultures being invented in these areas of poor opportunity. Two of these subcultures provide illegal avenues to success goals; these are the "criminal subculture" which contains rules for the pursuit of material gain by means such as theft, extortion, and fraud, and the "conflict subculture" which contains rules for the achievement of status through manipulation of force or the threat of force. The other subculture, the "retreatist subculture" contains rules favoring the consumption of drugs. The basic notion here is that the subcultures are invented when aspirations are frustrated and when the frustration is diagnosed as due to the conditions of the social order rather than to personal attributes of the interacting but frustrated population.[27]

If a delinquent subculture, once invented, is to persist, there must be devices for passing the norms, values, and "rules for delinquency" on to newcomers, whether these newcomers are children of the participants or immigrants from another area where the subculture did not exist. For example, the "criminal subculture" described by Cloward and Ohlin is rather stable, and one source of this stability is the network of bonds that exist between age-levels.[28] Children are linked with adolescent delinquents and share their normative conflict; adolescent delinquents, in turn, are linked with young adult offenders, who in turn are linked with adult criminals. The delinquent subculture is carried by a broad, age-linked, population. On the other hand, the "conflict subculture" is less stable, probably because devices for socializing newcomers into it have not developed to the same degree. While any newcomer must learn the values of the conflict subculture, the subculture is carried by adolescents, not by children and adults. Accordingly, those persons who have been socialized do not move onward through a set of age-graded patterns; they tend to be guided by other values when they reach young adulthood, rather than

---

[27] Cloward and Ohlin, op. cit., pp. 111–124.

[28] Op. cit., p. 44. Cloward and Ohlin do not make a careful distinction between gang activities and the delinquent subcultures on which gang activities are based, with the result that it is difficult to determine when they are concerned with the invention of a delinquent subculture and when they are concerned with the distribution of the values of this subculture to individuals. See the discussion of gangs in Chapter 9, pp. 199–208, below. For an excellent study of the way the behavioral rules making up a deviant subculture get invented, see John K. Irwin, *Surfers: A Study of the Growth of a Deviant Subculture*, Unpublished Masters Thesis, Department of Sociology, University of California, Berkeley, 1965.

moving on to an "adult" form of violence. The population carrying the values of the conflict subculture is small and diffuse.

Discovery of the processes leading to the invention of delinquent and criminal subcultures whose existence establishes normative conflict in a society does not explain either the behavior of individual delinquents and criminals or the distribution of crime and delinquency rates. Even in societies disproportionately stressing success goals to the degree that delinquent subcultures are invented, most persons do not use illegitimate means for achieving the approved ends.[29] Rather, in a multi-group type of social organization, conflicting standards of conduct are possessed by various groups. Normative conflict is not distributed evenly throughout the society. An individual who is a member of one group will use one means for achieving the success goal, while an individual having membership in another group will use other means. McKay has pointed out that alternative educational processes are in operation and that a child may be educated in either "conventional" or criminal means of achieving success.[30] Cloward has shown that even unsanctioned means of attaining success are not available to everyone; some persons may be "double failures," in the sense that neither legitimate nor illegitimate means for achieving success are available to them: "Note, for example, variations in the degree to which members of various classes are fully exposed to and thus acquire the values, education, and skills which facilitate upward mobility. It should not be startling, therefore, to find similar variations in the availability of illegitimate means."[31]

MOBILITY.  The industrial and democratic revolutions were accompanied by increased mobility as well as by a conflict between increased aspirations and conditions of the social structure. The new condition of mobility was compatible with the individualistic ideology, and it was at the same time incompatible with political absolutism. In the first place, the large family and the homogeneous neighborhood, which had been the principal agencies of social control, disintegrated, primarily as the result of mobility.[32]

[29] Cf. Judith Blake and Kingsley Davis, "Norms, Values, and Sanctions," Chapter 13 in Robert E. L. Faris, Editor, *Handbook of Modern Sociology*, Chicago: Rand-McNally, 1964, pp. 456–484.

[30] Henry D. McKay, "The Neighborhood and Child Conduct," *Annals of the American Academy of Political and Social Science*, 261:32–42, January, 1949. See also, South Side Community Committee, *Bright Shadows in Bronzetown* (Chicago: Author, 1949), pp. 26–28.

[31] Richard A. Cloward, "Illegitimate Means, Anomie, and Deviant Behavior," *American Sociological Review*, 24:164–176, April, 1959. See also Albert K. Cohen and James F. Short, Jr., "Research in Delinquent Subcultures," *Journal of Social Issues*, 14:20–37, No. 3, 1958.

[32] See Kingsley Davis, *Human Society* (New York: Macmillan, 1949), pp. 392–429.

They were replaced by the small family consisting of parents and children, detached from other relatives, and by a neighborhood in which the mores were not homogeneous. Many family functions were transferred to other social institutions, resulting in a weak family unit in which the members had relatively few activities or interests in common. Similarly, the neighborhood ceased to function as an effective socializing agency in which the pressures for conformity were intimate, personal, and consistent.

Second, with increased mobility the problem of control was greatly intensified, for the boundaries of frequent and effective interaction were extended from the local community to nations and then to most of the earth in the form of commerce, travel, newspapers, and other means of communication. When interaction was confined to the local community, spontaneous and sentimental influences controlled behavior, for the effect of the behavior of a person was immediately apparent to himself and to others. When interaction extended beyond the area of intimate association, the effects of the behavior were not immediately discernible either to the members of any local community or to the participants in the broader area of interaction. Because of increased mobility, a condition of anonymity was created, and the agencies by which control had been secured in almost all earlier societies were greatly weakened. It is probable that the family and neighborhood would have been relatively impotent to control their members in activities with outsiders, even if they had been retained in their original strength, for these agencies cannot be effective in the control of behavior occurring far away from their location. A certain national loyalty, somewhat comparable to the loyalties in the earlier primary groups, flourished in connection with the doctrine of the divinity of royalty, but apparently the common people did not take this doctrine as seriously as did royalty, and when the belief in the doctrine disintegrated, no effective substitute was found.

We may conclude that mobility of persons and of commodities widens the area within which control becomes necessary and at the same time weakens the local agencies of control in the communities into which the migrants move. However, this conclusion is not based on sufficient evidence to justify a definitive statement regarding the significance of mobility to criminality. It is possible that rapid changes in technology may create conditions under which the criminal laws, written for social conditions as they existed before the technological changes, must almost necessarily be violated if the new technologies are to be retained.[33] Certain

[33] W. F. Ogburn, *Social Change* (Second Edition, New York: Viking Press, 1952), Part IV.

students of law, on the other hand, have insisted that the prevalence of crime is due to the fact that the law has been extended much more rapidly than the general mores, and that when the law is not thus supported by general mores it is relatively important and is violated frequently.[34] In either case, the most relevant variable is the normative conflict which has arisen to provide alternative patterns of conduct, some of which are clearly violations of the criminal law.

A few studies of the relationship between horizontal mobility and the crime rate have been made, but they have been directed toward analysis of the direct effects of mobility in a contemporary situation. They fail to measure the full significance of mobility, for the effects of this process on criminality are principally indirect and are diffused over a period of time and over a wide area. The data are presented, however, as illustrations of the first efforts to study this process. McKenzie found a correlation of 0.39 between juvenile delinquency and mobility by wards in Columbus, and Sullenger found a correlation of 0.34 in a similar study in Omaha.[35] Carpenter concluded that a criminal group studied in Buffalo was much more migratory than a control group in the same city.[36] Stuart, in a study in Berkeley, found that delinquents lived in areas which had high rates of mobility, but that they personally were less mobile than the average family.[37] Reiss showed that 39 percent of a group of delinquent probationers in Chicago had resided at the present address for less than three years, and the Gluecks found that 33.6 percent of their delinquents, as compared with only 14.8 percent of the nondelinquents, were at their present address for less than one year.[38] Hotels suffer loss by theft roughly in proportion to the transiency of their guests. One city hotel serving transients suffers a loss by theft of about 25,000 towels a year, and another hotel lost by theft within two years one-fifth of the pictures which had

[34] K. N. Llewellyn, "Law Observance versus Law Enforcement," *Proceedings of the National Conference of Social Work*, 1928, pp. 127–136; Jerome Frank, "Realistic Reflections on Law as a Constructive Social Force," *Proceedings of the National Conference of Social Work*, 1933, pp. 326–332; Herman Oliphant, "The Public and the Law," *American Bar Association Journal*, 18:787–791, December, 1932.

[35] R. D. McKenzie, "The Neighborhood," *American Journal of Sociology*, 28:166, September, 1921; T. E. Sullenger, *Social Determinants in Juvenile Delinquency* (New York: John Wiley and Sons, 1936), p. 179. See also his, "The Social Significance of Mobility: An Omaha Study," *American Journal of Sociology*, 55:559–564, May, 1950.

[36] Niles Carpenter and William M. Haenszel, "Migratoriness and Criminality in Buffalo," *Social Forces*, 9:254–255, December, 1930.

[37] Johannes Stuart, "Mobility and Delinquency," *American Journal of Orthopsychiatry*, 6:486–493, October, 1936.

[38] Albert J. Reiss, Jr., "The Accuracy, Efficiency, and Validity of a Prediction Instrument," *American Journal of Sociology*, 56:552–561, May, 1951. Sheldon and Eleanor T. Glueck, *Unraveling Juvenile Delinquency* (New York: The Commonwealth Fund, 1950), p. 80.

been hung on the walls at the time it opened.[39] These statistics give some understanding of the reason why the word "traveler" in medieval England was used in popular discourse to designate the thief. Such statistics, however, are entirely inadequate as demonstrations of the significance of horizontal mobility, for the important point is that mobility has affected all persons in modern society and not merely those who are non-residents at the time of a crime.

CULTURE CONFLICT.  Like "social disorganization," the concept "culture conflict" has been used to refer to social conditions characterized by a lack of consistency and harmony in the influences which direct the individual. The concept has not been clearly formulated, however, for it sometimes is used as a synonym for "normative conflict" and sometimes is restricted to only the normative conflict arising from migration of conduct norms from one area to another.[40] We shall use the term in the latter sense, to refer to a special kind of normative conflict. As we have seen, normative conflict can develop *within* a culture, without the introduction of norms from other cultural areas. It also can arise when the norms of one cultural area come into conflict with those of another. Most of the American research on the relationships between "culture conflict" and crime has been concerned with normative conflict arising in the latter process, the interpenetration of cultural codes. This emphasis no doubt reflects an interest in America's "immigrant problem."

Conflicts between the norms of behavior of divergent cultural codes may arise in at least three ways.[41] First, the codes may clash on the border of contiguous culture areas. Speck observed, for example, that:

Where the bands popularly known as the Montagnais have come more and more into contact with Whites, their reputation has fallen lower among the traders who have known them through commercial relationships within that period. The accusation is made that they have become less honest in connection with their debts, less trustworthy with property, less truthful, and more inclined to alcoholism and sexual freedom as contacts with the frontier towns have become easier for them.[42]

With increased mobility and the development of communication processes, the "border" between such divergent cultures has become extremely broad, for knowledge concerning divergent conduct norms no longer arises solely

[39] N. S. Hayner, "Hotel Life and Personality," *American Journal of Sociology*, 33:792, March, 1928; Margaret A. Barnes, "How We Behave Away from Home," *American Magazine*, 111:23, March, 1931.

[40] Sellin, *op. cit.*, p. 58.

[41] *Ibid.*, pp. 63–67.

[42] *Op. cit.* Reprinted by permission of the publishers.

out of direct personal contacts. The old social relations and standards of behavior which had been adequate for control while China was relatively isolated from the rest of the world have proved inadequate in more recent years, when the cultures of other groups have been introduced into China through impersonal means. Remarkable changes in criminality have occurred.[43] In the United States, Evelyn Crook found that 86 percent of the delinquent girls who were studied resided on racial or language "frontiers," where two or more racial groups came in contact, and only 14 percent resided in the interior of a racial or language group. The exact proportion of children residing on frontiers of this kind, which one should know in order to construct a rate of delinquency, was not available, but certainly it was much less than 86 percent.[44]

2) Second, in "colonization" the laws and norms of one cultural group may be extended to cover the territory of another, with the result that traditional ways of behaving suddenly become illegal. For example, when Soviet law was extended to Siberian tribes, women who obeyed the Soviet law and laid aside their veils were killed by their relatives for violating the norms of the tribes. Wearing a veil was illegal from the point of view of Soviet law, and not wearing a veil was illegal from the point of view of tribal law. Similarly, before French law was introduced in Algeria, the killing of an adulterous woman was the right and duty of the woman's father or brother; but under the French law such killing became a crime, punishable by death.

3) Third, when participants in one culture migrate to another culture, they may take with them ways of behaving which clash with the norms of the receiving culture. This process is the reverse of the one just discussed, and it occurs when the migrant group is politically weaker than the group whose territory is invaded. If the Algerians in the above illustration had moved to France, they would have introduced divergent norms in that nation. After a period of dominance by English customs and laws, many conflicting norms were introduced in the United States by this process. Generally, the immigrant population, having reached maturity in the Old World environment, remains relatively isolated and has a relatively low crime rate when the immigrants settle in America, but some studies show that the sons of immigrants have a much higher crime rate than their parents or the native-born of native parentage, apparently because the second generation, like the Siberian women, finds it difficult to identify

[43] Ching Yueh-yen, *op. cit.* This discussion refers to pre-Communist China.
[44] Evelyn B. Crook, "Cultural Marginality in Sexual Delinquency," *American Journal of Sociology*, 39:593–600, January, 1934.

the proper ways of behaving.[45] Also, some studies, though not all, have concluded that the native-born children with one parent native-born and the other foreign-born have a higher rate than native-born children with both parents foreign-born or both parents native-born, and this also seems to be due to the greater divergence of norms in those cases. Psychiatrists and social workers find these conflicts within the home to be highly significant in emotional disturbances of children, and they feel that the emotional disturbances are conducive to delinquency.[46]

TENDENCIES TOWARD INTEGRATION. The individualistic system in business and politics has been modified in the last generation or two in its material aspects. Free competition was ruining individuals and they were driven into corporate activities. Huge corporations, huge banks, chain stores, chain theaters, chain newspapers, and broadcasting companies have developed. Trade associations, trade unions, chamber of commerce, and many other associations have also been formed. To an increasing extent, the behavior and opportunities of individuals are determined and defined by these corporations and associations. Thus, the general development has been from feudalism and absolutism to individualism, and from individualism to private and public collectivism. But the transition from individualism has been confined principally to material effects. Corporations and associations have no more interest in general social welfare than did the competing individuals who preceded them. The ideology of individualism still remains in a world of corporate activity.[47] This may be seen in the frequency with which the directors and officers of corporations are traitors to their stockholders, in the competition between associations for financial advantages, and in many other ways.

Four tendencies toward social integration, aside from the corporate activities described above, may be discovered in the modern world. First, a wider uniformity of behavior and a greater degree of identification of self with others are secured by newspapers, radio, theaters, television, and public education. This interest, however, is restricted in scope or is concerned with ephemeral incidents. Its importance may be indicated in relation to

[45] E. D. Beynon, "Crime and Custom of the Hungarians of Detroit," *Journal of Criminal Law and Criminology*, 25:755–774, January–February, 1935; Rose H. Lee, "Delinquent, Neglected, and Dependent Chinese Boys and Girls of the San Francisco Bay Region," *Journal of Social Psychology*, 36:15–34, August, 1952. See below, pp. 152–158.

[46] John Levy, "Conflict of Cultures and Children's Maladjustments," *Mental Hygiene*, 17:41–50, January, 1933. See also Louis Wirth, "Culture Conflicts and Delinquency," *Social Forces*, 9:484–492, June, 1931; Eleanor T. Glueck, "Culture Conflict and Delinquency," *Mental Hygiene*, 21:46–66, January, 1937.

[47] Cf. Clinard, op. cit.

bribery of athletes. In 1919, when Arnold Rothstein, a notorious gambler and gangster, bribed some of the baseball players in the world series to "throw" the game, a tremendous pressure for punishment of the players and the briber was exerted. Bribery of a member of the President's cabinet provoked less popular antagonism than the bribery of these baseball players. An almost identical reaction to bribery of college basketball players occurred in 1950–1951. The players were dismissed, and in some states laws were enacted which made the penalty for giving bribes in athletic contests more severe than the penalty for robbery with a gun. On this point, the public or that part of it which counted in athletics presented a united front. It is possible that baseball or some other sport could become the nucleus around which public morality may be unified, as has been claimed of cricket in England; but in general the public interests, like the newspapers and other agencies of communication which largely create them, are fluctuating, unstable, and concerned with unimportant things.

2) A second tendency toward uniformity of thought and attitudes is seen in the recent artificial efforts to develop nationalism in Europe, as in the Nazi régime in Germany, Fascism in Italy, Sovietism in Russia, and dictatorships in other countries. These movements, like the New Deal in the United States, were gropings toward social organization to replace the individualism which had broken down or was breaking down economically, legally, and politically.

3) Third, the rise of suburban living in the United States, a leveling-off of the birth rate, and the near elimination of immigration should permit the development of a cultural homogeneity that has not been possible since the early nineteenth century. The passing of the population expansion phase of our history, together with industrial decentralization, may lead to a cessation of city growth, may permit the development of neighborhoods and residential suburbs of a primary-group type, and may reduce the speculative aspect of economic life.

4) A fourth tendency toward homogeneity may be found in the development of scientific activities and intellectual honesty. The number of scientific people in modern society is not large, but the results of science have permeated all society to a greater or lesser extent. The attitude of scientific inquiry is an important variable to be considered in analysis of changes in some of the old institutions. A characteristic of the changes in social organization described earlier was their incompatability with intellectual honesty.[48]

[48] P. W. Bridgman, "The Struggle for Intellectual Integrity," *Harpers*, 168:18–25, December, 1933.

## SUGGESTED READINGS

Arnold, Thurman, *The Folklore of Capitalism*. New Haven: Yale University Press, 1937.

Barron, Milton L., "Juvenile Delinquency and American Values," *American Sociological Review*, 16:208–214, April, 1951.

Bell, Daniel, "Crime as an American Way of Life," *Antioch Review*, 13: 131–154, June, 1953.

Blake, Judith, and Kingsley Davis, "Norms, Values, and Sanctions," Chapter 13 in Robert E. L. Faris, Editor, *Handbook of Modern Sociology*. Chicago: Rand-McNally, 1964, pp. 456–484.

Bordua, David J., "Delinquent Subcultures: Sociological Interpretations of Gang Delinquency," *Annals of the American Academy of Political and Social Science*, 338:119–136. November, 1961.

Clinard, Marshal B., *The Black Market*. New York: Rinehart, 1952.

Cloward, Richard A., "Illegitimate Means, Anomie, and Deviant Behavior," *American Sociological Review*, 24:164–176, April, 1959.

Cloward, Richard A., and Lloyd E. Ohlin, *Delinquency and Opportunity: A Theory of Delinquent Gangs*. Glencoe: The Free Press, 1960.

Cohen, Albert K., *Delinquent Boys: The Culture of the Gang*. Glencoe: The Free Press, 1955.

Cook, Fred J., and Gene Gleason, "The Shame of New York," *The Nation*, 189:261–321, October 31, 1959.

Crook, Evelyn B., "Cultural Marginality in Sexual Delinquency," *American Journal of Sociology*, 39:493–500, January, 1934.

Dewey, John, "Individualism, Old and New," *New Republic*, 61:239–241, 294–296; 62:13–16, 184–188, January–April, 1930.

Glueck, Eleanor T., "Culture Conflict and Delinquency," *Mental Hygiene*, 21:46–66, January, 1937.

Goode, William J., "A Theory of Role Strain," *American Sociological Review*, 25:483–496, August, 1960.

Hacker, Louis M., *The Shaping of American Tradition*. New York: Columbia University Press, 1947.

Hall, A. C., *Crime in Its Relation to Social Progress*. New York: Columbia University Press, 1902.

Henry, Andrew F., and James F. Short, Jr., *Suicide and Homicide: Some Economic, Sociological, and Psychological Aspects of Aggression*. Glencoe: The Free Press, 1954.

Kvaraceus, W. C., and Walter B. Miller, *Delinquent Behavior: Culture and the Individual*. Washington: National Education Association, 1959.

Levy, John, "Conflict of Cultures and Children's Maladjustments," *Mental Hygiene*, 17:41–50, January, 1933.

Llewellyn, K. N., "Law Observance versus Law Enforcement," *Proceed-*

ings of the National Conference of Social Work, 1928, pp. 127–136.

Matza, David, and Gresham M. Sykes, "Juvenile Delinquency and Subterranean Values," American Sociological Review, 26:712–719, October, 1961.

Oliphant, Herman, "The Public and the Law," American Bar Association Journal, 18:787–793, December, 1932.

Price, Maurice, "The Concept of Culture Conflict," Social Forces, 9:164–167, December, 1930.

Reifen, David, "Observations on the Juvenile Court in Israel," Social Service Review, 26:202–214, June, 1952.

Reinhardt, James M., "Crime in a Discordant Culture," Journal of Criminal Law and Criminology, 41:32–35, May–June, 1950.

Rhodes, H. T. F., The Criminals We Deserve. London: Methuen, 1937.

Sellin, Thorsten, Culture Conflict and Crime. New York: Social Science Research Council, 1938.

Veblen, Thorstein, Theory of the Leisure Class. New York: Macmillan, 1912.

Wirth, Louis, "Culture Conflicts and Delinquency," Social Forces, 9:484–492, June, 1931.

Wirth, Louis, "Urbanism as a Way of Life," American Journal of Sociology, 44:1–24, July, 1938.

Wood, Arthur L., "Political Radicalism in Changing Sinhalese Villages," Human Organization, 23:99–107, Summer, 1964.

# 6. PHYSICAL AND PHYSIOLOGICAL CONDITIONS AND CRIME

ALTHOUGH CRIME and criminality are by definition social phenomena, men have for centuries entertained the notion that they are the products of non-social causes. This notion has been expressed in many essays and research studies on the relationship between crime rates and certain physical conditions of the earth, and on the relationship between criminality and certain aspects of the biological make-up of the criminal. The data have been confined to arrest and incarceration rates and to criminals who are arrested and prosecuted; the white-collar criminal and the unapprehended criminal are not represented. This chapter reports on the more significant recent essays and studies and discusses the conclusions which may be drawn from them.

PHYSICAL ENVIRONMENT. For many generations, some scholars have attempted to discover and demonstrate physical determinants of criminal behavior. They have reported that crimes against property are more frequent in winter months and crimes against the person are more frequent in summer months; and, analogous to this, that crimes against property increase and crimes against the person decrease with the distance from the equator.[1] It has been reported also that crime rates vary with changes in barometric pressures and with direction of the wind.[2] Other scholars have

[1] The research studies on this point are reviewed by G. Aschaffenburg, *Crime and Its Repression* (Boston: Little, Brown and Company, 1913), pp. 16–30; Gerhard J. Falk, "Influence of Seasons on Crime Rate," *Journal of Criminal Law, Criminology, and Police Science*, 43:199–213, July–August, 1952; and Sidney J. Kaplan, "The Geography of Crime," in Joseph S. Roucek, Editor, *Sociology of Crime*, New York: Philosophical Library, 1961, pp. 160–192.

[2] C. A. Mills, "Suicide and Homicide in Their Relation to Weather Changes," *American Journal of Psychiatry*, 91:669–677, November, 1934; Manfred Curry, "The Relationship of Weather Conditions, Facial Characteristics, and Crime," *Journal of Criminal Law and Criminology*, 39:253–261, July–August, 1948; Y. S. Mehendale, "Physical Environment and Adolescent Crime," *Indian Journal of Social Work*, 16:146–152, No. 3, 1955.

reported that crimes are frequent in mountainous areas and infrequent in plains areas, or are frequent near the coast, and infrequent in the interior.

These reports and claims may be appraised in two propositions. First, the association between crime rates and these physical conditions at best is slight; in some cases not even a slight association has been demonstrated.[3] In general, many exceptions can be found, such as the fact that infant murders are highest in the winter, although most other crimes against the person are highest in the summer. Second, these physical conditions provide the habitat for human life and consequently may facilitate or impede contacts among human beings and perhaps in that sense be related to opportunities for criminal behavior.[4] For example, the greater frequency of crimes against the person in summer months is presumably due to the greater frequency of contacts among human beings in those months. Schmid reported that in Seattle homicides reach the maximum in the winter and explained that this was due to the influx of migratory laborers in the late autumn.[5] It has not been demonstrated that changes in physical conditions change the attitudes and values which are conducive to criminal behavior.

HEREDITY.   In the early part of the present century the discussion of causes of crime was concentrated on the controversy between heredity and environment and this controversy continues, with decreasing attention, in the present generation. Five methods have been used in the effort to reach conclusions on the question of whether criminality is hereditary: comparison of criminals with the "savage," family trees, Mendelian ratios in family trees, statistical associations between crimes of parents and of offspring, and comparison of identical and fraternal twins.

Lombroso and his followers used comparisons of criminals and "savages" as their method of studying inheritance of criminality.[6] They considered that the typical criminal was a born criminal and attributed this to atavism, or "throw-back" to lower animal and savage life. Their principal evidence that criminality was atavistic was the resemblance of the criminal subjects to the savage, but the characteristics of the savage were assumed, not determined by reliable methods. The result was that Lombroso had no significant proof or explanation of the inheritance of criminality.

[3] Ernest LaRoche and Louis Tilley, "Weather and Crime in Tallahassee," *Journal of Criminal Law and Criminology*, 47:218–219, July–August, 1956.

[4] Henry A. Bullock, "Urban Homicide in Theory and Fact," *Journal of Criminal Law and Criminology*, 45:565–575, January–February, 1955.

[5] C. F. Schmid, "A Study of Homicides in Seattle" *Social Forces*, 4:745–756, June, 1926.

[6] See above, pp. 56–57.

Family trees have been used extensively by certain scholars in the effort to prove that criminality is inherited. Perhaps the most famous of these is the study of the Jukes family by Dugdale and Estabrook, who reported that of about 1,200 members of this family, 140 were criminals; seven were convicted of murder, 60 of theft, and 50 of prostitution.[7] Often compared with the Jukes family were the descendants of Jonathan Edwards, a famous preacher in the colonial period; none of his descendants were found to be criminals, while many were Presidents of the United States, governors of states, members of the Supreme Court and of other high courts, and famous writers, preachers, teachers. The specific difficulty about this comparison is that some of Jonathan Edwards' ancestors did have criminal records; his maternal grandmother was divorced on the ground of adultery, his grand aunt murdered her son, his grand uncle murdered his own sister. If criminality be inherited, Jonathan Edwards and many of his descendants should have been criminals. The more general argument against a conclusion from the study of family trees is that it shows only that a trait appears in successive generations; this does not prove that the trait is inherited. The use of the fork in eating has been a trait of many families for several generations, but this does not prove that a tendency to use a fork is inherited. Every child in the Jukes family has been subject to the influences of social interaction as well as of heredity, and the culture of this family was customarily conducive to crime. Dahlström has shown that in a family of criminals whose records for four generations were known, six children removed from the family before the age of seven became respectable members of society and two removed after the age of seven became criminals.[8]

Some years ago, a German study of the family histories of 98 inmates of a penal institution led to the conclusion that criminality not only appears in successive generations but also that it appears in accordance with the expected Mendelian ratios.[9] The criminality in the families investigated by Dugdale, Estabrook, and others showed no resemblance to the Mendelian ratios. The fallacy in the German study is that the criminality of the offspring is used to determine the nature of the parent and then the nature of the parent is used to explain the criminality of the offspring. Since criminality is assumed to be a recessive trait, the trait of an ancestor (duplex, simplex, nulliplex) can be determined by assumption. There is a

[7] Richard Dugdale, *The Jukes, A Study in Crime, Pauperism and Heredity* (New York: Putnam, 1877). A. H. Estabrook, *The Jukes in 1915* (Washington: Carnegie Institution, 1916).

[8] Sigürd Dahlström, "Is the Young Criminal a Continuation of the Neglected Child?" *Journal of Delinquency*, 12:97–121, June, 1928.

[9] Carl Rath, *Ueber die Vererbung von Dispositionen zum Verbrechen* (Stuttgart: Spemann, 1914).

necessary defect in studies of this kind, for it is not possible to control the breeding of human beings for a sufficient period of time to determine whether a particular individual is "pure," as can be done for plants and insects.

4)   Goring attempted to prove by elaborate correlations that the criminalistic tendency is inherited and that environment conditions are of slight importance to criminality. He found that criminality, measured by imprisonment, of fathers and sons was correlated by a coefficient of +.60, which is very nearly the same as the coefficient for stature, span, length of forearm, eye color, diathesis of tuberculosis, insane diathesis, and hereditary deafness; and that brothers had a coefficient of correlation for criminality of +.45, which is approximately the same as for physical traits.[10] Goring realized that such correlations might be the result of either heredity or environment or both, and he attempted to eliminate the factor of environment on the hypothesis that if the influence of environmental factors is found to be very low, heredity will, by elimination, be the explanation. In order to do this, he divided environmental factors into "contagion" and "force of circumstances," and his argument regarding them is as follows: (a) The resemblance of fathers and sons regarding criminality is not due to "contagion." First, the coefficient of correlation is no higher in crimes of stealing, in which fathers are examples for their sons, than in sex crimes, which fathers ordinarily attempt to conceal from their sons and in which therefore they are not examples. Second, children taken away from the influence of parents at an early age, by imprisonment, become confirmed criminals to a greater extent than those taken at a later age. (b) This resemblance is not due to the "force of circumstances," such as poverty, standard of living, or ignorance, because, after the influence of defective intelligence is eliminated by the use of partial correlations, the correlation between criminality and "force of circumstances" is negligible.

The argument and methods that Goring used are open to criticism at a great many points. The following defects are found in his arguments: (a) He attempted to determine the importance of heredity by eliminating the influence of environment. If this were to be done accurately, it would be necessary to measure completely the influence of environment, but Goring considered only eight environmental factors, which are a relatively small part of the total environment. (b) He assumed that mental ability is not at all affected by environment, and by thus underrating the environment he overrated heredity. (c) His comparison of stealing and sex offenses is based on an assumption that parental contagion is restricted entirely to

[10] Charles Goring, *The English Convict* (London: His Majesty's Stationery Office, 1913), p. 369.

techniques of crimes, and he did not consider the possibility that transmission of more general values is more important. (d) The removal of a child from the home to prison at an early age does not remove the child from a criminalistic to a non-criminalistic environment, as Goring assumed. (e) He restricted his study to male criminals, although he mentions the fact that the ratio of brothers to sisters in respect to imprisonment is 102 to 6. If criminal diathesis is inherited to the same extent that color of the eyes is inherited, it must affect females to the same extent as males unless it is sex-linked. Since, according to Goring, the diathesis consists entirely of physical and mental inferiority, sex-linkage is not plausible. These defects in Goring's arguments undermine his conclusion so that it carries no weight as a demonstration of the inheritance of criminality.

The fifth method of measuring the relation of heredity to criminality is the comparison of identical twins, which are the product of a single egg, with fraternal twins, which are the product of two eggs fertilized by two sperms. Heredity is assumed to be identical in the former and different in the latter. Lange made a study of thirty pairs of adult male twins; thirteen of the pairs were identical twins and seventeen fraternal twins. One member of each pair was a criminal, and whenever the twin was also criminal the pair was termed "concordant." The problem was to determine whether concordance would be more frequent among the group of identical twins than among the group of fraternal twins. He found that 77 percent of the pairs of identical twins and only 12 percent of the pairs of fraternal twins were concordant, that is, both criminal. The similarity of identical twins with reference to criminality was thus 6.4 times as great as the similarity of fraternal twins.[11] This greater similarity was assumed to be a measure of the inheritance of criminality, but it is subject to scepticism on two points. First, the number of cases of each type is very small, and a shift of one or two cases from one category to the other would produce a significant difference in the conclusions. Second, the classification of a particular pair of twins as identical or fraternal must be doubtful in many cases, since evidence as to the birth process is seldom available.

Lange's work was hailed as proof of the inheritance of criminality. However, three later studies of twins in European countries by methods similar to those of Lange show for all the cases in the three studies that the frequency of similarity in criminal behavior among identical twins was only 1.4 times as great as the frequency among fraternal twins.[12] One of the

[11] Johannes Lange, Verbrechen als Schicksal (Leipzig: Thieme, 1919); translated by Charlotte Haldane with the title Crime and Destiny (New York: Boni), 1930.

[12] A. M. Legras, Psychose en Criminaliteit bei Tweelingen (Utrecht: Kemink, 1932); F. Stumpfl, Die Ursprünge des Verbrechens (Leipzig: Thieme, 1936); Heinrich Kranz, Lebensschicksale Krimineller Zwillinge (Berlin: Springer, 1936).

most extensive studies of the criminality of twins was later made by Rosanoff and others on adult criminality, juvenile delinquency, and child behavior problems. This study showed, for all types of cases combined, approximately three times as much concordance among identical twins as fraternal twins.[13] The procedures in this study, however, are so inaccurate that the conclusions are worthless. This may be illustrated with reference to the juvenile delinquents in the study. A juvenile delinquent was rigorously defined as a child under eighteen years of age brought before the juvenile court on a delinquency petition and either placed on probation or committed to a correctional institution. According to the brief descriptions given in the Rosanoff report, all delinquents of the fraternal type conform to this definition, while 9 of the 29 male juvenile delinquents of the identical-twin type fail to conform to the definition, and consequently should not be included as concordant cases. If correction be made for those cases which do not conform to the definition, concordance appears among identical twins only 1.1 times as frequently as it appears among fraternal twins. This difference is not sufficiently great to create a presumption of inheritance.

Even if a difference between the two types of twins in reference to concordance in criminality be accepted, the conclusion that criminality is inherited does not necessarily follow. The difference between the two types of twins may be explained in whole or in part by two other conditions. First, as compared to the homes of the fraternal twins, the homes of the identical twins seemed to be more frequently characterized by economic distress, illegitimacy, drunkenness, feeble-mindedness, and psychoses. In such homes, regardless of the nature of twinship, both members of the pairs of twins are more frequently delinquent than in homes not characterized by such conditions. This observation is based upon descriptions given in the Rosanoff report, but no explanation for this relationship between identical twins and poor homes is available. Second, the environments of identical twins are more nearly alike, psychologically, than the environments of fraternal twins. Because of the difficulty of distinguishing one identical twin from the other, the reactions of other persons toward identical twins will be more nearly alike than the reactions of others toward fraternal twins.[14] These reactions of others are the most important

[13] A. J. Rosanoff, Leva M. Handy, and Isabel A. Rosanoff, "Etiology of Child Behavior Difficulties, Juvenile Delinquency, and Adult Criminality," *Psychiatric Monographs*, No. 1 (Department of Institutions, California, 1941).
[14] Ernest R. Mowrer, "Some Factors in the Affectional Adjustment of Twins," *American Sociological Review*, 16:468–471, August, 1954; H. H. Newman, *Multiple Human Births: Twins, Triplets, Quadruplets, and Quintuplets* (New York: Doubleday, 1940), p. 160.

part of the "environment." In general, therefore, the study of twins has failed as completely as other procedures to demonstrate the inheritance of criminality.

Two positive propositions and one negative proposition can be stated as conclusions regarding the relation of heredity to crime. *First*, criminals, like all human beings, have some inherited traits which make it possible for them to behave like human beings. This proposition, however, does not aid in explaining why some human beings commit crimes and others do not. *Second*, some inherited characteristics may be significantly related to criminal behavior by virtue of the fact that members of a society have learned to react to them in a certain way. For example, the color of the skin of the Negro is reacted to in a certain way in the United States, and the crime rate is high among Negroes. But this proposition is not relevant to explaining criminality on the basis of heredity, for traits which are not inherited may be reacted to in a significant way and may likewise be associated with criminal behavior. The *third* proposition is that, except in the two senses previously stated, heredity has not been demonstrated to have any connection whatever with criminal behavior. If persons with certain inherited traits are more likely to commit crimes than persons with other inherited traits, these traits have not been identified, and their connection with criminal behavior has not been demonstrated.[15] It is obviously impossible for criminality to be inherited as such, for crime is defined by acts of legislatures and these vary independently of the biological inheritance of the violators of the laws.

ANATOMICAL CONDITIONS. Lombroso insisted that criminals differed from non-criminals with reference to certain physical traits which he called "stigmata of degeneracy." He found these physical deviations in all parts of the anatomy but placed particular emphasis on deviations in the shape of the cranium. Goring made careful measurements of several thousand prisoners in comparison with the general population and reached the conclusion that prisoners differed anatomically from the general population only in being slightly shorter in stature and slightly lighter in weight. Goring's work is generally accepted as having demolished the early Lombrosian view that criminals are characterized by certain stigmata and constitute an inferior biological type. However, in the late 1930's Hooton, an American anthropologist, attempted to revive the Lombrosian theory. He made elaborate measurements of thousands of prisoners and of a few non-

---

[15] Cf. M. F. Ashley-Montagu, "The Biologist Looks at Crime," *Annals of the American Academy of Political and Social Science*, 217:46–57, September, 1941; L. S. Penrose, "Genetics and the Criminal," *British Journal of Delinquency*, 6:15–25, No. 1, 1955.

prisoners. He found a few slight differences between the two classes and concluded that "the primary cause of crime is biological inferiority."[16] Three principal criticisms of Hooton's procedures and conclusions have been made. *First, his control groups are so small* and so selected that they are worthless as a sample of the non-criminal population, and consequently he has no means of showing that criminals differ from non-criminals. He used 29 Italian-Americans as a sample of the Italian-American non-criminal population, and about 150 Nashville firemen and 150 Boston outpatients, militiamen, and patrons of a bathhouse as a sample of the native-white-parentage, non-criminal population of the United States. The Nashville firemen differed from the Boston control group in more respects than either of these control groups differed from the prisoners. *Second, he* found few significant differences between criminals and non-criminals and used a surprisingly large number of measurements which were practically identical. Consequently his data give practically no basis for his conclusions. *Third,* he had no criterion of biological inferiority. He apparently assumed that persons who were imprisoned were inferior; by this logic males should be appraised as biologically inferior to females since a larger proportion of males are imprisoned. It has been pointed out by Merton and Montagu that Hooton's criminals differed from the anthropoid apes in more respects than did the control groups; if similarity to anthropoid apes be accepted as a criterion of inferiority, the non-criminals are the inferior group and the criminals the superior group.

Other studies have generally reached the conclusion that criminals are not significantly different in physical traits from non-criminals.[17] For example, a study by the Institute for Juvenile Research of approximately 4,000 school boys between the ages of six and sixteen in two delinquency areas in Chicago concluded that on the average delinquents had fewer "stigmata of degeneracy" than non-delinquents.[18] Red hair was classified by Lombroso as one of the stigmata in degeneracy, and interest in this

[16] E. A. Hooton, *Crime and the Man* (Cambridge: Harvard University Press, 1939), p. 130. See also E. A. Hooton, *The American Criminal: An Anthropological Study* (Cambridge: Harvard University Press), 1939. The most careful appraisals of Hooton's study are the following: Robert K. Merton and M. F. Ashley-Montagu, "Crime and the Anthropologist," *American Anthropologist*, 42:384–408, August, 1940; James S. Wallerstein and Clement J. Wyle, " 'Biological Inferiority' as a Cause for Delinquency," *Nervous Child*, 6:467–472, October, 1947; N. S. Timasheff, "The Revival of Criminal Anthropology," *University of Kansas Law Review*, 9:91–100, February, 1941; William H. Tucker, "Is There Evidence of a Physical Basis for Criminal Behavior," *Journal of Criminal Law and Criminology*, 31:427–437, November–December, 1940.

[17] The recent studies have been summarized by W. Norwood East, "Physical Factors in Criminal Behavior," *Journal of Clinical Psychopathy*, 8:7–36, July, 1946.

[18] This study was made by S. Boshes, S. Kobrin, E. Reynolds, and S. Rosenbaum. The statement above is taken from an abstract by M. F. Ashley-Montagu, *op. cit.*

trait was revived by Von Hentig, who presented some evidence to the effect that American outlaws were red-haired to an unusual extent. This was vigorously denied by Rasch, and the relation of red hair to criminality has certainly not been demonstrated.[19]

The general body-build or somatotype also has received considerable attention as a possible explanation of criminal behavior.[20] Kretschmer developed a classification of somatotypes in relation to psychoses and general personality. Attempts have been made to use Kretschmer's classification in the study of criminals but thus far no relationship has been found between his body types and criminal behavior.[21]

Sheldon has more recently made another attempt to differentiate criminals from non-criminals in respect to somatotype.[22] He found three somatotypes—the endomorphic which is round and soft, the mesomorphic which is round and hard, and the ectomorphic which is thin and fragile—and claimed that three temperamental types and three psychiatric types are closely related with their somatotypes. After making a study of 200 young adults in a Boston welfare agency, whom he described as "more or less delinquent," he concluded that delinquents are different from non-delinquents in their somatotypes and in their related temperamental and psychiatric types. Also he assumed that these differences are in the direction of inferiority and that the inferiority is inherited. His data, in fact, do not justify the conclusion that the delinquents are different from the non-delinquents in general, the conclusion that the difference if it exists indicates inferiority, or the conclusion that the inferiority if it exists is inherited. On the contrary, he found that body types of these delinquents are much like those of business and military leaders and of psychiatrists. He had no criterion of inferiority. His only evidence of inheritance was that sons resemble their parents, and this similarity obviously may be due

[19] Hans von Hentig, "Redhead and Outlaw," *Journal of Criminal Law and Criminology*, 38:1–6, May–June, 1947; Hans von Hentig, *The Criminal and His Victim* (New Haven: Yale University Press, 1948), pp. 50–57; Philip J. Rasch, "Red Hair and Outlawry," *Journal of Criminal Law and Criminology*, 38:352–357, November–December, 1947.

[20] An excellent summary and appraisal of the general morphological theories of criminal behavior has been made by William A. Lessa, "An Appraisal of Constitutional Types," *Memoirs of the American Anthropological Society*, No. 62. (*American Anthropologist*, Volume 45, No. 4, Part 2, 1943); and "Somatomancy—Precursor of the Science of Human Constitution," *Scientific Monthly*, 75:355–365, December, 1952.

[21] See, for example, S. Blinkov, "Zur Frage nach Körperbau des Verbrechers," *Monatsschrift für Kriminalpsychologie*, 20:212–216, 1929; G. J. Mohr, "Incidence and Test Performance of Kretschmer Types among Convicts," *Archives of Neurology and Psychology*, 18:485–488, 1927; M. Riedl, "Ueber Beziehungen von Geistig-Körperlischen Constitution zur Kriminalität und anderen Defecten," *Monatsschrift für Kriminalpsychologie*, 23:473–484, 1932.

[22] William H. Sheldon, *Varieties of Delinquent Youth: An Introduction to Constitutional Psychiatry* (New York: Harpers, 1949).

to social experience rather than heredity.[23] The Gluecks have used the logic of Kretschmer and Sheldon in a study of juvenile delinquents.[24] Like Sheldon, they have adopted a system characterized by a noted physical anthropologist as a "new Phrenology in which the bumps of the buttocks take the place of the bumps on the skull."[25]

PHYSICAL AND PHYSIOLOGICAL DEFECTS. Physical defects such as blindness, deafness, and lameness are sometimes regarded as important in relation to criminality. These physical defects may be due to heredity, to antenatal conditions, to difficulties in the birth process, and to postnatal conditions. Regardless of their origin, their frequency in the criminal population in comparison with the non-criminal population is not known. The Massachusetts Census of 1905 reported that blind persons were not over-represented in the delinquent and criminal population, but there was a considerable excess of lameness and deafness among the offenders. The definitions of these defects, however, were not standardized and the difference shown in this census is not clearly reliable. No other statistical material in the United States or European countries carry any greater confidence. Optometrists have reported wide difference between the delinquents and school children in respect to defective vision, and offer the explanation that children with defective vision are more likely to become delinquent because of the physical irritation caused by defective vision and because of the difficulty in reading, which drives them into truancy and gang activities. One study reported that 55 percent of a criminal group had "flap ears" as compared with 23 percent of a non-criminal group. This difference was explained as due to the ignorance or neglect of parents: children who are neglected are permitted to sleep with one ear twisted under the head. They become delinquent for the same reason that they develop "flap ears," namely, the ignorance and neglect of the parents.[26] A Norwegian study found that of all males born in Oslo in 1933, 5 percent had become registered lawbreakers by January 1, 1958. A comparison of the offenders' and non-offenders' conditions of health revealed only slight differences. For example, 12 percent of the offenders and 9 percent of the

[23] Edwin H. Sutherland, "Critique of Sheldon's *Varieties of Delinquent Youth*," *American Sociological Review*, 16:10–14, February, 1951.

[24] Sheldon and Eleanor T. Glueck, *Physique and Delinquency* (New York: Harper, 1956). See also Sanford J. Fox, "Delinquency and Biology," *University of Miami Law Review*, 16:65–91, Fall, 1961.

[25] S. L. Washburn, "Review of W. H. Sheldon, *Varieties of Delinquent Youth*," *American Anthropologist*, 53:561–563, December, 1951.

[26] T. W. Kilmer, "A Study of the Human Ear from the Standpoint of Identification in Criminology," *Correction* (New York State Department of Correction), 2:12, November, 1932.

non-offenders had been given medical discharges from military service, and there were insignificant differences in regard to other medical decisions. The differences were all in the same direction, however: The offenders were placed in somewhat lower "grades" of physical fitness. The offenders were slightly shorter than non-offenders, but when educational level was held constant this difference disappeared. The differences in height among non-offenders of differing educational levels were much greater than the differences between offenders and non-offenders on the same educational level.[27]

Though physical defects have not been shown to be present in criminal populations to a significantly higher degree than in non-criminal populations, they are significant in some individual cases. However, this significance depends upon the reactions of other persons toward the defects.[28] The child with enlarged tonsils who consistently holds his mouth open, the child with crossed eyes, and the child who stutters or lisps may or may not meet ridicule and suffer loss of social status which leads him to identification with delinquents. Both the person with a physical defect and other persons are likely to find the defect irritating, and for the person with the defect the sequence may be of irritation, retardation and dissatisfaction with school or work, truancy, association with delinquents, and a general view of one's self as an outcast.

Undernourishment, disease, and poor health are sometimes reported to be found among criminals in excessive proportions, while in other investigations no significant difference is found between criminals and non-criminals.[29] In some studies, recidivists are reported to be in better health than first offenders. While there is no reason to minimize the importance of good health, it is apparent that the connection between crime and physical ailments is not close or necessary. Many criminals are quite healthy; many non-criminals have physical ailments. Even if a statistical difference could be shown, the criminality would not be demonstrated to be a product of the poor health rather than of the conditions which produced the poor health or other conditions.

Other physiological abnormalities which are less evident have also been regarded as important by some writers. During the decade of the twenties popular and semi-popular writers placed much emphasis on the endocrine

---

[27] Nils Christie, *Unge Norske Lovovertredere* (Young Norwegian Lawbreakers), Oslo: Universitetsforlaget, 1960, pp. 211–219, 306–307.
[28] R. S. Banay, "Physical Disfigurement as a Factor in Delinquency and Crime," *Federal Probation*, 7:21 ff., January, 1943; Raymond J. Corsini, "Appearance and Criminality," *American Journal of Sociology*, 65:49–51, July, 1959.
[29] These studies are reviewed by W. Norwood East, *op. cit.*

glands as determiners of personality and of criminal behavior.[30] Endocrinologists in general have been much more cautious than these popular writers, and they generally state that no conclusion has been reached regarding the relation between the endocrine glands and criminal behavior.[31]

AGE RATIOS IN CRIME.    Despite all their limitations, statistics on crime give information important to our understanding of crime and to hypotheses and theories about it. Similarities and differences in crime rates for certain categories of persons are so consistent that a gross relationship between the category and crime can reasonably be concluded to exist. In these cases, it is practical to assume that if the part of an observed relationship which is due merely to the methods of collecting statistics were eliminated, a real relationship would still remain. After specifying this assumption, we can go ahead and use the statistics. Even if they are gross, relationships which consistently appear and which cannot be readily "explained away" by citing the inadequacy of crime statistics must be taken into account in any theory of crime and criminality. There are at least six types of such consistent relationships that are of great theoretical significance to students of crime and criminality. Age and sex will be discussed here, race and nativity in Chapter 8, size of community in Chapter 9, and social class in Chapter 11.

Many varieties of statistics, in many jurisdictions, in many different years, collected by many types of agencies, uniformly report such a high incidence of crime among young persons, that it may reasonably be assumed that there is a statistically significant difference between the rate of crime among young adults and the rate among other age groups. Statistics are likely to exaggerate the crime rate of young adults: old people may have prestige enough to avoid fingerprinting and arrest, and young children might not be arrested as readily as either young adults or old adults, leaving young adults to bear the responsibility for more than their share of all the crimes committed. But there does seem to be a difference, even if it is not as great as the statistics indicate when they are taken at face value. In this sense, there are two general relationships between age and criminality.

[30] The following are some of the more extreme exponents of the determination of personal behavior by endocrine glands: Louis Berman, *The Glands Regulating Personality* (New York: Macmillan, 1931); I. G. Cobb, *The Glands of Destiny* (London: Heinemann, 1927); Adolf Lenz, *Grundriss der Kriminalbiologie* (Vienna: Springer, 1927); Max G. Schlapp and Edward H. Smith, *The New Criminology* (New York: Boni, 1928), p. 72. A more conservative statement is given by Leizer E. Grimberg, *Emotion and Delinquency* (New York: Brentano's, 1928).

[31] See, for example, R. G. Hoskins, *Endocrinology* (New York: Norton, 1941), p. 348; and Edward Podolsky, "The Chemical Brew of Criminal Behavior," *Journal of Criminal Law and Criminology*, 45:675–678, March–April, 1955.

*adolescence*

A. The age of maximum general criminality is probably during or shortly before adolescence. English statistics show that the age of maximum convictions for indictable crimes is 12 or 13 for males and 16 or 17 for females. While American statistics place this age higher, ranging from 18 to 24, these statistics are based on fingerprints submitted by local police departments to the Federal Bureau of Investigation, and American police departments seldom take fingerprints of young people. Similarly, in Scandinavian Countries, 13–15 is the age of maximum criminality.[32]

*not under all cond.*

B. The age of maximum criminality is not the same under all conditions. The extent to which the crime rate among young persons exceeds the crime rate among other age groups varies by offense, sex, place, and time.

*variants 1) type*

1. The age of maximum criminality varies with the type of crime. For example, males aged 15–19 have higher arrest rates for auto theft and burglary than does any other group of males. Table VIII presents some recent data on the percentages of all arrests which were arrests of young persons. The table shows, for instance, that murders and embezzlements are committed by persons who are much older, on the average, than are the persons committing automobile theft and burglary. In a study of homicides committed in Philadelphia between 1948 and 1952, Wolfgang found that the age group 20–24 predominated, with a homicide rate of 12.6 per 100,000; the median age of the offenders was 31.9.[33]

*2) sex*

2. The age of maximum criminality varies by sex. Generally speaking, females commit crimes at later ages than do males. In 1957, for example, 74 per cent of the males arrested for larceny were under 25 years of age, but only 69 per cent of the females arrested for the same offense were under 25. Yet sex offenses, narcotic drug offenses, crimes against family and children, driving while intoxicated, and homicide and forgery appear earlier in the lives of women than in the lives of men. In 1957, 46 per cent of the females and 30 per cent of the males arrested for forgery were under age 25.[34]

*3) place*

3. The age of first delinquency varies from place to place. In areas of high rates of delinquency, the children who become delinquent do so at an

---

[32] Knut Sveri, *Kriminalitet og Alder* (Criminality and Age), Stockholm: Almquist and Wiksell, 1960, pp. 80, 161. See also Knut Sveri, "Barnekriminaliteten: Dens Omfang, Art og Betydning" (Child Criminality: Its Extent, Nature, and Significance) *Nordisk Tidsskrift for Kriminalvidenskap*, 47:132–147, 1959.

[33] Marvin E. Wolfgang, "A Sociological Analysis of Criminal Homicide," *Federal Probation*, 25:48–55, March, 1961.

[34] Computed from data supplied by the Federal Bureau of Investigation to supplement Tables 42 and 43 in *Uniform Crime Reports for the United States*, Federal Bureau of Investigation, Vol. 28, No. 2 (1957), pp. 115–17.

# TABLE VIII

NUMBER AND PERCENTAGE OF ARRESTS OF PERSONS UNDER 18,
UNDER 21, AND UNDER 25 YEARS OF AGE, 1964

| Offense Charged | Total Number of Persons Arrested | Percentage | | |
|---|---|---|---|---|
| | | Under 18 | Under 21 | Under 25 |
| Total | 4,685,080 | 20.5 | 30.3 | 41.0 |
| Murder | 6,412 | 8.5 | 18.3 | 32.8 |
| Forcible rape | 9,450 | 18.8 | 39.9 | 61.6 |
| Robbery | 39,134 | 27.6 | 47.5 | 67.7 |
| Aggravated assault | 79,895 | 14.8 | 25.2 | 39.9 |
| Burglary—breaking or entering | 187,000 | 51.4 | 67.5 | 79.9 |
| Larceny—theft | 358,569 | 54.0 | 66.5 | 75.3 |
| Auto theft | 97,356 | 64.4 | 80.1 | 88.8 |
| Other assaults | 191,455 | 14.0 | 24.2 | 39.4 |
| Arson | 5,220 | 63.5 | 71.5 | 78.0 |
| Forgery and counterft. | 30,637 | 10.2 | 23.5 | 41.7 |
| Fraud | 45,998 | 2.9 | 9.6 | 24.7 |
| Embezzlement | 8,610 | 2.2 | 9.1 | 25.5 |
| Stolen property; buying, receiving, etc. | 18,152 | 34.7 | 49.2 | 62.9 |
| Vandalism | 76,814 | 77.3 | 85.0 | 89.7 |
| Weapons; carrying, possessing, etc. | 47,287 | 20.4 | 34.7 | 51.1 |
| Prostitution and commercialized vice | 28,190 | 1.9 | 13.1 | 42.8 |
| Other sex offenses | 58,082 | 23.6 | 35.2 | 49.4 |
| Narcotic drug laws | 37,802 | 8.7 | 23.3 | 46.1 |
| Gambling | 103,814 | 2.2 | 6.2 | 15.9 |
| Offenses against family and children | 57,454 | 1.4 | 9.3 | 25.9 |
| Driving under the infl. | 225,672 | .8 | 5.3 | 16.0 |
| Liquor laws | 153,829 | 26.0 | 62.8 | 70.5 |
| Drunkenness | 1,458,821 | 1.5 | 5.2 | 12.5 |
| Disorderly conduct | 475,756 | 15.8 | 29.3 | 43.7 |
| Vagrancy | 132,955 | 6.8 | 19.2 | 30.6 |
| All other offenses (except traffic) | 510,624 | 29.3 | 41.8 | 54.6 |
| Suspicion | 102,106 | 19.3 | 38.5 | 55.8 |
| Curfew and loitering law violations | 64,784 | 100.0 | 100.0 | 100.0 |
| Runaways | 70,517 | 100.0 | 100.0 | 100.0 |

Source: Federal Bureau of Investigation, *Uniform Crime Reports for the United States,* 1964 (Washington: Government Printing Office, 1965), p. 111.

earlier age than do the children living in areas with low rates of delinquency.[35]

4. The type of crime most frequently committed by persons of various ages varies from place to place. In some areas of Chicago, delinquent boys between 12 and 13 years old commit burglaries, while in other areas delinquent boys of those ages commit petty larcenies or engage in gang violence. In rural areas, offenders of any specified age are likely to be convicted of crimes different from those committed by offenders of the same age who live in urban areas.

5. For all crimes, and for each specific crime, the rate decreases steadily from the age of maximum criminality to the end of life. This conclusion is derived from the general statistics of many nations, although Pollak has found some conflicting statistics in a study of criminals in Pennsylvania.[36] In the United States, burglary and automobile theft decrease rather regularly after ages 15–19, as does the crime rate generally; homicide decreases rather regularly after ages 20–29, where it is concentrated. Consistently, several studies have shown that the number of first offenders per 1,000 persons of any given age decreases regularly after ages 15–19.[37] Some crimes decrease more dramatically with increasing age than do others; for example, the evidence is fairly conclusive that larceny decreases in old age more than do sex offenses.[38]

6. The crime rates among different age groups vary from time to time. In England the crime rate for persons over 60 decreased more between 1911 and 1928 than did the crime rate for any other age group, and this was explained as probably due to the system of old age pensions.[39] On the other hand, juvenile delinquency rates seem to have increased enormously during the last 20 years in proportion to the crime rates at older ages.

7. Both the probability that a crime will be repeated and the length of time between first and second offenses vary with the age at which the first offense is committed. Generally speaking, the younger a person is when he commits his first offense, the higher the probability that he will

[35] See Ernest Manheim, Youth in Trouble (Kansas City, Mo.: Department of Welfare, 1945), pp. 66–67.

[36] Otto Pollak, "Criminality of Old Age," Public Charities Association [of Pennsylvania] Herald, 22:4, November, 1945. See also Otto Pollak, "The Criminality of Old Age," Journal of Criminal Psychology, 3:213–235, October, 1941.

[37] Gunnar Dahlberg, "A New Method of Crime Statistics Applied to the Population of Sweden," Journal of Criminal Law and Criminology, 39:327–341, September–October, 1948; W. Norwood East, "Crime, Senescence and Senility," Journal of Mental Science, 90:835–850, October, 1944.

[38] David O. Moberg, "Old Age and Crime," Journal of Criminal Law, Criminology, and Police Science, 43:764–776, March–April, 1953; V. Fox, "Intelligence, Race, and Age as Selective Factors in Crime," Journal of Criminal Law and Criminology 37:141–152, July–August, 1946.

[39] East, "Crime, Senescence and Senility," op. cit.

commit a second offense and the shorter the interval between first offense and second offense.[40]

8. Juvenile delinquency is probably related in some manner to adult criminal behavior, but it is not correct to say that the juvenile delinquent of today is the adult criminal of tomorrow, as has frequently been stated. The error is due to the fact that practically all juveniles commit delinquencies, but not all of them develop into adult criminals. Moreover, many persons acquire their first formal record of crime after passing the juvenile age. Frum found that the criminal histories of 46 percent of the 319 recidivists in the Indiana Reformatory and State Prison officially started prior to age eighteen.[41] There is evidence, also, that after about age 25 the percentage of criminals who are first offenders increases with increasing age.[42]

In sum, the available statistics on crime tell us that young persons have higher crime rates than older persons but that there are variations in the ratio of young persons to old persons in the criminal population. Thus, crime rates vary with age, but in any age group the rates vary with specific social conditions. Age appears to have an important effect, directly or indirectly, on the frequency and type of crime committed.

One of the theories presented as an explanation of the age ratios in crime is that they are due directly to biological traits such as physical strength and vigor: crimes are committed frequently by persons who are strong and active and infrequently by persons who are weak and passive. Another biological theory is that crimes are concentrated in three periods, ages 3 to 6, 14 to 16, and 42 to 45, and that these periods are products of libidinal tides due to changes in the ego strength.[43] A third biological theory is that inheritance is the direct cause; Goring stated that persons predisposed by heredity to crime commit crime at a very young age, while those with a weaker tendency delay longer.

These biological theories obviously provide no explanation of many of the variations in the age ratios in crime; indeed, it may be said that they do not explain even one of the facts outlined above when that fact is considered in its ramifications. On the other hand, all of these facts are consistent with the general theory that crime and criminality are products of

---

[40] Thorsten Sellin, "Recidivism and Maturation," *National Probation and Parole Association Journal*, 4:241–250, July, 1958; Hermann Mannheim and Leslie T. Wilkins, *Prediction Methods in Relation to Borstal Training* (London: Her Majesty's Stationery Office, 1955), p. 64.

[41] Harold S. Frum, "Adult Criminal Offense Trends Following Juvenile Delinquency," *Journal of Criminal Law and Criminology*, 49:29–49, May–June, 1958.

[42] Thorsten Sellin, *The Criminality of Youth* (Philadelphia: The American Law Institute, 1940), p. 108.

[43] This theory was stated by Phillip Roche, Secretary of the Philadelphia Psychiatric Society, in an address to the Pediatric Department of the Germantown Dispensary and Hospital, January 26, 1947.

social experiences and social interaction. It must be agreed, however, that the sociological theories of crime causation have not been sufficiently demonstrated as to any of these facts.[44]

SEX RATIOS IN CRIME. Sex status is of greater statistical significance in differentiating criminals from non-criminals than any other trait. If an investigator were asked to use a single trait to predict which persons in a town of 10,000 population would become criminals, he would make the fewest mistakes if he simply chose sex status and predicted criminality for the males and non-criminality for the females. He would be wrong in many cases, for most of the males would not become criminals, and a few of the females would become criminals. But he would be wrong in more cases if he used any other single trait, such as age, race, family background, or a personality characteristic. As is the case with age, there are two general relationships to be observed between crime and sex status.

A. The crime rate for men is greatly in excess of the rate for women—in all nations, all communities within a nation, all age groups, all periods of history for which organized statistics are available, and for all types of crime except those peculiar to women, such as infanticide and abortion. In the United States at present, the rate of arrest of males is about ten times the rate of arrest for females; about 15 times as many males as females are committed to correctional institutions of all kinds; and about 20 times as many males as females are committed to state and federal prisons and reformatories housing serious offenders. Approximately 85 percent of the delinquency cases in juvenile courts are boys. While these statistics certainly reflect a bias in favor of females, they are supported by statistics from sources other than the police and the courts.[45] Death certificates indicated that males committed 88 percent of the 821 homicides occurring in ten North Carolina counties in one 11-year period; 83 percent of the males and 71 percent of the females killed males.[46] A questionnaire study of 2,000 school children resulted in the conclusion that girls have a stronger sense of honor than boys.[47] Even if correction could be made for

[44] See below, pp. 158–159.
[45] W. E. McClure, "Characteristics of Problem Children," *Journal of Juvenile Research*, 13:124–140, April, 1929; C. M. Whitlow, "Attitudes and Behavior of High School Students," *American Journal of Sociology*, 40:489–494, January, 1935; Edward E. Schwartz, "A Community Experiment in Measurement of Juvenile Delinquency," *National Probation Association Yearbook*, 1945, pp. 157–181; James F. Short, Jr., and F. Ivan Nye, "Extent of Unrecorded Juvenile Delinquency: Tentative Conclusions," *Journal of Criminal Law and Criminology*, 49:296–302, November–December, 1958.
[46] Harold Garfinkel, "Research Note on Inter- and Intra-Racial Homicides," *Social Forces*, 27:369–381, May, 1949. See also Edwin D. Driver, "Interaction and Criminal Homicide in India," *Social Forces*, 40:153–158, December, 1961.
[47] Robert Clark, "A Direct Study of the Child's Sentiment of Honor," *International Journal of Ethics*, 42:454–461, July, 1932.

the statistical bias in favor of females, the male crime rate probably would still greatly exceed that of females.[48]

B. The extent to which the crime rate among males exceeds the crime rate among females is not the same under all conditions. There are variations in the sex ratio in crime, just as there are variations in the age ratio in crime:

1. The extent to which the rate for males exceeds the rate for females varies from one nation to another. Male criminals are 342 times as numerous as females in Belgium and 2,744 times as numerous in Algiers and Tunis in proportion to the populations of the several groups. In Ceylon, 98 percent of the delinquents placed on probation in 1946–1956 were male.[49] The sex ratio among 177,000 Japanese juvenile delinquents in 1959 was 1,725; among the 2,624 delinquents accused of robbery, only 18 were girls, a sex ratio of 14,477.[50] The female crime rate shows some tendency to approach closest to the male in countries in which females have the greatest freedom and equality with males, such as Western Europe, Australia, and the United States, and to vary most from the male rate in countries in which females are closely supervised, such as Algiers.[51] If countries existed in which females were politically and socially dominant, the female rate, according to this trend, should exceed the male rate.

2. The extent to which the rate for males exceeds the rate for females varies with the social positions of the sexes in different groups within a nation. An analysis of statistics in pre-war Poland indicated sex ratios that ranged from 176 to 1,163 in 42 groups in categories according to age, province of residence, rural-urban residence, religion, and civil status.[52] In the United States, the sex ratio is less extreme among Negroes than it is among whites, and it is probable that Negro males and females more closely resemble each other in social standing than do white males and

[48] Cf. Otto Pollak, *The Criminality of Women* (Philadelphia: University of Pennsylvania Press, 1950), pp. 44–56, 154; and Bertha J. Payak, "Understanding the Female Offender," *Federal Probation*, 27:7–12, December, 1963.

[49] Ceylon Department of Census and Statistics, *Juvenile Probationers in Ceylon* (Ceylon: Government Press, 1957), p. 10.

[50] National Police Agency, *Juvenile Delinquency in Today's Japan and Its Countermeasures*, Tokyo: Author, 1960, p. 21.

[51] E. Hacker, *Kriminalstatistische und Kriminalaetiologische Berichte* (Miskolc: Ludwig, 1941); Commonwealth Immigration Advisory Council, *Third Report of the Committee Established to Investigate Conduct of Migrants* (Canberra: Commonwealth Government Printer, 1957), p. 14. Severi, op. cit., p. 50.

[52] L. Radzinowicz, "Variability in the Sex Ratio of Criminality," *Sociological Review*, Vol. 29 (January, 1937), pp. 76–102. The sex ratio always is expressed as the number of males per 100 females. A ratio over 100, thus means that males exceed females, while a ratio less than 100 means that females exceed males.

females. In 1957, the sex ratio among Negroes committed to New York state prisons was 1,075, but the ratio among whites was over 3,000.[53]

*SIZE*      3. The extent to which the rate for males exceeds the rate for females varies with the size of community of residence. In Americans cities the crime rate of females is closer to the crime rate of males than is the case in rural areas and small towns. The ratio of male arrests to female arrests for crimes against the person in Massachusetts in 1963 was 36 to 1 in "towns," most of which have less than 12,000 population, and 14 to 1 in cities above 12,000; for offenses against property the ratio was 21 to 1 in towns and 10 to 1 in cities.[54]

*AGE*      4. The extent to which the crime rate among males exceeds the crime rate among females varies with age. In the United States, the sex ratio among persons committed to penal institutions tends to increase with increasing age. At ages 15–17 the sex ratio is about 1,300, while at 60–64 it is about 2,500. The English statistics of convictions for indictable crimes in 1958 show a sex ratio of 772 for all ages; however, for the ages under 17 the ratio is 1,266, for the years 17–21 it is 850, and for the ages 21 and over it is 589.[55] In earlier years, these data were compiled for all age groups, and they indicated that after age 10 the two sexes became progressively more alike with advancing age until the age of 40, with little change thereafter. Hacker's statistics of convictions in eight European nations show the greatest difference between the sexes in the young-adult ages with smaller differences after 40 or 45 and with early childhood in two cases intermediate between the young adults and the older ages.[56] On the other hand, Dahlberg reports that in Sweden the sexes differ least in the rate of first convictions in the age period 20–25, when males have 6 times as many first convictions as females, that the difference becomes steadily greater with increasing age to the age 40–45, when males have 24 times as many first convictions, and that the ratio is irregular after the age 45, perhaps because of the small number of cases at those later ages.[57] For Norway in 1959, the male rate per 1,000 population of the same age was only three times the female rate at age 60 and over, eight times the female rate at ages 40–59, and 12 times the female rate at ages 25–39. The

[53] New York State Commission of Correction, *Thirty-First Annual Report, 1957* (New York: Sing Sing Prison Press, 1958), p. 405.

[54] *Statistical Reports of the Commissioner of Correction, 1963* (Boston: Massachusetts Public Document No. 115, 1964), p. 58. Communities of less than 12,000 are "towns," but a community with more than 12,000 becomes a city only if it chooses to give up the "town" designation.

[55] Great Britain Central Statistical Office, *Annual Abstract of Statistics*, Volume 95. (London: Her Majesty's Stationery Office, 1958), p. 71.

[56] Hacker, *Kriminalstatische und Kriminalaetiologische Berichte*, op. cit.

[57] Dahlberg, op. cit.

greatest differences were at ages 9, 12, and 24, where the male rate exceeded the female rate by 30 times, 36 times, and 30 times, respectively.[58]

*Area* 5. The extent to which the crime rate among males exceeds the crime rate among females varies with area of residence within a city. Generally, the higher the crime rate of an area the lower the sex ratio in crime. However, it has been shown that some areas with high delinquency rates also have unusually high sex ratios among their delinquents.[59]

*Time* 6. The extent to which the crime rate among males exceeds the crime rate among females varies with time. There is some evidence that the sex ratio is decreasing. The percentage of girl arraignments to all arraignments in the Children's Court of New York City increased from 12.7 in 1907–1914 to 27.1 in 1923–1930. In 1938, females were 5 percent of the persons under age 18 whose arrests were reported to the FBI; in 1947 females were 10 percent; in 1957 they were 12.7 percent; and in 1964 they were 16 percent. On the other hand, Hacker's study of the Canton of Zurich for the period 1834–1936 showed many variations but no unified trend for adult females; the percentage of female delinquents to all delinquents decreased generally from 1855 to 1875, increased generally from 1875 to 1915, and then decreased from 1915 to 1936.[60] In war years, when women take over the occupations of men and in other ways approach social equality with men, the female crime rate increases. Women in Germany and Austria had a conviction rate for theft during World War I which was higher than the conviction rate of men for theft in the same countries in prewar years, and during World War II female crime rates increased tremendously in the United States, Sweden, England, and Denmark.[61]

7. Among young criminals, the extent to which the crime rate for males exceeds the crime rate for females varies with the degree of integration in the family. Among delinquents from broken homes, the sex ratio is lower than it is among delinquents from unbroken, "integrated" homes.[62] Further, there is some evidence from specialized studies that the sex ratio in delinquency is lower in families in which male children outnumber the females than in families in which the number of each sex is more nearly equal.[63]

[58] Sveri, *op. cit.*, p. 84.

[59] E. Manheim, *Youth in Trouble, op. cit.*, pp. 64–65.

[60] E. Hacker, *Die Kriminalität des Kantons Zürich* (Miskolc: Author, 1939), pp. 241–247. See also Pollak, *The Criminality of Women, op. cit.*, p. 61.

[61] Franz Exner, *Krieg und Kriminalität in Osterreich* (Vienna: Hölder-Pichler-Tempsky, 1927); Moritz Liepmann, *Krieg and Kriminalität in Deutschland* (Stuttgart: Deutsche Verlagsanstalt, 1930); Pollak, *op. cit.*, pp. 64–75.

[62] J. Toby, "The Differential Impact of Family Disorganization," *American Sociological Review*, 22:505–512, October, 1957.

[63] R. F. Sletto, "Sibling Position and Juvenile Delinquency," *American Journal of Sociology*, 39:657–669, March, 1934.

As indicated, no other trait has as great statistical importance as does sex in differentiating criminals from non-criminals. But no one feels that he has an explanation of criminality when he learns that the criminal is male. Some scholars have claimed that the higher rate of delinquency of the male sex is due to the biological characteristic of the male. This conclusion has no more justification than the conclusion that a death rate of males by lightning six times as high as of females is due to the biological differences between the sexes. The variations in the sex ratio in crime are so great that it can be considered that maleness is not significant in the causation of crime in itself but only as it indicates social position, supervision, and other social relations. Moreover, since boys and girls live in the same homes, in equal poverty, and with equally ignorant parents, and have the same neighborhoods which are equally lacking in facilities for organized recreation, these conditions of the social environment cannot be considered as causes of delinquency. The significant difference is in the social positions of the girls and women as compared with the boys and men, and the difference in social positions either determines the frequency and intensity of the delinquency and anti-delinquency patterns which impinge upon them or determines the frequency of opportunities for crimes which are available to them.[64] Probably the most important difference is that the girls are supervised more carefully and behave in accordance with anti-criminal behavior patterns taught to them with greater care and consistency than in the case of boys. From infancy, girls are taught that they must be nice, while boys are taught that they must be rough and tough; a boy who approaches the behavior of girls is regarded as a "sissy." This difference in care and supervision presumably rested originally on the fact that the female sex is the one which becomes pregnant. The personal and familial consequences of illicit pregnancy leads to special protection of the girl not only in respect to sex behavior but also in respect to social codes in general.[65] Grosser has shown that stealing has a different functional significance for boys and girls; it can be integrated with and can express features

[64] Cf. Pollak, The Criminality of Women, op. cit., pp. 137–148.

[65] Talcott Parsons has presented the thesis that girls are less delinquent than boys partially because the girls receive an apprenticeship training from their mothers for the careers into which they are to enter, while boys remain during the same age isolated from the occupational activities of their fathers and that this leads to frustration of the boys and consequent delinquency. If this thesis were valid, the delinquency rates of the two sexes should be more nearly alike in rural districts, where both boys and girls receive this apprenticeship training, than in urban districts, where the girls alone receive it. But Toby has shown that the delinquency rates are more nearly the same for the two sexes in the urban districts where the training in this respect differs more widely. See Talcott Parsons, Essays in Sociological Theory (Glencoe: The Free Press, 1949), pp. 219 and 257–259. Jackson Toby, op. cit.

of the masculine adolescent role, but it cannot do so for the basic features of the feminine role.[66]

CONCLUSION. The general conclusion from this survey of the facts regarding physical and physiological conditions is that these conditions have not in any case been demonstrated to be a direct force in the production of crime or delinquency. On the contrary, it is apparent that these conditions are significant in crime causation only to the extent that they affect social interaction.

*affect social interaction*

## SUGGESTED READINGS

Bullock, Henry A., "Urban Homicide in Theory and Fact," *Journal of Criminal Law, Criminology, and Police Science,* 45:565–575, February, 1955.

Corsini, R., "Season of Birth and Mental Ability of Prison Inmates," *Journal of Social Psychology,* 23:65–72, February, 1946.

Curry, Manfred, "The Relationship of Weather Conditions, Facial Characteristics, and Crime," *Journal of Criminal Law and Criminology,* 39: 253–261, July–August, 1948.

East, W. N., "Crime, Senescence and Senility," *Journal of Mental Science,* 90:835–850, October, 1944.

East, W. N., "Physical Factors in Criminal Behavior," *Journal of Clinical Psychopathy,* 8:7–36, July, 1946.

Fink, Arthur E., *Causes of Crime, Biological Theories in the United States, 1800–1915.* Philadelphia: University of Pennsylvania Press, 1938.

Fox, Sanford J., "Delinquency and Biology," *University of Miami Law Review,* 16:65–91, Fall, 1961.

Foxe, A. N., "Heredity and Crime," *Journal of Criminal Law and Criminology,* 36:11–16, May–June, 1945.

Glueck, Sheldon and Eleanor T., *Physique and Delinquency.* New York: Harper, 1956.

Howells, W. W., "A Factorial Study of Constitutional Type," *American Journal of Physical Anthropology,* 10:91–118, March, 1952.

Hunt, E. E., Jr., "Human Constitution: An Appraisal," *American Journal of Physical Anthropology,* 10:55–73, March, 1952.

La Roche, Ernest, and Louis Tilley, "Weather and Crime in Tallahassee," *Journal of Criminal Law, Criminology, and Police Science,* 47:218–219, July–August, 1956.

Lessa, William A., "An Appraisal of Constitutional Types," *Memoirs of the American Anthropological Society,* No. 62; *American Anthropologist,* Volume 45, No. 4, Part 2, 1943.

[66] George H. Grosser, *Juvenile Delinquency and Contemporary American Sex Roles,* Unpublished Ph.D. Dissertation, Harvard University, 1952.

Moberg, David O., "Old Age and Crime," *Journal of Criminal Law, Criminology, and Police Science,* 43:764–776, March–April, 1953.

Montagu, M. F. Ashley, "The Biologist Looks at Crime," *Annals of the American Academy of Political and Social Science,* 217:46–57, September, 1941.

Payak, Bertha J., "Understanding the Female Offender," *Federal Probation,* 27:7–12, December, 1963.

Pollak, Otto, *The Criminality of Women.* Philadelphia: University of Pennsylvania Press, 1950.

Toby, Jackson, "The Differential Impact of Family Disorganization," *American Sociological Review,* 22:505–512, October, 1957.

Wolfgang, Marvin E., "A Sociological Analysis of Criminal Homicide," *Federal Probation,* 25:48–55, March, 1961.

Wolfgang, Marvin E., "Pioneers in Criminology: Cesare Lombroso (1835–1909)," *Journal of Criminal Law, Criminology, and Police Science,* 52:361–391, December, 1961.

# 7. CRIME IN RELATION
# TO RACE AND NATIVITY

WE PREVIOUSLY EXAMINED the age and sex ratios in crime, described certain variations in the ratios, and made a preliminary attempt to explain the ratios and the variations. In this chapter we shall consider the variations in two more ratios, the race ratio and the nativity ratio. Any general theory of criminal behavior should explain all the ratios and, also, the variations in the ratios. A theory which makes sense of the sex ratio and its variations, for example, should also explain the age ratio, the race ratio, and the nativity ratio.

RACE RATIOS AND CRIME.   Crimes are sometimes regarded as a direct product of racial traits, and racial traits are regarded as biologically determined. For example, some persons believe that Negroes are a primitive race and are innately inclined toward crime. This belief is composed of two constituent notions: that Negroes cannot control their emotions and consequently have a high rate of crime against the person, and that they have no moral sense regarding property rights and consequently have a high rate of crime against property.[1] A survey of the facts regarding the crimes of various races in the United States should indicate whether such biological notions are valid, but it is difficult to obtain the facts. The statistics on the crimes of various racial groups must be interpreted with greatest caution.

In the first place, arrests are reported for selected areas in the United States, and the population of the several races in those areas cannot be determined. The arrest rate for a racial group must necessarily be computed by taking the arrests in these particular areas in proportion to the population of that race in the entire United States. A comparison of this nature is justified only if the several races whose arrests are recorded are

---

[1] Gunnar Myrdal, An American Dilemma (New York: Harpers, 1962, revised ed.), p. 655.

found in the selected areas in the same proportions as in the entire United States; this is decidedly unlikely.

A second error arises because the statistics on arrests, published by the Federal Bureau of Investigation, do not include arrests by federal agents. Since Indians are under the supervision of the federal government in unusual ways, their official arrest rate is lower than it would be if all arrests were included in the statistics.

A third error in the statistics arises because the procedures used in the administration of criminal justice are frequently biased against minority groups. A number of studies have shown that in the United States, Negroes are more likely to be arrested, indicted, and convicted than are whites who commit the same offenses.[2] Similarly, it has been shown that Negroes have less chance than whites to receive probation, a suspended sentence, parole, commutation of a death sentence, or a pardon.[3] Thus, almost any "index" of the crime rate is likely to exaggerate the rate for Negroes, as compared with the rate among whites. Myrdal concluded that one could merely "suspect" that Negroes commit more crimes than whites. However, it is also true that many crimes committed by Negroes against other Negroes receive no official attention from the police or criminal courts, and this practice of overlooking some crimes offsets to some unknown degree the bias in other arresting, reporting, and recording practices. It is probable that some crimes of other minority groups are also overlooked. At least four localized studies have shown that the racial membership of the victim is of great importance in determining the official reactions to crimes committed by Negroes.[4] Moses states that for the persons in his study there was "no reason even to suspect that Negroes were more

[2] See, for example, Edwin M. Lemert and Judy Rosberg, "The Administration of Justice to Minority Groups in Los Angeles County," *University of California Publications in Culture and Society*, Vol. 2, No. 1 (1948), pp. 1–28.

[3] Thorsten Sellin, "Race Prejudice in the Administration of Justice," *American Journal of Sociology*, 41:212–17, September, 1935. Also Sidney Axelrad, "Negro and White Institutionalized Delinquents," *American Journal of Sociology*, 57: 569–74, May, 1952; and Marvin E. Wolfgang, Arlene Kelly, and Hans C. Nolde, "Comparison of the Executed and the Commuted Among Admissions to Death Row," *Journal of Criminal Law and Criminology*, 53:301–311, September, 1962.

[4] Guy B. Johnson, "The Negro and Crime," *Annals of the American Academy of Political and Social Science*, 217: 93–104, September, 1941. James D. Turner, *Differential Punishment in a Bi-Racial Community*, unpublished M.A. dissertation, Indiana University, 1948. James D. Turner, *Dynamics of Criminal Law Administration in a Bi-Racial Community of the Deep South*, unpublished Ph.D. dissertation, Indiana University, 1956. Henry A. Bullock, "Significance of the Racial Factor in the Length of Prison Sentences," *Journal of Criminal Law and Criminology*, 53:411–417, December, 1961.

readily convicted than whites."[5] However, Bullock found that juries tend to give Negro prisoners convicted of murder shorter sentences than whites, while Negroes convicted of burglary received longer sentences than whites. Murder by Negroes tends to be an intra-racial crime, while burglary by Negroes is mainly inter-racial.[6]

Despite the limitations of the official indexes of the crimes committed by members of the various races, it seems reasonable to assume that in the United States the general crime rate among Negroes is considerably higher than the rate among whites. If we make this assumption, then we can observe that there are two general relationships between crime and race, just as there are two general relationships between crime and age, and between crime and sex. The "races" which are numerically most significant in the United States as minority groups and which are identified in crime statistics are Negroes, Indians, Chinese, Japanese, and Filipinos. We shall focus on a comparison of the rates of Negroes and of whites.   *Race*

A. The general crime rate of Negroes exceeds the rate among whites. *black > white* The official statistics of arrest per 100,000 population of the same race 15 years of age and over for the entire United States, show that Negroes have arrest rates approximately three times that of the white population. The rate of commitment of Negroes to state and federal prisons is about six times the white rate. The arrest rates of Indians and Chinese are also about three times the rate of whites, but the Japanese have a rate slightly lower than that of whites. The commitment rates of Indians and Chinese are also similar to the rate of Negroes; the rate for Filipinos is a little more than twice as high as the rate for whites, but the commitment rate for Japanese is only about half that of whites.

B. The extent to which the crime rate among Negroes exceeds the *varies Social Conds.* crime rate of whites varies with social conditions. In some conditions the rate for Negroes is not as far in excess of the rate for whites as it is in other conditions, and in still other conditions the rate for Negroes is lower than the rate for whites.

1. The extent to which the rate for Negroes exceeds the rate for whites varies with regions of the United States. The excess is highest in the *regions* Western states and lowest in the Southern states, with Northern states

---

[5] Earl R. Moses, "Differentials in Crime Rates Between Negroes and Whites," *American Sociological Review*, 12:411–420, August, 1947. See also William H. Kephart, *Racial Factors and Urban Law-Enforcement* (Philadelphia: University of Pennsylvania Press, 1957), pp. 174–175.

[6] Bullock, op. cit.

occupying an intermediate position.[7] In Philadelphia in 1954, Negroes made up 20 percent of the population but accounted for 50 percent of the arrests;[8] in Michigan and Ohio at about the same time Negroes were 7 percent of the population and about 40 percent of the prison population.[9] The differences in rates are not distributed in the same way for all offenses; for homicide, for example, the difference is greatest in the South and least in New England. Similarly, Hayner has shown that the crime rate of one Indian tribe is quite different from that of another, and the variations are related to their contacts with white civilization and to their economic resources.[10]

2. The extent to which the crime rate of Negroes exceeds the crime rate of whites varies with sex status. In 1964, 49 Negro women were convicted in 88 United States district courts for each 100 white women convicted, but 412 white men were convicted for each 100 Negro men. Although rates cannot be calculated because the exact numbers of the four categories of persons in the general population are unknown, it is probable that the excess of crime among Negro women was much greater than the excess among Negro men. In 1964, 716 Negro men were convicted in U.S. district courts for each 100 Negro women convicted; 1,466 white men were convicted for each 100 white women.[11] Wolfgang studied all criminal homicides occurring in Philadelphia between January 1, 1948, and December 31, 1952; the rate per 100,000 by race and sex of offenders showed the following rank order: Negro males—41.7, Negro females—9.3, white males—3.4, and white females—.4.[12]

3. The extent to which the crime rate of Negroes exceeds the crime rate of whites varies with the offense. When based on imprisonment rates, the excess is greatest for assault and homicide and lowest for rape. Of those persons whose arrests were reported to the Federal Bureau of Investigation

---

[7] The high ratio in the West may be due in part to the fact that Negroes in that area tend to be unduly concentrated in the young-adult group and in cities, both of which have high crime rates.

[8] William H. Kephart, "The Negro Offender," American Journal of Sociology, 60:46–50, July, 1954.

[9] Vernon Fox and Joan Volakakis, "The Negro Offender in a Northern Industrial Area," Journal of Criminal Law and Criminology, 46:641–647, February, 1956; Ohio Legislative Service Commission, Capital Punishment, Staff Research Report No. 46 (Columbus: Author, 1961), p. 62.

[10] Norman S. Hayner, "Variability in the Criminal Behavior of American Indians," American Journal of Sociology, 47:602–613, January, 1942. See, also, Hans Von Hentig, "Delinquency of the American Indian," Journal of Criminal Law and Criminology, 36:75–84, July–August, 1945.

[11] Administrative Office of the U.S. Courts, Federal Offenders in the United States District Courts, 1964 (Washington, 1964), p. 42.

[12] Marvin E. Wolfgang, "A Sociological Analysis of Criminal Homicide," Federal Probation, 25:48–55, March, 1961.

in 1964, 27 percent were Negro. At the same time, about 10 percent of the total United States population was Negro. In 1964, this proportion of the population comprised about 56 percent of the persons arrested for murder and non-negligent manslaughter, 45 percent of those arrested for forcible rape, 54 percent for robbery, 31 percent for burglary, and 26 percent for automobile theft.[13] It also is known that the excess of crime among Negroes is higher for second offenses than it is for first offenses. One study indicated that in Virginia the rates for forgery and for drunken driving actually are lower among Negroes than among whites, but this does not take into account the fact that literacy and automobile ownership are probably less frequent among Negroes.[14] McKeown correlated arrest rates for specified crimes in 1930 and in 1939 in 55 cities of 100,000–250,000 population and 36 cities over 250,000 with the percentage of Negro population in those cities. For murder and non-negligent manslaughter the coefficients of correlation range from +.67 to +.87 in the two years and the two classes of cities; these high correlations justify a conclusion that cities which have a large percentage of Negro population have high rates of murder and non-negligent manslaughter. The coefficients for other types of crimes vary widely from one year to the other or from one class of cities to the other, and justify no conclusion regarding the relation between Negro population and crime rates of cities. Moreover, it has been shown that in Southern cities, which have large percentages of Negroes, the white populations have very high rates of murder and manslaughter; consequently, the relatively high murder and manslaughter rates in the cities which have large proportions of Negroes cannot be attributed to a racial factor.[15]

4. The extent to which the crime rate of Negroes exceeds that of whites varies with the area of residence within a city. Studies of Houston and Baltimore show that the Negro delinquency rate is lowest in those areas having the greatest proportion of Negroes in their populations, and highest in those areas with relatively low proportions of Negroes to whites.[16] Although these data do not necessarily indicate that the excess of crime is

[13] Federal Bureau of Investigation, United States Department of Justice, *Uniform Crime Reports for the United States, 1964* (Washington: Government Printing Office, 1965), p. 114.

[14] Workers' Writers Program, *The Negro in Virginia* (New York: Hastings House, 1940), p. 341.

[15] James E. McKeown, "Poverty, Race, and Crime," *Journal of Criminal Law and Criminology*, 39:480–483, November–December, 1948.

[16] *The Houston Delinquent in His Community Setting* (Houston: Bureau of Research, Council of Social Agencies, 1945), pp. 22–45; Bernard Lander, *Towards an Understanding of Juvenile Delinquency* (New York: Columbia University Press, 1954), p. 82.

greatest in areas where whites and Negroes are not segregated, this is probably the case. However, the juvenile delinquency rate of Negroes decreases regularly from the center of the city to the outer zones of the city, as shown by studies in Chicago and other cities.[17] The change in delinquency rates as the residential areas change is substantially the same for Negroes as for white children.

5. The extent to which the crime rate of Negroes exceeds the crime rate of whites varies with time. There is no precise evidence on this point, but it seems probable that the amount of excess has been increasing. An earlier study indicated that in three decades the Negro juvenile delinquency rate in Chicago increased seven times, while the Negro population increased only three times.[18] The comparable data on the rate and population increases for whites are not available. Negro children have a relatively low delinquency rate when they first settle in a deteriorated area, but their delinquency rate increases with length of residence until a peak is reached; this generally has taken about five years.[19]

6. The extent to which the crime rate of Negroes exceeds that of whites varies with educational status. Older studies indicated little crime among graduates of Negro colleges, but it is likely that educated Negroes have been increasingly convicted of crime in recent years, while small semi-rural Negro communities with high degrees of illiteracy have remained relatively free of crime.[20] Nevertheless, the crime rates of highly educated Negroes is much lower than the rate of poorly educated whites.

In short, such statistics as are available indicate that Negroes have higher crime rates than whites but that the ratio of crime rates among Negroes to crime rates among whites varies with specific social situations. These variations cannot be explained by biological differences among the races. They can be explained only by social interaction. The specific theory of social interaction which explains these racial ratios in crime has not been determined.

One theory is that the minority group status, as such, produces a high crime rate. The low crime rate of the Japanese is a sufficient refutation of that theory, for this minority group has a lower crime rate than the majority group.

[17] Hugh P. Brinton, "Negroes Who Run Afoul of the Law," *Social Forces*, 11:96–101, October, 1932; E. Franklin Frazier, *The Negro Family in the United States* (Chicago: University of Chicago Press, 1939), pp. 371–374.

[18] Earl R. Moses, "Community Factors in Negro Delinquency," *Journal of Negro Education*, 5:220–227, April, 1936.

[19] *Ibid.* See also Earl R. Moses, "Differentials in Crime Rates Between Negroes and Whites," *op. cit.*

[20] E. Franklin Frazier, "Theoretical Structure of Sociology and Social Research," *British Journal of Sociology*, 4:293–311, December, 1953.

A second theory is that the high crime rate of minority groups is due to    *No*
frustrations produced by discriminations. Again, the Japanese meet discrimination and are presumably frustrated, but they do not have a high
crime rate. Furthermore, while frustration is a vague term which cannot be
measured or even defined, the feeling of frustration is probably more pronounced in the upper socio-economic class of Negroes, whose crime rate is
low, than in the lower class of Negroes, whose crime rate is high.

A third theory is that it is the economic status of the minority group,    *No*
which is a product of discrimination, that explains the high crime rate of
the minority group. Blue has shown in a statistical study of delinquency of
Negro and white children by census tracts in Detroit that when economic
status is held constant the partial correlation between race and juvenile
delinquency is +.52, while when race is held constant the correlation between economic status and juvenile delinquency is −.59.[21] This indicates
that economic status is slightly more closely related to juvenile delinquency
than is race. However, the non-economic conditions associated with race
are also important. Further, the Japanese resemble other minority races in
their low economic position but differ from them in crime rates. Finally,
economic determinism is not a satisfactory general explanation of criminal
behavior.[22]

A more specific theory is limited to the high rate of assaults and homicides by Negroes. This theory is that Negroes build up a great feeling of
anger because of the discriminations against them, that they do not dare
express their anger against the powerful white population, and that they
release this anger in attacks on their fellow Negroes. This theory, which is
a theory of displacement of emotion, has been stated by Dollard[23] and
apparently accepted as valid by Myrdal. The difficulty in the theory is that
it cannot be proved or disproved.

According to the differential association theory, the race ratios in crime
result from differential associations with criminal and anti-criminal patterns. In the United States, race may be related to associations in either or
both of two ways. First, the inheritance of certain characteristics may deter-    *)*
mine the social and economic level at which members of a race must live
and thus possibly throw them into situations where certain criminal patterns impinge upon them with great frequency and intensity. Negroes do
not commit white-collar crimes as frequently as do whites, because they

21 John T. Blue, "The Relationship of Juvenile Delinquency, Race, and Economic
Status," *Journal of Negro Education,* 17:469–477, Fall, 1948. See also Kenneth Polk,
"Juvenile Delinquency and Social Areas," *Social Problems,* 5:214–217, Winter, 1957.
22 See p. 240, below.
23 John Dollard, *Caste and Class in a Southern Town* (New Haven: Yale University
Press, 1937).

are not as frequently in white-collar jobs; they commit crimes which are typical of that part of the society with which they come in contact. Second, confinement of a race to a given locale may mean that the members of the race can hardly escape the traditions which are characteristic of the locale.[24] The traditions may be in conflict with the laws under which the race is expected to live, or they may be essentially anti-criminal. Thus, the experience of the race may be such that there is much or little conflict between its traditional ways of behaving and the laws under which it is expected to live.

NATIVITY RATIOS AND CRIME. While assimilation of vast numbers of immigrants is no longer a serious social problem in the United States, analysis of data on the nativity of criminals remains a problem of great theoretical significance. During the years when immigration was at its height many persons argued that immigration was the chief cause of crime. The mechanisms by which immigration produces crime were not specified, but the following were suggested: (a) Immigrants come from inferior "racial stock," or there is a larger proportion of inferior individuals in the "racial stock" of immigrants than among native whites. (b) Immigrants are not trained in the codes and ideals of America and are, therefore, not adjusted. (c) Immigrants are frequently poverty-stricken and this condition of poverty and the resulting frustration creates personal maladjustments of various kinds. (d) Immigrants are highly mobile and, hence, isolated from the inhibiting and restraining influences of primary groups. Each of these notions is based upon the assumption that there is an excessive rate of criminality among the immigrants. Many research studies have been conducted on the crime rates of immigrants, and these studies have yielded a set of statistical data about the nativity ratio in crime and about the variations in this ratio. Consideration of these data should throw light on the validity of the various notions. As is the case with age, sex, and race, there are two general relationships between crime and nativity.

A. Computed on the basis of population numbers only, the native-white rates of arrest and imprisonment in the United States are approximately two times as high as the rates for foreign-born whites. Similarly, the crime rate for native Australians is about twice the rate for immigrants arriving after World War II.[25] When correction is made for the fact that the age

---

[24] See Marvin E. Wolfgang, *Patterns in Criminal Homicide* (Philadelphia: University of Pennsylvania Press), 1958, pp. 65–70, 180–181; and Mozell Hill, "The Metropolis and Juvenile Delinquency Among Negroes," *Journal of Negro Education*, 28:277–285, 1959.
[25] Commonwealth Immigration Advisory Council, *Third Report of the Committee Established to Investigate Conduct of Migrants* (Canberra: Commonwealth Government Printer, 1957), p. 4.

and sex distributions of the populations are not the same, the rates of the two groups become nearly equal, but still show less crime among immigrants than among native whites.[26] For example, 52.5 percent of the immigrants in Australia and only 29 percent of the native Australians are in the "crime-committing ages" (15 to 35), so the correction for age gives the immigrants an even lower comparative crime rate. In the earlier studies it was often concluded that immigrants contributed more than their quota of crime, but the present findings rebut this conclusion.[27]

B. The extent to which the crime rate of native whites exceeds the rate among immigrants is not the same under social conditions:

1. The extent to which the crime rate among native whites exceeds the crime rate of the foreign born varies with offenses. Certain types of crime are characteristic of one immigrant group, while another type of crime is characteristic of a different immigrant group. Some groups have high rates for drunkenness and other misdemeanors, and low rates for felonies, while other groups have high rates for felonies and low rates for misdemeanors. A high rate of commitment to jails and workhouses, as in the case of the Irish and Finnish immigrants, is usually an expression of the drinking habits and extent of intoxication in those groups. Of German immigrants committed to federal and state prisons in 1932–1936, 4.5 per cent were committed for homicide, 3.6 percent for assault, and 14.3 percent for burglary, while of Italian immigrants the percentages were 10.7, 9.4, and 7.1; that is, the Italians had twice the proportion of homicides and assaults, and half the proportion of burglaries. Thus certain crimes or groups of crimes are characteristic of certain national groups. These same types of crimes are, usually, characteristic of the home countries, also. The Italian immigrants have an extraordinarily high rate of conviction for homicide, and also Italy has had the highest rate of homicide of any of the nations in Western Europe. Italians in America have a low rate of arrest for drunkenness, and drunkenness is comparatively absent in Italy. The traditions of the home country are transplanted to America and determine the

[26] C. C. Van Vechten, "The Criminality of the Foreign-Born," *Journal of Criminal Law and Criminology*, 32:139–147, July–August, 1941.

[27] For examples of the earlier studies, see United States Immigration Commission, "Immigration and Crime," *Report*, Vol. XXXVI (Washington: Government Printing Office, 1910); Chicago City Council, *Report of the Commission on Crime* (Chicago: Author, 1915), pp. 51–56; Joseph M. Gilman, "Statistics and the Immigrant Problem," *American Journal of Sociology*, 30:29–48, July, 1924; H. H. Laughlin, "Analysis of America's Modern Melting Pot," *Hearings before the Committee on Immigration and Naturalization* (House of Representatives, 67th Congress, November 21, 1922); Edwin H. Sutherland, "Is There Undue Crime Among Immigrants?" *Proceedings of the National Conference of Social Work*, 1927, pp. 572–579.

relative positions of the immigrant groups with reference to the types of crimes.[28]

2. The extent to which the crime rate of native whites exceeds the rate among foreign born persons varies from one immigrant group to another. In 1955, Eastern European immigrants in Australia had crime rates about three times as high as Southern European immigrants and almost twice as high as Northern European immigrants.[29] Similarly, in the United States in the years when immigration was at its height, persons of Irish nativity had crime rates three to five times as high as German immigrants. The crime rate among Japanese immigrants was exceptionally low.[30] The rate among the children of these immigrants was also exceptionally low, but the grandchildren are now beginning to take on the crime rates of the areas where they reside.[31] A recent study of our adult Puerto Rican citizens in Brooklyn showed, similarly, that the crime rates are disproportionately low.[32] Another study shows that Puerto Rican children are not over-represented in New York City's juvenile courts.[33]

3. The extent to which the crime rate of native whites exceeds the rate among the foreign born varies from one native white group to another. The native white sons of immigrants tend to have crime rates higher than those of their fathers but lower than other native whites. Even this variation changes with specific circumstances. Sometimes the rates for the children of immigrants are higher than for those of native whites of native parentage. Among the 8,615 juvenile delinquents referred to the Los Angeles County Probation Department in 1956, 34 per cent were identified as Mexican-Americans, which probably means that they were the children of immigrants from Mexico. The rate for the Mexican-Americans was three times the rate for "Anglos" (whites who are not of Mexican or Oriental descent) and slightly higher than the rate for Negroes.[34] Ogburn found

[28] Cf. Earnest A. Hooton, Crime and the Man (Cambridge: Harvard University Press, 1939), pp. 204–252.

[29] Commonwealth Immigration Advisory Council, op. cit., p. 18. This publication does not specify the nations involved. For a summary of research on the crime rates of various immigrant groups in America, see Arthur Lewis Wood, "Minority Group Criminality and Cultural Integration," Journal of Criminal Law and Criminology, 37:498–510, April, 1947.

[30] Norman S. Hayner, "Delinquency Areas in the Puget Sound Area," American Journal of Sociology, 39:314–328, November, 1936.

[31] Gerald H. Ikeda, "Japanese Americans Fight Delinquency," California Youth Authority Quarterly, 12:3–6, Summer, 1959.

[32] Julius Alter, Crimes of Puerto Ricans in Brooklyn (Unpublished Masters' thesis Department of Sociology, Brooklyn College, 1958).

[33] Clarence O. Senior, Strangers—Then Neighbors (New York: Anti Defamation League of B'nai B'rith, 1961), p. 31. See also New York City Board of Education, The Puerto Rican Study, 1953–1957 (New York: Author, 1958). p. 120.

[34] Joseph W. Eaton and Kenneth Polk, Measuring Juvenile Delinquency (Pittsburgh: University of Pittsburgh Press, 1961), pp. 20, 28.

that crimes known to the police have a negative correlation with the number of children of immigrants in three groups of cities, and that the negative association persists when other factors are held constant; the coefficients of correlation in the three groups of cities range between −0.34 and −0.54.[35] The Bureau of the Census, in its *Report on Federal and State Prisons* for 1933, presented a table regarding nativity of prisoners in 26 states in which reports regarding nativity were complete enough for comparison. In seventeen of these states the children of immigrants had a rate of commitment lower than that for native whites of native parentage, while in the other nine states their rate of commitment was higher. Taft made an analysis of this table, with corrections for variations in age distribution, and concluded that the states in which the second generation had lower rates were those in which the older immigration was predominant, and the states in which they had higher rates were those in which the newer immigration was predominant.[36] Taft's study showed, also, that the children of immigrants had higher rates of commitment than their parents in all except one of the 26 states, and that offspring of mixed parentage had lower rates of commitment than offspring of foreign parentage in seventeen states and higher in nine states.

4. The amount of the excess of crime among the native born varies with age. Among immigrants who arrive in the United States when they are in early childhood, the crime rate is higher than among immigrants arriving in middle age.[37] Young immigrants take on the relatively high crime rate of native whites to a greater extent than do middle-aged immigrants. Further, the sons of immigrants tend to change from the types of crime characteristic of their parents to those characteristic of the native born. This is illustrated in Table IX, a comparison of the Irish immigrants of the first and second generations and the native whites of native parentage with reference to a few crimes of which they were convicted in the New York Court of General Sessions in 1908–1909.[38] The same tendency appears, also, in a comparison of the first and second generations of Italian immigrants with reference to crimes of personal violence in Massachusetts, as

35 William F. Ogburn, "Factors in the Variation of Crime among Cities," *Journal of the American Statistical Association*, 30:21–24, March, 1935. See also McKeown, *op. cit.*, and Hans von Hentig, "The First Generation and a Half: Notes on the Delinquency of Native Whites of Mixed Parentage," *American Sociological Review*, 10:792–798, December, 1945.

36 D. R. Taft, "Nationality and Crime," *American Sociological Review*, 1:724–736, October, 1936.

37 Van Vechten, *op. cit.*

38 U. S. Immigration Commission, *op. cit.*, p. 14; see also pp. 14–16 and 67–86.

## TABLE IX

### RATE OF CONVICTION OF SPECIFIED GROUPS

| Offense | Irish | | Native White or Native Parentage |
|---------|-------|------|----------------------------------|
|         | Immigrants | 2nd Generation |                          |
| Homicide | 2.3 | 1.0 | 0.5 |
| Rape     | 0.0 | 0.3 | 0.7 |
| Gaming   | 1.2 | 2.7 | 3.6 |

shown in Table X.[39] This seems to show that the tendency to commit crimes of personal violence which is seen so clearly in the Italian immigrants is a matter of tradition—a tradition which is not passed on to the second generation.

5. The extent to which the crime rate of native whites exceeds that of immigrants varies with the length of time the immigrants have been in the host country. Both immigrants and their sons tend to take on the crime rate of the specific part of the community in which they locate. The delinquency rates of the second generation are comparatively low when the immigrant group first settles in a community, and they increase as contacts with the surrounding culture multiply. The rate remains low in those foreign colonies which are comparatively isolated from the surround-

## TABLE X

FREQUENCY OF COMMITMENTS TO STATE PRISON AND STATE REFORMATORY OF MASSACHUSETTS FOR MURDER, MANSLAUGHTER, AND ASSAULT, IN SPECIFIED GROUPS, 1914–1922, PER 100,000 IN EACH GROUP IN 1915

| Nativity and Parentage | Number Committed for Specified Offenses |
|------------------------|------------------------------------------|
| Born in Italy | 192 |
| Native-born, one or both parents born in Italy | 24 |
| Native-born, of native parentage | 24 |
| Native-born, one or both parents born in any foreign country | 22 |

[39] Computed from reports of the Massachusetts Department of Correction, 1914–1922; population was secured from the Massachusetts State Census of 1915; the Census of 1920 does not give the necessary information; Italians of all ages were included, and native-born, both white and colored, of all ages, were used in computation of the native white rate. A similar analysis for the state of New Jersey has been made by Stofflet. E. H. Stofflet, "A Study of National and Cultural Differences in Criminal Tendency," *Archives of Psychology*, No. 185, 1935.

ing culture. However, the rate is lowest in the heart of the colony and increases on the borderlines where the group comes into contact with other groups. Moreover, the rates are comparatively low in the immigrant groups which have moved away from the areas of deterioration into better residential areas. Even the immigrant group itself tends to approach the crime rate of the host country.[40] A study of crime rates in France in the nineteenth century indicated that migrants moving from one province to another changed their crime rates in the direction of the rate of the host province, whether the rate in the host province was higher or lower than the rate in the province from which they migrated.[41] In the first five years of residence in an area of high delinquency in Los Angeles, 5 percent of the children in an immigrant group appeared before the juvenile court; after five more years, 46 percent appeared; and after another ten years 83 percent of the children came before the court.[42] The delinquency rate increased with length of stay in the area, presumably because the immigrant group was assimilating that part of American culture which it experienced, including the delinquency rates. It is safe to assume, on the basis of the study of France, that if the immigrant group had had a high crime rate and had settled in an area of low delinquency rates, their rate would have decreased with increased length of stay.

Taken together, the above variations in the nativity ratio force a rejection of each of the four theories described above; each theory is contradicted by at least one of the variations. Also, the fact that there is generally no undue amount of crime among the foreign-born undermines the assumption on which each of the theories is based.

The variations can be explained in terms of differential associations with criminal and anti-criminal behavior patterns. Since immigrants often live in poverty, are mobile, and are affected by many other conditions which are described as "criminogenic," it has been argued that their apparently low general crime rate must be due to statistical errors.[43] There is no necessary conflict here, however. Most immigrants have developed respect

[40] Evelyn B. Crook, "Cultural Marginality in Sexual Delinquency," *American Journal of Sociology*, 39:493–500, January, 1934; Norman S. Hayner, "Delinquency Areas in the Puget Sound Region," *American Journal of Sociology*, 39:314–328, November, 1933; Andrew W. Lind, "The Ghetto and the Slum," *Social Forces*, 9:206–215, December, 1930; Andrew W. Lind, "Some Ecological Patterns of Community Disorganization in Honolulu," *American Journal of Sociology*, 36:206–220, September, 1930; Helen G. McGill, "The Oriental Delinquent in the Vancouver Juvenile Court," *Sociology and Social Research*, 22:428–438, May, 1938.

[41] Henri Joly, *La France Criminelle* (Paris: Cerf, 1889), pp. 45–46.

[42] Pauline V. Young, "Urbanization as a Factor in Juvenile Delinquency," *Publications of the American Sociological Society*, Vol. 24 (1930), pp. 162–66.

[43] Donald R. Taft, "Does Immigration Increase Crime?" *Social Forces*, 12:69–77, October, 1933.

for law in their home countries, and these habits, ideals, and codes persist after they reach America so that they are not so criminalistic as native Americans. They are, nevertheless, affected by the behavior patterns of the people living in the areas where they settle, and these patterns are likely to involve norms conducive to delinquency and crime.[44] The comparatively low crime rate of recent southern European migrants in Australia has been attributed to the fact that most such migrants enter Australia under the sponsorship of a member of their own family already in Australia; the migrants who had spent many years in displaced persons camps in Europe made up the group responsible for the greatest number of crimes committed by aliens.[45] Thus, the important variables in the differential crime rates of the several nationality groups are the strength and consistency of the traditions which they assimilated in their home countries and the strength and consistency of the traditions with which they come in contact in the new country.[46] These traditions, also, explain the differences in the types of crime characteristics of the various immigrant groups, and the variations in the types of crime and crime rates of the second generation immigrants as compared with their parents.

SUMMARY AND CONCLUSIONS. In this chapter and in Chapter 6 we have considered some of the facts about the relationship of crime and delinquency to age, sex, race, and nativity. Although these are only some of the social conditions with which crime rates vary, the list is sufficiently long to enable us to draw the important conclusion that crime is social behavior that is closely associated with other kinds of social behavior. In Chapters 9 and 11 we will consider additional sets of facts, those pertaining to relationships between crime and size of community and between crime and social class. Here, we need only observe that one set of facts indicates that the crime rate is higher for young adults than for persons in later life, higher for men than for women, higher for Negroes than for whites, and higher for native born than for foreign born. Such differences may be described as ratios—the age ratio in crime, the sex ratio in crime, etc. A second set of facts shows that these ratios are not constant. They vary in definite ways, depending on social conditions.

These ratios, and variations in ratios, make up some of the facts that a general explanation of crime must fit. They may be called definitive facts,

[44] See Elena Padilla, Up From Puerto Rico (New York: Columbia University Press, 1958), p. 229; Richard A. Cloward and Lloyd E. Ohlin, Delinquency and Opportunity (Glencoe: The Free Press, 1960), pp. 194–211; and Daniel Bell, "Crime as an American Way of Life," Antioch Review, 13:131–154, June, 1953.
[45] Commonwealth Immigration Advisory Council, op. cit., pp. 5, 18.
[46] Cf. Wood, op. cit.

for they define or limit the explanations of crime that can be considered valid. For example, an explanation that attributes crime to poverty helps make good sense out of the overrepresentation of Negroes in the general criminal population, but the theory falls flat when it is recalled that women, who are equal in poverty with men, have very low crime rates; when it is recalled that immigrants, who are probably at least as poor as their sons, sometimes have crime rates lower than their sons; when it is recalled that even poor Negroes do not have high crime rates in their old age, and so on. Similarly, an explanation of crime in terms of a hereditary characteristic, or of a psychological trait such as aggression must show that the characteristic is much more frequent among men than among women, among Negro women than white women, among young persons as compared to old persons, among native whites as compared to immigrants; and it must show that the trait occurs very infrequently among some immigrant groups, among Negroes who live in segregated areas, among Southern European immigrants in Australia, etc.

None of the general explanations of crime makes good sense of all the ratios and variations in ratios. Some of them explain one set of facts, and others explain another set of facts, but none of them explains all the facts. However, the theory of differential association, and concordant sociological theories that have as their general point the observation that crime and criminality are products of social experience and social interaction, makes better sense out of more of the facts than do other general theories.

$$Crime = SE \times SI$$

## SUGGESTED READINGS

Axelrad, Sidney, "Negro and White Institutionalized Delinquents," *American Journal of Sociology*, 57:569–574, May, 1952.

Beach, Walter C., "Oriental Crime in California," *Stanford University Publications in History, Economics, and Political Science*, Volume III, No. 3, 1932.

Bonger, W. A., *Race and Crime*. Translated by Margaret M. Horduk. New York: Columbia University Press, 1943.

Bullock, Henry Allen, "Significance of the Racial Factor in the Length of Prison Sentences," *Journal of Criminal Law, Criminology and Police Science*, 52:411–417, December, 1961.

Caldwell, Morris G., "Personality Trends in Youthful Male Offenders," *Journal of Criminal Law, Criminology, and Police Science*, 49:405–416, January–February, 1959.

Eaton, Joseph W., and Kenneth Polk, *Measuring Juvenile Delinquency*. Pittsburgh: University of Pittsburgh Press, 1961.

Eisenstadt, S., "Delinquency Group Formation Among Immigrant Youth," *British Journal of Delinquency*, 2:34–45, July, 1951.

Finestone, Harold, "Cats, Kicks and Color," *Social Problems*, 5:3–13, July, 1957.

Fox, Vernon, and Joan Volakakis, "The Negro Offender in a Northern Industrial Area," *Journal of Criminal Law, Criminology, and Police Science*, 46:641–647, January–February, 1956.

Goldberg, N., "Jews in the Police Records of Los Angeles, 1933–1937," *Yivo Annual of Jewish Social Science*, 5:266–291, 1950.

Hayner, Norman S., "Social Factors in Oriental Crime," *American Journal of Sociology*, 43:908–919, May, 1938.

Hentig, Hans von, "The First Generation and a Half: Notes on the Delinquency of Native Whites of Mixed Parentage," *American Sociological Review*, 10:792–798, December, 1945.

Johnson, Guy G., "The Negro and Crime," *Annals of the American Academy of Political and Social Science*, 217:93–104, September, 1941.

Kephart, William H., "The Negro Offender," *American Journal of Sociology*, 60:46–50, July, 1954.

Kitano, Harry, "Differential Child-Rearing Attitudes Between First and Second Generation Japanese in the United States," *Journal of Social Psychology*, 53:13–19, 1961.

Ross, Harold, "Crime and the Native Born Sons of European Immigrants," *Journal of Criminal Law and Criminology*, 28:202–209, July–August, 1937.

Rudwick, Elliott M., "Race Labeling and the Press," *Journal of Negro Education*, 31:177–181, 1962.

Stofflet, E. H., "The European Immigrant and His Children," *The Annals of the American Academy of Political and Social Science*, 217:84–92, September, 1941.

Van Vechten, C. C., "The Criminality of the Foreign Born," *Proceedings of the American Prison Association*, 70:505–516, 1940.

Wolfgang, Marvin E., Arlene Kelly, and Hans C. Nolde, "Comparison of the Executed and the Commuted Among Admissions to Death Row," *Journal of Criminal Law, Criminology and Police Science*, 53:301–311, September, 1962.

Wolfgang, Marvin, *Crime and Race: Conceptions and Misconceptions*. New York: Institute of Human Relations Press, 1964.

Wood, Arthur Lewis, "Minority-Group Criminality and Cultural Integration," *Journal of Criminal Law and Criminology*, 37:498–510, March–April, 1947.

Young, Pauline V., *Pilgrims of Russian-Town*. Chicago: University of Chicago Press, 1932.

# 8. PSYCHOPATHY AND CRIME

A WIDELY HELD BELIEF is that criminal behavior is due to some characteristic or trait of the personality and that this trait is in the nature of a pathological condition which exists prior to the criminal behavior and is the cause of it. The Lombrosian notion that criminals constitute a distinct physical type has continued as a neo-Lombrosian notion that maintains the same logic but substitutes psychopathological type for physical type. Some scholars have found the explanation of crime in mental defectiveness, others in schizophrenia, others in psychopathic personality, and others in a composite group of emotional disturbances. However, psychiatrists differ as to the importance of these pathological traits; some assert that practically all criminals are psychopathic, others assert that 10 percent or even less are psychopathic.

The mental pathologies have been classified in many ways. One of the simpler classifications includes three groups, namely, mental defect or feeble-mindedness, psychosis or insanity, and neuropathic conditions, which include epilepsy, post-encephalitic personality, psychopathic personality, and the psychoneuroses.

MENTAL DEFECT. Mental defect was once used almost as a specific explanation of crime. The explanation was explicitly stated in propositions that all or almost all criminals are feeble-minded. It also was stated implicitly in the proposition that feeble-minded persons commit crimes, in the absence of special inhibiting conditions, because they do not have sufficient intelligence to appreciate the reasons for laws and the consequences of violations of law; in the proposition that feeble-mindedness and, thus, the tendency to commit crimes is inherited as a unit character in accordance with Mendel's law of heredity; and in the proposition that a policy of sterilization or segregation of the feeble-minded is the only effective method of preventing crime and of dealing with criminals.

This statement of the propositions does not include the many exceptions made by various authors, and perhaps is unfair even to Harry H. Goddard, who was in the early period the most extreme adherent of the idea that mental defect causes crime. He stated in 1919:

Every investigation of the mentality of criminals, misdemeanants, delinquents, and other antisocial groups has proven beyond the possibility of contradiction that nearly all persons in these classes, and in some cases all, are of low mentality. . . . It is no longer to be denied that the greatest single cause of delinquency and crime is lowgrade mentality, much of it within the limits of feeble-mindedness.[1]

And in another connection, he said that the feeble-mindedness of a delinquent *fully* explained the delinquency.[2]

An attempt was made in 1928 and 1929 to assemble the results of all intelligence tests of criminals and determine what conclusions were justified.[3] The following conclusions were derived from an analysis of approximately 350 reports of this nature, which included tests of approximately 175,000 criminals and delinquents. *First*, the proportion of delinquents diagnosed feeble-minded decreased from more than 50 percent in the average study made in the period 1910–1914 to 20 percent in the period 1925–1928. *Second*, wide variations are found in the results of tests given over a period of two decades, variations which are more likely to reflect differences in the methods of the testers than differences in the intelligence of the persons tested. *Third*, when allowance is made for the selection involved in arrest, conviction, and imprisonment, the distribution of intelligence scores of delinquents is very similar to the distribution of intelligence scores of the general population. Zeleny, after equating the procedures of different testers, concluded that the ratio of delinquents and general population in respect to mental deficiency was about 1.2 to 1.[4] *Fourth*, the studies of groups of feeble-minded persons in the community do not show an excess of delinquency among them, as compared with the normal population. *Fifth*, feeble-minded prisoners have about the same disciplinary records in prisons as other prisoners. *Sixth*, feeble-minded offenders are successful on parole about as frequently as other parolees. *Seventh*, feeble-

[1] H. H. Goddard, *Human Efficiency and Levels of Intelligence* (Princeton: Princeton University Press, 1920), pp. 73–74. Reprinted by permission of the publishers.
[2] H. H. Goddard, *Juvenile Delinquency* (New York: Dodd, Mead, 1921), p. 22.
[3] Edwin H. Sutherland, "Mental Deficiency and Crime," Chapter XV in Kimball Young, Editor, *Social Attitudes* (New York: Henry Holt, 1931), pp. 357–375.
[4] L. D. Zeleny, "Feeble-mindedness and Criminal Conduct," *American Journal of Sociology*, 38:564–578, January, 1933. See also Simon H. Tulchin, *Intelligence and Crime* (Chicago: University of Chicago Press, 1939); Edward A. Ferentz, "Mental Deficiency and Crime," *Journal of Criminal Law and Criminology*, 45:299–307, September–October, 1954; and Mary Woodward, "The Role of Low Intelligence in Delinquency," *British Journal of Delinquency*, 5:281–303, April, 1955.

minded offenders become recidivists with about the same frequency as other offenders. *Eighth*, persons convicted of sex crimes are more likely to be feeble-minded than persons convicted of other crimes. In general, this analysis showed that the relationship between crime and feeble-mindedness is comparatively slight. Certainly intelligence is not as closely correlated with crime as are age and sex. This does not, however, mean that it may not be a very important condition in individual cases.

An extensive survey of the literature on the general relation between morality and intellect concluded that the relation is positive but low, with correlations usually between 0.10 and 0.39. The only significant point of difference from the analysis described above is on the fourth point, for the survey reports that feeble-minded groups in the community have an unusually large number of delinquencies.[5] Further evidence on this point has been supplied by Kennedy, who compared 256 morons and a matched control group of 129 non-morons and concluded that morons had a higher rate of arrest and also of recidivism than had non-morons.[6] The difficulty with this study, however, is that the parents and other family members of the morons also had a higher arrest rate than the family members of the non-morons. Thus the control group was not matched with the moron group in certain essential respects and the higher arrest rate of the morons may be due to their family associations rather than to their I.Q.'s.

The proposition that feeble-mindedness is inherited as a unit characteristic has now been generally abandoned. Intelligence as measured by tests has been proved to be modifiable, as is shown both by retesting of identical individuals and by comparisons of foster children reared in different environments.[7] Recent psychological thought regarding the relationship between mental deficiency and crime tends to parallel that of Coleman, who makes the following statement:

Popular opinion, based on outdated psychological findings, has it that the great majority of inmates of penal institutions are mentally defective and that mentally defective individuals are especially prone to criminal behavior. Indeed, one of the major reasons why institutionalization was first recommended for the mental defective was to protect society from his supposed "criminal propensities." More recent psychological evidence

[5] Clara F. Chassell, *The Relation between Morality and Intellect* (New York: Columbia University Press, 1935), p. 133.

[6] Ruby Jo Reeves Kennedy, *The Social Adjustment of Morons in a Connecticut City* (Hartford: Commission to Survey the Human Resources of Connecticut, 1948). See also Austin E. Grigg, "Criminal Behavior of Mentally Retarded Adults," *American Journal of Mental Deficiency*, 52:370–374, April, 1948.

[7] See Kenneth Eells, *Intelligence and Cultural Differences: A Study of Cultural Learning and Problem Solving* (Chicago: University of Chicago Press, 1951).

has conclusively demonstrated, however, that inferior mentality is neither the specific cause nor the outstanding factor in crime and delinquency. Although a higher percentage of delinquent children come from the ranks of the mentally defective, particularly from those of borderline intelligence, it is not the mental deficiency per se but the inability of the child to make adequate school or social adjustments that usually results in his delinquency.[8]

PSYCHOSES. Although mental disease has been studied for many generations, much disagreement still prevails regarding definitions, classifications, causes, methods of diagnosis, therapy, extent in the general population, and frequency in the criminal population. It probably is improper to speak of adjustment problems as "disease" or even "illness."[9] However, if the disease analogy is used, then the phenomenon is not one disease but a large number of diseases, differing from each other as much as bronchitis differs from tuberculosis. Paresis is a fairly well-established disease with clear symptoms and demonstrable organic origin, but schizophrenia is extremely indefinite in regard to both symptoms and origin. Increasing emphasis is being placed on the role of social relations in the etiology of many of the psychoses. In a pioneering work along this line, Faris and Dunham studied the residences of psychotic patients received in the public and private hospitals of Illinois and showed a definite relationship between social organization and the incidence of psychoses. Generally, they found that the previous places of residence clustered around the center of the city and decreased in frequency toward the city limits. Moreover, they found that all psychoses did not follow the same pattern of distribution, that one type of social organization tended to produce schizophrenia, another type to produce manic-depressive disorders.[10] A more recent study shows a close relationship between social class position and various kinds of mental disturbance.[11] Another investigator has emphasized that delusional ideas and abnormal reaction patterns are transferred from one person to another, and that this phenomenon is found among persons in

[8] From Abnormal Psychology and Modern Life, pp. 476–477, by James C. Coleman. Copyright, 1950, by Scott, Foresman and Company and reprinted with their permission. See also Franco Ferracuti, "Il Contributo Die Tests Psicologici Alle Teorie Criminologiche Ed Alla Diagnosi Dei Criminali Mentalmente Anormali," Quaderni Di Criminologia Clinica, 2:495–506, December, 1960.

[9] Thomas S. Szasz, The Myth of Mental Illness: Foundations of a Theory of Personal Conduct (New York, Hoeber-Harper, 1961). See also Thomas S. Szasz, Law, Liberty, and Psychiatry: An Inquiry into the Social Uses of Mental Health Practices, (New York, The Macmillan Company, 1963).

[10] R. E. L. Faris and H. W. Dunham, Mental Disorders in Urban Areas: An Ecological Study of Schizophrenia and Other Psychoses (Chicago: University of Chicago Press, 1939).

[11] August B. Hollingshead and Frederick C. Redlich, Social Class and Mental Illness (New York: Wiley, 1958).

close and prolonged personal contact, even when there is no blood relationship.[12]

The major characteristic which psychotics have in common is complete breakdown or severe impairment of the means of communication; they lose contact with "reality." They sometimes are completely isolated from the values of their social groups and, in fact, do not maintain membership in social groups. In other cases, the isolation is less extreme. Naturally, many psychotics do not manage their lives in a way considered satisfactory by most persons, and they sometimes get into trouble with the law. The psychoses may produce social harms in various ways. A hallucinatory voice may repeat a command to kill and the voice may finally be obeyed. An innocent person may be attacked as a means of revenge for or defense against an imagined misdeed. However, only some of the persons classed as psychotic are dangerous, and certainly not all psychotic persons are hospitalized.

Psychiatric examinations of criminals on admission to state prisons generally show not more than 5 percent to be psychotic, and in many institutions less than 1 percent. This variation is affected both by the preconceptions of the examiners and by variations in the manner of handling defendants who plead that they are "insane," not "criminal." In one clinic, no delinquent was diagnosed as "normal," on the strange ground that "normality is a vague concept because everybody simply projects his own ideal of perfection into it."[13] Offenders admitted to houses of correction and to jails have a slightly higher rate of psychoses than those admitted to prisons. Even so, the rate is seldom higher than 5 percent of the admissions and in many studies is reported to be about 2 percent. The offenders in these institutions often have alcoholic psychoses, from which they may quickly recover. Moreover, when the harms committed are not serious, the court is not as likely to declare a defendant "insane" and commit him to a hospital rather than to a penal institution. The fact that a criminal is psychotic does not mean that his crime was due to his psychosis. Silverman reported that the social backgrounds of 500 psychotic inmates of the Federal Medical Center were remarkably similar to those of non-psychotic federal prisoners.[14] However, he did find that psychotic

12 Alexander Gralnick, "Folie a Deux—The Psychosis of Association; a Review of 103 Cases and the Entire English Literature, with Case Presentations," *Psychiatric Quarterly*, 16:230–263, September, 1942.

13 Pierre Rube, "Psychiatric Clinic for Adolescent Delinquents," *Quarterly Journal of Child Behavior*, 4:24–56, January, 1952.

14 Daniel Silverman, "The Psychotic Criminals: A Study of 500 Cases," *Journal of Clinical Psychopathology*, 8:301–327, October, 1946. See also Daniel Silverman, "Psychoses in Criminals: A Study of 500 Psychotic Prisoners," *Journal of Criminal Psychopathology*, 4:703–730, April, 1943.

prisoners were considerably different from psychotic persons outside prisons. This suggests that the social backgrounds which produced criminal
behavior in the non-psychotic prisoners also produced criminal behavior
in the psychotic prisoners.

Many psychotic persons do not commit crimes or legal harms of any
kind. This has been demonstrated in two organized research studies. Dunham in a study of 870 male schizophrenic patients aged 15–29 in Illinois
hospitals, found that only 24 percent had records of juvenile delinquency
or adult crime and a large proportion of these records were for minor
offenses; approximately 20 percent of these records were in connection
with the current commitment to the hospitals; the paranoid had a significantly higher rate of crime than the catatonic[15] A similar study of
1,262 patients in the Eloise State Hospital in Michigan showed that 21.1
percent had records of definite crimes, and an additional 4.4 percent had
records of threatened or attempted crimes, making a total of 25.5 percent
for whom such behavior was recorded; of these 39 percent had the recorded behavior before the recognized onset of mental disease, 61 percent
after the onset.[16] The law-abiding behavior of most psychotics is explained
partly by the types of psychoses, partly by the fact that their characters
and inclinations were law-abiding prior to the onset of the psychosis and
somehow persisted after the mental disturbance occurred.

Research on the exact role of psychoses in crime is complicated by the
fact that a person who is "insane" at the time he commits a legally-for-
bidden harm does not commit a crime. A person charged with a crime
may defend himself in court by showing that he was insane at the time
the act occurred, just as another person may plead that his act occurred
in self defense. This means, for example, that one who is insane at the
time he kills another has committed no crime; he is committed to a hospital for treatment rather than to a prison for punishment. Hence, if the
legal concept "insanity" were synonymous with the psychiatric term "psychosis" there would be no problem regarding the role of the psychoses in
criminality, for persons would be either psychotic or criminal. In the current medico-legal situation, however, "insanity" differs from what many
psychiatrists have in mind when they speak of "psychoses." Consequently
a court may find a defendant to be criminal (i.e., "not insane" and guilty),
while a psychiatrist may diagnose the same defendant as schizophrenic or,
generally, psychotic.

[15] H. Warren Dunham, "The Schizophrene and Criminal Behavior," *American Sociological Review*, 4:352–361, June, 1939.
[16] Milton H. Erickson, "Criminality in a Group of Male Psychiatric Patients,"
*Mental Hygiene*, 22:459–476, July, 1938.

Generally, "insanity" is used to describe legally harmful behavior perpetrated under circumstances in which the actor did not know the nature or quality of his act or did not know right from wrong. This rule for determining insanity was formulated in England in 1843 and is known as the "M'Naghten Rule." Most psychiatrists hold that it does not incorporate the many advances in their profession since that time. The most frequent argument against it is that in some kinds of behavior the actor does know right from wrong but nevertheless exhibits the harmful behavior because it is prompted "from within" by a force which he is powerless to resist.[17] This argument has had some effect on criminal law theory, for at present the courts of about 14 states hold that punishment for perpetration of a legal harm can be avoided by showing that, while the defendant knew right from wrong, his behavior was prompted by an "irresistible impulse."[18] In 1954 the Court of Appeals in the District of Columbia rejected the M'Naghten Rule for determining insanity, holding simply that a defendant is not criminally responsible if his act was the product of "mental disease or mental defect."[19] In most states, however, the vagueness of both the criminal law concepts and psychiatric concepts allows some criminals to be declared "insane," and thereby to escape punishment; and it allows some psychotics to be punished for crime rather than treated for mental disease.

During the last generation, development of the electroencephalograph technique, a recording of a so-called "brain wave," has enabled researchers to compare delinquents and criminals with psychotics without actually declaring the delinquents to be psychotic or insane. The results of the tests of delinquents and criminals have been inconclusive, some studies reporting that almost all of the delinquents tested showed abnormal electroencephalograms, other studies reporting no significant differences between delinquents and non-delinquents.[20] Silverman found that electroencephalo-

---

[17] See Manfred S. Guttmacher and Henry Weihofen, *Psychiatry and the Law* (New York: Norton, 1952), pp. 401–423; and Donald R. Cressey, "The Differential Association Theory and Compulsive Crimes," *Journal of Criminal Law, Criminology, and Police Science*, 45:29–40, May–June, 1954.

[18] E. R. Keedy, "Irresistible Impulse as a Defense in Criminal Law," *University of Pennsylvania Law Review*, 100:956–993, May, 1952.

[19] Durham v. United States, 214 F 2d 862–876.

[20] See R. L. Jenkins and B. L. Pacella, "Electroencephalographic Studies of Delinquent Boys," *American Journal of Orthopsychiatry*, 13:107–120, January, 1943; Frederick A. Gibbs, B. K. Bagchi, and Wilfred Bloomberg, "Electroencephalographic Study of Criminals," *American Journal of Psychiatry*, 102:294–298, November, 1945; C. A. Miller and Margaret Lennox, "Electroencephalography in Behavior Problem Children," *Journal of Pediatrics*, 33:753–761, December, 1948; R. S. Hodge, "Delinquency and Epilepsy: A Clinical and Electrophysiological Note," *Journal of Mental Science*, 94:439–443, April, 1948; Dennis Hill and D. A. Pond, "Reflections on 100 Capital Cases Submitted to Electroencephalography," *Journal of Mental Science*, 98:23–43, January, 1952; Sara G. Geiger, "Organic Factors in Delinquency," *Journal*

gram abnormalities were no more frequent among psychotic criminals than among non-criminal psychotics and concluded that the electroencephalogram was therefore not significant in relation to criminality.[21]

POST-ENCEPHALITIC PERSONALITY. Epidemic encephalitis or encephalitis lethargica is relatively recent as a classified disease. This disease produces lesions in the central nervous system and aftereffects in the form of behavior problems, especially if the patient is a child. The primary effect is lethargy, retardation, and irritability. Quarrels, thefts, truancy, and other disorders of behavior are reported frequently. There is, however, little evidence regarding the proportion of cases of this disease in which behavior disorders appear and continue beyond the period of the primary sickness. It has been believed by some psychiatrists that subsequent behavior disorders are almost universal, and they have suggested that many other delinquents may have become disorganized as a result of the disease, though the disease was not recognized as such. If this be true, it is possible that many other children may have had the disease, not recognized as such, and have had no sequelae in the form of behavior problems.

This disease is regarded as very significant because it is taken as evidence that injuries to the neural system produce delinquency. As a matter of fact, however, the explanation is not simple. There is the direct physiological theory that the lesions in the central nervous system produce irritability and reduce efficiency and inhibitions, and consequently the child acts impulsively. These effects persist beyond the acute stage of the disease because of habit formation. A second is that the inferiority resulting from the lesions in the central nervous system lowers the status of the child, and the criticisms of parents and teachers when the child does not do as well as previously drive the child desperate. When the child is placed in a group of other post-encephalitic children, from whom less is expected, the feeling of inferiority is overcome and the behavior improves.[22] Another theory is that those encephalitic patients who manifest subsequent behavior difficulties are members of families or groups which manifest behavior problems such as psychosis, drunkenness, and criminality. In fact, explana-

---

of Social Therapy, 6:224–237, 1960; J. R. Hughes, "A Controlled Study on the Behavior Disorders Associated with the Positive Spike Phenomenon," Electroencephalography and Clinical Neurophysiology, 18:349–353, 1965.

[21] D. Silverman, "The Electroencephalogram of Criminals," Archives of Neurology and Psychiatry, 52:38–42, December, 1944.

[22] For a description of an interesting experiment in the re-education of post-encephalitic children, see Earl D. Bond and Kenneth E. Appel, The Treatment of Behavior Disorders Following Encephalitis (New York: Commonwealth Fund, 1931). Earl D. Bond and L. H. Smith, "Post-encephalitic Behavior Disorders, American Journal of Psychiatry, 92:17–31, July, 1935.

tion of the behavior disorders following this disease is not certain, though the injury to the nervous system is evidently of great significance. Also, it is probable that the person's behavior is affected by emotional changes and the reactions of others to these changes, rather than by intellectual deterioration.[23]

PSYCHOPATHIC PERSONALITY.   The terms "psychopath," "psychopathic personality," and "constitutional psychopathic inferior" are used with little or no differentiation to refer to persons who are regarded as emotionally abnormal but who do not manifest the break with reality that characterizes psychotics. Some psychiatrists have classified psychopathic personalities in three groups—the egocentric, the inadequate, and the vagabond—and many descriptive terms have been applied to each category. Others classify them into schizoid types, paranoid types, cyclothymic types, sexual deviants, alcoholics, and drug addicts.[24] The method of diagnosing psychopathic personality is not at all standardized or objective; consequently, a person may be psychopathic or not, depending upon the preconceptions of the person making the examination. Because it is difficult to define or identify a psychopath, the label "psychopathic personality" can be applied to almost anyone. Investigators who are convinced that all, or almost all, criminals must have "bad" personalities can attribute the criminality of persons showing no ordinary psychoses or neuroses to psychopathic personality. Indeed, "delinquency of one kind or another constitutes the most frequently utilized symptomatic basis for diagnosis of psychopathic personality."[25] The concept is often designated a "waste-basket category" into which not-otherwise-explicable criminal behavior is tossed. Preu has made the following statement regarding the concept:

The term "psychopathic personality," as commonly understood, is useless in psychiatric research. It is a diagnosis of convenience arrived at by a process of exclusion. It does not refer to a specific behavioral entity. It serves as a scrapbasket to which is relegated a group of otherwise unclassified personality disorders and problems.[26]

[23] M. Molitch, "Chronic Post-Encephalitic Behavior Problems," *American Journal of Psychiatry*, 91:843–861, January, 1935. For a similar conclusion regarding epilepsy, see L. E. Keating, "Epilepsy and Behavior Disorder in Children," *Journal of Mental Science*, 107:161–180, 1961.

[24] Walter Bromberg and Charles B. Thompson, "The Relation of Psychosis, Mental Defect and Personality Types of Crime," *Journal of Criminal Law and Criminology*, 28:1–22, May–June, 1937.

[25] P. W. Preu, "The Concept of Psychopathic Personality," in J. McV. Hunt, Editor, *Personality and the Behavior Disorders* (New York: Ronald Press, 1944), Vol. II, pp. 922–937.

[26] *Ibid.* Reprinted by permission of the publishers. See also Jack V. Wallinga, "The Psychopath: A Confused Concept," *Federal Probation*, 20:51–54, September, 1956.

The vagueness of the term as used in criminology is indicated by the fact that under the administration of one psychiatrist 98 percent of the inmates admitted to the state prison of Illinois were diagnosed as psychopathic personalities, while in similar institutions with different psychiatrists not more than 5 percent were so diagnosed. Vagueness in diagnosis also has been indicated by Sheldon who, speaking of 200 boys in a social agency in Boston, declared that it was not uncommon to find that as many as a dozen different psychiatric diagnoses and interpretations had been made on a youngster. Moreover, diagnoses of some boys were contradictory, and others had been given "all the possible diagnoses."[27] Numerous persons have attempted to define the concept "psychopathic personality" with some degree of rigor and to account for the formation of psychopathic personalities.[28]

The most careful investigations of psychopathic personalities among criminals have been made by Cason. In reviewing the literature, he found 202 terms which have been used more or less synonymously with the term "psychopath."[29] He then counted 55 "traits or characteristics" which are generally held to be present among psychopaths, and 30 behaviors which are frequently characterized as "forms of psychopathic behavior." A study of the inmates held at the Psychopathic Unit of the Federal Medical Center revealed that some inmates exhibited many of the 30 different forms of psychopathic behavior, and some had few of the behaviors. He selected two groups—the 23 inmates having the largest number of the psychopathic behaviors and the 29 inmates having the smallest number—and determined the frequency with which each of the 55 traits or characteristics appeared in each group. He found that 47 of the 55 traits had no statistical significance in differentiating the most psychopathic from the least psychopathic, and of the eight remaining traits six were just barely significant. With the exception of the two traits—intolerance and making threats—the traits which are generally regarded as characterizing the psychopaths were not as

[27] William H. Sheldon, Varieties of Delinquent Youth: An Introduction to Constitutional Psychiatry (New York: Harper, 1949), p. 42. See also Nathan W. Ackerman, "Psychiatric Disorders in Children—Diagnosis and Etiology in Our Time," in Paul H. Hoch and Joseph Zubin, Editors, Current Problems in Psychiatric Diagnosis (New York: Grune and Stratton, 1953), pp. 205–231.

[28] See K. A. Menninger, "Recognizing and Renaming 'Psychopathic Personalities'," Bulletin of the Menninger Clinic, 5:150–156, December, 1941; G. S. Sprague, "The Psychopathology of Psychopathic Personalities," Bulletin of the New York Academy of Medicine, 17:911–921, December, 1941; J. M. Caldwell, "Neurotic Components in Psychopathic Behavior," Journal of Nervous and Mental Disease, 99: 134–148, July, 1944; H. F. Darling, "Definition of Psychopathic Personality," Journal of Nervous and Mental Disease, 101:121–126, May, 1945; M. D. Gynther, "Crime and Psychopathology," Journal of Abnormal and Social Psychology, 64:378–380, 1962.

[29] Hulsey Cason, "The Psychopath and the Psychopathic," Journal of Criminal Psychopathology, 4:522–527, January, 1943.

useful in differentiating the most psychopathic from the least psychopathic as were the facts that a person was born in the Eastern states, had engaged in farming, or had violated the Dyer Act against automobile thefts.[30] These studies seem to justify a conclusion that the concept "psychopathic personality" is as useless in the interpretation of criminal behavior as was the older concept "moral imbecile" which has been completely discarded by scholars in this field.

In another study, Cason and Pescor compared 500 prisoners in the Federal Medical Center who had been diagnosed as psychopaths with all federal prisoners and with the civilian population of the United States. Among other things, they found that the psychopathic prisoners were very much concentrated in the age group 20–29, in comparison both with all federal prisoners and with the civilian population.[31] This is highly significant, for it indicates that people cease to be psychopathic after they pass the age of thirty, or that psychopathic persons stop committing federal crimes after the age of thirty, or that psychiatrists do not characterize older persons as psychopaths as readily as they do younger persons. No theory of psychopathy adequately accounts for the first two interpretations. Gough's theory that the psychopath is deficient in role-playing abilities probably offers the most promising research leads in this connection.[32]

During the years immediately following World War II, several states became panic-stricken because of a small number of serious sexual attacks, and their legislatures hurriedly enacted "sexual psychopath" laws, which spread through certain sections of the United States. Because no one has been able to identify a sexual psychopath any more than any other psychopath, the laws have been absurd in principle and futile in operation.[33]

OTHER PERSONALITY DEVIATIONS. Emotional instability and other traits of personality have been studied independently of the concept of psychopathic personality, and delinquent behavior is frequently attributed to one or more of these traits. One of the principal research procedures has been

[30] Hulsey Cason, "The Symptoms of the Psychopath," *Public Health Reports*, 61:1833–1868, December 20, 1946.

[31] Hulsey Cason and M. J. Pescor, "A Statistical Study of 500 Psychopathic Prisoners," *Public Health Reports*, 61:557–574, April 19, 1946; see also Hulsey Cason and M. J. Pescor, "A Comparative Study of Recidivists and Non-recidivists among Psychopathic Federal Offenders," *Journal of Criminal Law and Criminology*, 37:236–238, September–October, 1946.

[32] Harrison G. Gough, "A Sociological Theory of Psychopathy," *American Journal of Sociology*, 53:359–366, March, 1948.

[33] See Edwin H. Sutherland, "The Sexual Psychopath Laws," *Journal of Criminal Law and Criminology*, 40:534–554, January–February, 1950; Edwin H. Sutherland, "The Diffusion of Sexual Psychopath Laws," *American Journal of Sociology*, 56:142–148, September, 1950.

PRINCIPLES OF CRIMINOLOGY

to give a personality test to a group of delinquents and then to compare
their scores with the scores of a control group composed of non-criminals.
Dozens of tests, rating scales, and other devices for measuring these traits
have been used. Studies have been made of instincts, emotions, moods,
temperaments, moral judgments, ethical discriminations, as well as of such
specific tendencies as aggressiveness, caution, conformity, conscientious-
ness, deception, self-assurance, social resistance, suggestibility, and many
others. Thomas stated that if these tests had really measured the things
they were intended to measure, our knowledge of and control over human
nature would be nearly complete, but that as a matter of fact the units are
not adequately defined, the tests do not measure the things they purport
to measure, and the results have not been validated by reference to other
data.[34] Some psychiatrists who have attempted to avoid the vagueness of
the psychopathic personality concept have merely substituted personality
deviations of various kinds. For example, of the 2,537 individuals coming
before the Psychiatric Clinic of the New York City Court of General Sessions in 1948, 19.4 percent were diagnosed as psychopathic, but 76.1
percent were found to have personality deviations such as aggressiveness,
emotional instability, and shiftlessness.[35] However, no personality tests
were utilized, and the technique for locating such deviations is not precisely described. Moreover, there is no assurance that the deviations found
among the criminals would not also be found among the general population.

Schuessler and Cressey in 1950 summarized the results of all studies in
which the personality test scores of delinquents and criminals were compared with the scores of control groups. In the 113 studies of this kind, the
whole range of traits was included and also the whole range of tests, including the Rorschach and other projective tests. One conclusion of their
analysis was that not a single trait was shown in this series of studies to be
more characteristic of delinquents than of non-delinquents. The general
observation was that "the doubtful validity of many of the obtained differences, as well as the lack of consistency in the combined results, makes
it impossible to conclude from these data that criminality and personality
elements are associated."[36] Recent studies using the Minnesota Multi-

[34] W. I. Thomas and Dorothy S. Thomas, The Child in America, New York:
Knopf, 1936, p. 263.
[35] Walter Bromberg, "American Achievements in Criminology," Journal of Criminal
Law, Criminology, and Police Science, 44:166–176, July–August, 1953.
[36] Karl F. Schuessler and Donald R. Cressey, "Personality Characteristics of Criminals," American Journal of Sociology, 55:476–484, March, 1950. Essentially the same
conclusion was reached by Lawson G. Lowrey, "Delinquent and Criminal Personalities," in J. McV. Hunt, op. cit., pp. 794–821.

phasic Personality Inventory have shown differences between delinquents and non-delinquents in some instances but not in others.[37]

A thoughtful study of delinquents from the point of view of personality has been made by Jenkins and Hewitt, who found various kinds and degrees of "inhibition" among their subjects.[38] The inadequacy of this study from the point of view of a theory of criminal behavior is that it is not directed at an explanation of the delinquent behavior. A similar analysis of non-delinquents would probably result in the same finding of overinhibited and underinhibited persons, and persons inhibited with reference to ingroups but not to others. Consequently, the study gives no aid in understanding which persons engage in delinquent behavior, although it should be useful in the efforts to rehabilitate delinquents and non-delinquents.[39]

One of the concepts which is most frequently used in connection with deviations in personality, regardless of whether these are labeled psychopathy or not, is frustration. It is assumed that a person is frustrated, that frustration results in emotional disturbance which produces aggression, and that delinquency is the consequence. The belief that aggression is a necessary consequence of frustration is certainly incorrect,[40] and the belief that aggression has some necessary connection with delinquency is equally incorrect. If one were to select the tenth of the population which is most aggressive, assuming that aggression could be measured, it is not at all certain that this aggressive population would contain an unusual proportion of criminals.

The best general study of personal traits in relation to delinquency was made by Healy and Bronner.[41] This was an analysis of 105 delinquents treated over a three-year period in three clinics, in comparison with 105 non-delinquent siblings who lived in the same homes and neighborhoods and were matched with the delinquents, so far as possible, by age and sex. This study resulted in the finding that 91 percent of the delinquents and only 13 percent of their non-delinquent siblings had deep emotional disturbances. This difference is striking and has been regarded as final proof

[37] S. R. Hathaway and Elio D. Monachesi, *Analyzing and Predicting Delinquency with the MMPI* (Minneapolis: University of Minnesota Press, 1953); Arthur P. Volkman, "A Matched-Group Personality Comparison of Delinquent and Non-delinquent Juveniles," *Social Problems*, 6:238–245, Winter, 1959; George B. Vold, *Theoretical Criminology* (New York: Oxford University Press, 1958), pp. 131–138.

[38] R. L. Jenkins and Lester Hewitt, "Types of Personality Structure Encountered in Child Guidance Clinics," *American Journal of Orthopsychiatry*, 14:84–94, January, 1944.

[39] See Albert J. Reiss, Jr., "Social Characteristics of Psychological Types of Delinquency," *American Sociological Review*, 17:710–718, December, 1952.

[40] E. Faris, "Some Results of Frustration," *Sociology and Social Research*, 31:87–92, November, 1946.

[41] William Healy and Augusta F. Bronner, *New Light on Delinquency and its Treatment* (New Haven: Yale University Press, 1936).

that delinquency is due largely to emotional disturbance. However, this
interpretation is open to question for the following reasons: *First*, the
difference between the delinquents and their non-delinquent siblings is
probably exaggerated. The staff in these clinics was composed almost entirely of psychiatrists and psychiatric social workers, who have been predisposed to an interpretation of delinquency in terms of emotional disturbance. Since tests of emotional disturbance are not standardized, these
staff members cannot easily check on their preconceptions. Also, the staff
became much better acquainted with the delinquents than with the non-
delinquents, since they carried on three-year treatment programs for
delinquents and on that account would be more likely to discover the
emotional disturbances of the delinquents. The inadequacy of the investigations of the non-delinquents is revealed by the report that only 21
percent of them were "even mildly delinquent."[42] In a sample of university
students in classes in criminology over a fifteen-year period at least 98 percent report that they were at least "mildly delinquent" in childhood.
*Second*, the emotional disturbance, even if not exaggerated, is not demonstrated to be the cause of the delinquent behavior; the delinquent behavior
may cause the emotional disturbance. No organized effort was made in
this study to determine whether the emotional disturbance preceded the
delinquent behavior. *Third*, the process by which emotional disturbance
produces delinquent behavior is not adequately investigated. The argument is: a child is emotionally disturbed, so he commits a delinquent act.
Emotional disturbance, however, does not in itself explain delinquent behavior, as is shown by the 13 percent of the non-delinquents who were
emotionally disturbed, and by the fact that there is no correlation between
the frequency of emotional instability among school children and delinquency rates of school districts.[43] The alternative hypothesis is that emotional disturbance produces delinquency when it isolates a person from the
law-abiding group and decreases the prestige of this group, or when it
throws an individual into contact with delinquent groups. Under the same
conditions of association, delinquent behavior results in those who are not
emotionally disturbed. The girls in these homes are presumably emotionally
disturbed as frequently as the boys, but they are not so frequently delinquent.

ALCOHOLISM. Alcoholism is significant in criminology in two respects.
First, it may be a crime in itself or may be directly related to violations of

[42] *Ibid.*, p. 54.
[43] G. E. Swanson, "The Disturbance of Children in Urban Areas," *American Sociological Review*, 14:676–678, October, 1949.

certain laws such as those prohibiting public intoxication and drunken driving. Second, it may indirectly contribute to the violations of other laws, such as those prohibiting murder, rape, assault and battery, vagrancy, and non-support of families.[44] A questionnaire study of 2,325 male felons committed to California's Department of Corrections indicated that 98 percent had used alcoholic beverages, while the usage in the United States population of males 21 years of age and older was estimated at 70 percent. Twenty-nine percent of the alcoholic beverage users claimed they were intoxicated at the time they committed the offense for which they were sent to prison. The proportion of who had been intoxicated varied with the type of crime committed, from the high of 50 percent for automobile theft to the low of 10 percent for narcotics offenses.[45]

Two major problems for a theory of criminal behavior are posed by the alcoholic criminal. The first of these is whether a person who is under the influence of alcohol will violate laws which he would not violate if he were not under that influence; if he does violate the law under such circumstances, he may not be acting under the influence of differential association. No clear-cut research work has been done on this problem, and no definite answer can be given. However, considerable information which points in the direction of a negative answer is available. It is known that when people in certain areas become intoxicated, they are almost certain to start fights and violate criminal laws; this is particularly true of the lower socioeconomic class. On the other hand, intoxication in other parts of American society may result only in singing, exchange of dirty stories, or crying. These differences appear to operate in larger groups and do not merely differentiate one person from another. Furthermore, it may be said that even if a person, without change in his associations, acts differently when under the influence of alcohol than at other times, this may conceivably be because he has learned from associations with others certain ways of acting when intoxicated. He may have learned that when he is becoming intoxicated he should act gay and consequently he begins to sing, or he may have learned that he should act tough and consequently he picks a fight. And he may have learned that intoxication is a good excuse or rationalization for behavior which would he regarded as inexcusable otherwise.

The second problem is whether alcoholism is a form of psychopathy. Many psychiatrists in making classifications of psychopathies interpret alco-

---

[44] Marvin E. Wolfgang and Rolf B. Strohm, "The Relationship Between Alcohol and Criminal Homicide," *Quarterly Journal of Studies on Alcohol*, 17:411–425, No. 3, 1956.

[45] State of California, Department of Public Health, Division of Alcoholic Rehabilitation, *Criminal Offenders and Drinking Involvement*, Publication No. 3, 1960, pp. 7, 14.

*psychopathy*

holism as a form of vagabondage, or an abnormal method of escaping from reality. Scores of papers have been written from the point of view of this interpretation, and it may be regarded as a generally accepted belief of psychiatrists. As a matter of fact, it has never been demonstrated, and the concept of escape is so vague that it cannot readily be tested. Moreover, it has been believed that the person who becomes alcoholic does so because of certain traits in his personality. An analysis has been made, however, of all the available studies in which alcoholics have been given personality tests in comparison with non-alcoholics or with the general population, and one conclusion from this analysis is that the alcoholics have not been demonstrated to have any trait or traits which differentiate them from non-alcoholics. Particularly, the Rorschach tests, which have been used more frequently than any other tests in studies of alcoholics, fail completely to arrive at any consistent result. Another conclusion which may be drawn from the studies is that there is no such thing as a pre-alcoholic personality, that is, a type of person who is more likely than others to become an alcoholic.[46] Further evidence that alcoholism is not primarily an expression of personal pathology is found in the fact that the Alcoholics Anonymous organization has had some success in treating alcoholics. Although it can be argued that only the alcoholics without personal pathologies join the organization, those who do interact with ex-alcoholics gain assistance in overcoming their craving for alcohol. Alcoholics Anonymous has demonstrated that it is not necessary to attempt to find and treat some underlying defect in the alcoholic's personality. Another method of dealing with alcoholism is a drug called antibuse. Although some psychiatrists insist that this drug must always be administered along with accompanying psychiatric treatment in order to be successful, evidence is accumulating that the drug is quite as successful when no attention is paid to personality as when accompanied by psychiatric treatment.

NARCOTIC DRUGS.  Drug addiction, like alcoholic intoxication, is often regarded as a symptom of psychopathy; drug addiction is presented in some reports as one of the classes of psychopathies, co-ordinate with paresis and schizophrenia. The discussion of narcotic addiction is included in this chapter on psychopathic traits and criminal behavior as a matter of convenience rather than of logic, for narcotic addiction is certainly not one of the psychopathies. Lindesmith has shown conclusively that no distinction can be made between psychopathic and normal persons in the genesis of

[46] Edwin H. Sutherland, H. G. Schroeder, and C. L. Tordella, "Personality Traits and the Alcoholic: A Critique of Existing Studies," *Quarterly Journal of Studies on Alcohol*, 11:547–561, December, 1950.

drug addiction. Any person may begin to use narcotic drugs casually, either from motives of curiosity and observance of folkways in variant cultures or in complete ignorance of the fact that he is using narcotic drugs, which happened especially in earlier generations in connection with medical prescriptions and patent medicines for digestive ailments. Any person, regardless of the traits of his personality, who thus uses narcotic drugs casually until he suffers distress when the drugs are withdrawn and who becomes aware of the relation between his distress and the withdrawal of the drugs is a drug addict. Psychopathic and normal persons behave in uniform ways in this respect.[47]

Narcotic drugs are often said to be factors in the genesis of criminal behavior. The general tendency during the last generation has been to minimize the importance of narcotic drugs in this respect, especially so far as serious crimes are concerned. Sandoz was able to secure the life histories of 60 persons addicted to morphine. Of these, 42 had never been arrested before addiction to drugs, and after addiction had an average number of arrests of 8.2 each; the other eighteen persons had an average of 2.8 arrests prior to addiction and 8.3 after addiction. For the group as a whole, the average number of arrests prior to addiction was 0.8 each, after addiction 8.2 each, of which 5.5 were for offenses other than violation of the drug law.[48] These arrests for other offenses than violation of the drug law were principally for petty thefts and vagrancy. More recent studies have also suggested that in America, where addicts must almost necessarily become underworld figures, and where underworld figures are over-represented in the addict population, crime rates are increased considerably by drug addiction. This is not true in nations that handle drug addicts in such a way that they are not forced into intimate association with criminal behavior patterns.[49]

A precise definition of the process by which narcotic drugs are related to criminal behavior has not been made. The popular belief that these drugs make their users reckless and violent is certainly not correct. The opiates, in fact, have the opposite effect. Cocaine, which should be distinguished

[47] A. R. Lindesmith, *Opiate Addiction* (Bloomington: Principia Press, 1947); A. R. Lindesmith, "Dope Fiend Mythology," *Journal of Criminal Law and Criminology*, 31:199–208, July–August, 1940; T. Michelson, "Lindesmith's Mythology," *Journal of Criminal Law and Criminology*, 31:375–400, November–December, 1940; A. R. Lindesmith, "The Drug Addict, Patient or Criminal?" *Journal of Criminal Law and Criminology*, 31:531–535, January, 1941; A. R. Lindesmith, "Can Chimpanzees Become Morphine Addicts?" *Journal of Comparative Psychology*, 39:109–117, April, 1946.

[48] C. E. Sandoz, "Report on Morphinism to the Municipal Court of Boston," *Journal of Criminal Law and Criminology*, 13:43, May–June, 1922.

[49] Alfred R. Lindesmith, *The Addict and the Law* (Bloomington: Indiana University Press, 1965), pp. 124–128.

from the opiates, is an excitant and it is reported that gangsters sometimes take this drug prior to their crimes for the purpose of driving them into reckless behavior. Even though this be true, the criminal behavior is established before the drug is used. Moreover, in comparison with the opiates, cocaine is rarely used. A second process which has been suggested is that narcotic addiction produces physical and mental deterioration and therefore reduces the addict's income; at the same time the drug habit demands a continuous supply of expensive drugs, with food and other necessities sacrificed in order to secure the drugs. The petty thefts by drug addicts are therefore said to be due to economic necessity. It is doubtful whether this simple explanation is adequate. All persons have needs; some persons satisfy their needs by legal methods and some by illegal methods and neither the fact nor the size of the need seems to differentiate the illegal methods from the legal methods. A third hypothesis is that the person who becomes a drug addict loses his economic efficiency and his previous associates; he is driven into the underworld in order to secure a supply of narcotic drugs and there he associates with criminalistic values which enable him to engage in petty larceny and other illegal methods by which he can acquire a supply of drugs. If he were driven into the underworld for any other reason, he would have the same associates and the same tendencies to commit crimes.

PSYCHOANALYTIC THEORY. A large proportion of professional persons working with delinquents and criminals use some form of psychoanalytic theory in their explanations of criminality. There really are many psychoanalytic theories; not one, but all emphasize unconscious emotional difficulties of some kind in the causation of crime.[50] The conventional Freudian theory contends that the mind is composed of three portions or parts: id, ego, and super-ego. The id consists of instincts, "original tendencies," or "impulses" which are possessed at birth. The id impulses are not adapted to social life and must be repressed or expressed in socially acceptable ways if one is to maintain himself in social life. Basically, this is a frustration of drives common to all men. The super-ego is the embodiment of the moral codes of society, and the id impulses are directed in view of the super-ego by the ego. The id usually is tamed, but often the impulses remain in the unconscious; the ego represses or forces them into the unconscious because they are painfully in conflict with social conventions. They get into consciousness only in symbolic

[50] For an excellent summary of psychoanalytic explanations of delinquent acts and of delinquent types of personality, see Nigel Walker, *Crime and Punishment in Britain* (Edinburgh: University of Edinburgh Press, 1965), pp. 69–72.

form, as in dreams or in overt behavior which does not mean what, on its face, it seems to mean. The criminal is a person who has failed to tame the impulses sufficiently, or who has failed to transform them into socially acceptable ways of behaving. Criminal behavior, therefore, may be the direct expression of instinctual urges, it may be symbolic expression of repressed desires, or it may be the result of an ego which has become maladjusted because of the conflicting forces exerted on it by the id and the super-ego.[51]

The Oedipus complex concept, for example, is based on the premise that incest is a basic desire of human beings—every male loves his mother and is jealous of his father because of the father's sex relations with the mother. In this situation, the id could take over, and the father would be murdered and the mother raped. Or the id urges may be repressed or in-hibited because of the strong social taboos against their expression. Or they may be partially repressed, in which case the person may murder his father in some symbolic way, or he may commit an act which is symbolic of the act of sexual intercourse with his mother. Either kind of symbolic act may be a crime—he may "murder" his father by forging checks on his bank account, or he may "rape" his mother by burglarizing a dwelling house. But crime may arise in another way also. Whenever the id domi-nates the super-ego, as in instances where it asserts itself through uncon-scious wishes and desires for intercourse with the mother, the ego feels guilty, for the super-ego is always operating. To get rid of the guilt feelings the ego may seek punishment, and, since punishment follows crime, a crime may be committed. The existence of clues to detection and apprehension such as a fingerprint left at the scene of a crime, is inter-preted as evidence of this phenomenon.[52]

The major difficulty with such theory is the fact that the variables can-not be studied scientifically. There is no way to prove or disprove the theory, for the elements of it cannot be observed or measured. From the point of view of a non-believer the symbolism often is fantastic, and the psychoanalysts have no way of demonstrating the relation between the symbols and the things they are supposed to represent. Moreover, one who argues that psychoanalytic theory is scientifically invalid in many

[51] For detailed discussion of psychoanalytic theory in criminology and for examples of research based upon it, see David Abrahamsen, *Crime and the Human Mind* (New York: Columbia University Press, 1945); Kate Friedlander, *The Psychoanalytic Ap-proach to Juvenile Delinquency* (New York: International Universities Press, 1947); Franz Alexander and Hugo Staub, *The Criminal, the Judge and the Public, a Psycho-logical Analysis*, Revised Edition (Glencoe: The Free Press, 1956); August Aichorn, *Wayward Youth* (New York: Viking Press, 1925); Robert Lindner, *Rebel Without Cause* (New York: Grune and Stratton, 1944).

[52] See. S. Glover, *The Roots of Crime* (London: Imago, 1960), p. 302.

respects is sometimes psychoanalyzed by the defenders of the theory, on the assumption that he himself must necessarily be expressing some deeply hidden, secret, emotional conflict rather than a worthwhile criticism.[53]

**CONCLUSIONS REGARDING CRIME AND PSYCHOPATHY.** The neo-Lombrosian notion that crime is an expression of psychopathy is no more justified than was the Lombrosian notion that criminals constitute a distinct physical type. Some studies have found a large proportion of criminals to be psychopathic, but it is possible that these findings arise from poor standardization in methods of diagnosis of psychopathy. The preconception of this school of thought is shown in extreme form in a report by psychiatrists on the medical aspects of crime to the effect that a diagnosis of mental disease "is permissible even when the criminal has shown no evidence of mental disease other than his criminal behavior."[54] According to this recommendation, the psychopathy which is to be used as the explanation of criminal behavior may be inferred from the criminal behavior which it explains; psychopathy and criminal behavior would necessarily be associated according to that circular method of reasoning. Perhaps this is why one psychiatrist has been able to say, "In all my experience I have not been able to find one single offender who did not show some mental pathology . . . The 'normal' offender is a myth."[55]

The fact which stands out most clearly from the organized research studies which have been conducted by scholars representing different schools of thought is that no trait of personality has been found to be very closely associated with criminal behavior. No consistent statistically significant differences between personality traits of delinquents and personality traits of non-delinquents have been found. The explanation of criminal behavior, apparently, must be found in social interaction, in which both the behavior of a person and the overt or prospective behavior of other persons play their parts.

## SUGGESTED READINGS

Alexander, Franz, and Hugo Staub, *The Criminal, the Judge, and the Public.* Revised Edition. Glencoe: The Free Press, 1956.
Ball, John C., *Social Deviancy and Adolescent Personality: An Analytic*

[53] Cf. Ernest Jones, *The Life and Work of Sigmund Freud*; Volume II, *The Years of Maturity*, 1901–1919 (New York: Basic Books, 1955), p. 127.
[54] Quoted by M. Ploscowe, "Some Causative Factors in Criminality," National Commission on Law Observance and Enforcement, *Report No. 13, Report on Causes of Crime*, Vol. I (Washington: Government Printing Office, 1931), p. 57.
[55] David Abrahamsen, *Who Are the Guilty? A Study of Education and Crime* (New York: Rinehart, 1952), p. 125. See also Benjamin Karpman, "Criminal Psychodynamics: A Platform," *Archives of Criminal Psychodynamics*, 1:3–100, Winter, 1955.

Study with the MMPI. Lexington: University of Kentucky Press, 1962.

Banay, Ralph S., "Alcoholism and Crime," *Quarterly Journal of Studies on Alcohol*, 2:686–716, March, 1942.

Bates, Jerome, "Abrahamsen's Theory of the Etiology of Criminal Acts," *Journal of Criminal Law and Criminology*, 40:471–475, November–December, 1949.

Board, Richard G., "Operational Criteria for Determining Criminal Responsibility," *Columbia Law Review*, 61:221–232, 1961.

Bromberg, Walter, and Hervey M. Cleckley, "The Medico-Legal Dilemma, a Suggested Solution," *Journal of Criminal Law, Criminology, and Police Science*, 42:729–745, March–April, 1952.

Cason, Hulsey, "The Psychopath and the Psychopathic," *Journal of Criminal Psychopathology*, 4:522–527, January, 1943.

Cressey, Donald R., "The Differential Association Theory and Compulsive Crime," *Journal of Criminal Law, Criminology, and Police Science*, 45:29–40, June, 1954.

Ferentz, Edward A., "Mental Deficiency and Crime," *Journal of Criminal Law, Criminology, and Police Science*, 45:299–307, September–October, 1954.

Foxe, A. N., "Freud's Contribution to an Understanding of Delinquency," *Journal of Orthopsychiatry*, 10:863–865, October, 1940.

Friedlander, Kate, *The Psychoanalytic Approach to Juvenile Delinquency*. New York: International Universities Press, 1944.

Gibbens, T. C. N., D. Pond and D. Stafford-Clark, "A Follow-Up Study of Criminal Psychopaths," *Journal of Mental Science*, 105:114–124, 1959.

Gough, Harrison G., "Theory and Measurement of Socialization," *Journal of Consulting Psychology*, 24:23–30, 1960.

Hakeem, Michael, "A Critique of the Psychiatric Approach to the Prevention of Juvenile Delinquency," *Social Problems*, 5:194–206, Winter, 1957.

Hakeem, Michael, "A Critique of the Psychiatric Approach to Crime and Correction," *Law and Contemporary Problems*, 23:650–682, Autumn, 1958.

Hathaway, S. R., and E. D. Monachesi, *Analyzing and Predicting Juvenile Delinquency with the MMPI*. Minneapolis: University of Minnesota Press, 1953.

Healy, William, and Augusta F. Bronner, *New Light on Delinquency and its Treatment*. New Haven: Yale University Press, 1936.

Hollingshead, August B., "Some Issues in the Epidemiology of Schizophrenia," *American Sociological Review*, 26:5–13, February, 1961.

Lindesmith, A. R., *Opiate Addiction*. Bloomington: Principia Press, 1947.

Lindesmith, A. R., *The Addict and the Law*. Bloomington: Indiana University Press, 1965.

Reiss, A. J., Jr., "Social Correlates of Psychological Types of Delinquency," *American Sociological Review*, 17:710–718, December, 1952.

Schuessler, Karl F., and D. R. Cressey, "Personality Characteristics of Criminals," *American Journal of Sociology*, 55:476–484, March, 1950.

Sewell, William H., "Infant Training and the Personality of the Child," *American Journal of Sociology*, 58:150–159, September, 1952.

Sewell, William H., and Archie O. Haller, "Social Status and Personality Adjustment of the Child," *Sociometry*, 19:114–125, June, 1956.

Shulman, Harry M., "Intelligence and Delinquency," *Journal of Criminal Law and Criminology*, 41:763–781, March–April, 1951.

Stafford-Clark, D., D. Pond, and J. W. L. Doust, "The Psychopath in Prison: A Preliminary Report of a Co-operative Research," *British Journal of Delinquency*, 2:117–129, October, 1951.

Sutherland, Edwin H., "Mental Deficiency and Crime," in Kimball Young, Editor, *Social Attitudes*. New York: Henry Holt, 1931, pp. 357–375.

Sutherland, Edwin H., H. G. Schroeder, and C. L. Tordella, "Personality Traits and the Alcoholic: A Critique of Existing Studies," *Quarterly Journal of Studies on Alcohol*, 11:547–561, December, 1950.

Volkman, Rita, and Donald R. Cressey, "Differential Association and the Rehabilitation of Drug Addicts," *American Journal of Sociology* 69:129–142, September, 1963.

Wooton, Barbara, *Social Science and Social Pathology*. London: Macmillan, 1959.

# 9. CULTURE AREAS AND CRIME

IN THE DIFFERENT CULTURE AREAS of the earth, crime rates have ranged between zero and one hundred percent. Some isolated nonliterate tribes are, according to reports of ethnologists, completely free from violations of their own laws, while other groups have almost universal violations of laws. These standards of behavior, whether lawful or unlawful, are transmitted as traditions over many generations. Most cultural areas, of course, have crime rates between these two extremes, but wide variations exist. Like the variations in the age, sex, race, and nativity ratios in crime, the variations in crime rates from area to area pose challenging problems for a general theory of criminal behavior.

REGIONAL DISTRIBUTIONS.  Crime rates not only vary from one nation to another, but also generally among the several sections of each nation. Ferri reported that the rate of convictions for homicides per million population varied widely in different provinces in each of the principal European countries. In Italy, twenty-seven provinces had rates of less than fifty, while thirteen provinces had rates of more than two hundred. Convictions of homicide in Sardinia were more than fourteen times as frequent in proportion to population as in Lombardy.[1] Aschaffenburg found the offenses against the person were much higher in East Prussia, Bavaria, and the Palatinate than in the other German provinces. He found also that convictions for larceny were much higher in the provinces adjoining the Russian frontier than elsewhere in Germany, while resistance to or attack on officers were most frequent in seaports and in manufacturing districts.[2] The rate of indictable crimes known to the police in England is highest in the counties containing and adjacent to London, next in the counties

---

[1] E. Ferri, L'omicido nell' antropologia criminale (Torino: Bocca, 1895), pp. 241–325.
[2] G. Aschaffenburg, Crime and Its Repression (Boston: Little, Brown, 1913).

containing the principal seaports, next in the manufacturing counties in the central part of England, and lowest in the agricultural and mining counties. This same distribution was found in 1893, except that the south-western agricultural counties, which had a low general rate for indictable offenses, had the highest rate of any section of the country for offenses against morals. At an earlier period, according to Pike, the counties in England in which crime was most prevalent were those adjoining Scotland, because of the lack of organized government in those counties, and this continued until the final amalgamation of the counties.[3]

Joly found similar variations among the 86 departments in France, and he made an analysis of internal migration in relation to crime rates. He found, for instance, that the Corsicans were prosecuted more often when living in their native department than when living elsewhere in France. When the crime rate of Corsica was considered as the number of prosecutions in Corsica of persons born in Corsica, the department had next to the highest rate of the 86 departments; it dropped to sixty-fifth position when the crime rate was considered as the number of prosecutions of persons born in Corsica regardless of whether the prosecutions were in Corsica or in other departments. Similarly, the department which was next to the lowest in its rate at home rose to the thirty-sixth rank when prosecutions away from home were included. Some departments retained the same rank in the two methods of computing the rates, but others showed these very significant changes.[4]

The *Uniform Crime Reports* data presented in Table XI show the variations in the frequency of specific types of crime in different regions of the United States.[5] Subject to the qualifications mentioned earlier, the statistics indicate that New England had the lowest rates for homicide, rape, robbery, and aggravated assault. The East South Central region (Alabama, Kentucky, Mississippi, and Tennessee) had the lowest burglary, larceny, and automobile theft rates. The highest rates for burglary, larceny, and automobile theft were found in the Pacific states (Alaska, California, Hawaii, Oregon, Washington); the highest homicide rate appeared in the South Atlantic region (all East Coast states south of Pennsylvania); the highest robbery rate was in the East North Central states (Illinois, Indiana, Michigan, Ohio), and the highest forcible rape rate was in the Mountain states. By individual states, Vermont in 1964 had the lowest homicide and robbery rates, Hawaii the lowest rape rate, New Hampshire the lowest rate of aggravated assault. North Dakota had the lowest rate

[3] Luke O. Pike, A *History of Crime in England* (London: Smith, Elder, 1873–76).
[4] Henri Joly, La *France Criminelle* (Paris: Cerf, 1889), pp. 45–46.
[5] *Uniform Crime Reports*, 1964, pp. 50–53.

## TABLE XI

CRIME RATES, 1964, BY GEOGRAPHICAL DIVISION

(Offenses per 100,000 inhabitants)

| Division | Homicide | Forcible Rape | Robbery | Aggravated Assault | Burglary | Larceny Over $50 | Auto Theft |
|---|---|---|---|---|---|---|---|
| United States | 4.8 | 10.7 | 58.4 | 96.6 | 580.4 | 368.2 | 242.0 |
| New England | 1.7 | 5.6 | 21.2 | 37.0 | 469.9 | 294.4 | 314.4 |
| Middle Atlantic | 3.9 | 8.7 | 51.7 | 85.1 | 483.3 | 386.7 | 247.5 |
| East North Central | 3.7 | 11.2 | 90.6 | 88.2 | 510.9 | 336.5 | 261.4 |
| West North Central | 2.9 | 8.7 | 41.9 | 52.3 | 493.7 | 277.0 | 171.2 |
| South Atlantic | 8.2 | 10.1 | 51.0 | 145.8 | 586.5 | 329.5 | 193.2 |
| East South Central | 7.4 | 9.5 | 29.6 | 98.7 | 454.9 | 253.6 | 127.4 |
| West South Central | 7.3 | 10.9 | 43.0 | 114.3 | 574.3 | 305.7 | 191.9 |
| Mountain | 4.3 | 13.0 | 48.0 | 78.2 | 651.4 | 486.0 | 255.3 |
| Pacific | 3.7 | 17.4 | 85.3 | 117.3 | 973.2 | 601.2 | 368.8 |

for burglary, West Virginia for larceny, and Mississippi for automobile theft. Mississippi also had the highest homicide rate. Illinois had the highest robbery rate, North Carolina the highest aggravated assault rate, Alaska the highest rape rate, and California the highest burglary, larceny, and automobile theft rates.

Lottier analyzed sectional crime rates in the United States and reported a center of concentration for murder in the Southeastern states, with somewhat regular gradients to the north and west; robbery was concentrated in the Middle Central states, with an axis running from Tennessee and Kentucky to Colorado, and with decreasing rates on either side of this axis. Shannon repeated this study fifteen years later and found essentially the same pattern. The rate for crimes against the person showed definite regional concentration, but crimes against property did not show such marked concentration, probably because they were not based on the total property values in the states in question.[6]

Certain types of towns, also, have high crime rates. Lombroso reported that in every province in Italy certain villages had acquired reputations for special crimes; one was noted for murder, another for robbery, and another for swindling. Artena, for instance, had thirty times as many highway robberies as the average community in Italy, and had been noted as a home of robbers since the twelfth century.[7] Similarly, certain types of towns in

[6] Stuart Lottier, "Distribution of Criminal Offenses in Sectional Regions," *Journal of Criminal Law and Criminology*, 29:329–344, September–October, 1938. Lyle W. Shannon, "The Spatial Distribution of Criminal Offenses by States," *Journal of Criminal Law and Criminology*, 45:264–273, September–October, 1954.

[7] C. Lombroso, *Crime, Its Cause and Remedies* (Boston: Little, Brown, 1911).

America have been noted for high crime rates for short periods. Frontier towns, river towns, and resort towns are somewhat outstanding in this respect. Mining towns generally have higher rates than agricultural towns of the same size, and the mining counties of a state generally have higher rates than the agricultural counties.[8]

Such broad comparisons of crime rates have been made in many countries over a long period of time. In general, the various geographical divisions hold nearly the same ranks year after year. For regions, the ranks remain nearly the same whether the crime rates are computed for the the larger cities or for the smaller cities in the regions. Various attempts have been made to explain the differences. Aschaffenburg believed that the explanation of the differences in rates of crimes against the person in different provinces in Germany were related to the consumption of alcohol, while larceny was related to poverty, and crimes against public officials to the heterogeneity of population. Niceforo concluded that the differences in the crime rates in Sardinia were due to differences in racial origin of the population. The high crime rates in the Southern states are generally interpreted as due to the large number of Negroes, but it is evident that homicides, at least, cannot be explained so simply, for the death rate by homicide for white persons in the South is approximately five times as high as in New England, and the Negro homicide rate in New England is slightly lower than the white homicide rate in the same area.[9]

Professor Reckless has attributed these variations to differences in community organization and traditions of orderliness.[10] Such explanation is consistent with the differential association theory, which predicts that if the ratio of criminal behavior patterns to anti-criminal behavior patterns in a region remains approximately the same, the crime rate will remain approximately the same. Once started, a tradition of violence or theft is passed on to generation after generation. For example, in Upper Egypt, as in Sicily, a tradition which requires that revenge be taken for insults and other harms has given this region extraordinarily high homicide rates for centuries. On the other hand, the same region has extraordinarily low rates of conviction for drunkenness, owing to a strong anti-alcohol tradi-

[8] Helen L. Yoke, "Crime in West Virginia," *Sociology and Social Research,* 16:267–273, January, 1932; Mary Phleger and E. A. Taylor, "An Ecological Study of Juvenile Delinquency and Dependency in Athens County, Ohio," *Publications of the American Sociological Society,* 26:144–149, 1932.

[9] H. C. Brearley, *Homicide in the United States* (Chapel Hill: University of North Carolina Press, 1932).

[10] Walter Reckless, *The Crime Problem,* Second Edition, (New York: Appleton-Century-Crofts, 1955), pp. 63–65.

tion stemming from the Islam religion. An illustration of such traditions in exaggerated form was found in the thievery patterns of the criminal tribes of India:

The Bhamptas are a tribe who give an infinity of trouble. Their home is in the Decan; but there is no limit to their field of operations. They work all over India, traveling even to Assam; and no railway is exempt from the Bhampta pest. . . . The Bhampta is a marvellously skillful pick-pocket and railway thief. He frequents fairs, landing-places, bazaars, temples—any place, in fact, where there is a crowd. He is always on the lookout for his prey. . . . The Bhamptas are trained to crime from their earliest childhood, so it is not wonderful that they should become very expert. The children are initiated into the profession of their life by lessons in the pilfering of shoes, cocoanuts, and any odds and ends that they may come across. If they are slow or stupid they are encouraged to improve by the application of a stick. The boys soon become adept. . . . Adults generally work in small gangs of three or four. One of them stealthily removes an ornament from some one in the crowd, or adroitly picks a pocket, or, jostling the victim, boldly snatches his bag or satchel, and instantly passes his booty to one of his accomplices, who in turn passes it on to another; and in an incredibly short space of time the stolen property is far away. . . . Again a Bhampta sees a well-to-do person in the street. He makes a great show of brutally beating a small boy. The boy screams and yells and rushes for protection to the prosperous-looking stranger, who shields the child and expostulates with the Bhampta. The latter in apparent anger snatches away the boy from his protector, while the young rascal, who has been well trained, kicks and struggles for all that he is worth. The sympathizer has had enough of it, and is glad to let the youngster go. Later on he realizes that his purse has disappeared.[11]

RURAL-URBAN DISTRIBUTIONS. Statistics from many countries, and in many periods of time, indicate that urban areas have higher crime rates than rural areas. Two general types of relationship between crime and size of community can be observed, just as two types of relationship were observed between crime and age, sex, race, and nativity.

A. Official statistics indicate that the number of serious crimes per 100,000 population tends to increase with the size of the community. In 1964, the rate of robberies known to the police varied from 11.7 in towns of less than 10,000 population to 173.4 in cities of over 250,000. This trend is roughly the same for other types of crime and in other years, except

[11] Edmund C. Fox, *Police and Crime in India* (London: S. Paul, 1911), 234–237. See also Paul F. Cressey, "The Criminal Tribes of India," *Sociology and Social Research*, 20:503–511; 21:18–25, July–September, 1936.

that the rates in cities over 250,000 are sometimes less than in cities of 100,000–250,000. Similar tendencies have been reported for certain European countries and for Canada.[12] Of all the males born in Norway in 1933, 5.08 percent had become registered offenders by January 1, 1958. Among the boys living in Oslo, however, nine percent had become offenders, as compared to eight percent of the residents of other cities and four percent of the country residents.[13] Among a sample of 3,032 Danish men who in 1953–1954 were 21 years of age or more, 9.6 percent were violators of the criminal code. Thirteen percent of the men living in Copenhagen were violators, as compared to 8.8 percent of those living in towns with populations of 2,000–19,000, and to 6.2 percent of those living in rural districts and small towns with less than 2,000 inhabitants.[14] Offenses committed by rural criminals might not be reported or recorded as readily as offenses committed in urban areas, but the urban rate generally so far exceeds the rural rate that it is reasonable to conclude that there is in fact a great excess of crime in urban places. Moreover, a large proportion of urban crime also is overlooked, and it is not at all certain that this proportion is any less than the proportion of rural crimes that is overlooked.

B. The extent to which the crime rate in urban areas exceeds the crime rate in rural areas is not the same under all conditions. In some rural areas the crime rate, especially for some types of offenses, is higher than the rate in urban areas:

1. The amount of the excess of crime in urban areas varies by offenses. In American cities of over 250,000, murder and rape rates are about four times as high as the rates in towns of 10,000; burglary and larceny rates are about three times as high; aggravated assault and automobile theft about five times as high, and robbery about 15 times as high. In certain respects, the number of crimes decreases as the distance from the large city increases. Burglaries or robberies were committed against 59.6 percent of the stores belonging to a chain in the city of Chicago in the years 1931 and 1932, while only 29.8 percent, or exactly one-half the proportion, were burglarized or robbed in the suburban area within 25 miles from the center of Chicago in the same period. Moreover, the proportion of stores burglarized or robbed decreased by 25-mile zones steadily until it reached 6.2

---

[12] P. Sorokin and C. C. Zimmerman, *Principles of Rural-Urban Sociology* (New York: Henry Holt, 1929), Chapter 16; R. E. Watts, "The Influence of Population Density on Crime," *Journal of the American Statistical Association,* 26:11–20, March, 1931; E. Hacker, *Kriminalstatistische und Kriminalaetiologische Berichte* (Miskolc: Ludwig, 1941), pp. 113–114.

[13] Nils Christie, *Unge Norske Lovovertredere* (Young Norwegian Lawbreakers), Oslo: Universitetsforlaget, 1960, pp. 76, 304.

[14] Preben Wolf, "Crime and Social Class in Denmark," *British Journal of Criminology,* 13:5–17, July, 1962.

percent in the zone 100–125 miles away from the city. If the suburban cities above 20,000 population are eliminated, the trend remains the same. Similarly, while 57.9 percent of the stores in a chain of drugstores were burglarized or robbed in Chicago in 1927–1932, only 21.4 percent of the stores in this chain in the suburban area within 100 miles of the city were burglarized or robbed. The banks in Chicago, East St. Louis, and Wichita were less frequently burglarized or robbed than suburban banks outside those cities but within 25 miles of the center of the city, but otherwise the rate of burglaries and robberies of banks decreased as the distance from the city increased. Similarly, in the period 1924–1929, 19.5 percent of the suburban banks within 25 miles of the center of Chicago were burglarized or robbed, while only 5.6 percent of those 75 to 100 miles away were burglarized or robbed.

Lottier, in a more extensive analysis of the distribution of crimes, found that murders, assaults, rapes, and robberies known to the police decreased consistently in the commutation area of Detroit to a distance of 20 miles from the city hall, but that burglaries, auto thefts, and larcenies did not show a consistent decrease. He also found the same crimes against the person decreasing in the entire metropolitan area of Detroit within a radius of 200 miles, but again the crimes against property showed no such consistent decrease. He suggested that the difference in the two types of crimes may be due to the fact that crimes against the person were calculated in proportion to the number of persons, but crimes against property were not calculated in proportion to the amount of property. To illustrate this point, he calculated the ratio of chain-store burglaries to the number of chain stores in a zone and found that the burglaries of stores decreases steadily by zones from 1.87 burglaries per store in the first five-mile zone to .07 in the zone 45–55 miles from the city hall, rising in the next zone to .44 per store.[15] For the United States as a whole, however, the rural rates are slightly higher than the urban rates for homicide, about equal for rape, about one-half as high for assault, and from about one-fourth to about one-third as high for robbery, burglary, larceny, and auto theft.

2. The amount of the excess of crime in urban areas varies by area. In an earlier period, frontier towns, river towns, and resort towns were noted for high crime rates, despite the fact that they were not large in size. Further, Radzinowicz has demonstrated that in the southern districts of Poland the crime rates decrease as communities increase in size, that even in other sections of Poland many small communities have higher crime rates than many large communities, and that communities of the same size

[15] Stuart Lottier, "Distribution of Criminal Offenses in Metropolitan Regions," *Journal of Criminal Law and Criminology*, 29:37–50, May–June, 1938.

vary immensely in crime rates.[16] Also, in some other European countries
the larger city rates have been shown to be lower than the rural rates.[17]
Christie's study of all males born in Norway in 1933 showed a clear overrepresentation of offenders in the most densely populated areas, which
also had the highest number of policemen per 1,000 inhabitants. However,
the most sparsely populated area—Finnmark, the northernmost county in
Norway—had an offender rate which was approximately the same as that
of the densely populated industrial areas. Finnmark, which is populated by
Lapps as well as by Norwegians, also has one policeman for each 500
inhabitants, as compared to a ratio of 1 to 12,000 in other sparsely populated counties and to a ratio of 1 to 400 in Bergen and Oslo.[18]

Studies in Iowa and Kansas have indicated regular increases in delinquency rates from the most rural to the most urban counties.[19] However,
a study of the distribution of delinquency in Wisconsin indicated that the
counties containing cities have high delinquency rates, but that certain isolated rural logging counties also have high rates.[20] Wiers found in Michigan
that the most urban county had the highest delinquency rate, but that the
sparsely settled logging counties had higher rates than the southern agricultural counties.[21] Similarly, in West Virginia the mining communities
have higher crime rates than the agricultural communities. It must be concluded that certain contemporary rural sections have special criminalistic
traditions, just as in an earlier period certain frontier areas had such traditions.

3. The amount of excess of crime in urban areas varies in time. There is
evidence that as improved communication and transportation have reduced
the differences between urban and rural districts, the differences in the
crime rates of the two areas have decreased. In Sweden, the conviction
rate in rural districts steadily approached the conviction rate in city districts from 1879 to 1935. The same trend is found in France, but the
opposite trend is found in Finland. An analysis of the conviction rate in

[16] Leon Radzinowicz, "Criminality by Size-Groups of Communities," Mss., 1946.
[17] Hans von Hentig, "Der kriminelle Aspekt von Stadt und Land," Monatsschrift
für Kriminalpsychologie, 23:435–436, July, 1932; Hans von Hentig, "Die Gross-stadt
und das kriminelle Land," Monatsschrift für Kriminalpsychologie, 18:203–205, July,
1927.
[18] Christie, op. cit., pp. 78–80, 305.
[19] Charles N. Burrows, "Criminal Statistics in Iowa," University of Iowa Studies in
the Social Sciences, Vol. 9, No. 2, 1930; Mapheus Smith, "Tier Counties and Delinquency in Kansas," Rural Sociology, 2:310–322, September, 1937.
[20] M. G. Caldwell, "The Extent of Juvenile Delinquency in Wisconsin," Journal of
Criminal Law and Criminology, 32:145–157, July–August, 1941.
[21] Paul Wiers, "Juvenile Delinquency in Rural Michigan," Journal of Criminal Law
and Criminology, 30:211–222, July–August, 1939; see also Paul Wiers, Economic
Factors in Michigan Delinquency (New York: Columbia University Press, 1944).

Iowa for the period 1865–1925 showed that the rural rate had been consistently lower than the urban rate and did not show any significant tendency to approach the urban rate.[22] In Hutchinson County, South Dakota, the percentage of the total population convicted of crime rose steadily from the 1890–1900 decade to an all-time high between 1920–1930 and then receded slightly in the following ten years. In the earlier years the rate was higher among farm than town populations; in the recent years the crime rate of the towns has been twice that of the agricultural areas. These trends have been attributed to the enactment of laws running counter to the local mores.[23] The *Uniform Crime Reports* data indicate that, since about 1945, the rural rate in the United States has increased more rapidly than the urban rate. Consequently, the expected trend is found, but it is not consistent in all counties and areas.

It has been suggested that the excessive criminality of the city is due to the selective migration from the country of those who are most likely to commit crimes. Kinberg gave statistics that in Sweden about half the vagrants were born in the country and half in the towns, but that the persons who became vagrants migrated from the country to towns four times as frequently as the general population did and migrated from towns to country less than half as frequently as the general population did.[24] Also, the excessive criminality of the city has been explained as due to the impersonality of city life in comparison with rural life.[25] But criminals tend to migrate to areas in which other criminals operate, and these other areas may be cities in some countries and rural districts in other countries. Further, patterns of criminal behavior have become established in some rural districts, and persons migrating to those districts tend to become criminals, just as do persons migrating to urban areas in which criminal behavior patterns are prevalent. Thus, the significant conditions are the area's ratio of anti-criminal behavior patterns to pro-criminal behavior patterns, and the nature and extent of participation in these behavior patterns. It should be noted, however, that relatively little organized research work has been done on rural criminality. Clinard has made one of the best studies, concluding that rural criminality is explained by the person's identification with delinquents and his conception of himself as

[22] Thomas P. Monahan, *The Trend in Rural and Urban Crime*, Mss., 1937, based principally on the data in Charles N. Burrows, *op. cit.*

[23] John Useem and Marie Waldner, "Patterns of Crime in a Rural South Dakota County," *Rural Sociology*, 7:175–185, June, 1942.

[24] O. Kinberg, "On So-Called Vagrancy," *Journal of Criminal Law and Criminology*, 24:552–583, September–October, 1933; see also Hacker, *op. cit.*, Heft 5, pp. 5–7.

[25] See Marshall B. Clinard, "The Process of Urbanization and Criminal Behavior: A Study of Culture Conflicts," *American Journal of Sociology*, 48:202–213, September, 1942.

reckless and mobile, an explanation which is consistent with differential association.[26]

INTRA-CITY DISTRIBUTIONS.  It has been evident for many decades that criminals and delinquents are much more numerous in some city areas than in others. Shaw, McKay, and their collaborators have amplified this information and organized it in relation to the general pattern of the large American city. By an analysis of the rates of delinquency in various areas of Chicago and other cities they reached the following five conclusions: *First,* the rates of delinquency vary widely in different neighborhoods. None of the boys residing in some areas are arrested, while in other neighborhoods more than one-fifth of the boys are arrested in one year.[27] This variation has been found in each of fifteen cities, and the neighborhoods with the highest rates have been designated "delinquency areas." *Second,* the rates are generally highest in the low-rent areas near the center of the city and decrease with the distance from the center of the city. Also, the rates are high near large industrial or commercial sub-centers of the city and decrease with distance from those sub-centers. *Third,* the areas which have high rates of truancy also have high rates for all juvenile court cases, for all boys' court cases, and for all adult commitments to the county jail. The areas which have high rates for boy delinquencies also have high rates for girl delinquencies. *Fourth,* the areas which had high rates in 1930 also had high rates in 1900, although in the meantime the national composition of the population of the area had changed almost completely. When Germans and Swedes occupied an area near the center of the city their children had high rates of delinquency; when they were replaced by Polish, Italian, or other national groups, the juvenile delinquency rates in the area were essentially the same. *Fifth,* the delinquency rate of a particular national group such as German or Polish shows the same general tendency as the delinquency rate for the entire population, namely, to be high in the areas near the center of the city and low toward the outskirts of the city.[28]

[26] *Ibid.* See also Marshall B. Clinard, "Rural Criminal Offenders," *American Journal of Sociology,* 50:38–45, July, 1944; William P. Lentz, "Rural-Urban Differentials in Juvenile Delinquency," *Journal of Criminal Law and Criminology,* 47:311–339, September–October, 1956; and Marshall B. Clinard, "A Cross-cultural Replication of the Relation of Urbanism to Criminal Behavior," *American Sociological Review,* 25:253–257, April, 1960.
[27] See Henry D. McKay, *Rate of Delinquents by Communities in Chicago, 1953–1957* (Chicago: Institute for Juvenile Research, 1959. Mimeographed).
[28] Clifford R. Shaw and Henry D. McKay, *Juvenile Delinquency and Urban Areas* (Chicago: University of Chicago Press, 1942); Clifford R. Shaw and others, *Delinquency Areas* (Chicago: University of Chicago Press, 1929). For an excellent summary of research on delinquency areas, see Terrence Morris, *The Criminal Area* (London: Kegan Paul, 1958).

The conclusions above have been criticized on the ground that the statistics from which they were drawn were not valid measures, but the conclusions have been substantiated by studies in other localities by other authors. The question which has been raised most persistently, perhaps, is whether the statistics of arrests or of juvenile court appearances do not give a biased measure of delinquencies because of the poverty of the families in the area which are reported as having the highest delinquency rates.[29] Wealth and social position, to be sure, do provide a certain degree of immunity against arrest and incarceration.[30] Also, certain national or religious groups maintain welfare agencies which take problem cases that would otherwise be referred to the police or to the juvenile court, while other national and religious groups have no agencies of this nature.[31] Even when allowance is made for these probable statistical biases, some concentration of ordinary crime and delinquency seems to remain. In the District of Columbia the juvenile court statistics showed less concentration of cases in the high-delinquency areas than did the unofficial statistics of other agencies.[32] Of course, white-collar crime is not concentrated in the areas which have the highest official delinquency rates. The "concentration," it should be noted, is a concentration of the residences of criminals and delinquents, rather than of the crimes and delinquencies themselves. Generally, the places at which crimes are committed are close to the residences of the criminals. This is especially characteristic of crimes against the person, for the offender and the victim are usually of the same race, the same economic class, and also of the same neighborhood.[33] A study of Indianapolis indicated that petty crimes against property are concentrated near the places of residence of criminals, but that the more serious crimes against property are committed some distance from the places of residence of criminals.[34] A more recent study of Seattle indicated that even the serious property crimes, such as larceny and robbery, tend to occur in the central segment of the city, and are perpetrated by persons residing in that

[29] Christen T. Jonassen, "A Re-evaluation and Critique of the Logic and Some Methods of Shaw and McKay," *American Sociological Review*, 14:608–617, October, 1949; and Jackson Toby, "The Differential Impact of Family Disorganization," *American Sociological Review*, 22:505–512, October, 1957.

[30] James F. Short, Jr., and F. Ivan Nye, "Reported Behavior as a Criterion of Deviant Behavior," *Social Problems*, 5:205–213, Winter, 1957.

[31] Sophia M. Robison, *Can Delinquency Be Measured?* (New York: Columbia University Press, 1936).

[32] Edward E. Schwartz, "A Community Experiment in the Measurement of Juvenile Delinquency," *National Probation Association Yearbook*, 1945, pp. 157–181.

[33] Henry A. Bullock, "Urban Homicide in Theory and Fact," *Journal of Criminal Law and Criminology*, 45:565–575, January–February, 1955.

[34] R. Clyde White, "A Study of Residence and Place of Offense of Felons in Indianapolis," *Social Forces*, 10:498–509, May, 1932.

segment of the city. For example, 63 percent of the robberies and 40 percent of the burglaries were committed in the central segment, and 41 percent of those arrested for robbery and 34 percent of those arrested for burglary resided in the central segment.[35]

Though the concentration of the residences of delinquents and ordinary criminals near the industrial and commercial centers is demonstrated in an adequate sample of large American cities, the centers of concentration are not the same in European, Asiatic, or Latin American cities. In fact, a study of residences of criminals in Peiping indicates a concentration in the slum areas at the gates of the city rather than in the center of the city, and much the same distribution is reported in the older European cities, although special studies of residences of delinquents have not been made. Hayner found that in Mexico City crime is concentrated both in the central zone and in the peripheral zones.[36] In some smaller cities in the United States, the residences of delinquents are in the low-rent areas adjacent to the railway tracks or to the "dumps" on the outskirts of town. Because of the rapid expansion of American cities, especially those east of the Rocky Mountains, the areas of poverty in these cities tend to be located near the center. Thus, the high delinquency areas tend to be concentrated in the areas of greatest poverty, whether those areas are near the center of the city or on the outskirts.[37] It is not correct, however, to conclude from this that poverty is the cause of crime. In a study of offenses known to the police of Seattle, Schmid found that the census tracts with high crime rates tended to be characterized by low family status, low occupational status, low economic status, and a high rate of population mobility.[38]

Two principal interpretations of the concentration of delinquents have been presented. The first is in terms of social organization in the neighborhood. The areas of concentration in large American cities, and especially Chicago, where the problem has been studied most intensively, are areas of physical deterioration, congested population, decreasing population, economic dependency, rented homes, foreign and Negro population, and few

[35] Calvin F. Schmid, "Urban Crime Areas: Part II," *American Sociological Review*, 25:655–678, October, 1960.

[36] N. S. Hayner, "Criminogenic Zones in Mexico City," *American Sociological Review*, 11:428–438, August, 1946; see, also, Theodore Caplow, "The Social Ecology of Guatemala City," *Social Forces*, 28:113–133, December, 1949.

[37] Bernard Lander, *Towards an Understanding of Juvenile Delinquency* (New York: Columbia University Press, 1954), p. 87; Morris, op. cit., pp. 129–130; and John Mack, "Full-time Miscreants, Delinquent Neighbourhoods, and Criminal Networks," *British Journal of Sociology*, 15:38–53, March, 1964.

[38] Calvin F. Schmid, "Urban Crime Areas: Part I," *American Sociological Review*, 25:527–542, August, 1960.

institutions supported by the local residents. Lawlessness has become traditional; adult criminals are frequently seen and have much prestige. Gangs
have continued to exist, with changing personnel, for 50 years in some of
these areas. At a particular time the gang may have a senior, junior, and
midget branch. The techniques, codes, and standards are transmitted from
older to younger offenders. Delinquencies begin here at an early age, and
maturity in crime is reached at an early age. Boys 14 or 15 years of age
steal automobiles and commit robberies, while in other areas delinquents
of the same age are committing petty thefts. They not only acquire skill
in the execution of crimes, but also prepare for avoidance or mitigation of
penalties. They know the techniques of "fixing," of intimidating witnesses,
of telling plausible stories in court, of appeals to sympathy. Consequently
the influences toward delinquency there are strong and constant.

At the same time the anti-delinquent influences are few, and organized
opposition to delinquency is weak. Parent-teacher associations do not exist
nor do other community organizations which are supported principally by
the people of the neighborhood. Because the population is mobile and
heterogeneous, it is unable to act with concert in dealing with its own
problems. The school, the social work agencies, and the church are supported by people who reside elsewhere, and these agencies are for the most
part formal and external to the life of the neighborhood.

The residents of these neighborhoods probably know much better than
do the members of the upper classes the details of any graft and dishonesty
in the city's politics. The American culture which they see is a culture of
competition, grasping greed, deceit, graft, crime, delinquency, and immorality. They see practically nothing of the culture of cooperation, decency, and law-abidingness in which some Americans are immersed from
infancy. Thus they come in contact with a disorganized and rather lawless
neighborhood, and the rather dishonest public culture of America, but are
isolated from the predominantly law-abiding culture of the primary groups
in the middle-class American population.[39] That they would behave differently if they came into contact with a different culture pattern has been
shown in a comparison of a delinquency area of Boston with a delinquency
area of Cairo. In the Boulac area of Cairo, a high delinquency area, 35
percent of the delinquents arrested in 1952 had committed crimes against
the person, while in the Roxbury section of Boston the comparable percentage was eight. Similarly, 65 percent of the Roxbury delinquents, but
only 25 percent of the Boulac delinquents, admitted crimes against property. These variations are the result of cultural differences in what Ameri-

[39] Edwin H. Sutherland, "Social Process in Behavior Problems," *Publications of the
American Sociological Society*, 26:55–61, August, 1932.

can and Egyptian slum dwellers learn about an individualistic orientation to life—that is, to what they know is true about the role of "fate" in their personal affairs, as compared to the role of other persons. Boulac residents have learned that people have caused one's misfortunes. They behave accordingly: "In Boulac society, the individualism of Roxbury society is lacking . . . Persons, in themselves, are more important to an individual than his belongings. When an individual's success, or his status, or his recognition is hindered or threatened, he usually thinks in terms of some person or persons hindering his success, or threatening his status, or discouraging his recognition. Thus he may try to revenge himself by removing the cause—in this case, the person concerned."[40]

The second interpretation is that competitive processes select out constitutionally inferior, or psychologically inferior, persons who would have high delinquency and crime rates wherever they lived. As a matter of fact, those who reside in the areas of high delinquency rates at a particular time are of three types: recent immigrants, remnants of the earlier residential groups, and failures in the better residential districts who have been forced to move back into the cheaper rent areas. A study of Danville, Illinois, supported the selective migration interpretation by finding that while the residences of adult criminals were concentrated near the center of the city, very few criminals had been reared in that area.[41] However, most of them had been reared in families in which other members were delinquent, which might mean merely that they were reared in the delinquency areas of other cities. The most important evidence on this point is Shaw and McKay's finding that the delinquency rate remained practically constant over a 30-year period despite an almost complete change in the national composition of the population. This indicates that the delinquency rate is more likely to be a function of social pressures in an area than of the biological or psychological traits of people who reside there. Consistently, a detailed study showed that when an immigrant group first settled in Los Angeles, only 5 percent of the children of juvenile court age appeared in juvenile courts; five years later this percentage had increased to 46, and after another decade 83 percent of their children appeared in the juvenile court.[42] The stock in this case remained constant but the opportunities for assimilation of the culture of the American city increased, and in their

---

[40] Saied Euwies, "A Comparative Study of Two Delinquency Areas," *The National Review of Criminal Science* (U.A.R.), 2:1–15, November, 1959.

[41] D. R. Taft, "Testing the Selective Influence of Areas of Delinquency," *American Journal of Sociology*, 38:699–712, March, 1933.

[42] Pauline V. Young, "Urbanization as a Factor in Juvenile Delinquency," *Publications of the American Sociological Society*, 24:162–166, 1930; Pauline V. Young, *The Pilgrims of Russia-Town* (Chicago: University of Chicago Press, 1932).

neighborhood this meant assimilation of delinquency and crime. Similarly it has been reported that when a national group, such as the Greeks or Mexicans, first settles in an area of deterioration, the children do not play with the children of other residents and do not become delinquent, but as contacts develop in five to ten years the delinquency rates increase.

The location of delinquency areas near the commercial or industrial centers is related to the rents in those centers. Rents are low because accommodations are poor, and the accommodations are not improved because of the expectation that the commercial and industrial activities will expand and the near-by areas will be annexed to the business sections. Consequently they are areas of deterioration, for there is little expectation of permanence or provision for the future as residence sections. When poor migrants arrive, they settle in those districts where the rents are low, but some of them move out to better residential districts as soon as they accumulate sufficient capital. In this case, their delinquency rates go down. Negroes, Italians, Puerto Ricans, and Mexicans have dispersed less than other national or racial groups, and for that reason are likely to continue to have problems of delinquency.

Although the areas of high delinquency contain an abundance of pro-delinquent behavior patterns, many persons residing in them are not delinquent, and these persons live under the same conditions of poverty as do the delinquents. For example, within any given area, the female delinquency rate is customarily much lower than the male delinquency rate, although the wealth of parents, housing conditions, and many other external conditions are the same for girls and boys. Furthermore, in areas with relatively high delinquency rates, less than half of the boys can be identified as past or present delinquents, and about half are engaged in regular school work or occupations and show no sympathy whatever for the delinquent boys. Mack found that in a Scottish city, the precinct with the highest crime rate produced an annual average of 11 offenders per 100 households during the years 1948–60; the highest density street in this precinct produced 20 offenders per 100 houses per year. For this street, 32 percent of the households produced two or more offenders over a period of ten years, and another 7 percent of the households had a record of only one offense in the period. Thus, three out of five households in the most criminal area of the city had no criminal record at all, and only one out of three was "criminally active" in the sense that two or more offenders were produced in ten years.[43]

One explanation of the presence of non-delinquents in areas of high delinquency is the limitation on contact with delinquency patterns, even

[43] Mack, *op. cit.*, p. 44.

in the most delinquent areas. A delinquency area is practically never solidly delinquent; rather, there are certain streets or parts of streets on which at a particular time most delinquents reside, and on other streets the children may associate with each other in relative isolation from the behavior patterns of delinquents. Sometimes one or more national groups within a general residential area are isolated from the rest of the population, or a few members of one such group may be isolated within a larger area of another nationality. For example, in Seattle the delinquency rate in the Japanese colony, which is in a very deteriorated, high delinquency area, is lower than in the best residential areas.[44] Further, some children are kept from frequent or intimate contact with delinquency patterns because of their retiring, quiet, and unaggressive dispositions, and others, especially girls, are kept from such associations by careful and capable parents or siblings. Some children may refrain from delinquency because they have formed attachments at school with teachers, or at other agencies with other leaders; and their interests have been developed and their lives organized around lawful activities.[45]

A second, but consistent, explanation is that punishment of delinquents makes the career of a delinquent unattractive to some of the children in the areas of high delinquency. Of the young adults in the so-called Forty-Two Gang in Chicago in the 1930's, about one-third were killed by the police or by private parties, and another third were committed to prisons or reformatories. Killing young criminals or committing them to prison is a dramatic, but generally ineffective, way of presenting anti-criminal behavior patterns to those who remain behind. Nevertheless, some of the boys in the vicinity must have avoided delinquency because of the outcomes of the older boys in the Forty-Two Gang. Yet punishment sometimes inadvertently operates as a pro-delinquent influence, despite the attempt to use it as a device for presenting anti-criminal behavior patterns. All children are somewhat delinquent, but only some are caught, punished, and thus, publicly defined as delinquents. This first public appearance as a delinquent or criminal is highly critical, for thereafter the child's associations with law-abiding persons are restricted and he is thrown into intimate association with the behavior patterns of other delinquents. A boy who is consistently criminal is not defined as law-abiding if he commits a single lawful act, but a boy who is consistently law-abiding is likely to be publicly defined as a criminal if he is caught committing a single criminal act.

[44] N. S. Hayner, "Delinquency Areas in the Puget Sound Area," *American Journal of Sociology*, 39:314–328, November, 1933.
[45] See William Foote Whyte, *Street Corner Society* (Chicago: University of Chicago Press, 1943), pp. 104–108.

It is clear that even in the areas of highest delinquency many non-delinquent and anti-delinquent behavior patterns are available.[46] Whether a particular child becomes delinquent or not depends upon the ratio of his participation in this kind of behavior pattern, as compared with pro-delinquency behavior patterns, just as is the case with a child that lives in a more affluent area. The difference is the availability of the two kinds of behavior pattern, not in the process by which they are learned.[47]

THE GANG.   Among the influences in a neighborhood, the mutual stimulation of children in association is one of the most important. Many studies have shown that delinquencies are generally committed by two or more children acting together. Of 500 delinquents studied by Glueck, 492 or 98.4 percent chummed largely with other delinquents, while despite the fact that the 500 non-delinquents used as a control group lived in similar neighborhoods, only 37 or 7.4 percent of them had intimates among delinquents.[48] Shaw and McKay found by a study of the juvenile court records in Chicago that 88.2 percent of the boys had been engaged in delinquencies in company with others, and that 93.1 percent of those engaged in stealing had been in company with others.[49] The number of participants known to the juvenile court was two in 33.0 percent of the cases, three in 30.9 percent, four in 11.8 percent, and more than four in 13.3 percent. Lentz found that 22 percent of a group of rural training school boys were known to be members of delinquent gangs, while 87 percent of the urban boys were members of such gangs.[50] In a study of the first delinquencies of boys admitted to the Ohio Boys Industrial School, it was found that the median age of the first contact with the police or courts for delinquency was 13.1 years. Of boys whose first official delinquency occurred before this age, 77 percent were with companions when the act occurred; of those whose first delinquency occurred after the age of 13.1, 73 percent were with companions.[51]

In some areas of high delinquency, the boys are organized for crime in definite working groups, which they call "cliques" or "gangs," in which the

[46] Cf. Solomon Kobrin, "The Conflict of Values in Delinquency Areas," *American Sociological Review*, 16:653–661, October, 1951.

[47] See Jon E. Simpson, Simon Dinitz, Barbara Kay, and Walter C. Reckless, "Delinquency Potential of Pre-Adolescents in High-Delinquency Areas, *British Journal of Delinquency*, 10:211–215, January, 1960.

[48] Sheldon and Eleanor Glueck, *Unraveling Juvenile Delinquency* (New York: The Commonwealth Fund, 1950), p. 164.

[49] Shaw and McKay, *op. cit.*, pp. 193–199.

[50] Lentz, *op. cit.*, p. 335.

[51] Thomas G. Eynon and Walter C. Reckless, "Companionship at Delinquency Onset," *British Journal of Criminology*, 12:162–170, October, 1961.

*gangs* ⌐ labor is precisely divided. In robbery, for example, one boy drives the car, a second carries the gun and acts as lookout, while a third has the principal responsibility for entering the store. The assignment of tasks, of course, varies with the type of offense. This kind of organization is comparable to the division of labor among professional pickpockets. The term "gang" or "delinquent gang" is generally used for a somewhat larger and less definite group. The definition of "gang" is not clear. Inquiries among university students indicate that more than two-thirds of the men had, during childhood, been members of groups which were called gangs and that approximately a third of the women had such memberships. Most of these groups were described as harmless in their activities, though inclined to mild rowdyism, and the name "gang" was applied largely in a spirit of bravado. Bloch and Niederhoffer attribute gang behavior of this kind to the problems arising in the transition from the status of child to adult; they find gang behavior in many cultures.[52]

These childhood gangs are different from neighborhood delinquent gangs. In some areas of high delinquency, all the boys who live on one street, or the boys of one ethnic group, belong together for the purposes of fights and are known by a common name. Frequently a portion of the neighborhood boys of about the same age and with somewhat similar attitudes toward delinquency or toward "play" (which might involve delinquency) have a common meeting place on a corner and engage in many common activities without any other formal organization. A stranger would not be permitted to associate with these groups, and certain boys in the neighborhood might be ostracized, but otherwise the group is inclusive. Other gangs are much more formally organized, with names, leaders, passwords, and slogans, and they may persist with changing personnel for several decades. A "delinquent gang in this sense is a means of disseminating techniques of delinquency, or training in delinquency, of protecting members engaged in delinquency, and of maintaining continuity in delinquency."[53] It is not necessary that there be bad boys inducing good boys to commit offenses. It is generally a mutual stimulation, as a result of which each boy commits delinquencies which he would not commit alone.

So far as structure is concerned, then, neighborhood delinquent gangs may consist of loosely federated small cliques, or street clubs with rather informal and rapidly changing leadership, or of organizations with an age

---

[52] Herbert A. Bloch and Arthur Niederhoffer, *The Gang: A Study in Adolescent Behavior* (New York: Philosophical Library, 1958).

[53] Cf. John B. Mays, "A Study of a Delinquent Community," *British Journal of Delinquency*, 3:5–19, July, 1952.

hierarchy and specific leadership.[54] Among 225 gangs studied in Warsaw in 1953–1955, only 24 percent had an age hierarchy and specific leadership; another 24 percent was said to have "rudimentary organization," and the remaining 53 percent were "non-organized."[55] One analysis has characterized both the loose federations of cliques and the street clubs as "near groups," rather than as groups.[56] The argument underlying this characterization is that these gangs are merely loose federations of individual boys who are trying to work out their own emotional problems in gang activities. There is little consensus, little identification with the group, and rapidly changing leadership. Thrasher observed the unstable quality of Chicago delinquent gangs in the 1920's.[57] It is not at all certain, however, that emotionally disturbed boys are attracted to delinquent gangs in a disproportionate degree. One study of street clubs in Chicago found only about ten percent of the members emotionally disturbed enough to be referred to a casework agency.[58] It appears, however, that even the gangs that are highly organized for some purpose such as protection of their "turf" from invading gangs, and which have "Senior," "Junior," and "Midget" sections, are so poorly integrated that the gang may disintegrate if a leader is arrested or moves out of the neighborhood.

Delinquent gangs may be classified according to activities as well as according to the type of organization involved. One such classification developed from observations of the kinds of delinquent gangs arising in the slum areas of large American cities: gangs oriented to criminal activities, gangs oriented to conflict and violence, and gangs oriented to the use of drugs.[59] This classification refers to gangs in different locations and in different periods of history. In 1963, Short and his co-workers could find no criminally oriented gangs in Chicago, and it took more than a year of

[54] Ruth Shonle Cavan, *Juvenile Delinquency* (Philadelphia: Lippincott, 1962), p. 164.

[55] A. Pawelczyńska, "Grupy nieletnich przestepców," *Archives Kryminologi*, 1:113–163, 1960.

[56] Lewis Yablonsky, "The Delinquent Gang as a Near-Group," *Social Problems*, 7:108–117, Fall, 1959.

[57] Frederic M. Thrasher, *The Gang* (Chicago: University of Chicago Press, 1927), pp. 35–37.

[58] Charles H. Shireman, *The Hyde Park Youth Project, May 1955–May 1958* (Chicago: Welfare Council of Metropolitan Chicago, n.d.), p. 147.

[59] Richard A. Cloward and Lloyd E. Ohlin, *Delinquency and Opportunity: A Theory of Delinquent Gangs*, (Glencoe: The Free Press, 1960). See also Yablonsky's classification: delinquent gangs, violent gangs, and social gangs. The latter are not delinquent. Lewis Yablonsky, *The Violent Gang* (New York: Macmillan, 1962), pp. 149–150. Cohen and Short stimulated classifications of these kinds by identifying three kinds of male delinquent subcultures: the "parent" subculture, the conflict-oriented subculture, and the drug addict subculture. Albert K. Cohen and James F. Short, Jr., "Research in Delinquent Subcultures," *Journal of Social Issues*, 14:20–37, 1958.

extensive inquiries to locate a drug-oriented group.[60] It should be emphasized, moreover, that no classificatory system is airtight—the gangs that
steal also fight occasionally, and gangs involved in the pursuit of "kicks"
also engage in various forms of theft, as well as in violence.[61]

In all three types of gang described by Cloward and Ohlin, members of
the gangs are committed to a set of norms in opposition to those held by
law-abiding groups of the larger society. They have "withdrawn their at-
tribution of legitimacy to certain of the norms maintained by law-abiding
groups of the larger society and have given it, instead, to new patterns of
conduct which are defined as illegitimate by representatives of official
agencies."[62] The activities of gangs follow rules which are specifically
provided and supported by the delinquent subcultures described in Chapter 5, but the activities of the members, and of the gangs themselves,
should not be confused with the delinquent subcultures. Because of inconsistencies in the general social structure, certain forms of delinquent
activity become essential requirements for the performance of some social
roles. This kind of delinquent activity is subcultural delinquency, and the
"rules for delinquency" which underlie it constitute a delinquent subculture.
However, explanation of the process by which the "rules for delinquency"
come into existence, develop, and change, is different from explanation of
the behavior of delinquents, whether these delinquents perform their delinquencies alone or in gangs.

The delinquent gang is, above all, an important agency for diffusion of
the values that make up delinquent subcultures. Acts of delinquency which
have the support of a gang are likely to recur with great frequency, for
delinquent behavior is a prerequisite for acceptance and status in the
gang.[63] In gangs oriented to criminal activities, this means that a boy's
social position in the gang can be maintained only if he can "score" now

---

[60] James F. Short, Jr., Ray. A. Tennyson, and Kenneth I. Howard, "Behavior
Dimensions of Gang Delinquency," American Sociological Review, 28:411–428, June,
1963.

[61] James F. Short, Jr., "Street Corner Groups and Patterns of Delinquency: A Progress Report," American Catholic Sociological Review, 24:13–32, Spring, 1963.

[62] Cloward and Ohlin, op. cit., p. 19.

[63] The following material is based on Cloward and Ohlin, op. cit., pp. 10–11, but
it stresses the difference between gang activities and the delinquent subcultures on which
gang activities are based. Cloward and Ohlin are vague about whether theirs is a theory
about the behavior of delinquents, a theory about delinquent gangs, or a theory about
the origin of delinquent subcultures. Their use of the terms "gang" and "subculture"
synonymously contributes to this vagueness. We consider as primary the problem of
explaining how delinquent values come into existence, and we view the problem of how
these values are diffused as secondary. Cloward and Ohlin state that they are concerned with the first problem: "Why do delinquent norms, or rules of conduct, develop?" (P. ix.) However, their book is devoted principally to discussion of how delinquent rules of conduct, once they are in existence, get distributed to individuals.

and then, and if he can exhibit the behavior patterns of a "real man" or a "thief."[64] In street gangs devoted primarily to fighting and violence, a member's social position depends upon frequent exhibitions of "heart," and skill in the use of violence. Fighting gangs are almost constantly engaged in negotiations with each other, and as demonstrations of strength many agreements, alliances and contracts are made. "These are generally pseudobargains, which serve as means for gang members to flex muscles they are unsure they have."[65] In gangs oriented to the use of drugs, the individual member can lay claim to "rep" only if he frequently displays his ability to obtain drugs and to increase the experience of the "kick."

Gang activities furnish continuity between criminal activities as a juvenile and criminal activities as an adult. Not all gang members become adult criminals, by any means, but gang activities sometimes afford the young an opportunity to acquire the values and skills that are necessary to becoming a competent adult criminal. A study of 711 active Negro male gang members in Philadelphia indicated that the rate for each type of delinquency rose gradually each year from the average age of first contact with the police (13.4 years) to a peak at 15–16 years, and then decreased in the last year of juvenile status.[66] The average time between the first and second contacts with the police was fourteen months, while the average interval between the ninth and tenth contacts was 3.6 months. Of 580 gang members who moved out of juvenile status between January 1 and October 15, 1962, 41 percent acquired criminal records in this period. These data indicate that once gang delinquencies begin there is a chain reaction in which each delinquent act becomes a stimulus for commission of another act within a briefer period, indicating gang members' increasing acceptance of the norms and values of the gang. Further, participation in gang activities makes a delinquent difficult to change, for his behavior belongs to an explicit network of expectations and obligations. Most delinquent and criminal behavior is the property of groups rather than of individuals, in the way the French language or English language is the property of collectivities rather than of individuals, but in the case of gang behavior, the ownership of the delinquency is more explicit and obvious. Accordingly, efforts to induce a member to feel shame or guilt are blocked by the rationalizations and reassurances which the group provides.

The member of a delinquent gang organized primarily for pursuit of material gain by such illegal means as theft, fraud, and extortion adopts

---

[64] See John Irwin and Donald R. Cressey, "Thieves, Convicts and the Inmate Culture," *Social Problems*, 10:142–155, Fall, 1962.

[65] Yablonsky, *The Violent Gang, op. cit.*, p. 157.

[66] Gerald D. Robin, "Gang Member Delinquency: Its Extent, Sequence, and Typology," *Journal of Criminal Law and Criminology*, 55:59–69, March, 1964.

values which regard members of the conventional world as "suckers," which see the world of business as a world of rackets and the world of politics as a world of graft. However, the solutions to problems of lower-class boys provided by delinquent gangs are primarily *status* rewarding, rather than economically rewarding.[67] In conflict gangs, for example, the role-model is the "bopper" who displays the courage and bravery of the hero, the successful warrior. A youth can obtain "rep" in such a gang if he is tough and destructively violent; he must not be weak. Short and Strodtbeck have shown that leaders of conflict gangs often respond to status threats by instigating aggression against persons outside the gang.[68] In "retreatist" gangs oriented to drug use, the member learns that to be important he must be a "cat," a "hipster" who is detached from the life-style and everyday activities of "squares." A "cat," moreover, "hustles," and this means that he lives by his wits rather than by routine labor. By begging, cheating, pimping, or stealing he can live in idleness and give his entire attention to the "kick."[69] The retreatist gang thus provides each of its members with a system for achieving status in a group which the gang views as "elite," a group which assigns prestige to those who can cultivate the hustle and the kick.

Cloward and Ohlin's thesis is that gang behavior is motivated by failure, or the anticipation of failure, in achieving success-goals by socially-approved means.[70] This thesis is similar to that of Albert K. Cohen, who stresses the function of the gang in resolving the status frustrations of working-class boys.[71] Lower-class male adolescents find themselves at a competitive dis-advantage in gaining access to legitimate routes to success. If they attribute their failure to injustice in the social system, rather than to their own in-adequacies, they may (a) bend their efforts to reforming the social order, (b) dissociate themselves from it, or (c) rebel against it. "Democratizing the criteria of evaluation without at the same time increasing the oppor-tunities available to lower-class youngsters will accentuate the conditions that produce feelings of unjust deprivation."[72] A sense of injustice, then, springs from a sense of being discriminated against. It should not be con-cluded, however, that persons with limited opportunities or persons who are discriminated against perceive these restrictions as status deprivation.

---

[67] Short, "Street Corner Groups and Patterns of Delinquency," op. cit., p. 22.

[68] James F. Short, Jr., and Fred L. Strodtbeck, "The Response of Gang Leaders to Status Threats: An Observation on Group Processes and Delinquent Behavior," *American Journal of Sociology*, 68:571–579, March, 1963.

[69] Harold Finestone, "Cats, Kicks and Color," *Social Problems*, 5:3–13, July, 1957.

[70] *Op. cit.*, p. 110.

[71] Albert K. Cohen, *Delinquent Boys: The Culture of the Gang* (Glencoe: The Free Press, 1955).

[72] Cloward and Ohlin, op. cit., p. 121.

Using a crude measure of perceived status deprivation, Reiss and Rhodes found that only 28 percent of a sample of delinquents and 16 percent of a sample of non-delinquents perceived that their clothing and housing were not as good as that of their fellow students.[73] Similarly, an Ohio State study found only slight association between delinquency proneness and perception of limited opportunity, and a Chicago study indicated that many of the values of members of delinquent gangs closely resemble the values of the middle class.[74]

The gang-formation process is initiated when the individual frustrated delinquent finds encouragement and reassurance for his acts of deviance by "searching out others who have faced similar experiences and who will support one another in common attitudes of alienation from the official system."[75] The gang of peers forms a new social world in which the legitimacy of the individual's delinquent conduct is strongly reinforced.

Once individuals start seeking support from others who feel alienated from the prevailing social norms, a gang has begun to form. But before gang activities can begin, there must be effective interaction between the actors in a collective problem-solving process.[76] Cohen describes this problem-solving process as a "conversation of gestures," which serves at least four important functions.[77] *First,* it permits the gang members to explore the extent to which each is willing to go in accepting alternative rules for action. *Second,* it enables them to explore the extent to which they can rely on each other for support if they take a daring, rebellious, or delinquent path. *Third,* it gives each member an opportunity to test the degree to which his techniques for neutralizing the influences of law-abiding society[78] are accepted by others. *Fourth,* it enables the gang collectively to try out various courses of delinquent action and to judge the commitment that each member of the gang is willing to make to each type of action.

This process of alienation is abetted by the very processes by which

---

[73] Albert J. Reiss, Jr., and A. Lewis Rhodes, "Status Deprivation and Delinquent Behavior," *Sociological Quarterly,* 4:136–149, Spring, 1963.

[74] Judson R. Landis, Simon Dinitz, and Walter C. Reckless, "Implementing Two Theories of Delinquency: Value Orientation and Awareness of Limited Opportunity," *Sociology and Social Research,* 47:408–416, July, 1963; Robert A. Gordon, James F. Short, Jr., Desmond S. Cartwright, and Fred L. Strodtbeck, "Values and Gang Delinquency: A Study of Street-Corner Groups," *American Journal of Sociology,* 69:109–128, September, 1963. See also Delbert S. Elliott, "Delinquency and Perceived Opportunity," *Sociological Inquiry,* 32:216–226, Spring, 1962.

[75] Cloward and Ohlin, *op. cit.,* p. 126.

[76] Cohen, *op. cit.,* p. 59.

[77] *Ibid.,* pp. 60–61. Cf. Cloward and Ohlin, pp. 140–142.

[78] Gresham M. Sykes and David Matza, "Techniques of Neutralization: A Theory of Delinquency," *American Sociological Review,* 22:664–670, December, 1957.

law-abiding society attempts to deal with delinquent activities. Tannenbaum referred to these processes as a "dramatization of evil":

> The first dramatization of "evil" which separates the child out of his group for specialized treatment plays a greater role in making the criminal than perhaps any other experience. It cannot be too often emphasized that for the child the whole situation has become different. He now lives in a different world. He has been tagged. A new and hitherto nonexistent environment has been precipitated out for him.
>
> The process of making the criminal, therefore, is a process of tagging, defining, identifying, segregating, describing, emphasizing, making conscious and self-conscious; it becomes a way of stimulating, suggesting, emphasizing, and evolving the very traits that are complained of.[79]

Consistently, one of the earliest studies of delinquent gangs pointed out that the societal reactions to gang behavior make gang members more acutely aware of the gang's isolation from the values of the law-abiding community:

> It does not become a gang, however, until it begins to excite disapproval and opposition, and thus acquires a more definite group-consciousness. It discovers a rival or an enemy in the gang in the next block; its baseball or football team is pitted against some other team; parents or neighbors look upon it with suspicion or hostility; "the old man around the corner," the storekeepers, or the "cops" begin to give it "shags" (chase it); or some representative of the community steps in and tries to break it up. This is the real beginning of the gang, for now it starts to draw itself more closely together. It becomes a conflict group.[80]

The specific direction taken in a gang's activities depends upon access to various directives for illegal actions, as well as upon accessibility to directives for legal actions. Thus, a gang, like a person, takes a delinquent course rather than a non-delinquent course because a delinquent subculture in the form of rules, norms, values and beliefs is more readily available than an anti-delinquent culture with its norms, values and beliefs. In this connection, Miller maintains that the dominant motivation underlying gang behavior is the attempt by gang members to achieve standards of value as they are defined in lower-class urban areas.[81] By the same token, a gang moves into one kind of delinquency rather than another because of the norms, values, and beliefs available to it.

[79] Frank Tannenbaum, *Crime and the Community* (New York: Ginn, 1938), pp. 19–20.

[80] Thrasher, *op. cit.*, p. 30.

[81] Walter B. Miller, "Lower Class Culture as a Generating Milieu of Gang Delinquency," *Journal of Social Issues*, 14:5–19, 1958.

An individual frustrated by his condition of poverty may relieve his tension by accepting a non-delinquent solution, such as renouncing all worldly things and becoming a hermit, or moving into the political arena to effect economic reforms. Alternatively, he may simply work harder, holding down two jobs at the same time.[82] Or he may solve the problem by adopting any of a number of delinquent solutions, one of which might be a burglary pattern, or a shoplifting pattern, or even an embezzlement pattern. Which of the delinquent solutions are adopted by the individual depends upon their availability to him. Similarly, whether a delinquent gang composed of persons dissatisfied with their lot in life moves in the direction of a particular kind of delinquency depends upon the availability of directives for action, and of training for action. In this connection, Cloward and Ohlin say that "the individual must have access to appropriate environments for the acquisition of values and skills associated with the performance of a particular role, and he must be supported in the performance of the role once he has learned it."[83]

Negatively, this means that gangs oriented to stealing will not develop where values favorable to stealing are not readily available, that gangs oriented to violence will not develop where behavior patterns favorable to violence are scarce, and that gangs oriented to drug use will not develop in areas where drugs and knowledge about their "good" effects are rare. Positively, gangs oriented to property offenses develop in areas in which the criminality of adults makes the values conducive to property offenses, and the opportunities for displaying adoption of these values, both readily available. Gangs oriented to conflict arise in areas where access to legitimate channels to success-goals are denied, where the opportunity to learn values conducive to renouncing the importance of "success" and values conducive to theft also are denied, and where values supporting violent actions are available. Thus, the conflict gang is composed of young men who are unable to "make it" legitimately, but also are unable either to "make it" by theft or to "explain away" their failure, and who are able to seize upon patterns for manipulation of violence as a route to high status. Some support for this point is found in Short's observation that of 16 Chicago gangs, containing a total of 598 members, the six gangs most oriented to conflict, and three of the four gangs least oriented to conflict, were Negro.[84] This suggests that the status deprivation of Negroes produces conflict-oriented gangs only when the conflict values available to be

[82] Harold L. Wilensky, "The Moonlighter: A Product of Relative Deprivation," *Industrial Relations*, 3:105–124, October, 1963.
[83] *Op. cit.*, p. 148.
[84] Short, Tennyson, and Howard, *op. cit.*, p. 425.

learned outweigh the non-conflict values. As Short and others have said: "Given culturally supported requirements for aggressive responses, such characteristics of lower-case life as public drinking, milling behavior, and a high incidence of guns may precondition the occurrence of acts of violence which involve individuals who could not have been differentiated from their peers by any personality assessment, even an hour before the occurrence of violence."[85] Gangs oriented to retreatism in the form of drug use occur among persons faced with failure in the use of both legitimate and illegitimate means for achieving success goals, and they occur in areas where the opportunities for obtaining drugs and for learning how to use them are available.[86]

In sum, delinquent gangs provide alternative channels for gaining status or symbols of status. Whether the kinds of opportunities provided by gangs are present in an area of a city, and whether specific forms of illegitimate channels of opportunity are present, depends upon the traditions of the people in the area—traditions of beliefs, values, and rules of conduct that are integrated closely enough so that they can be called a "subculture." Yablonsky, like Cloward and Ohlin, has argued that gang members are boys who have been satiated with delinquency behavior patterns and, at the same time, alienated from anti-delinquency behavior patterns.[87] Nettler, like Sykes and Matza, has argued that the behavior of gang members, like that of other delinquents, is based on values extending from those held by most members of the society and that delinquency, therefore, is better understood as a form of conformity than as a form of deviation.[88]

NEIGHBORHOOD AGENCIES. Individuals and institutions in the neighborhood may disseminate delinquent and criminal behavior patterns, intentionally or inadvertently. The following excerpt describes the rare case of

[85] James F. Short, Jr., Fred L. Strodtbeck, and Desmond S. Cartwright, "A Strategy for Utilizing Research Dilemmas: A Case from the Study of Parenthood in a Street Corner Gang," Sociological Inquiry, 32:185–202, Spring, 1962.

[86] Richard A. Cloward, "Illegitimate Means, Anomie, and Deviant Behavior," American Sociological Review, 24:164–176, April, 1959. See also Howard S. Becker, "Marihuana Use and Social Control," Social Problems, 3:25–44, July, 1955; and "Becoming a Marihuana User," American Journal of Sociology, 59:235–242, November, 1953.

[87] The Violent Gang, op. cit., pp. 170–194. See also Martin R. Haskell, "Toward a Reference Group Theory of Juvenile Delinquency," Social Problems, 8:220–230, Winter, 1961.

[88] Gwynn Nettler, "Good Men, Bad Men, and the Perception of Reality," Sociolmextry, 24:279–294, September, 1961; David Matza and Gresham M. Sykes, "Juvenile Delinquency and Subterranean Values," American Sociological Review, 26:712–719, October, 1961.

an adult turning many children in the direction of delinquency for a profit:

In one neighborhood in Boston there was a modern Fagan, called "The Lobster" by the children in the neighborhood. He lived in a rickety, disreputable dwelling, facing the alley, in which was a running sewer, infested with rats and vermin. . . . For many years his ramshackle house has been the rendezvous for the boys and girls of the surrounding neighborhood, and he had displayed an aptitude that might well be termed genius, in discovering and developing the peculiar weakness of the individual child, and then twisting and further distorting that trait, till the child was prepared to enter upon a career of juvenile delinquency. With fiendish precision and ingenuity he had planned his illicit laboratory, carefully planting and fostering various vices and apportioning that iniquity to the individual child that best suited its characteristics. Therefore, in his gang were juvenile offenders of all types and kinds, and in proportion as they flourished and prospered, so his finances increased, as he permitted them to keep but a fraction of their peculations and ill acquired booty.[89]

The "fence," the junk-man, and other persons who are willing to purchase stolen goods stimulate delinquencies both by failing to present antidelinquency patterns to children who present stolen goods for sale, and by presenting the pro-criminal behavior patterns implicit in their purchase of the goods. Sometimes the person who influences the standards of the children may be another child. The following account was written by a middle-aged student regarding his own childhood. It shows the effect of one new arrival in the community upon the lives of the juvenile inhabitants.

I lived near the edge of a town of about 15,000 population. My father was a lawyer. My chief companions were boys of about my own age, one being the son of a Methodist preacher, one the son of a Baptist preacher, and one the son of the fireman at the Tuberculosis Sanitarium. The son of the Methodist preacher knew much more about the world than the rest of us did. He told us a great deal about sex matters and about Jesse James. Under his guidance we built a cave, secured some detective stories, and had what we regarded as a regular den of iniquity in the cave. Eventually, with the help of a few others, we constituted a small gang which threw rocks at the street cars, broke windows in empty houses, shot pigeons belonging to other boys, stole fruit from orchards and candy from stores and flipped the trains. We did not learn all of these things from the son of the

[89] S. Drucker and M. B. Hexter, *Children Astray* (Cambridge: Harvard University Press, 1923), p. 77.

Methodist minister; he undoubtedly learned much from the rest of us. We worked out our plans together. But our delinquent tendencies started soon after he arrived in the neighborhood and ceased soon after his father was called to another church.

Illegal agencies ordinarily are located in a neighborhood against the wishes of the members of that neighborhood. To a degree, this is true of gambling houses and "bookie joints," but often such institutions depend on their neighbors for patronage, and it cannot then be said that the neighbors really do not want them in the area. Houses of prostitution are another matter, for their patrons ordinarily do not come from the local area. The neighbors oppose them, but they are unable to produce the legal and political pressures necessary to force them to move. Negroes and other minority groups suffer most from such vice districts. A situation existing in Chicago a half-century ago continues today in many American cities:

The chief of police [of Chicago] in 1912 warned prostitutes that so long as they confined their residence to districts west of Wabash Avenue and east of Wentworth Avenue, they would not be disturbed. This area contained at that time the largest group of Negroes in the city, with most of their churches, Sunday Schools and societies. . . . That many Negroes live near vice districts is not due to their choice, nor to low moral standards, but to three causes: (1) Negroes are unwelcome in desirable white residence localities: (2) small incomes compel them to live in the least expensive places regardless of surroundings; while premises rented for immoral purposes bring notoriously high rentals, they make the neighborhood undesirable and the rent of other living quarters there abnormally low; and (3) Negroes lack sufficient influence and power to protest effectively against the encroachments of vice.[90]

Such agencies are not likely to produce sexual delinquencies because of the sex standards involved, but they contribute to more general crime and delinquency rates in three interrelated ways. First, the district of vice is frequently the district of organized criminals who share in the control of gambling, of the distribution of narcotic drugs, and of various rackets, as well as of prostitution. They have their headquarters or hangouts in such sections and by their opulence they demonstrate to the people of the neighborhood that crime does pay. Second, by their very presence such institutions demonstrate the existence of a rich vein of corruption in political and law-enforcement organizations, making it difficult for parents to convince their children that people get ahead in the world by good, hard, honest labor in the service of country, man, and God. Third, the presence

[90] Chicago Commission on Race Relations, A Study of Race Relations and a Race Riot (Chicago: Author, 1922), pp. 343–344.

of such agencies in a neighborhood lowers the status of the people in the ³⁾
district, just as do conditions of squalor, with the result that anti-criminal
admonitions become less effective—the people have less to lose if convicted of crime.[91]

Recreational agencies also contribute to the delinquency of the children
in the neighborhood. It has become commonplace to state that most of
the delinquencies of children occur in the search for recreation. One general notion in this regard is that the only recreations generally available
in deteriorated neighborhoods are those furnished by commercial concerns.
Since these concerns are interested primarily in securing a profit, they offer
whatever recreation produces the largest revenue, regardless of the welfare
of the patrons. The result is that many of the neighborhood dance-halls,
pool-rooms, school-stores, and other recreational institutions are "injurious"
to many juveniles. A more realistic interpretation is that such institutions
merely serve as gathering places for neighborhood youth, thus providing
opportunities for dissemination of delinquent attitudes and standards. The
same process of dissemination occurs when youth gather on street corners
or in public playgrounds.

Another notion is that the absence of places of organized public recreation, particularly playgrounds, somehow contributes to the delinquency
rate of a neighborhood. A great proportion of the studies of the relation
between recreation and delinquency have been conducted by persons or
agencies who have a stake in the promotion of recreational programs, and
the methods used to reach the conclusion that "lack of wholesome recreation" is a cause of delinquency are dubious. It is obvious that delinquency,
like baseball or swimming, is a "spare-time" activity, but this does not
mean that delinquency results from an absence of baseball fields or swimming pools.

From the point of view of the differential association theory, there are
three possible ways in which playground participation may be related to
delinquent behavior. *First*, the activities may have little effect on the
participant's attitudes regarding delinquency but may keep him from
committing delinquencies during some of his waking hours; he cannot
play baseball and participate in burglaries at the same time. *Second*, the
participant may come into contact with delinquent behavior patterns; the
playground may become the gathering place of the delinquents in the
neighborhood and may, in fact, serve to promote a strong in-group feeling
among them. *Third*, the playground director may be able to present anti-

[91] Jackson Toby, "Social Disorganization and Stake in Conformity: Complimentary
Factors in the Predatory Behavior of Hoodlums," *Journal of Criminal Law and
Criminology*, 48:12–17, May–June, 1957.

delinquent behavior patterns to the participant, or the participant may in other ways come into contact with anti-delinquent behavior patterns. Thus participation in the playground activities may be neutral, or it may be conducive to either delinquency or non-delinquency, depending upon the nature of the associations experienced. If the neighborhood baseball team is made up of delinquents, then an excellent and enthusiastic baseball player is more likely to become delinquent than a boy who abhors baseball, other things being equal. On the other hand, if the members of the neighborhood baseball team are anti-delinquent in their attitudes and behavior patterns, then the probability that a good and enthusiastic baseball player will become delinquent is lower than the probability that a boy who abhors baseball will become delinquent, other things being equal.

"Other things" may not be equal, however. The boy who hates baseball may be an excellent and enthusiastic pool player in a neighborhood where pool players view stealing as a form of play, thus increasing the probability of his delinquency if he engages in his favorite form of recreation. But if the values of the pool players are anti-delinquent, then the probability of his delinquency is diminished. The process of "selecting" delinquent or anti-delinquent companions depends in part, then, on the person's recreational interests and abilities. Yet it would be absurd to explain a person's delinquency or non-delinquency in terms of referring to his pool-playing or baseball-playing ability. Further, selection or rejection of de-linquent or anti-delinquent companions is itself a function of previous associations with anti-delinquent and delinquent behavior patterns. An excellent baseball player with strong anti-delinquent identification and intimate association with anti-delinquent behavior patterns may give up baseball rather than play with delinquents. A boy without such strong counter-acting values may join the team and become delinquent. More-over, a person with reference groups which are anti-delinquent in their behavior patterns may join a baseball team made up of delinquents and not become a delinquent himself. In this sense, an individual's "selection" of a delinquent, non-delinquent, or anti-delinquent play group depends on his prior associations with delinquent and anti-delinquent behavior patterns, just as does his delinquency itself. As Sherif has said:

As he, [man] passes from one group situation to another from time to time, he reacts to the demands, pressures, and appeals of new group situations in terms of the person he has come to consider himself and aspires to be. In other words, he reacts in terms of more or less consistent ties of belongingness in relation to his past and present identifications and his future goals for security of his identity, and also status and prestige concerns. . . . The groups to which an individual relates himself need not always be the groups in which he is actually moving. His identifications need not always be with groups in which he is registered, is seen to be, or announced to be a member. . . . In many cases, of course, the individual's reference groups are at the same time his membership groups. However, in cases where the individual's membership groups are not his reference groups, it does not follow that the groups in which he actually interacts will not have an effect on him.[92]

The facilities for sports and other recreational activities certainly are relatively inadequate in delinquency areas, and this may be detrimental to the health and safety of many children, delinquents and non-delinquents alike. But provision of such facilities does not assure that boys reared in a delinquent culture will use them. Children often prefer free play to more formalized recreation, especially if it is necessary to be "good" in order to participate in the latter and if the program is administered by "outsiders." Tappan has made the following generalizations about play activities and delinquency:

1. Being a good athlete is no deterrent at all to delinquency.

2. Experience in team play through recreation can have no significant amount of carry-over to general character traits or conduct patterns.

3. Even highly organized recreational activities do not absorb enough of the energy or time of a child to reduce appreciably his opportunities to engage in delinquency.

4. In fact a play group may itself help to stimulate its members to illegal activities, engaged in "for fun" after their games are over; the probability of this is increased when there are delinquent or near-delinquent members in the group.

5. Many of the recreational programs do not in any event reach those children who are presumed to need them most because of their problems of health or delinquency.

6. If a child is disposed toward law violation because of the influences of his family and neighborhood, his early training, his personality distortions, or his attitudes toward authority, it will require much more than games and sports to do anything effective about it.

7. Where children have come to enjoy their delinquencies as games— so commonly the case—the thrills thus provided are usually greater than those which organized recreation can provide.[93]

[92] M. Sherif and C. W. Sherif, *Groups in Harmony and Tension* (New York: Harper, 1953), pp. 160–161. See also Robert K. Merton and A. S. Kitt, "Contributions to the Theory of Reference Group Behavior," in Robert K. Merton and Paul Lazersfeld, Editors, *Continuities in Social Research: Studies in the Scope and Method of the American Soldier* (Glencoe: The Free Press, 1950), pp. 40–105.
[93] Paul W. Tappan, *Juvenile Delinquency* (New York: McGraw-Hill, 1949), p. 150. Reprinted by permission of the publishers.

## SUGGESTED READINGS

Blake, Judith, and Kingsley Davis, "Norms, Values, and Sanctions," Chapter 13 in Robert E. L. Faris, Editor, *Handbook of Modern Sociology.* Chicago: Rand-McNally, 1964, pp. 456–484.

Charlesworth, James C., Editor, *Leisure in America: Blessing or Curse?* American Academy of Political and Social Science, Monograph No. 4, 1964.

Clinard, Marshall B., "A Cross-cultural Replication of the Relation of Urbanism to Criminal Behavior," *American Sociological Review,* 25:253–257, April, 1960.

Cloward, Richard A., and Lloyd E. Ohlin, *Delinquency and Opportunity: A Theory of Delinquent Gangs.* Glencoe: The Free Press, 1960.

Cohen, Albert K., *Delinquent Boys: The Culture of the Gang.* Glencoe: The Free Press, 1955.

Cohen, Albert K., and James F. Short, Jr., "Research in Delinquent Subcultures," *Journal of Social Issues,* 4:20–37, No. 3, 1958.

Cook, Waldo L., "Murders in Massachusetts," *Publications of the American Statistical Association,* New Series, No. 23, September, 1893.

Delaney, Lloyd T., "Establishing Relations with Anti-Social Groups and an Analysis of Their Structure," *British Journal of Delinquency,* 5:34–45, July, 1954.

Finestone, Harold, "Cats, Kicks and Color," *Social Problems,* 5:3–13, July, 1957.

Hawley, Amos H., "Ecology and Human Ecology," *Social Forces,* 22:398–405, May, 1944.

Kobrin, Solomon, "The Conflict of Values in Delinquency Areas," *American Sociological Review,* 16:653–661, October, 1951.

Longmoor, E. S., and Erle F. Young, "Ecological Interrelationships of Juvenile Delinquency, Dependency, and Population Mobility," *American Journal of Sociology,* 41:598–610, March, 1936.

Morris, Terrence, *The Criminal Area.* London: Kegan Paul, 1958.

Polk, Kenneth, "Juvenile Delinquency and Social Areas," *Social Problems,* 5:214–217, Winter, 1957.

Reckless, Walter C., Simon Dinitz, and Ellen Murray, "The 'Good' Boy in a High Delinquency Area," *Journal of Criminal Law, Criminology, and Police Science,* 48:18–25, May–June, 1957.

Robin, Gerald D., "Gang Member Delinquency: Its Extent, Sequence, and Typology," *Journal of Criminal Law, Criminology, and Police Science,* 55:59–69, March, 1964.

Robinson, W. S., "Ecological Correlations and the Behavior of Individuals," *American Sociological Review,* 15:351–357, June, 1950.

Schmid, Calvin F., "Urban Crime Areas," *American Sociological Review,* 25:527–542 and 25:655–678, August and October, 1960.

Shannon, Lyle W., "The Spatial Distribution of Criminal Offenses by States," *Journal of Criminal Law, Criminology, and Police Science*, 45: 264–273, September–October, 1954.

Short, James F., Jr., "Street Corner Groups and Patterns of Delinquency: A Progress Report," *American Cotholic Sociological Review*, 24:13–32, Spring, 1963.

Toby, Jackson, "Social Disorganization and State in Conformity: Complementary Factors in the Predatory Behavior of Hoodlums," *Journal of Criminal Law, Criminology, and Police Science*, 48:12–17, May–June, 1957.

Vold, George B., "Crime in City and Country Areas," *Annals of the American Academy of Political and Social Science*, 217:38–45, September, 1941.

Whyte, William F., *Street Corner Society*. Chicago: University of Chicago Press, 1943.

# 10. THE HOME AND FAMILY
# IN RELATION TO CRIME

SINCE THE family has almost exclusive contact with the child during the period of greatest dependency and greatest plasticity, and continued intimate contact over a subsequent period of several years, it plays an exceptionally important role in determining the behavior patterns which the child will exhibit. No child is so constituted at birth that it must inevitably become a delinquent or that it must inevitably be law-abiding, and the family is the first agency to affect the direction which a particular child will take. Probably it is for this reason that a large proportion of the criminological research and thinking during this century, and especially in the 1930's, has been concerned with the relationship between crime and delinquency on the one hand and various kinds of home conditions and child-rearing practices on the other hand.

Although the family units are expected to train their children in some efficient way, so that they will not become delinquent, there is no real science of child rearing, and such knowledge as is developed is not available to or utilized by many families. The task of child training was comparatively simple in early society but has become extremely difficult in modern life. In preliterate life both parents were reared in a rather simple, harmonious culture, as were also the grandparents, other relatives, and neighbors. The result was a steady and harmonious pressure upon the child which formed his character without difficulty and with a minimum of conflicts. This is impossible in modern society, where the persons in charge of the training of the child cannot be consistent.[1] Parents are in conflict with each other, with grandparents, with school teachers, and with movie actors. Moreover, parents are in conflict, probably more than previously, for the affection of the child. In this situation the harmonious pressure of consistent authorities is impossible. It is not even possible for one parent to be

[1] See W. H. Sewell, P. H. Mussen, and C. W. Harris, "Relationships Among Child Training Practices," *American Sociological Review*, 20:137–148, April, 1955.

consistent with himself, for he does not have the support of a consistent culture to keep his policies stable. These inconsistencies undoubtedly affect the degree of obedience which parents can exact from children and, generally, the degree to which children can be controlled. Further, obedience and control depend largely upon the prestige of the parents, and these are affected by both the consistency of the demands they make upon a child and their status in the community.[2] The poverty, physical features, competitive ability and comparative attainments, language and social status of the parents in comparison with other persons with whom the child is acquainted, may destroy the prestige of the parents so that the behavior patterns presented are relatively ineffective.[3]

TYPES OF HOMES AND OF FAMILY RELATIONSHIPS. The homes from which delinquent children come are frequently characterized by one or more of the following conditions: (a) other members of the family criminalistic, immoral, or alcoholic, (b) absence of one or both parents by reason of death, divorce, or desertion, (c) lack of parental control through ignorance, blindness or other sensory defect, or illness, (d) home uncongeniality, as evidenced by domination by one member, favoritism, oversolicitude, overseverity, neglect, jealousy, crowded housing conditions, interfering relatives, (e) racial or religious differences, differences in conventions and standards, foster home, or institutional home, (f) economic pressures, such as unemployment, insufficient income, mother working out.

Three general methods have been used in the effort to determine the importance of these conditions as "factors" in delinquency. One of the methods is to evaluate the home as a whole, by means of some rating device or scale. The home is customarily appraised by setting a "normal" standard for homes and concluding that the home conditions are the cause of delinquency if most delinquents come from homes below this normal. In an earlier period, the "Whittier Scale for Grading Home Conditions" was utilized; this scale has a maximum grade of five on each of five items: necessities, neatness, size, parental conditions, and parental supervision. The median score of 162 delinquents on this scale was 14, while the median score of 50 non-delinquents in a control group was 22; the range of scores for delinquents was 5 to 25, of non-delinquents 4 to 25.[4] After a short period of

[2] See David C. Sottong, "The Dilemma of the Parent as a Culture Bearer," *Social Casework*, 36:302–306, July, 1955; and Bernard C. Rosen, "Conflicting Group Membership: A Study of Parent-Peer Group Cross-Pressures," *American Sociological Review*, 20:155–161, April, 1955.

[3] Cf. Albert J. Reiss, Jr., "Delinquency as the Failure of Personal and Social Controls," *American Sociological Review*, 16:196—208, April, 1951.

[4] J. H. Williams, "The Whittier Scale for Grading Home Conditions," *Journal of Delinquency*, 1:273–286, November, 1916; J. H. Williams, *The Intelligence of the Delinquent Boy* (Whittier, California: Whittier State School, Department of Research,

use, the Whittier score card and others designed for the same purpose seem to have disappeared. Children who get into the juvenile courts come, in more than fair proportion, from homes that are ranked as "poor" or "bad," but none of the children in some homes of this kind, and not all of the children in other homes, get into the juvenile court, while on the other hand some delinquent children come from homes that are ranked as "good." Moreover, the rating of a home as "bad" or "good" is to a large extent determined by the values and the social class position of the investigator.

A second method is the evaluation of the influence of the home by a general study of individual cases. By this method Healy judged that the home was a major "factor" in delinquency in 19 percent of a series of one thousand cases studied in Chicago and a "minor factor" in 23 percent, and that home conditions constituted 22 percent of the entire number of major and minor factors; 23 percent of these delinquents came from homes having "extreme lack of parental control."[5] In a study of a second series of one thousand cases in Chicago Healy found that 46 percent came from homes having "extreme lack of parental control."[6] This method permits the investigator to evaluate the meaning which a particular set of home conditions has for the specific child, and to thereby make allowances for the fact that "bad" homes do not always produce delinquent children. However, the method is subjective, and the findings are likely to reflect the preconceptions of the investigator. During a period when rather strict discipline is the fad in child rearing, homes without such discipline are likely to be designated as delinquency-producing; but when permissiveness is the fad in child rearing, then the homes using strict discipline are likely to be so designated. Furthermore, whether the home is designated as a "factor" in the delinquency of a child may depend on the likelihood that the home can be modified by welfare agencies—a home which can be modified may more readily be designated as a factor than one which apparently cannot be modified.

A third method is statistical. The technique varies from simple calculation of the comparative incidence of certain home conditions among delinquents and non-delinquents to more sophisticated techniques of holding certain variables constant while determining the degree of association be-

---

1919), pp. 167–173. See also Mabel R. Fernald, Mary H. S. Hayes, and Almena Dawley, A Study of Women Delinquents in New York State (New York: Century, 1920), p. 216.

[5] William Healy, The Individual Delinquent (Boston: Little, Brown, 1915), pp. 130–131, 134.

[6] William Healy and Augusta F. Bronner, "Youthful Offenders," American Journal of Sociology, 22:50, July, 1916.

tween delinquency and one other variable. Thus the method aims at the identification of certain specific home conditions which are associated with delinquency, rather than at measuring the influence of the home as a whole. This is the most popular method currently in use, and it will be illustrated in the sections which follow.

CRIMINALITY IN THE HOME.   One of the most obvious elements in the delinquency of some children is the criminalistic behavior of other members of the child's family. Burt concluded from his study in England that vice and crime were present five times as frequently in the homes from which delinquents came as in the homes of non-delinquents.[7] The Gluecks report that 84.8 percent of the offenders released from the Massachusetts Reformatory had been reared in homes in which there were other criminal members; also they found that 86.7 percent of the juvenile delinquents and 80.7 percent of the women delinquents whom they studied were from such homes.[8] Barker, however, found in Chicago that the several areas varied widely in the extent to which the delinquency of a child was associated with the delinquencies of other children in the family and concluded that the association between these two variables is a function of the community.[9] In their most recent study the Gluecks found drunkenness, crime, or immorality in the homes of 90.4 percent of 500 delinquent boys and in the homes of only 54 percent of the 500 non-delinquents comprising the control group.[10] McCord found that the sons of criminals had a higher rate of criminality than did the sons of non-criminals.[11] Interestingly enough, however, the sons of criminals who had been rejected by their fathers had higher crime rates than those who did not. Johnson hypothesizes that this difference comes about because "rejection by the father creates aggressive tendencies which are channeled into crime because the father serves as a role model,"[12] an interpretation which is consistent with the theory of differential association.

[7] Cyril Burt, *The Young Delinquent*, Fourth Edition (London: University of London Press, 1944).

[8] Sheldon and Eleanor T. Glueck, *Five Hundred Criminal Careers* (New York: Knopf, 1930), pp. 111–112; *One Thousand Juvenile Delinquents* (Cambridge: Harvard University Press, 1934), p. 79; *Five Hundred Delinquent Women* (New York: Knopf, 1934), p. 72.

[9] Gordon H. Barker, "Family Factors in the Ecology of Juvenile Delinquency," *Journal of Criminal Law and Criminology*, 30:881–891, January–February, 1940.

[10] Sheldon and Eleanor Glueck, *Unraveling Juvenile Delinquency* (New York: The Commonwealth Fund, 1950), pp. 110–111.

[11] Joan McCord and William McCord, "The Effects of Parental Role Model on Criminality," *Journal of Social Issues*, 14:66–75, 1958.

[12] Elmer H. Johnson, *Crime, Correction, and Society*, (Homewood, Illinois: Dorsey Press, 1964), p. 188.

Thus the homes in which delinquents are reared are to a significant degree situations in which patterns of delinquency are present. These patterns do not generally result in exact copies by the children; rather it is the attitudes toward obeying the law which are likely to be most significant. It has been shown that farm boys who prefer farming as an occupation, as compared with farm boys who prefer non-farm occupations, more frequently have participated in a family value system functionally related to farming.[13] There is no reason to believe that boys participating in a value system functionally related to crime should not, similarly, enter criminality more frequently than those not participating in such direct, primary-type influences. Two psychiatrists have concluded that parents' unwitting sanction or indirect encouragement is a major cause of, and the specific stimulus for, truancy and various kinds of delinquency."[14] Wolfgang has shown that a "subculture of violence" exists in the urban lower class, and this subculture is carried by families as well as by other groups.[15] As Taft and England have said, "A boy brought up on kicks, slaps, and crude language may transfer this mode of interaction to the larger world, some segments of which—for example, a high school teacher assaulted by an angry teenage slum boy—define such behavior as 'criminal'."[16]

THE BROKEN HOME.    The modification of home conditions by death, divorce, or desertion has generally been believed to be an important reason for delinquency of the children. This belief is found even in nonliterate tribes, for the Ama-Xosa, a Bantu tribe in southern Africa, have a proverb, "If the old bird dies, the eggs are addled." Research reports indicate that from 30 to 60 percent of delinquents come from broken homes, but the percentages tend to cluster around 40 percent. The proportion of delinquent girls coming from broken homes is greater than the proportion of delinquent boys coming from such homes, and the proportion of delinquent Negroes is greater than the proportion of whites.[17] Polk has shown that the judicial process tends to select children from broken homes;

[13] Murray A. Strauss, "Personality Characteristics and Functional Needs in the Choice of Farming as an Occupation," *Rural Sociology*, 21:257–266, December, 1956; see also A. O. Haller, "The Occupational Achievement Process of Farm-Reared Youth in Urban-Industrial Society," *Ibid.*, 25:321–333, September, 1960.

[14] Adelaide M. Johnson and S. A. Szurek, "Etiology of Antisocial Behavior in Delinquents and Psychopaths," *Journal of the American Medical Association*, 154:814–817, March 6, 1954.

[15] Marvin Wolfgang, "Subculture of Violence: An Interpretive Analysis of Homicide," paper read at the meetings of the American Sociological Association, New York, August, 1960.

[16] Donald R. Taft and Ralph W. England, Jr., *Criminology*, Fourth Edition (New York: Macmillan, 1964), p. 137.

[17] Thomas P. Monahan, "Family Status and the Delinquent Child: A Reappraisal and Some New Findings," *Social Forces*, 35:250–258, March, 1957.

among the cases of male juveniles which the Los Angeles Probation Department closed at intake in 1956, 43 percent were from broken homes, while 50 percent of those placed on probation and 58 percent of those institutionalized came from broken homes.[18] Similarly, Nye found that 24 percent of the most delinquent boys in a high school came from broken homes, while 48 percent of the boys in a training school came from such homes, indicating that a selective principle was operating.[19]

Such statistics are meaningless except in comparison with similar percentages of the non-delinquent children or for the total population. About 11 percent of all American children under age 18 are living in broken homes, but the percentage probably is higher in the working class.[20] Burt found about twice as many broken homes in a delinquent group than he did in a control group in England, and the Gluecks found a ratio of 1.8 to 1 among a group of delinquent boys and a control group in the United States.[21] On the other hand, Slawson found a ratio of 1.5 to 1 in comparing the institutions for delinquents in New York State with the public school in New York City which had children of the lowest social status,[22] and this same ratio was found among delinquent and non-delinquent boys in Spokane.[23] Barker found that the coefficient of correlation between the juvenile delinquency rate of an area and the percentage of parents divorced was +.79 ±.04, which could mean that both the delinquency rate and the divorce rate are determined largely by other conditions, such as the local community culture.[24] Shaw and McKay compared delinquent boys with school boys of the same age and national derivation and found that 42.5 percent of the delinquent boys and 36.1 of the school boys came from broken homes, or a ratio of 1.18 to 1.[25] Christie studied all males born in Norway in 1933; by January 1, 1958, five percent of these males were registered offenders. In the country as a whole, the homes of 17.4 percent of the offenders and 12.7 percent of the non-offenders were broken by

[18] Kenneth Polk, "A Note on the Relationship Between Broken Homes, Disposition, and Juvenile Delinquency," manuscript.

[19] F. Ivan Nye, *Family Relationships and Delinquent Behavior* (New York: Wiley, 1958), pp. 43–44, 47–48; see also Philip M. Smith, "Broken Homes and Juvenile Delinquency," *Sociology and Social Research*, 39:307–311, June, 1955.

[20] Computed from Metropolitan Life Insurance Company, "Statistical Bulletin," February, 1955, p. 5, by Donald R. Taft and Ralph W. England, Jr., *op. cit.*, p. 142.

[21] Glueck and Glueck, *Unraveling Juvenile Delinquency*, *op. cit.*, p. 122.

[22] John Slawson, *The Delinquent Boy* (Boston: Badger, 1926), pp. 354–366.

[23] H. Ashley Weeks and Margaret G. Smith, "Juvenile Delinquency and Broken Homes in Spokane, Washington," *Social Forces*, 18:48–55, October, 1939.

[24] *Op. cit.*

[25] Clifford R. Shaw and Henry D. McKay, "Social Factors in Juvenile Delinquency," *Report on the Causes of Crime*, National Commission on Law Observance and Enforcement, No. 13, Vol. II (Washington: Government Printing Office, 1937), pp. 261–284.

death, divorce, or separation, a ratio of 1.36 to 1. Among the persons whose parents were still alive, six percent of the homes of offenders and three percent of the homes of non-offenders were broken by divorce or separation.[26] This indicates that the broken home is not closely linked with the delinquency of adolescent males. A study by similar methods of delinquent girls in Chicago yielded the conclusion that 66.8 percent of the delinquent girls and 44.8 percent of the school girls came from broken homes, or a ratio of 1.49 to 1. This indicates that a break in the home has a greater influence on girls than on boys.[27]

Various explanations of this difference between boys and girls in respect to the incidence of broken homes have been suggested. Weeks found that the type of delinquency must be held constant when comparing the incidence of broken homes among boy and girl delinquents. The boy and girl delinquents in this study came from broken homes in approximately the same proportion when the delinquency was ungovernability, running away, or immorality. Girls are more frequently referred for this type of offense, and cases of this type were referred to the juvenile court largely from sources other than the police, indicating that the broken home probably has more to do with referral of cases to the court than with actual causation of delinquency. The broken home had essentially the same significance for boys and for girls when comparison was restricted to similar delinquencies.[28]

Toby has suggested that such weak control is exercised over adolescent males in American families that there is little difference between supervision in a well-integrated family and a disorganized one. Hence, there is no appreciable relationship between broken homes and delinquency among adolescent males. But for girls and pre-adolescents the well-integrated family gives firm supervision, whereas the disorganized family is unable to do so. Therefore, girls and pre-adolescents from disorganized households are more likely to be exposed to criminogenic influences than girls and pre-adolescents from well-integrated households. This differential exposure, then, may account for the apparent positive relationship between broken homes and delinquency observed in these populations.[29] The same inter-

[26] Nils Christie, *Unge Norske Lovovertredere* (Young Norwegian Lawbreakers) (Oslo: Universitetsforlaget, 1960), pp. 105, 111.

[27] See Margaret Hodgkiss, "The Influence of Broken Homes and Working Mothers," *Smith College Studies in Social Work*, 3:259–274, March, 1933. See, also Monahan, *op. cit.*

[28] H. Ashley Weeks, "Male and Female Broken Home Rates by Types of Delinquency," *American Sociological Review*, 5:601–609, August, 1940.

[29] Jackson Toby, "The Differential Impact of Family Disorganization," *American Sociological Review*, 22:505–512, October, 1957; cf. Christie, *op. cit.*, pp. 111–112, 305.

pretation could be given to Polk's finding that 69 percent of a group of Negro delinquents placed on probation came from broken homes, as compared with 46 percent of the white cases.[30]

DISCIPLINE AND TRAINING.   Burt concluded that the most important difference between the situations of delinquent and non-delinquent children was in the home discipline. Defective discipline was present 6.9 times as frequently in the homes of delinquents as of non-delinquents. It appeared in the following forms: parental indifference to discipline; physical, intellectual, or moral weakness of parent which made discipline weak; lack of discipline due to absence of parent; disagreement about the control of the child; and overstrict discipline. Discipline was four times as important as poverty in the home in relation to delinquency.[31] Glueck found "unsuitable" supervision by the mother in the homes of 64 percent of the delinquent children and in the homes of only 13 percent of the non-delinquents; also, discipline by the mother was "lax" in 57 percent of the delinquents' homes and in 12 percent of the non-delinquents' homes.[32] Bandura and Walters found that parents of aggressive-destructive boys, relied, to a greater extent than did the parents of a control group, on disciplinary methods involving ridicule, physical punishment, and deprivation of privileges.[33]

The home discipline fails most frequently because of indifference and neglect. While it cannot be concluded that children of working mothers are necessarily neglected, the fact that a mother works often affects the training of the child.[34] In some of the homes of working mothers, like some of the homes of non-working mothers, the children are thrown on their own resources as soon as they are physically able. As a result they are brought into contact with the behavior patterns of persons outside the home. Whether they become delinquent or not depends upon the community patterns encountered. However, neglect of training by parents is probably more extensive in slum areas than in middle-class residential areas, and in American cities slums are areas of delinquent subcultures. Consequently, the probability that a neglected child will come into contact with an excess of delinquent behavior patterns is high.

Many of the complaints in juvenile courts originate with the parents who

[30] Polk, *op. cit.*

[31] Burt, *op. cit.*

[32] Glueck and Glueck, *Unraveling Juvenile Delinquency, op. cit.,* pp. 113, 131.

[33] Albert Bandura and Richard H. Walters, "Dependency Conflicts in Aggressive Delinquents," *Journal of Social Issues,* 14:52–65, 1958.

[34] Elizabeth Herzog, *Children of Working Mothers* (Washington: Department of Health, Education, and Welfare, 1960), pp. 18–20; Eleanor E. MacCoby, "Children and Working Mothers," *The Child,* 5:83–89, June, 1958.

charge their own children with ungovernability. This public accusation against a child by his own parents weakens the subsequent influence over the child, while at the same time it throws the child into association with delinquent behavior patterns. This behavior of parents is due in part to the lack of affection and concern for the child, in part to exasperation which is expressed violently and inconsistently. Moreover, this behavior of parents seems to be concentrated largely in the lower socio-economic classes, where there is a relative lack of non-judicial resources for dealing with the problem behavior of children. Porterfield has reported that 100 percent of 437 college men and women reported delinquencies in their pre-enrollment years of the same types as those for which children were before the juvenile court of Fort Worth, Texas. However, while these persons had engaged in much the same delinquent behavior as the children who appeared before the juvenile court, their own parents and others did not make formal complaints against them and they did not develop into consistent delinquents in the manner in which the children who appeared before the court did.[35] The child who appears in the juvenile court, in spite of legal theory to the contrary, is branded as a criminal and as a result he is impeded in adjusting to the larger society, and the society is impeded in adjusting to him. The inadequacy of the home throws a burden on the community, and the community has not developed methods of discipline and training which are equal in efficiency to those of the adequate home.

A special problem of training and discipline appears in the immigrant family. Parents who were effective in training their children in the peasant communities of Europe find themselves incompetent in the strange American city. A part of the explanation of their difficulty is their ignorance regarding the conditions of social life in America and the greater speed of their children in acquiring this knowledge, with the result that the children may look on their parents with contempt. It is therefore difficult for the parents to make the home attractive to the children, or to control the children. As a result of such home conditions in immigrant families the children are often thrown upon their own resources or the resources of the delinquent subcultures which surround them.[36] Thomas and Znaniecki

[35] Austin L. Porterfield, "Delinquency and Its Outcome in Court and College," *American Journal of Sociology*, 49:199–208, November, 1943; Austin L. Porterfield, "The Complainant in the Juvenile Court," *Sociology and Social Research*, 28:171–181, January, 1944.

[36] See S. N. Eisenstadt, "Delinquency Group-Formation Among Immigrant Youth," *British Journal of Delinquency*, 2:34–45, July, 1951; and Richard A. Cloward and Lloyd E. Ohlin, *Delinquency and Opportunity* (Glencoe: The Free Press, 1961), pp. 194–211.

stated that because the immigrants do not have the support of the larger family and of the community, they cannot control their children.[37]

Another special problem of training and discipline occurs with respect to institutionalized children. Of 500 delinquent girls in an institution in New York City, 100 had been in orphanages or other child-caring institutions for periods ranging from one to twelve years.[38] Slawson found that 13.3 percent of a group of delinquents had been at one time in an orphanage, as compared with 1.8 percent of an unselected group of New York City school children.[39] Another study indicated that of 84 foster children who had reached the age of eighteen who had never been in orphanages, 82 percent had made satisfactory adjustments, while of 96 children of the same kind who had been in orphanages for five years or more only 66 percent had made satisfactory adjustments.[40] Institutional children frequently do not acquire the feeling of security and self-esteem which comes from membership in a strong primary group, and at the same time many of them are thrown with few inhibitions into association with patterns of delinquency.[41] Neither of these is a necessary outcome of institutionalization, however.

Foster children are often believed to be more inclined toward delinquency than are other children. The truth of this belief cannot be determined, for there are no good comparisons of the two kinds of groups on this point and it would be extremely difficult to select adequate samples for such comparisons. Probably the belief is based on occasional observations of foster children who become delinquent and on *a priori* beliefs. Certainly only a small minority of foster children become delinquent.

GENERAL PROCESSES.    From the preceding analysis of home conditions in relation to delinquency, five principal processes appear. First, a child may assimilate within the home by observation of parents or other relatives the attitudes, codes, and behavior patterns of delinquency. He then becomes delinquent because he has learned delinquency at home. However, other children of the same age and sex probably are more important than parents in presenting patterns of behavior, whether the patterns presented are delinquent or anti-delinquent.

Second, parents determine both the geographic and the social class locus of the home in the community, and the locus of the home, in turn, largely

----

[37] W. I. Thomas and F. Znaniecki, *The Polish Peasant in Europe and America* (Chicago: University of Chicago Press, 1918), Vol. I, p. 711.

[38] Anne T. Bingham, "Determinants of Sex Delinquency in Adolescent Girls," *Journal of Criminal Law and Criminology*, 13:505, January–February, 1923.

[39] Slawson, *op. cit.*, p. 379.

[40] Sophie V. Thais, *How Foster Children Turn Out* (Albany: 1924), p. 151.

[41] Cf. Reiss, *op. cit.*

determines the kind of behavior patterns the child will encounter. If the home is in a high delinquency area, the probability that the child will encounter many delinquent patterns is higher than it is if the home is located in a low delinquency area. Similarly, being a member of a lower socio-economic class may greatly affect the child's denial or acceptance of the dominant values of the society.[42]

Third, the home may determine the prestige values of various persons and also the type of persons with whom intimacy later develops. The child may learn to reject members of certain minority groups, policemen, social workers, or others. He learns to appraise persons by their bearing, clothing, language, or occupation as important or unimportant, and this appraisal later affects his acceptance or rejection of the behavior patterns which are presented. He learns, in other words, to pay little attention to the behavior patterns, whether criminal or anti-criminal, presented by some persons, and to pay close attention to those presented by other persons.

Fourth, a child may be driven from the home by unpleasant experiences and situations or withdraw from it because of the absence of pleasant experiences, and thus cease to be a functioning member of an integrated group. Nye found that delinquency is higher in unbroken but unhappy homes than it is in broken homes.[43] The important element is that isolation from the family is likely to increase the child's associations with delinquency behavior patterns and decrease his associations with anti-delinquency behavior patterns. However, it is entirely possible that the reverse sometimes takes place: the child could become isolated from the patterns of the delinquent home and thereby increase his associations with anti-delinquent behavior patterns.

Fifth, the home may fail to train the child to deal with community situations in a law-abiding manner. That is, delinquency patterns may not be present in the home, but the home may be neutral with respect to delinquency of the child. This failure to present anti-delinquency patterns may be due to neglect of training because of the absence of the parents or because of the unconcern of parents, or it may be due to overprotection in the form of failure to acquaint the child with the kinds of delinquencies he will be expected to resist or with the taboos of the outside world. In either case he fails to develop inhibitions against delinquency, which are

[42] Albert K. Cohen *Delinquent Boys: The Culture of the Gang* (Glencoe: The Free Press, 1955); Solomon Kobrin, "The Conflict of Values in Delinquency Areas," *American Sociological Review*, 16:653–661, October, 1951; and Walter B. Miller, "Lower Class Culture as a Generating Milieu of Gang Delinquency," *Journal of Social Issues*, 14:5–19, 1958.

[43] *Op. cit.*, p. 47.

supposed to be developed in the family life. Again, whether such a "neutral" child becomes delinquent or not will depend upon his associations with delinquent and anti-delinquent patterns outside the home.

Most of the conditions which have been found to be associated with delinquency can be interpreted in relation to the fourth and fifth of the processes which have been outlined. The fact that the mother works away from home, that the father is dead, that the housing facilities are very inadequate, that the parents are unconcerned with the behavior of the child or are extremely harsh in their discipline—all of these may fall within the framework of the fourth and fifth processes. In both of those processes, the active condition is assimilation of delinquent behavior patterns from associates. These two processes are important because they increase the probability that a child will come into intimate contact with delinquents and will be attracted by delinquent behavior. If the family is in a community in which there is no pattern of theft, the children do not steal, no matter how much neglected or how unhappy they may be at home. There are cases in which parents neglect and abuse their children, are in dire poverty, are frequently intoxicated, and in many respects are vicious; in spite of such home conditions, the children may engage in practically no delinquencies.

A sixth process also has been suggested. This is the persistence in the general community of habits of disobedience formed in the home. This notion is frequently discussed in common-sense terms of the failure of the child to develop habits of obedience. It also is discussed in psychiatric terms of resentment of authority. Both views assume that there is a generalized attitude toward authority. That is questionable, for disobedience of one kind or another develops in a large proportion of the children in the modern home, due to the impossible demands made on them and to the inconsistency in the enforcement of home regulations. Psychoanalysts have emphasized the Oedipus complex as an important source of delinquency. This complex consists of hatred of the father because of rivalry for the affections of the mother; because the father is the authority in the home, the boy transfers hatred of authority when he becomes active in the outside community. It is difficult to determine the extent to which such transference occurs. Children who are very disobedient at home are frequently well behaved in the home of a neighbor or in school. A study of 74 adult male prisoners found no correlation between the subjects' attitudes toward public law and morality and their attitudes toward their parents.[44]

[44] Norman Watt and Brendan A. Maher, "Prisoner's Attitudes Toward Home and the Judicial System," *Journal of Criminal Law and Criminology*, 49:321–330, November–December, 1958.

A seventh process also is frequently suggested: psychological tensions and emotional disturbances in the home. There is no doubt that tensions accompanying or resulting from favoritism, rejections, insecurity, harshness, rigidity, irritation, and other conditions characterize many homes and affect many children. Observation of such home conditions among delinquent groups has resulted in the proposition: "The problem child is a child with problems." The delinquent is considered as emotionally disturbed, and his emotional disturbance is considered the product of emotional disturbances in his home. Psychiatrists and psychoanalysts have recently brought this notion into prominence, and it probably is the most popular interpretation of juvenile delinquency at present.[45] However, it is not at all certain that there is an undue incidence of emotional disturbances among delinquents or in the homes of delinquents. Furthermore, a most significant theoretical question regarding this interpretation of delinquency has not been adequately answered. Granted that juvenile delinquents sometimes come from homes characterized by family tensions and emotional disturbances, how do these tensions produce delinquency? Obviously, they may produce delinquency through the fourth and fifth processes described above; that is, through increasing the probability of contacts with delinquency behavior patterns or through failure of the family to acquaint the child with the taboos of the community. Psychological tensions and emotional disturbances at home may drive the child away from home and into contact with delinquents. Slawson found that 54 percent of the delinquents he studied had run away from home, as compared with 4 percent of the school children on a low economic level. A girl who finds no affection at home may find affection in illicit relations with boys or she may find it in nondelinquent activities in the school or community. A child does not necessarily become delinquent because he is unhappy. Children in unhappy homes may take on delinquency patterns if there are any around for them to acquire. Certainly they will not start giving away their personal possessions according to the custom of some Indian tribes, for this pattern is not present in urban America.[46]

DELINQUENT AND NON-DELINQUENT SIBLINGS. It might be expected that all children in the homes in which the processes described above apparently are operating would become delinquent. As a matter of fact, many

---

[45] For an illustration of this viewpoint see David Abrahamsen, "Family Tension, Basic Cause of Criminal Behavior," *Journal of Criminal Law and Criminology*, 40:330–343, September–October, 1949; and Beatrice R. Simcox and Irving Kaufman, "Treatment of Character Disorder in Parents of Delinquents," *Social Casework*, 37:388–395, October, 1956.

[46] H. Warren Dunham and Mary E. Knauer, "The Juvenile Court in Its Relationship to Adult Criminality," *Social Forces* 32:290–296, March, 1954.

of the children in such homes are not delinquent. One study found that in 372 two-child families in which one child was delinquent, the other child was delinquent in 20 percent of the families, and the character was not known in 2 percent. In 333 six-child families in which one child was delinquent, 12 percent of the siblings were known delinquents, 82 percent non-delinquents, and 6 percent unknown.[47] This shows a relatively small proportion of the siblings delinquent, and indicates that the home conditions as such do not completely determine behavior. It is probable, however, that some of the siblings were too young to be involved in delinquencies and the proportion delinquent might be increased if the figures were restricted to children above the age of ten years. Moreover, the home changes greatly in some cases by reason of the death of a parent, a change in economic status, formation or discontinuance of habits and attitudes by parents, or other conditions; thus the home of one child is not the same as the home of another child in the same family. Also, parental affection and supervision vary considerably in a home at a particular time for the different children, so that a child may not, on that account, have the same home as his brother. Finally, many of the associations which an individual has with delinquent and anti-delinquent behavior patterns outside the home are adventitious. It is not necessary to believe that every turning point in the life of an individual is a choice directed by a deep-seated and fundamental trait of personality.

ORDER OF BIRTH IN RELATION TO CRIME. Many studies have been made of the relation of order of birth to achievement, intellectual ability, psychopathy, aggressiveness, and other traits of personality and of behavior. The earlier studies generally showed inferiority in the first-born child, but the later studies have reduced this difference, due principally to an improvement in the statistical procedures. The result is that it is now doubtful whether order of birth has any association with traits of personality or behavior. Two explanations have been offered for the difference which has been found or has been assumed. One of these is biological and is to the effect that the first-born child is inferior because of the greater difficulty of his birth process. The other explanation is in terms of social relations and includes undeveloped skill of parents in training the child, oversolicitude of parents because of the newness of the experience, and conflict for the child in passing from a favored position as an only child to a subordinate position when a second child is born.

Studies of delinquents have been made from these points of view, but

---

47 William Healy and Augusta F. Bronner, *Delinquents and Criminals: Their Making and Unmaking* (New York: Macmillan, 1926), p. 104.

most of them have been limited to a small number of cases. Levy in New York and Goodenough and Leahy in Minneapolis found the first-born child delinquent in a disproportionately large number of cases, but Rosenow has questioned the validity of this finding.[48] A study of two groups of juvenile probationers in England showed an over-representation of intermediate-aged children, as compared with oldest and youngest in the family.[49] On the other hand, a study of all Norwegian offenders and non-offenders born in 1933 showed an underrepresentation of youngest sons among the offenders. Thirteen percent of the offenders and ten percent of the non-offenders were only children; 23 percent of the offenders and 19 percent of the non-offenders came from families with two children.[50] Parsley studied 361 delinquent girls in comparison with an equal number of non-delinquent girls of the same ages and nationalities, and found no significant difference in regard to the proportions of first-born, but did find that a significantly smaller proportion of the non-delinquents were youngest children.[51] This indicates that the youngest child is less likely to become delinquent and this conclusion applies equally to the native white and the Polish groups, but no significant difference was found in the Negro cases. In general, there are variations of such size and types that a conclusion on the significance of ordinal position seems unjustified.

Sletto has made an investigation of a different nature on this topic. He compared 1,145 juvenile delinquents in Minneapolis with an equal number of school children matched for age, sex, and sibling position. The problem was to determine whether an undue number of the delinquents had older brothers, younger brothers, older sisters, young sisters, or various combinations of these. He found that for boys the delinquency rates were highest among those with both older brothers and younger brothers but no sisters, lowest among those with both older brothers and older sisters but no younger siblings, and intermediate among those with other combinations of brothers and sisters. For girls, the rates were highest among those with a combination of older brothers, younger brothers, and younger sisters, lowest among those with both older brothers and older sisters but no younger siblings, and intermediate among those with other combinations

---

[48] John Levy, "A Quantitative Study of Behavior Problems in Relation to Family Constellation," *American Journal of Psychiatry*, 10:637–654, January, 1931; Florence Goodenough and Alice Leahy, "The Effect of Certain Family Relations upon the Development of Personality," *Pedagogical Seminar*, 34:69, March, 1927; Curt Rosenow and Anne P. Whyte, "The Ordinal Position of Problem Children," *American Journal of Orthopsychiatry*, 1:430–434, July, 1931.

[49] J. P. Lees and L. J. Newson, "Family or Sibling Position and Some Aspects of Juvenile Delinquency," *British Journal of Delinquency*, 5:46–65, July, 1954.

[50] Christie, op. cit., pp. 117–122.

[51] Mannie Parsley, "The Influence of Ordinal Position and Size of Family," *Smith College Studies in Social Work*, 3:274–283, March, 1933.

of siblings. Moreover, it was found that girls who have brothers and no sisters have a higher delinquency rate than girls who have sisters and no brothers. Apparently a girl with no siblings of the same sex is likely to approach the delinquency standards of the brothers. A boy who has sisters and no brothers does not show a consistent tendency of an analogous kind.[52] Sletto's study, in general, justifies a conclusion that social relations are affected by the ordinal position and that the social relations are important in delinquency.

The "only child" is generally supposed to be extraordinarily prone to delinquency. The studies which have been made do not consistently bear this out. To cite only a few of the studies, Bohannon, Burt, Slawson, and Parsley, found a disproportionate amount of delinquency among "only children,"[53] while Levy, Goodenough and Leahy, and Ward did not find this disproportion.[54] Shield and Gregg found that undue proportions of Virginia State Prison inmates were first-born, last-born, or only children.[55] On the contrary, the Gluecks found that their group of delinquent boys contained lower proportions of first children, youngest children, or only children than did the control group.[56] Nye found that oldest and only children show less delinquency behavior than intermediate and youngest children.[57] Wattenberg reviewed the studies of delinquency and only children and concluded that the meaning of being an only child varies among different national, racial, religious and economic groups, and that, consequently, the status of only child has no consistent relationship to delinquency or other behavior problems.[58]

MARITAL STATUS.  The marital status of the adult person appears to have considerable significance in relation to crime. The rate of commitment to prisons and reformatories per 100,000 population of the same marital status is lowest for the married, next to the lowest for widowed, next for the single, and highest for the divorced. These ranks, however, are affected in

[52] R. F. Sletto, "Sibling Position and Juvenile Delinquency," *American Journal of Sociology*, 39:657–669, March, 1934.

[53] E. W. Bohannon, "The Only Child in a Family," *Pedagogical Seminar*, 5:475–496, April, 1898; Burt, *op. cit.*, pp. 91–92; Slawson, *op. cit.*, pp. 398–409; and Parsley, *op. cit.*

[54] Levy, *op. cit.*; Goodenough, *op. cit.*, and Anne Ward, "The Only Child," *Smith College Studies in Social Work*, 1:41–65, January, 1930.

[55] J. A. Shield and A. E. Gregg, "Extreme Ordinal Position and Criminal Behavior," *Journal of Criminal Law and Criminology*, 35:169–173, September–October, 1944.

[56] Glueck and Glueck, *Unraveling Juvenile Delinquency*, *op. cit.*, p. 120.

[57] Nye, *op. cit.*, p. 37; see also Raymond A. Mulligan, "Family Relationships and Juvenile Delinquency," *Pacific Sociological Review*, 1:40, Spring, 1958.

[58] William W. Wattenberg, "Delinquency and Only Children: A Study of a 'Category,'" *Journal of Abnormal and Social Psychology*, 44:356–366, July, 1949.

part by age. Divorced persons have the highest commitment rate at each age, and this is true for each of the sexes. Divorced males 20 to 24 years of age have a rate of commitment about six times as high as either single males of the same age or married males of the same age, while divorced females of that age have a rate about ten times as high as either single females or married females of the same age. Married males have a lower commitment rate than single males in all age groups except fifteen to nineteen; the rate is only slightly lower in the age 20 to 24, but is significantly lower in later ages. For females, however, the married women have a higher commitment rate at each age except twenty-five to thirty-four but the difference is not very great except in the age group fifteen to nineteen. These statistics, which are based on commitments to prisons in the United States, are in substantial agreement with the statistics from European countries. It has been found, also, that married persons succeed on parole more frequently than persons of any other marital class, and that those who are compatibly married succeed more often than those incompatibly married.[59] Gillin made a study of 172 prisoners in comparison with their non-criminal brothers and found that the prisoners had the following characteristics more frequently than their brothers: single or divorced; did not have harmonious relations with wife; did not come from same nationality, religion, educational, or economic status as wife.[60] It is not possible, however, to conclude from these statistics that marital status is a direct causative "factor" in crime. It can be concluded from these statistics that marital status is important to criminality and non-criminality because it determines the kinds of behavior patterns with which a person comes in contact.

## SUGGESTED READINGS

Abrahamsen, David, "Family Tension, Basic Cause of Criminal Behavior," *Journal of Criminal Law and Criminology,* 40:330–343, September–October, 1949.

Barker, Gordon H., "Parental Organizational Affiliation and Juvenile Delinquency," *Journal of Criminal Law, Criminology, and Police Science,* 44:204–207, July–August, 1953.

Burt, Cyril, *The Young Delinquent,* Fourth Edition. London: University of London Press, 1944.

Cohen, Albert K., *Delinquent Boys: The Culture of the Gang.* Glencoe: The Free Press, 1955.

Davis, Allison, and R. J. Havighurst, "Social Class and Color Differences

[59] Sheldon and Eleanor T. Glueck, *Five Hundred Criminal Careers,* op. cit., p. 269.
[60] John L. Gillin, "Backgrounds of Prisoners in Wisconsin State Prison and of Their Brothers," *American Sociological Review,* 2:204–212, April, 1937.

in Child Rearing," *American Sociological Review*, 11:698–710, December, 1946.

Eisenstadt, S. N., "Delinquency Group-Formation Among Immigrant Youth," *British Journal of Delinquency*, 2:34–45, July, 1951.

Healey, William, *The Individual Delinquent*. Boston: Little, Brown, 1915.

Healy, William, and Augusta Bronner, *New Light on Delinquency and its Treatment*. New Haven: Yale University Press, 1936.

Kobrin, Solomon, "The Conflict of Values in Delinquency Areas," *American Sociological Review*, 16:653–661, October, 1951.

Lees, J. P., and L. J. Newsom, "Family or Sibling Position and Some Aspects of Juvenile Delinquency," *British Journal of Delinquency*, 5:46–65, July, 1954.

Monahan, Thomas P., "Family Status and the Delinquent Child: A Reappraisal and Some New Findings," *Social Forces*, 35:250–258, March, 1957.

Nye, F. Ivan, *Family Relationships and Delinquent Behavior*. New York: Wiley, 1958.

Reiss, Albert J., Jr., "Delinquency as the Failure of Personal and Social Controls," *American Sociological Review*, 16:196–208, April, 1951.

Shield, J. A., and A. E. Gregg, "Extreme Ordinal Position and Criminal Behavior," *Journal of Criminal Law and Criminology*, 35:169–173, September–October, 1944.

Shulman, Harry M., "The Family and Juvenile Delinquency," *Annals of the American Academy of Political and Social Science*, 261:21–31, January, 1949.

Sletto, R. F., "Sibling Position and Juvenile Delinquency," *American Journal of Sociology*, 39:657–669, March, 1934.

Sottong, David C., "The Dilemma of the Parent as a Culture Bearer," *Social Casework*, 36:302–306, July, 1955.

Straus, Murray A., "Power and Support Structure of the Family in Relation to Socialization," *Journal of Marriage and the Family*, 26:318–326, August, 1964.

Toby, Jackson, "The Differential Impact of Family Disorganization," *American Sociological Review*, 22:505–512, October, 1957.

Wattenberg, William, "Delinquency and Only Children: A Study of a 'Category,'" *Journal of Abnormal and Social Psychology*, 44:356–366, July, 1949.

Weeks, H. A., and Margaret G. Smith, "Juvenile Delinquency and Broken Homes in Spokane, Washington," *Social Forces*, 18:48–55, October, 1939.

Weeks, H. A., "Male and Female Broken Home Rates by Types of Delinquency," *American Sociological Review*, 5:601–609, August, 1940.

Witmer, Helen L., Editor, *Parents and Delinquency*. Washington: Department of Health, Education, and Welfare, 1954.

# 11. SOCIAL INSTITUTIONS AND CRIME

MANY EFFORTS have been made to determine the effects on criminal behavior of the general social institutions. The basic social institutions—such as family, economics, government, education, and religion—are organized systems for meeting societal needs. Each organizes some aspects of the individual's behavior, and each is necessary to the continued existence of a society. There are many variations in the specific form and content of the institutions as we move from society to society, and these variations conceivably are linked to variations in crime rates among societies. As was indicated in Chapter Five, however, intersocietal comparisons of institutional structure and functioning, like intersocietal comparisons of crime rates, are very difficult and hazardous. Consequently, most of the research on the subject in the United States has been directed at analysis of the role of the various institutions in determining the variations in crime and criminality in our own society. That is, "family factors," "economic factors," "political factors," etc., in crime have been sought. The family institution, which was discussed in the last chapter, and the economic institution, especially as it affects the distribution of wealth, have received more explicit attention than the other institutions.

THE ECONOMIC INSTITUTION. Many studies have been made of the relation between crime and poverty, an economic condition. These have been directed at two principal questions: Do people of lower economic status commit more crimes than people of higher economic status? And, do crime rates increase when poverty increases in periods of economic depression? A survey will be made of the principal findings of these studies, their limitations, and the conclusions that seem warranted.

Studies of the economic status of criminals have indicated that the lower economic class has a much higher official crime rate than the upper economic class. This conclusion has been derived from two types of data:

those on the social class membership of criminals and delinquents, and those on delinquency and crime rates of persons living in areas of poverty, as compared to the rates of persons living in other areas of cities.

*Variations by social class.* The reliability of the official statistics on the socio-economic class backgrounds of criminals has been questioned even more severely than have statistics on variables like age, race, and area of residence. Many persons maintain that the law-enforcement processes tend to select working-class persons, just as they tend to select Negroes. Thus it is believed that if a member of the working class and a member of the upper class are equally guilty of some offense the person on the lower level is more likely to be arrested, convicted, and committed to an institution. Further, some white-collar crimes are not included in sets of official crime statistics. It is not possible at present to compile quantitative data regarding the white-collar crime rate, and therefore it is not possible to make accurate comparisons of the total criminal behavior of the several classes. When white-collar crimes are taken into account, however, they throw doubt on the conclusion that crime is concentrated in the lower economic classes. Reckless is confident that if statistical procedures could be corrected the distribution of crime by social classes in the United States would show a bi-modal curve, with high peaks for members of the upper class and lower class, and a low valley for members of the middle class.[1] Even for ordinary crimes, the administrative processes are more favorable to persons in economic comfort than to those in poverty. One study found that lower-class boys were significantly overrepresented in the population of training schools; however, when high school students were asked to report on their delinquencies, no significant differences in the delinquency of boys and girls in the different socio-economic classes was found.[2] However, the statistics on ordinary crime so consistently show an overrepresentation of lower-class persons that it is reasonable to assume that there is a real difference between the behavior of members of this class and the members of other social classes, so far as criminality is concerned. If this assumption is made, the following two observations are warranted.

A. In the United States, official statistics indicate that the largest proportion of delinquent and criminal populations come from the working class, and there is some evidence that the delinquency rate and crime rate of working-class persons exceed the rates of other persons. In institu-

[1] Walter C. Reckless, *The Crime Problem*, Second Edition (New York: Appleton-Century-Crofts, 1955), pp. 28–30.
[2] F. Ivan Nye, James F. Short, Jr., and Virgil J. Olson, "Socioeconomic Status and Delinquent Behavior," *American Journal of Sociology*, 63:381–389, January, 1958. For a study with contradictory findings, see footnote 13 below.

## TABLE XII

PERCENTAGE DISTRIBUTION OF THREE SERIES OF OFFENDERS, BY ECONOMIC
STATUS OF PARENTAL FAMILIES

| Parental Families: Economic Status | 1,000 Juvenile Delinquents | 500 Young-Adult Male Delinquents | 500 Women Delinquents |
|---|---|---|---|
| Dependent | 8.1 | 14.8 | 13.3 |
| Marginal | 63.2 | 56.4 | 78.0 |
| Comfortable | 23.7 | 28.8 | 8.7 |
| Total | 100.0 | 100.0 | 100.0 |

tionalized populations, about two-thirds to three-fourths of the men, and about nine-tenths of the women, are members of the working class. Caldwell, using an occupational rating scale, found that 33.4 percent of the parents of boy delinquents and 52.7 percent of the parents of girl delinquents in Wisconsin correctional institutions were unskilled, in comparison with 11.8 percent of the entire employed population of the state.[3] Similarly, data gathered on 761 delinquents in Passaic, New Jersey, indicated that their fathers' occupational ratings were considerably lower than the rating for the general population of the city.[4] The economic status of the parents of three series of offenders studied by Sheldon and Eleanor Glueck is presented in Table XII.[5] This shows that 71.3 percent of the offenders in one series and 91.3 percent in the series at the other extreme were below the "comfortable level," which was defined as possession of sufficient surplus to enable a family to maintain itself for four months without going on relief. Comparisons of the occupational status of adult criminals likewise shows a disproportionately large representation of unskilled and semiskilled occupations. Warner and Lunt found that while the two lower classes constituted only 57 percent of Yankee City's population, 90 percent of the arrests during a seven-year period were arrests of members of these two classes.[6] Seventy-three percent of a sample of the children placed on probation in Ceylon in 1944–1956 were classed as

[3] M. G. Caldwell, "The Economic Status of Families of Delinquent Boys in Wisconsin," American Journal of Sociology, 37:231–239, September, 1931.

[4] W. C. Kvaraceus, "Juvenile Delinquency and Social Class," Journal of Educational Sociology, 18:51–54, September, 1944.

[5] Sheldon and Eleanor Glueck, One Thousand Juvenile Delinquents (Cambridge: Harvard University Press, 1934); Five Hundred Criminal Careers (New York: Knopf, 1930); Five Hundred Delinquent Women (New York: Knopf, 1934). See also Maud A. Merrill, Problems of Child Delinquency (Boston: Houghton Mifflin, 1947), pp. 77–78.

[6] William Lloyd Warner and Paul S. Lunt, The Social Life of a Modern Community (New Haven: Yale University Press, 1941), pp. 373–377.

"poor" or "very poor."[7] A study in Denmark indicated that 10 percent of a group of offenders came from the upper or middle class, while 27 percent of the general population was in these classes.[8] Many other studies have shown the same tendency for adult and juvenile delinquents to be concentrated in the lower economic class.[9] One study indicated that prisoners rank themselves lower than they rank their fathers on socio-economic status, perhaps indicating that the prisoners were unable to maintain the family level of status, let alone improve it through upward mobility.[10]

B. The extent of overrepresentation of working-class persons in the criminal population is not the same under all conditions. In some situations, working-class people have crime rates lower than those of other classes.

1. The ratio of working-class persons to other persons in the criminal population varies by social group. In the Japanese colony in Seattle prior to World War II the children had a very low delinquency rate, despite the fact that the residents were of the working class and were in as great poverty as residents of the area surrounding the colony, who had high rates. Moreover, residents of certain rural areas may be in extreme poverty with little incidence of crime. Shaw found that for the 87 counties of Minnesota the correlation between crime rates and the percentage of the populations on relief combined with the percentage of the populations seeking work was only +.213. By way of contrast, he found a correlation of +.717 between the degree of urbanization of the counties and their crime rates.[11] Sheldon discovered no close relationship between the indexes of economic status and juvenile delinquency when other factors were held constant, but found a significant relationship between indexes of social disorganization and juvenile delinquency when economic factors were held constant.[12] Clark and Wenninger studied the self-reported crimes of public high school students, sixth through twelfth grades, in four communities chosen

[7] Department of Census and Statistics, Juvenile Probation in Ceylon (Ceylon: Government Press, 1957), p. 24.

[8] Preben Wolf, "Kriminalitet og Social Klasse," Sociologiske Meddeleser, 3:3–7, April, 1957. See also Preben Wolf, "Crime and Social Class in Denmark," British Journal of Criminology, 13:5–17, 1962.

[9] See, e.g., Hermann Mannheim, John Spencer, and George Lynch, "Magisterial Policy in the London Juvenile Courts," British Journal of Delinquency, 8:13–33, and 8:119–138, June and October, 1957; and Terrence Morris, The Criminal Area (London: Kegan Paul, 1958), pp. 164–181.

[10] Harold Bradley and Jack D. Williams, Intensive Treatment Program: Second Annual Report (Sacramento: Department of Corrections, 1958), p. 16.

[11] Van B. Shaw, "The Relationship Between Crime Rates and Certain Population Characteristics in Minnesota Counties," Journal of Criminal Law and Criminology, 40:43–49, May–June, 1949.

[12] Henry D. Sheldon, "Problems in the Statistical Study of Juvenile Delinquency," Metron, 12:201–223, 1934.

to represent four class levels—rural farm, lower urban (mostly unskilled occupations), industrial city, and upper urban (mostly executive and professional). They found that the incidence of self-reported crimes became greater as one moved from rural farm to upper urban to industrial city to lower urban.[13] Also, girls in the areas of poverty in the typical American city are in as great poverty as boys but their delinquency rate is much lower than the delinquency rate of boys. Similarly, members of groups in extreme poverty have literally starved to death rather than violate laws. The following is a report on a period of famine in India in 1943:

Through all these months the white Brahmin cattle wandered by the hundreds through the streets of Calcutta, as they always have, stepping placidly over the bodies of the dead and near-dead, scratching their plump haunches on taxi fenders, sunning themselves on the steps of the great Clive Street banks. No one ever ate a cow; no one ever dreamed of it. I never heard of a Bengali Hindu who would not perish with all his family rather than taste meat. Nor was there any violence. No grocery stall, no rice warehouse, none of the wealthy clubs or restaurants ever was threatened by a hungry mob. The Bengalis just died with that bottomless docility which, to most Americans, is the most shocking thing about India.[14]

2. The ratio of working-class persons to other persons varies by offense. The kind of crime, as contrasted with the fact of crime, is very significantly related to economic status. One's position in the economic structure determines opportunities, facilities, and the requisite skills for specialized crimes.[15] Most studies showing high ratios of working-class persons have concentrated on crimes against property, such as larceny and burglary. There is some evidence, however, that the ratio is somewhat lower for sex offenses, and in fact the crime rate of the working class may be lower than those of other classes for some sex offenses.[16] Similarly, a study conducted in Detroit indicated that working-class persons are not as overrepresented in the population of automobile thieves as they are in other delinquent and criminal populations.[17] And of course working-class persons have

[13] John P. Clark and Eugene P. Wenninger, "Socio-Economic Class and Area as Correlates of Illegal Behavior Among Juveniles," American Sociological Review, 27:826–834, December, 1962.

[14] John Fischer, "India's Insoluble Hunger," Harper's, 190:438–445, April, 1945.

[15] See Donald R. Cressey, "Application and Verification of the Differential Association Theory," Journal of Criminal Law, Criminology, and Police Science, 43:72–80, June, 1952.

[16] A. C. Kinsey, W. B. Pomeroy, and C. E. Martin, Sexual Behavior in the Human Male (Philadelphia: Saudners, 1948), pp. 327–393.

[17] William W. Wattenberg and James Balistrieri, "Automobile Theft: A 'Favored-Group' Delinquency," American Journal of Sociology, 57:575–579, May, 1952.

lower crime rates than other persons for such offenses as embezzlement, misrepresentation in advertising, violation of anti-trust laws, and issuing worthless stocks.

*Variations by area.*[18] Ogburn found a significant association between poverty and crime in a comparison of 62 cities.[19] Shaw and McKay compared residential areas within each of twenty-one cities and found a large and consistent relationship between crime and poverty; they also found very high positive correlations by residential areas between boy delinquency and girl delinquency rates, and also between boy delinquency rates and adult crime rates.[20] In an English city, Morris found a correlation of +.74 between delinquency rates and percentage of over-crowded homes, and a correlation of −.76 between delinquency rates and the percentage of middle class households.[21] Correlations between crime rates and other indexes of poverty also indicate that crime is associated with areas of poverty. For instance, the economic values of houses in a delinquency area are low, the delinquency rate is higher among renters than among property owners, and the physical condition and equipment of houses in delinquency areas is poor.[22] Reiss and Rhodes studied 9,238 white male Tennessee delinquents of all social classes and found, among other things, that (1) both in areas of high delinquency and in areas of low delinquency, the low-status boy has the greatest chance of becoming delinquent, (2) no matter whether he is of high status, middle status, or low status, the chances that a boy will be a delinquent are greater if he resides in a high-delinquency rate area than if he resides in a low-delinquency rate area, (3) the more the lower-class boy is in a minority in the school and residential community, the less likely he is to become a delinquent.[23] All these findings are consistent with the implication, in the theory of differential association, that socio-economic status is important to delinquency and crime primarily as it affects the probability of association with delinquent and criminal behavior patterns.

*Variations in time.* The relation between crime rates and economic

[18] See the discussion of intra-city distributions in Chapter 9, pp. 192–199, above.

[19] W. F. Ogburn, "Factors in the Variation of Crime Among Cities," *Journal of the American Statistical Association*, 30:12–34, March, 1935. See also James E. McKeown, "Poverty, Race, and Crime," *Journal of Criminal Law and Criminology*, 39:480–483, November–December, 1948.

[20] Clifford R. Shaw and Henry D. McKay, *Juvenile Delinquency and Urban Areas* (Chicago: University of Chicago Press, 1942), pp. 141 ff.

[21] Morris, op. cit., p. 169.

[22] Howard Harlan and Jack Wherey, "Delinquency and Housing," *Social Forces*, 27:58–61, October, 1948.

[23] Albert J. Reiss, Jr. and Albert Lewis Rhodes, "The Distribution of Juvenile Delinquency in the Social Class Structure," *American Sociological Review*, 26:720–732, October, 1961.

conditions also has been studied by examination of data on the relationship between fluctuations in business conditions and fluctuations in crime
rates. Here, poverty is measured by the poor business conditions constituting an economic depression, rather than by socio-economic class or by
area of residence. Studies of this kind, which have been under way for more
than a century, have been summarized and appraised by Sellin.[24] The
methods which have been used have seldom been carefully devised and the
indexes of both crime and business conditions have varied widely, with the
result that no positive, definite, and valid generalizations can be made. The
following are the closest approximations to conclusions from the studies.

1. Serious crimes have a slight and inconsistent tendency to rise in
periods of depression and fall in periods of prosperity. Dorothy Thomas
found a correlation of —.25 between all indictable crimes and economic
prosperity in England and Wales for the period 1857–1913, Ogburn a
similar coefficient —.35 in New York State for the period 1870–1920, and
Phelps a coefficient of —.33 in Rhode Island for the period 1898–1926.[25]

2. The general crime rate does not increase significantly in periods of
depression.[26]

3. Property crimes involving violence show a tendency to increase in
periods of depression, but property crimes involving no violence, such as
larceny, show only a very slight and inconsistent tendency to increase in
depression periods.[27] Radzinowicz found a clear-cut increase in crimes
against property in Poland in the depression years of the early thirties.[28]
None of the studies which cover longer periods of time has shown such
significant relationship, perhaps because extraneous factors, such as variations in laws and in administration of the laws, play less part in the longer
period.

4. Drunkenness tends to increase in periods of prosperity according to
some studies but shows no significant change according to others. Dorothy

[24] Thorsten Sellin, *Research Memorandum on Crime in the Depression* (New York:
Social Science Research Council, 1937). See also W. A. Bonger, *Criminality and
Economic Conditions* (Boston: Little, Brown, 1916).

[25] Dorothy S. Thomas, *Social Aspects of the Business Cycle* (London: Routledge,
1925), pp. 143–144; W. F. Ogburn, "Business Fluctuations as Social Forces," *Social
Forces*, 1:73–78, January, 1923; H. A. Phelps, "Cycles of Crime," *Journal of Criminal
Law and Criminology*, 20:107–121, May–June, 1929. See also George B. Vold, *Theoretical Criminology* (New York: Oxford University Press, 1958), pp. 177–181.

[26] Albert H. Hobbs, "Relationship Between Criminality and Economic Conditions,"
*Journal of Criminal Law and Criminology*, 34:5–10, May, 1943; James F. Short, Jr.,
"A Note on Relief Programs and Crimes During the Depression," *American Socio-
logical Review*, 17:226–229, April, 1952.

[27] For a recent study on this point, see James F. Short, Jr., "A Social Aspect of
the Business Cycle Re-examined: Crimes," *Research Studies of the State College of
Washington*, 20:36–41, 1952.

[28] L. Radzinowicz, "The Influence of Economic Conditions on Crime," *Sociological
Review*, 33:1–36, 139–153, January–May, 1941.

Thomas found a correlation of $+.34$ between prosecutions for drunkenness and prosperity in England in 1857–1913;[29] Winslow found no significant relation in Massachusetts between prosecutions for drunkenness and unemployment.[30]

5. Crimes against the person show no consistent relationship to the business cycle. Some studies have reported increases in crimes against the person in periods of prosperity and find, also, that the consumption of alcohol accompanies the increase in crimes against the person.

6. Juvenile delinquency tends to increase in periods of prosperity and to decrease during periods of depression.[31] A recent study suggests that combining statistics on juvenile crime with statistics on adult crime may give the erroneous impression that the general crime rate (all ages) does not change in periods of depression.[32]

*Conclusions.* Before a general positive conclusion about the relationship between poverty and crime is derived from these three kinds of studies, two negative conclusions should be drawn. *First,* the official criminal statistics, being biased as to class by the exclusion of white-collar crimes and by differences in arresting practices, exaggerate the extent to which crimes are concentrated in the lower class; excessive criminality of the lower class except in the official crime records has not been demonstrated. *Second,* even if the official statistics are accepted, they give conflicting evidence. Criminal behavior is related consistently to poverty and low economic status according to studies which compare residential areas of criminals and non-criminals, but is related inconsistently or not at all to poverty and low economic status when chronological periods are compared.

The conflicting kinds of evidence suggest that poverty has certain social accompaniments when considered geographically which are lacking when considered chronologically, and that it may be these accompaniments of poverty rather than the economic need which result in criminal behavior. Poverty in the modern city customarily means segregation in low-rent areas, where people are isolated to a considerable degree from

[29] D. Thomas, *op. cit.,* pp. 143–144.

[30] Emma A. Winslow, "Relationships between Employment and Crime Fluctuations as Shown by Massachusetts Statistics," *Report on the Causes of Crime,* National Commission on Law Observance and Enforcement, No. 13, Vol. I (Washington: Government Printing Office, 1937), pp. 257–333.

[31] J. O. Reinemann, "Juvenile Delinquency in Philadelphia and Economic Trends," *Temple University Law Quarterly,* 20:576–583, April, 1947; Lowell J. Carr, *Delinquency Control* (New York: Harper, 1950), pp. 83–89; Paul Wiers, "Wartime Increases in Michigan Delinquency," *American Sociological Review,* 10:515–523, August, 1945; Paul Wiers, *Economic Factors in Michigan Delinquency,* New York: Columbia University Press, 1944; David Bogen, "Juvenile Delinquency and Economic Trend," *American Sociological Review,* 9:178–184, April, 1944.

[32] Daniel Glaser and Kent Rice, "Crime, Age and Employment," *American Sociological Review,* 24:679–686, October, 1959.

anti-criminal patterns and forced into contact with many criminal behavior patterns. It generally means a low social status, with little to lose,
little to respect, and little to sustain efforts at self-advancement. It generally means bad housing conditions, poor health, and invidious comparisons in other physical and physiological conditions. It may mean that
both parents are away from home during most of the hours the children
are awake, and are fatigued and irritable when at home. It generally means
that the child is withdrawn from school at the earliest permissible age to
enter an unskilled occupation which is not interesting or remunerative
and which offers few opportunities for economic advancement. Poverty
in a small town may have few of those accompaniments. On the other
hand, a depression does not modify significantly the associations of many
persons, for rents decrease and families generally occupy the same houses
and have the same neighbors as formerly[33] Poverty may, therefore, be
significant because of the social accompaniments of poverty. The general
conclusion is that poverty affects crime and criminality as it determines
associations with criminal behavior patterns or isolation from anti-criminal
behavior patterns.

THE INSTITUTION OF GOVERNMENT.    There has been much speculation but
relatively little research on the institution of government and the political
processes in relation to criminal behavior. Two possibilities for research
may be suggested. First, various forms of government might be compared,
as the capitalist democracy and the communist "dictatorship of the pro-
letariat." Other comparisons, with less economic involvement, might be
made between a democratic system and an absolute monarchy, a dictatorship, or a system of government by tribal council, with the objective of
determining the extent to which criminal behavior is related to the general
form of the political institution. The reason no organized research work
has been done on this problem and the reason such research is infeasible
need hardly be mentioned—the lack of comparable statistics for different
nations and systems. Second, comparison might be made of specific
political variables within a nation, such as a Democratic administration
with a Republican administration, or the particular policies of one administration with those of another. Discussion of this subject has resulted in
many conflicting claims, but the problem seems peculiarly insusceptible
to scientific research. In fact, the crime statistics inadequately represent
the true crime picture in the United States partly because various political
administrations juggle the figures so as to "prove" that their policies have

[33] Ruth Shonle Cavan and Katherine H. Ranck, *The Family and the Depression*,
(Chicago: University of Chicago Press, 1938).

reduced crime while the policies of the opposition have increased or would increase crime. Because of the absence of organized research on the influence of government on crime rates, analogous to that in the area of economic conditions, this problem can be discussed only in general terms.

A prominent theory is that crime is due to the lack of enforcement of laws, and that the solution of the problem of crime is pressure upon the police and courts to enforce the laws strictly. Strict enforcement of laws would certainly reduce crime, but strict enforcement of laws is extremely difficult because the agencies of justice have been kept weak by the same conditions which have produced high crime rates.[34]

A few centuries ago government had prestige because it was based on the divine right of the sovereign. General opposition to strong government developed because of the necessity of breaking away from the regulations which persisted from the feudal period, because of the democratic fear of absolutism, and because of the new problems of the frontiers. In spite of this distrust, the widening area of social interaction and the deadly effects of competition drove many groups to appeal to government for assistance. Many laws have been passed for the purpose of controlling behavior in these impersonal situations but the legislation has not been supported by a cohesive body of opinion and sentiment. The result has been the anomalous condition of a great amount of legislation and little respect for legislation. Each group rebels against the legislation forced upon it by other groups, and each group attempts to secure legislation to regulate other groups. It is easy to break laws derived from a source that one does not respect greatly and it is easy to manipulate policies in the interest of one's group when few people have an intense interest in the larger group. Clinard has indicated that in America the general public attitude toward law obedience is that all laws except those dealing with very serious offenses should be violated if one can get away with it, or that laws should be selectively obeyed according to one's interests.[35] The first can be seen in the attitudes toward tax evasion and manipulation, the patronage of gambling establishments, the failure to obey traffic regulations, and public intoxication. The second can be seen in the selective obedience of laws governing business, labor, and agriculture.[36]

[34] *Cf.* Mabel A. Elliott, "Perspective on the American Crime Problem," *Social Problems*, 5:184–193, Winter, 1957.

[35] Marshall B. Clinard, "Secondary Community Influences and Juvenile Delinquency," *The Annals of the American Academy of Political and Social Science*, 261:42–54, January, 1949.

[36] For examples of selective obedience see Marshall B. Clinard, *The Black Market* (New York: Rinehart, 1952); Robert E. Lane, "Why Businessmen Violate the Law," *Journal of Criminal Law, Criminology, and Police Science*, 44:151–165, July–August, 1953; and Erwin O. Smigel, "Public Attitudes Toward Stealing as Related to the Size of the Victim Organization," *American Sociological Review*, 21:320–327, June, 1956.

The general disrespect for law and disrespect for those who make and enforce laws is seen not only in the fact that people break laws but also in the attitudes of those who do not break laws. Legislative bodies, considered as corporate bodies rather than as individuals, are generally considered with contempt, suspicion, and distrust. Novels dealing with legislatures in the United States over the last four generations have presented these bodies as corrupt, boss-ridden, and inefficient. Similarly, the police are generally regarded as brutal, corrupt, and inefficient. The public attitude toward the courts is perhaps a little more favorable but inclines toward ridicule and contempt for the lower courts for defects of dishonesty, individual inefficiency, and squalid surroundings. The lack of respect was illustrated recently when a club woman who was the complaining witness in a burglary case notified the police that she could not be in court at the hour set for trial because she had an appointment for tea with a prominent visitor.

Officials charged with the enforcement of laws may avoid their responsibility altogether or may enforce the laws only sporadically. The cyclical pattern of "reform" so common to American municipalities is partly a function of sporadic enforcement. The citizens, however, are indirectly responsible for the lack of enforcement; the laws are not enforced because the officials are fearful of arousing public antagonism.[37] In many groups, individuals would generally prefer to be caught breaking almost any of the non-felony laws rather than be detected eating potatoes with a knife, and in certain groups even felonies are less serious than breaches of etiquette. Prohibition probably made a generous contribution to the development of a code of selective obedience of law.

When one is caught, the problem is to "fix" things. This occurs very commonly in the so-called law-abiding groups in relation to traffic violations, gambling, smuggling, liquor, and certain other crimes. In other circles it occurs in relation to shoplifting, picking pockets, robbery, burglary, and murder. There is a prevalent belief among prisoners that their own cases could have been "fixed" if they had had sufficient money. According to that belief, the only reason for being arrested or convicted is poverty. It is probable that no part of the population is better acquainted with the corruption and graft in the legislative, judicial, and police systems, so far as they exist, than are the professional criminals.

Some cities are under the control of political machines, and these are sometimes bipartisan and continue their control regardless of the party in power. The political party is an agency for predatory control. It can

[37] Cf. Anonymous (an ex-mayor), "Are You Sure You Want an Honest Mayor?" Collier's, October 30, 1953, pp. 64–67.

retain its position only by rendering services to one special group or another, or to the general society. It must serve the general society, but service to the general society is a means to its own welfare. *In the first place*, the ordinary individual does not want to be bothered with political activity and does not have the initiative to get the government to act. He wants to permit someone else to do the work, and the politician steps in and meets this need. *In the second place*, ordinary citizens who do have initiative and force in relation to government generally have an individual interest to promote; it may be a financial return to themselves, a crank's utopian scheme, or a fanatic's hostility to existing practices. It is necessary to have some person or group to weigh these many demands against each other and work out compromises that will give some satisfaction to the discontented groups. The politicians, being essentially amoral, calculate these demands in terms of returns to their own welfare. These calculations do produce a balancing of extremes, and this is a service to the general society. *In the third place*, the politician is generally a personal friend and benefactor of the people in his immediate district. He renders many services to them in a warmhearted manner and without antagonizing them. Even though his benefactions may come from the public treasury, he acts as a personal friend in the midst of a huge impersonal society. One writer has made the following general observation:

The political party in our society is an extralegal development but obviously a very indispensable one. This can be explained by the fact that constitutional provisions originally localized and split up power into units and fractions in such a way as to make government unworkable without it. The party supplies the important unity and dynamic which make government move past dead-center equilibrium and function in a positive manner.[38]

Among the services which the political machine renders and from which the politicians are most likely to derive their own direct financial gains, those which are rendered to persons who violate the law or who wish to prevent the enactment of laws injurious to them are very important. It is these services which are generally regarded as corruption. The first of these services, which is generally known as political corruption, is protection of law-violators. The political machine provides immunity for prostitution, gambling, and violation of liquor laws.[39] This, in fact, is so important

[38] Edwin M. Lemert, *Social Pathology* (New York: McGraw-Hill, 1951), p. 61. Reprinted by permission of the publishers.
[39] Cf. Virgil W. Peterson, "Chicago's Crime Problem," *Journal of Criminal Law and Criminology*, 35:3–15, May–June, 1944.

that the leaders in these vices are generally either themselves in positions of importance in the local political machine or else are the heaviest contributors to the party treasury in return for their immunity. Consequently an individual policeman is completely unable to take action regarding these violations of law; and furthermore, the chief of police is equally impotent, for he himself is under the control either directly or indirectly of the same machine. This immunity, moreover, is extended to the organized vices even when it becomes evident that this means protection of groups which are engaging in bank robberies, kidnapings, and other serious crimes, as was the case in many of the organized bootlegging groups during the period of national prohibition. Equally important is the immunity granted to many huge and respectable business concerns who violate the laws regarding fire hazards, safety devices, obstruction of sidewalks, and other dangers and inconveniences. Certainly a large part of the campaign contributions come from those who expect immunity in the violation of the law, and not all of the persons who expect immunity belong to the underworld.

Second, political machines receive support because of the protection they can furnish against injurious legislation. This protection is sometimes sought by organized vice and crime, but, generally, it is more useful to business and labor interests. Public utilities and liquor groups have been particularly active in this sphere. Many industries make huge contributions to political campaigns in order that they may have the good will of those who regulate the legislatures and may thus prevent the enactment of legislation that these industries regard as injurious. This is a form of bribery only slightly concealed.

A third form of corruption is through contracts for public works and the franchises which are granted to public utilities and other concerns. Every public contract is regarded as an opportunity for money-making by those who are engaged in it. Some politicians get rich by letting these contracts for buildings, parks, pavements, and purchase of coal. This, also, is a form of embezzlement, generally known as graft. It is a means of enriching the politicians either as individuals or as a machine. The extent to which persons in important political positions become wealthy after securing office is evidence of the extent of this collusion with private contractors to rob the public treasury.

A fourth form of political corruption is the patronage system. In some organizations each candidate for an elective office, including the governor of the state, is required to agree in advance that the appointive offices will be filled by the organization. A patronage secretary or a patronage committee may be publicly recognized as in charge of this function. The principal opposition to a state patronage system comes from the township and county politicians, who insist that patronage is the function of the local organization rather than of the state organization. It is important to the organization, whether national, state, or local, that it control the patronage, for it is through patronage that many of its services are rendered to individuals and groups. First, it may thus reward its members who have rendered services in elections; the result is that a large proportion of offices are filled by inferior persons whose principal loyalty is to the political machine and whose salaries frequently are an incidental part of their incomes. Second, through control of patronage the organization can control the activities of the officeholders. Third, as a specific form of the second value, the organization can thus grant immunity, in return for campaign contributions, to the agencies which violate the law or are in other ways injuring the community. One of the members of the patronage committee in Illinois some years ago was the president of one of the principal banks of the state and he had membership on that committee because the banks, utility companies, insurance companies, and similar concerns were interested in the selection of bank examiners, public utility commissioners, and other similar officers, who would be friendly and could be controlled. Patronage is the most obvious indication of the fact that the political organization is interested primarily in its own welfare, and only secondarily in the welfare of the state.

A fifth important method of insuring the control of the political machine is fraud in voting. In a recount of votes in Chicago in 1933, fraud was discovered in 29 percent of the ballot boxes and in some wards in every box. In Kansas City 275 election officials and other party workers were indicted for fraud in connection with the election of 1936. A 1948 congressional race in Kansas City culminated in the theft of ballots from the Jackson County courthouse.[40]

As a result of these influences which corrupt politics, the honest operation of the police and of the courts is limited. An honest official must make many compromises with the party machine if he is to get along at all, for the system has been operating for many decades and no person can change it very much. Corrupt politics probably has more significance in relation to the vices, organized crime, and white-collar crime than it does in relation to juvenile delinquency and the adult crimes for which persons are committed to prison. In any case, juvenile delinquency and adult violations of the criminal code seem related most intimately to the politics of the local community.

[40] Estes Kefauver, *Crime in America* (New York: Doubleday, 1951), p. 261.

THE INSTITUTION OF RELIGION.   Since the church has been instrumental in developing and maintaining a sacred morality among mankind, and since crime often involves violation of this standard of morality, it may rightfully be concluded that a close relationship exists between crime and the religious institution. From one point of view, criminality represents a failure on the part of the church to train members of society to behave morally, and from this it is easy to conclude that "lack of religious training" is the basic cause of crime. However, this conclusion merely emphasizes the fact that some persons do commit crime, and it does not really explain why they do so. To the extent that criminality and immorality are synonymous, the problem in criminology is to explain or account for the fact that some persons behave immorally and some do not, and it is not sufficient to state merely that the absence of morality is the cause of immorality. There is no specific evidence regarding the effect of religion, considered as something different from anti-criminal values, on crime. Certain external expressions of religion, however, are found to be slightly and inconsistently related to crime.

Church members are committed to prison slightly less often than are persons who are not members, but the relationship is not entirely consistent.[41] One study indicated that delinquents had more favorable attitudes toward religious issues than did non-delinquents.[42] A study of 915 girls attending classes in religious instruction revealed that the training "did not contribute to the subjects' ability to apply the principles of moral law to life situations."[43] Similarly, whether children attend Sunday School or not seems to bear only a slight relationship to delinquency. Kvaraceus found that 91 percent of 761 delinquent children were affiliated with some church and that 54 percent attended church regularly, that 20 percent attended occasionally, and that only 26 percent rarely visited a church.[44] Wattenberg found in Detroit that 69 percent of 2,137 male delinquents attended church regularly or occasionally; of the recidivists 65 percent attended regularly or occasionally, as compared to 71 percent of the non-recidivists.[45] The Gluecks discovered that 39 percent of the delinquents

[41] John R. Miner, "Church Membership and Commitment to Prisons," *Human Biology*, 3:429–436, September, 1931.

[42] Warren C. Middleton and Paul J. Fay, "Attitudes of Delinquent and Non-Delinquent Girls Toward Sunday Observance, the Bible, and War," *Journal of Educational Psychology*, 32:555–558, October, 1941.

[43] Carmen V. Diaz, *A Study of the Ability of Eleventh Grade Girls to Apply the Principles of Moral Law to Actual and Hypothetical Life Situations* (Unpublished Ph.D. Dissertation, Fordham University, 1952).

[44] William C. Kvaraceus, "Delinquent Behavior and Church Attendance," *Sociology and Social Research*, 28:284–289, March, 1944.

[45] William W. Wattenberg, "Church Attendance and Juvenile Misconduct," *Sociology and Social Research*, 34:195–202, January, 1950.

studied attended church regularly, 54 percent attended occasionally, and 7 percent never attended; among the non-delinquents in the control group, 67 percent attended regularly, 29 percent attended occasionally, and 4 percent never attended.[46] However, while a survey of 162 delinquent girls in a private institution indicated that 76 percent claimed church affiliation, only 2 percent attended church regularly.[47] These studies, of course, do not indicate the percentage of regular church attendants who commit delinquencies, and this percentage is a necessary prerequisite to a detailed analysis of the relationship between church attendance and delinquency.

Among adult offenders, one study of 45 prisons by two Catholic priests revealed that 87 percent of the prisoners indicated some religious affiliation, as compared with about 40 percent in the general population of the United States at the time.[48] This finding probably indicates more about the unreliability of prisoner's statements than it does about church membership—on the chance that parole board members will hear about it and react favorably inmates have been known to make false statements about church membership, to put in routine appearances at the prison chapel, to join the prison choir, to recite the Bible to guards, and to change their religious preference. Most of the Catholic prisoners interviewed by Kalmer and Weir, for example, were not considered true Catholics. Those prisoners who attended church regularly prior to the crimes of which they were convicted succeed on probation or parole more frequently than those whose attendance has not been regular. Compulsory church attendance, however, has produced negativistic reactions as a rule,[49] so that it presumably is not church attendance as such but the group relationship of those who attend church which are influential in this respect.

A similar observation may be made regarding the denominational or religious affiliations of criminals. In America the Baptists and the Catholics have the highest rate of commitment to those prisons which report religious affiliations. However, a survey showed that two-thirds of the membership in the Roman Catholic and Baptist churches comes from the lower class.[50] Both in the United States and in Europe, Jews have low crime

[46] Sheldon and Eleanor Glueck, *Unraveling Juvenile Delinquency* (New York: The Commonwealth Fund, 1950), p. 166.

[47] M. Dominic, "Religion and the Juvenile Delinquent," *American Catholic Sociological Review*, 15:256–264, October, 1954.

[48] Leo Kalmer and Eligius Weir, *Crime and Religion* (Chicago: Franciscan Herald Press, 1936), p. 19.

[49] John L. Ernst, "An Analysis of the Religious and Ethical Habits of a Group of Convicts," *University of Pittsburgh Bulletin*, 27:47–53, November 15, 1930. See also Richard V. McCann, "The Self-Image and Delinquency," *Federal Probation*, 20:14–23, September, 1956.

[50] Philip M. Smith, "Organized Religion and Criminal Behavior," *Sociology and Social Research*, 33:362–367, May, 1949.

rates, and this condition has attributed to the close family and community ties among members of this group.[51] Similarly, an intensive analysis of the differences in crime rates of the several denominations in Hungary resulted in the conclusions that these differences were due not to the differences in the creeds but to the differences in the economic, educational, and family status of the members, to the differences in places of residence, and to the differences in age and sex.[52] A census taken in the penal institutions of the Netherlands in 1955 showed that Protestants and Catholics were slightly overrepresented, as compared with the general population of the Netherlands, while "other denominations" were slightly underrepresented.[53]

THE EDUCATIONAL INSTITUTION. Since the school has been assigned a major role in training children for adult life, crime and delinquency often are attributed to "poor education" or "failure of the schools," just as they have been attributed to "bad homes" and "poor family training." Schools do not have the specific function of preventing delinquency, but they, like the family, are now expected to inculcate juveniles with certain values of a law-abiding society and are expected to provide interesting activities for the child. Probably delinquency and crime are related to the school in much the same way they are related to family conditions, namely through the effects which school activities have on the students' associations with delinquent and anti-delinquent behavior patterns.[54]

On the basis of very inadequate and unreliable statistics, which do not include white-collar crimes, it appears that crime decreases with the amount of formal education. In 1931 MacCormick estimated that about 17 percent of all prisoners could not read a newspaper or write a letter,[55] and in 1951 it was estimated that "from 10 to 30 percent of the admissions

---

[51] N. Goldberg, "Jews in the Police Records of Los Angeles, 1933–1947," *Yivo Annual of Jewish Social Science*, 5:266–291, 1950; A. J. Jaffe and Saul D. Alinsky, "A Comparison of Jewish and Non-Jewish Convicts," *Jewish Social Studies*, 1:359–366, 1939; Liebman Hersh, "Delinquency among Jews," *Journal of Criminal Law and Criminology*, 27:515–538, 857–873, November–December, 1936, and April–May, 1937. This study refers to Poland.

[52] Ervin Hacker, *Der Einfluss der Konfession auf die Kriminalität in Ungarn* (Miskolc: Jun, Ludvig, Janovits, 1930).

[53] W. H. Nagel, "Criminality and Religion," *Tidschrift voor Strafrecht*, 69:263–291, 1960.

[54] Cf. Albert K. Cohen, "The Schools and Juvenile Delinquency," in Subcommittee to Investigate Juvenile Delinquency, *Education and Juvenile Delinquency, Interim Report, 84th Congress* (Washington: Government Printing Office, 1956), pp. 50–60; Albert J. Reiss, Jr., "Juvenile Delinquency and the Schools," *Ibid.*, pp. 63–68; and I. J. Croft and T. G. Gryier, "Social Relationships of Truants and Juvenile Delinquents," *Human Relations*, 9:436–466, No. 4, 1956.

[55] Austin H. MacCormick, "Education in the Prisons of Tomorrow," *Annals of the American Academy of Political and Social Science*, 157:72–73, September, 1931.

to correctional institutions throughout the country are illiterate."[56] Of 4,000 inmates over age 17 admitted to the Texas prison system, 5 percent had not completed the first grade, 44 percent had not completed the eighth grade, 89 percent had not completed high school, and 99+ percent had not completed college; the comparable percentages for prisoners admitted to the New Jersey State Prison in 1955 were 3.6, 41, 91, and 99+.[57] Kvaraceus reported that all Passaic, New Jersey, delinquents studied had repeated one or more grades and that most of them did not go beyond junior high school.[58] It is probable that this level of educational achievement of criminals and delinquents is lower than the level among non-offenders, but comparable data for the general population or for control groups are needed.

In 1940, 3.9 percent of the male population over twenty-five years of age had not completed the first grade of school, 35.3 percent had completed only the seventh or eighth grade, 12 percent had completed only the twelfth grade, and 5.4 percent had completed college. Among all males over twenty-five years of age in prisons and reformatories in 1940, 7.5 percent had not completed the first grade, 22.9 percent had completed only the seventh or eighth grade, 5.6 percent had completed high school only, and .9 percent had graduated from college. The median grade of school completed was 8.3 for the civilians and 7.4 for the prisoners.[59] Per 100,000 population twenty-five years of age and over of the same educational status, the number of prisoners with no schooling was approximately 700, of persons who finished only the seventh or eighth grade was 300, of persons who finished high school 170, and of those who finished college 60. Thus in proportion to their numbers about four times as many persons with no schooling as persons who had completed high school, and about twelve times as many persons with no schooling as college graduates, were in prison. Among the males who were born in Norway in 1933 and who had become offenders by January 1, 1958, 32 percent had some education beyond elementary school, as compared to 52 percent of the non-offenders who were born in 1933. Two percent of the offenders and 10 percent of the non-offenders had four or more years of education beyond elementary

---

[56] Price Chenault, "Education," in Paul W. Tappan, Editor, *Contemporary Correction* (New York: McGraw-Hill, 1951), pp. 224–237.

[57] Subcommittee to Investigate Juvenile Delinquency, *op. cit.*, pp. 106, 110. See also Albert D. Ullman, Harold W. Demone, Jr., A. Warren Stearns, and Norman F. Washburne, "Some Social Characteristics of Misdemeanants," *Journal of Criminal Law and Criminology*, 48:44–53, May–June, 1957.

[58] William C. Kvaraceus, *Juvenile Delinquency and the School* (Yonkers: World Book Company, 1945). See also R. W. Edmiston and E. H. Swaim, "Juvenile Delinquency and Provisions for Education," *School and Society*, 55:195, February, 1942.

[59] Joseph D. Lohman, Lloyd E. Ohlin, and Dietrich C. Reitzes, *Description of Convicted Felons as a Manpower Resource in a National Emergency* (Springfield: Illinois Division of Correction [mimeographed, n.d.]), p. 24.

school.[60] A large proportion of delinquents are failures in school, and they are retarded in reading, writing, and arithmetic.[61] A low level of education has also been observed among a group of delinquents which was compared with a control group. Five years after a group of delinquents and a group of controls were first observed by Merrill, 70 percent of the delinquents and 31 percent of the controls were no longer in school. Of the delinquents who had left school, 29 percent left after completing only the eighth grade and 77 percent left before finishing high school; the comparable percentages for the control group were 6 and 39.[62]

These differences do not prove that formal education, in itself, deters from crime, for the formal educational level may merely reflect the economic status, home conditions, and several other conditions which affect the probabilities for contacts with delinquent and criminal behavior patterns. Like the home, the school may be located in a delinquency area, may affect the prestige values of various types of persons the child later will encounter, may fail to present anti-delinquency behavior patterns, or may provide pleasant or unpleasant experiences which affect the child's associations with delinquency behavior patterns. Perhaps the school's influence on delinquency rates has been largely through the last process. The fact that truancy and delinquency are closely correlated by area, and the fact that truancy so frequently precedes delinquencies involving theft is evidence of this. Among some groups of juveniles appearing before juvenile courts, as many as 60 percent have truanted habitually.[63] Of 2,021 prisoners investigated in one study, 40 percent had first been committed to an institution because of truancy.[64] Frum found that 23 percent of 148 cases of adult recidivism started with juvenile truancy or incorrigibility,[65] and another author estimates that 61 percent of the delinquents aged 8–17 are not in school.[66] The fact that some children dislike school and play truant is undoubtedly related to family conditions and to other conditions out-

[60] Nils Christie, Unge Norske Lovovertredere (Young Norwegian Law-Breakers) (Oslo: Universitetsforlaget, 1960), pp. 144–147.

[61] Bruce Balow, "Delinquency and School Failure," Federal Probation, 25:15–17, June, 1961; George C. Brook, "High School Drop-Outs and Corrective Measures," Federal Probation, 23:30–35, September, 1959.

[62] Maud A. Merrill, Problems of Child Delinquency (New York: Houghton Mifflin, 1947), pp. 101–105.

[63] A. C. Johnson, Jr., "Our Schools Make Criminals," Journal of Criminal Law and Criminology, 33:310–315, November–December, 1942.

[64] Justice and the Child in New Jersey, Report of the New Jersey Juvenile Delinquency Commission, 1939, p. 110, cited by John R. Ellingston, Protecting Our Children From Criminal Careers (New York: Prentice-Hall, 1948), p. 277.

[65] Harold S. Frum, "Adult Criminal Offense Trends Following Juvenile Delinquency," Journal of Criminal Law and Criminology, 49:29–49, May–June, 1958.

[66] Samuel M. Brownell, "Delinquency, an Important Problem in Education," School Life, 36:52–53, January, 1954.

side the school as well as to the school program itself.[67] A study of 21,720 boys and girls in grades seven through twelve in the schools of Nashville indicated that delinquents and truants are more likely to want to quit school and accept the conforming goal of getting a job than they are to want to quit school because they regard the norm of compulsory school attendance as coercive.[68] This suggests that "rebellion" represented by truancy might be ameliorated for some truants and delinquents by an opportunity to undertake a productive role in the labor force. However, the nature of the activities provided by the school probably greatly affects the truancy rate, and truancy, except that it is itself frequently defined as delinquency, probably is important to delinquency largely to the degree that it increases the probabilities of contacts with delinquency behavior patterns. One study of 42 cities indicated that in general the greater the number of days that the schools are in session each year the lower the delinquency rates.[69]

In reference to adults, the schools have been criticized severely by certain persons because the difference in criminality between the educated and uneducated is not greater than it is. This criticism usually is based on the observation that the school fails to present its charges with anti-criminal behavior patterns and, instead, remains rather neutral in respect to criminality, concentrating on dissemination of academic and technical skills.[70] Eighty-nine percent of 202 school superintendents stated that primary and elementary teachers should have additional training in recognizing and understanding signs of maladjustment.[71] Ordinarily, the criticism is stated in terms of the school's failure to supply the nation's youth with moral and democratic ideals.[72] The failure to present sufficient anti-criminal attitudes and ideals is related to the kinds of functions which have been assigned the school by society. It is only in rather recent years that schools have been expected to take over many of the socializing functions formerly assigned to the family and other primary groups.[73] More-

[67] Cf. P. Kamerdze, *A Study of the Major Sociological Aspects of Truancy Within Selected Census Tracts of Washington, D.C.* (Washington: Catholic University of American Press, 1955), pp. 3–6, 16–17.

[68] Albert J. Reiss, Jr. and Albert Louis Rhodes, "Are Educational Norms and Goals of Conforming, Truant and Delinquent Adolescents Influenced by Group Position in American Society?" *Journal of Negro Education*, 28:252–267, Summer, 1959.

[69] Edmiston and Swaim, *op. cit.*

[70] See Harry E. Barnes and Negley K. Teeters, *New Horizons in Criminology,* Third Edition (New York: Prentice-Hall, 1959), pp. 607–608.

[71] Commonwealth of Massachusetts, *Special Report of the Division of Youth Service,* House Document No. 3025 (Boston: Legislative Printers, 1957), p. 33.

[72] See, for example, Mabel A. Elliott, "Can Your Community Control Delinquency?" *National Parent-Teacher,* 38:4–6, December, 1943.

[73] See the discussion by Frank J. O'Brien, "The Role of Social Services in Education," *National Probation and Parole Association Yearbook,* 1944, pp. 120–133.

over, urban areas, which have the best educational facilities, have higher crime rates than rural areas.[74]

WAR. Many persons have asserted that crimes increase during war and postwar periods. This assertion has a certain amount of truth, but it over-simplifies the situation. The following propositions are a more adequate statement of the facts.

First, the official statistics on juvenile delinquency show a general trend toward an increase in wartime.[75] This is shown in Figure I. The trend, however, is a statistical artifact: rates go down in many communities, while going up in a larger number of communities. Furthermore, the statistics of arrests and convictions of juveniles are not a certain meas-ure of the delinquent behavior of juveniles. Arrests and convictions of juveniles are not only an indication of delinquent behavior of juveniles, but are also an indication of reactions of officials and other adults toward that delinquent behavior. In Liverpool, England, the number of convic-tions of juveniles increased during the First World War, but the number of unofficial actions in the form of warnings decreased by approximately an equal amount. Since army officials and community officials in the vicin-ity of army camps were vigorous in their attacks on sex offenses during the Second World War, it is possible that a large part of the increase in arrests for sex offenses by girls may reflect that change in policy rather than an increase in sex delinquency.

Several explanations of the increase in juvenile delinquency in wartime have been suggested. One is that the increase is due to an increase in a "contagion of violence." Children in wartime develop an admiration for the soldier. They play war games and in other ways take over the patterns of warfare into their own lives. If this theory were correct, it would be expected that assaults and similar crimes of violence would show the great-est increases, but they do not. A second explanation, popular between the wars, was that the increase in delinquency is due to an increase in economic hardships due to blockades, rationing systems, and reduced earnings. The inadequacy of this explanation is seen in the United States, where during World War II delinquency increased in the midst of unusual prosperity. A third explanation is that the increase in juvenile delinquency is due to emotional strain in wartime. The inadequacy of this explanation is seen in the fact that some kinds of delinquency increase and some kinds decrease,

[74] See Terrence Morris, op. cit., pp. 49–50.
[75] See Edward R. Schwartz, "Statistics of Juvenile Delinquency in the United States," Annals of the American Academy of Political and Social Science, 261:9–13, January, 1949; Martin H. Neumeyer, "Delinquency Trends in Wartime," Sociology and Social Research, 29:262–275, March, 1945; Walter C. Reckless, "The Impact of War on Crime, Delinquency and Prostitution," American Journal of Sociology, 48:378–386, November, 1942.

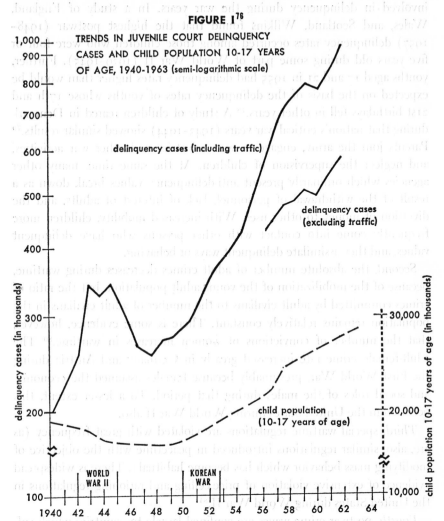

FIGURE 1[76]

TRENDS IN JUVENILE COURT DELINQUENCY
CASES AND CHILD POPULATION 10-17 YEARS
OF AGE, 1940-1963 (semi-logarithmic scale)

delinquency cases (including traffic)

delinquency cases
(excluding traffic)

delinquency cases (in thousands)

child population 10-17 years of age (in thousands)

child population
(10-17 years of age)

WORLD
WAR II

KOREAN
WAR

[76] U.S. Department of Health, Education and Welfare, *Juvenile Court Statistics,*
1963 (Washington: Children's Bureau Statistical Series, No. 79, 1964), p. 14. Also
see Table V, p. 38 above.

and in the fact that the variations in delinquency rates are not uniform. It
is difficult to understand why emotional strain should produce an increase
in one kind of delinquency and a decrease in another kind. A fourth explanation, which seems to best fit the facts, is that juvenile delinquency increases in wartime as a result in changes in the family and other local community institutions.[77] It has been determined, moreover, that these changes
also affect the postwar delinquency rates of children too young to get very

[77] See E. Abbott, "Juvenile Delinquency During the First World War: Notes on the
British Experience, 1914–1918," *Social Service Review,* 17:192–212, June, 1943.

involved in delinquency during the war years. In a study of England, Wales, and Scotland, Wilkins found that the highest postwar (1948–1957) delinquency rates occurred among those children who were four or five years old during some part of World War II (1939–1945). Further, youths aged 17 and 21 in 1955 had delinquency rates higher than would be expected on the basis of the delinquency rates of youths whose 17th and 21st birthdays fell in other years.[78] A study of children reared in Denmark during that nation's critical war years (1943–1944) showed similar results.[79] Parents join the army, engage in war industries and other war activities, and neglect the supervision of children. At the same time, many other agencies which ordinarily present anti-delinquency values break down as a result of the withdrawal of personnel, lack of interest of adults, and the diversion of money to other uses. With increased mobility, children more frequently come into contact with other persons who have delinquent values, and they assimilate delinquent ways of behaving.

*Second*, the absolute number of adult crimes decreases during wartime, because of the mobilization of the young-adult population, but the ratio of crimes committed by adult civilians to the number of adult civilians in the population remains relatively constant. There is some evidence, however, that the number of convictions of women increases in wartime.[80] The adult-female crime rate increased greatly in Germany and Austria during the First World War, presumably because females assumed the economic and social roles of the males during that period. To a lesser extent, this occurred in the United States during World War II also.

*Third*, special wartime regulations are violated with great frequency (as are, also, similar regulations introduced in peacetime with the objective of modifying mass behavior which has become habitual). There is widespread evidence of extensive violation of price-ceiling and rationing regulations in the United States during World War II.[81]

*Fourth*, postwar crime waves are confined largely to countries which suffer rather complete disintegration of their economic, political, and social systems as a result of the war. Earlier studies have shown that serious crimes increased significantly in France after the Revolution of 1884, in the

[78] Leslie T. Wilkins, *Delinquent Generations* (London: Home Office Studies in the Causes of Delinquency and the Treatment of Offenders, Report No. 3, 1961), pp. 3, 7–9.

[79] Karl O. Christiansen, "Delinquent Generations in Denmark," *British Journal of Criminology*, 3:259–264, January, 1964.

[80] Edwin H. Sutherland, "Crime," in William F. Ogburn, Editor, *American Society in Wartime* (Chicago: University of Chicago Press, 1943), pp. 185–206.

[81] Frank E. Hartung, "White-Collar Offenses in the Wholesale Meat Industry in Detroit," *American Journal of Sociology*, 56:25–35, July, 1950; Clinard, *The Black Market, op. cit.*, pp. 28–50, 115–204.

United States after the Civil War,[82] in Germany and Austria after the War of 1866, in Germany and France after the Franco-Prussian War of 1870–71, and in Germany and Austria after the First World War.[83] But in nations which did not experience a great disintegration of social institutions, such as England after World War I and the United States after World War II, the crime rates seem to remain rather constant in prewar, war, and postwar periods. This seems to be adequate rebuttal of the argument that young men who have engaged in physical violence during wars will continue similar activities when they return to civilian life. Furthermore, after World War I it was observed that when former servicemen were committed to prison they were most likely, in comparison with those who had not seen war service, to be committed for fraud, embezzlement, and nonsupport, and least likely to be imprisoned for homicide, burglary, assault, and rape. After World War II this same tendency was found. James V. Bennett, Director of the United States Bureau of Prisons, reported that the offenses most commonly committed by veterans committed to federal prisons were embezzlement, fraud, and forgery, while "robbery and homicide, the violent crimes for which one might expect a high proportion of veterans, were well down the list."[84] Bennett indicated further that the imprisonment rate for veterans in all age groups from 25 to 54 was lower than the rate for non-veterans; the 20–24 age category, however, had a larger proportion of veterans among the prisoners than were in the general population. He explains these variations in terms of the selective processes of the Armed Forces.

PUBLIC AGENCIES OF COMMUNICATION. A Gallup Poll conducted in 1954 indicated that about 70 percent of a nation-wide sample placed some of "the blame" for teen-age crime on comic books; an identical percentage placed some of "the blame" on crime and mystery programs on television and radio.[85] Little support for this accusation can be found in the statistical data of delinquency and crime rates. People all over the United States read the same comics, see the same movies and television shows, and listen

[82] Edith Abbott, "The Civil War and the Crime Wave of 1860–1870," *Social Service Review*, 1:212–234, June, 1927.

[83] Franz Exner, *Krieg und Kriminalität in Oesterreich* (Vienna: Hölder-Pichler-Tempsky, 1927); Moritz Liepman, *Krieg und Kriminalität in Deutschland* (Stuttgart: Deutsche Verlagsanstalt, 1930).

[84] James V. Bennett, "The Ex-GI in Federal Prisons," *Proceedings of the American Correctional Association*, 1953, pp. 131–136; and "The Criminality of Veterans," *Federal Probation*, 28:40–42, June, 1954. See also John C. Spencer, *Crime and the Services* (London: Routledge and Kegan Paul, 1954); and Harry Willbach, "Recent Crimes and the Veterans," *Journal of Criminal Law and Criminology*, 38:501–508, January–February, 1948.

[85] *Los Angeles Times*, November 22, 1954.

to the same crime broadcasts, but they differ among themselves greatly in regard to criminality. Even when the communicator deliberately intends to modify people's attitudes, which is certainly not the case among the personnel of the communication agencies which are said to contribute to crime, there is a great deal of variation in the response. Berelson has said that "effects upon the audience do not follow directly from and in correspondence with the intent of the communicator and the content of the communication. The predispositions of the reader or listener are deeply involved in the situation, and may operate to block or modify the intended effect or even to set up a boomerang effect."[86] This is the same thing as saying that only "some kinds of communication on some kinds of issues, brought to the attention of some kinds of people under some kinds of conditions, have some kinds of effects."[87] The relationship of the various media of mass communication of crime and delinquency is discussed below.

*Newspapers and crime.* American newspapers have been generally and severely criticized for the part they play in relation to crime. The following charges are made against them. *First,* they promote crime by the constant advertising of crime, by glorifying the criminal leaders and acting as press agents for them, and by a jocular method of presenting crime news which takes away the dignity of the police and court proceedings. *Second,* they interfere with justice by "trial by newspaper," by distortion of news, and by providing advance information to the public, including the criminals, regarding the plans of the police and prosecutors. *Third,* they produce a public panic in regard to crime which makes consistent and sober judicial and preventive procedures difficult.

The desirability of publishing crime news is not here in question. Rather it is the amount and style of the crime news. The English newspapers publish crime news in the form of brief factual statements. The American crime news is presented vividly and sometimes not distastefully to the reader.[88] Because nothing is said about the millions of persons who lead a consistently law-abiding life, the impression is created that crime is the customary mode of life. Conceivably, this publicity given to crime creates and perpetuates an attitude of indifference to ordinary criminal offenses among persons who are not the direct victims of them. On the other hand, the publicity given to certain sensational crimes does rouse the public to

[86] B. Berelson, "Communications and Public Opinion," in W. Schramm, Editor, *Communications in Modern Society* (Urbana: University of Illinois Press, 1948), pp. 168–185.

[87] *Ibid.* Reprinted by permission of the publisher.

[88] See Paul S. Deland, "Crime News Encourages Delinquency and Crime," *Federal Probation*, 11:3–6, April, 1947.

action, and this action could culminate in the creation of strong anti-criminal influences in the community. Usually, however, the public action merely consists of requesting the legislatures to increase the severity of punishments for the type of crime in question, after which the whole thing is forgotten.[89] Newspapers could play, and sometimes do play, an important role in mobilizing the public to a more significant kind of anti-criminal organization.

Moreover, the effect of the constant presentation of crime news to the public certainly cannot be demonstrated in specific criminal cases. Occa-sionally, a criminal states that he got the idea for a crime from a news-paper account of the activities of another criminal. But the publicity given to the activities of that other criminal may also on occasion prove to some persons that it would be foolhardy to attempt repetition of such activities. Most "crime waves" are fabrications of the press: a sensational crime is committed and given wide publicity in one community, that type of crime becomes "news," editors begin publicizing hitherto unnoticed crimes of the same type in other parts of the country, and newspaper readers get the impression that the influence of the criminal whose offense was first pub-licized is spreading throughout the country. Criminals read the crime news and may be quick to attribute their own criminality to some case currently in the headlines.[90]

Newspapers do on occasion glorify specific criminals and, consequently, increase their prestige among other criminals and among certain boys resid-ing in delinquency areas. Newspaper publicity, like commitment to a prison for adults, contributes immensely to one's status in some delinquent groups. Further, newspaper accounts contribute considerably to the self-esteem of professional criminals, who generally are among the most en-thusiastic readers of the newspapers. When a newspaper carries the story that a certain criminal is the worst, or the best, or the most dangerous, or some other superlative appellation, it is one of the few consolations this criminal will have, in case of conviction, while he is in prison. However, this glorification probably has little or no effect on persons whose attitudes have been previously determined by membership in intimate, personal groups which are anti-criminal.

Newspapers sometimes carry advance information to criminals regard-ing the plans of the police and the prosecutors. During 1933, one of the Chicago newspapers contained an announcement with big headlines

[89] See Edwin H. Sutherland, "The Diffusion of Sexual Psychopath Laws," *American Journal of Sociology*, 56:142–148, September, 1950.

[90] Joseph L. Holmes, "Crime and the Press," *Journal of Criminal Law and Crimi-nology*, 20:258, July–August, 1929.

that twenty police squads were watching two buildings, the addresses of which were printed in the article, because of information that a notorious criminal who was being hunted used these places as hangouts. The announcement would certainly destroy completely the efficiency of the police work. Such items appear frequently. Though they are sometimes a camouflage of the real plans of the police, they are frequently secured from subordinates by bargains, bribery, or threats. One of the ransom notes in a kidnaping case threatened the death of the child if information were given to police or newspapers. A reporter for a New York City paper secured verification of the kidnaping story by representing himself over the telephone to be an agent of the kidnapers, and his paper printed the story. The dead body of the child was found later. Federal agents have threatened reporters with arrest for obstructing justice in kidnaping cases because the reporters persisted in interfering with the investigations. As justification for their activities newspaper personnel frequently point to our tradition of "freedom of the press," and also insist that police corruption is minimized when publicity is given to the police activities.

Also, newspapers sometimes interfere with the course of justice by what has been called "trial by newspaper." Prior to the trial, the reporters present such evidence as they have, which is likely to be partisan information, again and again, until the public accepts the implied verdict of the newspaper and thereafter cannot easily be shaken in its opinion. The newspaper's sources of information are almost always the office of the prosecuting attorney or the police; the defendant's version of the case is ignored until the time of the trial itself. A fair trial under such circumstances becomes almost impossible, especially in communities where the judges are elected and where they are afraid of arousing public antagonism. It is quite certain that under such circumstances many innocent persons are convicted and that many persons who are punished severely would otherwise be given light penalties. The number of cases which attract this detailed and continued attention is probably not large. Any case may be selected for this presentation because some detail is sufficiently striking to make a good story. A man was killed in a drunken brawl; the murderer had previously had a good reputation but was not prominent in any way. The case would probably have passed with the customary procedure as a manslaughter case with imprisonment for, perhaps, three years except that a reporter happened to learn that the murderer had the nickname "Banjo Ben." That trivial point made a good story of it. It was written up at length and repeated frequently. Consequently this offered an opportunity for the prosecutor to build up publicity for the next election. The offender was convicted of murder and sentenced to prison for 199 years.

Crime news sometimes throws the public into a panic. Newspapers learned during the flu epidemic in 1917 that it was dangerous to publish colorful stories about an epidemic of disease and they customarily kept such information entirely out of their columns, especially when a convention or fair is imminent or in progress. Similarly, newspapers sometimes refuse to publish information regarding the poor financial condition of a bank for fear that a panic which might produce public injury will ensue. The newspapers in England deal with crime news as they do with sickness and financial dangers, that is, quietly and factually. The American newspapers on the other hand, have not realized the dangers of panics of this nature and continue to make the crime stories as colorful as possible. The public gets outmoded notions of "inborn criminality," distorted notions about the nature and success of probation and parole, and sensational, "tough" punitive policies rather than a constructive approach to problems of crime causation, law enforcement, and crime control.[91] Taft and England have observed that reporters have a tendency to find trivial motives for crime because the more shockingly trivial the alleged motive, the more newsworthy it becomes, especially when heinous offenses are involved— "I wanted to see what it was like to kill someone," "I stabbed Pa because he was always criticizing me," "We set fire to the school because the gym teacher bawled us out."[92] Newspapers are concerned with arousing emotions rather than giving the reader an understanding of the crime situation because they are business concerns, operated for the purpose of profits. Their primary interest is circulation, and public welfare is secondary.

Perhaps the major effect of crime dramatization and publicity is the creation and perpetuation of an attitude of indifference to ordinary criminal offenses among persons who are not the direct victims of them. Because little is said about the millions of consistently law-abiding citizens, the impression is created that crime is frequent and usual, and the reading public becomes indifferent even to the sensational, violent crimes, and even less concerned with ordinary offenses such as burglary and larceny. Thus, dramatization of crime appears to minimize public indignation when crimes are committed and, perhaps, to contribute indirectly to high crime rates. A population for whom crime has become usual cannot present a consistent front against crime. On the other hand, it has not been demon-

[91] See F. Perry Olds, "The Place of the Press in Crime Control," *National Probation and Parole Association Yearbook*, 1947, pp. 245–259; Bruce Smith, "Enforcement of the Criminal Law," *Annals of the American Academy of Political and Social Science*, 217:12–18, September, 1941.

[92] Donald R. Taft and Ralph W. England, Jr., *Criminology*, Fourth Edition (New York: Macmillan, 1964), p. 211. See also Britt-Mari Persson Blegvad, "Newspapers and Rock and Roll Riots in Copenhagen," *Acta Sociologica* (Copenhagen), 7:151–178, 1964.

strated that exposure through newspapers to the constant dramatization of crime is effective in changing individuals from non-criminal to criminal.[93]

The comics. Judicial, psychological, sociological, and literary "experts" are in almost complete disagreement regarding the effect of the "comics" on delinquency, just as a few generations ago they were in disagreement as to the effects of "dime novels" and "pulp magazines." The erotic and "blood-and-thunder" literature in these magazines has been severely denounced because of the continued direction of attention to sex and brutality and the continued presence of sex imagery. A noted psychiatrist who is an ardent opponent of the comics has listed the following objections:

They often suggest criminal or sexually abnormal ideas; create a mental preparedness or readiness for temptation; suggest the forms a delinquent impulse may take; may act as the precipitating factor of delinquency or emotional disorder; may supply rationalization for a contemplated act which is often more important than the impulse itself; set off chains of undesirable and harmful thinking in children; and create for young readers a mental atmosphere of deceit, trickery, and cruelty.[94]

Another author, however, has asserted that "no one has conclusively demonstrated that comic books are detrimental in any way."[95]

One study compared 235 delinquents and a comparable group of non-delinquents matched in general for age, sex, school level, and socio-economic status. The delinquents were found to read the "harmful" and "questionable" books more often than did the non-delinquents, although there was little difference as to reading "harmless" comics.[96] In another study, 972 high school students were asked to report on their delinquencies, on the extent to which they read crime and horror comics, and on the extent to which they associated with delinquents. A correlation of +.19 between reading comics and delinquency was found for girls. How-

[93] See Stafford Derby, "Crime News Writing and Its Role as a Crime Stimulant," National Probation and Parole Association Journal, 4:320–327, October, 1958.

[94] Marjorie Bell, "The NPPA at the Congress of Correction," Focus, 27:175–179, November, 1948, summarizing the remarks made by Fredric Wertham. Reprinted by permission of the publisher. See also Fredric Wertham, "The Comics . . . Very Funny," Saturday Review of Literature, May 29, 1948, pp. 6–7; Judith Crist, "Horror in the Nursery," Collier's, March 27, 1948, pp. 22 ff.; Fredric Wertham, "What Parents Don't Know About Comic Books," Ladies Home Journal, November, 1953, pp. 48 ff.; Fredric Wertham, Seduction of the Innocent (New York: Rinehart, 1954); and Fredric Wertham, "It's Still Murder—What Parents Don't Know About Comic Books," The Saturday Review, April 9, 1955, pp. 11 ff.

[95] John R. Cavanagh, "The Comics War," Journal of Criminal Law and Criminology, 40:28–35, May, 1949.

[96] Thomas Ford Hoult, "Comic Books and Juvenile Delinquency," Sociology and Social Research, 33:279–284, March, 1949.

ever, this relationship was attributable to the group of girls who reported association with delinquents (+.25); for the group of girls not reporting such associations, the correlation was not significant (+.11). For boys, there was no significant correlation between reading comics and delinquency in either the group reporting associations with delinquents (+.12) or the group reporting no such association (.04). There was a positive correlation between delinquency and association with delinquents for both girls (+.29) and boys (+.40).[97] Comic books are a relatively ineffective medium for presenting behavior patterns, as compared to the effectiveness of intimate, personal groups.

In individual cases, tendencies toward delinquency which have been derived from other sources may be re-enforced by the crime stories in comic books, and in some cases specific techniques of delinquency are thus learned. But whether a behavior pattern is followed and whether a specific criminal technique is used will depend upon the child's prior associations with delinquent and anti-delinquent behavior patterns in his primary groups.

*Movies, television, and radio.* Criticism of comic books as contributors to delinquency has waned since the arrival of television, which now is faced with almost the same charges once hurled at comic books and, before that, at movies and radio. Similarly, arguments used to answer the charges made against radio are now being used to answer the charges against television. Movies, television, and radio unquestionably glamorize life and stimulate desires for a life of luxury. Movies and television probably are most effective in this regard, because of the vivid visual imagery, together with the decisiveness and unambiguity of the films or programs. Hollywood stories are more likely to be accepted as correct and authoritative than radio stories. They provide people with temporary philosophies of life, with ideas of their rights and privileges, with fashions in dress, language, etiquette, and child-rearing. They also teach children the words of popular songs, techniques of love-making, and certain criminal techniques. Children impersonate actors in their play, and both children and adults imitate them in their everyday language and conduct. However, what persons perceive when they watch movies or listen to the radio varies with socio-economic, ethnic, religious, and cultural background.[98] Also,

---

[97] Edwin H. Pfuhl, Jr., "The Relationship of Crime and Horror Comics to Juvenile Delinquency," *Research Studies of the State College of Washington*, 24:170–177, June, 1956.

[98] Theodore M. Newcomb, *Social Psychology* (New York: Dryden: 1950), pp. 90–96. See also Eunice Cooper and Helen Dinerman, "Analysis of the Film 'Don't Be a Sucker': A Study in Communication," *Public Opinion Quarterly*, 15:243–264, 1951.

many children play as gangsters or robbers after seeing a gangster or crime show, but they also play as gangsters or robbers after seeing a love-story or musical. And many adolescents make love after seeing gangster movies as well as after seeing pictures of romantic love-making. The techniques of crime which are presented are used by only a very few children, just as the criminal techniques known to the police are used by very few policemen.

In the most careful study on the subject of movies and delinquency made to date, the authors summarize their findings as follows:

It seems clear that the motion pictures were a factor of importance in the delinquent or criminal careers of about 10 percent of the male and 25 percent of the female offenders studied. . . . Several important indirect influences disposing or leading persons to delinquency or crime are discernible in the experiences of male offenders. Through the display of crime techniques and criminal patterns of behavior; by arousing desires for easy money and luxury, and by suggesting questionable methods for their achievement; by inducing a spirit of bravado, toughness, and adventurousness; by arousing intense sexual desires; by invoking daydreaming of criminal roles, motion pictures may create attitudes and furnish techniques conducive, quite unwittingly, to delinquent or criminal behavior. One may detect in the case of delinquent girls and young women influences similar to those spoken of in the case of young men. Motion pictures may play a major or minor role in female delinquency and crime by arousing sexual passion, by instilling the desire to live a gay, wild, fast life, by evoking longings for luxury and smart appearance, and by suggesting to some girls questionable methods of easily attaining them; by the display of modes of beautification and love techniques; by the depiction of various forms of crime readily imitated by girls and young women; and by competing with home and school for an important place in the life of the girls.[99]

This conclusion does not deny certain beneficial influences that movies have, does not deny that other social influences are significant in determining sensitivity to criminal and sexual patterns presented by the pictures, and does not show the process by which the movies may play a role in delinquency. An aroused desire for easy money and luxury, or a spirit of bravado and adventurousness, for example, could lead to increased activity in a legitimate economic enterprise as well as to delinquency. Which course is taken probably is most dependent upon the person's personal

[99] Herbert Blumer and Philip M. Hauser, *Movies, Delinquency and Crime* (New York: Macmillan, 1933), pp. 198–199. Reprinted by permission of the publishers. For a critique of this study, see Mortimer J. Adler, *Art and Prudence* (New York: Longmans, Green, 1937).

contacts and associations.[100] In fact, the general tendency seems to be that children who reside in areas where delinquency rates are high are influenced more significantly by crime and sex movies and radio crime dramas than are those who live in areas of low-delinquency rates.[101] This, in general, is what would be expected on the basis of the differential association theory.

CONCLUSIONS. The general argument of this chapter has been that the causes of crime lie primarily in the area of personal interaction, and that personal interaction is confined almost entirely to local communities and neighborhoods. Negatively, criminal behavior is not affected directly or significantly by variations in the form of the general social institutions— economics, government, religion, and education—or by the media of mass communication. This negative proposition does not deny that the general institutions and mass media have some significance for crime, and certain exceptions and qualifications should be noted. *First*, the crime rate does increase when the general institutions are suddenly disrupted, as in the Central European nations after the First World War. *Second*, the efficiency of the police system and of the entire system of criminal justice does have an effect on the crime rate. *Third*, the institutions have a very important indirect effect in that they determine the social organization of the local community.

## SUGGESTED READINGS

Bonger, W. A., *Criminality and Economic Conditions*. Translated by H. P. Horton. Boston: Little, Brown, 1916.

Clark, John P. and Eugene P. Enninger, "Socio-Economic Class and Area as Correlates of Illegal Behavior Among Juveniles," *American Sociological Review*, 27:826–834, December, 1962.

Cressey, Paul G., "The Motion Picture Experience as Modified by Social Background and Personality," *American Sociological Review*, 3:516–525, August, 1938.

Derby, Stafford, "Crime News Writing and Its Role as a Crime Stimulant," *National Probation and Parole Association Journal*, 4:320–327, October, 1958.

Dobbins, D. A., and Bernard M. Bass, "Effects of Unemployment on White and Negro Prison Admissions in Louisiana," *Journal of Criminal*

---

[100] Paul G. Cressey, "The Motion Picture Experiences as Modified by Social Background and Personality," *American Sociological Review*, 3:516–525, August, 1938.

[101] Ethel Shanas and C. E. Dunning, *Recreation and Delinquency* (Chicago: Chicago Recreation Commission, 1942); Howard Rowland, "Radio Crime Dramas," *Educational Research Bulletin*, 23:210–217, November, 1944.

Law, Criminology, and Police Science, 48:522–525, January–February, 1958.

Edmiston, R. W., and Swaim, E. H., "Juvenile Delinquency and Provisions for Education," School and Society, 55:195, February, 1942.

Elliott, Mabel A., "Perspective on the American Crime Problem," Social Problems, 5:184–193, Winter, 1957.

Glaser, Daniel, and Kent Rice, "Crime, Age and Employment," American Sociological Review, 24:679–686, October, 1959.

Henry, Andrew F., and James F. Short, Jr., Suicide and Homicide. Glencoe, The Free Press, 1954.

Hoskins, Percy, "The Press and the Administration of Justice," Federal Probation, 22:31–35, June, 1958.

Kefauver, Estes, Crime in America. New York: Doubleday, 1951.

Klapper, Joseph T., The Effects of Mass Communication. Glencoe: The Free Press, 1961.

Kvaraceus, W. C., "Delinquent Behavior and Church Attendance," Sociology and Social Research, 28:284–289, March, 1949.

Mannheim, Hermann, John Spencer, and George Lynch, "Magisterial Policy in the London Juvenile Courts," British Journal of Delinquency, 8:13–33, and 8:119–138, June and October, 1957.

Millspaugh, Martin, "Trial by Mass Media," Public Opinion Quarterly, 13:554–558, 1950.

Peterson, Virgil, "Chicago's Crime Problem," Journal of Criminal Law and Criminology, 36:3–15, May–June, 1944.

Reckless, Walter C., "The Impact of War on Crime, Delinquency, and Prostitution," American Journal of Sociology, 48:378–386, November, 1942.

Reiss, Albert J., Jr., and Albert Louis Rhodes, "Are Educational Norms and Goals of Conforming, Truant and Delinquent Adolescents Influenced by Group Position in American Society?" Journal of Negro Education, 28:252–267, Summer, 1959.

Reiss, Albert J., Jr., and Albert Louis Rhodes, "The Distribution of Juvenile Delinquency in the Social Class Structure," American Sociological Review, 26:720–732, October, 1961.

Sargent, W. E., "Religion and Delinquency," British Journal of Delinquency, 3:298–300, April, 1953.

Sellin, Thorsten, Research Memorandum on Crime in the Depression. New York: Social Science Research Council, 1937.

Short, James F., Jr., "A Note on Relief Programs and Crime During the Depression of the 1930's," American Sociological Review, 17:226–229, April, 1952.

Smith, Phillip M., "Organized Religion and Criminal Behavior," Sociology and Social Research, 33:262–267, May, 1949.

Steffens, Lincoln, Autobiography. New York: Harcourt, Brace, 1931.

Straus, Murray A., "Deferred Gratification, Social Class, and the Achievement Syndrome," *American Sociological Review*, 27:326–335, June, 1962.

Wattenberg, W. W., "Church Attendance and Juvenile Misconduct,"
*Sociology and Social Research*, 34:195–202, January, 1950.

Willbach, Harry, "Recent Crimes and the Veterans," *Journal of Criminal
Law and Criminology*, 38:501–508, January–February, 1948.

Wood, Arthur L., "A Socio-Structural Analysis of Murder, Suicide, and
Economic Crime in Ceylon," *American Sociological Review*, 26:744–
753, October, 1961.

Wright, Charles R., "Functional Analysis and Mass Communications,"
*Public Opinion Quarterly*, 24:605–620, Winter, 1960.

# 12. PROCESSES IN CRIMINAL BEHAVIOR

IN THE LIFE history of the criminal, in the interaction between criminals and the public, and in the interaction among criminals all of the processes seen in other social life may be discovered. Some of these processes have greater significance than others for the understanding of crime. One of the significant processes in the life history of the criminal is maturation. Segregation, conflict, and the competitive development of techniques of crime and of protection against crime appear in the interaction between criminals and the public. Fashion, organization, and professionalization appear in the interaction among criminals. These processes are discussed briefly in this chapter as illustrations rather than as a complete analysis of the topic.

MATURATION. A process which may be called "maturation" appears in the life history of persisting criminals. This means merely that criminality in such persons grows in a somewhat consistent course. It does not mean that an individual who starts on this course must follow it to the end, or that he may not begin at some other point than that at which most other criminals begin. Like other terms borrowed by the social sciences from biology, the term "maturation" is misleading but it is used in the absence of a better term.

A person's criminal age is determined by the point he has reached in this process of maturation. The process describes the development of criminality, with reference first to the general attitudes toward criminality, and second, to the techniques used in criminal behavior. A boy who is reared in an area of high delinquency might reach criminal maturity by age twelve or fourteen. He has reached criminal maturity because criminality has become an integrated part of his personality. He plans his offenses, knows how to "fix" things if caught, and thinks of himself as "delinquent" or "bad."[1] When convicted, he takes imprisonment philosophically as a part

[1] Walter C. Reckless, Simon Dinitz, and Ellen Murray, "Self-Concept as an Insulator Against Delinquency," *American Sociological Review*, 21:744-746, December, 1956.

of his life, just as a newsboy who has made what provision he can against the rain takes the rain as a part of his life. The embezzler, on the other hand, may be four times as old as this delinquent but he has made no provision for immunity in case of detection, and he has no philosophy to support him in his trial and punishment. His character is not integrated; he is immature.

The development of criminal methods in relation to chronological age varies in different crimes. Life histories of persons who in young adult life become robbers and burglars show that criminality proceeds from trivial to serious, from occasional to frequent, from sport to business, and from crimes committed by isolated individuals or by very loosely organized groups to crimes committed by rather tightly organized groups.[2] This process in crimes of violence reaches its height when the offender is about nineteen years of age and then remains constant for five or ten years, when it either changes into crimes which require less agility and daring, or into the quasi-criminal behavior connected with politics, gambling, liquor, and prostitution, or is abandoned entirely. Glueck reports in his study of five hundred graduates of the Massachusetts Reformatory that 31.3 percent of those 21–25 years of age at the beginning of the second five-year period after release committed crimes against property, while of those 36 years or over at this time 10.8 percent committed crimes against property.[3] The non-violent crimes of a professional nature are continued, however, to an older age.

The process in the life history of embezzlers is decidedly different. Persons who have previous histories of rectitude accept positions of financial trust with no intention of committing a crime, then later become embezzlers by criminally violating their positions of trust. The persons who occupy positions of financial responsibility seldom are psychopathic, feeble-minded, residents of deteriorated slum areas, or in other ways personally or situationally pathological. Consequently, few embezzlers have such characteristics. Usually embezzlements are committed by employees who have held positions of financial responsibility for many years, rather than by

See also Reckless, Dinitz, and Barbara Kay, "The Self Component in Potential Delinquency and Potential Non-Delinquency," *American Sociological Review,* 22:566–570, October, 1957; and Dinitz, F. R. Scarpitti, and Reckless, "Delinquency Vulnerability: A Cross Group and Longitudinal Analysis," *American Sociological Review,* 27:515–517, August, 1962.

[2] See Clifford R. Shaw, *The Jack-Roller* (Chicago: University of Chicago Press, 1930); Clifford R. Shaw, *The Natural History of a Delinquent Career* (Chicago: University of Chicago Press, 1931); Hutchins Hapgood, *The Autobiography of a Thief* (New York: Fox, Duffield, 1930); Stephen Burroughs, *Memoirs of the Notorious Stephen Burroughs of New Hampshire* (New York: L. MacVeagh, Dial Press, 1924); John Bartlow Martin, *My Life in Crime* (New York: American Library, 1952).

[3] Sheldon and Eleanor T. Glueck, *Later Criminal Careers* (New York: The Commonwealth Fund, 1937), p. 109.

recent recruits. Occasionally, embezzlers snatch a large sum of money, or whatever money is on hand, and abscond. The more usual procedure is to abstract relatively small sums over a long period of time. *First,* the potential trust violator defines a financial problem which confronts him as "unshareable," that is, as a problem which cannot be shared with persons who, from a more objective point of view, could aid in its solution. In many cases these unshareable financial problems arise from obligations incurred in gambling, extravagant living, or maintaining an extramarital establishment, but they also arise in other ways. *Next,* the potential trust violator realizes that he has the ability and opportunity to solve the un-shareable problem by violating his position of trust. He realizes that he can solve the un-shareable financial problem by using the same technical skills which he had been using in the legitimate aspects of his position. *Third,* he defines embezzlement in terms which enable him to look upon it as essentially non-criminal, as justified, or as part of a general irresponsibility for which he is not completely accountable.[4] One popular notion among embezzlers, for example, is that they are merely "borrowing," not "stealing," the entrusted funds. Use of this rationalization enables them to look upon themselves as borrowers and to take relatively small amounts of money over a period of time, always with the intention of repaying it. It is the popularity of this notion, in fact, which accounts for the relatively small proportion of "snatch-and-run" embezzlers. In some cases the embezzler repays the "borrowed" money and his embezzlement goes undetected. Among apprehended embezzlers, a few are found to have kept a careful record of the amount of the "indebtedness," but most state that after a few abstractions they lost track of the total amount of their "debt." A considerable amount of money may be taken before the embezzler realizes that he cannot possibly repay the amount taken. This realization, which is described by embezzlers as recognition of the fact that they are "in too deep," does not occur in all cases, since some violators are arrested before it takes place; and its absence enables these trust violators to continue rationalizing, even after apprehension, that they were merely borrowing. But when an embezzler discovers that he is "in too deep" he is forced to abandon the notion that he is borrowing and to face the fact that he, an "honest and respectable person," has committed a crime. By using the rationalization that they are borrowing, then, embezzlers are able to remain in full contact with the values and ideals of former and present associates who condemn crime, and when they find that they are "in too deep" and

---

[4] Use of such definitions has been described as a "technique of neutralization." See Gresham M. Sykes and David Matza, "Techniques of Neutralization: A Theory of Delinquency," *American Sociological Review,* 22:664–670, December, 1957.

have slipped into a category (criminal) which they know is regarded as undesirable according to that set of values and ideals, they rebel against it. They usually describe themselves as being extremely nervous, tense, emotionally upset, and unhappy. To get rid of these symptoms they may report their behavior to the police, quit taking funds, speculate or gamble wildly in an attempt to regain the stolen funds, or commit suicide. On the other hand, they may identify themselves with criminals and, thus, become reckless in their defalcations, taking larger amounts than formerly and with less attempt to avoid detection and with no notion of repayment. Thus, in the absence of the rationalization that he is borrowing an embezzler of this kind cannot reconcile the fact that he is converting money while at the same time he is an "honest and trusted person"; consequently, he either (a) readopts the attitudes of the non-criminal groups with which he identified himself before he violated his trust, or (b) adopts the attitudes of the new category of persons (criminals) with whom he now finds him- self identified. After apprehension, those embezzlers who finally come to look upon their behavior as criminal express general disapproval of crime and embezzlement, just as do non-prisoners. The crimes are generally com- mitted individually, but occasionally two or more persons are in collusion. Embezzlers are scorned by professional criminals but are regarded by prison officers as model prisoners. A comparatively small proportion of them become recidivists, for the discovery of an embezzlement generally pre- cludes further employment in positions of financial trust.[5]

Similarly, the processes in the life histories of other types of criminals might be described. The legal offense category probably is not the best unit to use in these descriptions. Rather, sociological categories which combine several legal categories could be used as the unit. After a sufficient number of such units have been defined and described, the types which appear can be differentiated from each other with little reference to the legal crime.[6]

A few statistical studies have been made from the point of view of the sequential relations between crimes. Grassberger made a study of the arrest records of habitual criminals in New York City which shows that the habitual criminal during his lifetime spreads his crimes over almost the entire field of illegality, and is not confined to a single specialty. This study, however, does not show the sequence of types of crimes.[7] Frum

---

[5] For an extended discussion of embezzlement, see Donald R. Cressey, *Other People's Money, A Study in the Social Psychology of Embezzlement* (Glencoe: The Free Press, 1953).

[6] See the discussion below, pp. 287–288.

[7] Roland Grassberger, "Gewerbs– und Berufsverbrechertum in den Vereinigten Staaten von Amerika," *Kriminologische Abhandlungen*, Vienna, No. 8, 1933.

found that 63 percent of 148 cases of adult recidivism began with some type of juvenile stealing, 23 percent with truancy or incorrigibility, 13 percent with drunk-vagrancy, and 1 percent with robbery.[8] Burkey found that boys of normal intelligence were more likely to begin with sex offenses, and that both the normal and the subnormal who begin with stealing are likely to continue that offense rather than turn to some other offense.[9] The assertion has been made frequently that problem children become delinquent children, and delinquent children become criminal adults. While there is some possibility that this is true, it has not been adequately demonstrated.[10]

Glueck has treated this process of maturation from a different point of view. He regards maturation as the underlying influence in reform. According to his conclusions the criminals became law-abiding as they matured chronologically; this process of reformation practically stopped at the age of thirty-five; further, he concluded that those who passed the age of thirty-five and had not reformed were much more frequently mental deviates. Thus his proposition is that age has a beneficent effect on those who are not mental deviates, so that they reform before the age of thirty-five; age has no such effect on the mental deviates and they continue in crime thereafter.[11] He reaches this conclusion, however, by two very questionable methods: first, a definition of mental deviate so broad that it could be made to include all persons whatsoever; second, a comparison of persons of a given age-span in the first follow-up period with another group of persons of the same age-span in the second follow-up period, and from this drawing conclusions regarding the effect of age.[12]

SEGREGATION.    Segregation may be observed in the interaction between criminals and the public. The extent to which segregation occurs is determined largely by the hatred the group has for the criminal. The sex offender was completely ostracized in many communities two generations ago, much less completely now. The person with a prison record is still completely ostracized in certain communities but he may become a politi-

[8] Harold S. Frum, "Adult Criminal Offense Trends Following Juvenile Delinquency," *Journal of Criminal Law and Criminology*, 49:29–49, May–June, 1958.

[9] Ruth E. Burkey, "A Statistical Study of the Sequence of Successive Delinquencies," *Journal of Juvenile Research*, 16:133–144, April, 1932.

[10] See Nathan Bodin, "Do Problem Children Become Delinquents and Criminals?" *Journal of Criminal Law and Criminology*, 27:545–559, November–December, 1936. Bodin reported that 92.5 percent of the problem cases in the Bureau of Research and Guidance in the Berkeley School had developed records of delinquency within the subsequent eight years. It should be noted, however, that slightly more than half of the children had juvenile court records prior to their reference to the Bureau.

[11] Glueck and Glueck, *op. cit.*, Chapters X–XI.

[12] *Ibid.*, p. 395.

cal leader in other communities. Thus segregation as a process does not apply universally to all criminals in all groups.

There is, however, a general portion of American society which may be called the underworld. Admission to this underworld is secured generally by personal introductions and can be secured only by those who are regarded as not dangerous to the criminals, quasi-criminals, and politicians who compose the underworld. This underworld has a general suspicion of respectable society, moves for the most part in different circles, and has its own meeting places. Criminal slang has developed and persisted in this underworld.[13]

In some of the earlier societies the criminals lived entirely apart from law-abiding society, in remote regions from which they might issue to make raids upon travelers or householders. Today most of the criminals live in the midst of society, in certain areas of the cities, where they are protected by collusion with predatory politicians and have developed a symbiotic relation with many kinds of businessmen.

PROGRESSIVE CONFLICT.    Criminals and the protective agents are engaged in continuous conflict. In this conflict each side tends to drive the other side to greater violence unless the conflict becomes stabilized, on a recognized level, as it has been in England for some years. In England the police and the criminals both go without guns and the danger of death is practically eliminated. Until the last decade in the American city, on the other hand, there has been progressive armament of both sides and progressive rapidity of shooting. Each side adopted the slogan "Shoot and shoot first." Each side felt that it was dangerous to give the other side a chance. This affected not only the police but also that part of the general public which was repeatedly victimized by criminals. The result was an increasing death rate on both sides. The number of policemen murdered annually in the course of duty increased in New York City from 1.8 per 10,000 members of the staff in 1906–1910 to 4.1 in 1926–1930, and in Chicago from 5.1 to 18.2 in the same years. The rate in Chicago in 1945–1958 was 2.8. The number of policemen murdered in Chicago in the course of duty increased from 47 in 1919–1925 to 62 in 1926–1931, and then decreased to 7 in 1946–50, 9 in 1951–55, and 9 in 1956–58. The number of Chicago criminals killed in connection with their crimes was 190 in 1919–1925, 314 in 1926–1931, 107 in 1946–50, 147 in 1951–55, and 99 in 1956–58. Approximately one-half of these criminals were killed by private citizens, and

---

[13] For illustrations of criminal slang, see Donald Clemmer, *The Prison Community*, New Edition (New York: Rinehart, 1958); and David W. Maurer, *The Big Con* (Indianapolis: Bobbs-Merrill, 1940).

one-half by the police.[14] The number of policemen killed decreased 85 percent between 1926–31 and 1945–1955, while the number of criminals killed decreased 53 percent during this period. When the police treat criminals violently, the criminals react violently when they have an opportunity. This spurs the police to greater violence, which again produces more violence by the criminals. It is not evident and perhaps makes no difference which side is responsible for the beginning of this process. The recent trends in murders of policemen and in violent deaths of criminals seem to indicate that the tradition of violence is being abandoned.

In the absence of settled traditions, this process of progressive conflict begins with arrest, which is interpreted as defining a person as an enemy of society, and which calls forth hostile reactions from representatives of society prior to and regardless of proof of guilt. It is not surprising that the arrested person reacts by further hostility. Thus, in certain areas where arrests are frequent, a tradition of hostility is developed and is assimilated by many persons who have had no personal experiences with the procedures of arrest. During the last generation, as the police have found it necessary to deal with more and more driving offenders and, thus, with a wider and wider cross-section of the society, rather widespread hostility toward the police has developed.[15]

COMPETITIVE DEVELOPMENT OF TECHNIQUES OF CRIME AND OF PROTECTION AGAINST CRIME. Both criminals and protective officers appropriate the inventions of modern science so far as these are useful to them. In early days both proceeded on foot or horseback, then both used bicycles, and now automobiles, with the occasional use of an airplane. In the early days both used clubs as weapons, and now both use guns and machine-guns, with an occasional survival of the knife among some national and racial groups. Both use bullet-proof vests and armored cars. Both on some occasions use tear-gas bombs, and both may be equipped with gas masks. Kidnapers use adhesive tape, which was practically unknown fifty years ago even to physicians, to bind the eyes, mouth, and hands of victims.

When the police develop an invention for the detection or identification of criminals, the criminals utilize a device to protect themselves. When the police began to use the fingerprint technique, criminals began to wear gloves and to wipe surfaces that had been touched by them. The police utilize the radio to notify squad cars of the location of a crime that is being committed and to direct those cars in the pursuit of crminals. The well-equipped burglars carry their own short wave radio sets with them,

[14] See Hans W. Mattick, *The Unexamined Death: An Analysis of Capital Punishment*, Chicago: John Howard Association, 1963, p. 19.

[15] For a history and analysis of motoring offenses, see T. C. Willett, *Criminal on the Road* (London: Tavistock, 1964).

tune them in while they are at work, and are informed of an alarm as quickly as are the police. The police are trying to perfect selective devices for radio calls which will restrict the calls to police cars, but it may be expected that if this difficulty develops the criminals will devise methods of overcoming it.

The history of the safe furnishes one of the best illustrations of this alternation of progress in the techniques of protection and of crime. The safe seventy years ago was locked with a key. Professional safe-burglars learned how to pick these locks, and then the combination lock was invented. The criminals rigged a lever by means of which the whole spindle of the combination could be pulled out of the safe. When correction was made to prevent this, the burglars drilled holes in the safe and inserted gunpowder or dynamite. Then the manufacturers made the safe drill-proof, and the burglars secured harder drills with more powerful leverage. The manufacturers used harder materials for the safe and therefore the burglars turned to nitro-glycerine, which could be inserted in minute crevices around the door where powder and dynamite would not enter. The safe-makers then developed doors which fitted so perfectly that a small piece of paper would prevent the door from locking, and this made it impossible to insert even nitroglycerine in the cracks. The burglars then adopted the oxyacetylene torch and turned it against the safe, and the manufacturers devised a compound which was proof against the torch. Somewhere in this process the burglars began to kidnap bankers and compel them to open the safe, regarding this as easier than mechanical methods of opening safes. To prevent this, the time-lock was invented so that the businessmen could not open their own safes until the appointed hour. Also, when the manufacturers made the safes difficult to open, the burglars began hauling the safes themselves away. The manufacturers countered by making the safes too heavy to move, and banks installed night depositories so that businessmen would not have to leave money in their own small safes. The safe-makers also experimented with safes which would release gas or great clouds of smoke when drilled. The burglars then went equipped with gas masks. Recently, an electronic lock for safes was invented, but the inventor declared that within a short time someone certainly would design tools and devices to pick it.[16] This process of alternations of techniques has given first one side and then the other the advantage. When the protective devices were ahead, some safe-burglars turned to other types of crimes. As the criminal technique was perfected it was adopted by others and the number of safe-burglars increased.

The tendency during the last generation has been to substitute robbery for burglary, for a criminal gang can reach a bank by automobile, rush into

[16] *Indianapolis Star*, April 20, 1950, p. 3.

the bank completely armed, make a raid in a few minutes, and rush away. The search for devices to prevent this type of crime is under way. Secret push-buttons to call guards have been developed. Also, secret push-buttons to release tear gas at the same time have been utilized. Efforts are being made to secure automatic photographs of the scene in order that the robbers may be identified. In general the protective devices in the larger banks, both against burglary and robbery, are so well developed that the criminals prefer to make attacks on the smaller banks which cannot afford such expensive equipment, although the prospective gains in these banks are less than in the impregnable banks. If the smaller banks improve their protective devices, the criminals will direct their attacks against other business or commercial concerns which do not have adequate protection. Thus, there is a selection and development of techniques of crimes and a selection of types of crimes in relation to the protective devices, and similarly there is a development of protective devices in relation to the methods used by criminals.

FASHIONS IN CRIME.    Certain types of crimes have disappeared almost entirely. This has generally been due to changes in the situation, other than the protective devices. Piracy has practically disappeared, and its disappearance was due to the development of steam ships which were too large and fast for attack by pirates. The development of the steamship did not occur, of course, as a protection against piracy. Train robberies, of the type in which a train was stopped and the mail car and the passengers were robbed, have been discontinued. Cattle stealing in the form of driving away a herd of cattle has ceased, but for it has been substituted the loading of two or three cows into a truck and delivering them in the city. The general situation may change and cause the disappearance of a crime.

In addition, however, the type and method of crime vary in ways which much resemble fashion in other affairs. A criminal makes an attack on a gambling place and within a short time dozens of other gambling places are attacked. Some criminal selects a hotel for robbery and quickly dozens of other hotels are robbed. A pickpocket secures a thousand dollars in a certain railway station, and the other pickpockets flock to that station. A criminal makes an unusually successful gain by a method which was not customary. Other criminals try the method. In recent years, robbery of banks by "lone wolf" criminals who demand the money in the cash box of a teller seems to have become fashionable.

ORGANIZATION OF CRIMINALS.    Organization develops in the interaction of criminals. This organization may be a formal association with recognized leadership, understandings, agreements, and division of labor, or it may be informal similarity and reciprocity of interests and attitudes. A group which has been formed for legitimate purposes may change into a criminal group, or individual criminals may organize an association for illegitimate purposes. The criminal tribes of India, the bandits of China, the brigands of southeastern Europe, the smugglers in America and in many European countries in earlier times, the Ku Klux Klan and the lynching mobs, guerrilla warfare and feuds were earlier forms of organized crime. The James gang in Missouri and the criminal organization in Italy were produced by wars and political differences and survived as organized criminals. The Chinese Tongs in America were primarily business associations but on occasions directed their activities along criminal lines.

Aside from these earlier forms of organized crime, the organization of criminals appears at present in the following forms: First, criminals form working groups, known as mobs or troupes, with understandings, division of labor, and sometimes with recognized leadership. The number of criminals in the mob is determined by the requirements of the work, but is generally restricted to two, three, four, or five members. Second, the underworld is bound together by a common hostility toward the law, and consequently the members co-operate in assisting and protecting each other. Third, within certain areas syndicates control gambling, prostitution, and sale of narcotics. Fourth, cooperation develops between each of the above-mentioned types of criminal organizations and the agencies whose legal business is enforcement of law. Large and strong criminal organizations cannot develop if the government is strongly organized. The strong criminal organizations in the past have generally been found during an interregnum, or on the borderline between conflicting police jurisdictions, or in inaccessible territory remote from the seat of government. The disorganization of the present American governments, however, is different from the early types of governmental disorganization. A few members of modern law-enforcement agencies cooperate with criminal organizations because they are under the control of politicians who are themselves criminals.

Small groups, organized for the execution of a particular type of crime, have existed for centuries. These groups during the Elizabethan period have been described with some detail.[17] Similar groups exist today for purposes of bank burglary, shoplifting, confidence games, picking pockets, and stealing automobiles. Frequently these groups cooperate with each other. A group of automobile thieves on the West Side in Chicago and another group on the South Side developed an exchange of information which enabled one group to steal cars from the neighborhood in which the other group lived.

17 A. V. Judges, *The Elizabethan Underworld* (London: Routledge), 1930.

Organization involves, also, the development of arrangements for the disposal of stolen goods. A "fence" or receiver of stolen goods is frequently consulted in advance of a crime, and a theft may be executed for the purpose of securing specific commodities desired by the "fence." In Los Angeles the "legitimate businessmen," mostly used car dealers, who purchased stolen automobile radios and other accessories had to be put out of the "fence" business before thefts from automobiles could be reduced.[18]

Protection against arrest and conviction is a necessary part of organized crime. The precautions that the individual criminal may take in order to escape detection are merely the beginning. Additional protection is secured by finding traitors among law-enforcement officers. The techniques of fixing crimes are as important as the techniques of executing crimes.[19] Fortunately for the criminals, the political machine in many cities stands ready to protect criminals if proper compensation in money or services is made. The fixing of cases involves, first, various methods of inducing victims not to testify and not to press the prosecution. These methods include persuasion, restitution of stolen property, frequently with additional compensation, intimidation, tricks, and murder. The police are sometimes the agents of the criminals in persuading victims to accept restitution. They inform the victim that a criminal trial will cause him great inconvenience and expense, and may be continued for many months, after which the victim will have no prospect of recovering his stolen goods. Sometimes the criminals themselves make the contact with the victim and present the same arguments, together with an offer of restitution. Second, the police are induced not to make complaint or, if the complaint has been made, not to testify truthfully. This result may be secured by direct bribery or by political orders. Third, the prosecuting attorney may be induced not to prosecute, or if prosecution is inevitable, to see that the evidence is presented badly so that the case against the offenders is not clear. In the modern court, the prosecutor has immense power in this respect. Immunity is secured in this manner in many cases, generally through the influence of a political leader, though the prosecutor generally secures financial compensation for his assistance either directly or indirectly. Fourth, the court may be induced not to convict. Immunity is less frequently secured at this stage, for the court is public and the judge or jury is subject to much criticism for open protection of the criminal. It is possible, however, for the judge to impose sentence for the sake of the public and then to modify the sentence in his chambers, or for him to commit an offender to a workhouse and then,

---

[18] Robert De Roos, "Car Clouting," Collier's, December 11, 1953, pp. 90–95.
[19] Erving Goffman, "On Cooling the Mark Out: Some Aspects of Adaptation to Failure," Psychiatry, 15:451–463, November, 1962.

within a short time, recall him and change the sentence to a small fine. *Fifth*, officers of corrupt city and county correctional institutions may be induced to release the offender immediately, for a suitable payment, but carry him on the books as an inmate of the institution until the end of his sentence. If this is too dangerous, they can at least give the criminal a comfortable position in the institution and recommend an early release on parole. It is probable, however, that there is less fixing of cases with the parole board, than at any other point in the whole judicial and penal procedure.

These cases of fixing as a part of organized crime are not glaring to the casual observer, for the organized criminals are a comparatively small part of the entire number who are arrested and prosecuted. Corrupt police, prosecutors, and judges, similarly, are only a small part of all such functionaries. Those who are corrupt can be severe with the friendless and unorganized criminals, who have no money and no political connections, making the favors granted to organized criminals less apparent.

Organization, in sum, involves association of a small group of criminals for the execution of a certain type of crimes, together with the development of plans by which detection may be avoided, and the development of a fund of money and political connections by means of which immunity or relative immunity may be secured in case of detection. In order that immunity may be secured in this manner it is necessary that a political machine be kept intact, and this requires, among other things, large campaign contributions from respectable as well as disreputable businesses. These campaign contributions are made in order that laws may not be passed or may not be enforced against the businesses which make the contributions, and often they are made to each of the opponents in an election campaign.

The most widespread organization of lawlessness is in connection with the vices. Relatively few people demand that burglars, pickpockets, and confidence men engage in crime, but many persons demand opportunities for illicit sexual intercourse, gambling, and consumption of narcotics. Perhaps the principal public demand comes from the underworld rather than respectable society, but at any rate the demand is insistent. This provides a basis for extensive organization which involves the places of vice, the patrons, the real estate dealers, the manufacturers of commodities used in the vices, the police and courts, the politicians, and sometimes a much wider public.

Organization of the vices in American cities has existed for several decades, at least. Laws designed to regulate the liquor traffic have been violated rather systematically in most American cities for at least a century.

This consistent violation has been possible only because the police do not try to enforce the laws or are not able to enforce them. The non-enforcement of laws sometimes is a service which is purchased by saloons, sometimes simply a function of a manpower shortage in a police department. During the period of national prohibition, the difficulties of enforcement were very great, to be sure, but the efforts at enforcement were frequently insincere. For a considerable part of the period of national prohibition the leading American manufacturer of intoxicating drinks was in charge of the enforcement of the law against the illicit manufacture and sale of intoxicating drinks. With comparative immunity from prosecution, with a somewhat widespread public demand for alcohol, and with huge profits, the supply was forthcoming. Almost from the first, the manufacture, distribution, and sale was in the hands of groups of people rather than of isolated individuals. These groups at first were generally based on neighborhood or national lines and reflected homogeneity of culture. They came into competition and by violent warfare were forced into larger units, and these larger units were again forced into huge syndicates. The process was exactly the same as in legitimate business, though the methods inclined somewhat more to violence and less to fraud than in legitimate business. While the organized syndicate was using warnings, destruction of property, and murder as means of preventing competition, the police, acting under orders of political leaders, were harassing any dealers or manufacturers who attempted to enter the liquor business. The organization was never secure, however, for subordinates were rebellious and ambitious, and since the entire business was illegal, control depended finally upon violence.

The process in the organization of gambling has been somewhat similar to that in liquor and there is some evidence that the bootleggers of the prohibition era went into the illegal gambling business when the sale of alcohol was made legal.[20] Gambling has existed in violation of law but with protection by officers of the law for many decades. The assistance of the officers of the law is secured by payments to them as individuals, or payments to the controlling officers, or by financial and political services to the politicians who control the higher officers. These arrangements were once generally confined to particular gambling places, and formal organization did not go much beyond that relationship with the officers of the law. This, however, was changed during the period of national prohibition. The liquor syndicate began to develop gambling as an organized business,

[20] Special Committee to Investigate Organized Crime in Interstate Commerce, *Third Interim Report*, U.S. Senate Report, No. 307, 82nd Congress (Washington: Government Printing Office, 1951).

depending especially upon slot machines. The number of the machines in a particular area was greatly increased, and the area under the control of the syndicate was increased, so that both intensive and extensive developments occurred. This, also, required collusion of the public officers and of the politicians and, as in the case of alcohol, this was easily secured.[21] Competition developed as the profits from this business became apparent, but competition was restrained both by the police and by destruction of property and life. Organized criminal syndicates in the United States now receive most of their income from gambling enterprises.[22]

In the early period, prostitution involved somewhat more organization than gambling did. Houses of prostitution were segregated in many cities to a much greater extent than were the gambling places. Individual houses and a particular area of prostitution were protected by the police, who, however, harassed competitors. Vice drives shortly before World War I broke up these segregated districts, which had never had a monopoly on prostitution. As early as that, also, girls were transported from place to place for purposes of prostitution and were held against their will in places of prostitution. The federal law against the white-slave traffic was directed at this development of the business but has never had much effect. The principal organization of the business of prostitution came, as did the organization of gambling, when it passed into the hands of the liquor syndicates. The organization which took over the payment of protection money for the liquor business could equally well make collections and payments for gambling and prostitution. Consequently most houses of prostitution in the cities passed into the control of the syndicate, and those prostitutes who attempted to ply their business outside of protected houses were harassed by the police, while those in the protected houses were secure. Thus the prostitutes were forced very generally into the organization.

There is sufficient evidence that many liquor gangs engaged in other types of crime, and also that they have entered many legitimate businesses. If the income from the liquor, gambling, and prostitution business was less than was needed at a particular time, a group of the regular staff of the organization would rob a bank or a hotel, enter into racketeering, or become involved in some other profitable type of crime. Since they had the support of the police and courts for their organized traffic in liquor, gambling, and prostitution, they were relatively immune even in cases of

21 See Virgil W. Peterson, "Chicago's Crime Problem," *Journal of Criminal Law and Criminology*, 35:3–15, May–June, 1944.
22 Mortimer M. Caplin, "The Gambling Business and Federal Taxes," *Crime and Delinquency*, 8:371–378, October, 1962.

robbery. In 1951, the Senate Special Committee to Investigate Organized Crime in Interstate Commerce found approximately fifty business enterprises which have been infiltrated by organized criminals. These include the legitimate liquor industry, transportation, steel, oil, banking and finance, the garment industry, and many others. Also, some trade union locals were captured by representatives of criminal syndicates. The syndicate developed protective organizations, which were based essentially on threat of violence if the person did not join. These organizations at first were in the weaker groups, but they spread to the groups which already had trade unions or trade associations, and have frequently involved both the trade union and the employers' association.[23]

PROFESSIONALIZATION. The term "professional" when applied to a criminal refers to the following things: the pursuit of crime as a regular, day-by-day occupation, the development of skilled techniques and careful planning in that occupation, and status among criminals.[24] The professional criminal is differentiated from the occasional criminal, the amateur criminal, the unskilled and careless criminal. The term "profession" does not carry with it the ideal of public service which is supposed to be characteristic of the legitimate professions, but the professional criminal argues that the ideal of public service is no more developed in the legal profession than in the criminal profession.

Certain types of crimes can be committed without previous experience in crime. Murder by shooting, for instance, may be committed by a person who had no previous experience in murder, even if he did have experience in shooting. Most crimes, however, require training. Boys in a delinquency area are taught how to commit thefts of various kinds. The boy who moves into an area at, say, the age of ten years without previous experience in stealing has to learn many things in order to keep out of difficulty. The other boys will show him how to steal articles from a department store, how to steal from a truck, how to steal an automobile. These are techniques which must be learned, but the training extends somewhat beyond the execution of the crime. It includes knowledge of methods of behavior in case one is caught, knowledge of when to cry and when not to cry, what types of lies to tell the police or the court. Although, from the standpoint of the mature professional criminal, such devices are on a relatively crude and low plane, as is the work of the older amateur burglars and robbers,

[23] See Malcolm Johnson, *Crime on the Labor Front* (New York: McGraw-Hill, 1950.
[24] Reckless has used essentially the same criteria to differentiate "career criminals." Walter C. Reckless, *The Crime Problem*, Second Edition (New York: Appleton-Century-Crofts, 1955), pp. 144–145, 148–150.

the criminal maturation of such trained criminals is much greater than that of episodic criminals such as murderers, embezzlers, and rapists.

The professional criminal has a highly skilled occupation. At one time the safe-breaker stood at the head of the criminal professions, for his skill was unusually great and his plans had to be made with unusual care. Thieves whose occupation requires skill in social manipulation also have high status. These include pickpockets, shoplifters, and confidence men. The crime of picking pockets requires manual skill, to be sure, but in addition it requires the proper diversion of attention at the crucial moment. Shoplifting may be of the casual amateur kind, but there is also a highly skilled technique, which requires that the thief give to the clerks in the store the impression that he is a respectable customer so that they dare not stop him for fear of insulting a regular customer. The confidence games are based essentially on salesmanship and generally involve a willingness on the part of the victim to engage in an illegitimate profit.[25]

The skill of the professional extends beyond the execution of the crime, however. It involves the prior location of "spots," and the prior preparation for escaping punishment in case of detection in crime. Arrangements are made in advance for bail, legal service, and fixing the case. It is in these advance arrangements quite as much as in the technique of executing the crime that professionalization is found. Professionalization will be discussed further in the next chapter.

THE CRIMINAL CODE. In connection with organization and professionalization, codes of behavior develop among criminals. The codes are not the same for all types of crimes or all types of criminals. There are, however, two very general rules. One is not to inform on another criminal, the other is to make an honest division of the loot with the companions or partners in crime. "Do not squeal" and "Do not burn your partner" are the basic commandments of thieves. Unquestionably these commandments are violated frequently among criminals, but on the other hand it is surprising how much pain many criminals will suffer rather than inform on other criminals. These commandments are enforced by direct and violent punishment in criminal groups. They are perhaps obeyed most strictly by professional criminals and least strictly by the occasional and amateur criminals.

In certain criminal groups, "toughness" must be displayed in dealing with the public. This is in part based on the segregation of criminals and of criminal behavior. Just as the businessman acts on the principle that

[25] Edwin M. Schur, "Sociological Analysis of Confidence Swindling," *Journal of Criminal Law, Criminology, and Police Science*, 48:296–304, October, 1957.

"business is business," so these criminals act on the principle "crime is crime." There is no place for sentiment in either case. In addition, however, there is a considerable amount of bravado involved in the displays. A group of young criminals make a successful daylight robbery of a store across the street from a police station and as they drive away in their automobile, they shoot several times through the window of the police station. A young criminal is angered at the way the police have treated his brother and he sets fire to a police automobile which is parked in front of the police station. Automobile thieves make a special effort to steal police automobiles. A criminal who is on trial in a courtroom filled with people and with policemen and bailiffs standing around secures a gun and tries to shoot his way out of the courtroom. Such acts are expressions of bravado. They give the criminal a thrill status in his group. Professional criminals are not likely to engage in such exploits. Professional pick-pockets, for instance, do not pick the pockets of policemen though they could easily do so. This would simply antagonize the police and the professional criminal wants to reduce antagonism.

Criminals who are considered crude by the professionals also display feelings in other ways. Robbers sometimes punish the man who has no money or very little money when he is searched. Similarly, burglars may destroy property in a store if they find no money. One burglary insurance company has suggested to its clients that they should always leave a small sum of money accessible in the till so that burglars will not destroy property. These expressions of resentment may be spontaneous, but they seem to some extent to vary in fashion-like manner. It is probable that as newspapers describe the expressions of resentment, other criminals read the accounts and imitate the procedure.

## SUGGESTED READINGS

Bolitho, W., "The Gangster Trauma," Survey, 63:661–665, March 1, 1930.

Bolitho, W., "The Natural History of Graft," Survey, 64:138–140, 170–176, May 1, 1930.

Bolitho, W., "The Psychosis of the Gang," Survey, 63:501–506, February 1, 1930.

Cameron, Mary Owen, The Booster and the Snitch: Department Store Shoplifting. New York: The Free Press of Glencoe, 1964.

Catton, Bruce, The War Lords of Washington. New York: Harcourt, Brace, 1948.

Cook, Fred J., "Gambling, Inc.," The Nation, 191:257–316, October 22, 1960.

Cooper, C. R., Here's to Crime. Boston: Little, Brown, 1939.

Cressey, D. R., *Other People's Money: A Study in the Social Psychology of Embezzlement.* Glencoe: The Free Press, 1953.

Edwards, Loren E., *Shoplifting and Shrinkage Protection for Stores.* Springfield, Ill.: Charles C. Thomas, 1958.

Gosnell, H. F., "The Political Party vs. the Political Machine," *Annals of the American Academy of Political and Social Science,* 169:21–28, September, 1933.

Hoover, J. Edgar, "White Slave Traffic," *Journal of Criminal Law and Criminology,* 24:475–482, July–August, 1933.

Hostetter, G. L., "Gangsterized Industry," *Survey,* 59:16–17, January, 1933.

Hynd, Alan, *The Giant Killers.* New York: McBride, 1945.

Irey, E. L., and W. J. Slocum, *The Tax Dodgers.* New York: Greenberg, 1948.

Johnson, Malcolm, *Crime on the Labor Front.* New York: McGraw-Hill, 1950.

Kefauver, Estes, *Crime in America.* New York: Doubleday, 1951.

Kennedy, Robert F., *The Enemy Within.* New York: Harpers, 1960.

Landesco, John, *Organized Crime in Chicago,* in Illinois Association for Criminal Justice, *Illinois Crime Survey.* Chicago: Author, 1929, Part III.

Lever, Harry, and Joseph Young, *Wartime Racketeers.* New York: Putnam, 1945.

Lindesmith, A. R., "Organized Crime," *Annals of the American Academy of Political and Social Science,* 217:119–127, September, 1941.

Lockwood, P. E., "How State and City Governments Deal with Racketeering," *Journal of Criminal Law and Criminology,* 32:130–138, May–June, 1941.

McCarthy, Katherine C., "Racketeering: A Contribution to a Bibliography," *Journal of Criminal Law and Criminology,* 22:578–586, November–December, 1931.

Manes, A., "Insurance Crimes," *Journal of Criminal Law and Criminology,* 35:34–42, May–June, 1944.

Merriam, Charles E., *Chicago, a More Intimate View of Urban Politics.* New York: Macmillan, 1929.

Murtagh, John M., "Gambling and Police Corruption," *Atlantic Monthly,* 206:49–53, November, 1960.

New York Legislature, *Report of the Joint Committee on the Government of the City of New York* (Hofstadter and Seabury Committee), 5 Volumes, Albany: State Printing Office, 1932.

New York Legislature, *Report and Proceedings of the Senate Committee on the Police Department of the City of New York* (Lexow Committee), 5 Volumes. Albany: State Printing Office, 1895.

Peterson, Virgil W., *Barbarians in Our Midst.* Boston: Little, Brown, 1952.

Ploscowe, Morris, Editor, *Organized Crime and Law Enforcement*. Two Volumes. New York: Grosby Press, 1952–1953.

Reckless, W. C., *Vice in Chicago*. Chicago: University of Chicago Press, 1933.

Robin, Gerald D., "Patterns of Department Store Shoplifting, *Crime and delinquency*, 163–172, April, 1963.

Roebuck, Julian B., "The Negro Numbers Man as a Criminal Type: The Construction and Application of a Typology," *Journal of Criminal Law, Criminology, and Police Science*, 54:48–60, March, 1963.

Steffens, Lincoln, *Autobiography*. New York: Harcourt, Brace, 1931.

Sullivan, E. D., *Rattling the Cup on Chicago Crime*. New York: Vanguard, 1929.

Tannenbaum, Frank, *Crime and the Community*. Boston: Ginn, 1938.

Tyler, Gus, *Organized Crime in America*. Ann Arbor: University of Michigan Press, 1962.

VanCise, Philip S., *Fighting the Underworld*. Boston: Houghton Mifflin, 1930.

# 13. BEHAVIOR SYSTEMS IN CRIME

MOST OF THE scientific work in criminology has been directed at the explanation of crime in general. Crime in general consists of a great variety of criminal acts. These acts have very little in common except the fact that they are all violations of law. They differ among themselves in the motives and characteristics of the offenders, the characteristics of the victims, the situations in which they occur, the techniques which are used, the damages which result, and the reactions of the victims and the public. Although burglary, robbery, embezzlement, and rape are all crimes, it is almost obvious that they are homogeneous with respect to etiology only in a general way. Even the legal definitions of specific crimes, such as kidnaping, do not always delimit categories of behavior which are homogeneous in regard to their specific causal or genetic characteristics.

Consequently, it is not likely that a general theory of crime can be sufficiently precise or specific to aid greatly in understanding or controlling all types of crime.[1] While a general theory of crime such as the differential association theory organizes criminological knowledge, and is therefore desirable, in order to make progress in the explanation of crime it is also desirable to break crime into more homogeneous units. In this respect, crime is like a disease. The germ theory of disease is a very useful general theory, but even this theory does not apply to all diseases. Progress in the explanation of disease is being made principally by the studies of specific diseases. Similarly, it is desirable to concentrate research work in criminology on specific crimes and on specific "sociological units" within the broad area of crime and within the legal definition of specific types of crime such as kidnaping and burglary.

[1] Cf. E. W. Burgess, "Discussion" of Frank E. Hartung, "White-Collar Offenses in the Wholesale Meat Industry in Detroit," American Journal of Sociology, 56:25–34, July, 1950; Don C. Gibbons and Donald L. Garrity, "Some Suggestions for the Development of Etiological and Treatment Theory in Criminology," Social Forces, 38:51–58, October, 1959.

Several procedures for studying such sociological units within the broad field of crime and within the definitions of specific crimes have been suggested. The typological approach is one such procedure. It has been used by Riemer and by Lottier to define homogeneous units within a specific offense category, embezzlement, and it has been used by Clinard and Wade to define a homogeneous unit, vandalism, as a specific type of delinquency.[2] A second procedure has been to combine legal categories of crime in such a way that some of the crimes in each of several legal categories are made into a sociological unit. In the course of an attempt to formulate a sociological theory of embezzlement, for example, it was discovered that the legal term "embezzlement" did not describe a homogeneous class of behavior. Persons whose illegal behavior was not covered by the legal definition were found to have been convicted of embezzlement, and the behavior of some persons who were convicted of offenses such as forgery and confidence game was found to come within the definition of embezzlement. Consequently, a new, sociological definition of the behavior under study was made. This definition enabled the investigator to study certain cases from each of several legal categories, including embezzlement, forgery, and confidence game, and to develop a causal theory about this new sociological unit.[3]

A third procedure suggested by sociologists for breaking crime into homogeneous units is the study of "behavior systems." Just as is the case when the typological approach is used, these systems of criminal behavior ordinarily have been defined in such a way that the behavior becomes homogeneous within the definition of a specific legal category. An example of this may be seen in the work of Jerome Hall, who found several behavior systems within the legal category of "larceny."[4] Perhaps this procedure holds the greatest promise for criminological research, for by taking the behavior system as the unit of study it is possible to break away from the legal limitations that have often impeded scientific work in criminology; the behavior system can be studied wherever it exists, whether as

[2] Svend Riemer, "Embezzlement: Pathological Basis," Journal of Criminal Law and Criminology, 32:411–423, November–December, 1941; S. Lottier, "Tension Theory of Criminal Behavior," American Sociological Review, 7:840–848 December, 1942; Marshall B. Clinard and Andrew L. Wade, "Toward the Delineation of Vandalism as a Sub-type in Juvenile Delinquency," Journal of Criminal Law and Criminology, 48:493–499, January, 1958.

[3] Donald R. Cressey, "Criminological Research and the Definition of Crimes," American Journal of Sociology, 56:546–551, May, 1951; and Guy Houchon, "Contribution a la Methode Differentielle en Criminologie," Revue Internationale de Criminologie et de Police Technique, 18:19–32, 1964.

[4] Jerome Hall, Theft, Law and Society, Second Edition (Indianapolis: Bobbs-Merrill, 1952).

crime or not crime. For this reason, the procedure will be discussed in more detail.

THE BEHAVIOR SYSTEM IN CRIME. The behavior system in crime may be described by its three principal characteristics. *First*, a behavior system in crime is not merely an aggregation of individual criminal acts. It is an integrated unit, which includes, in addition to the individual acts, the codes, traditions, *esprit de corps*, social relationships among the direct participants, and indirect participation of many other persons. It is thus essentially a groupway of life. Behavior systems in crime may be illustrated by professional theft, circus grifting, drug addiction, racketeering, fraudulent advertising, and manipulation of corporate securities as practiced by Insull, the Van Sweringens, and many others.

*Second*, the behavior which occurs in a behavior system is not unique to any particular individual.[5] It is common behavior. It operates in the same manner in a large number of persons and therefore it should be possible to find causal processes which are not unique to particular individuals.

*Third*, while common and joint participation in the system is the essential characteristic of a behavior system, it can frequently be defined by the feeling of identification of those who participate in it. If the participants feel that they belong together for this purpose, they do belong together. A professional confidence man and a professional forger would feel that they belonged together, even though they used different techniques, because they have many common interests and standards and can therefore participate in the same system. On the other hand an embezzler would not identify himself with an automobile thief. If these two should meet they would have no common reactions or sentiments growing out of their crimes except such as were common to practically all other persons who violate the laws. Ultimately a behavior system should be defined as a way of life which grows out of a unified causal process. A behavior system in this respect would be similar to a disease, which is differentiated from other diseases by the causal process common to it regardless of the person in whom it occurs.

If a behavior system can be isolated, the problem is to explain that system as a unit. This is similar to an attempt to explain baseball in America. This does not consist primarily of explaining why a particular person becomes a baseball player, and in fact the explanation of why a particular person becomes a ball player merely assumes the existence and persistence of baseball as a system. By taking the behavior system as a problem it is

[5] See Tamotsu Shibutani, "Reference Groups as Perspectives," *American Journal of Sociology*, 60:562–569, May, 1955.

possible to avoid some of the methodological difficulties which arise when the act of a specific person is taken as the problem.[6]

PROFESSIONAL THEFT AS A BEHAVIOR SYSTEM. Professional theft is presented as an illustration of a behavior system which can be defined and explained as a unit.[7] The principal genetic question regarding professional theft is: How does it originate and how is it perpetuated in our culture? A secondary question is: How does a particular person get into this professional group?

The principal, but not the only, rackets used by professional thieves are confidence games, shoplifting, and pocket-picking. Not all persons who commit these specific crimes are professional thieves. Professional thieves make a regular business of theft. They use techniques which have been developed over a period of centuries and transmitted to them through traditions and personal association. They have codes of behavior, esprit de corps, and consensus. They have a high status among other thieves and in the political and criminal underworld in general. They associate with each other and do not associate with outsiders on the same basis, and they carefully select their colleagues. They tend to look down upon amateur thieves, referring to them as "neurotic kids," because the crude crimes committed by amateurs arouse the public and make the professional practice of theft more difficult and less profitable.[8] Because of this differential association they develop a common language or argot which is relatively unknown to persons not in the profession. And they have organization.

A thief is a professional when he has these five characteristics: regular work at theft, technical skill, consensus, status, and organization. The amateur thief is not a professional; neither is the consistently dishonest bondsalesman. The case is not quite so clear for the professional burglar or robber, for there the principal differential is the nature of the technique and the identification. The techniques of the professional thief are much the same as those of the salesman and the actor; they consist of methods of manipulating the interests, attention, and behavior of the victim. The professional thief depends on cleverness and wits, while the robber or burglar resorts more frequently to force or threat of force. Professional thieves have their groupways of behavior for the principal situations which

[6] See Robert Dubin, "Deviant Behavior and Social Structure," *American Sociological Review*, 24:147–164, April, 1959; and J. Milton Yinger, "Contraculture and Subculture," *American Sociological Review*, 25:625–626, October, 1960.

[7] See Edwin H. Sutherland, *The Professional Thief* (Chicago: University of Chicago Press, 1937).

[8] See John K. Irwin and Donald R. Cressey, "Thieves, Convicts, and the Inmate Culture," *Social Problems*, 10:142–155, Fall, 1962.

confront them in their criminal activities. Consequently professional theft is a behavior system and a sociological entity.[9]

The motives of professional thieves are much the same as the motives of other occupational groups: they wish to make money in safety. These desires require no specific explanation. The specific problem is: How do professional thieves remain secure in their violations of the law? Many professional thieves have conducted their illegal activities for a normal lifetime and never been locked up longer than a few days at a time; others have had one or two terms over a period of twenty or thirty years.

Security in professional theft is attained in three ways. *First,* the thieves select rackets that involve a minimum of danger. The confidence game is relatively safe because the victim generally agrees to participate in a dishonest transaction and when he finds that he is the victim he cannot make complaint without disgracing himself. For example, the three principal types of big confidence game—the "wire," the "pay-off," and the "rag"— all involve victims who believe that they are defrauding someone. In the "wire" the confidence man convinces the victim that they can delay the telegrams of race results long enough so that the victim can make bets with bookmakers after the race is run, thereby defrauding the bookmakers; in the "pay-off" the victim believes he is defrauding a large racing syndicate; in the "rag" he believes he has "inside" information regarding the great value of apparently worthless stock.[10] Some confidence games do not depend upon the victim's willingness to do something dishonest, but all of them are quite safe.[11] In one recent version of an ancient confidence game, for example, the confidence man telephones the victim and represents himself as a radio announcer who is conducting a quiz program; after the victim answers a simple question the announcer tells him that he has won an amount of money equal to the amount of money he has in the house and asks him to name that amount; if $100 is mentioned the announcer says he will deliver that amount by messenger; when the messenger arrives he has two checks, one for $100 and the other for $200, and the latter is represented as a "double dividend" which the victim has won instead of the $100; after the victim gives the confidence man the $100 in cash, to prove that he actually had that amount in the house, he receives the bogus $100 check and a receipt for his money, plus the bogus check for the $200 prize; the confidence man then safely disappears. Similarly, shoplifting is

[9] See David W. Maurer, *Whiz Mob, A Correlation of the Technical Argot of Pickpockets with Their Behavior Patterns* (Gainesville, Florida: American Dialect Society, 1955), pp. 19–28; and Robert L. Gasser, *The Confidence World as a Criminal Behavior System,* unpublished Ph.D. dissertation, American University, 1955.

[10] David W. Maurer, *The Big Con* (Indianapolis: Bobbs-Merrill, 1940).

[11] See Fletcher Pratt, "The Grift Goes Legit," *Harper's* June, 1955, pp. 60–65.

relatively safe because the stores do not wish to run the risk of accusing legitimate customers of stealing, and the professional shoplifter makes it a point to look and act like a legitimate customer.[12] Picking pockets is relatively safe because the legal rules of evidence require direct evidence that the thief withdrew the money from the pocket, and that evidence is seldom secured.

Second, professional thieves develop clever and skilled techniques for executing the crimes they select. They do this through tradition, and tutelage. Cleverness and skill may merely mean brashness, as in the case of the thief who, in the sporting-goods section of a large department store, balanced an aluminum kayak on his head and walked out with it. Cleverness and skill also include such things as the utilization of one man to maneuver a victim so that another can pick his pocket, the dexterity required to steal a victim's wrist watch from his wrist, the device whereby one man distracts attention from a shoplifter by kicking or pinching a child so that he will set up a commotion, and the ability to identify, watch, and out-talk store clerks and detectives. Similarly, many ingenious devices for obtaining and carrying shoplifted goods have been invented. These include innocent-looking boxes with false bottoms so that they can be placed over counter merchandise, trousers with hidden pockets and linings, "belly pockets" worn around the waist, false arms, and rubber suction cups attached to strings and elastic bands.[13]

Third, the professional thief makes arrangements to fix those cases in which he may be caught. He expects to fix every such case. He generally does not fix the case himself but employs a professional fixer, for in a larger city one man generally does all of the fixing for all of the professional thieves. Whether the fixing is done by the thieves themselves or by their fixer, it is generally accomplished by the direct or indirect payment of money. Usually a promise is made to the victim that his stolen property will be returned, sometimes with a bonus, if he will refuse to push the prosecution or to testify in a way that would damage the thief. A large proportion of the cases are fixed in this manner, for the victim is generally more interested in the return of his stolen property than he is in seeing that justice is done to the thieves. If this fails, the police, prosecutor, bailiff, or judge may be bribed. The policeman may advise the victim to take his money back and not be bothered with a long trial; or he may give evidence which conflicts with that of the victim or other witnesses; or he

---

[12] See Mary Owen Cameron, *The Booster and the Snitch: Department Store Shoplifting*, New York: Free Press of Glencoe, 1964.
[13] See Lawrence Klingman, "The Booster, the Heel, and the Snitch," *Park East*, January, 1953, pp. 12–17.

may render other services. The prosecutor may refuse to push the prosecution or, if he is compelled to do so, he may make a very weak effort to bring out evidence which is damaging to the thief. As a last resort, the judge may be bribed to render a decision in favor of the thief, or to impose a minor penalty. It is not necessary that everyone of these officeholders act dishonestly. The only thing necessary is to find one of them who will twist or pervert evidence or decisions. As Maurer has said, "The dominant culture could control the predatory cultures without difficulty, and what is more, it could exterminate them, for no criminal subculture can operate continuously and professionally without the connivance of the law."[14]

The profession of theft, then, exists in modern society because victims are more interested in getting their property back than in abstract justice, because officeholders are under the control of a political machine or have predatory personal interests. Also, professional theft exists because business concerns are willing to purchase stolen commodities, and because lawyers are willing to defend professional thieves by every clever argument and device available. Professional theft exists not only because persons are willing to steal, but also because the rest of society does not present a solid front against theft. In other words, society is disorganized with reference to theft.

The entrance of a particular person into the professional group is of secondary importance, for the explanation of theft as a profession cannot be found in the life-history of one of the members of the profession. Rather it is necessary to understand the profession in order to explain the individual thief. For admission into the profession is not merely an act of will of a person who decides that he would like to be a professional thief. He can no more become a professional thief in that manner than he can become a professional ballplayer. Others must permit him to become a professional thief, just as they must permit a person to become a professional ballplayer. Members of the profession make their entrance by a process of mutual selection.

No one can acquire all of the skills and work safely in cooperation with others without training and tutelage. Lemert has pointed out that check forgery is now a crime committed principally by isolates, rather than a crime committed by professional criminals, as was the case in the nineteenth and early twentieth centuries, largely because the forger no longer needs tutelage by and cooperation with other forgers.[15] Tutelage in pro-

---

[14] *Op. cit.*, p. 129.
[15] Edwin M. Lemert, "The Behavior of the Systematic Check Forger," *Social Problems*, 6:141–149, Fall, 1958. See also his "An Isolation and Closure Theory of Naïve Check Forgery," *Journal of Criminal Law and Criminology*, 44:296–307, September–October, 1953.

fessional skills can be given only by those already in the profession. Consequently one gets into the profession by acceptance. If a neophyte satisfactorily performs his "apprentice" or "journeyman" tasks his responsibilities may be increased until he is finally given the same tasks as regular members of the profession.

Professional thieves do not extend this tutelage to everyone who would like to join them. They extend their assistance, of course, only to those with whom they come in contact in a friendly manner; that is, to fellow-lodgers in hotels, rooming-houses, or jails, and to waiters, cashiers, and taxicab drivers. The thieves get acquainted with most of these people in a legitimate manner, and confidence develops. They like a certain prospect, and he likes them. They may suggest that he join them, but more frequently he asks to join them because he wants more money than he can make at legitimate work and because their life looks attractive. Doubtless thousands of others with whom they do not come in contact in this manner have the abilities required for professional theft, but they do not happen to meet. Thus entrance into the profession is by selection. The selection is impersonal in the sense that a person must be in a position where he will come in contact with professional thieves in order to develop personal acquaintance. The selection is also personal in the sense that the thieves must be attracted to the prospect, and he must be attracted to them. He has a veto on joining the profession, but just as certainly they have a veto on him joining it.

CIRCUS GRIFTING. Circus grifting is a second behavior system in crime, which will be described as an illustration of this method of analysis. It consists principally of sure-thing gambling, as seen in the shell game, three-card monte, the eight-dice cloth, the cologne joint, and the spindle. In order that circus-grifting may be conducted satisfactorily and safely, four elements are necessary: grifters, victims, a dishonest circus management, and dishonest public officials. The behavior system is a combination of these four elements.

Circus grifters come from two principal sources. They may have been grifting previously in state fairs, resort communities, or carnivals, with methods somewhat similar to those used in the circus. Or they may have been living in the community in which the circus is playing, have been employed for a day as a shill or assistant in one of the games, have proved efficient, and have been taken along with the circus and trained in other details of the game. It is reported that a large proportion of the circus grifters originated in Indiana, where several circuses make their winter headquarters.

The circus grifters form a relatively cohesive group. They have a saying, "Once a circus grifter, always a circus grifter." The gambling games played in the circus are played elsewhere, but seldom with the same abandon. Many people who play one of these games elsewhere do not succeed in the circus, and many who are very successful in the circus are inefficient when they try to operate the same games elsewhere. The grifters in a particular circus are a somewhat exclusive group while the circus is on the road; the performers do not associate with them. In the early days the grifters rode in the "privilege car" of the circus train. This car was lined with steel to protect the occupants from attacks by angered residents of the community in which the gambling games had been operated. Also the grifters from all circuses associate during the winter season, for many of them spend the winter, or as much of it as their funds permit, in Hot Springs. The grifter in one circus will know the principal grifters in all of the other circuses. This exclusive association is a product of the necessity for training and tutelage in the operation of the gambling games.

Victims are available in practically every community. The general interest in gambling is the basis, but to this are added, first, the general atmosphere of make-believe and celebration connected with the circus, and second, the techniques used in appealing to spectators. One of these techniques is the example of the shill, who appears to be another spectator, but is actually an assistant in the game, and who plays and wins frequently. Another technique is an apparent opportunity for dishonesty; one of the shills raises one of the shells while the operator's back is turned and enables the other spectators to see the pea under the shell, or he bends the corner of the card in the monte game so that the spectator knows which card to select. Since this dishonesty seems to make the gamble absolutely certain, many spectators then try it, and lose. The suggestions and insistence of the operator and of other assistants who seem to be spectators are factors. Finally, the general method is to induce a spectator to make a start, even without paying, and he is then ashamed to stop after a loss or two.

Dishonest public officials can be found in a large proportion of the communities in which circuses appear. Gambling is at least winked at in most communities, and the officials feel that some gambling in connection with the celebration at the time of a circus can be condoned, especially in return for tickets or money.

Dishonest circus managers have been abundant. The circus fifty years ago generally depended on the return from grifting for a substantial part of its income. The circus manager employed a "privilege man" who had charge of all of the grifting, and who paid to the circus a percentage of everything taken in on all of the games. Many of the circus managers started as grifters, and were sympathetic toward the grifters.

These four elements are therefore the necessary characteristics of this behavior system. Circus grifting was authorized and flourished in practically all of the circuses in 1880, in all except Ringling's in 1900, and all except the largest circuses in 1930. In other words, circus-grifting is decreasing. The circus grifters explain that this decrease is not due to a reduction in the number of potential grifters, or in the number of potential victims, or in the number of dishonest public officials. They insist that the decrease is due entirely to the changed attitude of circus managers. Moreover, the changed attitude of the circus manager is not due to an increase in honest motives, but to a change in the economic relationships. In the earlier days the grifting circus could change its name and thus conceal its identity before returning to a community which had been angered by the gambling games on the last trip. As the circus increased in size, its name came to be an asset from the point of view of advertising and could not be changed without loss of prestige and therefore loss of income. The loss from the change of name would be greater than the gain from grifting, and therefore grifting was reluctantly abandoned. It is for that reason that grifting is now found only in the smaller circuses.

The principal question is: Why did the circus ever authorize and participate in grifting? The most immediate answer is that this was a specific manifestation of generally dishonest tendencies. Many circuses in early days were fences for stolen horses. Its employees have been notorious for thefts from clotheslines. The circus management has frequently dealt dishonestly with its employees, holding out a part of the wages, overcharging on expenses. The circus has been unfair in its competition with the other circuses. The men who put up posters in the early decades were necessarily sluggers who could fight with the bill plasterers of rival circuses. Many of the attractions have been frauds. The "garmagunt" with three heads and eight legs was made of sole leather. The Siamese twins were two separate persons with a flesh-colored belt holding them together during the time they were on exhibition. The "horse with its tail where its head ought to be" was discovered, after payment of ten cents, to be a horse with its tail toward the manger. The exhibit "for men only" proved to be a pair of suspenders. The emu eggs sold by the attendant to farmers for $1.50 each proved to be goose eggs. The man who sold balloons hired an assistant to go through the circus grounds and, with his mouth full of tacks, blow them at the balloons which had been purchased so that resales could be made. Hundreds of incidents of this nature are recounted in the histories of the circus.

This general dishonesty, in which the circus grifting was embedded, was a product of four conditions. *First,* the circus was a mobile organization. It seldom remained longer than one day in a community, and there were no permanent ties, duties, responsibilities, or relationships. The circus was regarded as queer by the community, and the community was regarded as queer by the circus people. *Second,* the community was hostile toward the circus in several respects. In some places the circus or any other exhibit was prohibited. The opposition was partly on the ground of morals. It was believed that the circus would corrupt the young people. In some communities it was customary for the preachers to agree to preach anti-circus sermons in all churches on the Sunday preceding the circus. To counteract this, Barnum advertised moral lectures as a part of the circus program, but the lectures bulked larger in the advertisements than they did in the program. The opposition was also on economic grounds. It was believed that the circus took away from the community money which should be spent in the community. *Third,* the people of the community frequently were dishonest in their dealings with the circus. The head of the department of streets in one city on the night before the appearance of the circus substituted old, worn-out manhole covers for the ones then in use, so that many of these covers would be broken by the heavy wagons in the circus parade. He then presented to the circus a bill for damages each year until the circus became suspicious and discovered the truth. A woman whose home was adjacent to the circus grounds claimed damages of fifty dollars because her laundry on the clothesline was spotted by flies attracted by the circus. The circus promised to give a free ticket to each child in an orphanage and to enough attendants to take care of the children; when the children arrived each one had an adult attendant. Thus the circus has been confronted with continuous efforts to impose upon it. *Fourth,* on the basis of this mobility, opposition, and community impositions, the circus personnel were undoubtedly selected. It was not a random assortment of the population of the country, but rather was selected for that type of life. They had had a hard, unsociable life, and they were hard, unsociable people. Out of this has grown the general dishonesty and grifting. It is reported that the English circus, which was much less mobile than the American circus, had very little dishonesty.[16]

[16] See Bert J. Chipman, "Hey Rube!" (Hollywood: Hollywood Print Shop, 1933); C. R. Cooper, Circus Day (New York: Farrar and Rinehart, 1931); E. C. May, The Circus from Rome to Ringling (New York: Duffield and Green, 1932); Gil Robinson, Old Wagon Show Days (Cincinnati: Brockwell, 1925); R. E. Sherwood, Hold Yer Hosses! The Elephants Are Coming! (New York: Macmillan, 1932); E. H. Smith, "Grift, An Account Based on Statement by Hoke Hammond," Collier's, 69:11–12, 20–21, April 8, 1922; M. R. Werner, Barnum (New York: Harcourt, Brace, 1923).

KIDNAPING.    Kidnaping is discussed here as an illustration of a legal entity which is not a sociologically homogeneous unit. As kidnaping is studied further, it is possible that behavior systems will be found, or that sociologically significant types of kidnaping will be identified, or that certain of the forms of kidnaping will be found to have characteristics in common with certain of the offenses described by another legal term, such as assault or murder.

As a legal entity, kidnaping consists of taking possession of the body of another person, against his will, by force or fraud and in violation of the law. Kidnaping appears in at least ten forms which are socially distinct and which generally involve different causal processes. *First*, kidnaping was the basis of the slave trade, and all those who participated in the slave trade and in slavery were accessory to kidnaping. *Second*, impressment was a form of kidnaping in which a sailor was forced to leave a ship in which he had a legal right to be, to board another ship and work there as a sailor. *Third*, men were shanghaied by force and compelled to work as sailors in ships. They received wages, but commissions for the crimps who had kidnaped them were deducted from their wages. *Fourth*, girls were kidnaped and used for prostitution. This aroused attention in the period before World War I under the name of white slavery. Probably few bona fide cases occurred, and at any rate the law which was enacted has been used extensively by "gold diggers" as a means of blackmailing their paramours. *Fifth*, underworld leaders were kidnaped by underworld criminals and held for ransom, especially during the prohibition period. Since the underworld leaders were not able to appeal to the law for support and did not wish to advertise their inability to protect themselves, these kidnapings aroused little public attention. *Sixth*, kidnaping of wealthy persons in the upperworld by members of the underworld for purposes of ransom developed extensively about 1930, so that newspapers announced a new crime in the making. While kidnaping of wealthy and respectable persons for ransom had occurred occasionally in the United States prior to this date, its prevalence increased at that time. But kidnaping for ransom was not new, and kidnaping for other purposes was not new. The only thing that was new was the importance of the victims. *Seventh*, offenders took possession of victims in connection with other crimes, such as robbery, as a means of security for themselves. This was temporary and the victim was released as soon as the offender was secure. *Eighth*, illegal arrest is a form of kidnaping. If a policeman takes possession of a person under conditions not authorized by law, he is committing the crime of kidnaping. In this sense, policemen have kidnaped many times as frequently as all other offenders combined. During the 1930's, a special form of this appeared in connection with strikes, when special police took pickets, reporters, stu-

dents, and others to the state line and pushed them across, with instructions not to return. *Ninth,* children have been kidnaped by lonesome and
probably psychopathic women in lieu of other methods of securing children of their own. *Tenth,* parents have kidnaped their own children who
have been assigned by the court to the other parent in divorce proceedings,
or under other circumstances. Doubtless other minor forms of kidnaping
could be found, but these ten are a sufficient number to show that kidnaping is not an entity in the causal sense.

These ten forms are, to be sure, somewhat interrelated. The first six
forms mentioned (slave trade, impressment, shanghaiing, white slavery,
underworld ransom cases, and upperworld ransom cases) all have financial
returns as the objective, while the last four do not have this objective.
Moreover, the six which have financial gain as the objective may be divided
into two groups: those in which there is a large demand for victims with
a small price per victim, and those in which there is a restricted demand
with a high price per victim; the latter cases are those in which ransom is
used. Also, they can be divided into kidnapings with respectable and important offenders and lowly, unimportant victims; and kidnapings with
underworld offenders and important victims. The only form of kidnaping
that has aroused great public antagonism is that in which the victims are
important and respectable; the much more extensive kidnapings in which
the victims were unimportant or not respectable continued for centuries
before enough opposition developed to stop the practices. Consequently,
explanation of the existence and continuance of one form of kidnaping is
likely to be different from explanation of another form.[17]

CONCLUSION. Professional theft and circus grifting have been described in
some detail as illustrations of the procedure for studying behavior systems
in crime. Neither of these topics has been investigated exhaustively and
the interpretations are therefore tentative and hypothetical. More intensive studies are needed of these two behavior systems and of other behavior
systems in crime before general propositions can be developed.

It is not understood that the entire area of crime can be covered in this
manner. Rather it is understood that certain crimes cluster in systems, are
organized, are combined with other behavior in such manner as to form
systems, and that certain other crimes stand somewhat isolated and outside
of systems. These behavior systems may be understood more readily than

[17] The following references on kidnaping are restricted principally to the recent
literature on kidnaping for ransom. Herbert Asbury, *Barbary Coast* (New York:
Knopf, 1933), pp. 199–231; Justine Mansfield, *True Tales of Kidnaping* (New York:
Business Bourse Press, 1932); Melvin Purvis, *American Agent* (Garden City: Double-
day, Doran, 1936), pp. 70–97, 117–174, 221–242; E. D. Sullivan, *The Snatch Racket*
(New York: Vanguard Press, 1932).

the isolated crimes, and therefore the study of them may yield general propositions that apply to a considerable part of criminal behavior. Then legal categories designating less systematic crimes, such as murder, embezzlement, and some forms of kidnaping, can be combined or redefined in such a way that the behavior designated by them can be studied scientifically and related to the general propositions.

## SUGGESTED READINGS

Asbury, Herbert, The Gangs of New York. New York: Knopf, 1928.

Barbash, James T., "Compensation and the Crime of Pigeon Dropping," Journal of Clinical Psychology, 8:92–94, October, 1951.

Becker, Howard S., Outsiders. Glencoe: The Free Press, 1963.

Black, Jack, "A Burglar Looks at Laws and Codes," Harpers, 160:306–313, February, 1930.

Burgess, E. W., "Discussion" of Frank E. Hartung, "White-Collar Offenses in the Wholesale Meat Industry in Detroit," American Journal of Sociology, 56:25–34, July, 1950.

Cameron, Mary Owen, The Booster and the Snitch: Department Store Shoplifting. New York: Free Press of Glencoe, 1964.

Clarke, Donald H., In the Reign of Rothstein. New York: Vanguard Press, 1929.

Debaun, Everett, "The Heist: Theory and Practice of Armed Robbery," Harpers, 180:69–77, February, 1950.

Dentler, Robert A., and Kai T. Erikson, "The Function of Deviance in Groups," Social Problems, 7:98–107, Fall, 1959.

Dubin, Robert, "Deviant Behavior and Social Structure," American Sociological Review, 24:147–164, April, 1959.

Gibbons, Don C., and Donald L. Garrity, "Definition and Analysis of Certain Criminal Types," Journal of Criminal Law, Criminology, and Police Science, 53:27–35, March, 1962.

Gordon, Milton, "The Concept of the Subculture and Its Application," Social Forces, 26:40–42, October, 1947.

Hall, Jerome, Theft, Law and Society, Second Edition. Indianapolis: Bobbs-Merrill, 1952.

Hamilton, Charles (Editor), Men of the Underworld: The Professional Criminal's Own Story. New York: Macmillan, 1902

Hapgood, Hutchins, Autobiography of a Thief. New York: Fox. Duffield, 1903.

Hentig, Hans von, "The Pickpocket: Psychology, Tactics, and Techniques," Journal of Criminal Law and Criminology, 34:11–15, May–June, 1943.

Hollingshead, August B., "Behavior Systems as a Field for Research," American Journal of Sociology, 4:816–822, December, 1939.

Hoover, J. Edgar, "Bankruptcy Frauds," *Journal of Criminal Law and Criminology*, 23:1073–1080, March–April, 1933.

Irwin, John K., *Surfers: A Study of the Growth of a Deviant Subculture.* Unpublished Master's Thesis, Department of Sociology, University of California, Berkeley, 1965.

Irwin, Will, *Confessions of a Con Man.* New York: B. W. Huebsch, 1919.

Kahn, E. J., Jr., "Annals of Crime," *The New Yorker*, April 11, 1959, pp. 120–153.

Jackman, Norman R., Richard O'Toole, and Gilbert Geis, "The Self-Image of the Prostitute," *Sociological Quarterly*, April, 1963, pp. 150–161.

John I. Kitsuse, "Societal Reaction to Deviant Behavior," *Social Problems*, 9:246–256, Winter, 1962.

Lemert, Edwin M., "An Isolation and Closure Theory of Naïve Check Forgery," *Journal of Criminal Law, Criminology, and Police Science*, 44:296–307, September–October, 1953.

Lemert, Edwin M., "The Behavior of the Systematic Check Forger," *Social Problems*, 6:141–149, Fall, 1958.

Lottier, S., "Tension Theory of Criminal Behavior," *American Sociological Review*, 7:840–848, December, 1942.

Martin, John Bartlow, *My Life in Crime.* New York: New American Library, 1952.

Maurer, David W., *The Big Con.* Indianapolis: Bobbs-Merrill, 1940.

Maurer, David W., *Whiz Mob, A Correlation of the Technical Argot of Pickpockets with Their Behavior Pattern.* Gainesville, Florida: American Dialect Society, 1955.

McKenzie, Donald, *Occupation: Thief.* Indianapolis: Bobbs-Merrill, 1955.

Peterson, Virgil W., "Chicago's Crime Problem," *Journal of Criminal Law and Criminology*, 36:3–15, May–June, 1944.

Riemer, Svend, "Embezzlement: Pathological Basis," *Journal of Criminal Law and Criminology*, 32:411–423, November–December, 1941.

Shibutani, Tamotsu, "Reference Groups as Perspectives," *American Journal of Sociology*, 60:562–569, May, 1955.

Simmons, J. L., "On Maintaining Deviant Belief Systems," *Social Problems*, 11:250–256, Winter, 1964.

Sterling, Stewart, "Stop That Shoplifter," *Saturday Evening Post*, October 22, 1949, pp. 19 ff.

Sutherland, Edwin H., *The Professional Thief.* Chicago: University of Chicago Press, 1937.

Sutherland, Edwin H., "The Professional Thief," *Journal of Criminal Law and Criminology*, 28:161–163, July–August, 1937.

Yinger, J. Milton, "Contraculture and Subculture," *American Sociological Review*, 25:625–626, October, 1960.

# part 2 THE CONTROL OF CRIME

# 14. VARIATIONS IN PUNITIVE POLICIES

WITH THIS chapter we begin the study of various methods of dealing with crime and with apprehended criminals. On a general level, these methods may be described as "societal reactions" to crime and criminality, and, as such, they are subject to analysis and explanation, just as are the criminal reactions themselves. However, social scientists have concentrated on understanding and explaining law-breaking itself rather than on understanding and explaining the societal reactions to law-breaking. Consequently, much available information about the societal reactions to law-breaking has not been organized or integrated, and theoretical problems in control of crime are not as sharply delimited as are theoretical problems in criminal etiology. Systematic organization of knowledge pertaining to crime control is a prerequisite not only for understanding and explanation of present and future control policies, but for their efficient direction and administration as well. As a preliminary step toward such integration, four general problems in the control of crime will be specified.

One general problem is closely analogous to the problem of observing variations in crime rates. Just as many variations in crime rates have been described, careful descriptions of variations in societal reactions to crime should be made. The varieties of methods and policies for control of crime are enormous, if they are considered in detail, and an important part of the problem is to classify and generalize these variations in a manner which will make them easier to study and understand. For instance, we can readily observe a great number of variations in reactions to law-breaking, not only in the United States at present, but in the history of mankind. In some social systems the reaction to law-breaking is annihilation, in some systems severe corporal punishments, in others imprisonment or probation, and so on. Similarly, the number of variations in the official policies for implementing the societal reactions to crime—such as policies for police, courts, prisons—is enormous. For example, in some prisons the inmates are tortured, in others they are studiously ignored except when they try to escape, and in others serious efforts are made to "treat" and rehabilitate them. These many variations can be classified tentatively according to their position on a scale ranging from a purely *punitive* reaction or policy to a purely *treatment* reaction or policy, although this classification does not summarize all of the differences. Some societal reactions to crime and, hence, some policies and organizations for control of crime, have been and are directed primarily by punitive considerations, others by treatment considerations, and a final category by a mixture of punitive and treatment considerations.

Second, the general problem of "efficiency" must be analyzed if the materials on control of crime are to be integrated. Is crime control "better" when punitive policies are used than when treatment policies are used? Official policies in recent times have shown a distinct trend toward treatment and away from punishment, but this trend is not based on a demonstration of the superiority of treatment methods. The criteria of efficiency have not been precisely established nor agreed upon, and "better control" cannot be established until such criteria are defined. One preliminary and general criterion is that the system is most efficient which results in the smallest number of crimes, other things being equal. A small number of crimes may result from either of two things: few people who commit crimes, or few repetitions of crimes by those who commit at least one crime. Hence, according to this criterion, an efficient system would reform those who commit crimes, so that they do not repeat often, and also it would keep others from committing their first crimes, either by "deterrence," which has to do with refraining from crime because of fear of punishment, or by "prevention," which has to do with refraining from crime for other reasons. This statement of the criterion of efficiency leaves many problems unsolved, such as the relation between efficient control of crime and efficiency in other respects, and the relation between reformation and deterrence.

In dealing with problems of efficiency the question also must be raised as to whether the most efficient method or policy for controlling crime in order to reduce crime rates has a chance of being adopted in a given society at a given time. For example, even if it were shown with complete certainty that crime would be greatly reduced by methods which are much closer to "pure" treatment (no punishment) than those now being used in the United States, this policy might not be adopted. In view of what appears to be a punitive societal reaction to law-breaking, our society probably would reject such a method. Similarly, a policy of extremely severe punishment might be rejected, even if it were shown to be the

most efficient method of dealing with criminals, for the society also possesses certain humanitarian attitudes. Or the society might formally adopt
the efficient policy of "pure" treatment or severe punishment, only to
wink at its enforcement. There is doubt as to whether such a policy would,
in the circumstances in which it would be expected to operate, be superior
to some other policy which could be carried out in a straight-forward
manner.

A third general problem is establishment of the relation of the varying
reactions to law-breaking and methods of control to the existing knowledge
of the causation of criminal behavior. Every method for control of crime
is based, implicitly or explicitly, on a theory of crime causation. However,
changes in policies do not immediately follow new discoveries about crime
causation, and it may be presumed that some present methods are inefficient because they are based on erroneous theories.[1] Many modifications would be made if police departments, courts, probation departments,
and prisons operated strictly in accordance with the criminological theory
of emotional disturbances, or with the theory of economic determinism,
or with the differential association theory.

The fourth general problem is not unlike the general problem of explaining crime and criminality. The problem may be summarized by the
question: *Why do the policies and methods in control of crime vary from
time to time and from place to place?* If changes in policies are to be controlled, not only the variations, but the causes of the variations must be
understood. One basic subsidiary problem in this area is that of accounting
for the origins and variations in general societal reactions to law-breaking,
such as the punitive reaction and the treatment reaction. More specific or
detailed subsidiary problems are the following: (a) Explaining the variations in the traditional "modalities" of punishment: severity, uniformity,
celerity, and certainty. In some societies punishments may be comparatively severe, uniform, swift, or certain, while in other societies the reaction
to law-breaking may be punitive but not so severe, uniform, *etc.* The
problem is to account for these differences. (b) Explaining variations in
specific methods of implementing the punitive reaction, such as the death
penalty, corporal punishment, imprisonment, and fines. In some societies
the punitive reaction may be implemented almost exclusively by imposing
punishment by imprisonment, while in other societies it may be implemented by imposing punishment corporally. (c) Explaining variations in
specific methods of implementing the treatment reaction, such as individual case work with criminals, group or community work, and group

[1] See Donald R. Cressey, "The Nature and Effectiveness of Correctional Techniques," *Law and Contemporary Problems*, 23:754–771, Autumn, 1958.

therapy. (d) Explaining the differences between the "official" or formal societal reactions to crime and the unofficial or informal reactions.

The present chapter supplies some of the data on variations in the general punitive reaction to crime, as well as on variations in the use of specific methods of punishment, in different times and places. Chapters 15 and 16 are concerned with variations in other specific aspects of the punitive reaction, with variations in the treatment reaction, with the comparative efficiency of punitive and treatment policies, and with explanation of variations in punishment and treatment. After this "introduction," the treatment and punitive aspects of the various agencies and institutions which deal with the criminal, from the time of his apprehension to the time of his discharge from parole, will be discussed.

DEFINITION OF PUNISHMENT.—Two essential ideas are contained in the concept of punishment as an instrument of public justice. (a) It is inflicted by the group in its corporate capacity upon one who is regarded as a member of the same group. War is not punishment for in war the action is directed against foreigners. The loss of status which often follows crime is not punishment, except in so far as it is administered in measure by the group in its corporate capacity. (b) Punishment involves pain or suffering produced by design and justified by some value that the suffering is assumed to have. If the pain or suffering is merely accidental, to be avoided if possible, it is not punishment. A surgical operation performed on a prisoner to correct a physical defect is not punishment, for the pain is not regarded as valuable or desirable. The confinement of a psychotic person may involve suffering for him, but it is not punishment. Many of the modern methods of dealing with criminals, especially juvenile court procedures, are not punitive. While any method used by the courts in dealing with criminals probably involves some suffering, it seems preferable to limit the punishment concept to the deliberate infliction of suffering regarded as valuable. This is the conventional conception as used in the criminal law.

VARIATIONS IN THE PUNITIVE REACTION TO LAW-BREAKING.  Many writers have maintained that punishment is an expression of an instinct of vengeance or the expression of a desire for vengeance which consists of a complex of instincts or processes. Undoubtedly some crimes and other acts which are regarded as wrong upset the equilibrium of society and the interests of individual members, and various punitive reactions which partially restore this equilibrium take place. There is, however, no evidence that these reactions are directed by an instinct of vengeance or by a basic desire for punishment of the offender. Furthermore, the punitive reaction

is only one of many reactions to law-breaking, and it is not at all important
in the reactions to offenses occurring among nonliterate peoples.

Three types of wrongs, followed by three types of reactions, no one of
which is clearly punitive, may be found in preliterate societies. The first includes tribal and sacral offenses, such as treason, witchcraft, sacrilege, and
poisoning. Although such offenses seldom occurred in small, homogeneous
groups, when they did occur the societal reaction was annihilation. The
group might annihilate the offender by either death or exile; both rendered
the offender nonexistent so far as the group was concerned. The reaction
of annihilation was closely related to war, social hygiene, and sacrifice. The
offender was regarded as an enemy and was treated as an enemy. He also
was considered to be polluted, and the tribe attempted to get rid of him
and of everything connected with him as a social hygiene measure. Thus,
in many societies witchcraft was followed by death, and the body of the
offender was thrown into the sea, which was supposed to have cleansing
power, or it was buried on foreign soil. His name could not even be mentioned for fear that it might carry pollution with it. An element of sacrifice
appears, also, in the reaction to these offenders; the reaction was designed
to please the gods.

The second group of wrongs were injuries to private individuals who
were not in the same family (gens, clan, etc.). The offenses would now be
defined as assault, murder, theft; generally, they provoked feuds between
families. The attitude in these feuds was largely vengeance, and severe
suffering was involved. But the reaction to the offense was not a societal
reaction; it was private, involving two private individuals and their relatives.
By and large, the general community was merely a spectator, although one
or the other of the opposing parties was likely to enjoy the approval or
tacit support of the disinterested remainder of his society.[2] This seems to
have been the origin of the system of payment of damages in civil courts,
but not of punishment by criminal courts.

The third group of wrongs consisted of injuries to other members of the
same family. These wrongs were neither regarded as crimes nor followed
by punishment in the sense that the word is used today. In the family, as
in the tribe generally, ridicule was the most powerful method of control
and was generally sufficient to secure observance of rules. This is illustrated
by the Andaman Islanders:

There is no such thing as the punishment of a crime by the society. If
one person injured another, it was left to the injured one to seek vengeance
if he wished and if he dared. There were probably always some who would

[2] E. Adamson Hoebel, *The Law of Primintive Man: A Study in Comparative Legal
Dynamics* (Cambridge: Harvard University Press, 1954), pp. 329–330.

side with the criminal, their attachment to him overcoming their disapproval of his actions. The only painful result of anti-social actions was the loss of the esteem of others. This in itself was a punishment that the Andamanese, with their great personal vanity, would feel keenly, and it was in most instances sufficient to prevent such actions. For the rest, good order depended largely on the influence of the more prominent men and women.[3]

Even if a person killed his father, which was in many preliterate groups regarded as a horrible offense, he was not punished by the other members of the family or by the tribe, the members of the family felt that since the family had already been weakened by the loss of one member, it would be foolish to weaken it still more by injuring the offender. They looked upon such acts, however, with great surprise and disgust.

Similarly, among modern non-literate peoples who are fairly well segregated from civilization, as among primitive peoples, punishment of children seldom occurs.

Travelers everywhere have remarked upon the extreme indulgence toward children. This is very marked among the Eskimos, though perhaps not more so than among the Fuegians of South America. Wherever we have data parents almost never punish or even severely reprove, but such pressure as may be needed is exercised by certain relatives. . . . Chastising the young seems to have been practised in the centres of higher culture, but outside of these limits was practically unknown. . . . In short, the same principles applied to control of the young as to adults, viz., admonition and ridicule. In fact, the whole control of the local group in aboriginal days seems to have been exercised by admonition and mild ridicule instead of by force and punishment.[4]

The Winnebago Indian had the following precepts:

"If you have a child and it is naughty do not strike it. In old times if a child was naughty the parents did not strike it but made it fast. When it is quite hungry it will reflect upon its disobedience. If you hit him you will merely put more naughtiness into him. It is said that mothers should not lecture the children, that they merely make the children bad by admonishing them."[5]

[3] A. Radcliffe-Brown, The Andaman Islanders (Cambridge: The University Press, 1922), p. 52.
[4] C. Wissler, The American Indian (New York: Oxford University Press, 1922), pp. 177–178. Reprinted by permission of the publishers.
[5] Paul Radin, Crashing Thunder: The Autobiography of a Winnebago Indian (New York: D. Appleton-Century, 1926), p. 463. Reprinted by permission of the publishers.

In these non-literate groups, therefore, we find certain motives and attitudes which apparently preceded the punitive reaction to law-breaking but were not, in themselves, punishment: desire to annihilate an enemy of the group, sacrifice to appease or fend off the wrath of the gods, social hygiene measures to rid the community of pollution, self-redress in cases of private injury, and surprise and disgust at the person who injured his own family. Deliberate and "just" infliction of pain by the group in its corporate capacity was not invented until later.

With the rise of kingship and the king's authority, disposition of wrongdoers became a public matter. The "court" arose and was backed by the central authority. The reaction to wrongs became collective or social rather than private, and wrongs were viewed as crimes—that is, as offenses against the group as well as against the victim.[6] The reaction approached the punitive reaction as we now know it, for severe corporal punishments were inflicted by the group, but the notion that the pain imposed by the group has some value in itself was not necessarily present. This kind of reaction is illustrated in the following statement about the Anglo-Saxon period in England:

A detected criminal was either fined, mutilated, or killed, but punishment, as we now understand the term, was seldom inflicted; that is to say, the dominant idea was neither to reform the culprit nor to deter others from following in his footsteps. If a man was killed it was either to satisfy the bloodfeud or to remove him out of the way as a wild beast would be destroyed; if a man was mutilated by having his fore-finger cut off or branded with a red-hot iron on the brow, it was done not so much to give him pain as to make him less expert in his trade of thieving and to put upon him an indelible mark by which all men should know that he was no longer a man to be trusted; if a fine were levied, it was more with a view to the satisfaction of the recipients of the money or cattle or what not, than with the intention of causing discomfort or loss to the offender.[7]

It was not until the modern period that the clearly punitive reaction to crime—the purposive infliction of pain on the offender because of some assumed value of the pain—became popular. Debates regarding the wisdom and efficiency of this societal reaction and of specific policies and

[6] *Cf.* E. Faris, "The Origin of Punishment," *International Journal of Ethics,* 25:54–67, October, 1914; Max Radin, "Enemies of Society," *Journal of Criminal Law and Criminology,* 27:328–356, September–October, 1936; Hans von Hentig, *Punishment, Its Origin, Purpose and Psychology* (London: William Hodge, 1937).

[7] W. L. M. Lee, *History of Police in England* (London: Methuen, 1901), p. 10. See also Linton C. Freeman and Robert F. Winch, "Societal Complexity: An Empirical Test of a Typology of Societies," *American Journal of Sociology,* 62:461–466, March, 1957.

methods consistent with it gave rise to three schools of penology: the classical, the neo-classical, and the positive or Italian. The principal arguments of these schools will be used here as illustrations of variations in the punitive reaction to crime, on the assumption that each of the schools arose as a result of or in connection with a variation in general societal reaction to crime, rather than on the assumption that the arguments of the schools caused the variations. The societal reactions reflected in the writings of the members of the neo-classical and the positive schools are conflicting, but both are characteristic of the United States at the present time. They were discussed earlier in the section on schools of criminology.

1) The classical school, to which Beccaria made one of the first significant contributions and to which Rousseau, Montesquieu, and Voltaire belonged, maintained the doctrine of psychological hedonism, that the individual calculates pleasures and pains in advance of action and regulates his conduct by the results of his calculations. The implication of the doctrine was that the societal reaction to crime should be the administration of a measured amount of pain. The general proposition of the classical school was that it is necessary to make undesirable acts painful by attaching punishment to them and to make the amount of pain thus attached entirely definite, so that the prospective criminal could make his calculations on it, and to make it just sufficient so that the pain would exceed the pleasure. Since the punishment must be one that can be calculated, it must be the same for all individuals, regardless of age, mentality, social status, or other conditions. The question of individual responsibility was not considered, just as it had not been considered in the earlier period when the offender was annihilated.[8] Bentham, the great reformer of the criminal law in this period, tried to extend hedonistic calculus by working out precise mathematical laws for the infliction of punishment.

2) The neo-classical school, which arose at the time of the French Revolution and the period immediately following, maintained that while the classical doctrine was correct in general it should be modified in certain details: since children and "lunatics" cannot calculate pleasures and pains they should not be regarded as criminals or be punished. This principle

---

[8] In the earlier period this lack of consideration for responsibility can best be shown by the penalties imposed upon inanimate objects, insects, and lower animals. Ives reports a number of instances in which inanimate objects were punished, and Evans collected a mass of materials regarding the medieval and modern practice of punishing animals. Much doubt has been cast on the authenticity of Evans's account by Liquori, however, and it is highly probable that the few cases which may have occurred have little significance from a theoretical point of view. George Ives, A History of Penal Methods (London: Stanley Paul, 1914), p. 254; E. P. Evans, The Criminal Prosecution and Capital Punishment of Animals (London: W. Heinemann, 1906), pp. 143, 175; Sister Mary Liquori, "The Trial and Punishment of Animals," America, February 1, 1936, pp. 395–396.

was to some extent extended to others, also, by the system of taking into account certain "mitigating circumstances." The reaction to crime, therefore, was no longer purely punitive; punishment were imposed on some law-breakers but not on others.[9] By recognition of the exceptions, individual responsibility was taken into account and subsequently it was necessary for administrators of justice to consider the psychology and sociology of crime. The neo-classical argument became the basic principle of the judicial and legal system of Western civilization during the last century.

The positive school denied individual responsibility and reflected an essentially non-punitive reaction to crime and criminality. Since the criminal was held to be not responsible for his acts, he was not to be punished. The adherents of this school maintained that a crime, as any other act, is a natural phenomenon, just like a tornado, a flood, a stroke of lightning, or the striking of a snake.[10] In self-protection, the group might put the criminal to death or incarcerate him, but these precautions were not punishment. Criminals who could be reformed were to be reformed and those who could not be reformed were to be segregated or killed. Denial of individual responsibility seriously affects the accused criminal's rights to a jury trial, to counsel, to confront witnesses, and to other safeguards of "due process of law."[11]

In contrast with the societal reactions to crime reflected in these three earlier schools of penology, two present-day reflections of a distinctly "treatment" reaction to law-breaking are appearing. The first of these is treatment by individual case work, which is based upon the premises of the positive school, although differing from it as to procedures. The second cannot be easily named, but it involves a belief that crime is an expression of a situation, generally involving a group, and cannot be "treated" effectively by isolating particular persons for case work but must be treated

---

[9] In general until the last two centuries, intent was not considered in the treatment of criminals, or was considered only occasionally or incidentally; little interest in the question of responsibility appeared. Intensive studies of particular communities indicate, however, that generalizations of this nature are subject to many exceptions. For instance, in Basel criminal responsibility was emphasized considerably by the beginning of the fourteenth century, and the law took into account youthful age, mental disease, drunkenness, force, accident, and negligence as factors involved in the responsibility. Karl Metzger, *Die Verbrechen und ihre Straffolgen im Basler Recht des späteren Mittelalters* (Basel: Helbing, Lichtenhahn, 1931).

[10] In Europe, recent attempts to introduce this idea into penal legislation are properly characterized as pleas for "social defense" against criminals. For a history of the "new social defense" movement, see Marc Ancel, "Défense Sociale et Prophylaxie Criminelle," pp. 141–152 in *Hommage a Georges Heuyer Pour Un Humanisme Médico-Social* (Paris: Presses Universitaires de France, 1961).

[11] Cf. Jerome Hall, "Science and Reform in Criminal Law," *University of Pennsylvania Law Review*, 100:787–804, April, 1952.

as a situation or group problem. This might be called group work, but it is different from the group work of most social workers. These two procedures and the societal reaction of which they are a part will be discussed later.[12]

**VARIATIONS IN USE OF METHODS FOR IMPLEMENTING THE PUNITIVE REACTION.** Like the general punitive reaction to law-breaking, the usage of specific techniques for implementing or expressing the punitive reaction has varied from time to time and place to place. During the history of mankind four principal methods of implementing the punitive policy have been used, but there has been no distinct "evolution" of any one system from the others. Removal from the group by death, by exile, or by imprisonment; physical torture; social degradation; and financial loss all have been used differentially in various historical periods, and they are used differentially today. While it cannot be maintained that any one type of punitive reaction is exclusively characteristic of any one historical period or of any one society, certain emphases upon the different methods can be observed. In the United States at present, for example, all four of the systems are used to some degree, but certainly fines and removal from the group by imprisonment are emphasized.

*The death penalty.* The prevalence of death penalties has varied a great deal in different societies.[13] Such techniques of inflicting death as burning, boiling in oil, breaking at the wheel, the iron coffin, drowning, and impaling have had their greatest frequency not in the earliest or in the more recent societies, but in the society of the medieval period. Impaling and immuring were practiced in Switzerland until about 1400, and death by drowning until about 1600. The last case of burning at the stake in Berlin was in 1786. In Frankfort a. M. the number of executions was 317 in the fifteenth century, 248 in the sixteenth, and only 140 in the seventeenth.[14] In the cantons of Zürich and Schwyz 572 executions occurred in the sixteenth century, 336 in the seventeenth, and only 149 in the eighteenth.[15]

In England, however, the situation is somewhat different, for there were only 17 capital offenses in the early part of the fifteenth century, about 350

[12] See below, pp. 375–380 and 673–680.
[13] As indicated above, it is not always clear that execution of a criminal is punishment in the strict sense of the word. A rather intensive study of the circumstances of the executions must be made to determine whether the executions in certain historical periods were punishments. Such a study has not been made and it will be necessary, therefore, to accept the uncritical statements now available.
[14] G. L. Kriegk, *Deutsches Bürgerthum im Mittelalter* (Frankfurt, a. M.: Rütten und Löning, 1868–1871), Vol. I, pp. 200–201.
[15] Karl L. von Bar, *A History of Continental Criminal Law* (Boston: Little, Brown, 1916), p. 299.

in 1780, and then, by 1839, the number was reduced again to about the same as it had been four centuries before.[16] In the earlier part of this period in England, the death penalty was frequently inflicted for religious offenses, but most of the later inflictions were for offenses against property, and many of them for very trivial offenses. In 1814 three boys—aged eight, nine, and eleven—were sentenced to death for stealing a pair of shoes.[17] This was not unusual. During the early part of the modern period the corpse was gibbeted, that is, remained hanging in chains, and was sometimes soaked in tar so that it would remain for a long time as a warning to evil doers. These objects were seen so frequently that landscape painters considered them an essential part of the scenery and not infrequently introduced them into their landscapes.[18]

Under the leadership of Romilly, Bentham, Peel, McIntosh, Montagu, Cruickshank, and others, and as the power of the common people increased, the use of capital punishment decreased. But as late as 1814, Romilly tried in vain to substitute simple hanging for treason in place of the existing penalty of hanging, cutting down alive, disemboweling, cutting off the head, and quartering the body. Although the latter penalty was not actually carried out, members of Parliament were afraid that treason would be greatly increased if the law were modified.

During the course of the last century, a very distinct trend away from the death penalty has occurred. About thirty-five countries have abolished it entirely, and in other countries the offenses for which it may be imposed have been generally limited to murder.[19] Of the fifty-two jurisdictions in the United States in 1965, only one (the District of Columbia) had a mandatory death penalty, forty two had a permissive death penalty, and nine jurisdictions did not permit the death penalty. The states which do not permit the death penalty are Alaska, Hawaii, Michigan, Minnesota, North Dakota, Oregon, Wisconsin, Maine and Rhode Island.

[16] See Leon Radzinowicz, *A History of English Criminal Law and Its Administration from 1750* (New York: Macmillan, 1948), Volume I, pp. 42–79, 611–659.

[17] "Punishment of Death," *Philanthropist*, 4:190, 1814.

[18] W. Andrews, *Old-Time Punishments* (London: Hull, W. Andrews, 1890), pp. 211–212.

[19] At least six, and probably eight, of the countries which abolished the death penalty have later restored it. Four of the six countries known to have restored the penalty did so under dictatorial governments, and the two countries for whom definite information on restoration is not available are also presently governed by dictators. See Frank E. Hartung, *On Capital Punishment* (Detroit: Wayne University Department of Sociology and Anthropology, 1951), p. 2; Lee Emerson Deets, "Changes in Capital Punishment Policy Since 1939," *Journal of Criminal Law and Criminology*, 38:584–594, March–April, 1948; Peter P. Lejins, "The Death Penalty Abroad," *Annals of the American Academy of Political and Social Science*, 284:137–146, November, 1952; and James McCafferty, "Major Trends in the Use of Capital Punishment," *Federal Probation*, 25:15–21, September, 1961.

Several variations may be observed in the use of the death penalty in the United States during the last century. *First,* there has been a slight and fluctuating tendency to abolish it. Between 1847, when the first state abolished the death penalty, and 1876 four states prohibited capital punishment; one addition to this list was made in 1907 and another in 1911. From 1913 to 1918 seven other states were added, but five of them restored the penalty after an average experience of two and a half years. Delaware joined the abolition states in 1958, the first state to do so since 1918. However, in 1961 Delaware restored the death penalty. Alaska and Hawaii both abolished capital punishment in 1957, and Oregon abolished it in 1964. There are periodic attempts to abolish capital punishment in those states retaining it, and to restore it in those states which have abolished it. In Michigan, for instance, capital punishment has been an issue before the legislature at least twenty-five times since 1885.[20]

*Second,* a more pronounced recent variation has been the substitution of a permissive death penalty for the mandatory death penalty. Courts and juries have been given the power of deciding whether one who has committed a capital offense must be executed. In 1918, the death penalty was mandatory on conviction for capital crimes in twelve states, in 1938 in five states, and in 1964 in none of the states. Of the forty-one states which permit capital punishment, an average of fourteen states each year have no executions. In 1945–1959, Illinois imposed the death penalty on only 1.2 percent of those eligible for it.[21] Maryland in 1936–1961 executed 56 percent of those sentenced to death; in 1936–1940 this percentage was 69; in 1946–1950 it was 56, and in 1956–1960 it was 23.[22] In 1964 there were no executions by the federal government or by thirty-four of the states which permitted the death penalty.[23] Thus, to some extent the introduction of permissive clauses has been a technique for abolishing capital punishment in practice while retaining it in law. A nationwide poll conducted in the United States in 1958 indicated that 42 percent of the people favored execution of persons convicted of "the worst crimes, like murder." Fifty percent were against the death sentence, and eight percent had no opinion.[24]

*Third,* the number of capital crimes has been reduced. There are in the

[20] Frank E. Hartung, "Trends in the Use of Capital Punishment," *Annals of the American Academy of Political and Social Science,* 284:8–19, November, 1952.

[21] Daniel Glaser, *Survey of the Death Sentence in Illinois* (Chicago: John Howard Association, 1959. Mimeographed.).

[22] Legislative Council of Maryland, *Report of the Committee on Capital Punishment* (Baltimore: Author, 1962), p. 54.

[23] Federal Bureau of Prisons, "Executions, 1930–1964," *National Prisoner Statistics,* No. 37, April, 1964.

[24] Hans W. Mattick, *The Unexamined Death* (Chicago: The John Howard Association, 1963), p. 29.

fifty states only twelve capital offenses, and no one state has declared all of these to be capital offenses. Only one crime is punishable by death in fourteen states, two in eight states, and only nine states have as many as six capital crimes.[25] In practice, however, there are in the United States very few executions except for murder and rape.

*Fourth,* over the last century the annual number and proportion of executions has decreased, largely as a result of the changes mentioned above. The number of executions in the United States has decreased rather consistently each year since 1935. Table XIII shows that in Ohio the number of death sentences decreased very greatly in proportion to the number of admissions to prison for first degree murder, while the percent of the death sentences which were actually executed decreased from 1900 to 1915, increased decidedly until 1925, and then remained fairly constant.

*Fifth,* executions have been closed to the public. While executions were at one time public spectacles, today the number of witnesses is highly restricted.

*Sixth,* in place of prolonged torture, the method of execution has been made as swift and painless as possible in a large proportion of the states. Electrocution was adopted in New York in 1888, and by 1952 this method was being used by twenty-four states. Eleven states now provide for execution by lethal gas, while six still use hanging and one (Utah) offers a choice between hanging and firing squad.

In 1930–1964, 3,849 executions by civil authorities occurred in the United States of which 86 percent were for murder and 11 percent for rape. Of the executed persons, 45 percent were white, 54 percent Negro, and 1 percent other races. Approximately .7 percent were female. About sixty percent of the executions carried out each year since 1930 have occurred in seventeen southern and southwestern states, which in 1950 contained about one-third of the nation's population.[26]

*Physical torture.* Most societies have to some extent implemented the punitive reaction by corporal punishment. Branding, stocks, pillory, mutilation, confinement in irons and cages, and whipping were used extensively in the medieval and early modern periods. Such penalties, in general, have increased and decreased in prevalence with the death penalty.

Whipping is the only one of the many varieties of corporal punishment

[25] The exact number of capital offenses is difficult to determine because of the tendency to specify subcategories; for example, Ohio specifies first degree murder as a capital offense, but it also specifies that killing of a policeman (a form of first degree murder) is a capital offense. See Leonard D. Savitz, "Capital Crimes as Defined in American Statutory Law," *Journal of Criminal Law and Criminology,* 46:355–363, Sept.–Oct. 1955.

[26] Ohio Legislative Service Commission, *Capital Punishment* (Columbus: Author, Staff Research Report No. 46, 1961), p. 20.

## TABLE XIII

ADMISSIONS TO OHIO PENITENTIARY FOR FIRST DEGREE MURDER, PERCENT
OF THESE WITH DEATH SENTENCES, AND PERCENT OF DEATH
SENTENCES EXECUTED, BY FIVE-YEAR PERIODS, 1896–1960[27]

| Years | Number of Admissions for First Degree Murder | Percent of First Degree Murder Admissions with Death Sentences | Percent of Death Sentences Which Were Executed |
|---|---|---|---|
| 1896–1900 | 33 | 58 | 58 |
| 1901–05 | 44 | 43 | 74 |
| 1906–10 | 55 | 40 | 59 |
| 1911–15 | 43 | 21 | 45 |
| 1916–20 | 118 | 27 | 59 |
| 1921–25 | 151 | 41 | 82 |
| 1926–30 | 197 | 26 | 69 |
| 1931–35 | 189 | 31 | 78 |
| 1936–40 | 178 | 21 | 84 |
| 1941–45 | 110 | 21 | 87 |
| 1946–50 | 229 | 21 | 77 |
| 1951–55 | 167 | 12 | 60 |
| 1956–60 | 102 | 25 | 54 |

which has been officially retained in Western civilization, and the trend of opinion is very much against it. In Great Britain it was a legal penalty for certain adult crimes and juvenile delinquencies until 1948.

In the United States, whipping is authorized in only one state. Until 1952 it could be used on wife-beaters in Maryland, but it seldom was actually inflicted. It is authorized in Delaware for several crimes. Of the 7,302 offenders convicted in Delaware in 1900–1942 for crimes which called for whipping, 22 percent were actually whipped; this percentage was 70 in 1900, 55 in 1910, 30 in 1921, 15 in 1930, 7 in 1940. Few floggings have taken place in this state since 1950.[28]

Agitation for the authorization of the penalty of whipping developed in several states subsequent to World War I, but the bills all failed. One of the more extreme bills was introduced in Minnesota in 1925. It provided

[27] 1896–1930 data compiled by the Ohio Institute; 1931–1960 data compiled by the Bureau of Research and Statistics, Ohio Department of Mental Hygiene and Correction. Some imprecision in column four is introduced by the fact that the persons executed in any five-year period are not necessarily the same persons admitted during that period.

[28] Robert G. Caldwell, Red Hannah, Delaware's Whipping Post (Philadelphia: University of Pennsylvania Press, 1947), pp. 69–70; Robert G. Caldwell, "The Deterrent Influence of Corporal Punishment," American Sociological Review, 9:171–177, April, 1944.

for whipping as a mandatory penalty, in combination with imprisonment or fine, for twelve offenses, ranging from murder to drunken driving. However, the bills introduced in the Delaware legislature to abolish this penalty have failed by large majorities, and in fact in 1920 the number of offenses for which whipping might be used was increased.

*Social degradation.* Shame and humiliation have been used to impose suffering by reduction of the social status of the offender, sometimes temporarily, sometimes permanently. In general, this method of punishment flourished from the beginning of the sixteenth to the end of the seventeenth century, but it is not absent even today. Many techniques for reducing prestige have been used in various societies. Some of them were used extensively in the societies in which physical torture was the primary method for implementing the punitive reaction. For example, the ducking stool, the stocks, the pillory, the brank, and other devices were not only instruments for corporal punishment, but were used to reduce the status of the offender as well. They were used for minor offenses, such as scolding, giving short weights, forgery, and blasphemy. In the seventeenth century one offender who had stolen cabbages from his neighbor's garden in New York was ordered to stand in the pillory with the cabbages on his head, and in addition was banished from the colony for five years.[29] The brank was a cage-like device placed over the head and provided with a bar which was thrust into the mouth of the offender, thus holding down the tongue; occasionally this bar had spikes on it to prevent any effort to use the tongue. This device was regarded as superior to the ducking stool in dealing with scolds, because the scold could talk between ducks.

The marks of degradation, temporary or permanent, inflicted in an effort to reduce the social status of the offender often did not deter him from further crimes. An English statute of 1698 which provided for branding on the left cheek was repealed after eight years with the explanation that this penalty

> . . . had not had its desired effect of deterring offenders from the further committing crimes and offenses but, on the contrary, such offenders, being rendered thereby unfit to be entrusted in any service or employment to get their livelihood in any honest and lawful way, become the more desperate.[30]

Another way of degrading criminals is to deprive them of rights of various kinds following commission of "infamous" and certain other crimes.

[29] Phillip Klein, *Prison Methods in New York State* (New York: Columbia University Press, 1920), p. 23.
[30] Luke O. Pike, *A History of Crime in England* (London: Smith, Elder, 1873–1876), Vol. II, p. 280.

In the Roman Republic infamy as the result of the conviction of crime meant loss of the right to vote, to hold office, to represent another in the courts, to be a witness, to manage the affairs of another, and the abridging of the right to marry. During the early modern period, also, certain crimes resulted in infamy. This infamy was produced to some extent merely by the publicity of the trial, but also by the subsequent loss of rights of citizenship. In addition, offenders were branded or mutilated, so that everyone might know that they had been guilty of crimes and thus would suffer infamy. Loss of rank, mutilation of the body after death, and other methods were used to produce a greater infamy than the public would naturally or ordinarily attribute to the offender. During the feudal period, by bills of attainder, persons convicted of treason or felony might be deprived of their real and personal property, their right to inherit or transmit property, and all rights in the courts. This was known as "civil death." In Idaho at present there is "civil death" for those sentenced to imprisonment in the state prison for life.

The general weight of opinion at the present seems to be that infamy attaches only to the punishment, not to the crime as such, so that the degradation can occur only in conjunction with other punitive methods.[31] In the American colonies any corporal punishment rendered the offender infamous. Later, imprisonment at hard labor was included as an infamous punishment, presumably because hard labor was regarded as a corporal punishment. By implication, then, imprisonment in a state prison, in which hard labor was generally required, came to be regarded as an infamous punishment, while imprisonment in a local workhouse or jail, in which hard labor was seldom required, was not an infamous punishment, even though the particular institution to which commitment was made did require hard labor of all its inmates who were able to work.

The following are the principal rights which, at the present, may be lost in various states by the commission of infamous crimes. (a) The right to vote is lost by conviction for almost all felonious or infamous crimes in all states except Indiana, Massachusetts, New Hampshire, and Vermont.[32] (b) The right to hold public office is lost in most states. Public offices are generally restricted to electors and therefore the loss of suffrage carries with

[31] However, Schofield showed that in some jurisdictions, at least, and for some deprivations the infamy is due to the nature of the crime, not to the nature of the punishment. If the infamy attached only to the punishment it could be wiped out by a pardon; but many civil rights, for example, may be lost by infamous crimes and not restored by a pardon. See Henry Schofield, *Essays on Constitutional Law and Equity* (Boston: Chapman Law Publishing Company, 1921), Vol. I, pp. 421–456.

[32] Federal Probation Officers Association, *A Compilation of State and Federal Statutes Relating to Civil Rights of Persons Convicted of Crime* (Detroit: Author, 1960. Mimeographed.).

it the loss of the right to hold office. In addition, certain other restrictions are specified in some states, such as incapacity to serve on a jury or to testify as a witness. (c) The right to practice certain professions or occupations. In addition, in a few states the convicted felon loses the right to make a contract, to marry, or to migrate to a foreign country.[33]

Somewhat related to the loss of civil rights is the deprivation of a license which is required for many activities at the present time. A person convicted of violating traffic regulations may be deprived of his driver's license, and a person convicted of violating game laws may be deprived of the right to secure another hunting license.

The original purpose of infamous punishments was to isolate the offender. It was designed to produce somewhat the same result as banishment, namely, increased social distance between the offender and the law-abiding citizen. In recent society an evident desire to protect the social and political institutions plays a part, and the suffering of the offender from the loss of rights may be becoming secondary.

*Banishment* and *transportation.* Practically all societies have banished some criminals, especially political criminals, but wholesale deportation of offenders is a rather recent invention. Banishment was used in early societies and in Ancient Rome, where it was either a prohibition against coming into a specified territory, generally the city of Rome, or a prohibition against going outside a specified territory, such as an island to which the offender had been removed; in either case, banishment might be for life or for a short time. After a long period during which this method for expressing the punitive reaction to crime was seldom used, the method was revived. In England the first modern legalization of transportation was in 1597, and concerned "rogues, vagabonds, and sturdy beggars." However, it is probable that the law was not used a great deal until the period during which America was colonized. From that time until the American Revolution a considerable proportion of England's criminal population was sent to America, although the practice was strenuously opposed by most of the colonies.[34] In 1786, after the colonies had become independent, the policy of transportation to Australia was adopted, and this practice continued until 1867. The total number transported during this period was 134,308, but the average number per year was 474 during the period 1787–1816, and

[33] See Negley K. Teeters, "The Loss of Civil Rights and Their Reinstatement," *Prison Journal,* 25:77–87, July, 1945. The disabilities produced as the result of infamy are terminated automatically in some states when the sentence is served; in other states they are terminated if the person is not indicted or convicted for another crime within a specified time after the completion of his sentence. In most states the disabilities are removed only by pardon, and in some of them not even by pardon.

[34] See Abbott E. Smith, *Colonists in Bondage* (Chapel Hill: University of North Carolina Press, 1947).

about 3,000 between 1816 and 1838. In England in 1834, the sentence of transportation was imposed on 4,053 persons, death on 480, and imprisonment on 10,716. This shows that at the time transportation, though at its height, was not being used as frequently as imprisonment. But all except 314 of those sentenced to prison had terms of one year or less, which means that imprisonment was used almost entirely for the relatively trivial offenses.

Transportation was abandoned by England because it was found not to be a good method of reformation or deterrence, because it was expensive, and primarily because it was strenuously opposed by the Australian colonies. John Mitchel, a convict transported for aiding in the Irish rebellion, described the conditions in Australia in 1851 as follows:

There is but one political question now existing—the transportation system. Most of the decent colonists, having families growing up, and feeling the effects of the moral and social atmosphere that surrounds them, and the ignominy of having no country but a penal colony, no servants, no laborers, few neighbors even, who are not men fairly due to the gallows— ardently desire to use this new Constitution, such as it is, to make vigorous protest against the continuance of the penal system.[35]

Many other countries have used transportation in the modern period. Portugal in the sixteenth century sent criminals and women of ill-repute to Brazil and later sent criminals to Angola. Spain tried transportation in a limited way in the eighteenth century. Russia has used Siberia as a penal colony since 1823. Since 1865 Italy has transported some convicts to the islands along her coast, and France from 1763 to 1766, in 1824, and from 1851 to the present has used transportation to some extent.

Banishment, which is closely related to transportation, is still used as part of the penalty for certain types of crimes. In one of the earliest criminal prosecutions on American soil, the penalty inflicted in 1637 was that the defendant was to be "banished from out of our jurisdiction as being a woman not fit for our society."[36] In 1961–1964, 1,860 alien criminals were deported; in addition 783 were deported as narcotic addicts, as subversives or anarchists, or because they were immoral.[37] The Department of Labor, which formerly had the responsibility in this matter, explained that this policy is not used with greater frequency because the appropriation has been insufficient to pay the expenses of deportation, because governors of

[35] John Mitchel, Jail Journal (Dublin: J. Corrigan, 1864), p. 264.
[36] William O. Douglas, An Almanac of Liberty (New York: Doubleday, 1954), p. 135.
[37] Immigration and Naturalization Service Department of Justice, Annual Report, 1964 (Washington: Department of Justice, 1964), p. 73.

states frequently pardon criminal aliens who, then, cannot be deported, because many countries refuse to receive their nationals when deported from the United States for crime, and because it is difficult to prevent deported criminals from returning to the United States. On the other hand, the procedure used in deporting aliens, whether criminal or non-criminal, has been criticized frequently.[38]

A modified form of banishment also is used constantly in the United States at present. It consists of giving a person accused or convicted of an offense a specified number of hours in which to leave the county, town, or state. This method is used frequently in dealing with tramps or "floaters" and hence is called "floating."[39]

*Imprisonment.* (a) In ancient and medieval societies. In preliterate societies imprisonment was rarely used as a penalty. Similarly, the penalty of imprisonment hardly ever occurred in early Greece,[40] and it was not used at all in the Roman Republic but was used for minor offenses in the Empire. Von Bar stated that "the penalty of imprisonment was almost unknown in France in the later Middle Ages."[41] The last code of laws in France previous to the Revolution was made in 1670 and contained no mention of imprisonment as a penalty. Incarceration was sometimes used in France and other countries, however, either as a means of enforcing the payment of fines or as a commutation of death sentences when mitigating circumstances were found. In the first part of the sixteenth century in Frankfort it was ordered that for certain offenses "the criminal shall be imprisoned and forgotten for a time."[42]

In England, imprisonment was used in a few cases in the Anglo-Saxon period, as in the law of Æthelstan, which provided that persons convicted of murder or theft should be imprisoned for 120 or 40 days respectively, before they could be redeemed by their kinsmen. Henry II provided a penalty of imprisonment for one year for perjury in a grand assize, and Henry III provided the same penalty for breaches of the forest law. In 1241 some Jews convicted of circumcising a Christian child were ordered either to pay twenty thousand marks "or else be kept perpetual prisoners." But it was in the reign of Edward I in the latter half of the thirteenth century

[38] Reuben Oppenheimer, "Report on the Administration of the Deportation Laws of the United States," National Commission on Law Observance and Enforcement, *Report No. 13* (Washington: Government Printing Office, 1931); Jane P. Clark, *Deportation of Aliens from the United States to Europe* (London: P. S. King, 1931).

[39] See Caleb Foote, "Vagrancy-Type Law and Its Administration," *University of Pennsylvania Law Review,* 104:603–650, March, 1956.

[40] P. Vinogradoff, *Outlines of Historical Jurisprudence* (London: Oxford University Press, 1920–1922), Vol. II, p. 190.

[41] Von Bar, *op. cit.,* p. 191.

[42] Kriegk, *op. cit.,* Vol. I, p. 262.

that incarceration came into extensive use in England, though even in this period it was used primarily as a "squeezer" or means of securing fines.

Thus, in general, until about the last part of the thirteenth century in England and probably a little later in some of the Continental countries imprisonment as a penalty was used only for very restricted groups of offenders. It is, therefore, a comparatively modern method of dealing with offenders, though its roots run back to the earliest societies.

(b) Imprisonment by the church. The early church authorities did use imprisonment, partly because they were not permitted by law to use the death penalty, and partly because they had an appreciation of the value of withdrawal from association with others. In 1283, a certain Brother John had bitten his prior's finger "like a dog" and the bishop gave orders to

. . . keep the said Brother John in prison under iron chains in which he shall be content with bread, indifferent ale, pottage, and a pittance of meat or fish (which on the sixth day he shall do without) until he is penitent.[43]

Though this method was used by the church as early as the fifth century, it was used most extensively during the Inquisition, when it was the most severe penalty that could be inflicted for any offense on those who professed conversion. In 1229, Gregory IX ordered that all who were converted after arrest because of fear of death should be imprisoned for life; this rule was stated by several councils, also. In the Inquisition of Toulouse from 1246 to 1248, of 192 known sentences all were imprisonment except 43 death penalties imposed on persons who refused to appear; of the 149 prison sentences, 127 were for life, 6 for ten years, and 16 for an indefinite period. Of the 636 sentences imposed by Bernard Giu from 1308 to 1322 (of which 88 were imposed on persons already dead), 300 were imprisonment. Many of these sentences were commuted, however. Of the 300 persons imprisoned by Bernard Gui, 119 were released on commutation. Such releases were necessary in part because of the lack of prisons, but in general the idea of reformation was taken into account. Chrysostom said:

I require not continuance of time, but the correction of your soul; demonstrate your contrition, demonstrate your reformation, and all is done.[44]

This ecclesiastical imprisonment varied from strict confinement in absolute solitude, known as "in pace," to congregate life in the corridors of the prisons, with occasional retirement to a cell, which was known as "murus largus." As a matter of fact there was much association between prisoners

[43] Quoted by Ives, op. cit., p. 43.
[44] Ibid., p. 38.

in many institutions, some gambling and feasting, and some "grafting" by jailers who kept the money of prisoners or food that had been sent to the prison for them, and ordered supplies for prisoners who had long been dead.

(c) Imprisonment in the galleys. The galleys were used considerably as places of confinement for criminals from about 1500 to the early part of the eighteenth century. This practice was a revival of the ancient method of forced labor, although in the earlier period the slaves were not necessarily criminals. It continued until the large sailing vessels were developed to such an extent as to make the galleys unsuitable for competition. In 1602, Queen Elizabeth appointed a commission to make arrangements for commuting other penalties to galley labor, so that offenders may be

In such sort corrected and punished that even in their punishment they may yeld more profitable service to the Common welth.[45]

In the seventeenth century in France, the courts were ordered to refrain from other methods of punishment as much as possible in order to provide crews for galleys. Those who could not work in the galleys, such as women, aged, and infirm, were frequently imprisoned on land during this period, and when the galleys were abandoned many former slaves were transported or were held in hulks on the shores or in arsenals.[46]

(d) Imprisonment in houses of correction.[47] The house of correction appeared in England about the middle of the sixteenth century, when, on the petition of Bishop Ridley of London for help in dealing with the "sturdy vagabonds" of the city, the King gave his palace at Bridewell to be one of the "hospitals of the city," for the "lewd and idle" and a place for the employment of the unemployed and the training of children. By act of 1576, Parliament provided that a house of correction should be erected in each county, and in 1609 provided penalties for counties failing to erect such institutions. The assumption was that hard work at rather unpleasant

---

[45] *Ibid.*, pp. 103–104.

[46] See W. Branch-Thompson, *The English Prison Hulks* (London: Christopher Johnson, 1957).

[47] It is necessary to make a distinction between the house of correction and the workhouse. Technically the workhouse was an institution in which employment was furnished to those able and willing to work, and industrial training was furnished for the young; consequently, it was a part of the poor-relief system. The house of correction, on the other hand, was a part of the penal system, designed to protect the poor-relief funds against encroachments by those able but unwilling to work. Thus, the house of correction was designed to compel "sturdy beggars" to work. But as a matter of fact, the two institutions are hardly distinguishable during the larger part of their history in England and America, and no attempt is made in the present discussion to differentiate them precisely; no attention is paid, however, to the workhouse in its pure form.

tasks would reform criminals, but the possibility of profits was not over-looked. Also, in addition to punitive labor, corporal punishments were used. Justices were ordered to search for "rogues, vagabonds and idle persons" and commit them to institutions, but the institutions also were used for confinement of "lewd women" with illegitimate children who might become a charge on the community and for men who deserted their families. By an act of 1711 the maximum period of confinement in these houses of correction was fixed at three years, and by subsequent legislation the number of offenses for which persons might be committed was greatly enlarged. Webb stated that by the early part of the eighteenth century the house of correction and the common jail were practically the same in discipline and character of inmates.[48]

This system for implementation of the punitive reaction to law-breaking also was used on the Continent during the same period. It began a little later, but was used more extensively than in England. In 1669 one Peter Rentzel established a workhouse in Hamburg at his own expense because he had observed that thieves and prostitutes were made worse instead of better by the pillory, and he hoped that they might be improved by work and religious instruction in the workhouse.[49] A house of correction was established in Waldheim in 1716 with the lower floor for criminals and the upper floor for paupers and orphans, and with complete separation of the sexes on both floors. On entrance the criminals received a "welcome" of ten lashes; work was compulsory and silence was the rule. The staff of the institution included a chaplain, a teacher, and a physician, which was distinctly noteworthy at that time. During the first century of its history this institution received 13,954 persons, of whom 7,921 were criminals, 4,642 paupers, and 1,391 orphans. Almost half of the criminals were convicted of theft, a fourth of begging and vagrancy, and an eighth of sexual offenses; 270 of them were convicted of homicide, which was usually infanticide.[50] Perhaps the most famous house of correction on the Continent was the one established in Ghent in 1775.[51]

(e) Early prison reforms. The early "prison reform" movement, which reached its peak in the last part of the eighteenth century and the first part of the nineteenth century, actually was a movement for the popularization

---

[48] Sidney and Beatrice Webb, *English Prisons Under Local Government* (London: Longmans, Green, 1922), pp. 16–17.

[49] F. H. Wines, *Punishment and Reformation* (New York: Crowell, 1895), pp. 115–116.

[50] Otto Glauning, "Das Zucht-, Armen-, und Waisenhaus zu Waldheim wahrend den ersten 100 Jahre des Bestehens" (1716–1816), *Monatsschrift für Kriminalpsychologie*, 10:32–43, April, 1913.

[51] See E. C. Wines, *State of Prisons and Child-Saving Institutions in the Civilized World* (Cambridge: J. Wilson and Sons, 1880), pp. 10–11.

of a relatively new punitive method: imprisonment as a system of punishment. Although imprisonment as punishment was in part the basis of the system of committing offenders to houses of correction, jails, and hulks in the seventeenth and eighteenth centuries, the primary use of imprisonment at that time was for persons awaiting trial. The "reforms" advocated and accomplished were primarily in reference to the prison as a place of detention, and they may be seen best in England and America. Chapter 22 will be devoted to changing societal reactions to crime in America.

In England, from the middle of the sixteenth century there had been considerable publicity regarding prison practices and various suggestions for methods of improvement. Geoffrey Mynshal, committed to prison as an insolvent debtor, while in prison wrote "Certain Characters and Essays of Prison and Prisoners," which was published in 1618. Wines calls this the first regular treatise on prison "abuses"; it describes most of the practices and conditions of prison life which John Howard found a century and a half later. In 1699, the Society for the Promotion of Christian Knowledge, with a committee on prisons, was formed. This committee visited many prisons and presented a report in 1702, under the title "Essay towards the Reformation of Newgate and other Prisons in and about London." The following conditions are mentioned: the old criminals corrupt the new; swearing, blasphemy, and gambling; unlimited use of intoxicating liquors; personal lewdness of officers and keepers; and the co-operation of officers with the prisoners in their vices. The committee suggested methods of reducing these conditions as follows: separate confinement in cells, labor while in prison, regular religious services, abolition of fees, prohibition of liquor in prison, retention of hardened offenders until evidence is furnished that they will secure decent employment when released and until they give security for good behavior, and advertisement to the public of the names of those prisoners who have lived decently in prison with the object of securing the help of good people for these prisoners after their release.

During the next century investigations, reports, and discussions continued; a few laws were passed; a few individuals in control of prisons undertook to make improvements as suggested by committees. In 1773, Parliament authorized magistrates to appoint chaplains in their jails. This was the first official recognition of the desirability of attempting to reform the prisoners. But in some institutions as late as 1808 the felons were not permitted to attend the religious services.

The great prison reformer of England was John Howard, who wrote "The State of Prisons in England" in 1777, after a personal investigation

of practically all the prisons of England. This book contains, after a short
summary, a description of each prison, so that it is a mass of concrete details. His general conclusion was:

If it were the wish and aim of magistrates to effect the destruction
present and future of young delinquents, they could not devise a more
effectual method, than to confine them so long in our prisons, those seats
and seminaries . . . of idleness and every vice.[52]

Howard's work was supplemented by that of other leaders, and several societies for prison reform were formed. Substantial changes were made in
prisons, as may be determined by a comparison of Dixon's account of the
prisons in 1850[53] and Howard's account in 1777. In fact, Beaumont in 1821
lamented because that prisons had changed so much they were no longer a
deterrent and that workmen preferred prison life to the life of freedom; he
urged a return to the earlier methods.[54] And another author berated justices of the peace for indulging

In such costly fads as the separation of male prisoners from females, of
adults from children, and of the convicted from the unconvicted, whilst
altogether disapproving the extravagant cubic space required either for the
cellular confinement or for the useful employment of any prisoners.[55]

This sketch of imprisonment shows that imprisonment as a method of
implementing the punitive reaction to law-breaking rarely occurred in earlier societies. It was adopted by the church and used quite extensively, and
then common jails and special prisons for larger and larger proportions of
criminals arose, until in the early nineteenth century imprisonment came
to be the principal method of punishing serious offenders. In England
there has been an unbroken downward trend in the use of imprisonment
by Superior Courts since 1900. For example, such courts gave prison sentences to 89 percent of the felony sexual offenders in 1909–13, and to 47
percent in 1951–54.[56]

*Financial penalties.* Reaction to criminality by general confiscation
of property or by imposition of a fine has existed in most literate societies,
but there have been great variations in the emphasis placed upon this sys-

[52] John Howard, *The State of Prisons in England and Wales,* Second Edition (London: Cadell and Conant, 1780), p. 13.
[53] W. Hepworth Dixon, *The London Prisons,* London (Jackson and Walford, 1850).
[54] B. Beaumont, "Essay on Criminal Jurisprudence," *Pamphleteer,* 1873 ff., 1821.
[55] Edward Mullins, *A Treatise on the Magistracy of England* (London, 1836).
[56] Hermann Mannheim, "Comparative Sentencing Practices," *Law and Contemporary Problems,* 23:557–582, Summer, 1958.

tem. The practice developed somewhat as the general punitive reaction developed. When an individual was injured by another, he might claim damages, the amount depending on the injury done and the social position of the injured party. Then the king claimed a part of this payment or an additional payment for the participation of the state in the trial and for the injury done to the state by the disturbance of the peace. About the twelfth century, the victim's share began to decrease and the exactions of the king to increase, until finally the king took the entire payment. These payments were one of the principal sources of revenue, and imprisonment was used largely at this time as a means of compelling the defendant to pay the fine. Fines, therefore, developed out of private damages or civil actions and were in their origin a part of the civil law rather than of the criminal law.[57]

This method became frequent only at the end of the last century, and the current trend toward its greater use is apparent in the following statistics.[58] In Germany in 1882, fines were 22.2 percent of all penalties imposed, in 1934, 54.7 percent; in France in 1900, 35.8 percent, in 1934, 47.8 percent; in Belgium in 1905, 48.0 percent, in 1933, 66.5 percent. In Sweden in 1953, and in Finland in 1959, fines were 95 percent of all sentences imposed.[59] In the United States at present, the imposition of a fine is by far the most frequent method of reacting punitively to crime; probably more than 75 percent of all penalties imposed are fines. This recent trend may be partly due to the increase in trivial offenses growing out of an increased number of technical regulations, but if a particular crime is taken, the same trend is apparent. In Germany, of all penalties for fraud, 11.0 percent were fines in 1882, and 47.5 percent were fines in 1932. In Finland in 1935, 23 percent of the persons convicted of drunkenness were fined; by 1959 the percentage had increased to 58.[60] Fines, then, are being substituted for other penalties.

The court at present is generally given authority to impose fines within maximum and minimum limits set by the legislatures. Sometimes only the maximum level is fixed, sometimes only the minimum. The constitutions of the several states provide that fines "shall not be excessive."

At common law, fines were enforced by executions against property, but now an offender is generally imprisoned in a jail or house of correction in

---

[57] L. T. Hobhouse, G. C. Wheeler, and M. Ginsberg, *The Material Culture and Social Institutions of the Simpler Peoples* (London: Chapman and Hall, 1915), pp. 86–119.

[58] George Rusche and Otto Kirchheimer, *Punishment and Social Structure* (New York: Columbia University Press, 1939), pp. 147–150.

[59] Thorsten Sellin, *The Protective Code: A Swedish Proposal* (Stockholm: Department of Justice, 1957), p. 17; and Inkeri Anttila, "Fines for Drunkenness—An Expensive and Ineffective System," *Alkoholpolitik* (Finland), 3:2–3, 1960.

[60] Antilla, op. cit.

default of payment of the fine. About 60 percent of the persons committed to the Baltimore City Jail in 1940 were committed for non-payment of fines. In 1933, 31 percent of those persons committed to all jails on sentences were committed in default of payment of fines. Ten percent of the 152,000 persons fined in Finland in 1959 went to jail for inability to pay the fine; persons convicted of drunkenness were disproportionately represented among the prisoners serving sentences in default of fines.[61] These offenders "lie out" the sum at some specified rate, such as $1.00 a day. This brings in practically no income and is a very considerable expense because the community not only fails to collect the fines but spends large sums to support the prisoners and their families.

Currently, when a fine is imposed it is tantamount to a declaration that neither the safety of the community nor the welfare of the offender requires the imprisonment of the offender and that the assumed values of punishment can be accomplished without imprisonment. Imprisonment for failure to pay fines is therefore only a means of collecting a debt to the state.[62] From early times efforts have been made to avoid the great expense of collecting such debts. In New Jersey in 1775, the offender who could not pay his fine might be sold for a term not to exceed five years to any person willing to pay the fine, and a similar provision was made in Louisiana in 1804. A Connecticut law in 1841 provided that an offender sentenced to pay a fine might, if unable to pay the fine, be released on his note. An English law of 1905 authorized the courts to permit installment payment of fines without imprisonment unless the installments were defaulted. Little use was made of this law, however, and in 1914 it was made mandatory for the court to accept installment payments of fines with certain exceptions. Largely as a result of this law, the number of persons imprisoned in default of fine decreased from 107,555 in 1904 to 12,497 in 1930. Several states in America have authorized the installment method of paying fines, and it is used quite extensively in connection with probation.

The justifications given for this method of implementing the punitive reaction have varied, but at present they consist of the following. First, the fine is the most easily and thoroughly remissible of any of the penalties; capital punishment, whipping, or imprisonment once administered cannot be remitted effectively, but a fine that has been paid can be repaid. Second, the fine is a most economical penalty; it costs the state practically nothing when used without imprisonment for default. Third, the fine is easily divisible and can be adjusted to the enormity of the offense, the character and

---

61 Ibid.

62 See Charles H. Miller, "The Fine: Price Tag or Rehabilitative Force?" National Probation and Parole Association Journal, 2:377–384, October, 1956.

wealth of the offender, the state of public opinion, and other conditions more easily than any other penalty. *Fourth, it does not carry with it the* 4) public stigma and disgrace that imprisonment does, and therefore does not hamper reformation of the offender. *Fifth, it affects one of the most gen-* 5) eral interests of mankind and causes a kind of suffering that is universal; therefore it is efficacious in dealing with the great majority of mankind. 6) *Finally, it provides an income* for the state, county, or city.

Restitution and reparation. In the previous discussion it was observed that the imposition of financial penalties appeared in a clear-cut form when the state appropriated all of the payment made by the offender; what had previously been a combination of civil and criminal procedures became thereby distinctly a criminal procedure. The offense came to be regarded as an offense against the state alone; the victim had to initiate a separate civil action to recover damages for the injury done to him.[63] It was found in practice, however, that the injured party had very little success in securing damages under this system, because of the insolvent condition of the ordinary criminal and the opportunity to hide or transfer his property. Consequently, victims usually made no effort to recover by civil process, or settled out of court by threatening to report the crime to the criminal court if the civil damages were not paid.

For nearly a century, opinion has been developing in favor of reparation or restitution by order of the criminal court. This kind of reaction to crime is essentially non-punitive, and it probably is a system for implementation of the general non-punitive reaction which was characteristic of the positive school and which has been gaining popularity in recent times. Several American states at the beginning of the nineteenth century had laws which provided that a person convicted of larceny should return to the owner twice the value of the property stolen. Bonneville de Marsangy outlined a definite plan for a system of reparation in 1847, and in the late nineteenth century several international prison congresses passed resolutions advocating re-establishment of restitution.[64] Later Garofalo became the foremost advocate of this method, seconded by Ferri, Fioretti and others. Their plan for enforcing reparation or restitution is as follows: If the offender is solvent, his property should be attached at the time proceedings are started, so that he can be compelled by order of the court to make restitution. If he is insolvent, he can be compelled to devote a part of his income to restitution. The amount to be paid in this way never should be greater than the total amount of the injury (including the cost to the state for arrest

[63] Stephen Schafer, *Restitution to Victims of Crime* (London: Stevens and Sons, 1960), pp. 3–7.
[64] *Ibid.*, pp. 9–10.

and prosecution) and never so great as to cause undue injury to the offender or his dependents. If the offender fails or refuses to pay the assessment, or if he is not dependable, he should be made a state workman, to receive wages for his work; a part of the wage would be retained by the state and paid into the compensation fund.

It is argued, first, that this method enables the injured party to recover, which is almost impossible when the criminal is imprisoned. Under the current system, the state undertakes to protect the public against crime and then, when a loss occurs, takes the entire payment and offers no effective remedy to the victim. Second, it is argued that this system has a greater reformative effect on many offenders than do other methods, because the result of the offenses is more clearly recognized and no stigma is attached to make reformation difficult. Third, it relieves the state of the great financial burden of supporting in institutions those guilty of minor offenses.

It is probable that the system of restitution and reparation is used much more frequently than official records indicate. One of the prevalent methods used by professional thieves when they are arrested is to suggest to the victim that the property will be restored if the victim refuses to prosecute. This results in release in a large proportion of cases, for most victims are more interested in regaining their stolen property than in "seeing justice done." Also, many persons are protected against crime by insurance. The insurance company is interested primarily in restitution, and in many cases the crime probably is not reported, or criminal prosecution is not urged, if restitution is made. Similarly, there are thousands of cases of shoplifting, embezzlement, and automobile theft annually which are not reported to the police by the victim because restitution or reparation is made.

Restitution and reparation are most frequently used, both officially and unofficially, in connection with minor cases. In the United States, the official method of demanding restitution is used in connection with probation, one condition of the latter often being that the offender make restitution.[65] Probation departments often are primarily collection agencies. The probation department of New York collects about $500,000 a year from probationers for restitution.

CONCLUSION. The general theme of this chapter has been that neither the punitive reaction to law-breaking nor any specific method of implementing that reaction is rooted in the human organism or in universal traits of human nature. On the contrary, reactions to crime are seen to change with variations in the culture. Some kind of reaction to criminal behavior is uni-

---

[65] For a summary of American laws, and of the laws of twenty-eight other nations, see Schafer, op. cit.

versal, but the reaction may be either punitive or non-punitive. Even when the societal reaction is punitive there are great variations in the specific methods used to implement the reaction.

## SUGGESTED READINGS

Aschaffenburg, G., *Crime and Its Repression*. Boston: Little, Brown, 1913.

Bamford, Paul W., "Procurement of Oarsmen for French Galleys, 1600–1748," *American Historical Review*, 65:31–48, October, 1959.

Bedau, Hugo A., "A Survey of the Debate on Capital Punishment in Canada, England, and the United States, 1948–1958," *Prison Journal*, 38:35–45, October, 1958.

Brown, Julia S., "A Comparative Study of Deviations from Sexual Mores," *American Sociological Review*, 17:135–146, April, 1952.

Bye, R. T., *Capital Punishment in the United States*. Philadelphia: The Committee on Philanthropic Labor of the Philadelphia Yearly Meeting of Friends, 1919.

Caldwell, Robert G., *Red Hannah, Delaware's Whipping Post*. Philadelphia: University of Pennsylvania Press, 1947.

Evans, E. P., *The Criminal Prosecution and Capital Punishment of Animals*. London: W. Heinemann, 1906.

Garfinkel, Harold, "Conditions of Successful Degradation Ceremonies," *American Journal of Sociology*, 61:420–424, March, 1956.

Hall, Jerome, "Science and Reform in Criminal Law," *University of Pennsylvania Law Review*, 100:787–804.

Hentig, Hans von, *Punishment, Its Origin, Purpose and Psychology*. London: Hodge, 1937.

Hoebel, E. Adamson, *The Law of Primitive Man: A Study in Comparative Legal Dynamics*. Cambridge: Harvard University Press, 1954.

Ives, George, *A History of Penal Methods*. London: Stanley Paul, 1914.

Maestro, M. T., *Voltaire and Beccaria as Reformers of the Criminal Law*. New York: Columbia University Press, 1942.

Margolin, A. D., "The Element of Vengeance in Punishment," *Journal of Criminal Law and Criminology*, 24:755–767, November–December, 1933.

McCafferty, James A., "Major Trends in the Use of Capital Punishment," *Federal Probation*, 25:15–21, September, 1961.

Mead, G. H., "The Psychology of Punitive Justice," *American Journal of Sociology*, 23:577–602, March, 1918.

Oppenheimer, H., *The Rationale of Punishment*. London: University of London Press, 1913.

Radzinowicz, Leon, *A History of English Criminal Law*. Volume I. New York: Macmillan, 1948.

Rusche, George, and Otto Kirchheimer, *Punishment and Social Structure*. New York: Columbia University Press, 1939.

Saleilles, R., *The Individualization of Punishment*. Translated by R. S. Jastrow. Boston: Little, Brown, 1911.

Savitz, Leonard D., "Capital Crimes as Defined in American Statutory Law," *Journal of Criminal Law, Criminology, and Police Science*, 46: 355–363, September–October, 1955.

Schafer, Stephen, *Restitution to Victims of Crime*. London: Stevens and Sons, 1960.

Sellin, Thorsten, "Correction in Historical Perspective," *Law and Contemporary Problems*, 23:585–593, Autumn, 1958.

Sellin, Thorsten, *The Death Penalty*. Philadelphia: The American Law Institute, 1959.

# 15. PUNITIVE POLICIES AND SOCIAL STRUCTURE

IN THE previous chapter we were primarily concerned with general variations in the punitive reaction to crime and with variations in specific methods of expressing that reaction. Here we will be concerned with the extent
to which official reactions are the actual reactions to law-breaking and with
variations in the justifications given for the punitive reaction. In the final
pages, several theories which have attempted explanation of the wide range
of variations will be reviewed.

VARIATIONS IN EXECUTION OF OFFICIAL PUNITIVE REACTIONS.  In the period during which the theories of the classical school were most popular it
was argued that if every crime were followed immediately by extreme suffering on the part of the criminal, crime would almost entirely disappear.
The ideal was a punitive societal reaction which would approach as closely
as possible an assumed law of nature. The attributes of punishment which
were considered desirable were uniformity, certainty, celerity, and severity,
and there was an attempt to make these the characteristics of the official,
legal, system of dealing with law-breakers. With the rise of the positive
school, on the other hand, any method of punishment was regarded with
considerable scepticism. The positivists pointed to intoxication which often
is rather promptly followed by suffering, but which is continued nevertheless. They maintained that a society has the amount of crime it deserves
in view of its biological composition and its economic conditions, and that
the policy used in dealing with criminals is relatively unimportant in determining behavior. Perhaps the same set of social conditions which gave life
to the positive school in the first place also effectively blocked the development of a uniform, certain, swift, and severe punitive reaction to law-
breaking.
   Uniformity in the classical system referred to the similarity of punishment of all persons who violated a particular law. This uniformity was jus-

tified on the ground that it was necessary to have a definite predetermined penalty in order that prospective offenders might take it into their calculations of the pleasures and pains which would result from criminal acts. The pride of the system was its impersonality. In reacting to crime, society was to give no consideration to social status, wealth, religion, previous behavior, age, sex, or any other element or circumstances of the person. The emphasis on uniformity was an expression of the spirit of democracy then strong in European countries.

Certainty of punishment refers to the frequency with which violators are detected, identified, convicted, and punished. Certainty cannot be attained in modern society, especially for such crimes as larceny and burglary, although there probably are great variations in its approximation. Many of these variations were discussed earlier, when it was observed that the value of crime statistics decreases as the distance from the crime in terms of procedure increases.[1] In general, the number of arrests for larceny and burglary probably is not more than 10 percent of the number committed, but this varies from society to society.

Severity and celerity of punishment have, of necessity, varied with uniformity and certainty; and, in fact, it seems impossible to separate any one of these attributes from the others. Many observations of severity have been attempted in support of arguments for and against its effectiveness as a deterrent, but such arguments never have been supported by conclusive evidence, probably because the relationship of severity to the other attributes cannot be controlled. Perhaps severe and swift punishment would be effective in deterrence and reformation if all offenders were punished in the same way. Also, it is likely that even mild punishments would be effective deterrents for many crimes, especially white-collar crimes, if they were swift and certain. Putthamer has argued that punishment has never been given a really fair chance to demonstrate just how much it can accomplish, because we have tended to assume that severe punishment will deter, even if it is not imposed certainly.[2] When one offender is punished severely and ninety are not even detected in their crimes, then the effects of an official policy of severity cannot be determined. Officially-prescribed punishments, whether severe or not, were not imposed certainly or with any fixed degree of uniformity during earlier historical periods, and surely they are not imposed certainly or uniformly in the United States at the present. This can be observed in the practice of mitigating official penalties and in the practice of imposing punitive policies differentially.

*Mitigation of penalties.* Penalties officially prescribed as a part of the

[1] See Chapter Two, pp. 27–32.
[2] Ernest W. Putthamer, *Administration of Criminal Law* (Chicago: University of Chicago Press), 1953, pp. 16–18.

general punitive reaction to law-breaking have been mitigated in various ways. One of the early methods used for this purpose was "securing sanctuary." In the thirteenth century, a criminal could avoid punishment by claiming refuge in a church for a period of forty days, at the end of which time he was compelled to leave the realm by a road or port assigned to him. In the early sixteenth century, instead of being permitted to leave the realm a criminal who had secured sanctuary might be compelled to spend the rest of his life in an assigned locality in England, the name of which was branded on his thumb for identification. The entire system of securing sanctuary began to decline in the last part of the fifteenth century, and by the middle of the sixteenth century murder, rape, burglary, arson, and a few other offenses no longer carried the right of sanctuary. The whole system was abandoned when the monasteries were broken up.

A second system for mitigation of penalties was "right of clergy." This grew out of the original demand of the church to try its own officers. To be tried by an ecclesiastical court was a distinct advantage, for the church was not permitted to impose the death penalty during a part of the period of its supremacy, and its penalties in general were less severe except for the offenses of heresy and witchcraft. The "clergy" were defined at first in the strict sense, but later the term came to include all who had the clerical tonsure, then all who could read. The test used in determining whether a person could read was generally the first verse of the fifty-first psalm, and a little coaching would enable almost anyone to pass this test. Finally the peers who could not read received the same benefit of clergy by nature of their position. This was a device by which those who were culturally similar to the lawmakers were made exempt from the more severe penalties. Those who were responsible for expression of the official punitive reaction did not inflict severe penalties upon their own members but reserved these punishments for the lower classes. While the number of persons who could claim right of clergy increased, the number of times a person could claim the right and the number of offenses for which this right could be claimed were gradually reduced. Thus penalties came to be more nearly the same for those who had the benefit of clergy and those who did not. An act of 1705 provided that even those who claimed the right of clergy might be punished by the secular authorities at least to the extent of confinement in a house of correction for not less than six months or more than two years. By the end of the eighteenth century the right of clergy meant nothing.[3]

A third method of mitigation of penalties was the pardon. The pre-

[3] See Jerome Hall, *Theft, Law and Society*, Second Edition (Indianapolis: Bobbs-Merrill), 1952, pp. 110–118, 356–363; and George Dalzell, *Benefit of Clergy* (Winston-Salem: Blair, 1955).

## TABLE XIV

CHANGES IN THE PROPORTION OF CAPITAL
PENALTIES EXECUTED

| Years | Percent |
|---|---|
| 1689–1718* | 52.6 |
| 1755–1784* | 28.3 |
| 1785–1814* | 25.6 |
| 1815–1819 | 10.5 |
| 1820–1826 | 6.9 |
| 1827–1833 | 4.1 |

\* Counties of Essex, Herts, Kent, Surrey, and Sussex only.

scribed penalties were severe, but the king was permitted to relax the severity in individual cases. Our present system of pardoning probably grew out of this practice. In the modern period, the courts were authorized to fix penalties within limits set by the legislatures, and in this manner to adjust the penalty to the needs of individual offenders.

A fourth method of mitigating penalties was the simple refusal to execute the punishments officially prescribed and imposed. In the seventeenth and eighteenth centuries in England, a period of rapidly shifting standards, property owners demanded severe penalties as a means of protection. But because the common people were increasing in political and social power these sentences, though imposed, were not executed in a large proportion of the cases, as is shown by the statistics for England in Table XIV.[4]

Corporal punishments disappeared from England, just as did the death penalty, because even when courts imposed the sentences, public sentiment prevented their execution. In the last part of the eighteenth century Bentham made the following statement regarding the penalty of branding:

Burning in the hand, according as the criminal and the executioner can agree, is performed either with a cold or a red-hot iron; and if it be with a red-hot iron, it is only a slice of ham which is burnt; to complete the farce, the criminal screams, whilst it is only the fat which smokes and burns, and the knowing spectators only laugh at this parody of justice.[5]

Similarly, as opposition to the policy of quartering the corpse after execution developed the method became more and more symbolic until in 1820 "quartering" consisted merely of scratching a cross on the neck of the

---

[4] See also Leon Radzinowicz, A History of English Criminal Law and its Administration from 1750 (New York: Macmillan, 1948), Volume I, pp. 143–164.

[5] Jeremy Bentham, "Principles of Penal Law," in John Bowring, Editor, The Works of Jeremy Bentham (Edinburgh, W. Tait, 1843), p. 550.

corpse. Some of the corporal punishments at present are also merely symbolic:

The laws of Delaware provide that the warden must whip certain offenders. The warden explained that "the law doesn't tell me how hard to whip. Here's the way I whip . . . ," slowly, gently, almost doubtfully, the warden's right arm swung back and forth, like the pendulum of a clock deciding to cease to work.[6]

Even fines may be remitted by executive or judicial acts. In general at present the governor alone has power to remit fines in state cases, but some variations are found. A practice has developed in some courts of imposing a fine and then, in chambers, allowing motions in mitigation, by which the fines are reduced. This was a favorite method in Cleveland during national prohibition; publicity was secured by imposing very heavy fines, and friends were secured by secretly reducing the fines. Of 131 fines involving over $200 each in Cleveland liquor cases originating in January, 1921, motions in mitigation were allowed in 85, for a total reduction of $39,150, or 52 percent of the amount of the fines.[7]

*Differential imposition of punishments*. There is a great deal of evidence that current official punitive policies for dealing with law-breaking are not imposed in all cases of law-breaking, and this would indicate that the actual, unofficial, societal reactions to crime are not precisely reflected in the laws governing the administration of justice. The unofficial reactions to the crimes of persons of one status are different from the reactions to the crimes of persons of another status. Discriminations have been made and are made because of the age, sex, wealth, education, political prestige, race, nationality, and other characteristics of the offender. For example, in the United States female offenders are less likely than men to be arrested, and female prisoners are held in prison on the average about two-thirds as long for a specified type of offense as male prisoners. It is very difficult to convict females of capital offenses when the death penalty is mandatory, for juries refuse to find them guilty. In fact, for most major crimes the ratio of convictions to arrests is lower for females than for males.[8]

Powerful groups are often punished less frequently and severely than less powerful groups, as may be observed in the differential punishments of

   [6] O. F. Lewis, "Delaware's Prison—a Paradox," *Survey*, 46:465–467, July, 1921. See also Robert G. Caldwell, *Red Hannah, Delaware's Whipping Post* (Philadelphia: University of Pennsylvania Press, 1947), pp. 53–55.
   [7] R. H. Smith and H. B. Ehrmann, "The Criminal Courts," in Roscoe Pound and Felix Frankfurter, Editors, *Criminal Justice in Cleveland* (Cleveland: Cleveland Foundation, 1922), Part I, p. 58.
   [8] Otto Pollak, *The Criminality of Women* (Philadelphia: University of Pennsylvania Press, 1950), pp. 4–5.

white-collar criminals compared with other criminals.[9] Also, numerous studies have shown that the official punitive policy is more frequently applied to law-breaking by Negroes than it is to law-breaking by whites. The following conclusions have been drawn by one or more investigators: (a) Negroes are more liable to arrest than whites. (b) Negroes have less chance of not being indicted and of having their cases nolle prossed, passed to files, or disposed of in a miscellaneous fashion than do whites.[10] (c) Negroes have a higher conviction rate than whites. (d) Negroes are often punished more severely than whites, but this is not true for all crimes. (e) Whites are more likely to receive probation and suspended sentences. (f) Negroes receive pardons less often than do whites. (g) Negroes have less chance of having a death sentence commuted than do whites.[11] Similarly, the foreign-born when sent to prison are likely to go with heavier sentences than are the native-born.[12] Lemert and Rosberg analyzed the records of the Los Angeles Superior Court for 1938 and found that both conviction and probation depend to some extent upon minority group membership. Of 100 persons of specified groups arrested on felony charges, the following proportions were convicted: Negroes 7.7, Filipinos 5.7, Mexicans 5.3, Japanese and Chinese 3.7, and whites 2.7. Of persons convicted on felony charges, the following proportions were placed on probation: Mexicans 8.8, Negroes 10.6, and whites 23.5.[13]

VARIATIONS IN THE JUSTIFICATIONS OF PUNITIVE REACTIONS. Not only have both formal and informal societal reactions to crime varied, but the rationale given for those reactions has varied as well. At various times and places expiation, deterrence, retribution, reformation, income for the state, restoring or promoting the solidarity of the group, and other things have been offered as justifications for the punitive reaction. The justifications are not merely ex post facto rationalizations but, instead, are the reasons or motives men have for punishing in the first place. The particular form the punitive reaction takes depends upon the reasons offered for it or, in

[9] See Edwin H. Sutherland, White Collar Crime (New York: Dryden, 1949).

[10] James D. Turner, Differential Punishment in a Bi-Racial Community (unpublished Master's Thesis, Indiana University, 1948).

[11] Frank E. Hartung, "Trends in the Use of Capital Punishment," Annals of the American Academy of Political and Social Science, 284:8–19, November, 1952; and Marvin E. Wolfgang, Arlene Kelly and Hans C. Nolde, "Comparison of the Executed and the Commuted Among Admissions to Death Row," Journal of Criminal Law and Criminology, 53:301–311, September, 1962.

[12] Thorsten Sellin, Culture Conflict and Crime (New York: Social Science Research Council, 1938), p. 73.

[13] Edwin M. Lemert and Judy Rosberg, "The Administration of Justice to Minority Groups in Los Angeles County," University of California Publications in Culture and Society, Vol. II, No. 1, 1948, pp. 1–28.

other words, upon the kind of value which the punishment is assumed to have. No consistent course of development can be discerned, and certainly at any given time, especially at the present, all the members of a given society do not have the same reason for using the punitive reaction, even if they agree that such a reaction is desirable. Even individuals probably have more than one motive for punishing. Usually investigators infer merely that one or more of the motives is dominant, but not exclusive, in a society. Thomas and Znaniecki, for example, argued that among the Polish peasants studied the motive for punishment of crime was the restoration of the situation which existed before the crime and renewal of the solidarity of the group, and that revenge was a secondary consideration.[14]

Exner said, "So far as we can look back, men have always punished and have never ceased to dispute their reasons for so doing."[15] After the early attempts to rationalize punishments by considerations of a transcendental nature, the leading writers in this field insisted that certain social benefits resulted from punishment and constituted the justification of punishment. But little of this literature faced the issue of punishment versus other methods of dealing with criminals. It was assumed without argument that punishment was necessary, and the problem was to formulate an acceptable statement of this necessity. Thus, the controversy was largely between adherents of rival concepts of punishment, not between the adherents and opponents of punishment. The political philosophers were concerned, also, principally with the abstract right of the state to punish for crime. Even if one admits that the state has such a right in general, the further problem remains of determining whether punishment is economical in the larger sense. Moreover, the philosophical discussions have been concerned primarily with the purpose or aim of punishment and with the amount and nature of punishment, not with its value in comparison with other methods of dealing with criminals. The following values of punishment have been indicated by those who insist on the desirability of punishment.

*Punishment as retribution.* At least since the formulation of Hammurabi's code (in about 1875 B.C.) of "an eye for an eye and a tooth for a tooth," it has been urged by leaders and accepted by the general public that the criminal deserves to suffer. The suffering imposed by the state in its corporate capacity is considered the political counterpart of individual revenge. Sir James Stephen stated:

[14] W. I. Thomas and F. Znaniecki, *The Polish Peasant in Europe and America* (Chicago: University of Chicago Press, 1927), Vol. II, pp. 1254–1255. See also George H. Mead, "The Psychology of Punitive Justice," *American Journal of Sociology*, 23:577–602, March, 1918.
[15] Franz Exner, *Gerechtigkeit und Richteramt* (Leipzig: F. Meiner, 1922), p. 6.

Criminal procedure is to resentment what marriage is to affection: namely, the legal provision for an inevitable impulse of human beings.

This actually is a statement of the aim or purpose of punishment, and not a justification of punishment in terms of the social utilities produced by it. Dewey argued that we are not relieved of the responsibility for the consequences of our procedure by the fact that the offender is guilty.[16] A justification of punishment must be stated in terms of the future effects of the punishment on criminals. The future is not often considered by those who insist that the criminal deserves to be punished. It is urged that unless the criminal gets the punishment he deserves, one or both of the following effects will be produced: the victim will seek individual re-venge, which may mean lynch-law if his friends co-operate with him; or the victim will refuse to make complaint or offer testimony and the state will therefore be handicapped in dealing with criminals.

*Punishment as a deterrent.* Among those who advocate punishment because of its social utility, some claim that the infliction of pain upon those convicted of crime serves to deter others from crime, and that it has great value for that reason, even if some individuals are not deterred. Generally, the notion that punishment reduces crime is based on the hedonistic assumption that people regulate their behavior by calculation of pleasure and pain. In the recent period this assumption has been seriously challenged. Dewey stated the general fallacy in the assumption in the following proposition.

Deliberation no more resembles the casting-up of accounts of profit and loss, pleasure and pain, than an actor engaged in a drama resembles a clerk recording debit and credit items in his ledger.[17]

Some criminals never consider the penalty. Sometimes this is because they are psychopathic or feeble-minded or acting under the stress of a great emotion. Sometimes the penalty merely makes the prohibited act more alluring. Münsterberg sums up the reasons for believing that the deterrent power of punishment is limited as follows:

The hope of escaping justice in the concrete case will easily have a stronger feeling tone than the opposing fear of the abstract general law. The strength of the forbidden desire will narrow the circle of association and eliminate the idea of the probable consequences. The stupid mind

[16] John Dewey, *Human Nature and Conduct* (New York: Henry Holt, 1930), pp. 18–19.

[17] Dewey, *op. cit.,* p. 199. Reprinted by permission of the publishers.

will not link the correct expectations, the slow mind will bring the check too late, when the deed is done, the vehement mind will overrule the energies of inhibition, the emotional mind will be more moved by the anticipated immediate pleasure than by the thought of a later suffering. And all this will be reinforced if overstrain has destroyed the nervous balance, or if stimulants have smoothed the path of motor discharge. If the severity of cruel punishment has brutalized the mind, the threat will be as ineffective as if the mildness of punishment had reduced its pain. And, worst of all, this fear will be ruled out if the mind develops in an atmosphere of crime where the child hears of the criminal as a hero, and looks at jail as an ordinary affair, troublesome only as most factors in his slum life are troublesome; or if the anarchy of corruption or class justice, of reckless legislation or public indifference to law defeats the inhibiting counter idea of punishment and deprives it of its emotional strength.[18]

However, a refutation of hedonistic psychology and its conceptions is probably not sufficient to justify the rejection of the broader aspects of the deterrence argument. In a broader perspective, the criminal law and its application by police and courts probably have great effects upon public morality. Although specific severe punishments may have little immediate demonstrable effect in deterring specific criminals, the existence of the criminal code with its penal sanctions probably has a long-run deterrent effect upon the development of criminalistic ideologies. By means of the criminal law and the procedures for implementing the criminal law, including the imposition of swift and certain punishments, the undesirability and impropriety of certain behavior is emphasized.

Not the crimes punished, but the crimes prevented should measure the worth of the law. . . . If out of a score of law-abiding persons, only one obeys the law from fear of its penalties, it does not follow that the penal system occupies a correspondingly insignificant place among the supports of social order. For the rules of the social game are respected by the many good men chiefly because they are forced upon the few bad. If the one rascal among twenty men might aggress at will, the higher forms of control would break down, the fair-play instinct would cease to bind, and, between bad example and the impulse of retaliation, man after man would be detached from the honest majority. Thus, the deadly contagion of lawlessness would spread with increasing rapidity till the social order lay in ruins. The law, therefore, however minor its part at a given moment in the actual coercion of citizens, is still the cornerstone of the edifice of order.[19]

18 H. Münsterberg, *On the Witness Stand* (New York: McClure, 1908), pp. 258–260.

19 E. A. Ross, *Social Control* (New York: Macmillan, 1916), p. 125. Reprinted by permission of the publishers.

When deterrence was regarded as the principal purpose of punishment, penalties were made as public and as brutal as possible—witness the ducking stool, the stocks, the pillory, the public hangings, and the gibbeting of the body so that it might remain as long as possible as an example to the public. The radio has been used in a few recent cases to carry to the public the specific details of the punishment. Whenever the fiction known as a "crime-wave" is heralded, a demand for an increase in the severity of penalties arises, based on the assumption that the more severe the penalty, the more effectively it will deter others from similar crimes. These demands ordinarily are based on a confusion of penal sanctions as general expressions of hostility to crime on the one hand, and severe punishments as deterrents of specific persons who might be contemplating prohibited acts on the other hand.

*Punishment as a means of reformation.* It is maintained also that punishment tends to reform criminals and that it accomplishes this by creating a fear of repetition of the punishment, by creating a conviction that crime does not pay, or by breaking habits that criminals have formed, especially if the penalty is a long period of imprisonment which gives the habits no opportunity for expression. Such illustrations as the following are given in support of this argument: If the bees swarm out of their hive and sting the boy who molests them, they will not be troubled by him in the future; if they should fly from the hive on the approach of the boy and leave their honey at his disposal, they would be troubled again and again. Moreover, attention is called to the fact that experiments with animals have shown that animals frequently learn an operation more quickly when they are punished for failure than when they are not punished. A city attorney, speaking in defense of punishment, stated:

> You must inflict pain to get results. It was that way with me when I was a boy: I had been misbehaving and my father gave me an awful "whaling" and he had to do it only once. I had the same experience in dealing with my son. It is the same way with criminals. You must inflict pain to get results.

Recently, objective tests and measurements have been used in the effort to determine the values of punishment in learning, and these studies are pertinent to the discussion of reformation of criminals since reformation involves a learning process. Experiments are set up in order to measure the relative values of rewards and punishments in relation to animal and human learning and performance. Chase summarized the results of many of these experiments and concluded that the number of studies which showed that punishment was more effective than reward was greater than the number of studies which showed the opposite, but that punishment was not clearly superior in learning by human beings.[20] The effects of punishment, therefore, even in these experimental situations cannot be stated as a simple proposition. A mild punishment may promote learning but a more severe punishment may cause terror and panic which interfere with the whole learning process. These experiments, however, have no great significance for purposes of social control. The social situations in which punishments for crime are inflicted are much more complex and involve elements which are lacking in punishments in experimental laboratories.[21]

Changes in school children's behavior in spite of, or because of, the disappearance of corporal punishment is much more significant than laboratory experiments. According to Barnard, a Suabian school teacher left an itemized list of 1,423,100 corporal punishments which he had inflicted on school children during his career.[22] The average number of whippings per day in 1845 in a school of about 250 pupils near Boston was 65.6. The principal part of the teachers' time in almost all schools of that period was devoted to the maintenance of order and infliction of punishments. In spite of this, nearly four hundred schools in Massachusetts were broken up in the year 1837 because the teacher was unable to maintain discipline. The behavior of school children in modern schools in which corporal punishment is seldom inflicted is much better than in the schools of a century ago, when corporal punishment was extremely frequent. It is evident that the effect of punishment on reformation depends very much on the situation in which the punishment is inflicted.[23]

*Punishment and social solidarity.* It is also asserted that respect for law grows largely out of opposition to those who violate the law. The public hates the criminal, and this hatred is expressed in the form of punishment. In standing together against the enemy of their values, they develop group solidarity and respect for the orders of the group. Tarde said that crime will increase if we cease to hate the criminal. As indicated earlier, this may be so not because the punishment deters near-criminals but be-

[20] Lucille Chase, "Motivation of Young Children," *University of Iowa Studies in Child Welfare,* Vol. V, No. 3, March, 1932.

[21] For an analysis of the complexities in the effects of punishment see Laurence Sears, *Responsibility: Its Development Through Punishment and Reward* (New York: Columbia University Press, 1932), especially Part III, Chapter I.

[22] Henry Barnard, *English Pedagogy,* Second Series (Hartford: Brown and Gross, 1876), p. 327.

[23] See Johs. Andenaes, "General Prevention—Illusion or Reality?" *Journal of Criminal Law, Criminology and Police Science,* 43:176–198, July–August, 1952; George H. Dession, "Justice After Conviction," *Connecticut Bar Journal,* 25:215–235, September, 1951.

cause its use reaffirms law-abiding ideals and attitudes in the general public. Lundstedt maintained that fear of punishment is not the significant value in punishment but rather the legal sentiments, legal conscience, or moral feeling which have been developed in the general public by the administration of the criminal law during previous generations, and which have become so organized that they regulate behavior spontaneously almost like an instinct.[24] Professor Robert Park, a pioneering sociologist, made the following statement in lectures at the University of Chicago:

> Punishment of crime is a ceremonial affair, from which you get a new and more vigorous definition of the crime and make the public realize its gravity. When you talk of dealing with criminals as medical cases you are treating them not as human beings.

TESTING THE EFFECTIVENESS OF PUNISHMENT. Most of the justifications of punitive reactions and policies have not been made in the abstract but, instead, have been given as rather specific arguments for such methods as corporal punishment, the death penalty, or imprisonment. At present each of these methods is advocated by some on the ground that it has a deterrent effect, an effect on social solidarity, or other desirable effects, just as they were advocated a century or more ago. In the earlier period the arguments were challenged only by counterarguments, while in the recent period the challenges have been based at least in part upon examination and analysis of such empirical data as can be found. Such analyses of evidence amount to attempts to test the arguments, to treat them as hypotheses. This is a scientific procedure, and some of the arguments for the death penalty, together with some of the kinds of data used to refute the arguments, are presented here to illustrate the procedure. Arguments and data regarding the effectiveness of imprisonment will be given later.[25]

The most popular arguments currently made in favor of the death penalty are (a) it is more effective than any other penalty in deterring from murder; (b) it is more economical than imprisonment; (c) it is necessary in order to prevent the public from lynching criminals; and (d) it is the only certain penalty, for murderers who are sentenced to life imprisonment frequently secure pardons. On the other hand, those who oppose the death penalty argue that the death penalty is not more effective than imprisonment as a deterrent, that the abolition of the death penalty does not promote lynchings, that it reduces the certainty and speed of punishment, that by breaking down respect for human life it tends to

---

[24] A. V. Lundstedt, *Superstition or Rationality in Action for Peace?* (London: Longmans, Green, 1925), pp. 47–49, 190–192.
[25] See Chapter Twenty-three, 541–546.

promote murder, that errors of justice are irreparable, and that it has undesirable effects on the prisoners and the staff in institutions in which it
is inflicted.[26] Of these arguments, the one in regard to the deterrent effect
of the death penalty is by far the most important.

*The death penalty as a deterrent.* The most common method of
testing the deterrent effect of the death penalty is to compare the homicide rate in states which have abolished the death penalty with states
which retain it. In general, such comparisons show that in abolition states
the homicide rate is only about one-third to one-half as high as it is in the
other states. However, such comparisons are somewhat biased because
the death penalty is authorized in all of the Southern states, and the
Southern states have the highest homicide rate. A more justifiable comparison is between states in a particular section of the United States.
Figures II-V show that there is no significant difference in the homicide
rates of the states which have abolished the death penalty and the adjoining states which have retained the death penalty.[27] The significant difference is not between states which have the death penalty and those
which do not, but between the different sections of the country, regardless of whether the states have or do not have the death penalty. The
composition of the population and the general culture of the section is
much more important than the presence or absence of the death penalty
in determining homicide rates. Similar differences are found within states.
Vold found in 1932 that the average homicide rate in the southern tier
of ten Iowa counties was 3.9 and in the northern tier of eight Missouri
counties was 3.5, but in the southern tier of twelve Missouri counties was
10.5. The northern tier of Missouri counties is very similar to the southern
tier of Iowa counties in culture and composition of the population, but
the southern tier of Missouri counties is significantly different. Both states
have the death penalty. Thus the difference in the rate of homicides is due
to things other than the death penalty.[28]

The data on which the preceding analysis is based are not completely
adequate. The homicide rate is different from the murder rate. First-degree
murders, for which the death penalty may customarily be imposed, probably constitute not more than 10 percent of the homicides. Massachusetts,
which had a mandatory death penalty for first-degree murder until 1951

---

[26] An excellent bibliography on capital punishment appears in Hugo A. Bedau, "A
Survey of the Debate on Capital Punishment in Canada, England, and the United
States, 1948–1958," *Prison Journal*, 38:35–45, October, 1958.

[27] Figures II–V are reproduced from Thorsten Sellin, "Capital Punishment,"
*Federal Probation*, 15:3–11, September, 1961.

[28] G. B. Vold, "Can the Death Penalty Prevent Crime?" *The Prison Journal*, October, 1932, pp. 3–8.

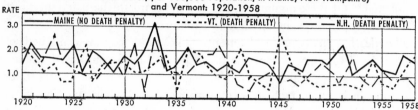

**FIGURE II**

Homicide Death Rates, per 100,000 Population, in Maine, New Hampshire, and Vermont: 1920-1958

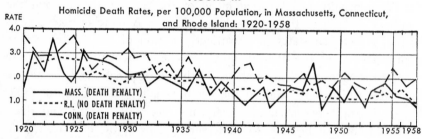

**FIGURE III**

Homicide Death Rates, per 100,000 Population, in Massachusetts, Connecticut, and Rhode Island: 1920-1958

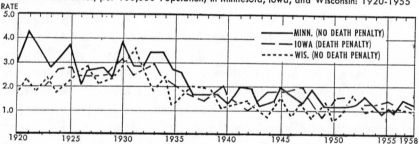

**FIGURE IV**

Homicide Death Rates, per 100,000 Population, in Minnesota, Iowa, and Wisconsin: 1920-1955

and now has a permissive death penalty for that offense, has a higher homicide rate than Rhode Island, which does not have the death penalty. But it is not certain that Massachusetts has more first degree murders than Rhode Island. It is highly probable, on a *priori* grounds, that the refinement of the homicide rate by eliminating the less serious homicides, such as "non-negligent manslaughter," would not alter the results of the comparisons previously presented, but this refinement is not possible at present and therefore the conclusion is somewhat questionable.

A second method for testing the deterrent effect of the death penalty is comparison of crime rates just before and just after one or more executions has taken place. If the death penalty has any deterrent value it presumably lies in its actual execution rather than in the legal possibility of

**FIGURE V**

Homicide Death Rates, per 100,000 Population, in Michigan, Indiana, and Ohio: 1920-1958

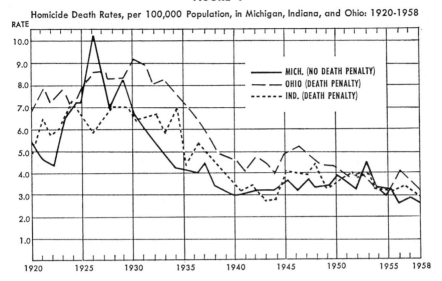

execution. Sections in which murderers are actually executed should be compared with sections in which the law prohibits such executions. Moreover, the sections should be sufficiently small (say, counties), so that an execution will produce some influence on the potential murderers in that section. No significant difference was found in this respect in a study of homicide rates sixty days prior and sixty days subsequent to five executions in Philadelphia.[29] In another Philadelphia study, Savitz analyzed the rate of capital crimes for a period of eight weeks just before and eight weeks after the sentencing of four men to death. He hypothesized that the greatest deterrence would occur in the locality where the crimes were committed and where the criminal was known. The four cases were selected because the sentencing was given great publicity in the newspapers. No significant increase or decrease in the murder rate occurred; there was no pattern that would indicate deterrence.[30] Similarly, a Chicago study indicated that homicide fluctuates independently of news coverage, executions, and commutations of sentences in capital cases.[31]

The results of the relatively crude comparisons in the United States are reenforced by comparisons in European countries. On the average, the European states which have abolished the death penalty have lower homi-

[29] Robert H. Dann, "The Deterrent Effect of Capital Punishment," *Friends' Social Service Series*, Bulletin No. 29, 1935.

[30] Leonard D. Savitz, "A Study of Capital Punishment," *Journal of Criminal Law, Criminology and Police Science*, 49:338–341, December, 1958. See also Schuessler, *op. cit.*

[31] Hans W. Mattick, *The Unexamined Death* (Chicago: John Howard Association, 1963), pp. 11–12.

cide rates (which generally means lower murder rates in Europe) than states which retain the death penalty. The Scandinavian countries, which have abolished the death penalty, have homicide rates about one-half as high as England, which retained the death penalty until recently.

A third method for testing the deterrent value of the death penalty is by comparing, in the states which have abolished the death penalty, the homicide rates before and after the abolition. The general conclusion from such comparisons is that the states which abolished the death penalty have had no unusual increase in homicide rates. Ten states abolished the death sentence only to restore it after a few years, on the ground that the murder rate had increased greatly after the abolition. The statistics show, however, that the changes in homicide rates were almost exactly parallel in other states which made no changes in their laws regarding the death penalty. For instance, Missouri abolished the death penalty in 1917 and restored it in 1919 on the ground that murders had increased greatly. But the changes in the homicide rate in Missouri from 1910 to 1924 were almost exactly the same in direction and amount as in Ohio, which retained the death penalty throughout this whole period, and were very much like the changes in the United States in general. Similarly, Kansas abolished the death penalty in 1907 and restored it in 1935. The annual average homicide rate in Kansas was 6.2 in 1931–1935, 3.6 in 1936–1940, and 3.0 in 1941–46. However, an identical trend characterized the states bordering Kansas. For example, Missouri's rate was 11.1 in 1931–35, 6.6 in 1936–40, and 5.3 in 1941–46. Comparison of the "before and after" homicide rates of European countries which have abolished the death penalty also shows that the presence or absence of the death penalty has no perceptible effect on the incidence of murder.[32]

The available statistics do not justify an absolute conclusion regarding the value of the death penalty as a deterrent. The evidence, such as it is, shows a relatively unimportant relation between the murder rate and the death penalty. The argument that the death penalty is an effective deterrent is not, at least, substantiated by the data available. It is based on preconceptions rather than on data, and the preconceptions are taken from the hedonistic psychology which assumes that the psychological processes are much less complex than they are in fact. Even premeditated murders are generally committed under the stress of a great emotion, and the penalty is seldom considered.[33]

The death penalty and certainty of punishment. The advocates of

[32] Schuessler, op. cit.
[33] See Marvin E. Wolfgang, Patterns of Criminal Homicide (Philadelphia: University of Pennsylvania Press, 1958), Chapter 10.

the death penalty argue that it is more certain than imprisonment, because imprisonment is frequently terminated by escape, pardon, or parole. Actually, the death penalty is very uncertain, because it is so seldom imposed even when it is authorized. For example, in 1964 there were only 15 executions carried out in the United States.[34] Also, the argument is made that juries are less willing to convict and witnesses less willing to testify when the penalty is death than when it is a less irreparable penalty. Calvert cites a petition by English bankers in 1830 for abolition of the death penalty for forgery on the ground that convictions could not be secured because of the severity of the death penalty and for the authorization of a less severe penalty in order that their property might be protected more adequately.[35] Bye found that a slightly larger proportion of convictions were secured in murder cases in states which had abolished the death penalty than in states which retain it.[36] However, in death penalty states prospective jurors who are opposed to the death penalty are excused from serving in capital cases, and in some instances this weeding-out process may produce juries which are most likely to convict the accused. Moreover, the percentage of defendants found guilty in murder cases, and the percentage of defendants convicted of first degree murder, varies widely from county to county even in states which have the death penalty. For example, during the period 1925–1941 Middlesex County, Massachusetts, found 16.8 percent of its cases guilty of murder in the first degree, while in adjacent Suffolk County the corresponding percentage was only 3.9.[37] Of 1,628 persons convicted of homicide in 29 states in 1936, only 4 percent were sentenced to death, and ten years later, in 1946, of 1,923 persons convicted of homicide only 4.6 percent were given death sentences.[38] As indicated, however, homicide is not synonymous with murder and perhaps not more than one-tenth of the persons committed to prison for homicide have been found guilty of premeditated murder. In Ohio, only 1.2 percent of the persons convicted of nonnegligent homicide were executed during the fifty-year period 1910–1959.[39]

The uncertainty of the death penalty also is indicated by the fact that

[34] Federal Bureau of Prisons, "Executions, 1930–1964," *National Prisoner Statistics,* No. 37, April, 1964.

[35] E. R. Calvert, *Capital Punishment in the Twentieth Century* (London: Putnam's Sons, 1927), p. 15.

[36] R. T. Bye, *Capital Punishment in the United States* (Philadelphia: The Committee on Philanthropic Labor of Philadelphia Yearly Meeting of Friends, 1919), pp. 47 ff.

[37] Herbert B. Ehrmann, "The Death Penalty and the Administration of Justice," *Annals of the American Academy of Political and Social Science,* 284:73–84, November, 1952.

[38] Frank E. Hartung, *On Capital Punishment* (Detroit: Wayne University Department of Sociology and Anthropology), 1951, p. 22.

[39] Ohio Legislative Service Commission, *Capital Punishment* (Columbus: Author, 1961, Staff Research Report No. 46, 1961), p. 36.

many of the persons sentenced to death are not executed. Of those persons sentenced to death for murder in the courts of 25 states during the period 1933–1939, 80 percent were executed; during the period 1940–1945, 81 percent were executed.[40] Of the 101 persons convicted of first degree murder between 1900 and 1959 in Massachusetts, which had a mandatory death penalty until 1951, 65 were executed, 35 were given life imprisonment, and one committed suicide.[41] In Maryland in 1936–1961, 59 percent of those sentenced to death for murder and 51 percent of those sentenced to death for rape were executed.[42] In Texas in the period 1924–1952, 21 percent of the death sentences for murder, 7 percent of the death sentences for rape, and 63 percent of the death sentences for armed robbery were commuted to life imprisonment.[43] While it is clear that imprisonment is not a completely certain penalty, it is clear, also, that the death penalty is not a certain penalty until it is actually executed.

Schuessler devised an index of the certainty of the death penalty and showed that the relative occurrence of murder has a slight tendency to decrease as the probability of execution increases. He found that among the death-penalty states, those which executed the largest proportion of the persons convicted of homicide in the period 1937–1949 generally had the lowest homicide rates. However, the correlation coefficient of −.29 was not statistically significant. Nor did the homicide rate drop consistently as the risk of execution increased. Also, he found that when a state executes a relatively large proportion of its murderers in one year, the homicide rate does not necessarily drop during the following year.[44]

The death penalty and financial economy. The death penalty often is defended on the ground that it is less expensive than life imprisonment. The per capita cost of imprisonment is perhaps $1500 per year, and the life term may amount to an average of twenty years, making a total of $30,000. If it is true that an execution costs less than this, the demand for execution would apply equally well to the non-criminal insane, to the feeble-minded, and to criminals who have committed offenses less serious than murder; for execution of such persons also would be cheaper than their maintenance in an institution. But there is some doubt as to whether execution actually is

[40] Schuessler, op. cit.

[41] Special Commission to Investigate and Study the Abolition of the Death Penalty in Capital Cases, *Report and Recommendations* (Commonwealth of Massachusetts, House Document No. 2575, December 30, 1958), p. 29.

[42] Legislative Council of Maryland, *Report of the Committee on Capital Punishment* (Baltimore: Author, 1962), p. 35.

[43] G. I. Giardini and R. G. Farrow, "The Paroling of Capital Offenders," *Annals of the American Academy of Political and Social Science*, 284:85–94, November, 1952.

[44] Op. cit. See Savitz, "A Study in Capital Punishment," op. cit.

cheaper than imprisonment. First, the trials of death penalty cases are ordinarily much longer than trials of other cases. Often as many as 1,000 jurors are examined before 12 can be chosen, and a year or more intervenes between arrest and sentence.[45] Second, although the maintenance cost per prisoner may be high, this does not mean that it would increase appreciably if those now executed were committed to prisons. Third, in considering cost of executions, the expenditures for death houses and for the closer custody which must be maintained are usually not computed. It costs $25,000 a year for the custodial officers in the death house of the New Jersey State Prison.[46]

*The irreparability of error with the death penalty.* Those who advocate capital punishment consider wrongful conviction as only a remote possibility. But although most mistakes are prevented by the judicial system or by executive clemency, some occur, due to mistaken identification, inadequate circumstantial evidence, framed and simulated evidence, perjury, unreliable expert evidence, overlooking and suppressing of evidence, and excessive zeal on the part of investigators and prosecutors.[47] Lawes has pointed out that between 1889 and 1927, 50 (12.3 percent) of the 406 persons sent to Sing Sing for execution were found, upon reconsideration, to have been sentenced in error.[48] Hartung found that in Michigan, which does not have the death penalty, judges and juries erred in 10.9 percent of 759 life imprisonment convictions for murder in the first degree in 1942–1951.[49]

**THEORIES OF PUNISHMENT.** Our previous discussion has indicated that there has been no constant desire to make all criminals suffer and that the system used for inflicting suffering on those criminals considered as deserving of suffering has changed from time to time. The punitive reaction to law-breaking has not been present in all societies, the methods for implementing the punitive reaction which are predominant in some societies are not predominant in other societies, the extent to which official punitive policies are carried out in practice varies from time to time even within a given society, and the rationale for punishment has taken many forms. A

45 Cf. Ehrmann, *op. cit.*

46 New Jersey Council to Abolish Capital Punishment, *Thirty-Seven Questions on Capital Punishment* (Indianapolis: John Woolman Press, 1963), pp. 10–11.

47 Charles E. O'Hara and James W. Osterburg, "Some Miscarriages Of Justice Analyzed in the Light of Criminalistics," Chapter 47 of *An Introduction to Criminalistics* (New York: Macmillan, 1959), pp. 680–685.

48 Lewis E. Lawes, *Twenty Thousand Years in Sing Sing* (New York: R. Long and R. R. Smith, 1932), pp. 146–147, 156.

49 Hartung, *op. cit.* See also Otto Pollak, "The Errors of Justice," *Annals of the American Academy of Political and Social Science*, 284:115–123, November, 1952; and Jerome Frank and Barbara Frank, *Not Guilty* (New York: Doubleday, 1957).

theory which precisely explains or accounts for all of these variations has not been developed. Preliminary attempts to account for at least some of the variations have been made, however, and the major cultural, psychoanalytic, and sociological explanations will be described briefly.

*Cultural consistency.* One theory which partially accounts for the many variations in the presence and implementation of the punitive reaction to law-breaking may be termed a theory of "cultural consistency." The societal reactions to law-breaking and the methods used to implement or express that reaction show a general tendency to be consistent with other ways of behaving of the society. This may be observed in a number of ways. *First,* two centuries ago criminals were disemboweled, quartered, hung in chains, branded, pilloried, ducked, and in other ways tortured, mutilated, and shamed. These practices occurred in a culture in which physical suffering was regarded as the natural lot of mankind and in which the means of preventing pain were not well developed. Today safeguards against physical suffering have been provided in other fields; a policy of physical torture of criminals cannot be harmonized with the general interest in the reduction of suffering, and the reaction toward crime is away from the strictly punitive. *Second,* the price system developed during the modern period, and the methods of punishment have developed somewhat consistently with the price system. Hence, perhaps, came the monetary implications in such phrases as "debt to society" and "pay the price." Just as a price is assumed to bear a constant relation to a commodity, so, it was assumed, the penalty should bear a constant relation to the crime. The aim was "to let the punishment fit the crime." The classical economists insisted that reward should be commensurate with service; the classical criminologists concluded that punishment should be commensurate with disservice or crime. *Third,* the ideal of uniformity in the treatment of offenders was stated about the time of the French Revolution when democracy meant the equality of all classes. Democracy has been re-interpreted since that time and the policy of uniform penalties has been similarly modified. Again, uniformity developed at the time when one cure was used by physicians for all kinds of diseases and all kinds of patients. *Fourth,* individualization in medical treatment has developed during the last two centuries and with it individualization in penal treatment. The positive school, which at first was a biological school, insisted that criminals, like patients, differ and that the offender rather than the offense should be the object of attention. The general trend at the present is toward the individualization which the positive school outlined. If this policy of individualization tends to result in a uniform reaction to criminality, it is a uniformity of reaction to all criminals who are similar in type of personality or in situation rather than uniformity based on the type of crime committed. It is a uniformity like that in medicine. *Fifth,* only a few generations ago punishment was emphasized in the home, school, and the church and, necessarily, the system for handling of offenders by the state was consistent. When penal methods were generally abandoned by the home, school, and church, it became difficult for the state to continue exercising penal policies successfully. Now the offender often gets more support and the state less support when the official reaction is severely punitive. *Finally,* the penalties tend to be more certain and severe for acts which endanger the values which are highly regarded, and these values change.[50] Perhaps it is for this reason that in several states at present the minimum official penalty for bribing an athlete is greater than for robbery with a gun.

Somewhat more specifically, two general changes in the method of implementing the punitive reaction have taken place in the last few centuries, and they seem to be correlated: imprisonment has been used more frequently, physical torture and death less frequently. The explanation for this decrease in the use of the methods of torture and killing and for the substitution of imprisonment is not entirely clear, but certain elements of the explanation stand out.

First, negatively, imprisonment on extensive scale was practically impossible in the earlier period. No institutions secure enough for imprisonment for large numbers of people had been constructed, and the difficulty of building such institutions made their development impractical. More important, with the many wars, the changes in control, and the lack of police and other guardians, such institutions, even if constructed, would have been relatively useless; it was necessary for social life to become more settled before imprisonment could become a general policy.

Second, more positively, a greater appreciation of freedom developed in the modern period, and restriction of freedom came to be regarded as suffering. During the medieval period, with the intense interest in theology, suffering could be imposed by excommunication. Similarly, during the modern period, with the interest in democracy and freedom, the loss of freedom means more than it did previously. In the earlier period prisoners of war and religious prisoners were ordinarily confined in castles, and the life of one imprisoned for crime would not have been significantly different from the life of many persons who had not committed crimes. Many castles of the time were no more pleasant than the prisons; in fact many castles were turned into prisons and then later used as castles again. Because of

50 *Cf.* F. Znaniecki, *Social Actions* (New York: Farrar and Rinehart, 1936), pp. 344–408; Arthur Lewis Wood, "The Alternatives to the Death Penalty," *Annals of the American Academy of Political and Social Science,* 284:63–72, November 1952.

the increased valuation of freedom, the loss of freedom has come to be regarded as sufficiently punitive for the worst criminals.

Third, labor power has been appreciated more in the recent period. Imprisonment developed at about the time of the waning of the slave labor system. Because of the higher valuation of labor power, it became necessary to conserve it instead of destroying it by death or mutilations. Life became valuable.

Finally, the more brutal punishments flourished at a time when the social distance between those who imposed the punishment and those who suffered it was very great. The situation changed in this respect in the modern period by the development of democracy and the means of communication. Democracy was important in this way because it meant that the control was secured by persons who had much the same experiences as the defendants; one was tried by his peers who understood his situation and looked upon him as a human being like themselves. The development of the means of communication was important because it brought about an increasing number of contacts between those who committed crimes and others. This enabled a larger proportion of the population to appreciate the situation of those who committed offenses, so that the imposition of pain or suffering was no longer similar to the injury of an animal or of a foreign enemy but was the injury of an other human being like themselves. Although limitations were imposed by color of skin and other differentiae, contacts that were frequent and intimate increased, with the result of greater understanding and a keener sympathy for criminals.

*The scapegoat theory.* Psychoanalysts have advanced a theory which correlates the many variations in the punitive reaction with variations in the alternative systems for satisfying aggressive and libidinal instincts. The general notion is that these instincts must be expressed in some fashion and that the criminal serves as a scapegoat for their legitimate expression. Thus, it is maintained that in punishing criminals society expresses the same urges which are expressed, among criminals, in committing crime.

One form of this theory holds that the urge to punish criminals is closely related to sexuality and that the variations in the punitive reaction to lawbreaking tend to follow the variations in social prohibitions against sexual behavior. In societies in which sex taboos are few and lax, punishment is absent or lenient; in periods when sex and sexuality are loudly declaimed, punishment is frequent, open, and severe; in periods when sex becomes more suppressed as a topic of public discussion punishment is suppressed or hidden. One author accounts for variations in the methods of implementing the punitive reaction in terms of the suppression of a rather fixed amount of libidinal "urge" which is assumed to be present in the human organism. It is his contention that in the recent period the punitive reaction to law-breaking is as prevalent as it was in the period when corporal and capital punishments were most popular but that the method of punishment has merely gone underground. Thus, we no longer openly whip or torture criminals but, instead, torture them secretively, behind prison walls.[51]

A more popular version of this theory deals more directly with aggression. Again, the essential notion is that the human organism, because of unconscious conflicts, contains a fixed amount of aggression, which must be expressed. It may be expressed in criminality, it may be expressed in punishment of criminals, or it may be expressed in other ways.[52] Variations in the punitive reaction to crime, then, would depend upon the availability of alternative outlets for aggressions. The reverse is also thought to be true: limitations on the expression of aggression through punishment of law-breakers would result in the expression of aggression in other ways, perhaps in criminality itself. It has been intimated that the First World War (aggression) was a substitute for punitive aggression against criminals. That is, the punitive reaction of aggression could not be expressed during the period just prior to the war, but since the aggression had to be expressed, enemies, rather than criminals, became the scapegoat.[53] Hence, it is concluded that societies need criminals for emotional reasons, and they organize the fight against them in such a way that crime is actually maintained.[54]

Punishment of criminals, then, is considered a system for sublimation of aggression tendencies; persons who are aggressive secure satisfaction in the punishment inflicted, and this satisfaction is socially proper. In this way, many persons can avoid illegal aggressions, just as they avoid them by other kinds of sublimation.[55] The analogy here is with the psychoanalytic theory of the development of the individual. Society is considered to have advanced through the same three stages as are assumed to be present in the psychological development of the human organism. First, there was in social life a stage in which there was free expression of the instincts of sexuality and aggressiveness, and this was the period of no punishment. Next, the expression of the instincts was repressed and, hence, the instincts obtained their outlet in superego activities, directed against their original

[51] Charles Berg, "The Psychology of Punishment," *British Journal of Medical Psychology,* 20:295–313, October, 1945.
[52] David Abrahamsen, *Who Are the Guilty: A Study of Education and Crime* (New York: Rinehart, 1952), p. 287.
[53] Paul Reiwald, *Society and Its Criminals* (New York: International Universities Press, 1950).
[54] *Ibid.,* p. 235.
[55] F. Alexander and H. Staub, *The Criminal, the Judge, and the Public,* Revised Edition (Glencoe: The Free Press, 1956), pp. 213–223; Robert Kann, "Criminal Law and Aggression," *Psychoanalytic Review,* 28:384–406, July, 1941.

form; this was the period of severe and open punishments. In the third stage there has been a further degree of repression, and an open expression of the libidinal and aggressive instincts is no longer tolerated, even in the indirect or symbolic form of punishment. Just as the libidinal and aggressive instincts are said to be repressed and hidden in the unconscious of the individual, the societal expression of such instincts is repressed and hidden behind prison walls. "Inside the prison—the objective equivalent of the unconscious—the same process [instinctual expression] goes on unseen by consciousness and inaccessible to ego-interference."[56]

3) Social structure theories. A few social scientists, largely European, have attempted to relate the many variations in the punitive reaction and its expression and implementation to variations in social structure. The variations have been accounted for by the availability of labor supply, the presence of the lower middle class, the division of labor, and social disorganization.

(a) Punishment and economic conditions. One theory of punishment is analogous to, or a part of, the economic theory of crime causation. The general notion is that both the punitive reaction itself and the specific methods of implementing that reaction are very affected, if not determined, by the general economic conditions of the society. Rusche, for example, has advanced the thesis that the primary determinant of the societal reaction to crime is the condition of the labor market.[57] He contends that when the labor market is glutted and labor therefore cheap the reaction to law-breaking tends to be punitive, but when the labor supply is scarce and labor therefore at a premium the reaction becomes non-punitive. Also, the methods of implementing the punitive reaction are thought to vary with the condition of the labor market. For instance, it is observed that the galleys were substituted for corporal and capital punishment when it was necessary to secure men for rowing, that the workhouse developed when the state did not have sufficient labor, that transportation began as a means of providing labor for the colonies and stopped because of increased demand for labor at home, that solitary confinement was abandoned because under that system the labor of the prisoners could not be utilized, and that fines developed as revenue measures.[58] The basic assumption in this theory is that crime is a lower-class phenomenon and that the societal reaction is a phenomenon of the upper

---

[56] Berg, op. cit.

[57] George Rusche, "Arbeitsmarkt und Strafvollung," Zeitschrift für Sozialforschung, 2:63–78, May, 1933. Cited and discussed by Thorsten Sellin, Research Memorandum on Crime in the Depression (New York: Social Science Research Council, 1937), pp. 8–9.

[58] George Rusche and Otto Kirchheimer, Punishment and Social Structure (New York: Columbia University Press, 1939).

classes, who have political power. When economic conditions are poor and the labor market is glutted the upper classes impose severe punishments upon the lower classes; but when the economic need of the upper classes for labor cannot be satisfied they impose few and mild punishments. Actually, the theory breaks down into two arguments, the second of which is as follows: When economic conditions are good there is no economic need to commit crime and the crime rate is low, but when there is widespread unemployment the temptation to commit crime is great. If, the upper classes believe, in times of unemployment criminals can illegally obtain economic necessities in exchange for mild punishments the crime rate will be high. Therefore, the upper classes impose severe penalties in order to counteract the temptations of the lower classes.

When the two arguments are put together, the formula takes the following form: When poverty increases crime increases and, also, the labor market is glutted; and when crime increases and the labor market is glutted the societal reaction to crime is punitive rather than non-punitive. Whether it is the crime rate or the condition of the labor market which determines the societal reaction, then, is not clear. However, most economic determinists are not concerned with this lack of clarity, for it is their contention that it is general economic conditions which determine both crime and unemployment rates and, thereby determine the societal reaction to crime and the means used to implement that reaction. The studies of the crime rate in relation to business cycles throw much doubt upon this assumed relationship between economic conditions, crime, and punishment.[59]

(b) Punishment and the middle class. Another theory of punishment relates variations in the punitive reaction to the presence or absence of the lower middle class. The chief proponent of this theory, however, uses the term "middle class" in a sense uncommon in the United States, and also there is some doubt as to whether he is considering the middle class or something else. The theory is summarized in the following statement.

The disinterested tendency to inflict punishment is a distinctive characteristic of the lower middle class, that is, of a social class living under conditions which force its members to an extraordinary high degree of self-restraint and subject them to much frustration of natural desires.[60]

This statement actually has three component parts: (i) The punitive reaction to law-breaking ("the disinterested tendency to inflict punishment") grows out of the moral indignation of the public; it does not grow out of

---

[59] Cf. L. T. Stern, "The Effect of the Depression on Prison Commitments and Sentences," *Journal of Criminal Law and Criminology*, 31:696–711, March–April, 1941.
[60] Svend Ranulf, *Moral Indignation and Middle Class Psychology: A Sociological Study* (Copenhagen: Levin and Munksgaard, 1938), p. 198.

the indignation of the person who has been injured by a crime. (ii) Moral indignation is found almost exclusively in the lower middle class and is the product of their self-imposed frustration. (iii) The punitive reaction increases in frequency and severity when the lower middle class is in control and decreases when the lower middle class decreases in power.

In connection with the second point, moral indignation, which is the emotion behind the disinterested tendency to inflict punishment and is a kind of disguised envy, is assumed to be caused by a repression of natural desires. The natural desires of lower middle class persons are repressed, the members of the class are morally indignant when crime occurs, and lower middle class persons react punitively to law-breaking. In this view, the theory is not a social structure theory but, instead, a variation of the scapegoat theory.

However, in connection with the third point it is argued that even if the above psychological interpretation is omitted, a correlation between the presence of the lower middle class and the frequency and severity of the punitive reaction to law-breaking still can be observed. At least the literature suggests that the punitive reaction has always been popular in that social class, which may be loosely described as the "petit bourgeoisie," and that it does not prevail in communities where this social class is of little significance. The punitive reaction to crime is said to have been absent among the Teutons, the Chinese, the Hindus, and among primitive groups, which had no class of this kind. Among the Israelites, the punitive reaction did develop strongly, but not until a social class comparable to the lower middle class in modern Europe had grown influential.[61]

One difficulty with this suggestive theory is the lack of precision in the definition of the lower middle class. Ranulf does not define this term precisely, and consequently it is not possible to appraise the theory. Probably what he means by "middle-class psychology" is similar to what is meant by "Puritanism" or "Victorianism." If this is true, then recent variations in the punitive reaction and the methods of implementing it could be related to the rise of the Protestant ethic, in much the same way that Max Weber linked the rise of the spirit of capitalism to the Protestant ethic.[62] The development of an appreciation of the value of labor was shown by Weber to be correlated with the rise of Protestantism, especially Calvinism, and it is not inconceivable that the workhouses and other systems for utilizing the labor of criminals developed along with Calvinism, which emphasized the spiritual value of labor.

[61] *Ibid.*, pp. 174–186.
[62] For a discussion of Weber's work see Talcott Parsons, *Structure of Social Action* (New York: McGraw-Hill, 1937), Chapters 14–17.

(c) Punishment and the division of labor. Durkheim attributed the fluctuations in the punitive reaction to changes in the division of labor of society. His theory may be stated briefly in three propositions. (i) Offenses which attack the collective values of a society elicit more severe punitive reactions than those which attack individual values. Such offenses are treason, heresy, or crimes in which force is used. (ii) Punishments for crime are ordered by tribunals made up of all the people or of only a select number, and they are imposed primarily for the purpose of re-enforcing the collective values, not for vengeance, intimidation, or reformation. "We must not say that an action shocks the common conscience because it is criminal, but rather that it is criminal because it shocks the common conscience."[63] (iii) As the principle of social organization changes from mechanical solidarity to organic solidarity the punitive reaction to lawbreaking tends to disappear and in its place is substituted restitution and reparations.

The final proposition is the one used to account for many of the variations in the punitive reaction to crime. The type of societal reaction to crime is determined by the social structure, and the important aspect of the social structure is the complexity of the division of labor. When a society has mechanical solidarity, a solidarity based not upon division of labor but upon similarity of behavior and attitudes, the reaction to legal wrongs is punitive. This punitive reaction is formalized in the criminal law. But in societies in which the solidarity is organic, a solidarity based upon specialization or division of labor, then the reaction is non-punitive, for the desire is to return things to the condition they were in before the offense. However, society in this case is not merely a sort of third-party arbitrator, intervening to compromise disputes between individuals, but applies general and traditional rules of law to particular cases. This non-punitive restitutive reaction is formalized in the rules of civil law, procedural law, administrative law, and constitutional law. Since organic solidarity is becoming more and more the essential characteristic of the social structure of modern societies, repressive law and the punitive reaction is decreasing in use, and the restitutive law and non-punitive reaction is increasing in frequency.

(d) Punishment and social disorganization. Another theory which attempts to account for many of the variations in the punitive reaction is stated in terms of the heterogeneity of societies. In general, the notion is that in homogeneous societies the punitive reaction is infrequent and mild, while in heterogeneous societies it is frequent and severe. While hetero-

---

[63] Emile Durkheim, *The Division of Labor in Society*, translated by George Simpson (Glencoe: The Free Press, 1947), p. 81. See also Durkheim, "Deux lois de l'evolution penale," *L'Anne Sociologique*, 14:65–95, 1900.

geneity does not necessarily imply social disorganization, heterogeneous societies are often considered as being in a condition of social disorganization, and homogeneous societies are considered as organized.

Sorokin has stated a "social disorganization" theory which is somewhat consistent with Rusche's theory and somewhat inconsistent with Durkheim's theory.[64] He refers to variations in the "ethico-juridical heterogeneity and antagonism" of social groups, and argues that whenever this heterogeneity increases, whatever the reason for the increase, the frequency as well as the severity of the punitive reaction to law-breaking increases. The greater the increase in the heterogeneity and antagonism, the greater is the increase in the punitive reaction, as formalized in the imposition of punishments by one part of the group upon the other.[65] The ethico-juridical heterogeneity and antagonism is increased by social crises, including the economic.[66]

In simple statement, this theory is that the quantity and severity of punishments tend to vary directly with the heterogeneity and antagonism within a society. When a society has homogeneous morality, violations of that morality are infrequent, they do not greatly endanger the group, and the societal reaction to them is essentially non-punitive. But when this network of social relations is broken up and there is an increase in moral and legal heterogeneity, a condition which may be called disorganization, the societal reaction to violations becomes punitive.

The evidence advanced in support of this explanation of variations in the punitive reaction is largely the fluctuations of the reaction in periods of revolution, when heterogeneity increases and the punitive reaction increases. Following the revolution, heterogeneity decreases and the punitive reaction decreases. In periods of revolution the use of death penalties, imprisonments, banishment, transportation, confiscation of property, and all other methods of implementing the punitive reaction increases enormously. For example, in Russia the number of executions averaged about 10 to 20 per year in the years 1880–1905, during the revolution of 1905–1907 they were up to about 500 per year, and even to about 1300 in 1908, thereafter dropping to about 100.[67] The same is true in most other revolutions.[68]

These theories are all based on the assumption that certain characteris-

[64] Pitirim A. Sorokin, *Social and Cultural Dynamics* (New York: American Book Company, 1937), Vol. II. pp. 523–632.

[65] *Ibid.*, p. 595.

[66] Cf. Gaston Richard, "Les Crises Sociales et les conditions de la criminalité," *L'Anne Sociologique*, 4:17, 1900. Cited by Thorsten Sellin, *Research Memorandum on Crime in the Depression*, op. cit., p. 9.

[67] Sorokin, op. cit., p. 601.

[68] See in this connection John N. Hazard, "Trends in the Soviet Treatment of Crime," *American Sociological Review*, 5:566–576, August, 1940.

tics of the general culture or social structure determine the general way that
criminality is handled in a society. While this assumption is undoubtedly
correct, none of the theories specify the process by which certain social
conditions produce the societal reactions. For example, the cultural consistency theory does not indicate how culture "works" to change the reactions to crime and criminality, just as the economic determinism theory of
crime causation does not indicate how poverty "works" to produce criminality in individuals. On another theoretical level, the process by which
persons learn to react differentially to crime could be studied, and the
punitive or non-punitive reaction of an individual could be considered the
product of his prior associations with punitive and non-punitive behavior
patterns. One learns to react punitively or in some other way just as he
learns to speak English, German, or Japanese. It could be maintained,
then, that the "societal" reactions to crime represent a summation of or
compromise between learned individual reactions to crime. This application of the differential association principle would place the emphasis upon
the study of the process by which societal reactions to criminality change;
it would supplement the theories outlined, and it would not necessarily
contradict any of them.

## SUGGESTED READINGS

Andenaes, Johs., "General Prevention—Illusion or Reality?" *Journal of
Criminal Law, Criminology and Police Science,* 43:176–198, July–
August, 1952.

Ball, John C., "The Deterrent Concept in Criminology and the Law,"
*Journal of Criminal Law, Criminology and Police Science,* 46:347–354,
September–October, 1955.

Bedau, Hugo A., "A Survey of the Debate on Capital Punishment in
Canada, England, and the United States, 1948–1958," *Prison Journal,*
38:35–45, October, 1958.

Dalzell, George, *Benefit of Clergy in America.* Winston-Salem: Blair,
1955.

Durkheim, Emile, *The Division of Labor in Society.* Translated by George
Simpson. Glencoe: The Free Press, 1947.

Freeman, Linton C., and Robert F. Winch, "Societal Complexity: An
Empirical Test of A Typology of Societies," *American Journal of Sociology,* 62:461–466, March, 1957.

Garfinkel, Harold, "Conditions of Successful Degradation Ceremonies,"
*American Journal of Sociology,* 61:420–424, March, 1956.

Hall, Jerome, *Theft, Law and Society,* Second Edition. Indianapolis:
Bobbs-Merrill, 1952.

Hazard, J. N., "Trends in the Soviet Treatment of Crime," *American Sociological Review*, 5:566–576, August, 1940.

Johnson, Elmer H., "Selective Factors in Capital Punishment," *Social Forces*, 36:165–169, December, 1957.

Kirchwey, G. W., "Crime and Punishment," *Journal of Criminal Law and Criminology*, 1:718–734, January–February, 1911.

Levitt, A., "Some Societal Aspects of the Criminal Law," *Journal of Criminal Law and Criminology*, 13:90–104, May–June, 1922.

Mannheim, Hermann, *Criminal Justice and Social Reconstruction*. New York: Oxford University Press, 1946.

Moore, U., and C. C. Callahan, *Law and Learning Theory: A Study in Legal Control*. New Haven: Yale Law Journal Company, 1943.

Saleilles, R., *The Individualization of Punishment*. Translated by R. S. Jastrow. Boston: Little, Brown, 1911.

Schuessler, Karl F., "The Deterrent Influence of the Death Penalty," *Annals of the American Academy of Political and Social Science*, 284:54–62, November, 1952.

Sharp, F. C., and M. C. Otto, "A Study of the Popular Attitude Toward Retributive Punishment," *International Journal of Ethics*, 20:341–357, 438–453, April, July, 1910.

Thomas, Paul A., "Murder and the Death Penalty," *American Journal of Correction*, 19:16–17 ff., July, 1957.

Wines, F. H., *Punishment and Reformation*. New York: Crowell, 1895.

Wolfgang, Marvin E., *Patterns of Criminal Homicide*. Philadelphia: University of Pennsylvania Press, 1958.

Wood, Arthur Lewis, "The Alternatives to the Death Penalty," *Annals of the American Academy of Political and Social Science*, 284:63–72, November, 1952.

# 16. THE TREATMENT OF CRIMINALS

IN EARLIER societies there were few alternatives to the punitive reaction, so that usually criminals either were punished or nothing was done to them. At present, however, when the punitive reaction decreases, a "treatment" reaction usually increases. While in some cases there still is no positive alternative to the punitive reaction, the trend during the last century has been toward a societal reaction in which the criminal is treated rather than punished. The personality of the offender and the social situation in which he became a criminal are studied and, by means of knowledge thus secured, an attempt to modify his behavior is made. The reaction is, by analogy with medicine, considered scientific. A positive or constructive program is implied, in contrast with the rather negative or neutral program of punishment. However, if the criminal fails to respond to the constructive program by acquiring anti-criminal attitudes, society protects itself from him by segregating him.

If there is one key to understanding present-day practices in the control of crime it is the conflict between this treatment reaction and the punitive reaction. Most of the practices of all agencies whose responsibility it is to apprehend and care for criminals are affected by this conflict, whether or not the agencies have an official policy of treatment rather than punishment. One approved reaction to crime is hostility, with insistence that the criminal be made to suffer. Every criminal law specifies a penalty for violation, and almost everyone convicted of violating the law must be at least threatened with punishment. As we have seen, the suffering is justified in various ways: vengeance, retribution, deterrence, reformation. The following statement is a present-day reflection of the punitive reaction:

I warn you to stay unswerving to your task—that of standing by the man on the firing line—the practical, hard-headed, experienced honest policemen who have shown by their efforts that they, and they alone, know the answer to the crime problem. That answer can be summed up in one sentence—adequate detection, swift apprehension, and certain, unrelenting punishment. That is what the criminal fears. That is what he understands, and nothing else, and that fear is the only thing which will force him into the ranks of the law-abiding. There is no royal road to law enforcement. If we wait upon the medical quacks, the parole panderers, and the misguided sympathizers with habitual criminals to protect our lives and property from the criminal horde, then we must also resign ourselves to increasing violence, robbery, and sudden death.[1]

The other approved reaction is one of inquiry designed to secure comprehension of criminal behavior and to work out methods of control based on this comprehension. Suffering may be necessary in the process of control through treatment, but the suffering is incidental, not a direct aim of the process. This second reaction is now most evident in the juvenile court procedure, and it is rapidly being extended into the criminal courts, prisons, and reformatories, and the systems of probation and parole. It is reflected, in extreme form, in the following statement:

Imprisonment and punishment do not present themselves as the proper methods of dealing with criminals. We have to treat them physically as sick people, which in every respect they are. It is no more reasonable to punish these individuals for behavior over which they have no control than it is to punish an individual for breathing through his mouth because of enlarged adenoids. . . . It is the hope of the more progressive elements in psychopathology and criminology that the guard and the jailer will be replaced by the nurse and the judge by the psychiatrists, whose sole attempt will be to treat and cure the individual instead of merely to punish him. Then and only then can we hope to lessen, even if not to entirely abolish, crime, the most costly burden that society has today.[2]

It has been argued that these conflicting reactions could and should be combined, the idea being that punishment should be retained but that the pain should be inflicted in a spirit of love rather than hatred. However, Professor Mead long ago pointed out that such a combination is logically impossible.

[1] J. Edgar Hoover, "Patriotism and the War Against Crime," an address given before the annual convention of the Daughters of the American Revolution, Washington, D. C., April 23, 1936. Quoted by permission of Mr. Hoover.
[2] Benjamin Karpman, "Criminality, Insanity, and the Law," *Journal of Criminal Law and Criminology* (Northwestern University School of Law), 39:584–605, January–February, 1949. Reprinted by permission of the publishers. See also John B. Waite, "Revenge Costs too Much," *Harper's*, 194:466–472, May, 1946.

The two attitudes, that of control of crime by the hostile procedure of the law, and that of control through comprehension of social and psychological conditions, cannot be combined. To understand is to forgive, and the social procedure seems to deny the very responsibility which the law affirms, and, on the other hand, the pursuit by criminal justice inevitably awakens the hostile attitude in the offender and renders the attitude of mutual comprehension practically impossible.[3]

In connection with discussions of the problem of trying to implement this view, it is sometimes argued that it is necessary either to retain punishment and abandon the effort to understand and treat criminality or abandon the punitive reaction and continue the effort to understand and treat. One can agree that the two reactions are logically incompatible while at the same time using both of them in practice. In fact, the theory of differential association implies that this seemingly contradictory position is the correct one. The implication is that crime in the generic sense, as well as individual criminal acts, must be understood in order to develop effective policies of control, and that the most important conditions in causing or preventing crime are the reactions of other persons toward crime and criminality. The reactions which are most effective in preventing crime are expressions of antagonism and hostility, and those which are most effective in causing crime are expressions of appreciation. This principle supports either punitive policies or more effective systems for expressing disapprobation, just as it supports programs for expression of appreciation of non-criminal and anti-criminal attitudes.[4] Thus, it is possible to combine the attitude of understanding crime in general and the attitude of hostility toward crime in general. Furthermore, acts may remain as punishable by law even if the actual program for changing criminals is one of treatment. Most of the agencies for control of crime have found it necessary to effect a compromise, on a practical level, between the two reactions.

TREATMENT AND THE STUDY OF CRIME CAUSATION. The development of causal explanations of crime probably is more a part of than an explanation for the development of the treatment reaction. Nevertheless, on a formal level it may be observed that attempts to explain criminal behavior have greatly abetted at least the official use of the treatment reaction. In

---

[3] G. H. Mead, "The Psychology of Punitive Justice," *American Journal of Sociology*, 23:577–602, March, 1918. Reprinted by permission of the publishers.

[4] Cf. Johs. Andenaes, "General Prevention—Illusion or Reality?" *Journal of Criminal Law, Criminology and Police Science*, 43:176–198, August, 1952; and Lloyd W. McCorkle and Richard Korn, "Resocialization within Walls," *Annals of the American Academy of Political and Social Science*, 293:88–98, May, 1954.

the eighteenth and early nineteenth centuries the will, assumed to be isolated from all other psychological conditions and from social processes and conditions, was practically the only element considered in discussions of behavior, both criminal and non-criminal. The Lombrosian school of criminologists denied the doctrine of freedom of the will and attempted to explain crime in terms of causal relationships. Their explanation was not at all satisfactory, but it resulted in a demand that crime be regarded as any other natural phenomenon and dealt with as such. Accordingly, the validity or efficiency of the punitive reaction was denied, and what is now called the treatment reaction was supported. To the argument of the Lombrosian school has been added the immense weight of authority in the last half century. By many methods, a valid explanation of crime and criminality is being developed, and the factors associated with crime are being isolated. Accompanying this natural science view of crime and criminality is the natural science view that these phenomena must be controlled by comprehension of the processes involved. The emphasis on feeble-mindedness, psychopathy, and differential association as explanations of crimes during the last fifty years has undoubtedly helped establish the view that if criminals are to be reformed they should be studied, understood, and helped. Further, since legal policies have been based on the doctrine of freedom of the will, the conclusion that crime and criminality must be understood and explained has created a great deal of controversy regarding use of the official punitive policies. One effect of the development of theories of crime and criminality has, therefore, been modification of procedures for dealing with criminals. Nettler found that determinists are less likely than indeterminists (free will) to recommend disinterested punishment in response to deviations.[5]

It is important to note, however, that the historical development has not been a simple matter of changing practices to fit changes in ideology and theory. Criminological theory has also been greatly affected by changing methods of dealing with crime and criminals. A bit at a time, the methods used in correctional practice for implementing the treatment reaction have encroached on the methods used to implement the punitive reaction, and it has appeared that some of them apparently are no less successful than the punitive policies of earlier days. Then, in the effort to account for the success of the new methods, new criminological theory has been organized. The development has taken on a kind of spiral effect, beginning with modifications in practice, which were not always recognized as in conflict with either the previous methods or theories. Next, new theory was de-

[5] Gwynn Nettler, "Cruelty, Dignity, and Determinism," *American Sociological Review*, 24:375–384, June, 1959.

veloped to account for the apparent success of the new practices. Then, with the gradual increase in the popularity of the new theory, deliberate attempts were made and are being made to replace punitive methods with practices consistent with theory. This process can be illustrated by observation of the relationship between development of the juvenile court and changing ideas about delinquency causation. With invention of the juvenile court, non-punitive methods to accompany the punitive methods of dealing with delinquents under the age of sixteen were introduced. New causal theories of delinquency developed, and they maintained, essentially, that delinquent behavior is a product of emotional maladjustments which can be modified only by the non-punitive methods used by the juvenile court. It then was said that if 16-year-old delinquents could be handled non-punitively, older persons could be similarly handled. Many persons now argue that the court would be more effective if the accompanying punitive methods were completely abolished. *Both functional ways of behaving in soc*

### THE CONFLICT BETWEEN PUNITIVE AND TREATMENT REACTIONS. Because

the punitive reaction is still very popular, many people assert that the fact that we are now using treatment methods in dealing with juvenile delinquents and to an increasing extent in dealing with adults, does not cast doubt upon the social utility of the punitive reaction. On the contrary, they argue for the social utility of the punitive reaction by maintaining that we have an increasing amount of crime as a result of the shift toward the treatment reaction to crime. Actually, there is no available proof that the change toward treatment methods has either increased or decreased crime rates. It is just as logical to assert that crime rates are high because of the survival of the punitive reaction.[6] Although many of the arguments against treatment are mere reiterations of the justifications for punishment which were used when treatment was not an alternative, a more detailed consideration of some of the objections may assist in clarifying the general conflict.

(1) It is asserted by those whose reaction to crime is punitive that the general public cannot be prevented from engaging in a general debauch of crime except by fear of punishment; we must keep punishment in order to deter from crime. The reply to this objection is that not all of the unpleasantness and suffering would be removed even if the present form of punishment for criminals were completely abandoned. On the basis of the experience when Denmark was without police during a part of the time the Nazis occupied the country, it may be concluded that the penal

[6] See Donald R. Cressey, "The Nature and Effectiveness of Correctional Techniques," *Law and Contemporary Problems*, 23:754-771, Autumn, 1958.

process, including arrest, does deter.[7] However, complete substitution of a treatment reaction for the punitive reaction does not mean that the police and other protective agencies will be abolished. There will always be some stigma connected with crime, regardless of the official treatment of offenders. But the real reason for believing that the substitution of treatment for punishment would not result in a debauch of crime is that the control, after all, lies in the group pressure, the recognition and response secured by lawful conduct rather than the direct fear of punishment. Not the fear of legal penalties, as such, but the fear of loss of status in the group is the effective deterrent. But this is not really fear; what really occurs is that the person feels that doing a specified thing in violation of the group standard, which also happens to be in violation of the law, would not be in harmony with his personality, would lower him. It does not occur to him to do such a thing. He would feel uncomfortable in violating such a law and would secure no satisfaction from it. This is the principal method of control whether the conduct is regulated by law or is not. One who would not think of breaking into a jewelry store and robbing a private merchant will smuggle jewelry into his country in violation of the law, or will violate the child-labor law or the tax law, or will engage in an illegal civil rights demonstration or in preventing a Negro from voting; his group does not regard such violations as beneath the dignity of one of its members. Regardless of the official methods of dealing with criminals we shall retain this method of control by group pressure.

One of the weaknesses of the legal system at present is the dependence on the threat of punishment for the enforcement of the law. It is much more efficient to develop an attitude of appreciation of the values before the law is passed, and then perhaps the law will be unnecessary. Although society can emphasize the necessity for conformity by threatening to punish non-conformists, it is certainly possible to develop the attitudes of appreciation more effectively than has been done to date.[8] Sweden's Penal Code Commission has abandoned the word "punishment" and replaced it with a neutral word meaning, literally, "something that follows something."[9]

(2) A second objection is that, if the criminal is not punished, the victim will take the law into his own hands and this will mean either self-

---

[7] Jorgen Trolle, *Syv Maaneder under Politi* (Seven Months Without Police), Copenhagen, 1945.
[8] See Johannes Andenaes, "Punishment and the Problem of General Prevention," paper read at the meetings of the International Criminological Association, Montreal, September, 1965.
[9] Thorsten Sellin, *The Protective Code: A Swedish Proposal* (Stockholm: Department of Justice, 1957), p. 10.

redress or lynch-law. This assertion is based on the belief that there is an unalterable demand for vengeance which will be satisfied by illegal means if it is not satisfied by legal means, and it is consistent with the "scape-goat" theory described in the previous chapter. There is probably no one who would not demand vengeance under certain circumstances. In offenses involving the relations of whites and Negroes in the South, in certain horrible sex offenses, and in offenses involving the relations of different social classes, a rather general demand for vengeance may arise and the individual who takes the law into his own hands may receive the support of the group. But a very large proportion of crimes—probably more than 75 percent—arouse the resentment of no particular individual. And when resentment is aroused it is generally confined to a very small number of persons, and today their resentment is counteracted by other members of the group.[10]

The vengeance reaction is quite certainly the product of social contacts and interactions. The difference between the crimes of Italian immigrants and their native-born offspring, studies of lynch mobs, and the fact that the treatment reaction exists all show this.[11] Even if an instinct of vengeance be admitted, the instinct certainly is not fixed in its method of expression. One may secure revenge by a blow with the fist, by spitting, by calling names, by shooting with a gun, by spreading calumny, by voting, and perhaps by bringing the offender to trial and assisting the state to use methods that will reform him.

(3). It is believed that the victim will be unwilling to testify or make complaint if he cannot see his opponent suffer; if there is no alternative to the treatment reaction he will take the loss and remain silent rather than go to the trouble of court procedure that will yield him no satisfaction. Against this objection it may be stated, first, that if the treatment reaction were used alone the victim would still secure the satisfaction of seeing his aggressor put to the trouble of a trial and would secure the satisfaction of a conviction; this would show that the public was on his side, would vindicate him, and would perhaps grant him all the satisfaction he wished. Second, he would secure satisfaction from the methods used in dealing with the offender, which might include permanent segregation. Third, at present when the punitive reaction occurs the friends of the criminal are likely to rally to his support in opposition to the hostile procedure of the law. If these friends had any reason to believe that the procedure was designed to improve the offender and would have some efficiency in this respect, they might be more inclined to assist in securing a

10 Cf. F. Znaniecki, *Social Actions* (New York: Farrar and Rinehart, 1936), p. 376.
11 See Alan Valentine, *Vigilante Justice* (New York: Reynal, 1956).

conviction for his own good.[12] *Fourth*, punishment of approximately 75 percent of the offenders does not give satisfaction to any private witness. For such offenses as drunkenness, prostitution, violations of traffic regulations, and vagrancy the complaint is made by a public officer and the testimony furnished by the same officer and others subpoenaed to appear in court. If we can depend on public prosecutors in such cases, it is reasonable to believe that testimony can be secured in the other offenses in which personal feeling is involved somewhat more.

(4) Another objection is that group solidarity and respect for the law, now developed by the punitive reaction, would decrease in the absence of this reaction.[13] As a matter of fact, group solidarity and respect for law can be developed in a great variety of other ways. They can be developed by collective action toward comprehending the causes of crime and controlling by means of knowledge thus obtained. The only thing needed is that something be presented on which the group can act collectively. Pursuit of the criminal might create social solidarity, but it also is created by collective action to cure disease, prevent catastrophes, save crops from insects, and other actions where comprehension and control, not punishment, are involved.

Moreover, it is doubtful whether at present crime upsets the equilibrium of the group or promotes much social solidarity through collective action. Punishment seldom restores the equilibrium of the group at present, because the equilibrium of the group is not much disturbed by crime. Crime is an impersonal event to be read about in the newspapers, and no direct collective reaction occurs. Also, when persons are protected against crime by insurance, the shock is taken from the crime and the burden is distributed over a period of years in the premium paid to the insurance company.[14] Even when the victim is not protected by insurance, he is generally willing to drop the case if he can secure restitution. The victim usually is interested only secondarily in the offense against the peace and dignity of the society. In general, whole communities are seldom disturbed by crimes or by high crime rates, and when punishment is inflicted it has little effect on the community except in spectacular cases.

As these opposing arguments show, punitive reactions and treatment reactions both are sanctioned ways of behaving in present-day society. For that reason, correctional procedures and programs are not exclusively

---

[12] *Cf.* Austin L. Porterfield, "The Complainant in the Juvenile Court," *Sociology and Social Research*, 28:171–181, January, 1944.

[13] See Arnold W. Green, *Sociology* (New York: McGraw-Hill, 1952), p. 36.

[14] See David Cort, "The Embezzler," *The Nation*, 188:339–342, April 18, 1959.

punitive nor exclusively treatment, even when they are formally set up to deal with criminals in one of the alternative ways.

LIMITATIONS OF PUNISHMENT.  As the treatment reaction to law-breaking has become more popular, many arguments (again usually based on very shaky empirical evidence) have been advanced in support of the general position that punishment is relatively ineffective as a reformative or deterrent device. It has been pointed out in this connection that punishment often has effects which are unanticipated, and that these effects are the opposite of those expected when the punishment was imposed. Thus, the general argument is that the treatment reaction should be substituted for the punitive reaction since it would not, at least to the same extent, produce these undesirable effects. The following are some of the types of unanticipated consequences produced by punishment:

(1) Punishment often isolates the individual who is punished and makes him a confirmed enemy of society, and his influence may extend to other individuals. When the sole reaction is punitive, criminals are isolated from law-abiding groups, and neither understand nor are understood by these groups. Hatred of the criminal by society results in hatred of society by the criminal. In this respect, the behavior is much like war, which produces a relatively complete isolation and dissociation of warring nations. When he is effectively ostracized, the criminal has only two alternatives: he may associate with other criminals, among whom he can find recognition, prestige, and means of further criminality; or he may become disorganized, psychopathic, or unstable. Our actual practice is to permit almost all criminals to return to society, in a physical sense, but to hold them off, make them keep their distance, segregate them in the midst of the ordinary community. Thus they are kept isolated from law-abiding groups. If they are to be turned into law-abiding citizens, they must be assimilated into society and treated as persons with the potential to be law-abiding citizens.[15]

(2) Punishment develops caution. Probably a painful experience, such as being punished or being stung by bees, will make the actor "think twice" before he repeats the behavior. But, in the case of the bees, "thinking twice" may be a means of securing immunity from the bees while molesting them. The actor has been made cautious by the previous suffering, but not "reformed." Similarly, an unanticipated consequence of

15 See Donald R. Cressey, "Changing Criminals: The Application of the Theory of Differential Association," *American Journal of Sociology*, 61:116–120, September, 1955; and Rita Volkman and Donald R. Cressey, "Differential Association and the Rehabilitation of Drug Addicts," *American Journal of Sociology*, 69:129–142, September, 1963.

current systems for punishing criminals might be cautiousness, not refor-mation. For example, professional and organized criminals have great skill in the execution of their crimes and in addition take many precautions to provide in advance for immunity in case they are caught. The result is that twenty-five amateur shoplifters who have stolen little articles in stores are likely to be convicted in a court while one professional shoplifter who steals hundreds of times as much as all of these amateurs escapes convic-tion. The amateur criminal, however, in the course of a few punishments of this nature acquires skill, largely in the penal institutions.

(3) Punishment creates other unanticipated attitudes. Even if some acts were known to be preventable by punishment, this prevention would not necessarily prove that punishment has promoted the social welfare. Whatever is accomplished by preventing that specific act may be more than off-set by general attitudes produced by it.[16] For instance, a child's practice of lying might be stopped by punishment. But as a result, the child might come to fear the parent who inflicted the punishment, and be estranged or alienated. If the parent is to have great influence over the child, he must keep the confidence of the child, and the relation between them must be very intimate and friendly, especially at the time when the child begins to be away from home many hours a day. Similarly, if the prevention of a particular delinquency results in loss of general control of the child, it is a doubtful gain. And thus the punitive reaction frequently creates other attitudes in criminals or in the public even when a particular crime is successfully forestalled—lack of respect for law, lack of patriotism, lack of willingness to sacrifice for the state, and lack of initiative. Perhaps the most serious consequence of punishment to the offender is loss of self-respect. Real efficiency in dealing with criminals involves not only the stopping of specific violations of law but the accomplishment of this result without the loss of other social values.

(4) Punishment often gives an offender high status. Among criminals, one's standing is frequently promoted by punishment. In states whose prisons are scaled from tough maximum-security institutions down to minimum-security institutions, youthful offenders frequently request as-signment to the maximum-security institutions, because such assignment will result in high status among their friends when they are released. They attempt to avoid assignment to reformatories and minimum-security insti-tutions, because incarceration there does not bring the desired prestige. Schrag has shown that within prisons positions of leadership go to men

[16] Kurt Lewin, *Die Psychologische Situation bei Lohn und Strafe* (Leipzig: S. Hirzel, 1931); Lucille Chase, "Motivation of Young Children," *University of Iowa Studies in Child Welfare*, Vol. V, No. 3, March, 1932.

convicted of serious offenses, such as robbery, and to men with long
punitive sentences.[17]

(5) Punishment generally stops constructive efforts. If the group, in a
spirit of hatred, inflicts punishment upon the offender, it generally sits
back, after the penalty is inflicted, with a sigh of relief and with a feeling
that the matter is now settled. But the situation remains, in general, just
as it was before the punishment was inflicted. Such a punitive reaction
may produce fear in the offender, but more than fear is required for an
alteration of character, personality, and behavior. Reformation involves
not only a determination to change one's behavior, but a constructive
process of organizing or reorganizing behavior. One must have stimula-
tions, patterns, suggestions, sentiments, and ideals presented to him. And
the individual must develop his definitions and attitudes by practice, generally in a slow and gradual manner.[18] One must have an appreciation of
the values which are conserved by the law, and this can be produced only
by assimilating the culture of the group which passed the law, or, stated
otherwise, only if the group which passed the law assimilates the criminal.
The negative act of prohibiting a thing is not sufficient because it is not
constructive and does not promote assimilation.[19]

## IMPLEMENTATION OF THE TREATMENT REACTION: INDIVIDUALIZATION.

The official policy of individualized treatment for criminals developed out
of the positive school's arguments against the practice of attempting to
impose uniform punishments on all persons violating a particular law. It
was, and is, argued that policies calling for uniform punishments are as
obviously ineffective as would be a policy calling for uniform treatment of
all medical patients, no matter what their ailments. This led some persons
to advocate that the type of punishment and the severity of punishment
should be adapted to the individual offender; even today "individualization" is sometimes used to refer to a system for imposing punishments.
However, as the treatment reaction has increased in popularity, "individualization" has come to designate a treatment process in which the
handling of each case of criminality includes expert diagnosis of individual
problems and needs, expert prescription of therapy, and expert therapy—
just as clinical medicine includes diagnosis, prescription, and therapy. This
is by far the most common meaning of the term in modern correctional

[17] Clarence Schrag, "Leadership Among Prison Inmates," *American Sociological
Review,* 19:37–42, February, 1954.
[18] See Jacob Chwast, "Reversibility-Irreversibility Problems in the Treatment of
Offenders," *American Journal of Psychotherapy,* 15:221–232, April, 1961.
[19] Cf. R. L. Jenkins, "The Constructive Use of Punishment," *Mental Hygiene,*
29:561–574, October, 1945.

parlance. By "individualization," then, is usually meant the general system for implementing the treatment reaction to law-breaking. Within this general system there are two major methods for administering treatment: case work on an individual or clinical basis, and case work on a group or situational basis. The methods are based upon different conceptions of the process by which criminality develops.

*The clinical method.* In the early part of the present century the system of individualized treatment for criminals was based almost exclusively on the principle that criminality is a strictly individual disorder which can, therefore, be treated in a clinic, just as syphilis can be treated in a clinic. The principal argument for the clinical method, which once was synonymous with "individualization," was that the processes of treating offenders should be analogous to the processes of treating medical patients. It was correctly pointed out that two or three centuries ago diseases were not differentiated from each other or explained as natural phenomena; bloodletting was almost the only treatment, varying in amount with the seriousness of the ailment. Since then the germ theory of disease and experimental methods have produced a great variety of treatment methods adapted to particular diseases. By analogy, until recently crime has been handled as sickness was handled two centuries ago —the methods of dealing with criminals consisted of imposing certain degrees of suffering upon them, depending upon their offense. The system of individualization was then introduced and this includes, first, an intensive study of the individual offender for the purpose of learning the cause of his criminality and, second, application of a program based on the knowledge of the offender and on knowledge previously secured regarding the effective methods of treating such cases. An entirely different program for each criminal was not implied, just as scientific treatment of diseases does not imply the use of an entirely different policy for each patient.[20] Also, when there was no known system for successfully treating an offender's difficulty he was to be segregated for the protection of society, just as dangerous psychotics are segregated for the protection of society. Furthermore, an attempt would be made to prevent criminality by methods based upon knowledge of crime causation, not by punitive methods alone.

But in the clinical method this medical analogy was then carried to its logical extreme. Because the original arguments for individualization were based on an analogy with clinical medicine, the theory used in diagnosing and treating cases of criminality were also closely analogous to theories

[20] See Marguerite Q. Grant, "Interaction Between Kinds of Treatments and Kinds of Delinquents," California Board of Corrections, Monograph No. 2, July, 1961, pp. 5–14; and Keiichi Mizushima and Richard L. Jenkins, "Treatment Needs Corresponding to Varieties of Delinquents," *International Journal of Social Psychiatry*, 8:91–103, 1962.

used in clinical medicine. That is, criminality was assumed to be treatable as an individual disorder independent of the offender's social groups, the diagnoses were very similar to the actual diagnoses of various medical ailments of patients, and the recommendations for treatment were very similar to the actual medical prescriptions for clinical treatment. Even today this interpretation of the individualization system has great popularity among correctional workers, a great many of whom assume that some cases of criminality, like some diseases such as anemia, are entirely individual disorders, but that most cases of criminality are like the infectious diseases such as syphilis. While group contacts of certain kinds are necessary to individual cases of syphilis and to some individual cases of criminality, both ailments can be "cured" in a clinic, without reference to those groups, just as anemia can be cured in a clinic. Individual psychotherapy, as a system for reforming criminals, is perhaps the best example of a current treatment method based upon this assumption. Social case work has been greatly influenced by psychiatry, and as a result most of the "diagnoses" made by social workers attached to courts, prisons, and other agencies dealing with criminals are made in clinical terms, just as are most of the diagnoses made by psychologists and psychiatrists. A diagnosis made in clinical terms will be followed, obviously, by clinical treatment of the individual.[21]

The following description of the method used in the New Jersey Home for Boys illustrates the clinical procedure. The assumption that the offender's difficulty can be cleared up by treating it as an almost completely individual disorder is apparent. Although the statement was made in 1921, it indicates the official method of treatment used by most prisons and by many other agencies today.[22]

First: We make a definite study of each boy when he enters the institution. This study extends over a period of several weeks and is conducted by trained people (psychiatrist, psychologist, director of education, etc.) . . . During the period of these examinations we secure from the Central Parole Bureau, probation officers and other sources, all the information possible about the ward's earlier history, his home and community relations and other vital facts.

Second: Once a week all of the people concerned with the examinations named in the last paragraph meet with the Superintendent for the purpose of comparing reports and consulting as to the best means of promoting the welfare of the ward while in the institution—this is called our Classification Meeting.

[21] See Michael Hakeem, "A Critique of the Psychiatric Approach to Crime and Correction," *Law and Contemporary Problems*, 23:650–682, Autumn, 1958.
[22] See the discussion below, pp. 522–530.

THIRD: We make a definite plan for the development and training of the boy. This plan, or parts of it, at least, are discussed with the boy. We try to secure his co-operation with us for his own development, with a definite purpose in his mind and ours of preparing him for a successful parole. Every boy's case is reconsidered by the Classification Committee within three months, and if the case presents unusual factors, it may be reconsidered several times.

FOURTH: As time for his parole approaches, each boy's case is taken up for pre-parole investigation. . . . Home investigations are made, employment and friendly counselors are secured; and the family prepared for the return of the boy. Sometimes the Central Parole Bureau has to prepare the neighborhood or move the family to a new locality, in order to further the interests of the boy.[23]

The group-relations method. The methods for implementing the punitive reaction were generally applied to the offender without regard for his relationships in social groups. He was assumed to have possessed the ability to refrain from criminality, regardless of the values of the groups in which he had membership. Similarly, the earlier treatment methods were applied to the criminal in isolation; criminality was considered an individual disorder and in the treatment process little consideration was given to the offender's group relations. Gradually, these treatment methods have been supplemented by methods based on an alternative principle, namely that criminality is social in nature and, therefore, can be modified in individual cases only if the criminal's relations with social groups are modified. The proponents of this principle have not abandoned the medical analogy which emphasized the importance of individualization in the treatment of criminals, but the analogy has not been extended to include the theory used in diagnosing, prescribing, and "treating." Rather, they contend, as is made explicit in the differential association theory, that persons become criminals principally because they have been relatively isolated from the culture of law-abiding groups, by reason of their residence, employment, codes, native capacities, or something else, or else have been in relatively frequent contact with a rival criminal culture. Consequently they are lacking in the experiences, feelings, ideas, and attitudes out of which to construct a life organization that the law-abiding public will regard as desirable. Criminality, which is the product of this isolation from law-abiding culture, will not be overcome by more isolation. Assimilation of such culture can come only by contact. As early as 1868 Desprez stated the argument against isolation, with special reference to isolation of prisoners from each other and from the public.

[23] New Jersey, *Report of State Home for Boys*, 1921, pp. 19–20.

All isolation, even if voluntary, is bad. There is no idea more fallacious than that isolation from the world by prolonged imprisonment will produce moral meditations in the culprit which will be the source of his reformation. It is not sufficient to place a person between four walls in order to improve him. . . . How is it possible to hope or believe for a single moment that gross natures, uncultured and degraded, can find in themselves the force to condemn and sincerely detest their faults, and maintain a firm resolution during the years of detention, in the midst of all the elements of corruption, if the imprisonment is in common, or in apathy and despair, if the imprisonment is in cells?[24]

In the group-relations method, then, diagnosis is directed at analysis of the criminal's attitudes, motives, and rationalizations regarding criminality, with recognition that the character of these behaviors depends upon the kinds of groups in which the individual has memberships, with which he identifies himself, and to which he owes allegiance and loyalty. If the criminality of an individual depends upon such group relations, then the prescription for "treatment" must be a prescription for modification of group relations.[25] As to the "treatment" itself, it is suggested that the group relations which support criminality cannot be directly modified in a clinic in the way that the condition of a person suffering from syphilis can be modified in a clinic; they can be modified only by providing the criminal with new social relations or in some way changing the nature of present group relations.[26]

Numerous policies or programs arising in correctional work during the last one hundred years have been explicitly or implicitly based upon recognition of the necessity for modifying criminality by changing the social relationships of criminals. Among these are probation, which permits or assists the offender to come in contact with law-abiding groups instead of isolating him behind prison walls; education and self-government in prison, which are attempts to develop social interaction even while the prisoners are physically isolated; parole, which acts in the same way as probation; and various other efforts to assist the offender after release from prison to gain or regain contacts with law-abiding groups.[27]

This method of implementing the treatment reaction by providing contact with the law-abiding culture is important, but it has two shortcomings.

24 E. Desprez, *De l'abolition de l'emprisonment* (Paris, E. Dentu, 1868), pp. 18–19.
25 Cf. Dorwin Cartwright, "Achieving Change in People: Some Applications of Group Dynamics Theory," *Human Relations*, 4:381–392, 1951.
26 Cf. Donald R. Taft, "The Group and Community Organization Approach to Prison Administration," *Proceedings of the American Prison Association*, 1942, pp. 275–284.
27 Cressey, "The Nature and Effectiveness of Correctional Techniques," *op. cit.*

*First,* the presence of a cultural pattern does not necessarily result in its adoption. Acculturation comes only as the result of contact, but contact does not necessarily result in acculturation. All persons are in contact with law-abiding culture, and all persons are in contact with criminal culture. Something more than contact is needed. Anthropologists have shown that cultural patterns are diffused among preliterate groups, not radially from a center as the result of spatial proximity, but in selected paths as the result of receptivity to the new patterns. Long-continued contact with a culture produces assimilation but it accomplishes this by affecting a large variety of elements of the culture. Immediate results in the reformation of an offender also require not only that the cultural pattern be present but also that the offender be made "receptive" to it.[28] *Second,* offenders frequently find great difficulty in securing intimate contacts with law-abiding groups. A boy who has been in a reformatory may not feel at home in a club, and the other members of the club do not feel comfortable in his presence. Neighbors may openly display prejudice against persons convicted of law violation, and law enforcement officers, fearful that offenders will repeat their crimes or will contaminate law-abiding citizens instead of the reverse, may hound criminals until they move from respectable neighborhoods. Employers will not give them jobs and even if they do the employees may threaten to strike if the ex-convict is not dismissed.

OBJECTIONS TO INDIVIDUALIZATION. Certain objections have been raised to the general system of individualization, as opposed to the general system of fixed penalties. The first objection is that individualization, except to a limited degree, is financially impractical. This conclusion is based on the assumption that individualization means a separate caretaker and a separate program for each offender. This is, of course, incorrect. Also, while individualized treatment is expensive initially, the great initial cost can be offset by the reduction in recidivism and the consequent reduction in crime.[29]

A second objection is that criminal justice is discredited in the eyes of the public because of the inequalities in suffering which individualization produces. But the public does not have much confidence in the administration of justice, no matter what the system. Such confidence as does exist is largely a hold-over from the time when courts were supposed to have some connection with divinity. Real confidence must be based on a belief in the scientific efficiency of the courts. It is logically impossible to adjust penalties to crimes; therefore a system based on fixed penalties never can be

[28] See the discussion in Chapter Twenty-nine, pp. 675–680.
[29] Cf. S. Queen, *The Passing of the County Jail* (Menasha, Wisconsin: Banta, 1920), pp. 142–153. The following discussion follows Queen's arguments very closely.

made scientifically efficient. There is at least a possibility that criminal justice can be made scientifically efficient if it is adjusted to the individual offender, by a policy of individualization.

A third objection is that criminals feel that they are treated unjustly; one burglar is placed on probation, another is held in prison for two years, another is held in prison for life. But the criminals who receive fixed punishments also feel that just such discriminations are made. And, because of the conflict between the punitive and treatment reactions, no well-organized method of adapting treatment to character, personality, and social situation actually is being used. Consequently, criminals have difficulty in appreciating the policy of individualization. But criminals can understand and appreciate such a policy and can be made to see the fallacy of fixed penalties.[30]

A fourth objection is that individualization endangers personal rights. This is not true if the usual legal procedures and safeguards are retained and used in the process of determining whether the accused person is "guilty."[31] Some authorities recommend that the whole court system be replaced by boards of experts who would determine what should be done with persons accused of crime; this system certainly would endanger personal rights, such as the right to be tried by a jury, to confront witnesses, and so on. However, the individualization system can be used in the administration of programs for offenders *after* they are found guilty, and in this system no personal rights are endangered. That is, acts can remain as punishable, and persons can be held accountable for the acts, even if punishments are rarely imposed. In the juvenile courts most procedural safeguards against injustices have been retained informally, although there has been considerable effort to abandon them officially.[32] The criminal has no personal right to receive a fixed penalty, regardless of the conditions which produced his criminality. Rather he has a right to receive such assistance, regardless of his crime, as will enable him to adapt himself to law-abiding society, if this is possible. It is true, of course, that abuses are found in the system of individualization, but this is true, also, when penalties are fixed in advance.

CONCLUSION. Punishment has evident values, but they are limited and are offset by unanticipated consequences. Punitive methods of dealing with criminals, then, seem relatively inefficient. Because of this apparent ineffi-

---

[30] For a general analysis of this fallacy, see W. I. Thomas and F. Znaniecki, *The Polish Peasant in Europe and America* (Chicago: University of Chicago Press, 1927), Vol. I, p. 12.

[31] *Cf.* Francis A. Allen, "Criminal Justice, Legal Values, and Rehabilitative Ideal," *Journal of Criminal Law, Criminology, and Police Science*, 50:226–232, October, 1959.

[32] See discussion below, pp. 456–467.

ciency, regardless of the right of the state to punish or the fact that the criminal may deserve to suffer, the scientific procedure of individualization is slowly being substituted. This procedure includes an attempt to understand the forces and mechanisms in crime and criminality and the development of an efficient method of control on the basis of such understanding. Our knowledge of human behavior is extending rapidly, and the success of treatment methods also seems to be increasing. The treatment reaction is being extended to larger and larger groups of offenders, and the trend is toward a method of treatment which is based upon recognition of the importance of social relations to criminality.

However, at present less than 10 percent of the 42,000 persons employed in prisons for adults are directly concerned with administration of treatment, education, or training.[33] In 1962 there were 52 psychiatrists, 664 social workers, 52 sociologists and 156 psychologists serving 206,550 adult prisoners, a ratio of one such professional employe to each 226 prisoners.[34] Assuming that these professional personnel work a forty-hour week and that they spend all their duty time in contact with inmates, the average amount of professional time available per prisoner each week was ten minutes; for psychiatrists, the time available to each prisoner was about half a minute per week. However, these personnel were not distributed evenly over the United States, with the result that the averages are, for some prisoners, deceptively high—thirty-six states had no full-time psychiatrist at all, twenty had no psychologist, and fifteen had no social worker or sociologist. We should not, therefore, assume that specific methods of treatment have been demonstrated to be superior to punishment, nor even that specific treatment methods have been utilized to any significant degree. There has been a widespread tendency to identify humanitarian handling of criminals with treatment of criminals and then to argue that this humanitarian handling is more effective in rehabilitating criminals than is less humane handling. There is no precise evidence on this point, principally because statistics on crime and recidivism rates are such that we cannot precisely measure the efficiency of various programs.[35] As McCorkle and Korn have said:

It is the tragedy of modern correction that the impulse to help has been confused with treatment and seems to require defense as treatment. One of

[33] Federal Bureau of Prisons, "Personnel, 1962," *National Prisoner Statistics*, No. 35, October, 1964, p. 5. See also Alfred C. Schnur, "The New Penology: Fact or Fiction?" *Journal of Criminal Law, Criminology and Police Science*, 49:331–334, December, 1958; and Elmer H. Johnson, "The Professional in Correction: Status and Prospects," *Social Forces*, 40:168–176, December, 1961.

[34] Federal Bureau of Prisons, *op. cit.*, p. 19.

[35] See Donald R. Cressey, "The State of Criminal Statistics," *National Probation and Parole Association Journal*, 3:230–241, July, 1957.

the more ironic difficulties with this position is that when one makes "rehabilitation" the main justification for the humane handling of prisoners one has maneuvered oneself into a position potentially dangerous to the humanitarian viewpoint. What if humane treatment [i.e., "handling"] fails to rehabilitate—shall it then be abandoned? The isolated survivals of flogging and other "tough" techniques which still disgrace American penology remain to remind us that this is no mere academic question. The bleak fact is that just as the monstrous punishments of the eighteenth century failed to curtail crime, so the more humane handling of the twentieth century has equally failed to do so.[36]

## SUGGESTED READINGS

Allen, Francis A., "Criminal Justice, Legal Values, and the Rehabilitative Ideal, Journal of Criminal Law, Criminology and Police Science, 50: 226–232, October, 1959.

Andenaes, Johs., "General Prevention—Illusion or Reality? Journal of Criminal Law, Criminology and Police Science, 43:176–198, July–August, 1952.

Buhler, Charlotte, "Goals of Life and Therapy," The American Journal of Psychoanalysis, 22:1–23, 1962.

Cantor, Nathaniel, "Conflicts in Penal Theory and Practice," Journal of Criminal Law and Criminology, 26:330–350, September–October, 1935.

Cartwright, Dorwin, "Achieving Change in People: Some Applications of Group Dynamics Theory," Human Relations, 4:381–392, 1951.

Cressey, Donald R., "Changing Criminals: The Application of the Theory of Differential Association," American Journal of Sociology, 61:116–120, September, 1955.

Cressey, Donald R., "The Nature and Effectiveness of Correctional Techniques," Law and Contemporary Problems, 23:754–771, Autumn, 1958.

Cumming, John, and Elaine Cumming, Ego and Milieu: Theory and Practice of Environmental Therapy. New York: Atherton Press, 1962.

Elliott, Mabel A., Conflicting Penal Theories in Statutory Criminal Law. Chicago: University of Chicago Press, 1931.

Elliott, Mabel A., Coercion in Penal Treatment. Ithaca: Pacifist Research Bureau, 1947.

Galtung, Johan, "Prison: The Organization of Dilemma," Chapter 3 in Donald R. Cressey, Editor, The Prison: Studies in Institutional Organization and Change. New York: Holt, Rinehart and Winston, 1961.

Green, Arnold W., "The Concept of Responsibility," Journal of Criminal Law and Criminology, 33:392–394, January–February, 1943.

Grusky, Oscar, "Role Conflict in Organization: A Study of Prison Camp Officials," Administrative Science Quarterly, 3:452–472, March, 1959.

[36] McCorkle and Korn, op. cit., pp. 94–95. See also Richard R. Korn and Lloyd W. McCorkle, Criminology and Penology (New York: Holt, 1959), pp. 474–476.

Jenkins, R. L., "The Constructive Use of Punishment," *Mental Hygiene*, 29:561–574, October, 1945.

Karpman, Benjamin, "Criminality, Insanity, and the Law," *Journal of Criminal Law and Criminology*, 39:584–605, January–February, 1949.

McCorkle, Lloyd W., and Richard Korn, "Resocialization Within Walls," *Annals of the American Academy of Political and Social Science*, 293: 88–98, May, 1954.

McWhinnie, James B., "The Treatment of Crime in Denmark," *Prison Service Journal* (England), 3:2–9, July, 1964.

Mechanic, David, "Sources of Power of Lower Participants in Complex Organizations," *Administrative Science Quarterly*, 7:349–364, December, 1962.

Penrose, L. S., "Mental Disease and Crime: Outline of a Comparative Study of European Statistics," *British Journal of Medical Psychology*, 18:1–15, March, 1939.

Penrose, L. S., "A Note on the Statistical Relationship Between Mental Deficiency and Crime in the United States," *American Journal of Mental Deficiency*, 47:462–466, April, 1943.

Rose, Gordon, *The Struggle for Penal Reform*. London: Stevens and Sons, 1961.

Saleilles, R., *The Individualization of Punishment*. Translated by R. S. Jastrow. Boston: Little, Brown, 1911.

Sellin, Thorsten, "Correction in Historical Perspective," *Law and Contemporary Problems*, 23:585–593, Autumn, 1958.

Vishinsky, Andrei, *The Law of the Soviet State*. New York: Macmillan, 1948.

Znaniecki, F., *Social Actions*. New York: Farrar and Rinehart, 1936.

# 17. THE POLICE

AFTER HE HAS been detected, a criminal could become, successively, the concern of many agencies which are organized for the direction and implementation of societal reactions to crime. Hypothetically, he could come into contact with, at least, the police system, the courts, the probation system, the prison system, and the parole system. However, most criminals do not participate in all the programs in the series. Many guilty persons are discharged by the police or courts, others succeed on probation and, consequently, do not come into contact with the prison system, others are sent to prison directly and have no contact with probation or parole agencies. In almost all instances, however, contact with the police system precedes contact with any subsequent agency or agencies. For this reason, and because in many cases contact with the police system is terminal, the police are in a strategic position with reference to the subsequent behavior of apprehended offenders. Implementation of a punitive reaction by the police undoubtedly will have important effects on the success of any subsequent attempts at treatment. Even if treatment methods are not used later, either because they are not available or because the guilty person does not encounter them, the methods used by the police in performing their functions will affect the probabilities for reformation or recidivism. In some instances police methods cause offenders to identify themselves with criminals and the underworld, and in other instances they cause them to abandon such criminal identifications as they may possess at the time of apprehension.

The police also are in a strategic position with reference to crime causation. Among both criminals and non-criminals they frequently are personified as "the law," and respect for law depends upon the behavior of the police more than on any other agents of the state. Most non-criminals have at least casual contact with the police, and in presenting anti-criminal behavior patterns to such persons or to apprehended offenders, the prestige of the police is affected by their prior conduct and by their efficiency in performing their duties.

COMPOSITION OF THE POLICE.  The term "police" refers primarily to agents of the state whose function is the maintenance of law and order and especially the enforcement of the regular criminal code. Each governmental unit, under the American constitution, may have its own police force. The city has a municipal police force, the small town has a marshal, and the township has a constable. The county may have an organized uniformed police force but usually it has only a sheriff and deputies. States now employ approximately 10,000 uniformed police, some of whom are limited to traffic regulation. In the United States there are about 40,000 law-enforcement agencies, employing approximately 200,000 policemen, sheriffs, constables, marshals, and similar officers. In 1964, there were 1.9 police department employees for each 1000 inhabitants of the 3,570 cities reporting to the F.B.I.[1] The police work of the federal government is centralized in the Federal Bureau of Investigation of the Department of Justice, but each federal department may have agents for enforcement of laws pertaining to it, including laws regarding the currency, narcotic drugs, internal revenue customs, immigration, and post office. The state militia and the army and navy may perform police functions in emergencies.

Two other types of agents are, however, included in the police system. The first of these is the private police. These are privately selected, privately financed, and privately controlled, although they are sometimes commissioned as public agents. A private industrial force, known as "the coal and iron police" existed in Pennsylvania for many years until prohibited by an act of 1935. Industrial corporations often organize private police forces because they feel that they are not fully protected by public police. In 1958, 1,821 uniformed private police and an unknown number of private detectives were employed in Los Angeles, where the strength of the city police force was 4,428. At present the railroad police of the United States and Canada comprise the largest privately supported police organization in the world. Four hundred different railroads are represented, and more than 8,000 persons hold commissions in more than 1,000 cities throughout the two nations. The work of these railroad police is co-ordinated by a central agency.[2] Such police protect the traveling public against pickpockets, confidence men, and sneak thieves, as well as protecting company property. Private detectives are also employed for the protection of race tracks, exhi-

[1] Federal Bureau of Investigation, *Uniform Crime Reports for the United States, 1964* (Washington: Government Printing Office, 1965), p. 144.
[2] William T. Faricy, "Functions of the Railroad Police," *Journal of Criminal Law and Criminology*, 42:385–391, September—October, 1951.

bitions, conventions, banks, department stores, jewelry stores, and other places of business.

The second type of special police consists of inspectors and examiners who are appointed by public authorities: game wardens, bank examiners, factory and dairy inspectors, and inspectors of weights and measures. The staffs of the Securities and Exchange Commission, the Federal Trade Commission, and analogous state and federal commissions perform police functions in relation to white-collar crimes. Broadly speaking, these special agents for the enforcement of trade regulations have been more efficient in law enforcement than have state and municipal agents. They are regarded with antagonism by many businessmen, who refer to the agents as "snoopers," just as the regular uniformed police are regarded with antagonism by pickpockets and burglars.[3]

CONFLICTS BETWEEN POLICE RESPONSIBILITY AND POWER. The American policeman is in a difficult position, for in order to do his work efficiently he must adopt more power than the law and the formal organization of his department permit. He is responsible for the enforcement of the criminal law and for the maintenance of order, yet he cannot meet these responsibilities under the power and authority granted him. At the same time, if he exceeds his authority in dealing with certain offenders he is subject to severe public criticism. He can safely exceed his legal authority only when he deals with people who are not powerful politically and who are, in one sense, helpless. Also, while he is expected to make crime dangerous for all, he also is expected to use discretion and to exercise certain judicial functions. He must not only know whether a certain act violates the law, but also whether it can be proved that the law has been violated. He must rigorously enforce the law, yet he also must determine whether a particular violation of law should be handled by warning or arrest, for the police are subject to informal rules which bar the arrest of some persons, and they are not expected to arrest everyone who is known to have violated a law. The courts would find it impossible to do their work if the police brought all cases into court, and the police would be in court so much of the time that the force would need to be enlarged enormously. Consequently, the police must judge and informally settle more cases than they take into court; but the processes by which such settlements are made are not within the scope of the policeman's formal authority.[4] There are numerous similar

---

[3] This chapter will be concerned with the work of the regular police and no further attention will be paid to the private police or the specialized public agents who perform police functions for the various divisions of the government.

[4] See Joseph Goldstein, "Police Discretion not to Invoke the Criminal Process: Low-Visibility Decisions in the Administration of Criminal Justice," *Yale Law Journal*, 69:543–594, March, 1960.

impediments to the performance of duties which the community ordinarily expects of the police. These include the assignment of administrative duties to the police, the law of arrest, antiquated legal systems, and political control of police activities.

Administrative tasks. Many administrative tasks are being imposed upon the police. Some of these are concerned primarily with public order, as in the direction of traffic (including installation and maintenance of traffic lights and signals, designation of one-way streets and of zones), granting permits or licenses for taxicabs, taxi-drivers, and taxi-stands, parades, and similar activities, restraining crowds at fires, and aiding in emergencies. Other tasks also are only indirectly concerned with the repression and prevention of crime. They include licensing of amusement parks, dance halls, theaters, concealed weapons, property for advertising purposes, auctioneers, places for handling explosives, and also inspecting motion pictures, weights and measures, and a great variety of other places and activities. The laws which require licensing and inspection are increasing rapidly, and in many places the enforcement of these laws is imposed upon the police. The budgets and staffs of police departments, however, are not being increased proportionately, so that inefficiency is almost a necessity. The police must select the laws they will enforce. Suggestions have been made that the regular police should confine their activities to the enforcement of laws against serious crimes, and that separate organizations should be developed for dealing with "morals," traffic, and licensing and inspection.

The public also has failed to recognize that the control of crime in modern times is extremely difficult and that it can be secured only by continuous, patient, effort. Such effort requires a large staff and expensive equipment. The development of modern means of transportation, and the resulting mobility of peoples have immensely increased the difficulties of control. People in a city are anonymous. Two generations ago criminals wore masks, but this practice occurs only infrequently today. The criminal is a stranger, and it is difficult to identify a stranger. The crowd on the city streets often facilitates escape. A professional burglar has stated that one block and around the corner in a city is as good as twenty miles in the country. Also, the very number of crimes impedes the solution of any one of them, yet the police are held responsible for the solution of all. In large cities a murder occurs, on the average, almost every day. A small, specialized homicide squad therefore has little time for study of a particular murder but must rush from one case to another. In England, on the other hand, where murders are less frequent, a specialized force can concentrate on one murder until it is solved. This difference would not be as significant if it were not for the public pressure in the United States to solve spectacular crimes. The pressure is instigated by the newspapers, and they, more than any other agency, make it impossible for the existing police to develop a policy of consistent work. Yet at the same time the public is indignant when a police force has left administrative work undone to concentrate on spectacular crimes.

The law of arrest. Arrests can be made on warrants, or written orders of the court, by anyone authorized to serve them. Upon application, a warrant may be obtained from a judge when the judge is convinced of the probability that a particular person is guilty of an offense. Under certain conditions, both private citizens and police officers can arrest without a warrant. Private citizens without a warrant, however, have no authority to arrest for misdemeanors, except in some states where they are allowed to arrest for a breach of peace committed in their presence. Officers can arrest for misdemeanors without a warrant if the misdemeanor is committed in their presence. For felonies, in some states arrest by a private person without a warrant is not lawful unless the arresting person (a) has reasonable grounds for believing the arrestee is guilty and (b) the arrestee is guilty. In a greater number of states a private citizen may arrest for a felony if (a) he has reasonable grounds for believing the arrestee is guilty and (b) a felony has been committed. In about five other states, a private person has the same powers as police officers generally have in regard to felonies: he can arrest for a felony whenever (a) he has reasonable grounds for believing that a felony has been committed and (b) reasonable grounds for believing that the arrestee committed it.[5] Under common law neither police officers nor private citizens could arrest for a felony without a warrant unless there were *positive* knowledge that a felony had been committed and there were reasonable grounds for believing that the arrestee was the guilty person.

The law is frequently violated by the police in making arrests. Most police departments, for instance, have rules which authorize officers to make arrests on suspicion quite in opposition to the law.[6] Most of the illegal arrests are designed to protect society. In rural areas where officers are paid by fees—one fee for making an arrest, another for discharging a person from jail, etc.—the police are induced to make unjustifiable and illegal arrests in order to get the fees. However, the thousands of unlawful arrests made by urban policemen in "drag-net raids," and in the arrests of drunk persons

[5] See Rocco Tresolini, Richard W. Taylor, and Elliott B. Barnett, "Arrest Without Warrant: Extent and Social Implications," *Journal of Criminal Law and Criminology,* 46:187–198, July–August, 1955.
[6] See Caleb Foote, "Vagrancy-Type Law and Its Administration," *University of Pennsylvania Law Review,* 104:603–650, March, 1956.

and vagrants, are not necessarily sinister. On the contrary, these arrests reflect, in many cases, "a praiseworthy zeal in the pursuit of the criminal, leading the zealous officer to chafe against, to strain, and occasionally to break the shackles which the law has thrown about his operations."[7] The number of illegal arrests probably would be even greater if more of the suspects made it necessary for a police officer to make an actual arrest before taking them to the police station for questioning or investigation. Often the officer merely says, "You had better talk to the captain about this," or "We had better take a ride down to the station," rather than actually placing the suspected person under arrest, but in many cases the person in question believes that he is being arrested.[8]

The police are severely criticized for making illegal arrests, and they are subject to damage suits by the illegally-detained persons. Yet they also are severely criticized for not arresting persons who apparently have violated the law. Under the law of arrest, if a thief were detained by a private citizen who saw him commit a misdemeanor and a policeman subsequently arrived on the scene and arrested the offender for the misdemeanor, the arrest probably would be illegal. But a policeman who did not arrest under such circumstances would be subject to severe criticisms, and it is not inconceivable that he would be accused of being in collusion with the offender. Persons charged with possessing concealed weapons are frequently discharged from court on the ground that the officer had no reasonable ground for making an arrest; the fact that concealed weapons were found in the search subsequent to the arrest is of no legal importance, for such evidence is held to have been illegally secured and therefore might not be introduced in the court. However, an officer who did not take such a suspect to court probably would lose his position on the police force. Police have resisted recent U.S. Supreme Court decisions holding that evidence secured through unreasonable search and seizure, in violation of the Fourth Amendment, shall not be admitted in court against the accused.[9]

Antiquated legal systems. Although the police are expected to control crime by enforcing the criminal law, thereby making crime dangerous, they are expected to do so within the framework of an antiquated system of criminal law and criminal procedure. Among students of the subject there is almost unanimous agreement that the criminal law and criminal proce-

---

[7] Lewis Mayers, The American Legal System, Revised Edition (New York: Harper and Row, 1964), p. 55.

[8] Clarence Alexander, The Law of Arrest in Criminal and Other Proceedings, (Buffalo: Dennis, 1949), Vol. 1, pp. 358–361.

[9] See O. W. Wilson, "Police Arrest Privileges in a Free Society: A Plea for Modernization, Chapter in Claude R. Sowle, Editor, Police Power and Individual Freedom: The Quest for Balance (Chicago: Aldine, 1962), pp. 21–28; and Caleb Foote, "The Fourth Amendment: Obstacle or Necessity in the Law of Arrest?" Ibid., pp. 29–36.

dure are inadequate for the purpose of controlling crime and administering justice. Not only is the law of arrest inadequate, as indicated above, but the police are expected to enforce laws which are unenforceable. The police are not taken into consideration when laws are passed and have no official vote in the determination of legislative policies. Many of the rules of evidence are not adapted to modern conditions, and frustrated police see many criminals escape conviction because of this system.

Moreover, the police are hampered by an antiquated system of local boundaries. In the area within 50 miles of the center of Chicago more than 400 independent police forces are operating with no central control or organization. In Cook County alone there are 11,000 police employed as members of over 200 separate and uncoordinated agencies.[10] The result is a system of duplicating and conflicting efforts which is necessarily inefficient.

Since the police are charged with the responsibility of controlling crime but are also thwarted in their attempts to do so by the existing legal system, they sometimes take it upon themselves to control by extralegal methods. For instance, the practice of wire-tapping by the Federal Bureau of Investigation has been justified by Director J. Edgar Hoover, who has stated, "I dare say the most violent critic of the FBI would urge the use of wire-tapping techniques if his child were kidnaped."[11] Similarly, when local boundaries hamper their efforts to control crime, police ignore them, or they devise summary methods of extradition, whereby the police in one bailiwick simply shove captured criminals across the boundary line into the arms of the police in the bailiwick in which the crimes were committed.

Also, violence which is not legally justified is sometimes used at the time of arrest or between the arrest and the court hearing. When such violence, including protracted questioning and various "psychological" tortures, is used to get confessions from suspected persons the Fifth, Sixth, and Fourteenth Amendments to the Constitution usually are violated. Those amendments safeguard the rights of suspected persons in courts and make it illegal for a state to deprive any citizen of life, liberty, or property "without due process of law." The methods by which these constitutional safeguards are violated are usually referred to as the "third degree." Third-degree practices are generally denied by police officials in their public statements, as might be expected, but in confidential conversations the policeman often

[10] Joseph D. Lohman, *Mid-Term Report* (Chicago: Cook County Sheriff's Office, 1956), pp. 12–13.

[11] Associated Press news dispatch, January 16, 1951. See also Edward D. Silver, "Legalized Wire-Tapping is Absolutely Necessary," *Police Review*, 22:3–16, Fall, 1959. For the opposite view, see Richard C. Donnelly, "Comments and Caveats on the Wire Tapping Controversy," *Yale Law Journal*, 63:799–810, April, 1954.

will ask, "If you caught one member of a kidnaping gang and had no information about the other members of the gang, would you not be inclined to use violence in forcing him to identify the other members?" It is not likely that violence is used frequently on professional thieves, or on the organized criminals in those occupations which are systematically protected by the police. Ordinarily, the methods are used against powerless and rather inconspicuous persons.

Some policemen have argued that it is impossible for the police to get along without third-degree methods, and there is some evidence that many citizens approve of the milder forms of the third degree.[12] Thirty-seven percent of the police officers questioned in one study believed that "roughing a man up" is justified if he has shown disrespect for the police and 19 percent believed that such violence is justified when the objective is to obtain information from the suspect.[13] A police inspector in New York City once said, "There is more law at the end of a policeman's night stick than in a decision of the Supreme Court," and a police captain published a defense of illegal violence.[14] The police commissioner of a large Eastern city stated, "I've sworn to protect this community against crime. If there has to be a choice between violating my oath of office and violating the Constitution, I'll violate the Constitution every time."[15] Ordinarily, when instances of brutality become public the police insist that they can be attributed to the behavior of a few sadistic officers, not to the nature of the police system.

The most injurious aspect of police violence is that it tends to alienate the public,[16] yet that same public applauds violence when it is used on the more unpopular criminals. A bill to ban third-degree tactics was passed by the lower house of an Eastern state, but it was killed when a state senator asked, "Are we to give the criminal an even break? Does the criminal give the law-abiding citizen an even break?"[17] The public, in a sense, also pro-

[12] Herman C. Beyle and Spencer D. Parratt, "Approval and Disapproval of Specific Third-Degree Practices," Journal of Criminal Law and Criminology, 28:526–550, November–December, 1938.

[13] William A. Westley, "Violence and the Police," American Journal of Sociology, 56:34–41, July, 1953.

[14] Cornelius W. Willemse, Behind the Green Lights (New York: Knopf, 1931).

[15] Quoted by Frederick G. Brownell, "It Could Happen to You," American Magazine, May, 1949, pp. 24 ff. Cf. William Seagle, Law, The Science of Inefficiency (New York: Macmillan, 1952), pp. 106, 109–110.

[16] August Vollmer and others, "Report on Police," National Commission on Law Observance and Enforcement, Report No. 14 (Washington: Government Printing Office, 1931), p. 45; Ernest J. Hopkins, Our Lawless Police (New York: Viking Press, 1931); E. H. Lavine, The Third Degree (New York: Vanguard Press, 1930); Audrey M. Davies, "Police, the Law, and the Individual," Annals of the American Academy of Political and Social Science, 291:143–151, January, 1954.

[17] Quoted by J. Edgar Hoover, "Third Degree," American Magazine, May, 1940, pp. 38 ff.

motes other illegal police methods by severely criticizing the police if they do not control crime, or do not quickly solve spectacular crimes, while at the same time granting them only inadequate legal powers to do so. For example, police may no longer stop and interrogate persons who seem suspicious, and they must immediately advise arrestees of their right to counsel, but these democratic rules do not silence democratic pleas for more security from "terror in the streets."

*Politics.* The most serious impediments to efficient crime control by the police are found in the system of political control of police organizations. In some cities the police force is under the control of politicians who do not wish and will not permit the enforcement of law and order. Appointments of commissioners and superintendents, and advancement of policemen from one rank to another are controlled largely by politicians. The politicians therefore control the fundamental policies and practices of the police department.[18] Formally, the police department is organized and operates for the welfare of society; informally, it is organized for the welfare of the politicians. This means both that some crimes must be overlooked and that some criminals must be protected by the police.

Under the control of corrupt politicians, police departments become systematically lawless. This does not mean that every policeman is lawless but that as a system the police operate in a lawless manner. Graft is one form of this lawlessness. Graft, in turn, is usually linked with collusion with professional and organized criminals. The investigations of the United States Senate Special Committee to Investigate Crime in Interstate Commerce revealed extensive collusion between criminals and law-enforcement officers and extensive evidence of graft by law-enforcement officers. For example, it was the committee's judgment that "outright payments for protection were most clearly established" in the case of a sheriff of Orleans, the parish in which the city of New Orleans is located.[19] The sheriff's divorced wife testified that in six years the sheriff had accumulated $150,-000 which he kept in a steel box in his home. She also testified that she had seen her husband receive money weekly from a slot-machine dealer and that she herself had received money every week from another slot-machine dealer. Another person, who reputedly ran a house of prostitution, came by on Saturdays, bringing "all the food for a week." Similarly, it was revealed that in Tampa a sheriff was the center of a criminal conspiracy to violate gambling laws and that he received direct payments of protection money. In Philadelphia there were direct payments of approximately $152,000 monthly, "not counting payments to higher-ups."

[18] See Virgil W. Peterson, "The Chicago Police Scandals," *Atlantic Monthly*, 206:58–64, October, 1960.
[19] Estes Kefauver, *Crime in America* (New York: Doubleday, 1951), pp. 175–176.

In New York City one bookmaking organization paid over $1,000,000 a year for police protection, and in Los Angeles an entry of $108,000 for "juice," the California term for protection money, was found in the books of a bookmaking organization.[20]

In many other cities evidence of a politico-criminal-police triumvirate was revealed.[21] In fact, the committee found evidence of corruption and connivance at all levels of government—federal, state, and local. In the federal government the corruption was found to be primarily in connection with the enforcement of income-tax laws, but evidence of illegal activities on the state and local levels took four different forms: (a) direct bribe or protection payments are made to the police by criminals; (b) politicians using their influence to protect criminals and further the interests of criminals; (c) police possessing unusual and unexplained wealth; and (d) police participating directly in the business of organized crime.[22]

Illegal activity in police departments is not a recent phenomenon. Federal and state investigating committees have revealed graft and collusion almost every time they have looked for them. The Lexow Committee in New York City in 1894–1895, for example, found that graft was characteristic of the police system rather than of isolated patrolmen.[23] The Seabury Committee a generation later found the same situation persisting.[24] In 1915 the Chicago City Council Commission on Crime found much evidence of collusion between police and professional criminals.[25] A Texas rancher who was swindled out of $45,000 in 1919 by a group of confidence men, pursued them for three years through Florida, California, Colorado, New York, and other states. His efforts were seriously hampered by the police in many cities, especially in Florida and California, and some of

---

[20] Special Committee to Investigate Organized Crime in Interstate Commerce, *Third Interim Report*, U. S. Senate Report No. 307, 82nd Congress (Washington: Government Printing Office, 1951), pp. 184–185. See also Norton Mockridge and Robert H. Prall, *The Big Fix* (New York: McGraw-Hill, 1957).

[21] For the Committee's findings in medium-sized cities, see its *Final Report*, U. S. Senate Report No. 725. 82nd Congress (Washington: Government Printing Office, 1951), pp. 37–62.

[22] *Third Interim Report*, pp. 183–184.

[23] New York Legislature, *Report and Proceedings of the Senate Committee Appointed to Investigate the Police Department of the City of New York* [Lexow Committee] (Albany: State Printing Office, 1895), Vol. V, pp. 5311–5388. For a brief description of this investigation, see Lincoln Steffens, *Autobiography* (New York: Harcourt, 1931), pp. 247–284.

[24] New York Legislature, *Report of the Joint Committee on the Government of the City of New York*, 5 Volumes (Albany: State Printing Office, 1932). This report has been summarized, interpreted, and amplified in several unofficial books, of which the following are the most important: W. B. Northrop and J. B. Northrop, *The Insolence of Office* (New York: Putnam's, 1932); Raymond Moley, *Tribunes of the People* (New Haven: Yale University Press, 1932); Norman Thomas and Paul Blanshard, *What's the Matter with New York?* (New York: Macmillan, 1932).

[25] Chicago City Council, *Report of the Commission on Crime* (Chicago: Author, 1915).

these interfering policemen were convicted as a result.[26] When the district attorney in Denver attempted to secure evidence against a ring of confidence men in 1922 he called in the state troopers to make arrests, and kept his prisoners confined in the basement of a church until the raid was complete, for he was afraid to let any of the city police learn of his plans.[27] For years, professional thieves have been able to work on the assumption that any case of theft by them in any American city can be "fixed" and that an arrest is merely a temporary discomfort from which no great inconvenience results. This kind of collusion does not involve the whole police system in the sense that graft connected with gambling or prostitution does, but it is a mistake to believe that graft is restricted to situations in which "morals" are regulated. The Lexow Committee found that the same system of bribery used by criminals was also used by commission merchants, contractors, pushcart vendors and bootblacks who wanted to use the public streets for private business, and others. The Seabury Committee reported that the bribery of public officers was the method used in securing special privileges regarding building zone ordinances, bus franchises, waterfront leases, condemnation cases, weights and measures, taxi regulations, and many other things. It is evident that bribery, graft, and corruption are not confined to the police department and in so far as found in the police department, are not confined to prostitution, gambling, and liquor. On the contrary, they may develop wherever business concerns or individuals see an opportunity for gain by bribery and wherever the police see an opportunity to force contributions from such concerns or individuals.

Another consequence of the fact that police departments sometimes are organized for the welfare of corrupt politicians, rather than of society, is inefficient and unqualified personnel. This is unquestionably linked with police dishonesty, since only police officers who are "right" can be employed by those in political control. Persons of low intelligence and with criminal records have been employed. Even civil service systems which have been set up for the selection and promotion of qualified men are sometimes ignored or circumvented.[28] The public loudly demands that the police control crime, yet it fails to see that policemen are selected carefully, to provide adequate training, to furnish adequate salaries and conditions

[26] J. F. Norfleet, *Norfleet: The Amazing Experiences of an Intrepid Texas Rancher*, Revised Edition (Sugar Land, Texas: Imperial Press, 1927); Philip S. Van Cise, *Fighting the Underworld* (Boston: Houghton Mifflin, 1936).

[27] Norfleet, *op. cit.*, pp. 314 ff.

[28] See Virgil W. Peterson, "Chicago's Crime Problem," *Journal of Criminal Law and Criminology*, 35:3–15, May–June, 1944. For illustrations of the process, see Jack Alexander, "Independent Cop," *The New Yorker*, October 3, 10, and 17, 1936, pp. 21–27, 24–28, 28–34; and David G. Wittels, "Why Cops Turn Crooked," *Saturday Evening Post*, April 23, 1949, pp. 26 ff.

of employment, and to make possible continuous policies. The average term of office of the chief official of police departments in American cities of a half-million population or more is only about two years, while in London it has been about fifteen years. Even when police are not selected on the basis of political patronage, directly or indirectly, the departments usually are inadequately staffed.

In general, the police are inefficient in performing their duties, as these duties are formally defined, but the inefficiency is due to the fact that the public fails to provide conditions which are essential to efficiency in the repression and prevention of crime. The police believe, for example, that a universal registration system would facilitate efficient police work. The ordinary American interprets this as an imposition on his personal liberty, although he makes no objection to submitting his fingerprints in other situations. In the same spirit, the public is unwilling to assist the police in other respects. It is extremely difficult for police officers to secure assistance from bystanders in the pursuit of a criminal or the detection of crime. The social conflicts and social disorganization which produce high crime rates also produce a police system which cannot deal effectively with crime under existing conditions. It cannot be properly said that the public wants the police to repress and prevent all crime.

THE PUNITIVE REACTION AND THE POLICE. From the time of the formation of the United States there has been a tradition of narrow and restricted authority and power on the part of administrators and executives, including the police. At the same time, the persons occupying such positions are expected to play skillfully their roles as administrators. Like other administrators—in the government, church, educational system, the army, and elsewhere—the police tend to take attitudes of superordination and to assume unofficial powers, often in opposition to the desires of many of their constituents, and in doing so they often adopt punitive measures. The police system is officially an agency which maintains order, serves the public, and captures suspected criminals and takes them to courts for trial. According to legal and political theory, the rights and duties of the police to inflict punishments are sharply limited.[29] Formally, authority to implement anything approaching a punitive reaction to law violation is restricted to three main areas. First, as noted previously, a limited judicial authority has been conferred upon the police, primarily in connection with minor offenses such as traffic violations, and the exercise of this authority often involves a punitive reaction to the offense. Second, police are expected to punish by destroying property which is prohibited by law, such

[29] See Jerome Hall, "Police and Law in a Democratic Society," *Indiana Law Journal*, 28:133–177, Winter, 1953.

as gambling devices and unregistered equipment for making alcohol. Third, police are authorized to confiscate or impound property which is being used in violation of law, with the result that the owner loses the property or is required to pay a fee for its recovery. This may be illustrated by the impounding of arms and by the towing away of illegally parked cars.

However, because they are expected to make crime dangerous, the police in fact implement a punitive reaction to crime in many additional ways. The third degree, which entails pain and suffering for the purpose of extorting a confession, is punitive in nature, as is collecting a bribe from a guilty person in lieu of arrest. Brutality in the process of arrest or detention is an expression of hatred and superiority. So far as brutality is defended by the police, it is said to be justified by the fact that many guilty persons escape conviction through technicalities or corruption and thus escape official punishment. The police say, in effect, "We will see that he gets this much punishment anyway."

Even when arrests and detention do not incorporate brutality they often include intentional imposition of suffering. Police are apt to be discourteous, sarcastic, or rude when arresting persons of lower socio-economic classes, but courteous and lenient when dealing with persons of high social status. The fact that courtesy was first emphasized in police departments when the police came into frequent contact with automobile drivers, who were not ordinarily of the lower classes, is evidence of this discrimination. In fact, until the police started dealing with automobile drivers they were mostly working men employed by the upper classes and middle classes to control other working men. The first police department, established in England in 1829, had something of this form, as did the first regular police forces in New York (1844) and Chicago (1855). The fact that Southern California, with the highest number of automobiles per capita in the world, also has the police with the highest average educational level in the world shows one effect of the encounter between the police and upper- and middle-class automobile drivers. Undoubtedly, the police make distinctions in favor of upper socio-economic classes because the making of such distinctions is part of our culture.[30] Similarly, the police use punitive methods because the punitive reaction to crime is popular in our culture.

It should not be concluded, however, that use of force and violence on the part of the police is necessarily "brutality," motivated by a desire to inflict punishment. Because some of the persons with whom the policeman deals are dangerous, he must be trained to fight, shoot, and use force.

[30] See Margery Fry, *Arms of the Law* (London: Gollancz, 1951), pp. 19, 97–98; and T. C. Willett, *Criminal on the Road* (London: Tavistock, 1964), pp. 4, 7, 65–109.

Confronting dangerous men and subduing them is a hazardous business, and policemen cannot be expected to be gentle at all times. When a policeman's life is at stake we cannot expect him to follow either the rules of boxing or the rules governing the behavior of television cowboys, both of which stress the propriety of fighting "fairly," like gentlemen. A policeman who fought by these rules would soon use up all his sick leave. The first chapter of a "practical handbook" for American police patrolmen is exclusively devoted to the use of force, and its instructions range from details about how to use an opponent's clothing to restrain him, to how to use a nightstick and how to kill with a gun.[31] On the latter point, the authors give policemen the following lesson:

You don't have to wait until a suspect is actually assaulting you before you draw your gun. In fiction and on film, the actor portraying a Western Marshal can afford to wait until his assailant has started to draw before he goes for his gun. You cannot. You are in a real-life drama; there are no rehearsals or retakes and mistakes can be fatal.[32]

*fundamentally punitive*

THE TREATMENT REACTION AND THE POLICE. Although the fundamental informal policy of police departments is punitive, during the last fifty years there has been a slight trend toward implementation of the treatment reaction to law-breaking. Changes in police departments in this connection, of course, correspond to changes in other agencies and in the society as a whole. As the treatment reaction has become more popular in the whole society it also has become popular in police organizations. However, like the implementation of the punitive reaction by the police, the implementation of the treatment reaction is largely unofficial. The activities of the police in this area are usually called "crime prevention"—discouraging or hindering crime by methods which are not designed to produce fear in the recipient. Most of the activities of crime-prevention divisions of police departments are directed toward what are considered the social conditions leading to delinquency and crime, but the treatment reaction also is implemented in other ways. In exercising their judicial authority, the police certainly screen offenders on the basis of whether or not it is thought that punishment is warranted, but they also sometimes evaluate offenders according to whether or not it is thought that treatment is needed. Especially in dealing with juveniles, the police screen offenders by using discretion as to whether a child should be released or referred to a guidance clinic for personality help, to a settlement for club contacts, to some other agency,

[31] David H. Gilston and Lawrence Podell, *The Practical Patrolman* (Springfield: C. C Thomas, 1959), pp. 5–28.
[32] *Ibid.*, p. 23.

or to a court, as a preliminary to institutionalization.[33] When the action of the police is expostulation rather than arrest, or referral to a social agency rather than referral to a court, guilt may or may not be assumed. But even if guilt is not assumed and the policeman makes his decision on the basis of mere probabilities or symptoms of delinquency, expostulation and referral are part of the treatment reaction to crime, just as the infliction of illegal punishments on innocent persons is part of the punitive reaction to crime.

In general, police departments have applied selected principles of social science to their work and, in so doing, they have put some emphasis upon treatment. But for the most part the police deal with persons who have not yet been convicted of crime, and they are expected to treat these persons as if they were innocent. While in a strict sense it is impossible to use such a policy, the possibility for development of treatment programs within police departments is severely limited by it. Some persons have, in fact, criticized the police for developing social work programs, on the ground that other agencies exist for this purpose and that such programs are extraneous to the official duties of the police.[34] This criticism is similar to the arguments of persons who criticize the police for unofficially inflicting punishments.

TRENDS IN POLICE WORK.   Plans for improving the efficiency of the police system have been developed by various persons and agencies, and there has been a slight and inconsistent trend toward following them. This program includes freedom from corrupt politics, larger territorial organization, improvements of personnel, systems of assignments, equipment and scientific techniques, the development of preventive police work, cordial relations between police and public, and the general development of police morale and of police work as a profession.

Politics.  The fundamental requirement for efficient police work is freedom from corrupt politics. The other parts of a program for the improvement of the police system are likely to be largely futile unless the impediments caused by corrupt politics are reduced, but the development of the other parts of this program may have an indirect influence in producing freedom from politics.

Freedom from corrupt politics does not, of course, mean freedom from all outside control. A police department cannot be a completely self-

[33] Citizens' Committee on Children of New York, *Police and Children* (New York: Author, 1951), p. 11. See also Nathan Goldman, *The Differential Selection of Juvenile Offenders for Court Appearance* (New York: National Council on Crime and Delinquency, 1963).

[34] See Herbert A. Bloch and Frank T. Flynn, *Delinquency* (New York: Random House, 1955), pp. 258–262.

governing organization. Moreover, freedom from corrupt politics does not mean freedom from pressures of various kinds. It may be expected that people will always continue to put pressure on the police department for special privileges, and for leniency in dealing with their friends. If the police are free to deal on their merits with these inevitable pressures, efficiency need not be decreased thereby.

Corruption in municipal politics seems to be decreasing. The strength of party affiliations and, therefore, the strength of local political control has diminished rather steadily since the Civil War, which left a heritage of party loyalty. Civil service measures have made great inroads on patronage in the last fifty years. Municipal, state, and federal welfare agencies now distribute goods and services to the needy, where forty years ago these things were distributed by political machines, in exchange for votes. Also, businessmen are beginning to revolt against the old system of corruption of government, especially local government, for special privilege.[35]

Further, the police may now secure a measure of freedom even in cities where politics remain corrupt. The executive officer of the police department was traditionally a political appointee, but such officers are increasingly being selected by civil service and given permanent tenure, subject to removal for cause. Furthermore, the police are inactive and uninfluential in politics in comparison with fifty years ago. For example, the Hatch Act forecloses political activity by federal police, and in many states police are forbidden by law or police regulations to participate in such activity. The Illinois State Police are by law 50 percent Democrats and 50 percent Republicans.[36] Also, graft has been increasingly centralized and syndicated with the result that the police secure little of the proceeds. Accordingly, the police are more inclined to view graft as crime. At the same time, police seem to be gaining a stronger voice in legislative and executive policies, enabling them to get the assistance of others in controlling crime. Similarly, the police are developing programs for educating the public about police problems. It has been argued that police unions can materially improve the conditions which make the policeman a ripe target for corruption.[37]

[35] The autobiography of Lincoln Steffens, the biography of Frank L. Smith, and an abundance of other evidence show that political corruption frequently emanates from large business concerns. See Lincoln Steffens, op. cit.; and C. H. Wooddy, The Case of Frank L. Smith (Chicago: University of Chicago Press, 1931).

[36] Donal E. J. MacNamara, "American Police Administration at Mid-Century," Public Administration Review, 10:181–189, Summer, 1950.

[37] Edmund P. Murray, "Should the Police Unionize?" The Nation, 188:530–533, June 13, 1959. For the opposite view, see Don L. Kooken and Loren D. Ayres, "Police Unions and Public Safety," Annals of the American Academy of Political and Social Science, 291:152–258, January, 1958.

*Regional and state police.* One reason for the inefficiency of both rural and urban police is the large number of small territorial units, each with its own police force. One of the fundamental elements of a program for efficient police work is the amalgamation and co-ordination of these forces. Three tendencies are apparent in this field. One is to develop a regular uniformed county police or else to place all of the constables and marshals of the county under the direction of the sheriff, so that at least within the county the police force will be organized, placed on a civil service basis, and become somewhat professional. A second trend is the development of a single police system for an entire metropolitan area. The large number and great variety of police forces in the area of a great city and its suburbs makes efficiency impossible. Co-operative efforts between the police forces in the metropolitan area of Chicago have been developed, while in Cincinnati a cooperative organization which includes counties in Ohio, Kentucky, and Indiana is now operating. Under a different arrangement, some small police jurisdictions now contract with larger jurisdictions for specific police services.[38]

A third trend, development of state police, is already well under way. In 1934, forty-seven state police systems were found in thirty-eight states, of which eleven were regular state police systems, nine highway police systems with general powers over crimes, twenty highway police systems with powers restricted to regulation of traffic, four state sheriffs, and three governor's reserves. By 1950, the police agencies in thirty-six states had substantially full law enforcement authority, whereas twelve were restricted to enforcement of traffic laws or to crimes committed on state highways.[39] The principal opposition to the extension of state police came from organized labor, which feared that they would be used as strikebreakers. Because of this opposition, many restrictions were placed on state police powers.[40]

Related to this development of regional and state police forces is the tendency toward increased participation of federal police in the administration of justice. Federal police go into operation only when the crimes are of an interstate nature or when federal activities are involved. But in recent years there has been a tremendous increase in the scope of federal criminal jurisdiction, brought about by new federal legislation enacted in response to the needs of a rapidly expanding nation. Federal action against crime

[38] Gordon Misner, "The Police Service Contract in California," *Journal of Criminal Law, Criminology and Police Science,* 52:445–452, December, 1961.
[39] MacNamara, *op. cit.*
[40] See Bruce Smith, *Police Systems in the United States,* Second Revised Edition (New York: Harper, 1960), pp. 193–196.

is made possible by the commerce clause of the Constitution and also by postal and taxing powers of Congress.[41]

An enormous amount of crime of an interstate nature was revealed by the Kefauver Committee in 1951.[42] Because of the mobility of professional and organized criminals the local agencies are seriously handicapped and a larger organization of police activities is needed. The Federal Bureau of Investigation claims that bank robberies have decreased 75 percent since 1934, when the crime was brought under federal jurisdiction. There is no logical reason why all serious crimes should not be defined by federal laws, as is done in Canada, and it is at least an open question whether much of the administrative work might not be transferred to the federal government to advantage.

*Personnel problems.* The efficiency of the police system depends upon a careful selection of policemen and adequate training, discipline, and remuneration. In about three-fourths of the cities at present policemen are at least selected by civil service examinations, though some cities still have a large turnover on change of political administration. Of the 3,714 men who applied for positions with the Detroit Police Department in 1964, only 4 percent were placed on the eligible list for appointment.[43] Police training, likewise, has developed extensively during the last fifty years. In a questionnaire study of cities of more than 250,000 in population, it was found that about 91 percent gave in-service or continuation training regularly to their police officers. One-half of these departments gave this training periodically, the other half on a part-time basis.[44] The majority of other large municipal and state police departments have in-service training programs of some kind, and many smaller departments provide advanced training. About fifty colleges or universities offer courses designed for police officers.[45] The Federal Bureau of Investigation organized a National Police Academy in 1935. This ordinarily has a session of twelve weeks, and in each session representatives from thirty-five to forty city, county, or state police departments are accepted for training.

[41] Albert J. Harno, "Some Significant Developments in Criminal Law and Procedure in the Last Century," *Journal of Criminal Law and Criminology*, 42:427–467, November–December, 1951. See also A. C. Breckenridge, "The Constitutional Basis for Co-operative Crime Control," *Journal of Criminal Law and Criminology*, 39:565–583, January–February, 1949.

[42] Special Committee to Investigate Organized Crime in Interstate Commerce, *op. cit.* See also Lohman, *op. cit.*

[43] Detroit Police Department, *1964 Annual Report* (Detroit: Author, 1965), p. 9.

[44] G. Douglas Gourley, "Recognition and Status for Rank and File Policemen," *Journal of Criminal Law and Criminology*, 40:75–84, May–June, 1949.

[45] MacNamara, *op. cit.* See also Donal E. J. MacNamara, "Higher Police Training at the University Level," *Journal of Criminal Law and Criminology*, 40:657–665, January–February, 1950; and Frank M. Boolesen, *Directory of University and College Criminology Programs*, Third Edition (Fresno: Fresno State College Department of Criminology, 1961).

*Assignments.* This assignment of police to specific tasks and the organization of work have changed significantly in the years since the automobile, the telephone, and the police radio became popular. August Vollmer developed a program for statistical and ecological studies of crimes as a basis of assignments. If the records of the police department indicate that robberies are concentrated in certain areas, at certain hours, and on certain days of the week the police force is also concentrated at those places and times. Further, the neighborhood patrolman is tending to disappear and specialized squads are increasing in number. The word "patrolman" is becoming little more than a designation of rank and no longer describes a type of work. The small number assigned to regular patrol duty is explained in part by the fact that a citizen in trouble can now telephone police headquarters, which can dispatch a radio car to his aid. Formerly, the patrolman had to be available on the beat if the citizen were to get aid. Improved communication and transportation have also made the use of specialized squads possible, while changes in the technology of police work have made them necessary.[46] The most important of these squads is the traffic squad. In some communities, regulation of traffic now occupies the time of as much as 25 percent of the police force. In addition, large cities have pickpocket squads, gunman squads, mendicant squads, narcotic squads, an aviation police squad, and other squads and divisions. Because the members of these squads are mobile experts, the neighborhood patrolman is less important. Some police authorities, however, continue to believe that the neighborhood patrolman is a necessary unit in police work and should not entirely disappear.

*Equipment.* The equipment of the police was once quite inadequate in comparison with the equipment of professional criminals. For example, a patrolman on foot was expected to catch a bandit in an automobile, and, generally, the criminals adopted new inventions before the police did. Now the police have taken the initiative and, by and large, American police departments are the best equipped of all police departments in the world. The most striking developments in the equipment of police departments have been in the means of transportation and communication. Flash and gong signals were once regarded as important innovations for communications with the patrolman on the beat. Now the teletype or telephone-typewriter has been developed for communication between stations, and the police radio for communication between stations and also between stations and cars, planes, boats, motorcycles, and foot patrolmen equipped with receiving sets.

[46] See Michael Banton, *The Policeman in the Community* (London: Tavistock, 1964), pp. 7, 127; and Elaine Cumming, Ian Cumming and Laura Edell, "Policeman as Philosopher, Guide and Friend," *Social Problems*, 12:276–286, Winter, 1965.

*Criminalistics.* About 25 percent of the arrests for the more serious crimes are made at the time of the commission of the crime. In the others, efforts are made to detect and identify the guilty party. This work is done in part by uniformed men, in part by the specialists making up the "detective division" of large departments. Detectives are increasingly coming to symbolize the "professional" policeman who has been trained in methods for utilizing knowledge of the physical, biological, and social sciences in the apprehension of criminals, and in some cities and other centers, scientific methods of crime detection have been developed.

A great variety of techniques for the study of the traces of crimes has been invented. Many of these are being used in the larger police departments, though they are generally regarded as useful in a very small proportion of the cases. These include the identification of arms and bullets, identification of clothes, hair, teeth, automobile tires, and many other objects.[47] The techniques of physics and chemistry have been applied to the detection of crime with remarkable success in a small number of cases. The "lie detector" and other devices for determining the truth of testimony are proving to have some value, though they are still definitely in the experiment stage. The Federal Bureau of Investigation has developed these methods further than any other agency in America.

The Bertillon system of physical measurements, started by Bertillon in France in 1883, was first used in America in 1893, and was regarded at the time as a great invention for purposes of identification. It has proved, however, to be difficult and expensive in operation and has been replaced by an organized system of fingerprints. The federal government has developed a central clearing house in Washington which had more than 8 million records in 1938 and over 30 million criminal and suspect records by 1958. In addition, many states have developed bureaus of identification. Thus a network of local, state, and federal bureaus is developing, by means of which the previous criminal records of persons arrested or convicted may be determined. Many police departments still fail to contribute their records to this system, and especially is this true in misdemeanor cases.

Another method of identification is known as the *modus operandi* system, which was devised by Major Atcherley of the English constabulary. This method is based on the principle that a criminal is likely to use the same technique repeatedly, and that an analysis and record of the technique used in every serious crime will provide means of identification in

[47] Recent developments in this area are reported in H. Söderman and John J. O'Connell, *Modern Criminal Investigation* (Chicago: Civil Service Book Sales, 1951); and in Charles E. O'Hara and James W. Osterburg, *An Introduction to Criminalistics* (New York: Macmillan, 1949).

a particular crime. Some burglars always enter through basement windows, some through doors, some through second-story windows; some always steal silver, some jewelry, some clothing, some money; some come in the afternoon, some in the evening, some in the early morning. An Oslo detective interviewed in 1965 claimed that when illegal entry to an automobile was made by breaking a window, he could study the window-breaking technique and correctly conclude that the culprit could only be one of four or five men. Most municipal departments make at least informal use of the method.

The police departments in some of the European countries are greatly assisted in their work by the system of registration of inhabitants. In many cities this includes a requirement that the inhabitant report to the police within a specified time after he arrives in a city. European detectives would generally be rather helpless if they did not have this information to assist them. In Argentina the inhabitant is required to carry a registration card which serves to identify him. The police associations in this country have urged the adoption of some universal system of registration, and some departments have to a slight extent implemented this policy by requiring the registration of all ex-convicts in their bailiwick. As a matter of fact, fingerprints are recorded in some places for a fairly large proportion of the male citizens, including the army and navy, United States civil service and some state and municipal civil service positions, depositors in the postal savings banks, illiterate depositors in many other banks, and employees of some of the larger corporations. More than 113 million fingerprints, representing about sixty million civilians, are now in a special file in Washington. Moreover, a very large proportion of the inhabitants of the country are recorded in some manner—in registers for election purposes, gas and electric light companies, the post office, social security, driving licenses, directories of telephone companies and of cities—and when the individual or family changes residence this is recorded by the same agencies, and also by trucking companies. If this information were organized in a central registration system, it would cause little inconvenience to the average citizen and might be of great assistance in dealing with criminals. One reason for the very large number of arrests on suspicion at the present time is the fact that the individual has no method of identification. There is a question whether in the present anonymous city life, some organized method of registration for purposes of identification is not essential. The objection which is usually raised against this system is that it is undemocratic, but it may be pointed out that Switzerland, which is a close approach to the ideal democracy, has a system of this nature.

*Preventive police.* In the last thirty years most large police departments have organized crime prevention divisions, and there has been a growing interest in prevention. With the development of the social sciences, police have come to have a better understanding of crime and delinquency, and this better understanding is undoubtedly related to the growth of prevention programs. However, the concept of preventive police work is not clearly defined.[48] As stated earlier, it often involves on-the-spot adjustment of individual cases. It also seems to include a great variety of activities, including "hounding the hoodlums," attacks on criminal hangouts, frequent patrolling, warning residents and business concerns to keep doors and windows locked, friendly acquaintance with the residents on the beat, friendly relations with boys' gangs, organization of recreational activities in areas where delinquency rates are high, concentrated and co-operative efforts to influence boys who are getting into trouble, and social service work with families or individuals in distress. Thus crime prevention is sometimes thought to include deterrent measures—control through force or fear—as well as other methods. It usually pertains to juveniles.

In some departments, crime-prevention bureaus or divisions are simply another name for women police. At present, policewomen are employed in more than 200 communities. While some of the preventive work evidently is done to advantage by women, policewomen also carry out many other duties in police departments. They act as matrons in jails and lock-ups, assist in traffic control and police investigations, detect runaway children, patrol department stores in an effort to apprehend shoplifters, and participate in many other activities. However, their primary duties are in connection with prevention of juvenile delinquency, and they use treatment methods much more extensively than do male police. Buwalda has stated that "it was the policewoman who brought a social work point of view with her into the police department."[49]

On the other hand, much preventive work is done by regular policemen, either in special divisions or as a part of the regular police program. This preventive work has been directed largely at establishing recreational and athletic programs. However, efforts also are being made to build up friendly relations with the schools, and to co-operate with the various social agencies which are interested in programs for individuals who seem inclined toward delinquency.

The police and the public. The police of the United States have

[48] For description of the preventive work of several police departments, see Pauline V. Young, Social Treatment in Probation and Delinquency, Second Edition (New York: McGraw-Hill, 1952), Chapter 21.

[49] Irma Wann Buwalda, "The Policewoman—Yesterday, Today, and Tomorrow," Journal of Social Hygiene, 31:290–293, May, 1945. For a brief history of police service by women, see Lois Higgins, "Historical Background of Policewomen's Service," Journal of Criminal Law and Criminology, 41:822–833, March–April, 1951.

been severely criticized, but, on the other side of the coin, the police have found the public to be indifferent to police problems. One of the reactions which criticism and indifference have produced is organized effort to develop friendly understanding with the public. In this effort, police departments have established "public relations" divisions and have attempted to develop methods which would reduce the amount of irritation provoked by existing procedures. The general aim is to insure that the behavior of police will not arouse public antagonism, either because the public understands the behavior or because the behavior itself is above reproach.

Direct efforts toward public understanding of police problems and, hence, of police behavior, have been made in numerous ways. For example, efforts have been made to improve relations with the press, which often arouses, rather than reflects, public sympathy or antagonism toward the police. Police departments recently have made sincere efforts to co-operate with reporters and to enlist the aid of reporters in publicizing police problems. Similarly, police departments have attempted to create confidence and respect by selecting members of the staff for full-time work in speaking to school assemblies, church groups, welfare clubs, and other organizations. Also, perhaps much of the recent effort to apply principles of biological, social, and physical science to police work has been aimed more at publicity than at efficiency. In this effort to establish amicable relations with the public through publicity there is no doubt that many police departments have become propagandists, which is perhaps necessary in the complex life of the present day.

It is probable, however, that mitigation of public indifference of antagonism will require more than education or propagandization of the public. It is being increasingly recognized by the police that education of the police is necessary as well. Methods of dealing with offenders and suspected offenders are changing. Many police departments, for example, now emphasize that their members must be polite and courteous, and attention is being paid to special problems of dealing with minority groups, labor groups, and people in traffic.[50] More fundamentally, however, demonstration of coordinated effort to protect society while at the same time efficiently protecting the civil liberties of individuals probably has more influence than anything else toward reducing public antagonism.[51]

[50] Raymond E. Clift, "Police, Press and Public Relations," *Journal of Criminal Law and Criminology*, 39:667–674, January–February, 1949. See also Joseph D. Lohman, *The Police and Minority Groups* (Chicago: Chicago Park District, 1947); and G. McManus, "Human Relations Training for Police," *Journal of Criminal Law, Criminology, and Police Science*, 46:105–111, May–June, 1955.

[51] See Don F. Kooken, "Ethics in Police Service," *Journal of Criminal Law and Criminology*, 38:61–74, 172–186, May–June, July–August, 1947; and G. Douglas Gourley, *Public Relations and the Police* (Springfield: C. C Thomas, 1953), p. 108.

One of the advantages which accrues from good relations with the public is high police morale. Present efforts toward professionalization of police service will succeed only if the officer is convinced that the public is supporting him in his work. More and more, high police morale is becoming dependent upon efficient public service rather than upon evidence of physical strength and courage.[52] In no other part of the entire field of criminal justice or of municipal administration is as much enthusiasm shown in regard to the possibility of developing scientific and professional methods as in the police field.

## SUGGESTED READINGS

Banton, Michael, *The Policeman in the Community*. London: Tavistock, 1964.

Beyle, H. C., and D. P. Spencer, "Approval and Disapproval of Specific Third Degree Practices," *Journal of Criminal Law and Criminology*, 28: 526–550, November–December, 1938.

Cumming, Elaine, Ian Cumming and Laura Edell, "Policeman as Philosopher, Guide and Friend," *Social Problems*, 12:276–286, Winter, 1965.

Donnelly, Richard C., "Police Authority and Practices," *Annals of the American Academy of Political and Social Science*, 339:90–110, January, 1962.

Ehrlich, H. J., J. W. Rinehart and J. C. Howell, "The Study of Role Conflict: Explorations in Methodology," *Sociometry*, 25:85–97, March, 1962.

Esselstyn, T. C., "The Social Role of the County Sheriff," *Journal of Criminal Law, Criminology, and Police Science*, 44:177–184, July–August, 1953.

Faricy, W. T., "Functions of the Railroad Police," *Journal of Criminal Law and Criminology*, 42:385–391, September–October, 1951.

Floch, Maurice, "Limitations of the Lie Detector," *Journal of Criminal Law and Criminology*, 41:651–653, January–February, 1950.

Goldman, Nathan, *The Differential Selection of Juvenile Offenders for Court Appearance*. New York: National Council on Crime and Delinquency, 1963.

Goldstein, Joseph, "Police Discretion not to Invoke the Criminal Process: Low-visibility Decisions in the Administration of Justice," *Yale Law Journal*, 69:543–594, March, 1960.

Gourley, Douglas, *Public Relations and the Police*. Springfield: C. C. Thomas, 1953.

[52] Robert L. Peabody, "Authority Relations in Three Organizations," *Public Administration Review*, 23:87–92, June, 1963, Robert L. Peabody, "Perceptions of Organizational Authority: A Comparative Analysis," *Administrative Science Quarterly*, 6:477–482, March, 1962; and R. A. Myren, "A Crisis in Police Management," *Journal of Criminal Law, Criminology and Police Science*, 50:600–604, January, 1960.

Hall, Jerome, "Police and Law in a Democratic Society," *Indiana Law Journal*, 28:133–177, Winter, 1953.

Harno, Albert J., "Some Significant Developments in Criminal Law and Procedure in the Last Century," *Journal of Criminal Law and Criminology*, 42:427–467, November–December, 1951.

Inbau, Fred E. and John E. Reid, *Lie Detection and Criminal Interrogation*. Baltimore: Williams and Wilkins, 1953.

Kadish, S. H., "Legal Norms and Discretion in the Police and Sentencing Processes," *Harvard Law Review*, 75:904–931, March, 1962.

Kefauver, Estes, *Crime in America*. New York: Doubleday, 1951.

Leonard, V. A., *Police Organization and Management*. New York: Foundation Press, 1951.

MacNamara, Donal E. J., "American Police Administration at Mid-Century," *Public Administration Review*, 10:181–189, Summer, 1950.

Mayers, Lewis, *The American Legal System*, Revised Edition. New York: Harper and Row, 1964.

Murray, Edmund P., "Should the Police Unionize?" *The Nation*, 188:530–533, June 13, 1959.

Nestle, William H., "Why the Sheriff?" *American Journal of Correction*, 17:15, January–February, 1955.

Peabody, Robert L., "Perceptions of Organizational Authority: A Comparative Analysis," *Administrative Science Quarterly*, 6:477–482, March, 1962.

Peterson, Virgil W., "An Examination of Chicago's Law Enforcement Agencies," *Criminal Justice*, January, 1950, pp. 3–6.

Pringle, Patrick, *Hue and Cry*. New York: Morrow, 1956.

Rolph, C. H., Editor, *The Police and the Public*. London: Heinemann, 1962.

Seagle, William, *Law, The Science of Inefficiency*. New York: Macmillan, 1952.

Smith, Bruce, *Police Systems in the United States*, Second Revised Edition. New York: Harper, 1960.

Söderman, Harry, and John J. O'Connel, *Modern Criminal Investigation*. Chicago: Civil Service Book Sales, 1951.

Sowle, Claude R., Editor, *Police Power and Individual Freedom: The Quest for Balance*. Chicago: Aldine, 1962.

Stern, Mort, "What Makes a Policeman Go Wrong?" *Journal of Criminal Law, Criminology and Police Science*, 53:97–101, March, 1962.

Vollmer, August, "Police Progress in the Past Twenty-Five Years," *Journal of Criminal Law and Criminology*, 24:161–175, May–June, 1933.

Westley, William A., "Violence and the Police," *American Journal of Sociology*, 56:34–41, July, 1953.

Willett, T. C., *Criminal on the Road*. London: Tavistock, 1964.

Wilson, James Q., "Generational and Ethnic Differences among Career

Police Officers," American Journal of Sociology, 69:522–528, March, 1964.

Wilson, O. W., Police Administration. New York: McGraw-Hill, 1950.

Winters, John E., "The Role of the Police in the Prevention and Control of Delinquency," Federal Probation, 21:3–8, June, 1957.

# 18. DETENTION BEFORE TRIAL

AFTER A suspected person has been arrested, it is the duty of the police to take him promptly to a magistrate. This duty often is ignored, and arrested persons are sometimes discharged by the police without a court appearance. If the alleged crime of the person taken before a magistrate is a minor one, the magistrate either discharges or convicts the accused. But if the alleged crime is serious the magistrate merely considers the conditions under which temporary release on bail or on the suspected person's own recognizance can be granted. Whether the person accused of serious crime is released on bail or not, he is entitled to a "preliminary hearing," also before a magistrate. At this hearing the magistrate determines whether the known evidence against the accused is sufficient to justify further legal proceedings. Defendants who have been denied bail or who cannot meet the requirements for bail must remain in custody while arrangements are made for this preliminary hearing, and the practice of holding accused persons in this way is detention.

The preliminary hearing is wholly for the benefit of the suspect and never results in a decision that the suspect is guilty. Its purpose is to save obviously innocent persons the expense and trouble of a lengthy trial. The magistrate makes no effort to obtain new evidence and deals only with probability of guilt or innocence. Six states bar newsmen from preliminary hearings, primarily because readers are likely to interpret a "probable cause" action as a finding of guilt.[1] If the known evidence against the accused is not sufficient to justify further court proceedings, he is discharged from custody or from the conditions of bail. However, if there is probability of guilt the accused person is held for further proceedings by a higher court or is temporarily released on his bail. The practice of holding suspected

[1] Gilbert Geis, "Preliminary Hearings and the Press," *U.C.L.A. Law Review*, 8:397–414, March, 1961.

persons for further legal proceedings after this preliminary hearing also is called detention.

RELEASE BEFORE TRIAL.   A person who has been arrested may be held at the police station for a few hours or days and then released without a court appearance, he may secure a release on a writ of *habeas corpus*, he may secure a temporary release on bail, giving financial security for his return, or he may secure temporary release on his own recognizance or promise to return.

*Unofficial release.*  Persons are frequently released by the police without court appearance. In some instances, such release follows illegal arrest and, hence, illegal detention, but in other cases it is considered the most practical system for dealing with persons rightfully arrested for minor offenses. Illegal arrests, for example, are arrests on suspicion, arrests made for failing to bribe an officer, arrests made for the purpose of forcing gambling places and houses of prostitution to pay graft, and arrests made when there is no evidence of crime. They are followed by illegal detention and, usually, release without trial. This system of release is also used in cases of intoxication, disorderliness, vagrancy, and other misdemeanors, and when so used it is known as the Golden Rule disposition. Intoxicated persons are often held in the police lockup only until they are sober; vagrants are held until they agree to leave the community; and disorderly persons are held until it is believed that their behavior will be orderly. Of 11,048 adults arrested for drunkenness in Detroit in 1958, 59 percent were charged with the offense, 40 percent were released under the Golden Rule, and 1 percent were released by the police under other conditions. Of a total of 26,830 arrests of adults for all other offenses (not counting city traffic offenses), 3,847 or 14.3 percent were released without prosecution. In addition, 666 persons were held as police witnesses and 26,176 persons were detained for investigation. In sum, of a total of 68,567 adult offenders officially handled by the Detroit police, 35,200 or 51.3 percent were released by the police without court appearance.[2] Reports from other cities indicate that the percentage in Detroit is not unusual. Formally, these releases are, with a few exceptions, unjustified. Informally, however, the unofficial release procedure often represents the selection of the best method available at the time. For example, the arrest and temporary detention of intoxicated persons protects them as well as the public. If these persons were taken into court they would either be dismissed or fined, and since most of them would be unable to pay fines they would be committed to a house of correction for a short period. None of these methods is of great value in solv-

[2] Detroit Police Department, *Annual Report, 1958* (Detroit: Police Record Bureau, 1959), pp. 48–52.

ing the problem of intoxication, but the police method of release probably makes as great a contribution as the alternative methods and is much cheaper. It is evident, however, that if the problems of intoxication are to be solved, more constructive methods must be made available. Some of the other unofficial releases are probably much like those which occur in cases of intoxication.

*Release by writ of habeas corpus.* So that citizens are protected against false arrest and illegal detention, *habeas corpus* writs may be obtained from courts to force the detaining officials to bring the arrested person before a magistrate immediately for a preliminary hearing. If no just reason for holding him can be shown, he must be discharged from custody. Although the arrested person usually must apply to the court for such a writ, some judges are known to have issued them informally from their homes, and writs also have been issued immediately after arrest. Some professional and organized criminals have attorneys constantly prepared to secure a writ of *habeas corpus*, and sometimes the attorney arrives at the police station with the writ even before the police arrive with the prisoner. The police, in order to prevent this system of "springing," in order to have an opportunity to question the arrested person, and for other reasons, frequently detain defendants incommunicado, sometimes for weeks. This is done by hiding the suspect in a "cold-storage" cell, or by shifting him frequently from one lockup to another. It is reported that some years ago a series of fifteen outlying station houses in Detroit constituted a "loop" and that prisoners were shifted from one to another of these stations for a period of a week or ten days and then released.[3] The abuse of the use of the *habeas corpus* writ by attorneys has, then, prompted police to use illegal methods to avoid its use.

*Release on bail.* The principal official method of securing release before trial is the use of bail. A promise is made to pay the state a specified sum of money if the accused person does not appear for trial. "Bail" is the name for the financial security which is pledged, but the term also is used to refer to the entire system whereby one is released after having given such security. The right to bail is guaranteed in the constitutions of thirty-five of the states in all cases except capital charges. As a general rule, magistrates are required by law to grant release on bail, but the law also gives them wide discretion as to the amount and character of the bail.[4] They can effectively prevent release by setting the bail at a high figure, or by requiring security of a kind which is extremely difficult to obtain.

In early English law a person charged with a crime could be released if a

[3] E. J. Hopkins, *Our Lawless Police* (New York: Viking Press, 1931), p. 126.
[4] Arthur E. Wood and John B. Waite, *Crime and Its Treatment*, New York: American Book Company, 1941, p. 407.

friend would act as his keeper and thus act as surety for his appearance in court. The person who acted as surety was liable for the punishment if the accused was not delivered. Later the surety pledged his property, which generally consisted of his house or land, but still remained essentially the keeper of the prisoner. The real estate of friends is still used as security in small towns and to some extent in cities, but in the city many defendants have no friends who own property available for bail. Professional bondsmen and corporate surety companies have filled this gap, and such agencies now provide surety. In New York City, from 40 to 50 percent of the pledges are made by surety companies, but in other cities such companies secure less of this business. In most places an accused person can pay a relatively small fee to a company or to a professional bondsman for providing the financial security necessary to his release. The security thus secured is called a bond or a "bail-bond," and it has become customary to refer to the status of one who has been released on bail as "out on bond." The usual bail for a person charged with burglary is about $5,000. Surety companies generally will provide a $5,000 bond for about $100 or $150, but in some communities the rates are much higher than this. In New York, surety companies and professional bondsmen are limited by law to fees equal to 3 percent of the bond. The Municipal Court of Chicago has set a maximum fee of 10 percent of the first $100 of the bond and 5 percent for each additional hundred dollars.

In some jurisdictions it has become common practice to require traffic offenders to provide what is called "cash bail." This is a sum fixed at an amount approximately equal to the fine customarily imposed for the offense of which the person is accused. If one who has paid such a sum desires a trial he appears in traffic court at a specified time, but if he does not desire a trial he simply does not appear, forfeiting the cash. The great majority of persons who post such sums forfeit them, and a large proportion of offenders consider them as fines. In practice, one who forfeits such a cash sum is absolved from further liability for the offense, forfeiture of the cash being tacitly accepted by the police and courts as satisfactory. Although it relieves the police and courts of a great deal of work, there is no real legal basis for this custom. Ordinarily, bail is in no sense a punitive measure, and the forfeiture of bail does not absolve the offender from prosecution. He can be re-arrested and tried, and even if he is acquitted the forfeited bail is not returned to him.

The ordinary system of providing financial security for persons charged with crimes has been criticized on several points. The chief criticism is that police departments and courts have inadequate facilities for determining whether financial security is needed, how much security is needed, and how adequate the security which is offered may be. The amount required is therefore generally determined by the charge against the defendant rather than by his character and responsibility. This bears heavily on the poor and makes bail practically prohibitive for them. A study of bail in New York City found that almost half of the accused persons could not obtain the funds for bail and that 38 percent of the persons unable to post bail were detained for from 50 to 99 days prior to the trial. The authors believed that bail was often intentionally set so high that the accused would not be able to obtain the necessary funds, so as to give the offender a "taste of jail" or to "protect society." This practice was condemned in the following terms:

It is fundamental that the state has no right to punish a person until his guilt has been established beyond a reasonable doubt. And there is no support in the law for the proposition that a person may be imprisoned because of the speculative possibility that he may commit a crime.[5]

In effect, therefore, a poor person of excellent character and responsibility charged with a crime of which he is completely innocent has no alternative to detention in an institution.[6] This hardship cannot be defended by the argument that poor persons should not commit crimes, for many of them are actually innocent. On the other hand, the financial security has little value if the defendant is not responsible and is not willing to return to court. Since the court has no facilities for investigating the security which is offered and since professional bondsmen as a group are closely allied with the underworld, the security is generally inadequate. Some years ago Moley described a professional bondsman in St. Louis who had been arrested twelve times but who was security for bonds aggregating $670,295, although his real property was worth not more than $20,000 and the encumbrances against this property were greater than its assessed valuation.[7] This is an exaggerated case so far as amounts are concerned, but is not exaggerated so far as the principle is concerned. Sometimes bondsmen do not even own the property they schedule. If one court refuses to accept the property as security, the bondsman "peddles" it to other courts until he finds one which will accept it. He feels secure in doing this because he

[5] Caleb Foote, James P. Markle, and Edward A. Wooley, "Compelling Appearance in Court: Administration of Bail in Philadelphia," *University of Pennsylvania Law Review*, 102:1031–1079, June, 1954. See also Charles Ares and Herbert Sturz, "Bail and the Indigent Accused," *Crime and Delinquency*, 8:12–20, January, 1962.

[6] See Caleb Foote, "The Bail System and Equal Justice," *Federal Probation*, 23:43–48, September, 1959.

[7] Raymond Moley, *Our Criminal Courts* (New York: Minton, Balch, 1930), pp. 49–50. See also Don T. Blackiston, *The Judge, the Defendant, and Criminal Law Administration* (unpublished Ph.D. dissertation, University of Chicago, 1952).

knows that relatively few bonds are forfeited and that even when they are forfeited the court does not force collection.

*2)* A second criticism of the bail system is that it involves collusion between the police, the courts, and the professional bondsmen. The occasional offender asks the police how he can secure bail, and the police suggest a bondsman or inform a runner for a bondsman that the defendant has no bondsman. Fees are then divided with officers of the police and courts. The bondsman also acts as "fixer" for professional criminals.

*1) / bureau* Several suggestions for improving the bail system have been made, and there has been a slight tendency to follow them in practice. First, it has been proposed that one bureau should have complete control of all the work of granting bail, recommending forfeitures, and collecting forfeited bonds in a city. This organization has been arranged in several cities with varying degrees of success. It results in better inspection of securities so that bonds can always be kept within the value of the securities listed, and it prevents bondsmen from "peddling" bonds from one court to another. It appears to have no effect on other aspects of the bail problem.[8] Second, *2) invest. char. of def.* it is argued that this bureau or a section of this bureau should be responsible for investigating the character of the defendant for the purpose of determining whether release should be granted without financial security, or under no conditions at all. Under present constitutional provisions an outright refusal of bail is not permissible in the United States in most cases, but such refusal is permissible in England. Probably a great proportion of offenders could be released on their own recognizance, a system which eliminates the necessity for bail and for detention. Under the sponsorship of the Manhattan Bail Project, law students interview and appraise the responsibility of adult prisoners appearing in Magistrates Felony courts and then either recommend or do not recommend that the man be released on his promise to return to court at a given time for trial. Of the first 275 defendants released under this system, only three did not fulfill *3) hearing promptness* their promises.[9] Finally, it has been suggested that bail would not be necessary if hearing and trials were more prompt.

As an alternative to the existing conditions of detention, bail has decided advantages. Perhaps the most important of these is that it permits persons who are merely accused of crime to avoid the financial hardships, the physical unpleasantness, and the punitive aspects of being detained in a police lockup or jail.

[8] "Detroit Solves the Bail Problem," *Journal of the American Judicature Society,* 16:143–149, February, 1933.
[9] Herbert Sturz, "An Alternative to the Bail System," *Federal Probation,* 23:12–17, December, 1962.

**PUNITIVE ASPECTS OF DETENTION.**   When a person is charged with a crime it is important that he should be available for trial. However, under the American system of government, the method of securing his presence at the trial should involve a minimum of hardship on him, since he might be innocent. The rule of presumption of innocence until guilt is proved, strictly speaking, refers only to the preponderance of evidence in a trial in court. The rule of evidence is that the defendant is assumed to be innocent rather than guilty, and the evidence must then be sufficient to convict. But this rule is, with limitations required by practical considerations, considered sound social policy in other situations. Of course, if the rule were made absolute there would be no justification even for arrest, let alone for detention before trial. For practical reasons it is necessary that the state apprehend and detain persons suspected of crime, thus at times imposing hardships upon persons who may be innocent.

The imposition of these hardships could be non-punitive, but it is, in fact, punitive. The constitutional view is that even when persons are actually guilty they are to be treated, so far as practicable, on the presumption of innocence. In this view, detention is something like confiscation of property for public purposes, or drafting men for the army in time of war, or requiring attendance at public schools, or summoning citizens for service on a jury, where the hardships are reduced to a minimum consistent with public purpose. Furthermore, it is observed that, especially for first offenders, the arrested person is in a very impressionistic condition and sympathetic handling and understanding will have great effect at this point, just as unnecessary and unwarranted hardships will be very damaging. In general, therefore, the official view is that those persons who are detained awaiting trial should be treated at least as well as those drafted into the army and that the conditions of life in a detention institution should be at least equal to those in an army camp.

In the same way that police have sometimes justified punitive methods in making arrests, the suggestion has been made that the hardships of detention should be severe and punitive. Generally, the argument is that a large proportion of guilty persons escape conviction and that they should at least suffer severe hardships in detention, as a deterrent to others or as a retributive or reformative measure. However, the hardships are imposed upon innocent as well as guilty persons, and no one has argued that people can be kept innocent by punishing the innocent. Even when this unofficial policy is not voiced it is the informal principle on which most detention institutions are operated. This may be observed in the types of institutions which are used as places of detention and in the manner in which these institutions are maintained and operated.

*Types of detention institutions.* The institutions used for detention are of the following four types: the station lockup, the small town municipal jail or lockup, the county jail, and the special detention institutions for women and children. Station lockups are maintained in connection with the precinct stations in large cities. Few criminals serve sentences in these institutions, and few suspected persons are held for court proceedings for more than a few days. Persons arrested in the precinct are kept in custody until arrangements for a preliminary hearing or a trial can be made, or they are released without trial after a few hours. Small town municipal jails usually are under control of police departments or marshals, and they resemble city police station lockups. However, in addition to persons awaiting hearings or trials these institutions are populated by offenders serving sentences, usually in lieu of payment of fines ordered by the court. Very frequently the personnel of these institutions make few, if any, distinctions between those persons awaiting court proceedings and those being punished. There are approximately 11,000 police and village lockups in the United States. About half of the persons detained in such lockups awaiting hearings or trials are not convicted.

County jails usually are under the control of the sheriff, and they generally are used for three different purposes. First, they serve as lockups for persons arrested by the sheriff's staff and awaiting trials or hearings. Second, they are used as penal institutions, ordinarily for misdemeanants whose sentences are under one year. No serious attempt is made to treat these offenders, and they are not ordinarily carefully segregated from those persons merely awaiting court proceedings. Third, county jails serve as detention institutions for persons who are accused of felonies and who, in preliminary hearings, have been bound over to a grand jury or ordered to await disposition by higher courts. Of 31,187 persons detained in Wisconsin county jails overnight or longer in 1956, only 6,811 were sentenced prisoners.[10] Ordinarily, if the court to which a person is taken after having been detained in a police, village, or county lockup has final jurisdiction, as in misdemeanor cases, it tries the case and either releases the individual or fixes a penalty; but if the court does not have final jurisdiction in a case and serves to provide a preliminary hearing only it may discharge the individual from custody, release him on bail, or commit him to the county jail to await further proceedings by a grand jury or a higher court. Persons held for trial in the federal courts usually are detained in county jails; in 1960 the average number of days of detention for all such persons aged 22 and over was 26; for persons aged 18–21 the average was 27, and for those

[10] Sanger B. Powers, "Day-Parole of Misdemeanants," *Federal Probation*, 22:42–46, December, 1958.

17 and under the average was 8.[11] No recent data on the period of detention of those awaiting trial in other courts are available. About one-third
of those in county jails are not convicted.

Special institutions and procedures for children have been developed in
some jurisdictions. Children within the juvenile court age are generally
permitted to remain at home after a complaint is made against them; a
summons is issued for the parents to bring the children to court at the
appointed time. But it is frequently necessary to detain children because
of the serious nature of the offense, the condition of the home, or the
possibility that the child will try to escape from the jurisdiction of the
court. Jails and lockups are frequently used as places of detention for juveniles, but in most states recent laws have placed restrictions on this use of
such institutions. In general practice, however, these laws are frequently
violated, especially in districts that do not have specially organized juvenile courts. A study of 118,772 children detained in various ways in the
fiscal year 1929–1930 showed that nearly 15 percent of them were detained
in jails and police stations; 65 percent in public detention homes; and the
others scattered in private orphanages, in shelters and homes, in boarding
homes, in hospitals and sanitoria, and in almshouses.[12] It has been estimated that between 50,000 and 75,000 children are still held annually in
county jails and police lockups,[13] and in April, 1950, a one-day check
showed 1,244 children under nineteen in detention homes and 6,681 in
local jails and workhouses.[14] Various arguments have been presented regarding the comparative values of public detention homes, private orphanages and shelters, and private boarding homes for the detention of children. The general criterion used for evaluation is the extent to which
effective physical detention is combined with a non-punitive program for
those detained. Thus some institutions of any one type may be satisfactory,
and other institutions of the same may be unsatisfactory. It is generally
agreed that specially designed and constructed institutions are most suitable to implementation of the treatment reaction to juvenile delinquency.[15]

[11] U.S. Bureau of Prisons, *Federal Prisons, 1960* (Washington: Department of
Justice, 1961), p. 60.
[12] Florence M. Warner, *Juvenile Detention in the United States* (Chicago: University of Chicago Press, 1933).
[13] Sherwood Norman, "New Goals for Juvenile Detention," in Paul W. Tappan,
Editor, *Contemporary Correction* (New York: McGraw-Hill, 1951), pp. 336–346.
[14] Herbert A. Bloch and Frank T. Flynn, *Delinquency* (New York: Random House,
1955), p. 269.
[15] A full discussion of specialized institutions for detention of juveniles will be
found in Sherwood Norman, *The Design and Construction of Detention Homes for
the Juvenile Court* (New York: National Probation Association, 1947); and Sherwood
Norman, *Detention Practices* (New York: National Probation and Parole Association,
1960).

The personnel of juvenile detention institutions usually consider mere detention to be insufficient, just as do the personnel of detention institutions for adults. The important difference between them is that in most adult institutions the desire is to supplement detention with punishment, while in most juvenile institutions the desire is to supplement detention with treatment.

*The maintenance and operation of detention institutions.* In general, the physical conditions in the county and city detention institutions are decidedly worse than the conditions in the state prisons where criminals are confined after conviction of serious offenses. Those who are officially presumed to be innocent, many of whom are actually innocent and almost all of whom are detained because they do not have the money or influence to obtain release on bail, are subjected to conditions much worse than those for persons already convicted of serious crimes. Criticisms of these conditions have been made for nearly a century, by both native and foreign observers. The president of the International Prison Congress in 1907 said that nothing as bad as the American jails had been known in the history of the world except in the prisons of Turkey in the thirteenth century. The conditions most frequently criticized at present are filth, vermin, fire hazard, inadequate food, inadequate plumbing, inadequate lighting and ventilation, lack of segregation of persons with infectious diseases, universal idleness, supervision of women prisoners by male attendants, lack of provision for medical care, special privileges for favored prisoners (sometimes including a key to the prison door), and inadequate security against escape. Fishman, who was inspector of jails for the federal government for some time, defined the jail thus:

*Jail:* An unbelievably filthy institution in which are confined men and women serving sentences for misdemeanors and crimes, and men and women not under sentence who are simply awaiting trial. With few exceptions, having no segregation of the unconvicted from the convicted, the well from the diseased, the youngest and most impressionable from the most degraded and hardened. Usually swarming with bedbugs, roaches, lice, and other vermin; has an ordor of disinfectant and filth which is appalling; supports in complete idleness countless thousands of able-bodied men and women, and generally affords ample time and opportunity to assure inmates a complete course in every kind of viciousness and crime. A melting pot in which the worst elements of the raw material in the criminal world are brought forth blended and turned out in absolute perfection.[16]

[16] Joseph F. Fishman, *Crucibles of Crime* (New York: Cosmopolis Press, 1923), pp. 13–14.

The federal government inspects county jails for the purpose of selecting institutions in which federal prisoners may be detained. In an inspection of 3,115 jails only 8 rated 80 or higher (100 was the perfect rating); 3,082 or 99 percent rated below 60; and 78 percent rated below 50.[17] In 1959 federal men inspected 641 jails in 45 states and rated 401 "fair" or better and 241 less than "fair."[18] State surverys generally show the same conditions. In 1956, California inspectors found that only five of the state's 58 county jails met a minimum standard, while thirty-three were rated "poor" or "very poor."[19] In a survey of Chicago's police lockups in 1946, 7 were rated "good," 10 "fair," and 22 "poor." The investigators reported the following:

Thirty-three lockups [studied] contain 336 cells, which housed 612 people on December 15, 1946. Eighteen of the 33 had repugnant odors. Some of the cell rooms were so malodorous as to affect the entire station. Twenty-six lockups had filthy walls which were also in need of major repairs. Two had as the only toilet facility a trough of constantly running water, which occasionally spread its contents over the entire floor area. . . . Twenty-five of the lockup keepers reported that their lockups were infested with vermin. Many reported that bedbugs, lice, cockroaches, mice and rats were so troublesome as to require the use of a gasoline torch to "burn them out." . . . With the exception of the women's lockups, prisoners are provided with two slices of bread, a slice of bologna, and a cup of black unsweetened coffee three times daily, if they desire.[20]

From the viewpoint of differential association, the fundamental criticism of the jail is that it permits association of convicted and unconvicted prisoners. Approximately half the inmates of county jails are awaiting trial, and most of the others are serving sentences imposed after conviction. The effect of this association with convicted prisoners not only leads the person accused of crime to identify with criminals, but such contacts often cause moral deterioration. The sheriff directing one of the nation's largest county jails, in Cook County, Illinois, criticized his own and other county jails as follows:

17 U.S. Bureau of Prisons, *Federal Prisons, 1950* (Washington: Department of Justice, 1951), p. 92.
18 U. S. Bureau of Prisons, *Federal Prisons, 1959* (Washington: Department of Justice, 1960), p. 13.
19 Special Study Commission, *The County Jails of California: An Evaluation* (Sacramento: Board of Corrections, 1957), p. 20.
20 Eugene S. Zemans, *Held Without Bail: Physical Aspects of the Police Lockups of the City of Chicago, 1947–1948* (Chicago: John Howard Association, 1949), pp. 42–43. Reprinted by permission of the publisher. See also B. Raymond Dejoie, *Chicago Police Lockups* (Chicago: John Howard Association, 1959).

County jails, as presently constituted, are for all practical purposes agencies for the creation of a community of interest on the part of those who violate the law. They establish contacts and a continuing association among law violators. They afford a machinery for perpetuating and transmitting the culture and tradition of crime. And they insure the maturation of delinquent and criminal attitudes as well as professional criminal skills among the young by the indiscriminate lodging of all types of persons under one framework of concrete and steel.[21]

It is possible to exaggerate the importance of contacts with convicted criminals, however. It is not clear that detention in a city police lockup in which no convicted prisoners are held is any less injurious than detention in a county jail in company with convicted prisoners. In the lockups, inmates with long prison records seldom are segregated from persons accused of their first crimes. And detention under existing conditions involves association with criminality even when it does not involve association with criminals.

EXPLANATIONS OF PUNITIVE CONDITIONS IN JAILS. Punitive and repulsive physical conditions in detention institutions have existed for centuries and have become traditional. In England, John Howard's investigations during the latter part of the eighteenth century, and Mrs. Fry's work during the early part of the nineteenth century, were investigations of institutions similar to our police lockups, for the prisons in those periods were used primarily for detention prior to trial. Criticisms of the jails in America— made three-quarters of a century ago, a half-century ago, and a quarter of a century ago, and only a few years ago—all sound very familiar.[22] The persistence of physically unpleasant and punitive conditions may be explained partially by the expense of improvements and by inertia among officials. As one authority states:

Jails mean jobs. Jails mean income. Jails mean power. Jails mean influence. Jails mean patronage. Jails mean votes. Against such a formidable defense the offense must devise an attack of atomic power.[23]

[21] Joseph D. Lohman, Mid-Term Report (Chicago: Cook County Sheriff's Office, 1956), p. 23. See also Vera Connolly, "Kangaroo Courts," Collier's, August 18, 1945, pp. 22 ff.
[22] E. C. Wines and T. W. Dwight, Report on the Prisons and Reformatories of the United States and Canada (New York State Assembly Document No. 35, 1867), Vol. II, pp. 314–336; New Jersey, Report of Prison Inquiry Commission (Trenton, 1917), Vol. II, pp. 321–325; Fishman, op. cit.; Louis N. Robinson, Jails: Care and Treatment of Misdemeanant Prisoners in the United States (Philadelphia: Winston, 1944).
[23] Roberts J. Wright, "The Jail and Misdemeanant Institutions," in Paul W. Tappan, Editor, Contemporary Correction (New York: McGraw-Hill, 1951), pp. 310–322. Reprinted by permission of the publishers.

Thus, sheriffs and other officials responsible for detention institutions resist change because the existing conditions are highly profitable, both in the form of influence and power and in income.[24] Jailers often are paid "turn-key" fees and are granted a certain sum for the daily maintenance of each prisoner in their custody. If the sum is one dollar and the daily costs can be reduced to 20 cents, the jailer is able to pocket 80 cents per prisoner per day. In some communities numerous arrests are made solely for the fees that the police and jailer can collect. While the incumbents have merely inherited, not created, such a system, it is understandable that they should resist attempts to improve the physical conditions in prisons by eliminating it.

However, resistance of officials is not a sufficient explanation; there is some popular sympathy with existing conditions. This sympathy takes two different forms. First, accusation is in fact taken as equivalent to proof of criminality. The person who is arrested and detained for court proceedings is identified with the persons already convicted of crime. Then, since the societal reaction to the crimes of persons confined in jails usually is punitive, those who are accused but not convicted are punished. But why does the public fail to make the distinction between those awaiting trial and those serving sentences? Perhaps it is because the public has so few contacts with either type of case. The agencies of mass communication ordinarily report in some detail the cases of persons who have been convicted, but only in the most sensational cases are acquittals reported. Also, many persons take the position that even one who is merely accused of crime is at fault and, hence, deserving of punishment. The argument used is that if the accused person has been leading an exemplary life he would not have been accused or would have been released by the police. Second, only the poor are held in jail for trial, and it is almost traditional to discriminate against the poor. A person in wealth or moderate comfort can secure release on bail in most instances. The attitude of the public is, then, one of indifference; it is not in touch with the situation, looks down upon those who get into jail, and does not suffer the hardships in person that would lead to insistence on modification. No matter how jails are operated the public is complacent. The poor do not have the power or influence to change the situation. Those who have been in jail, whether they were found guilty or not, try to conceal this fact rather than advertise it. Perhaps the situation will be improved in this country as in England, where Bernard Shaw said that the day of improvement was at hand because in a

[24] See E. R. Cass, "Jails for Profit," *Prison World*, 7:3 ff., September, 1945; Francis F. Kane, "House of Detention for Untried Prisoners," *Prison World*, 12:3-4, January, 1950.

short time every honest man would have spent some time in jail and would know what jails were like.

**ALTERNATIVES TO PRESENT-DAY DETENTION INSTITUTIONS.**   Many persons and agencies have suggested programs for modifying the methods of detention. In general, these suggestions have been made with consideration for the view that the methods of detention should conform to the constitutional notion that the accused should be treated as if they were innocent. Also, it is thought that certain modifications will reduce the crime rates by eliminating many contacts with criminal behavior patterns and by increasing the prestige of law-enforcement officers. Finally, it is believed that detention facilities for adults should, like the detention facilities for juveniles, adopt treatment methods which will at least assist accused persons with the problems arising from the fact that they have been detained. The following are some of the important suggestions which have been made:

(a) Bail and release on personal recognizance should be used more extensively, and the number of arrests should be reduced. It has been indicated previously that 60 percent of the arrests in certain cities result in release without prosecution. In addition, between a third and a half of the persons who are prosecuted are dismissed without conviction. It is not possible to determine what proportion of the dismissals results from inefficiency of the courts, but it is probable that both the courts and the police share responsibility. The summons may be substituted for arrest in many cases. Summonses are used now almost exclusively for violations of traffic regulations.

(b) The courts should dispose of cases more rapidly. The shorter the period of detention of the average prisoner, the smaller is the number detained at a particular time. The survey of the Cook County jail reported that the jail would contain only 29 people at one time if the average period of detention were one day, 200 if it were one week, 887 if it were one month, and 10,642 if it were one year. Experiences in several courts have demonstrated that speedier justice is possible without injury to defendants, and this will shorten the period of detention in jail.

(c) The physical conditions and the programs of jails and lockups should be improved. Perhaps this is the suggestion which is made most frequently. Even if the number of persons committed and the length of the period of detention were greatly reduced, it would still be sound policy to improve the health and sanitary conditions of the places of detention. However, this is not at all an easy suggestion to follow because the detained persons include many who are intoxicated at the time of arrest, or are habitual drunkards and vagrants, or are diseased, or are ignorant of the conditions of hygiene. But institutions can be made fireproof, sanitary plumbing can be installed, facilities for bathing can be made available, diseased persons can be segregated, organized activities can be provided. Some jails provide opportunity for voluntary but paid employment, recreational activities, reading, organized educational classes, moving pictures, and psychological counseling. The complete and practically universal idleness of the jail and lockup could be eliminated. It is suggested further that such standards should be maintained by a system of inspection by state officials, who would have authority to close the jails and lockups which do not meet requirements. Indiana, Minnesota, New Jersey, Oklahoma, and Wisconsin now have regular state supervision of jails and lockups, and certain other states inspect jails and lockups "on complaint." Virginia has adopted a plan whereby a state board is given almost complete control over jails and lockups; the board is authorized to prescribe minimum standards for the institutions and to prohibit the confinement of prisoners in institutions not meeting the standards. In Massachusetts, the state Division of Youth Services has these powers in reference to institutions for detention of children.

Also, it is pointed out that if the standards mentioned are to be maintained, it probably will be necessary to enlarge the geographical area served by particular detention institutions. The county apparently is too small a unit to maintain an institution of this nature, especially if the convicted prisoners and the responsible unconvicted prisoners are removed. Counties could combine, or the state could establish jail districts, or the state could own and operate the places of detention in which persons are held awaiting trial for longer than two or three days. Moreover, if larger units were organized, specialized institutions for special classes could be established. This has already started in the detention institutions for women and children but can be developed outside of the large cities only by state management of the places of detention.

(d) Persons awaiting trial should be separated from convicted criminals. Ordinarily, authorities believe that this could be best accomplished by maintaining convicted prisoners in one institution and detained persons in another.[25] Indiana, California, Wisconsin, Virginia, and numerous other states operate camps, farms, and colonies which take many of the convicted misdemeanants out of the county jails. Some cities and counties have provided farm work for the convicted prisoners, who are housed separately

[25] See Hans W. Mattick, *The Cook County Jail* (Chicago: Sheriff's Office, 1957), pp. 14–15; and Louis Partnow, "Detention and the Untried and Probation," *Prison Journal*, 38:22–26, April, 1958.

from those awaiting trial. Thirty-nine percent of the inmates sentenced to the fifty-eight county jails in California are assigned to camps and farms. Los Angeles County operates a 2,800-acre farm for about 1,000 men, and the city of Los Angeles maintains a 600 acre farm for alcoholics. Numerous jurisdictions have established "half-way houses" for chronic alcoholics, and it has been claimed that about a third of the men treated in such houses do not continue as problem drinkers.[26] Of 95 chronic alcoholics sentenced to the Seattle city jail and given special rehabilitative attention by the Seattle police, 38 percent avoided arrest during a six-month post-treatment period.[27] In Wisconsin, misdemeanants sentenced under the Huber law are permitted to work at regular jobs outside the jail.[28] If such state and county programs are to become widespread it will, again, be necessary to enlarge the geographical area served by a particular institution.

(e) Dependents of those detained in jail awaiting trial should be cared for by the state or other governmental unit in charge of the jail. If the state finds it necessary to detain in an institution a person against whom a charge of crime is made, the duty of providing for those dependent upon the detained person follows logically as a corollary. Whether the person is subsequently found guilty should make no difference in the care during the period of detention before trial.

(f) Those who are acquitted should be indemnified for financial losses suffered as the result of the detention. Such a system has prevailed for a long time in some of the European countries. By act of 1911, Massachusetts authorized indemnification, in case of acquittal or discharge, for financial losses if the detention awaiting trial exceeded six months. But there is no reason for such a long minimum period. The general arguments in favor of indemnification are as follows: First, when private property is taken for public use the owner is compensated; likewise when the state requires an individual to give his time or services to the state, he is compensated. The state does not compensate the person who is deprived of his property because the state was enriched but because the individual suffered a loss at the hands of the state. The person detained for trial is deprived of his liberty for the sake of public welfare; if the trial shows

26 Edward Blacker and David Kantor, "Half-way Houses for Problem Drinkers," Federal Probation, 24:18–23, June, 1960.

27 Joan K. Jackson, Ronald J. Fagan, and Roscoe C. Burr, "The Seattle Police Department Rehabilitation Project for Chronic Alcoholics," Federal Probation 22:36–41, June, 1958.

28 Wisconsin Service Associates, Wisconsin's Huber Law in Action (Milwaukee: Author, 1958); Martin E. Wyrick, "The Area of American Correction that Stood Still," American Journal of Correction, 20:7 ff., May–June, 1958; and Stanley E. Grupp, "Work Release in the United States," Journal of Criminal Law, Criminology and Police Science, 54:267:272, September, 1963.

that this detention was not justified, he should be compensated for the loss which he has suffered for the sake of public welfare. Second, in work-men's compensation laws the state has ruled that an employer, though he is not at fault, must compensate a workman for injuries. The principle involved in indemnification is the same as that of workmen's compensation laws—spread the loss on the public rather than impose it on one individual. Third, indemnification would be desirable because it would tend to prevent needless arrests, would tend to speed up the courts, and would tend to create a public opinion favorable to greater efficiency in police departments, detention institutions, and courts in general.

**DETENTION OF WITNESSES.** The material witness who is detained in a city or county jail awaiting trial has received little consideration until recently. Some years ago the newspapers reported a case of a person who was knocked down and robbed; he could not furnish financial security for his appearance at the trial and he was therefore detained in jail for three months as a material witness while the person accused of the crime was released on bail. During the fiscal year 1940–1941, 241 persons were detained in county jails in New York State as witnesses, and in 1958 the Detroit police detained 666 witnesses. Although witnesses make up an insignificant percentage of the persons handled by law-enforcement and detention personnel, it is important that their rights be respected. Performance of the task of testifying for purposes of public justice should not impose a hardship on these persons. They, like the persons accused of the crimes, are held at the demand of the state and should likewise not be detained unless the necessity is definite, and if detained should be treated in a decent manner. The American Law Institute has proposed that if a witness is unable within three days to secure financial sureties he be examined in the presence of the defendant and his deposition be authorized for use in the trial, in case he is not available at the time of the trial.

## SUGGESTED READINGS

Alexander, Myrl E., *Jail Administration*. Springfield: Thomas, 1957.

Ares, Charles, and Herbert Sturz, "Bail and the Indigent Accused," *Crime and Delinquency*, 8:12–20, January, 1962.

Babst, Dean V., and Joseph C. Gale, *Wisconsin County Jails, 1958–1960*. Madison: Wisconsin Division of Corrections, 1962.

Casey, Roy, "Catchall Jails," *Annals of the American Academy of Political and Social Science*, 293:28–34, May, 1954.

Deutscher, Irwin, "The Petty Offender," *Federal Probation*, 19:12–18, June, 1955.

Foote, Caleb, James P. Markle, and Edward A. Wooley, "Compelling Appearance in Court: Administration of Bail in Philadelphia," University of Pennsylvania Law Review, 102:1031–1079, June, 1954.

Gibson, Evelyn, Time Spent Awaiting Trial. Home Office Research Unit Report No. 2, London: Her Majesty's Stationery Office, 1960.

Grupp, Stanley E., "Work Release in the United States," Journal of Criminal Law, Criminology and Police Science, 54:267–272, September, 1964.

Hendrick, Edward J., "The House of Correction," American Journal of Correction, 20:3–6 ff., May–June, 1958.

Kane, Francis F., "Houses of Detention for Untried Prisoners," Prison World, 12:3–4, January, 1950.

Lewis, O. F., The Development of American Prisons and Prison Customs, 1776–1845. Albany: Prison Association of New York, 1922.

MacCormick, A. H., and J. H. Dooling, "Keeping Children Out of Jails: It Can Be Done," Federal Probation, 13:40–45, September, 1949.

Norman, Sherwood, "New Goals for Juvenile Detention," in Paul W. Tappan, Editor, Contemporary Correction. New York: McGraw-Hill, 1951, pp. 336–346.

Orfield, Lester B., Criminal Precedure from Arrest to Trial. New York: New York University Press, 1947.

Queen, S. A., The Passing of the County Jail. Menasha, Wisconsin: Banta, 1920.

Roberts, John W. and James S. Palermo, "A Study of the Administration of Bail in New York," University of Pennsylvania Law Review, 106:685–730, March, 1958.

Robinson, Louis N., "The Perennial Jail Problem," Journal of Criminal Law and Criminology, 35:369–374, March, 1945.

Stern, Leon T., "Jails: Yesterday and Today," Prison Journal, 25:88–89, July, 1945.

Sturz, Herbert, "An Alternative to the Bail System," Federal Probation, 23:12–17, December, 1962.

Wright, Roberts J., "The Jail and Misdemeanant Institutions," in Paul W. Tappan, Editor, Contemporary Correction. New York: McGraw-Hill, 1951, pp. 310–322.

Zeisel, Hans, Harry Kalven, Jr., and Bernard Buchholz, Delay in the Court. Boston: Little, Brown, 1959.

Zemans, Eugene S., Held Without Bail: Physical Aspects of the Police Lockups of the City of Chicago: 1947–1948. Chicago: John Howard Association, 1949.

# 19. THE CRIMINAL COURT

THE LAWS with which criminal courts are concerned all contain threats of punishment for infraction of specified rules. Consequently, the courts are formally organized primarily for implementation of the punitive societal reaction to crime. While the informal organization of most courts allows court personnel to use discretion as to which guilty persons actually are to be punished, the threat of punishment for all guilty persons always is present. Also, in recent years a number of formal provisions for the use of non-punitive and treatment methods by the criminal courts have been made, but the threat of punishment remains, even for the recipients of the treatment and non-punitive measures. For example, it has become possible for courts to grant probation, which can be non-punitive, to some offenders; but the probationer is constantly under the threat of punishment, for if he does not maintain the conditions of his probation he is imprisoned. As the treatment reaction to crime becomes more popular, the criminal courts may have as their sole function the determination of the guilt or innocence of accused persons, leaving the problem of correcting criminals entirely to outsiders. Under such conditions, the organization of the court system, the duties and activities of court personnel, and the nature of the trial all would be decidedly different from their current status.

ORGANIZATION OF THE AMERICAN COURT SYSTEM. Although there are variations among the states, the organization of the criminal courts includes the following types: (a) Inferior courts, such as justice of the peace courts, police courts, magistrate's courts, municipal courts, and recorder's courts. These inferior courts serve the dual purpose of rendering final decisions, subject to appeal, in minor cases and giving preliminary hearings in felony cases. They also consider release on bail or on the suspected person's own recognizance. (b) Trial courts, such as county courts, district courts, circuit courts, superior courts, and quarter sessions courts. The

*1) decide public hearing*
*2) dispose infer. c. cases*

*trial cout appeals*

county is usually taken as the unit, even when the circuit includes several counties. These courts render final decision, subject to appeal, in cases which have come up from the preliminary hearings, for trial. They also dispose of cases appealed from the inferior courts. (c) Specialized branches of the above-mentioned courts, such as traffic courts, morals courts, and domestic relations courts. These courts deal only with specified types of offenses. (d) Appelate courts and supreme courts. Such courts take cases on appeal from the trial courts, and have original jurisdiction in a restricted field.

Each of these courts is customarily a separate unit. The justices of the peace and the magistrates in a particular city ordinarily act without reference to each other or to other courts, except to consider the possibility of reversal of decisions by higher courts. The work is not well organized or coordinated. However, a slight trend toward coordination of the different courts is evident. For example, in 1905 the legislature of Illinois authorized a municipal court of Chicago to take the place of scattered and uncoordinated justices of the police and of police courts. The chief justice of this court has wide powers in regard to the assignment of judges and cases, and in regard to organization of work. Detroit in 1921 developed a somewhat similar organization, and other cities have done the same. The federal courts were unified in 1922. The development of state judicial councils is another example of the trend toward organization of court work. Such councils collect statistics and make suggestions for new legislation dealing with changes in court procedures and administration. Also, in some states associations of judges and of prosecuting attorneys have taken positive action toward coordination of the various units in the court system.

It has been suggested that all the work of criminal justice should be integrated. The police, the courts, the prisons, the probation and parole boards, and perhaps other related agencies would, according to this plan, be brought together under one director.[1] At present they are distinct units, in accordance with the theory that judicial and executive branches should be separate, and consequently they are frequently working at cross purposes.

INITIATION OF PROSECUTION AND THE GRAND JURY. Prosecution in misdemeanor cases is customarily initiated by complaint of a victim or witness of the offense; frequently the police officer who makes the arrest is the

---

[1] University of Chicago Conference on Probation, Prisons, and Parole, *Report of the Committee on Fair Hearings*, June 3, 1949 (mimeographed), p. 7.

complaining witness. The complaint and evidence are presented in the inferior court and the whole matter settled there, subject to an occasional appeal.

In felony cases the procedure is more complicated. The complaint is made by a victim or witness and the prosecutor or his assistant hears the evidence. If he decides that the case should be prosecuted, he must prepare the evidence of presentation before the inferior court where the defendant is arraigned. If the inferior court decides the evidence is sufficient, the prosecutor must in many states present the evidence again to the grand jury.[2] If the grand jury regards the evidence as sufficient, the offender is indicted, and the prosecutor must then present the evidence in the trial court. This involves one informal preliminary hearing of the evidence by the prosecutor and two formal preliminary hearings before the case goes to trial, and this whole procedure is sometimes necessary even if the accused person pleads guilty.

However, the tendency is toward permissive use of initiation by "information," rather than the absolute requirement of an indictment or the absolute prohibition of an indictment. At present only fifteen states require indictments in all felony cases. Twenty-three states permit the use of either the indictment or an accusation in writing, called an "information," by the prosecuting attorney in all felony cases. Ten states require indictments in certain felony cases but permit initiation of prosecution by information in other types of felony cases.[3] For almost a century, the State of Connecticut has permitted the initiation of prosecutions by information in most felony cases, and the tendency elsewhere has been toward elimination of the duplication found in the grand jury system. Those who favor the use of the information claim that the indictment does not protect the accused person, that it encumbers the whole process, that it delays decisions and thus facilitates the acquittal of the accused, that it is generally a perfunctory rubber-stamping of the prosecutor's evidence, and that it is a useless expense. Hall analyzed these criticisms and showed that their validity is by no means demonstrated.[4] The possibility of the indictment as

[2] The term "grand" came into use because in England the number of jurors, originally, was twenty-three, almost double the number composing the trial or "petit" jury, twelve. In some states, twenty-three is still the rule, but in other states, sixteen are required, while in two states the maximum size of the jury has been reduced to seven in one and five in the other. See Lewis Mayers, *The American Legal System*, Revised Edition (New York: Harper and Row, 1964), p. 67.

[3] R. Lee Benson, *The Grand Jury* (Baltimore: Research Division of the Legislative Council of Maryland, 1958), pp. 33–36.

[4] Jerome Hall, "Analysis of Criticisms of the Grand Jury," *Journal of Criminal Law and Criminology*, 22:692–704, January–February, 1932.

a check on the prosecutor's information is desirable, even if it is seldom used.[5]

The grand jury also has authority to initiate general investigations, but since the evidence in most cases must be collected and presented by the prosecutor, this work has not been very effective. A severe criticism of the grand jury from this point of view was made by the foreman of the Cuyahoga County Grand Jury, for the autumn term of 1933, in which he showed the helplessness of a grand jury which was anxious to make an investigation of banking practices, racketeering, police corruption, and other serious and organized forms of lawlessness. Because of the inactivity of the prosecutor in regard to these forms of lawlessness, the grand jury was confined to minor routine cases.[6]

Since about 1940 the United States Supreme Court has been holding that grand juries and trial juries alike ought to be bodies truly representative of the community, in the sense of being cross-sections or representative samples from the community. However, an analysis of grand jury service in the United States Criminal Court, Southern District of California, has shown that the principle of a representative jury has not been operative.[7] Instead, the membership of the grand juries shows considerable economic and social bias. During the years 1935 to 1947, the persons nominated for grand jury service included four times a representative number of proprietors, managers, and officials, and one and one-half times a representative number of professional and semiprofessional workers. On the lower economic levels, only 26 craftsmen, foremen, and kindred workers were nominated, whereas 167 would have been nominated if the panel had been representative. Similarly, the representative number of operatives was 198, but only two were nominated in the thirteen year period.

THE PROSECUTOR. The prosecutor is the most important person in the judicial system under present conditions. The prosecutor determines whether a particular case shall be prosecuted. He determines whether a compromise shall be accepted, which generally means a plea of guilt of a lesser offense in return for a recommendation for mitigation of penalty. He is responsible for the organization and presentation of evidence before the court, and upon his efficiency in doing this the decision of the court depends. He is generally very influential in regard to the disposition of cases, sug-

[5] A. A. Bruce, "The Judge and the Grand Jury," *Journal of Criminal Law and Criminology*, 23:10–19, May–June, 1932; Raymond Moley, *Politics and Criminal Prosecution* (New York: Minton, Balch, 1929), Chapter 6; Wayne L. Morse, "A Survey of the Grand Jury System," *Oregon Law Review*, 10:119–275, 1931.

[6] William Feathers, Grand Jury Report (Cuyahoga County, Ohio, December 21, 1933).

[7] W. S. Robinson, "Bias, Probability, and Trial By Jury," *American Sociological Review*, 15:73–78, February, 1950.

gesting to the judge or jury the appropriate penalty. Baker has given an interesting description of a typical day's work of a prosecutor in a city of medium size, showing the immense power of this officer and the conditions under which he works.[8]

At the same time this prosecutor is generally elected and, as is true of other elected officers, this means subservience to the wishes of the politicians. It also means distraction of attention from his official business for the sake of political activities. The prosecutor must be careful not to antagonize any large organized group, and his record must show a large proportion of convictions in cases which go to trial. It is customary in elections for the prosecutor to present statistics on this point, and James A. Reed included in his statement for Who's Who that as public prosecutor in Kansas City he secured 285 convictions in 287 cases that went to trial. The prosecutor's reaction to crime must be, and is, selectively punitive. That is, if he is to continue in his position or advance to a higher political office he must seek the severest punishments possible in most cases, but he must intentionally fail to prosecute other cases. He must be highly indignant about most crime, and this means that he must show that most offenders should be punished, not treated. Justice William O. Douglas of the Supreme Court has claimed that the quality of prosecutors has "markedly declined," and he observes that prosecutors "sometimes treat the courtroom not as a place of dignity, detached from the community, but as a place to unleash the fury of public passion."[9]

The assistant prosecutors, also, secure their positions in many cases because they have been active in political organizations, and their reactions to crime must be similar to those of the prosecutor. They are generally inexperienced in the work at the time they are appointed, and they are dismissed when the political administration changes. In 1932 when a Democrat replaced a Republican prosecuting attorney in Chicago all but 15 of about 85 assistants were replaced within six months, and the clerical staff experienced an almost complete turnover.[10] The Wickersham Report made this statement regarding the work of the prosecutor:

Taking the country as a whole, the features which chiefly operate to make the present-day criminal justice in the States ineffective are: Want of adequate system and organization in the office of the average prosecutor,

[8] N. F. Baker, "The Prosecutor—Initiation of Prosecution," *Journal of Criminal Law and Criminology*, 23:770–796, January–February, 1933. See also N. F. Baker and E. H. DeLong, "The Prosecutor and His Office," *Journal of Criminal Law and Criminology*, 23:926–963; 24:1025–1065; 25:358–400, 884–901; 26:821–846, March–April, 1933 to March–April, 1936.

[9] William O. Douglas, "A Challenge to the Bar," *Notre Dame Lawyer*, 28:497–508, Summer, 1953.

[10] Baker and DeLong, *op. cit.*, pp. 884–901.

decentralization of prosecution whereas law and order have come to be much more than local concern, diffusion of responsibility, the intimate relation of prosecution to politics, and in many jurisdictions no provision for a prosecutor commensurate with the task of prosecution under the conditions of today. . . . The system of prosecutors elected for short terms, with assistants chosen on the basis of political patronage, with no assured tenure, yet charged with wide undefined powers, is ideally adapted to misgovernment.[11]

The suggestion has been made that the prosecutor should be removed from this control of the political machine by providing for his appointment by the governor from a list nominated by the judicial council and for his removal by the governor on recommendation of the judicial council, but otherwise remaining in office for life. The prosecutors in this case would be assistants of the attorney general of the state.

The prosecutor is tending to become a criminal investigator, also. Several prosecutors have made great reputations by vigorous campaigns for law enforcement, in which they have made investigations, secured evidence, and initiated prosecutions. In many counties the prosecutor has his own staff of investigators. Also, the police departments in some jurisdictions assign a number of policemen to the prosecutor's office for this work, and the number thus assigned seems to be increasing. Students of the administration of criminal justice have generally opposed this trend toward expansion of the work of the prosecutor, because he already has an enormous task, because it produces friction between police and prosecutor, and because there is no reason to think the prosecutor will be more efficient than the police in making investigations.

THE LAWYER FOR THE DEFENSE. Legal defense for a person on trial was generally prohibited in early English law but has now become a general right. As early as 1701 the Pennsylvania legal code provided for the right of defendants to be represented by counsel.[12] A large proportion of criminal cases is in the hands of a small number of professional criminal lawyers. These lawyers are often recommended to the accused persons by the police and court attendants and in more general ways are dependent on cooperation of government officials. For example, they must deal with officials in arranging for interviews with their clients, in negotiating bail, in

[11] Alfred Bettman, "Report on Prosecution," in National Commission on Law Observance and Enforcement, Report No. 4 (Washington: Government Printing Office, 1931), pp. 11–12, 14.
[12] Richard L. Perry, Editor, Sources of Our Liberties (New York: Associated College Presses, 1960), pp. 325, 429.

bargaining for a sentence, and in many other ways. Accordingly, they tend to be more active in politics than are other lawyers, tend to find their friends among persons whose social status is lower than that of business-men, and tend to substitute social skills of dealing with officials for the professional technical skills of dealing with the law.[13] Criminal lawyers have been very influential as members of legislatures in preventing the en-actment of bills for the reform of criminal procedure and of court organi-zation. Gallison stated:

The preponderating cause of the failure of American justice is the Ameri-can lawyer. . . . Any system so constructed that improvement and sym-metrical growth are inimical to the material welfare of its personnel is fundamentally unsound. Alone among industrial and business enterprises and the "learned" professions, reform inevitably reacts to the material injury of the legal profession. Every proposal of value means loss of income, loss of power, and loss of position to the lawyer. Simply stated, the lawyer cannot reform the system nor permit others to reform it and survive.[14]

If the defendant is unable to hire his own lawyer, the court may assign one. All states make provision for an assigned counsel in capital cases, thirty-eight states make this provision for all felony cases,[15] and twenty-eight states make the provision for misdemeanor cases. In practice, how-ever, the person charged wth a misdemeanor seldom has an assigned counsel. A relatively capable attorney is frequently assigned in capital cases, but this is not true in other felony cases.[16] In a few cases, in recent years, state prisoners have won new trials after appeals based on the claim that though furnished counsel at the trial, the service rendered by such coun-sel was so incompetent that the petitioner was in effect without the assistance of counsel.[17] Sixty percent of the offenders defended by private counsel in the Cook County Criminal Court during the period September 1, 1945 through August 31, 1947 were represented by the same 35 attorneys. Eighty percent were represented by 42 attorneys.[18]

[13] Arthur Lewis Wood, "Informal Relations in the Practice of Criminal Law," *American Journal of Sociology*, 62:48–55, July, 1956. See also Arthur Lewis Wood, "Professional Ethics Among Criminal Lawyers," *Social Problems*, 7:70–83, Summer, 1959.

[14] I. P. Gallison, "A Layman Looks at Justice," *Journal of the American Judicature Society*, 16:176–181, April, 1933.

[15] See Emery A. Brownell, "Recent Developments in Legal Aid and Defender Services," *Federal Probation*, 23:41–44, March, 1959.

[16] Special Committee of the Association of the Bar of the City of New York and the National Legal Aid and Defender Association, *Equal Justice for the Accused*, (New York: Doubleday, 1959), pp. 63–68.

[17] Mayers, *op. cit.*, p. 30.

[18] Don T. Blackiston, *The Judge, the Defendant, and Criminal Law Administration* (unpublished Ph.D. Dissertation, University of Chicago), 1952.

Because of the inefficiency and unfairness of the system of assigned counsels, some states have authorized a special public defender who devotes his entire time to the defense of poor persons charged with crimes. The public defender was found in Ancient Rome, in the fifteenth century in Spain, and in many European countries in recent decades. In this country it was first adopted in Los Angeles in 1913 and since that time has been authorized in twenty-two states.[19] In most of these states, the legislation is merely "enabling," which means that a city or county can elect to set up a defender's office, but Connecticut and Rhode Island have established the public defender on a state-wide basis.[20] Fifty percent of the persons committed to the Illinois State Penitentiary from Cook County in 1945 were defended by public defenders.[21] In Los Angeles, the public defender's office defends approximately 5,000 persons annually, or about 60 percent of the criminal cases coming before the Superior Court.

The public defender system is superior to the system of assigned counsel. Delays are reduced, technical motions seldom made, and the expense to the state is reduced. At the same time they provide more efficient protection to the accused than do the assigned counsels. Because of their specialization they can help develop public opinion and criminal procedure as assigned counsels cannot.

Bar associations in some states, while recognizing the inefficiency of assigned counsels, have advocated voluntary defenders paid by the bar association or some other group as preferable to public defenders paid by the state. One of their arguments is that the defender and the prosecutor are likely to be members of the same political party and therefore both are under political control. Since most cases are settled in conference between the prosecutor and the defender, this is an important consideration.[22] It cannot be expected, however, that lawyers will bear the full financial burden of defending needy persons; the responsibility rests on the community, which must help support the volunteers.[23]

**THE JUDGE.** At present the trial judge has two rather separate duties. First, he must preside at the trial. If the case is tried before a jury he must supervise selection of jurors, enforce the rules of evidence, and declare law to

---

[19] Martin V. Callagy, "Legal Aid in Criminal Cases," *Journal of Criminal Law and Criminology*, 42:589–624, January–February, 1952; Lee W. Meyer, *Public Defenders* (New York: Institute of Judicial Administration, 1956), pp. 4–6, 37–38.

[20] See David Mars, "Public Defenders," *Journal of Criminal Law and Criminology*, 46:199–210, July–August, 1955.

[21] University of Chicago Conference on Probation, Prisons, and Parole, *op. cit.*, p. 10.

[22] Meyer, *op. cit.*, pp. 16–19.

[23] *Equal Justice for the Accused, op. cit.*, pp. 71–72, 95.

the jury. In the courts of some states he may even express to the jury his opinions about the innocence or guilt of the accused person, providing he makes it clear that the jury need not follow his opinion. He may order a jury to acquit a defendant, and when a jury returns a verdict of guilty, the judge, if he believes there is no evidence of guilt, may set it aside and order a new trial. However, he may not order a jury to convict nor can he set aside a verdict which is favorable to the defendant unless the verdict has been induced by fraud.[24] When the defendant pleads not guilty but waives jury trial the judge not only interprets the law and the rules of evidence, but he determines whether or not the defendant is guilty. Supreme court judges also determine guilt or innocence, without a jury, in cases appealed to them. The judge is well qualified, in general, to perform this first duty. When the courts are efficient, honest and capable judges are in control of a precise investigation to determine guilt or innocence. An approach to the Continental system, in which the judge actually directs the trial, would appear to be desirable. This method has been well developed in the juvenile courts and is being constantly extended in the courts for adults, particularly in the specialized courts.

The second duty of the judge is to impose just sentences according to the law, on those persons found guilty. When the influence of the classical school was at its height this imposition of sentences was considered as rather routine. Since the law ordained specific punishments for specific offenses, when it had been legally determined that the defendant had perpetrated an offense the judge simply ordered administration of the appropriate punishment. In theory, he had no choice in the matter, just as the present-day judge in some states theoretically has no choice about the imposition of the death penalty for some offenders. While there were many exceptions in practice, the offense, not the offender, was technically the object of attention. But with the recent changes in societal reactions to crime the offender has become more important, and the judge has been given a wide range of alternative methods for dealing with the offenders.

In general, unless he has some assistance the judge is not able to impose sentences effectively. The evidence in court is designed to show merely the fact of guilt or innocence; such evidence is not relevant to the purpose of determining which of various sentencing alternatives should be used in specific cases of persons who have been proven guilty. If sentences are to be "just" according to modern standards, it is necessary to know the background and character of the offender, and the possible effects of the different methods of dealing with him. In many cases the judge currently

[24] See Arthur E. Wood and J. B. Waite, *Crime and Its Treatment* (New York: American Book Company, 1941), p. 424.

must fix penalties or suggest treatment by guessing at the character of the person on the basis of his appearance and of incidental information that has come out during the course of the trial. It is said of some Philadelphia magistrate's courts that convictions of drunks and vagrants are "obtained by sight and smell alone" and that the magistrates are indifferent to the charges listed in the records.[25] On the other hand, a study of 1,437 convictions in the Philadelphia Court of Quarter Sessions concluded that the sentences were consistent with the criteria for sentencing established in the statutes.[26]

Judges vary immensely in their policies. One judge in New York placed 7 percent of those convicted on probation; another judge dealing with offenders of the same types placed 40 percent on probation. In New Jersey, six judges, rotating among the courts and dealing with the same types of cases, showed similar variation. One judge sentenced 57.7 percent of the convicted persons to imprisonment, and another judge sentenced only 33.6 percent to imprisonment; the first judge placed 19.5 percent on probation, the second 30.4 percent.[27] Ploscowe has pointed out similar disparities in the sentences imposed by Federal judges. In 1943 the judge in the Northern District of Alabama sentenced 78.7 percent of the offenders who came before him to prison terms of two years or over, while his colleague in the middle section of the state imposed such sentences on only 13.7 percent of the offenders coming before him. The judges assigned to the Eastern and Western Districts in Arkansas sentenced 69.1 and 10.2 percent, respectively, to terms of two years and over. In the Southern District of West Virginia 57.5 percent of the bootleggers and moonshiners were sentenced to prison terms of over two years, as compared with 2.3 percent in the Western District of that state, 86.2 percent in Northern Alabama, and 3.8 percent in Southern Alabama.[28] Green found that the Philadelphia judges favored females, youths and whites as compared to males, older offenders and Negroes, but he concluded that these differences were due

[25] Caleb Foote, "Vagrancy-Type Law and Its Administration," *University of Pennsylvania Law Review*, 104:603–650, March, 1956, at p. 612.

[26] Edward Green, *Judicial Attitudes in Sentencing*, (New York: St. Martin's Press, 1961), pp. 48–49.

[27] F. J. Gaudet, G. S. Harris, and C. W. St. John, "Individual Differences in the Sentencing Tendencies of Judges," *Journal of Criminal Law and Criminology*, 23:811–818, January–February, 1933. See also Harold E. Lane, "Illogical Variations in Sentences of Felons Committed to Massachusetts State Prison," *Journal of Criminal Law and Criminology*, 32:171–190, July–August, 1941; E. Frankel, "The Offender and the Court: A Statistical Analysis of the Sentencing of Delinquents," *Journal of Criminal Law and Criminology*, 31:448–456, November–December, 1940; Blackiston, op. cit.

[28] Morris Ploscowe, "The Court and the Correctional System," in Paul W. Tappan, Editor, *Contemporary Correction* (New York: McGraw-Hill, 1951), pp. 51–60. For a bibliography, see Institute of Judicial Administration, *Disparity in Sentencing of Convicted Defendants* (New York: Author, 1954).

to the crime rates among the various groups, rather than to bias among the judges.[29]

Attempts have been made to assist the judges by field investigations conducted by probation officers, by recommendations of psychiatrists, and in other ways. In California, judges must order an investigation by a probation officer before judgment is passed in felony cases, and pre-sentence investigations are similarly required in six other states.[30] It has been proposed that the data thus gathered be organized into prediction tables, to be used to supplement the judge's experience with various kinds of offenders.[31] If judges are to retain the sentencing power, they need assistance. Many people, however, believe that this function should be transferred entirely to a dispositions board composed of representatives of disciplines regarding human behavior, such as a psychologist, a psychiatrist, a sociologist, a social worker, and an educator.[32]

In thirty-eight states, judges are elected, and their terms are relatively short.[33] Voters cannot always know the qualities essential in a good judge, such as personal integrity, adequate legal training, and judicial temperament. Accordingly, some judges try to win votes by self-advertisement, by attending banquets, weddings, funerals, prize fights, and lodge entertainments, by sensational behavior on the bench, and in other ways. Judges have asked to be transferred from the civil to the criminal branch of the court shortly before elections because of the better opportunity for publicity in the criminal court. It is reported that one judge in New York offered a large sum of money to the district attorney in order to have a particular case tried before him, because of the publicity this trial would give him.

In some areas, bar associations try to assist the voters in the selection of judges by announcing preliminary rating of the candidates by the members of the association. This sometimes is effective, but sometimes it is not. The bar association recommended twenty judges in Chicago in 1933, of whom twelve were running on the Democratic ticket and eight on the

29 Green, op. cit., p. 63.
30 Will C. Turnbladh, "Probation and the Administration of Justice," *Prison World*, 12:11–12, November, 1950. See also Shlomo Shoham, "Sentencing Policy of Criminal Courts in Israel," *Journal of Criminal Law, Criminology and Police Science*, 50:327–337, December, 1959.
31 Sheldon Glueck, "The Sentencing Problem," *Federal Probation*, 20:15–25, December, 1960.
32 Nathaniel Cantor, "A Dispositions Tribunal," *Journal of Criminal Law and Criminology*, 29:51–61, May–June, 1931; Theodore Levin, "Sentencing the Criminal Offender," *Federal Probation*, 13:3–6, March, 1949; Richard A. Doyle, "A Sentencing Council in Operation," *Federal Probation*, 25:27–30, September, 1961; and John S. Palmore, "Sentencing and Correction: The Black Sheep of Criminal Law," *Federal Probation*, 26:6–14, December, 1962.
33 Council of State Governments, *Trial Courts of General Jurisdiction in the Forty-Eight States* (Chicago: Author, 1951).

Republican. Not one of the candidates on the Republican ticket was elected, although eight of the Democrats who were elected were rated by the bar association as very inferior. In 1940 Missouri adopted a plan whereby judges are nominated by a commission of outstanding citizens, including lawyers. The names of three nominees are submitted to the governor, who selects one. After a judge selected in this manner has served for one year his name is placed on the ballot and the voters decide whether he should be retained in office.[34] This plan does away with the defects and disadvantages of both the appointment system and the election system of selecting judges.

A judge's judicial behavior, like the behavior of other persons, is influenced by his participation in the social relationships that make up his experiences. His social class membership affects his interpretations of the law and colors his attitudes toward various types of offenses and offenders. His prior associations with punitive and non-punitive behavior patterns affect the particular way he reacts to a particular offender, and the general societal reactions to crime set the limits within which he must operate.[35] Some years ago an attempt was made to analyze the influences that entered into a decision in one case,[36] and Judge Cardozo made a more general analysis of decisions.[37] The judge's training as a lawyer does not ordinarily include studies in anthropology, psychology, and sociology, which would tend to promote an appreciation for the complicated variation found in the behavior of social groups other than his own. A recent study of the decisions of 313 state and federal judges indicates that decisions for or against the defense in criminal cases are significantly related to membership in various groups.[38] For example there was a greater tendency to decide for the defense among Democrats as opposed to Republicans, among nonmembers of the American Bar Association as opposed to members, among judges who had served as prosecutors as opposed to those who had not, and among Catholics as opposed to Protestants. On their responses to a mailed questionnaire, 119 of the judges were scored on "general liberalism" and on "criminal liberalism." The first score was determined by re-

[34] Harry E. Barnes and Negley K. Teeters, *New Horizons in Criminology*, Third Edition (New York: Prentice-Hall, 1959), p. 250. See also Lawrence M. Hyde, "The Missouri Plan for Selection and Tenure of Judges," *Journal of Criminal Law and Criminology*, 39:271–287, September–October, 1948.

[35] See the discussion above, pp. 298–307.

[36] T. Schroeder, "Psychologic Study of Judicial Opinions," *California Law Review*, 6:89–113, January, 1918.

[37] B. N. Cardozo, *The Nature of the Judicial Process* (New Haven: Yale University Press, 1922).

[38] Stuart S. Nagel, "Judicial Backgrounds and Criminal Cases," *Journal of Criminal Law, Criminology and Police Science*, 53:333–339, September, 1962; see also Stuart S. Nagel, "Testing Relations Between Judicial Characteristics and Judicial Decision-Making," *Western Political Science Quarterly*, 15:425–437, September, 1962.

sponses to questions measuring the degree of sympathy for less-privileged groups and the degree of acceptance of social change, while the second score was determined by the degree of agreement with the statement, "Our treatment of criminals is too harsh; we should try to cure, not punish them." Judges with a high "general liberalism" score had a significantly greater tendency to decide for the defense than did judges with low scores on this measure, and this was true also for judges with a high "criminal liberalism" score.

CLERKS AND ATTENDANTS.   The importance of clerks and attendants in the judicial process ordinarily is not recognized. Crime surveys show that these agents, like prosecutors and judges, are subservient to politicians and are sometimes the agents of corrupt bondsmen and fixers. The Seabury investigation revealed that clerks can manipulate complaint forms so that discharges result. Dates for which trials are set may be changed by clerks without the knowledge of the complaining witnesses so that the defendants will be discharged for lack of prosecution. Contents of indictments and of other secret papers may be revealed to the lawyers for the defense. In some cases the clerks actually advise the court. Some clerks and bailiffs steer cases to professional bondsmen and to lawyers who will split fees with them. In other ways these agents of the courts can be instrumental in implementing a selectively punitive reaction to crime.

THE TRIAL.   Except in very serious cases, such as capital offenses, a plea of guilty makes a trial unnecessary. If the defendant pleads not guilty he is entitled to a jury trial, but in many instances he can waive this right and stand trial before a judge. Recent statistics show that the trial plays a very small part in the system of criminal justice, and that the jury plays a small part in the trial. In 1964, 90.1 percent of those persons convicted in the United States District Courts were convicted on pleas of guilty, 6.7 percent on finding of a jury, and 3.2 percent on finding of the court.[39] Similarly, in New Jersey county courts, only 8.7 percent of the 1949–1954 cases were tried by juries; and in California 71 percent of the cases disposed of by Superior Courts in 1963–1964 were "dispositions before trial," and most of these were convictions on pleas of guilty.[40]

*The jury.*   The jury originated as a protection against the despotism of

[39] Administrative Office of the U.S. Courts, *Federal Offenders in the United States District Courts*, 1964 (Washington: Author, 1965), p. 15.

[40] Institute of Judicial Administration, *Law Enforcement Criminal Statistics Study*, New Jersey (New York: Author, 1955), Table 9; Judicial Council of California, *Twentieth Biennial Report* (Sacramento: Author, 1965), p. 151. See also Joseph Sherbow, "Waiver of Jury Speeds Criminal Trials in Baltimore Courts," *Journal of the American Judicature Society*, 31:150–152, February, 1951; and Henry P. Chandler, "Latter-Day Procedures in the Sentencing and Treatment of Offenders in the Federal Courts," *Federal Probation*, 16:3–12, March, 1952.

the king and frequently has been acclaimed as the "palladium of our liberties." According to legal theory, the business of the jury is to determine,
on the basis of evidence, a question of fact: Did the accused person commit the crime? It is supposed to be a problem in logic similar to the problem which confronts a scientist in a laboratory. In practice, however, the
prosecutor tries to select jurymen who will be antagonistic to the accused,
and the attorney for the defense tries to select jurymen who will be sympathetic. One tries to exclude all persons not of the same race, religion,
politics, or occupation as the accused, and the other tries to exclude all
persons who are of the same race, religion, politics, or occupation. A famous
criminal lawyer, Clarence Darrow, described the process of selecting a jury
in the following terms:

> Jurymen seldom convict a person they like, or acquit one that they dis-
> like. The main work of a trial lawyer is to make a jury like his client, or, at
> least, to feel sympathy for him; facts regarding the crime are relatively un-
> important.
>
> I try to get a jury with little education but with much human emotion.
> The Irish are always the best jurymen for the defense. I don't want a
> Scotchman, for he has too little human feeling; I don't want a Scandina-
> vian, for he has too strong a respect for law as law. In general I don't want
> a religious person, for he believes in sin and punishment. The defendant
> should avoid rich men who have a high regard for the law, as they make
> and use it. The smug and ultrarespectable think they are the guardians of
> society, and they believe the law is for them.
>
> The man who is down on his luck, who has trouble, who is more or less
> a failure, is much kinder to the poor and unfortunate than are the rich
> and selfish.[41]

In some cases, several thousand prospective jurors have been examined
before twelve were secured. In one Chicago trial 9,425 persons were summoned for jury duty and 4,821 were examined before 12 were finally selected. Ninety-one days were required to select a jury in one San Francisco
case. However, this procedure is not due to the jury system as such, for
there is evidence that in some courts, especially the federal courts, the jury
is generally selected expeditiously.

Jury trial is necessarily slower and more cumbersome than trial before a
judge, and about half the states have made legislative provision for waiver
of the jury trial and substitution of trial by the judge. Few cases go on trial

[41] From a statement made in an anniversary dinner at the Quadrangle Club, Chi-
cago, in 1933. Quoted by permission of the late Mr. Darrow. See also James A.
Dooley, "The Trial Court," The Law School Record (University of Chicago), Vol. 3,
No. 2, 1954, pp. 1 ff.

by jury in some states where this legislation has been in existence for some time. In United States District Courts in 1964, less than 7 percent of the defendants convicted of major offenses had jury trials.[42] Over 41 percent of the persons who pleaded not guilty in Massachusetts Superior Courts in 1963 waived the jury trial.[43] The weight of opinion is distinctly in favor of retaining the right to a jury trial but of facilitating the waiver of the jury.

Recent studies indicate both that juries tend to follow the technical instructions given them by the judges and that in jury-room deliberations the leaders are those who are most articulate and assertive, which means that the leaders tend to come from the upper socio-economic levels.[44] It also has been found that male jurors tend to try to complete the jury's task while female jurors tended more to react to the other jurors and to display social solidarity.[45]

*Evidence and testimony.* The great proportion of the evidence in a trial is furnished by the witnesses for the two sides. Several problems arise in regard to such evidence. The first is that it is very difficult to induce witnesses to appear in court and give testimony. In certain cases of a serious nature, terrorism may be involved. In other types of cases, witnesses are reluctant to go to court because of the great inconvenience involved. They may be required to go to court again and again, at great financial loss to themselves. Defense attorneys often attempt to obtain as many continuances as possible, on the theory that witnesses for the prosecution, including victims, eventually will grow tired of the inconvenience of coming to court. Consequently, many witnesses do not disclose to anyone the fact that they have important evidence, and many crimes are not reported to the police.

A second problem is the honest mistakes which witnesses frequently make. One sometimes remembers what he wants to remember. Also, his memory is a combination of what was witnessed and of other things that were heard or imagined subsequent to the occurrence. Delusions of perception occur also. Psychologists have been working for some time on the

---

[42] Administrative Office of the U.S. Courts, *Federal Offenders in the United States District Courts, 1964* (Washington, Author, 1965), p. 15. See also Frank W. Miller and Frank J. Remington, "Procedures Before Trial," *Annals of the American Academy of Political and Social Science*, January, 1962.

[43] Commissioner of Correction, *Statistical Reports* (Boston: Massachusetts Public Document No. 115, 1963), p. 66.

[44] Rita M. James, "Jurors Assessment of Criminal Responsibility," *Social Problems*, 7:58–69, Summer, 1959; and Fred L. Strodtbeck, Rita M. James, and Charles Hawkins, "Social Status in Jury Deliberations," *American Sociological Review*, 19:713–719, December, 1957; Rita M. James, "Status and Competence of Juries," *American Journal of Sociology*, 64:563–570, May, 1959.

[45] Fred L. Strodtbeck and Richard D. Mann, "Sex Role Differentiation in Jury Deliberations," *Sociometry*, 19:3–11, March, 1956.

comparative accuracy of replies to leading questions, and of narrative accounts on the part of various groups.[46] The only checks on mistakes in testimony in court is the testimony of other witnesses, but this adversary system places undue stress on the witness and makes it difficult for him to contribute in a meaningful way to the proceedings.[47] Under the heading "How to Humiliate and Subdue a Recalcitrant Witness," a book written for prosecutors and defense attorneys contains the following advice:

> When you have forced the witness into giving you a direct answer to your question you really have him under control; he is off-balance, and usually rather scared. This advantage should be followed up with a few simple questions such as, "You did not want to answer that question, did you?" If the witness says that he wanted to answer it, ask him in a resounding voice, "Well, why did you not answer it when I first asked you?" Whatever his answer is you then ask him, "Did you think that you were smart enough to evade answering the question?" Again, whatever the answer is you ask him, "Well, I would like for the jurors to know what you have behind all this dodging and ducking you have done!" . . . This battering and legal-style "kicking the witness around" not only humiliates but subdues him.[48]

A third problem is dishonesty in testimony. The only official check on dishonesty is the oath and the possibility of prosecution for perjury. In a few famous cases witnesses have not been permitted to testify because they were atheists to whom the oath would have no meaning. In general the oath probably has little significance to a large proportion of the witnesses in courts. Judges and others believe that there is an immense amount of perjury in testimony, but few persons are convicted of perjury.[49] In Cali-

[46] See, for example, Donald Slesinger and E. M. Pilpel, "Legal Psychology: A Bibliography and a Suggestion," *Psychological Bulletin*, 26:679–692, December, 1929; Alfred Kuraner, "The Consistency of Testimonial Accuracy," *Journal of Criminal Law and Criminology*, 22:406–413, September–October, 1931; H. E. Burtt, *Legal Psychology*, New York: Prentice-Hall, 1931; D. S. Gardner, "The Perception and Memory of Witnesses," *Cornell Law Quarterly*, 8:391–409, April, 1933; Manfred S. Guttmacher and Henry Weihofen, *Psychiatry and the Law* (New York: W. W. Norton, 1952), pp. 360–397; Maximilian Koessler, "Fallibility of Testimony and Judicial Accident Risk," *Case and Comment*, 62:12–16, November, 1957; Jack B. Weinstein, "The Law's Attempt to Obtain Useful Testimony," *Journal of Social Issues*, 13:6–11, No. 2, 1957; Henry A. Davidson, "Appraisal of Witnesses," *American Journal of Psychiatry*, 110:481–486, January, 1954; Israel Gerver, "The Social Psychology of Witness Behavior with Special Reference to the Criminal Courts," *Journal of Social Issues*, 13:23–29, 1957.

[47] Rudolph E. Morris, "Witness Performance Under Stress: A Sociological Approach," *Journal of Social Issues*, 13:17–22, 1957; see also Jack B. Weinstein, "The Law's Attempt to Obtain Useful Testimony," *Ibid.*, pp. 6–11.

[48] Lewis W. Lake, *How to Win Lawsuits Before Juries* (New York: Prentice-Hall, 1954), pp. 164–165.

[49] David Dressler, "Trial by Combat in American Courts," *Harper's*, 222:31–36, April, 1961.

fornia only twelve persons were sentenced to the penitentiary for perjury in the years 1945–1949.[50]

For some time efforts have been made to invent devices which will detect guilty knowledge. The "lie detector" currently has the best standing of any of these devices. This instrument registers the emotional changes which occur as the result of questions presented, but unfortunately the emotional changes are not necessarily due to lies. Probably the "lie detector" is of less value in the direct detection of lies than in the detection of emotional conditions which may be utilized by the examiner to induce a confession.[51] Various drugs are being used to some extent for the same purpose. It is reported that these drugs induce a state of semiconsciousness in which one will truthfully answer questions. This method, also, is still in the experimental stage and certainly should not be used as evidence in the courtroom.[52]

*Fixing the case.* The courts and other agencies of justice find constant pressure upon them by friends of the defendant. Members of the family, church, lodge, trade union, club, business firm, neighborhood, and other groups swear to the good character of the defendant and ask for leniency. This may be due to close personal friendship or may represent a desire to protect the reputation of the group. In any case it represents a personal and sympathetic appeal based on a non-punitive reaction to the offense. The alderman takes care of thousands of tickets for traffic violations, as a part of his preparation for the next election. Other political leaders, from the precinct up, perform similar services either directly or indirectly, and they extend their services to persons charged with serious crimes. In some cities at some point in the judicial process almost any case can be fixed, which means either that the case is dropped entirely, or the penalty is mitigated. Pressure is most frequently placed upon victims of crimes to induce them to refuse to prosecute and upon the police to induce them to present uncertain and confusing testimony. The inferior court or the magistrate's court is the place where most of these provisions for fixing operate. One of the Tammany leaders stated, "Give me ten magistrates and you can have the whole supreme court." The following statement, by a judge, refers to the inferior courts of New York City in 1932:

[50] Ronald H. Beattie, *California Prisoners, 1945–1949* (Sacramento: California Department of Corrections, 1951), p. 89.

[51] See Fred E. Inbau and John E. Reid, *Lie Detection and Criminal Interrogation,* (Baltimore: Williams and Wilkins, 1953).

[52] See C. W. Muehlberger, "Interrogation Under Drug Influence—the So-Called 'Truth Serum' Technique," *Journal of Criminal Law, Criminology and Police Science,* 42:513–528, Nov.–Dec. 1951.

It is a by-word in the corridors of the Magistrates' Courts of the City
of New York that the intervention of a friend in the district political club
is much more potent in the disposition of cases than the merits of the
cause or the services of the best lawyer and, unfortunately, the truth of
the statement alone prevents it from being a slander upon the good name
of the City.[53]

The "sporting theory" of justice. Formally, the essential business of
a trial is to determine a question of fact: Did the accused commit the
crime? In the performance of that duty, tricks and surprises are no more
justifiable than in determining a fact in a laboratory. In practice, however,
the criminal trial is regarded as a game between two lawyers. Large au-
diences were attracted in the past and in some sections of the country
criminal trials still are an important source of amusement. Each side tries
to win the case and takes advantage of every possible trick, surprise, and
technical device. It is not at all unusual for as many as fifteen formal
motions to be introduced in a case, each of which involves debate, possible
continuances, and decisions by the court. When a case is continued, witnesses disappear and public sentiments weaken, and the chance for conviction decreases. Moore has used an analogy with warfare, stating that the
trial involves scouting the enemy's position and strength, stratagems,
tactics, skirmishes, and battles. "Opposing counsel are charged with the
responsibility of so conducting their campaign that ultimate victory will
result."[54] It has been suggested that each side should be required to sub-
mit a list of witnesses who are to be called, with an abstract of the evidence to be presented. This would make it possible to reach a decision
without the surprises which are not a part of real justice. Since this suggestion and most other suggestions for the reform of criminal procedure
would strengthen the state in the trial, they are opposed by criminal
lawyers and have made little progress in the legislatures.

The "bargain theory" of justice. Many of the legal conflicts which
would have been conducted in the courtroom in earlier days in accordance
with the sporting theory of justice are now settled in the office of the
prosecutor by a process of bargaining. This, also, involves conflict between
the opposed attorneys, but it is not sport for there is no audience. Each
side tries to make the best possible bargain. The attorney for the defense
will go to trial, with certain exceptions, if he feels certain of acquittal. The

---

[53] New York Legislature, *Report of the Joint Committee on the Government of the
City of New York*, 5 Volumes (Albany: State Printing Office, 1932), Vol. II, p. 15.
[54] Leonard Moore, "Modern Practice and Strategy," *Practicing Law Institute*, 1946,
p. 1; quoted by Jerome Frank, *Courts on Trial*, Princeton: Princeton University Press,
1949, p. 8.

attorney for the state will go to trial, also with certain exceptions, if he
feels certain of a conviction. In the intermediate cases each is willing to
bargain, and this generally takes one of two forms. First, a plea of guilty to
a lesser offense than the one charged may be entered. Among prisoners,
this practice is known as "copping a plea." A charge of grand larceny may
be reduced to petty larceny, theft of an automobile may be reduced to
tampering with an automobile or theft of a tire, murder may be reduced
to manslaughter, and so on. In 1964, 71 percent of the offenders charged
with serious offenses in 1,751 cities were found guilty; of these, 96 percent
were guilty of the offense charged, 4 percent of a lesser offense. Of those
charged with rape, 46 percent were found guilty; 67 percent were guilty of
rape, 33 percent of a lesser offense.[55] In some instances, such reductions
represent informal attempts to mitigate severe penalties, but in many cases
they merely indicate a desire for expediency on the part of court personnel.
Sometimes the reduction is given as a reward to criminals who have testified against their partners in crime. A study of 1,336 cases, in which lesser
pleas were accepted and which were filed in New York City in the summer
of 1939, reveals the prosecuting attorney's officially-stated reasons for accepting lesser pleas.[56] In about 54 percent of the cases, mitigation of a
severe penalty was the stated reason for accepting the lesser plea, while in
36 percent the prosecutor reported that he had a weak case. In 4 percent
of the cases both a weak case and a desire for mitigation apparently were
involved, and in 6 percent no reason for the plea could be found. A plea
of guilty to a lesser offense satisfies the prosecutor, for he has an immense
burden of work and cannot go to trial on all cases, and the bargaining
enables him to settle the case expeditiously. He is able to record, for
purposes of coming elections, that he has obtained a conviction. However, it should be recognized that the acceptance of lesser pleas is not
necessarily inimical to justice. It would be physically impossible to try
all cases if guilty pleas were not obtained, and often the bargaining enables court personnel to modify the law informally so that it best suits the
individual case. The attorney for the defense is satisfied, for his client has
escaped a severe penalty which might have been inflicted.

In the second general form of bargaining, a plea of guilty to the offense
charged is entered in exchange for the prosecutor's promise of probation
or a light sentence. Even if he is guilty, the defendant has a legal and

---

[55] Federal Bureau of Investigation, *Uniform Crime Reports for the United States,*
1964, p. 101.
[56] R. G. Weintraub and R. Tough, "Lesser Pleas Considered," *Journal of Criminal
Law and Criminology,* 32:506–530, January–February, 1942. See also Samuel Dash,
"Cracks in the Foundation of Criminal Justice," *Illinois Law Review,* 46:385–406,
July–August, 1951.

moral right to plead not guilty if he believes that the state cannot prove its case against him. The prosecutor must not only know that the defendant committed the offense, but he must prove that fact. He usually is anxious to bargain for a guilty plea in cases in which proof would be difficult. It is the prosecutor's privilege to recommend a light or a heavy sentence to the judge, but the judge, of course, need not follow the recommendation. In practice, however, judges usually go along with the bargains made between the defendant and the prosecutor since considerable saving to the state is effected by a guilty plea, which makes a lengthy trial unnecessary. Many prisoners insist that prosecuting attorneys do not always keep their promises to recommend a light sentence, but, instead, merely use the bargaining system to trick the defendant into pleading guilty. Also, defendants who have bargained for a light sentence often are shocked when the judge imposes a heavier sentence than the one recommended by the prosecutor. While it would be difficult to prove, it is probable that a grave injustice is done to many defendants who insist on their right to a jury trial and refuse to bargain. An extreme penalty is sometimes ordered not solely because a crime has been committed but in part as punishment for refusing to plead guilty, thus causing the court personnel the inconvenience of holding a trial. For example, in 1950 two men who had refused to accept an offer of two year sentences in exchange for pleas of guilty to robbery were sentenced to twenty years by a Missouri trial judge. However, it should be pointed out that an identical sentence might have been imposed even if there had been no attempted negotiations of this kind.

It is not possible to determine what proportion of the reductions of charges and the promises of light sentences involve corruption. Not all of these bargains, however, are equally honest. In one study of 97 felony convictions, bargaining was admitted in 56.7 percent of the cases, but there was no evidence of bribery.[57] Neither is it possible to determine how much corruption is involved in the cases which are dismissed by motion of the prosecutor. Certainly corruption is involved in some of them, but it is equally certain that the prosecutor performs an important public service in sifting out the cases which should not go to trial, either because of the innocence of the accused, the triviality of the offense, or the inadequacy of the evidence.

"Cash register" justice. The "sporting theory" of justice and the "bargain theory" of justice, in general, apply to defendants who can afford to employ attorneys to secure justice for them. In other cases the accused

---

[57] Donald J. Newman, "Pleading Guilty for Considerations: A Study of Bargain Justice," *Journal of Criminal Law and Criminology*, 46:780–790, March–April, 1956.

are rushed through the court with scant attention, either of the prosecutor or the judge. This type of justice is well known in the traffic courts, where the whole procedure is mechanical. This procedure is perhaps inevitable in view of the large number of cases, but many citizens are irritated by it.[58] The poor and uninfluential persons accused of other minor offenses are rushed through the courts in exactly the same manner. In 1954, a Philadelphia court disposed of 55 cases of vagrancy, drunkenness, and disorderly conduct in fifteen minutes; four men were tried, found guilty, and sentenced in seventeen seconds.[59] It is difficult for a person to retain much respect for the system of justice after he sits in an inferior court for a few sessions and sees the inadequate information on which decisions are based. From the standpoint of the number of cases settled and the number of persons affected, these are the "supreme courts;" they are inferior courts only with reference to the character and training of the judges, the efficiency of the machinery, and the type of justice which is secured. At no point, in a very large proportion of cases, is there an opportunity for an adequate consideration of the facts in the case either by the prosecutor or by the court.

*The audience and publicity.* One of the rights for which the common people fought two centuries ago was the right to a public trial. This right is no longer highly prized by accused persons. On the contrary, at present one of the highly prized privileges which a few defendants secure is to be tried in the judge's chambers or to have the judge come to the courtroom at an unusual hour so that they may be protected against a public trial. The right to a private trial has been granted in the juvenile court and it has been argued that restrictions similar to those in the juvenile court should be authorized for all trials, so that the audience could be confined to those who have a particular and justified interest in the case. Many accused persons legitimately ask the question: When the state compels me to stand trial what right does it have to expose me to curiosity seekers? Many trials are unquestionably an invasion of the accused person's right to privacy. Probably the most notorious offenders in this respect are the reporters and photographers from the newspapers.[60] In some jurisdictions where the judges have little self-respect and are anxious for publicity, the constant flashing of the photographer's lights interferes seriously with the trial and certainly results in a lowering of the public's respect for the

[58] See Myron Stearns, "The Scandal of Our Traffic Courts," *Harper's*, 192:274–278, March, 1946.

[59] Foote, *op. cit.*, p. 605.

[60] Gilbert Geis and Robert E. Talley, "Cameras in the Courtroom," *Journal of Criminal Law and Criminology*, 47:546–560, January–February, 1957.

court.[61] Aside from this, the tendency is toward greater privacy, for the courtroom is generally arranged so that the audience hears almost none of the evidence except in jury trials.

### THE COURT AS A TREATMENT AND WELFARE AGENCY.

The conventional court system is an expression of a principle of conflict. The theory is that the state has been injured by a crime and in return should injure the offender by punishment, and also that the truth regarding guilt can best be determined by a conflict between opposed lawyers. The juvenile court, on the other hand, has been built on a different principle. Its work proceeds on the hypothesis that the delinquent child and the state have much in common and that the interests of both will be promoted by efforts to help or treat the child rather than injure him. Some branches of the criminal court, also, have adopted the principle that future crime can best be prevented by helping and treating the accused. Provisions for probation and psychiatric service are the best illustrations of this, and both have been adopted in many criminal courts in more or less restricted form. They are to be discussed in Chapter 21. The women's court and the boys' court are organized on somewhat the same principle as the juvenile court. The prosecutor frequently brings together persons who have been quarreling and by conciliation induces them to drop the prosecution. In many other branches of court work, generally those dealing with offenses toward which the punitive reaction is not aroused in the public, the court is endeavoring to use non-punitive and treatment methods either in co-operation with social welfare agencies or without assistance. It is certainly possible that this endeavor may become more prominent in several other branches of the court work in the future. However, criminal courts obviously cannot become generally non-punitive in their methods of dealing with criminals for punitive sanctions are an intrinsic part of the criminal law.

## SUGGESTED READINGS

Allen, Francis A., "The Supreme Court, Federalism, and State Systems of Criminal Justice," *The Law School Record* (University of Chicago), Special Supplement, 8:3–23, Autumn, 1958.

Beaney, William M., *The Right to Counsel in American Courts*. Binghampton, New York: Vail-Ballow Press, 1955.

Bok, Curtis, "The Jury System in America," *Annals of the American Academy of Political and Social Science*, 287:92–96, May, 1953.

[61] Foote, *op. cit.*, p. 607.

Brownell, Emery A., *Legal Aid in the United States.* Rochester: The Lawyers' Cooperative Publishing Company, 1951.

Cardozo, B. N., *The Nature of the Judicial Process.* New Haven: Yale University Press, 1921.

Foote, Caleb, "Vagrancy-Type Law and Its Administration," *University of Pennsylvania Law Review,* 104:603–650, March, 1956.

Frank, Jerome, *Courts on Trial.* Princeton: Princeton University Press, 1949.

Frank, Jerome, and Barbara Frank, *Not Guilty.* New York: Doubleday, 1957.

George, B. J., Jr., "Comparative Sentencing Techniques," *Federal Probation,* 23:27–31, March, 1959.

Green, Edward, *Judicial Attitudes in Sentencing.* New York: St. Martin's Press, 1961.

Hayner, Norman S., "Sentencing by an Administrative Board," *Law and Contemporary Problems,* 23:477–494, Summer, 1958.

James, Rita M., "Status and Competence of Jurors," *American Journal of Sociology,* 64:563–570, May, 1959.

James, Rita M., "Jurors' Assessment of Criminal Responsibility," *Social Problems,* 7:58–69, Summer, 1959.

Ladinsky, Jack, "Career of Lawyers, Law Practice, and Legal Institutions," *American Sociological Review,* 28:47–54, February, 1963.

Lemert, Edwin, "The Grand Jury as an Agency of Social Control," *American Sociological Review,* 10:751–758, December, 1945.

Mancusco, Edward T., *The Public Defender System in the State of California.* Chicago: National Legal Aid and Defender Association, 1959.

Mars, David, "Public Defenders," *Journal of Criminal Law, Criminology, and Police Science,* 46:199–210, July–August, 1955.

Mayers, Lewis, *The American Legal System.* Revised Edition. New York: Harper and Row, 1964.

Nagel, Stuart S., "Judicial Backgrounds and Criminal Cases," *Journal of Criminal Law, Criminology and Police Science,* 53:333–339, September, 1962.

National Parole Institutes, *The Sentencing and Parole Process.* New York: National Council on Crime and Delinquency, 1964.

Newman, Donald J., "Pleading Guilty for Considerations: A Study of Bargain Justice," *Journal of Criminal Law, Criminology, and Police Science,* 46:780–790, March–April, 1956.

Ohlin, Lloyd E., and Frank J. Remington, "Sentencing Structure: Its Effect Upon Systems for the Administration of Criminal Justice," *Law and Contemporary Problems,* 23:497–507, Summer, 1958.

Pound, Roscoe, *Criminal Justice in America.* Cambridge: Harvard University Press, 1945.

Powers, Edwin, "What's New In Sentencing?" *Correctional Research*

(United Prison Association of Massachusetts), Bulletin No. 7, October, 1957.

Robinson, W. S., "Bias, Probability, and Trial By Jury," *American Sociological Review*, 15:73–78, February, 1950.

Rubin, Sol, *The Law of Criminal Correction*. St. Paul: West Publishing Co., 1963.

Schulman, Sidney, *Toward Judicial Reform in Pennsylvania*. Philadelphia: University of Pennsylvania Law School, 1962.

Special Committee of the Association of the Bar of the City of New York and the National Legal Aid and Defender Association, *Equal Justice for the Accused*. New York: Doubleday, 1959.

Strodtbeck, Fred L., and R. D. Mann, "Sex Role Differentiation in Jury Deliberations," *Sociometry*, 19:3–11, March, 1956.

Strodtbeck, Fred L., Rita M. James, and Charles Hawkins, "Social Status in Jury Deliberations," *American Sociological Review*, 22:713–719, December, 1957.

Sunderland, E. R., "Qualifications and Compensation of Minor Court Judges," *Journal of the American Judicature Society*, 29:111–116, December, 1945.

Walker, Nigel, *Crime and Punishment in Britain*. Edinburgh: University Press, 1965.

Wood, Arthur Lewis, "Informal Relations in the Practice of Criminal Law," *American Journal of Sociology*, 62:48–55, July, 1956.

Younger, Richard D., "The Grand Jury Under Attack," *Journal of Criminal Law, Criminology and Police Science*, 46:26–49, May–June, 1955.

# 20. THE JUVENILE COURT

At COMMON LAW, a century and a half ago, children were tried and punished for violations of law in the same ways as adults, with the exception that a child under seven years of age was regarded as not responsible and therefore as incapable of committing a crime, while a child between the ages of seven and fourteen was regarded as having the possibility of such discernment as would make him responsible, and this was to be decided in each case by an examination. A child under seven years of age, therefore, could not be punished by order of the court, while a child between the ages of seven and fourteen could be subjected to all forms of punishment that were suitable for adults. In the course of time the maximum age was raised in some American states from seven to ten or some other age, but it still happens that children under fourteen years of age are arrested, held in jail, tried in court, and punished in the same ways as adult criminals. In 1963, almost 5 percent of the persons admitted to the three major Massachusetts prisons were 17 years of age or younger.[1]

ORIGINS AND DEVELOPMENT OF THE JUVENILE COURT. Differential reactions to the offenses perpetrated by children and those committed by adults have been developing for more than a century. While the societal reaction to the offenses of both groups has been slowly changing from a punitive to a treatment reaction, this change has been much more pronounced in the case of juveniles. At least the official policies for dealing with juvenile offenders have incorporated more treatment methods than have the official policies for dealing with adult offenders. As early as 1824 a juvenile reformatory was established in New York State so that children, after conviction, would not be confined with adult criminals. The laws of Illinois in 1831 provided that for certain offenses the penalties for minors

[1] Commissioner of Correction, *Statistical Reports* (Boston: Massachusetts Public Document No. 115, 1963), pp. 27–29.

might differ from those for adults. In 1861 the legislature of Illinois authorized the mayor of Chicago to appoint a commissioner before whom boys between the ages of six and seventeen could be taken on charges of petty offenses; this commissioner had authority to place the boys on probation, to send them to reform schools, and, generally, to use treatment methods. In 1867, this work was transferred to the regular judges of the courts. Separate hearings for juvenile offenders were required in Boston in 1870 and in all parts of the state of Massachusetts in 1872. In 1877, both Massachusetts and New York State authorized separate sessions with separate dockets and records for juvenile cases. During the last quarter of the nineteenth century, cases of truancy and incorrigibility of children were heard in some places by probate courts, without juries or the ordinary legal technicalities and formalities.[2]

These policies were combined and were supported by a consistent theory, which had been lacking in the earlier developments, and thus the juvenile court came into existence in 1899 in Chicago. The two significant points about this new court were: First, the age below which a child could not be a criminal was advanced from seven to sixteen years, which was in line with changes that had been made elsewhere. But whereas the previous law had made no definite provision for dealing with culprits below the age of responsibility, the new law did make provision for dealing with them under the softer name "delinquents." Second, the work of the court was placed under chancery or equity jurisdiction. For several centuries dependent children had been under chancery jurisdiction; in principle all children were wards of the state if their parents were not willing or able to care for them; in practice the protection of dependent children was confined almost entirely to those who had property. The juvenile court law of Chicago was merely a logical extension of this principle of guardianship by the court of chancery to all children who were in need of the protection and guardianship of the state, and thus was made to include delinquent children.

The juvenile court movement developed rapidly after the Chicago court was authorized. Twenty-two states had somewhat similar laws within ten years. By 1925 all except two states—Maine and Wyoming—had such laws, and by 1945, when Wyoming passed its law, all states had juvenile court laws. In 1932, a federal law authorized the federal courts to divert juvenile cases to the juvenile courts of the several states. The Federal Bureau of Prisons and the Federal Children's Bureau attempted to develop

[2] For an excellent discussion of the history, trends, and problems of the juvenile court, see Robert G. Caldwell, "The Juvenile Court: Its Development and some Major Problems," Journal of Criminal Law, Criminology and Police Science, 51:493–511, January, 1961.

the policy co-operatively, with the hope that most of the federal juvenile cases could be turned over to the states. But in the first two years very few of the federal juvenile cases were thus diverted, due principally to the fact that the maximum age jurisdiction of the juvenile courts in most of the states excluded a large proportion of the federal cases and partly to the fact that many of the states did not have adequate facilities for treating federal delinquents. Consequently, in 1938 the Federal government adopted a juvenile court act. The juvenile court movement has spread to other continents, and most of the civilized countries now have specialized juvenile courts.

The juvenile court movement has developed administratively as well as geographically. The age of the children coming under the court's jurisdiction has been raised from sixteen to seventeen or eighteen and in some places even to twenty-one. Adults who commit crimes against children or contribute to the delinquency or dependency of children are included in the jurisdiction of many juvenile courts. Many administrative tasks have been assumed by the juvenile court, including adoption proceedings, mother's pensions, recreational work, and educational work. These tasks are ordinarily administered as part of the preventive program of the court.

COMPARISON OF THE JUVENILE COURT AND CRIMINAL COURT. A comparison of the juvenile court with the criminal court is difficult because of the large number of variations in the procedure and organization of each court. At present, the actual practices of some juvenile courts do not differ a great deal from the practices of some criminal courts. Perhaps there is as much variation among juvenile courts as there is between juvenile and criminal courts. The following comparison refers to the conventional criminal court, without its recent modifications, and to the juvenile court in its ideal form.[3]

The juvenile court in most places and in many respects is significantly different from this description, and the criminal court in some respects has approached rather closely to the description of the juvenile court. Nevertheless, there is, characteristically, a significant difference between them: The expected reaction of the criminal court personnel to crime is punitive —they seek, with some exceptions, to implement a punitive reaction to an offense. In contrast, the expected reaction of the juvenile court personnel is that of treatment—they seek, with some exceptions, to implement a treatment reaction to the offender. The *ideal* of the juvenile courts is that

[3] For a more extended comparison, see Pauline V. Young, *Social Treatment in Probation and Delinquency*, Second Edition (New York: McGraw-Hill, 1952), pp. 226–229; and Herbert A. Bloch and Frank T. Flynn, *Delinquency* (New York: Random House, 1956), pp. 340–342.

| Criminal Court | Juvenile Court |
|---|---|
| 1. Trial characterized by contentiousness; two partisan groups in conflict. | 1. Hearing characterized by scientific methods of investigation. |
| 2. Purpose of trial to determine whether defendant committed the crime with which he is charged. | 2. Purpose of hearing to determine whether the child is delinquent and the general condition and character of the child. |
| 3. Little machinery for securing information regarding the character of the accused. | 3. Elaborate machinery for securing information regarding the character of the child. |
| 4. Such information, if secured, may not be introduced as a part of the evidence. | 4. Such information is the basis on which a decision is made. |
| 5. Punishment if convicted. | 5. Protection, guardianship, and treatment by the state if the existing conditions show the need. |
| 6. Correctional methods in a specific case determined not by the needs of the particular individual but by the legislature, in advance, for all who violate the law in question, with reference primarily to other actual or potential criminals. | 6. Correctional methods in a specific case determined by the needs of the particular individual without reference to other actual or potential delinquents. |

the personnel "are not looking outwardly at the act but, scrutinizing it as a symptom, are looking forward to what the child is to become."[4]

**CHARACTERISTICS OF THE JUVENILE COURT.** The characteristics of the juvenile court, stated in more detail, are as follows.

*Broad definition of delinquency.* A "blanket" definition of "juvenile delinquency" or of a "delinquent child" is provided. The State of Illinois, for example, uses the following definition of a delinquent child:

A delinquent child is any male who while under the age of 17 years, or any female child who while under the age of 18 years, violates any law of this state; or is incorrigible, or knowingly associates with thieves, vicious or immoral persons; or without just cause and without the consent of its parents, guardian or custodian absents itself from its home or place of abode, or is growing up in idleness or crime; or knowingly frequents a

[4] White House Conference on Child Health and Protection, *The Delinquent Child* (New York: Appleton-Century-Crofts, 1932), p. 257. Reprinted by permission of the publishers.

house of ill repute; or knowingly frequents any policy shop or place where any gambling device is operated; or frequents any saloon or dram-shop where intoxicating liquors are sold; or patronizes or visits any public pool room or bucket shop; or wanders about the streets in the night time without being on any lawful business or lawful occupation; or habitually wanders about any railroad yards or tracks or jumps or attempts to jump onto any moving train; or enters any car or engine without lawful authority; or uses vile, obscene, vulgar, or indecent language in any public place or about any school house; or is guilty of indecent or lascivious conduct.[5]

In the standard juvenile court law formulated by the National Probation Association, in California, and in the District of Columbia, the concept of delinquency is similarly avoided. These laws are even more general than the Illinois law, and they simply establish the fact that juvenile courts have jurisdiction over children who behave in certain general ways. For example, in the standard act jurisdiction is established over those "whose occupation, behavior, environment, or associations are injurious to his welfare," and those "who violate any state law or municipal ordinance."[6]

Definitions of the neglected child and the dependent child also are stated in general terms. The behavior of such children is quite different from behavior which, except for the age of the offender, would be crime. However, a careful distinction between the two kinds of behavior often is not made. As Tappan has said, "Whether a child be held delinquent, neglected, or dependent may depend chiefly on the petitioner and his motive rather than either the child's conduct or his more basic problem of adjustment."[7] It was not through oversight that the juvenile court was given jurisdiction over both delinquent and dependent children and uses essentially the same procedures for both. In dealing with either kind of case the purpose is supposed to be the same: to determine whether the child needs special guardianship by the state. The elements of guilt, responsibility, criminal intent, and punishment are, theoretically at least, not considered in either case. The omnibus definitions of delinquency are the logical extension of this theory. The assumption is that the results of contact with the juvenile court are beneficial, not harmful or punitive, and, consequently, precise descriptions of proscribed acts are not necessary.

[5] *Illinois Revised Statutes* (Chicago: Burdette Smith, 1949), pp. 1315–1316.
[6] National Probation Association, *A Standard Juvenile Court Act* (New York: Author, 1943), p. 10. For an enumeration of items mentioned in juvenile court laws as constituting delinquency, see Sol Rubin, "The Legal Character of Juvenile Delinquency," *Annals of the American Academy of Political and Social Science*, 261:1–8, January, 1949.
[7] Paul W. Tappan, *Juvenile Delinquency* (New York: McGraw-Hill, 1949), p. 20.

In practice, some criteria for distinguishing between delinquents and non-delinquents must be used by the courts, and, although the result is called "adjudication" or "finding" rather than "conviction" or "acquittal," the criteria used are very similar to those used in the criminal courts. For example, a juvenile court using the Illinois statute reprinted above would have to consider the question of guilt or intent in order to determine whether a child has *knowingly* associated with thieves or *knowingly* frequented a gambling house. Thus, "delinquency" becomes a mere softening of the word *crime*, for in distinguishing between delinquency and dependency the juvenile court in fact considers delinquents as "young" criminals." Perhaps the juvenile courts have assumed jurisdiction over neglected and dependent children in order to prevent such children from becoming "young criminals." In 1963, 72 percent of the 109,967 juvenile cases referred by California juvenile courts for probation handling were classed as "delinquent," meaning that they usually had committed acts which, except for their age, would be crime. Nineteen percent were cases of dependency, neglect, or parental abuse; and 9 percent were traffic or other cases.[8] In the United States, about 75 percent of the children referred to juvenile courts are delinquency cases, about twenty percent are dependency and neglect cases, and about five percent are involved in special proceedings, such as adoption.

*Equity or chancery jurisdiction.* Equity courts stand for flexibility, guardianship, and protection rather than rigidity and punishment. Consequently, friends of the juvenile court insist that children's cases should fall within the equity jurisdiction rather than the criminal jurisdiction. Supreme courts have approved of this in several decisions. But there is minority opinion. In the early period of the juvenile court movement, E. Lindsey, for instance, contended that there is no justification for placing the juvenile court under equity jurisdiction, and stated that the decisions of the supreme courts were due to the influence of public opinion and to the fact that few persons of wealth or influence had fought the question in courts.[9] More recently, Tappan has argued that the methods used in juvenile courts actually are not chancery procedures and that the analogy has been used merely to rationalize the abandonment of the basic elements of due process of law.[10] Diana has shown that in many jurisdictions almost all the procedural safeguards of the criminal law have been removed in

[8] Bureau of Criminal Statistics, *Delinquency and Probation in California,* 1963 (Scramento: Department of Justice, 1964), p. 100.
[9] E. Lindsey, "The Juvenile Court Movement from a Lawyer's Standpoint," *Annals of the American Academy of Political and Social Science,* 52:140–148, March, 1914.
[10] Tappan, *op. cit.,* pp. 204–205.

children's cases, so that the court has become a child-guidance agency whose decisions are supported by the coercive power of the state.[11]

Many courts that try children's cases do not have equity powers. Many of them have, nevertheless, adopted what is often called the equity procedure: informality in hearings, inquiries regarding character and general needs of the child, separate hearings, separate records, and so on. They are not distinguishable in procedure from the children's courts that operate under so-called equity jurisdiction.

3) *Informal procedures.* Whether the jurisdiction is that of equity or not, procedure in the juvenile court is generally required, by law, to be "summary" or informal. The proceedings begin with a *complaint* against a child. Ordinarily, this is called a "petition in behalf" of the child. He often is arrested, but he may be merely summoned to appear in court, or his parents may be summoned to bring him into court. The police are supposed to be more considerate and friendly when arresting juveniles, as compared with their attitudes toward adults. Next, the child is arraigned. This arraignment is similar to the preliminary hearing of an adult offender, except that the child has more privacy. He is told, in a more or less informal manner, of the charge against him. Following the arraignment, a *hearing* may be held immediately, or the court may adjourn until a social investigation has been made by a probation officer. In some courts this investigation is not held until after the court has indicated that a child is delinquent, but the trend is toward pre-hearing investigations.[12] The *investigations* involve not merely the questions of fact regarding a specified offense, but the whole social situation of the child—especially his home and neighborhood conditions. In many places physical, mental, and psychiatric examinations are made also. The information secured in this way is the basis of decisions and policies. Whether the adjournment of the court comes after an immediate hearing or before a hearing, the child is either placed in detention or released on his own recognizance, called "parole" in some juvenile courts. He usually is entitled to bail, but this procedure is seldom used.

Following the adjournment and the social investigation, a *hearing*, corresponding to the trial in adult courts, is held. The juvenile court judge may hear the case either in his chambers or in the courtroom, but the

[11] Lewis Diana, "The Rights of Juvenile Delinquents: An Appraisal of Juvenile Court Procedures," *Journal of Criminal Law and Criminology*, 47:561–569, January–February, 1957. See also Hercules Al Cavalier, "Juvenile Courts and Delinquents," *The Catholic World*, 181:110–115, May, 1955; Matthew J. Beemsterboer, "The Juvenile Court—Benevolence in the Star Chamber," *Journal of Criminal Law, Criminology and Police Science*, 50:464–475, January, 1960; and Frank E. Hartung, *Crime, Law and Society* (Detroit: Wayne State University Press, 1965), pp. 219–244.

[12] Tappan, *op. cit.*, pp. 187, 212–215.

courtroom is generally arranged so that spectators are so far removed from the bench or table at which the judge is sitting that they cannot hear the conversation. The records are customarily regarded as confidential, and some states prohibit the publication of information on juvenile court cases or printing a photograph of a child in the juvenile court.[13] The general practice in the hearings is to exercise care in weighing evidence, but without the same observance of forms as in the criminal courts. Ordinarily, it is necessary to show a specific violation of law, even of the blanket provisions; that is, it must be established by a preponderance of evidence, for example, that the child did violate a specific municipal ordinance or is in a specific way growing up in idleness or crime.[14] This specific proof is the basis of the whole treatment procedure. When the statutes are couched in vague and general terms, however, there is much room for disagreement on what constitutes "proof," and in some courts the specific charge is not considered as important as is the fact that a child might have a problem which must be discovered and treated. In many courts the entire hearing and adjudication process is avoided by dealing with the child unofficially, especially when there is no real evidence of delinquency. In recent years about half the cases reported to the U.S. Children's Bureau have been unofficial. Thus, the juvenile court acts as a social agency as well as a court.

Even in the juvenile courts which operate under equity jurisdiction many elements of criminal procedure may be found. First, the rights to counsel and trial by jury are retained, largely due to the fear that the supreme court might otherwise find the law unconstitutional.[15] However, the necessity of exercising such rights is minimized, and few children or parents demand an attorney or a jury trial. The National Probation Association stated that jury trials "are inconsistent with both the law and the theory upon which children's codes are founded." Second, juvenile court decisions may be appealed to the criminal courts. In forty states and the District of Columbia special provisions are made in the law for such appeals. A study of the appeals from the juvenile courts in Suffolk County, Massachusetts, from 1930 to 1935, revealed that the Superior Court filed, nol prossed, or discharged as not delinquent 46.1 percent of these appeal cases. Also, of 216 children who had been ordered to spend time in institutions by the juvenile courts only 9.3 percent were committed to institutions by the Superior Court. The reasons for these changes from the

---

[13] See Gilbert Geis, "Publicity and Juvenile Court Proceedings," *Rocky Mountain Law Review*, 30:1–26, February, 1958.

[14] Frederick B. Sussman, *Laws of Juvenile Delinquency* (New York: Oceana Publications, 1950), pp. 30–34.

[15] For a recent decision in a California case, see *In re Contreras*, 291 P. 2d 631 (March 18, 1952).

decision of the juvenile court is not necessarily that the higher court has a better basis for a decision than the juvenile court, but that the judge and the district attorney, struggling with an overload of work, regard the juvenile cases as trivial in comparison with the adult cases on which they are usually engaged, and as not deserving of serious consideration.[16]

*Third,* delinquency, while given a blanket definition by some phrases, is defined also by some specific phrases, in imitation of the criminal law. *Fourth,* the juvenile courts in their reports frequently classify offenses in terms of the criminal law, such as grand larceny, petty larceny, etc. Similarly, in an early New York case it was stated by a criminal court that an adult defendant charged with receiving stolen property could not offer the defense that since the property had been purchased from a "juvenile delinquent," not from a "thief" or a "criminal," it was not "stolen."[17] *Fifth,* most judges use methods that are distinctly those of the criminal court, including fines and short-term imprisonment. From the point of view of juvenile court theory, commitment to an institution is not an infliction of punishment but is a substitute for home training; in practice judges frequently order a delinquent child committed to an institution and then explain that the order will be suspended and the child will be given another chance on probation. Commitment to the institution is held over the child's head as a threat and is regarded as a punishment by the child, his parents, and the judge. The juvenile court is generally regarded, in spite of legal theory, as a place in which bad children are punished.[18] In the minds of the child, the parents, the neighbors, and others, juvenile court action is generally equivalent to a criminal process. The feeling is increased and justified by the fact that a very large proportion of the complaints against or petitions in behalf of delinquent children are filed by police officers. About 56 percent of the cases referred to Chicago's Family Court come from the police,[19] and in California 91 percent of the boy delinquency cases and 81 percent of the girl delinquency cases in 1963 were referred by police.[20]

*The court having jurisdiction.* Jurisdiction over children's cases varies widely from state to state and even from county to county within a state.

[16] Benedict S. Alper, "Juvenile Justice: A Study of Juvenile Appeals to the Suffolk County Court, Boston, 1930–1935," *Journal of Criminal Law and Criminology,* 28: 349–367, September–October, 1937.

[17] *Pollack vs. People,* Supreme Court of New York, Appellate Division, 1913. 154 App. Div. 716.

[18] *Cf.* John R. Erickson, *Some Parental Reactions to the Juvenile Court* (Unpublished M.S.W. Thesis, Simmons College School of Social Work, 1958).

[19] Harold P. O'Connell, "Role of the Family Court," in Joseph D. Lohman, Editor, *Searchlights on Delinquency* (Chicago: Cook County Sheriff's Office, 1955, mimeographed.)

[20] Bureau of Criminal Statistics, *op. cit.,* pp. 70–73.

The juvenile court is sometimes independent, sometimes a specialized part of another court. By 1947, independent juvenile courts had been created in 27 states and the District of Columbia, but in many of these states the juvenile court was independent only in certain counties.[21] The juvenile court usually is a specialized branch of some other court, generally a county court or a probate court. Lou described these juvenile courts as "designated courts," since they are appended to other court systems, and consist legally of special sessions or divisions or departments of some existing court.[22] Because county court judges preside over many of the independent juvenile courts, the independent courts are scarcely distinguishable from these designated courts.[23]

In thirty-seven states, the District of Columbia, and in parts of another state, the juvenile court, whether independent or designated, has exclusive jurisdiction in children's cases, with certain exceptions. In the other states the child may be taken either to the juvenile court or to a branch of the criminal court. Also, provision is frequently made in states in which the juvenile court has exclusive original jurisdiction that the judge may, at his discretion, transfer cases involving serious offenses to the criminal court. In eleven states and parts of another the juvenile court does not have any jurisdiction over juveniles charged with offenses which, if committed by adults, would be punishable by death or by life imprisonment, and similar limitations are made in five other states for serious offenses.[24] Good reasons exist for the opinion that the juvenile court should have original, exclusive, and complete jurisdiction over all cases of delinquency of children. The fact that in some states the jurisdiction of the juvenile courts and the criminal courts is concurrent, as well as the fact that serious offenses are excepted from the jurisdiction of the juvenile court, reveals that in some jurisdictions, at least, there is obvious confusion in the purposes of the juvenile statutes. It is asserted that the child is not responsible for crime and should not, therefore, be punished; yet violations which in the criminal law call for the most severe punishments are excepted.

The county generally is the territorial unit for the juvenile court system, but in some places the city is taken as the unit. The county system has many advantages at present, since most agencies co-operating with the court are organized along county lines. Also, when the city is taken as the unit, the rural parts of the county in which the city is located are left

[21] Figures based on National Probation and Parole Association, *Directory of Probation and Parole Officers*, 1947; computed by Negley K. Teeters and J. O. Reinemann, *The Challenge of Delinquency* (New York: Prentice-Hall, 1950), p. 295.

[22] Herbert H. Lou, *Juvenile Courts in the United States* (Chapel Hill: University of North Carolina Press, 1927), p. 34.

[23] See Gilbert Cosulich, *Juvenile Court Laws of the United States* (New York: National Probation Association, 1937), p. 13.

[24] Tappan, *op. cit.*, pp. 14, 18.

without provision for juveniles. In recent years even the county has been recognized as too small for efficient administration, and state-administered and state-financed courts are now operating in Connecticut, Utah, and Rhode Island.[25]

5) *Age jurisdiction.* Age jurisdiction also varies widely from state to state. In 1946 the maximum age for boys in juvenile courts was sixteen years in seven states, seventeen in eight states, eighteen in twenty-six states, nineteen in one state, and twenty-one in seven states. However, in six states the maximum age varied within the state. The maximum age for girls was sixteen in five states, seventeen in six states, eighteen in thirty-one states, and twenty-one in seven states. The maximum age for girls is higher than for boys in five states. In each of the seven states that extend jurisdiction to the age of twenty-one the criminal court has concurrent power to try serious cases.[26] In many states a child taken into the juvenile court before he reaches the maximum age of juvenile court jurisdiction remains within the jurisdiction of the juvenile court until a later age, generally until he reaches majority. In practice, however, few cases appear in the juvenile courts under this provision.

Many juvenile courts also have jurisdiction over certain adults. Forty-three states have laws which make it possible to deal through the courts with parents or others who contribute to the delinquency or dependency of children, and in thirty-one states and parts of six others it is the juvenile courts which have this jurisdiction, with limitations in some states. The juvenile court in a few states is given jurisdiction over the following specified groups: adults deserting or failing to support juveniles, adults accused of crimes against children, adults violating the child-labor law, parents failing to comply with the compulsory school law or concealing the birth of a child, adults aiding a child to escape from an institution, adults furnishing children in institutions with tobacco. Of 1,027 cases coming before the Domestic Relations and Juvenile Court of Toledo in the ten year period 1937–1946, approximately 50 percent were against parents, 76 percent of whom either pleaded or were found guilty.[27] However, the judge in this court has declared that its experiment in punishing parents for the crimes of their children is a failure.[28]

The justifications offered for extending the jurisdiction of these adults are that it keeps the child, even as a witness, out of the criminal court, that

[25] For a description of the Utah system, see John F. Larson, "Utah's State-Wide Juvenile Court Plan," *Federal Probation,* 13:15–17, June, 1949.

[26] Tappan, *op. cit.,* pp. 13–15. See also Sussman, *op. cit.,* p. 17.

[27] Paul W. Alexander, "What's This About Punishing Parents?" *Federal Probation,* 12:23–29, March, 1948.

[28] Paul W. Alexander, quoted in John and June Robbins, "Punishing Parents Doesn't Work," *This Week Magazine,* February 3, 1957, pp. 8–9 ff.

it is easier to deal with all the significant personnel together, and that judges in other courts hesitate to use the ordinary criminal sanctions in dealing with such offenders, and consequently discharge them with a futile warning. However, the informal procedures of the juvenile court do not safeguard civil rights, and many persons have therefore argued that the juvenile court hearing should not be used in dealing with adults. One judge has written, for example:

> The hearing, instead of remaining an investigation, would frequently become an inquisition; instead of impartial inquiry into the condition of a juvenile it might become a contested court trial with the judge as the accuser; instead of frankly admitting misconduct the child, probably cautioned or coached, would admit nothing and involve no one; instead of getting confidence and cooperation from parents, relatives and friends, one would be likely to find them on guard against being incriminated or incriminating anyone.[29]

6) The judge. The judge of the juvenile court is elected in certain cities or counties in six states, appointed by the governor in certain cities or counties in five states, and by the President of the United States in the District of Columbia. In by far the largest proportion of counties the judge is elected as judge of the ordinary local court, then later assumes the duties of a juvenile court judge. In most rural counties there is only one judge for all types of cases; the judge of the county, circuit, or district court, of which the juvenile court is a part, acts ex-officio as judge of the juvenile court. In the larger cities where the juvenile court is more completely separated from the court of which it is a branch, and one judge gives full time to juvenile court work, the judge of the juvenile court is appointed by his associates in most cases. When the appointment is not made in this way the judges frequently rotate, each one taking one month, or two months, or perhaps a year in the juvenile court. This method of rotation does not necessarily select judges who are best able to deal with juveniles, but one study indicated that Iowa Juvenile Court judges conceive of their role as one approximating the role defined in juvenile court philosophy, rather than as one approximating that of the criminal court judge.[30] Only two percent of all counties in the United States have full-time juvenile court judges, and one-third of these are not especially selected for the work.[31]

---

[29] G. Loevinger, "The Court and the Child." *Focus*, 28:65–69 ff., May, 1949. Reprinted by permission of the publisher.

[30] F. James Davis, "The Iowa Juvenile Court Judge," *Journal of Criminal Law and Criminology*, 42:338–350, September–October, 1951.

[31] Sol Rubin, "State Juvenile Court: A New Standard," *Focus*, 30:103–107, July, 1951.

Because the definitions of delinquency and the rules of law regarding juvenile court procedures are not precisely stated in most instances, the judge plays an exceedingly important role in the proceedings. It is his duty to order that the best available treatment procedures be applied to delinquents. At the same time, it is his duty to protect the rights of all children coming before the court and to declare children "delinquent" and, hence, subject to treatment, only when there are legal grounds for doing so. Familiarity with social science is necessary to the efficient performance of the first duty. For this reason, some persons have recommended that judges should be persons trained in principles of child welfare rather than in law. The second duty, however, requires decisions on issues of law, and other persons have argued that the judge must have adequate legal training.[32] Evidently it is desirable for the judge to have both legal training and knowledge of the behavior sciences. It is not possible to dispense with the legal character of the juvenile court or with the requirement that judges be trained in law.

It is possible, however, for very much of the work to be done under the supervision of the judge by persons who have not had legal training. Many cases are now settled by probation officers who have no legal training. In about one-third of the states the law gives juvenile court judges authority to appoint referees who make tentative disposals of cases, subject to the judge's subsequent approval. This power to appoint referees makes it possible for the judge to transfer all cases of girls involved in sex delinquency to a woman who, as referee, will make the decisions to be approved by the judge if desirable. This power is valuable, also, in extending the court to rural districts that are far from the place where the sessions of the court are held. If no such arrangement is made, offenses are passed over, if the injury is trivial, until it may become too late to modify the behavior of the offender, or the justice of the peace is appealed to for the exercise of his police power, or some other unsatisfactory method is adopted because of the inconvenience of attending the sessions of the juvenile court. This can be avoided by the appointment of several referees to act under the supervision of the judge. The same extension of the juvenile court may be found advantageous in the large cities.

1) **The disposition** The procedure called sentencing in the criminal courts generally is named "disposition" in the juvenile courts. The disposition of a case and the treatment of the child theoretically is determined by the whole investigation, of which the court procedure is only a part. In a very large proportion of the cases advice is given to the parents or to others

[32] See, for example, Paul W. Alexander, "Of Juvenile Court Justice and Judges," *National Probation Association Yearbook*, 1947, pp. 187–205.

and the case is dismissed; in some places such cases do not get to the judge at all, but are settled unofficially by the probation officers. No petition is filed, no court record or formal charge is made, and no hearing is held. Fifty percent of the delinquency cases reported to the Children's Bureau in 1963 were settled informally or unofficially.[33] The major methods used in disposing of official cases are continuance, probation, commitment, and referral to an agency or to an individual.

The continuance is designed as a test of the offender and his parents without special assistance or supervision by the court. It differs from dismissal of the petition (often called "adjustment" or "discharge") largely in that the judge feels that further action of the court might be necessary. It also differs from probation, which includes, theoretically at least, supervision and guidance by a probation officer. Probation is used in a large proportion of the cases in places where juvenile court methods have developed. But in places where the judge has had no special training in the problems of juvenile delinquency, where there are no social workers, psychologists, or psychiatrists, the child is either dismissed or committed to an institution. Referral to a social work agency, to a foster home, or to a qualified individual also is impossible in many small, rural, counties. Even when a child is placed on probation in such places, he generally is given no supervision or guidance. The difference between such places and those in which trained probation officers are employed may be illustrated by a comparison of the methods of disposing of juvenile court cases in California's seventeen largest counties and in the remaining 41 counties, which are more rural and which handle relatively few delinquents.[34] This is shown in Table XV.

Other methods used in making dispositions are the imposition of a fine, ordering of restitution or reparation, confinement in a detention home for a short period, and whipping. It is the general weight of opinion that each of these, with the exception of restitution and reparation, is a means of punishment and is hence inconsistent with the philosophy of the juvenile court. The committee on juvenile court standards recommends that "restitution or reparation should be required only in cases where they seem to have disciplinary value or to instill respect for property rights." The method of commitment to a detention home for a few days is much like commitment of adults to jails for a few days, and it is considered injurious. The

[33] U.S. Department of Health, Education, and Welfare, Welfare Administration, *Juvenile Court Statistics*, 1963, (Washington, U.S. Department of Health, Education, and Welfare, 1964), Statistical Series No. 79, p. 11.

[34] Bureau of Criminal Statistics, *Delinquency and Probation in California*, 1963 (Sacramento: Department of Justice, 1964), p. 104.

## TABLE XV

CALIFORNIA JUVENILE COURT DISPOSITIONS RESULTING FROM INITIAL PETITIONS
CITING BOYS FOR DELINQUENT ACTS, 1963

|  | 17 Counties Over 200,000 Population | 41 Other Counties |
|---|---|---|
| Number of cases | 24,156 | 3,833 |
| Dismissed | 13.5 | 16.7 |
| Transferred to other county | 1.9 | 7.3 |
| Remanded to adult court | .6 | 1.3 |
| Committed to Youth Authority | 2.3 | 3.0 |
| Placed on probation | 81.7 | 71.7 |

juvenile court in one state is authorized by law to order a delinquent child to be whipped, and this method is used in isolated instances in other states as well.

THE SUCCESS OF THE JUVENILE COURT. If it could be demonstrated that the juvenile offense rate in areas possessing juvenile courts is lower than the rate in areas without such courts, then, all other things being equal, there would be little question about the success of the juvenile court. This fact has not been demonstrated, however, for two reasons. First, in order to make such a study it would be necessary to locate two areas comparable in every significant respect, so that only the presence of a juvenile court was the differentiating factor. Second, it would be necessary to measure the amount of juvenile delinquency in each case. While the first difficulty could be partially surmounted by comparing an area before and after it established a juvenile court, experience in the past has indicated that judicial statistics do not precisely measure the amount of crime or delinquency. In Chicago, and probably to an equal extent in most other towns and cities, 95 percent of the children who commit delinquencies serious enough to result in arrests are kept at the police station and then unofficially released by the police. The Cambridge-Somerville Youth Study indicated that official action was taken in less than 1.5 percent of 6,416 infractions of the law by boys over a five-year period.[35] Also, broad definitions contribute to the difficulty of comparing the juvenile offense rates at various places and times. Consequently, the effects of juvenile court work must be measured in some other way.

Two alternative methods, both severely limited by the fact that many children under the care of the juvenile court commit delinquencies which

---

[35] Fred J. Murphy, Mary M. Shirley, and Helen L. Witmer, "The Incidence of Hidden Delinquency," *American Journal of Orthopsychiatry*, 16:686–696, October, 1946.

do not come to the attention of the juvenile court, have been used. *First*, several studies have been made of the subsequent "success" or "failure" of cases handled by juvenile courts. Healy and Bronner report that of 800 boys studied in Boston, 24.6 percent appeared subsequently in adult courts, and that of 420 boys studied in Chicago, 61 percent were failures subsequently, of whom 16 percent became professional criminals and 5 percent became murderers.[36] Sheldon and Eleanor T. Glueck found that of 1,000 juvenile delinquents in the Boston Juvenile Court and the Judge Baker Foundation 88.2 percent had additional delinquencies during the subsequent five years and that 70 percent of them had an average of 3.6 arrests each.[37] Dunham and Knauer found that 30.6 percent of 500 boys, a random sample of 6,976 cases, coming before the Detroit Juvenile Court in the period 1920–1940 were registered with the Detroit Police Department within five years of the time they left the jurisdiction of the juvenile court.[38] Of 101,043 children dealt with by the juvenile courts of Ohio during the five year period 1943–1947, 42.7 percent were repeaters.[39] A follow-up survey that yielded information on 257 of 300 cases originally studied by Merrill in California indicated that 47.9 percent were recidivists.[40] Of 1,275 children found guilty by the Glasgow, Scotland, juvenile court in 1946, 49 percent reappeared in court at least once between 1946 and 1953.[41] Also, dozens of boys have written life histories which describe many delinquencies after juvenile court appearances.

A *second* method of appraising the success of the juvenile court is by enumerating the offenders in adult courts or adolescents' courts who have previously been in juvenile court. Of 145 men committed to New York State Prisons and Reformatories, 42 percent had appeared at least once in juvenile courts.[42] Of 847 boys appearing in the Chicago Boys' Court during

---

[36] William Healy and Augusta F. Bronner, *Delinquents and Criminals, Their Making and Unmaking* (New York: Macmillan, 1926), pp. 245, 253.

[37] Sheldon and Eleanor T. Glueck, *One Thousand Juvenile Delinquents* (Cambridge: Harvard University Press, 1934), p. 167. See also their *Juvenile Delinquents Grow Up* (New York: The Commonwealth Fund, 1940), pp. 16, 26, 43, 59.

[38] H. Warren Dunham and Mary E. Knauer, "The Juvenile Court in Its Relationship to Adult Criminality," *Social Forces*, 32:290–296, March, 1954. See also LaMay Adamson and H. Warren Dunham, "Clinical Treatment of Male Delinquents: A Case Study in Effort and Result," *American Sociological Review*, 21:312–320, June, 1956.

[39] C. H. Growden, *A Group Study of Juvenile Homicide* (Columbus: State Bureau of Juvenile Research, Department of Welfare, 1949); cited by Teeters and Reinemann, *op. cit.*, p. 19.

[40] Maud A. Merrill, *Problems of Child Delinquency* (New York: Houghton Mifflin, 1947), p. 292.

[41] John A. Mack, *Delinquency and the Changing Social Pattern* (Glasgow: Charles Russell Memorial Lecture, 1956), pp. 3–4.

[42] New York Crime Commission, *Individual Studies of 145 Offenders* (Albany: J. B. Lyon, 1928), p. 22.

1924–1925, 24.5 percent had appeared previously in juvenile court.[43] Consequently it is evident that so far as official records are concerned, a very large proportion of first appearances occur after adolescence. Similarly, the Massachusetts prison reports show that approximately 27 percent of the offenders sentenced to the state prison and the state reformatories had previously been committed to institutions for delinquent children,[44] and a Michigan study indicated that 43 percent of the prison inmates studied had juvenile court records.[45]

Such statistical enumerations, of course, do not precisely test the effects of the juvenile court, since it is not clear what proportion of the subjects involved would have been recidivists if they had been dealt with in some other way. Also, insofar as the wards of the juvenile court refrain from subsequent delinquency, it is not clear why they do so. The assumption has been that the treatment methods used in connection with the juvenile court are the explanation. But serious questions have been raised regarding the validity of the belief that individualized treatment methods are valuable in a large proportion of cases.[46] For example, some years ago it was proposed that an intensive study be made of the Cincinnati court, which had a reputation for unusual success in turning delinquents from their careers, but a preliminary investigation showed that the court was far inferior to the Boston juvenile court in its standards of case work and facilities for case work although it secured at least equally successful results. Consequently, it was concluded that whatever degree of success the Cincinnati court might have could not be explained by its case work methods.[47]

On the basis of such information as has been presented, some of the leaders of the juvenile court movement have stated that the juvenile court is a dismal failure, while others have become convinced that it is highly successful. Those considering it a success point out that it is unfair to the court to test it in terms of absolute cessation of delinquency years after court treatment. Taft uses an analogy with a hospital, stating that "a hospital is not a complete failure if its patients leave in better health, even though they again contract the same disease for which they were treated."[48]

---

[43] Dorothy M. Burke, *Youth and Crime* (U.S. Children's Bureau Publication No. 196, 1930), pp. 96–102.

[44] *Commissioner of Correction, op. cit.*, pp. 36–37.

[45] H. A. Bears, *A Study of Selected Factors in the Prison Records of Five Hundred Inmates of the State Prison for Southern Michigan at Jackson* (Ypsilanti: University Lithoprinters, 1941).

[46] Richard C. Cabot, "Treatment in Social Case Work and the Need of Criteria and Tests of Its Success or Failure," *Proceedings of the National Conference of Social Work*, 1931, pp. 3–24.

[47] W. I. and Dorothy S. Thomas, *The Child in America* (New York: A. A. Knopf, 1928), p. 143.

[48] Donald R. Taft, *Criminology* (New York: Macmillan, 1950), p. 577.

Those who speak most frequently of the failure of the juvenile court probably would not prefer the old criminal procedures. They insist that the juvenile court has failed in order that a still better substitute for the criminal court may be developed. When considered as a substitute for the criminal court the juvenile court is regarded as a decided success, even if its greatest achievement is the mere recognition of the dignity and potentialities of children and adolescents.[49]

PROPOSED MODIFICATIONS. Among the plans suggested for changes, the two most important are (a) a merger of the juvenile court with a general family court and (b) a transfer of most of the work of the juvenile court to social welfare agencies or to the schools.

The suggestion that the juvenile court be merged with the general family court is made because of the conviction that the various problems of the family are related and should all be handled by one agency.[50] Family courts, or Domestic Relations Courts, would handle all cases of domestic difficulty, including non-support, desertion, paternity, divorce, alimony, custody of children, guardianship of children, adoption of children, juvenile delinquency, dependency, and contributing to the delinquency or dependency of children. A successful court of this kind has been operating in Cincinnati since 1914, and by 1947 such courts could be found in parts of at least eighteen states, chiefly in the larger urban areas, and throughout New Jersey and Virginia.[51] The National Probation Association, the American Institute of Criminal Law and Criminology, and the United States Children's Bureau all have recommended the amalgamation of juvenile courts with such courts.

It is evident that this procedure is, to some extent, in opposition to the earlier demand for separate hearings for children. The purpose of the separate hearings was not merely to keep the adult audience from the courtroom during the hearing of children's cases, but was rather to produce a complete separation in the mind of the child and the public between juvenile delinquency cases and crimes. When the child is taken into such a unified family court, dealing with many crimes of adults that affect family relations, this separation of juvenile delinquency from crime is not so complete. But, as indicated above, the separation in the juvenile court has been an aspiration rather than an actuality.

The second suggestion for the future is that the work of the juvenile

[49] William Healy, "Thoughts About Juvenile Courts," Federal Probation, 13:16–19, September, 1949.

[50] See, for example, Walter H. Beckham, "One Court for Family Problems," National Probation and Parole Association Yearbook, 1942, pp. 80–93.

[51] Alice Scott Nutt, "Juvenile and Domestic Relations Courts," Social Work Yearbook, 1947, pp. 270–276.

court be confined to the performance of judicial functions, and that all case
work functions be transferred to social work agencies. The suggestion is
contrary to the "social agency" view that as a public agency the court cannot refuse to accept any case which might come to it for aid, and it is an
endorsement of the legal view that the courts should limit their intake to
cases in which there is a specific issue of delinquency.[52] As early as 1903,
Aschaffenburg urged that the discipline of school age children should be
transferred to the schools and that they should not be tried at all in the
courts. In 1914, Eliot gave a more detailed argument in favor of this
transfer.[53] These earlier discussions have been supplemented by many
journal articles and conference papers. In recent years, the tendency is to
suggest that social welfare agencies, rather than the school, do the case
work and that it be co-ordinated by a council for a neighborhood or community.[54]

The argument for these transfers is based on the fact that the juvenile
court is doing an immense amount of administrative work at the present
which is extra-judicial. As has been indicated, of the cases which go to the
juvenile court the large proportion are settled unofficially, without an appearance before the judge. It is proposed, therefore, that all of this unofficial work be centralized in some agency or council of agencies which is de-
voting its energy to case work.[55] The proposal does not assume, of course,
that no cases need go to the juvenile court for adjudication and that no
delinquents need be committed to institutions. It is an expression of a belief that it is undesirable for a child to appear in a court of any kind,
juvenile or criminal, and that the number of such appearances should be
obviated as far as possible by the development of extra-court methods of
dealing with problem behavior.[56]

EXTENSION OF THE JUVENILE COURT. The statements made above regarding the characteristics of the juvenile court, as most other descriptions of
juvenile courts, give an incorrect impression of the present methods of
dealing with juvenile delinquents for the reason that attention is fixed on

[52] For discussion of these two views, see H. Warren Dunham, "The Juvenile Court:
Contradictory Orientations in Processing Offenders," *Law and Contemporary Problems*, 23:508–527, Summer, 1958.
[53] Thomas D. Eliot, *The Juvenile Court and the Community* (New York: Macmillan, 1914), pp. 152–153.
[54] See, for example, Alice Scott Nutt, "The Future of the Juvenile Court," *National
Probation Association Yearbook*, 1939, pp. 160–165; and Helen L. Witmer, "Social
Case Work in Juvenile Probation," *National Probation Association Yearbook*, 1941,
pp. 161–162.
[55] Alice Scott Nutt, "The Responsibility of the Juvenile Court and the Public Welfare Agency," *National Probation and Parole Association Yearbook*, 1947, pp. 206–
223.
[56] Thomas D. Eliot, "Case Work Functions and Judicial Functions," *National Probation Association Yearbook*, 1937, pp. 252–266.

the well-organized courts in a few large cities. But 90 percent of the courts that hear children's cases are in counties that have no city of more than 25,000 population, and in such areas few courts can afford even the bare essentials of a juvenile court; separate hearings for children, probation service, and records of social information. In a study made some years ago, it was found that hardly any counties containing cities with small populations had investigative and treatment facilities and that the large proportion of the counties with cities over 100,000 had such facilities.[57] While facilities in juvenile courts and the number of courts have increased greatly in recent years, the difference between the city and the smaller towns is still great.[58]

All this indicates that the great need of the juvenile court is the extension of its machinery and point of view to the rural sections. Thousands of children are deprived every year of rights which are guaranteed to them by law, the right not to be detained in jails with adult offenders, the right to a separate hearing, the right to be regarded as the ward of the court in need of protection and help rather than of punishment. The loss of these rights causes little protest because few people speak for such children; if the rights of a professional or other influential class were so denied or abridged, a howl of protest would compel the authorities to obey the law. It is this situation which has prompted proposals for organization of the juvenile court on a state-wide rather than on a county-wide basis.[59]

The problem of extending the juvenile court may be approached from another standpoint. Why should not the methods now used in juvenile courts be extended to adults? If we do this, does the separate existence of the juvenile court have an adequate justification?

Two principles have been used to justify the trial and treatment of juvenile offenders separately from adults:

(a) Juveniles lack responsibility and discernment. Since an essential element in crime is intent, the child has been regarded as not capable of committing crime because he does not have sufficient intelligence and experience to understand the situation adequately. But the juvenile court has retained the element of intent, to some extent, in the distinction between delinquency and dependency; both terms are defined very broadly, and whether a particular juvenile is treated as one or the other is determined largely by his intent. Moreover, if the child under sixteen or even under

[57] Evelina Belden, *Courts in the United States Hearing Children's Cases*, U.S. Children's Bureau Publication No. 65, 1920, pp. 41–65.

[58] See Lowell J. Carr, "Most Courts Have to be Substandard," *Federal Probation*, 13:29–33, September, 1949.

[59] National Probation and Parole Association, *Standard Juvenile Court Act* (New York: Author, 1949), pp. 339–340.

eighteen or twenty-one is by law incapable of having criminal intent, it would appear that many persons over the juvenile court age would be similarly incapable. No logical method exists for drawing a line between those who have responsibility and those who have not. A juvenile court based on the principle of lack of responsibility is, therefore, either not justified or else it indicates the necessity of similar methods for adults.

(b) Juvenile courts developed because it was felt that criminal courts were based on the assumption of vicious depravity of criminals and on the belief in the efficacy of severe penalties in deterring others from crime. It *guard kids* was insisted that the best policy in dealing with children would be to guard and protect them rather than punish them. But, in theory at least, the criminal law and criminal courts are making efforts to reform, protect, and assist adult criminals. Recent changes have made it impossible to state the function of the criminal court solely in terms of punishment; it is attempting to assist criminals to secure a better adjustment. While it may be observed that this is largely a formal change only and that in actual practice the object of the law is punishment, it may also be observed that in actual practice the object of most institutions and programs for juvenile delinquents is punishment, regardless of what the laws say about them. Certainly the differences between the criminal courts and the juvenile courts are not so great as they were thirty years ago.

Evidences of the change in attitudes and of the extension of juvenile court methods and procedure to courts for adults are numerous. In 1910, Judge Lindsey stated that juvenile court methods should be used in half the cases in criminal courts,[60] and similar statements have been made regularly by students of the subject down to the present. Jerome Hall has suggested that the procedure be adopted in a special court for thieves.[61] Certain laws also indicate a tendency to extend juvenile court procedures to adults. For example, pre-sentence investigations are required by law in the adult courts of at least seven states,[62] and in many states certain offenders, especially sex offenders, are accorded psychiatric treatment rather than punishment. Also, in many of the specialized courts, such as morals courts and domestic relations courts, the methods are very similar to those of the juvenile court.

But perhaps the best evidence of a changing attitude is the recent attempt to extend the juvenile court methods and ideology to young adults

---

[60] B. B. Lindsey and H. J. O'Higgins, *The Beast* (New York: Doubleday, 1910), p. 149.

[61] Jerome Hall, *Theft, Law and Society*, Second Edition (Indianapolis: Bobbs-Merrill, 1952).

[62] Will C. Turnbaldh, "Probation and the Administration of Justice," *Prison World*, 12:11–12, November, 1950.

by means of Youth Correction Authority Acts. The principle involved in this movement is that the juvenile court procedures might well be extended to the group 17–21 years of age, because such young adults are not held to be adults in the civil courts or at the polls. This movement was initiated by a report of a committee on delinquency appointed by two social welfare societies in New York City. The committee reported that the methods used in arresting, detaining, trying, and committing young adults were tending in many cases to perpetuate criminal behavior and suggested revisions in those procedures.[63] An advisory committee of the American Law Institute, consisting of outstanding lawyers, judges, psychiatrists, sociologists, and correctional workers, worked for two years on the careful formulation of a model act for dealing with young adults, and this model act was recommended to the states for legislative action in 1940. The stated purpose of this act is to substitute "for retributive punishment methods of training and treatment directed toward the correction and rehabilitation of young persons found guilty of violation of law." To this end, a committee called the Youth Correction Authority is established, and the judges of all courts except juvenile courts are instructed to commit almost all offenders up to the age of twenty-one to it. The Youth Correction Authority is given the power to determine what treatment, including probation, shall be given to each offender, to establish facilities for such treatment, and to retain offenders until there is a reasonable probability that discharge will result in no danger to the public. However, the offender may be held beyond age twenty-one only if his case is reviewed by the court. It is clear that the intent is to divide correctional procedure into two distinct parts—trial and treatment—and, hence, to limit the judiciary to the mere determination of whether or not the accused is guilty. Youthful offenders continue to be considered criminally responsible. Considerable controversy has developed as to the desirability of thus depriving the judge of the sentencing power.[64]

While such a proposal reveals a changing attitude toward young-adult offenders and a tendency to extend juvenile court procedures to them, the

[63] Leonard V. Harrison and Pryor M. Grant, *Youth in the Toils* (New York: Macmillan, 1938).

[64] See, for example, George W. Smyth, "Analyzing the Y.C.A. Act," *National Probation and Parole Association Yearbook*, 1941, pp. 241–246; Joseph N. Ulman, "The Youth Correction Authority Act," *National Probation and Parole Association Yearbook*, 1941, pp. 227–240; Joseph P. Murphy, "The YCA Act—Is it Practical and Needed?" *National Probation and Parole Association Yearbook*, 1941, pp. 247–260; John F. Perkins, "Defect in the Youth Correction Authority Act," *Journal of Criminal Law and Criminology*, 33:111–118, July–August, 1942; John B. Waite, "Judge Perkins' Criticisms of the Y. C. A.," *Journal of Criminal Law and Criminology*, 33:293–296, November–December, 1942; John F. Perkins, "Common Sense and Bad Boys," *Atlantic Monthly*, 173:43–47, May, 1944.

many modifications made as this act has been put into practice (in California, Illinois, Wisconsin, Minnesota, Massachusetts, Texas, and the federal government) indicate that the punitive reaction to young adult offenders still prevails.[65] For example, while the model act is designed to benefit young criminals, not juvenile delinquents, in all five states the enacted statutes are mainly instruments for handling juvenile delinquents only. The agency having authority powers in two states—Texas and Wisconsin—deals exclusively with juvenile delinquents, and 93 percent of the case load in Massachusetts and about two-thirds of the case load in California and Minnesota is made up of juvenile delinquents.[66] For the most part, the young adults continue to be handled in the traditional way. Similarly, the intent of the model act in regard to the powers of the court have not been carried out: under the enacted legislation the judge does not lose the sentencing power but commits a youth to the Authority only if he wants him incarcerated. Consequently, the Authority is largely restricted to handling persons committed to institutions.[67] Also, in some of the states it is doubtful whether the practices under the Youth Authority are any less punitive than they were before the Authority was established. It may be concluded that in practice "the Institute program has thus far done very little to better the correctional treatment of the age group which originally excited its interest and on whose behalf it originally launched the Authority program."[68]

In spite of this failure, some of the elements of the juvenile court seem to be applicable to the criminal court and probably would improve very greatly the work of that organization. Social investigations, use of summons, reformation as the ideal of treatment, informal procedures, and private sessions—all could be used advantageously by the criminal court. It is clear, however, that a blanket definition of "crime," corresponding to the broad definitions of delinquency, could not be used even if the juvenile court procedure were extended to adults. In designing the Model Youth Authority Act the committee made no attempt to modify the traditional

[65] For descriptions and the evaluations of established programs based on the model act, see Sol Rubin, "Changing Youth Authority Concepts," *Focus*, 29:77–82, May, 1950; Bertram M. Beck, *Five States, A Study of the Youth Authority Program as Promulgated by the American Law Institute* (Philadelphia: American Law Institute, 1951); James V. Bennett, "Blueprinting the New Youth Corrections Program," *Federal Probation*, 15:3–7, September, 1951; Jerome Hall, "Science and Reform in Criminal Law," *University of Pennsylvania Law Review*, 100:787–804, April, 1952; and Paul W. Tappan, "Young Adults Under the Youth Authority," *Journal of Criminal Law and Criminology*, 47:629–646, March–April, 1957.

[66] Beck, op. cit., p. 31. For description of California's program, see John R. Ellingston, *Protecting our Children from Criminal Careers* (New York: Prentice-Hall, 1948).

[67] Cf. Peter Lejins, "Is the Youth Authority Idea Really Paying Off?" *Proceedings of the National Conference of Juvenile Agencies*, 47:92, 1951.

[68] Beck, op. cit., p. 55.

"crime" concepts. Aside from the fact that there are prohibitions in existing law and in the constitutional safeguards ensuring due process of law, a
blanket definition of crime would be dangerous because of the many class
conflicts and differences in fundamental beliefs in modern society.

## SUGGESTED READINGS

Adamson, LaMay, and H. Warren Dunham, "Clinical Treatment of Male
  Delinquents: A Study in Effort and Result," *American Sociological Re-
  view,* 21:312–320, June, 1956.
Beck, Bertram M., *Five States, A Study of the Youth Authority Program
  as Promulgated by the American Law Institute.* Philadelphia: American
  Law Institute, 1951.
Beemsterboer, Matthew J., "The Juvenile Court—Benevolence in the Star
  Chamber," *Journal of Criminal Law, Criminology and Police Science,*
  50:464–475, January, 1960.
Breitenbach, H. Eugene, "Due Process of Law for Youthful Offenders,"
  *Journal of the State Bar of California,* 32:665–679, November, 1957.
Caldwell, Robert G., "The Juvenile Court: Its Development and Some
  Major Problems," *Journal of Criminal Law, Criminology and Police
  Science,* 51:493–511, January–February, 1961.
Diana, Lewis, "The Rights of Juvenile Delinquents: An Appraisal of
  Juvenile Court Procedures," *Journal of Criminal Law, Criminology, and
  Police Science,* 47:561–569, January–February, 1957.
Dunham, H. Warren, "The Juvenile Court: Contradictory Orientations in
  Processing Offenders," *Law and Contemporary Problems,* 23:508–527,
  Summer, 1958.
Geis, Gilbert, "Juvenile Justice: Great Britain and California," *Crime and
  Delinquency,* 7:111–120, April, 1961.
Geis, Gilbert, "Contributing to Delinquency," *St. Louis University Law
  Journal,* 8:59–81, Fall, 1963.
Hartung, Frank E., *Crime, Law and Society.* Detroit: Wayne State Uni-
  versity Press, 1965.
Healy, William, "Thoughts About Juvenile Courts," *Federal Probation,*
  13:16–19, September, 1949.
Hennings, Thomas C., Jr., "Effectiveness of the Juvenile Court System,"
  *Federal Probation,* 23:3–8, June, 1959.
Herman, Stephen M., "Scope and Purposes of Juvenile Court Jurisdic-
  tion," *Journal of Criminal Law, Criminology, and Police Science,*
  48:590–607, March–April, 1958.
Holton, Karl, "California Youth Authority," *Proceedings of the American
  Prison Association,* 1947, pp. 205–214.
Reinemann, John, "Fifty Years of the Juvenile Court Movement in the
  United States," *Mental Hygiene,* 34:391–399, July, 1950.

Rubin, Sol, "The Legal Character of Juvenile Delinquency," *Annals of the American Academy of Political and Social Science*, 261:1–8, January, 1949.

Rubin, Sol, "Protecting the Child in Juvenile Court," *Journal of Criminal Law, Criminology, and Police Science*, 43:425–440, November–December, 1952.

Shulman, Harry M., *Juvenile Delinquency in American Society*, New York: Harpers, 1961.

Sussman, Frederick B., *Laws of Juvenile Delinquency*. New York: Oceana Publications, 1950.

Tappan, Paul W., *Delinquent Girls in Court: A Study of the Wayward Minor Court of New York*. New York: Columbia University Press, 1947.

Waite, E. F., "How Far Can Court Procedure be Socialized without Impairing Individual Rights?" *Journal of Criminal Law and Criminology*, 12:339–348, November–December, 1921.

Younghusband, Eileen L., "Dilemma of the Juvenile Court," *Social Service Review*, 33:10–20, March, 1959.

Ziegler, John, "Right to Counsel in the Juvenile Court," *Michigan Law Review*, 54:1000–1004, May, 1956.

# 21. PROBATION

ALTHOUGH PROBATION is to a large extent a non-punitive method of handling offenders, it has developed within the framework of a legal system which is basically punitive. Probation methods represent a distinct break with the classical theory on which the criminal law is based, for an attempt is made to deal with offenders as individuals rather than as classes or concepts, to select certain offenders who can be expected, with assistance, to change their attitudes and habits while residing in the free community, and to use a great variety of non-punitive methods in rendering assistance to those offenders selected. Probation thus is a system for implementing the treatment reaction to law-breaking. It does not attempt to make the offender suffer; it attempts to prevent him from suffering. Some suffering results from having been placed in the "probationer" status but, in theory at least, this suffering is not intentional and is avoided as far as possible. Consequently there is no reason for insisting that probation is punishment, as some authors have done in an effort to win approval for the system.

THE NATURE OF PROBATION. From the constitutional point of view probation is the suspension of a sentence during a period of liberty in the community conditional upon good behavior of the convicted offender. The courts have without exception found the constitutional justification of probation in the right of the court to suspend sentence. But mere suspension of sentence is an act of mercy or judicial leniency which allows "hopeful cases" or first offenders "another chance." Probation is clearly different from the suspended sentence alone since it includes a positive method of dealing with the offenders. While a conditional suspension of sentence by the court is necessary, probation includes supervision, guidance, and assistance of the offender. This assistance has come to be the important part of the probation system.

The suspension of sentence, and hence the threat of punishment, is always present in probation, and it is a reflection of a punitive societal reaction to crime. However, in some states a suspended sentence now can be granted only if the offender is placed on probation; this notion that the offender should be guided and assisted is a reflection of a treatment reaction to crime. Probation, then, represents a kind of compromise between the punitive reaction and the treatment reaction. A definition of probation which reveals this compromise may be stated as follows: Probation is the status of a convicted offender during a period of suspension of the sentence in which he is given liberty conditioned on his good behavior and in which the state by personal supervision attempts to assist him to maintain good behavior. Court decisions based upon information obtained in pre-sentence investigations of the offender's personality and background are implied. The United States Supreme Court has stated that probation is to be used "to provide an individualized program offering a young or unhardened offender an opportunity to rehabilitate himself without institutional confinement under the tutelage of a probation officer and under the continuing power of the court to impose institutional punishment for his original offense in the event he abuses the opportunity."[1]

The suspension of sentence which permits positive action to be taken may be either a suspension of the imposition of the sentence or the suspension of the execution of the sentence. Most states suspend the execution, but others suspend the imposition, and others use both methods. In California in 1963, 70 percent of the probation grants to adults by Superior Courts were suspensions of the imposition of sentence, 24 percent were suspensions of the execution of a jail sentence, and 6 percent were suspensions of a sentence to prison.[2] If the judge imposes a sentence and then suspends the execution of the sentence, and if the offender violates the probation, the judge merely orders the execution of the original sentence. If the judge suspends the imposition of the sentence, he will in case of violation of probation have additional information on which to base a decision regarding the sentence which should be imposed.[3]

Whichever method of suspending the sentence is used, it is a method of suspending punishment, and it thus is a substitute for imprisonment or

[1] Roberts vs. United States, 320 U.S. 264, 272 (1943).

[2] *Delinquency and Probation in California*, 1963 (Sacramento: Department of Justice, 1964), pp. 180–181.

[3] Also it is argued that when the imposition of the sentence is suspended the status of the probationer is less likely to be considered infamous. See Richard Chappell, "Federal Probation Service: Its Growth and Progress," *Federal Probation*, 11:29–34, December, 1947.

some other penalty. Since probation incorporates assistance to the offender as well as a suspended sentence, it is to be regarded as a substitute for either of two other major methods currently used in dealing with convicted offenders: imprisonment or release without supervision. It is important to judge probation in relation to these two alternatives; it is frequently judged as though it were an alternative to imprisonment alone.

Some questions of law have arisen regarding probation. A federal court sentenced an offender to serve two years in a penitentiary and then provided that he be released on probation at the end of six months and kept on probation during the remainder of the two years. The higher court held that this was illegal because the court was really ordering the offender paroled and the court had no jurisdiction in regard to parole. Again, the court may convict an offender on two counts, then commit him to an institution on the first count and place him on probation on the second count. This, apparently, is not illegal, but it is contradictory to the principle that probation is to be used as a system for keeping offenders out of prison.[4] In some jurisdictions offenders frequently are granted probation with the stipulation that they spend part of the probationary period in the county jail. Forty-six percent of the persons granted probation by California Superior Courts in 1963 were given a jail sentence as part of the conditions of probation. Five counties gave jail sentences to over 80 percent of their probationers.[5]

THE ORIGIN, DEVELOPMENT, AND SCOPE OF PROBATION.   As was observed in Chapter Fifteen, the punitive reaction was at one time mitigated by methods such as securing sanctuary, right of clergy, judicial reprieve, and technical circumvention of statutes. Probation can be traced to such practices.[6] The common law practice of suspending sentences temporarily was extended, and courts began to suspend sentences indefinitely, permitting convicted offenders to remain at large on good behavior. Sometimes the offender was compelled to furnish financial guarantee that he would maintain good behavior, and in some instances restrictions were placed on his

[4] Sam B. Warner, "Some Legal Problems Raised by Probation," in Sheldon Glueck, Editor, Probation and Criminal Justice (New York: Macmillan, 1932), Chepter 2.

[5] Delinquency and Probation in California, 1963, op. cit., pp. 198–199. See also Special Study Commission on Correctional Facilities and Services, Probation in California (Sacramento: State Department of Corrections, 1957), pp. 33–34; Stuart Adams and Romey P. Narloch, Probation Standards in California, California Youth Authority Research Report No. 1, January, 1959; Richard Hartshorne, "The 1958 'Split-Sentence' Law," Federal Probation, 23:9–12, June, 1959; Kenyon J. Scudder, "In Opposition to Probation with Jail Sentence," Ibid., pp. 12–17.

[6] Frank W. Grinnell, "The Common Law History of Probation," Journal of Criminal Law and Criminology, 32:15–34, May–June, 1941.

freedom. Then volunteers began to assist such offenders during the period of the suspension of the sentence. Among the early volunteers was John Augustus, a shoemaker of Boston, who in 1841 secured the release of a confirmed drunkard from the police court of Boston by acting as surety for him. This offender turned out to be a "sober, industrious citizen" under his care. During the next seventeen years Augustus acted as surety for 1,152 males and 794 females and gave less formal aid to many others.[7] Such volunteers became more numerous and were, in effect, probation officers before probation had been authorized by statute.[8]

In 1869, a state visiting agency in Massachusetts was authorized by the legislature to accept the custody of juvenile offenders, with the right of placing them in private families. This amounted to probation, and 23 percent of the juvenile offenders convicted in the courts of Boston in the year 1869–1870 were dealt with in this manner. But the first statutory provision for probation with publicly paid officers was the Massachusetts law of 1878, which authorized the Mayor of Boston to appoint and pay a probation officer and authorized the municipal court to place offenders on probation. No restrictions were made, as in many subsequent probation laws, regarding the term of probation, the age, previous record, or other characteristics of the offender. The legislature extended this power to all other mayors of the state in 1880, and in 1891 it made mandatory the appointment of probation officers by lower court judges.

By 1917, twenty-one states had provided for adult probation and all states had authorized, at least, the suspension of sentences. The states which had the highest percentage of urban population developed probation first and it gradually spread to the more rural states. Probation was authorized in the federal courts in 1925, but those courts had used it without statutory authority for some years prior to that. Most European nations have provision for suspension and sentence and many have volunteer or philanthropic assistance for persons during the period of suspension of sentence, but few have provided for publicly-paid probation officers.

In 1953, all states had juvenile probation laws and Mississippi was the only state without an adult probation law.[9] However, use of probation in many of these states is limited by statute. Some states do not authorize

---

[7] *John Augustus, First Probation Officer* [reprint of a report by Augustus, with an introduction by Sheldon Glueck] (New York: National Probation Association, 1939), p. vi. See also N. S. Timasheff, *One Hundred Years of Probation* (New York: Fordham University Press, 1941).

[8] See Donald W. Moreland, "John Augustus and His Successors," *National Probation Association Yearbook*, 1941, pp. 1–22.

[9] Sol Rubin, "Legislation and Court Decisions," *National Probation and Parole Association Yearbook*, 1953, pp. 121–238.

paid probation officers, and in only thirteen states may probation be granted regardless of type of crime. Crimes of violence, crimes involving the use of a deadly weapon, and crimes carrying a certain penalty often are excepted. Furthermore, in some states probation may be used only by courts in cities or counties of a specified size, or by courts with specified types of jurisdiction. These statutory restrictions ordinarily are indicative of a conflict between the punitive and treatment reactions to crime, since they are based on the assumption that probation is mere judicial leniency which should not be available to certain offenders.

Evidence of the conflict also may be found in the failure of courts to appoint and pay authorized probation officers and in the failure to use probation when it is authorized by law and when probation officers are provided. About thirty percent of the counties in the United States have no probation service, and probation is seriously handicapped in many other counties by the limitation of part-time, ex-officio, and poorly-paid probation officers. The rural districts are far behind the urban communities in this respect. An Illinois survey made in 1948 revealed that in 90 down-state counties adult probation work was performed by full-time officers in only 20 counties; in 42 counties this work was done on a part-time basis by persons with other employment interests; and in 28 counties probation services were non-existent.[10] Similarly, a survey of California indicated that in some counties probation was used in less than 12 percent of the felony cases, while in other counties probation was used in over 80 percent of the cases.[11] A Pennsylvania survey revealed that only in a few counties did the courts consider any pre-sentence investigation necessary, that half a dozen counties had no probation service for adults, and that case loads of probation workers were many times higher than those generally considered as appropriate.[12]

No general statistics covering the entire United States are available. For 25 states in 1945, 31.6 percent of those convicted in courts of general jurisdiction were placed on probation or given suspended sentences; this percentage ranged from 64.6 and 49.8 in Rhode Island and New Hampshire to 15.7 and 13.0 in North Dakota and Iowa.[13] In the federal judiciary

[10] Division of Youth and Community Service, Illinois Department of Welfare, *Probation Survey* (unpublished); quoted in University of Chicago Conference on Probation, Prisons and Parole, *Report of the Committee on Probation*, June 3, 1949 (mimeographed).

[11] Special Committee on Governmental Administration, *Study of Building Needs of State Correctional Institutions* (Sacramento: State Senate, September 28, 1954).

[12] National Probation and Parole Association, *Probation Services in Pennsylvania* (Harrisburg: Governor's Commission on Penal and Corrective Affairs, 1957).

[13] Bureau of the Census, U.S. Department of Commerce, *Judicial Criminal Statistics, 1945* (Washington: Government Printing Office, 1947), p. 5.

## TABLE XVI

RATES PER 100,000 GENERAL POPULATION FOR CONVICTED OFFENDERS
GRANTED PROBATION, PAROLE OR SENTENCED TO PRISON IN
CENSUS YEARS, MICHIGAN, 1930–1960

| Census Years as of January 1 | Rates per 100,000 General Population for Offenders | | | |
|---|---|---|---|---|
| | Total | On Probation | On Parole | In Prison |
| 1930 | 270 | 72 | 38 | 159 |
| 1940 | 286 | 84 | 56 | 147 |
| 1950 | 299 | 105 | 59 | 135 |
| 1960 | 363 | 173 | 67 | 123 |

system in recent years, approximately 40 percent of those convicted in
district courts have been placed on probation. Since 1949, the District
Courts of Massachusetts have granted probation to approximately two-
thirds of the cases coming before them, and the Superior Courts have
used probation in 43 percent of their cases.[14] Probation probably is used
more generally in this state than in many others. In England's superior
courts there has been a steady increase in the proportion of offenders given
probation in this century; for example, one percent of the felony sex
offenders were given probation in 1909–1913, 15 percent in 1951–1954.[15]
Table XVI shows that in Michigan the number of prisoners per 100,000
population has decreased regularly since 1930, while the number of probationers per 100,000 population has steadily increased.[16]

ORGANIZATION OF PROBATION DEPARTMENTS. Two agencies have been
suggested as the proper bodies to control probation work: the court, and
an independent administrative body. Since probation originated in the
suspended sentence and hence is regarded as an extension of the judicial
function, the control of probation work usually is in the hands of the
court. This has carried with it the decision in some states that probation
officers can be appointed by no agency except the court. The stated objections to the method are: *First,* the work of supervision is essentially administrative, not judicial. There is no more reason for having probation
administered by the courts than for having prisons or reformatories so
administered. *Second,* the judge is not able to handle this administrative

[14] *Statistical Reports of the Commissioner of Correction,* 1963 (Boston: Commonwealth of Massachusetts Public Document No. 1151, 1964), p. 120.
[15] Hermann Mannheim, "Comparative Sentencing Practices," *Law and Contemporary
Problems,* 23:557–582, Summer, 1958.
[16] Robert J. Glass, *Review of Trends in Adult Corrections over Thirty Years*
(Lansing: Michigan Department of Corrections, 1961), Table A-3 (Mimeographed).

work efficiently. He has other duties which interfere with his supervision of probation, and the probation department really becomes an independent administrative body. Consequently there has been a trend toward the other method of appointment and supervision of probation officers. The Los Angeles County Probation Department, for example, is completely separate from the courts and is under the control of a County Board of Supervisors. It serves the juvenile courts as well as the adult courts. In at least thirteen states probation officers are appointed and paid by a state board.[17]

Probation, like the maintenance of detention institutions and the administration of juvenile courts, is primarily a muncipal or county responsibility. But approximately half the states have a state board which either administers or assists in the administration of probation. Rhode Island first developed state supervision in 1899; five states had state supervision by 1910, nine by 1920, and twenty-seven by 1931. In many of these states, however, county probation departments also serve the criminal courts. Most probation workers argue that administration of probation should be a function of the state, and in states which have a strongly centralized system the probation system has operated most effectively. Many counties cannot support the services of full-time probation officers, and in other counties there are so few criminal cases that employment of a full-time paid worker is not justified. Since parole is almost always administered on a state-wide basis, some states have integrated probation with the parole service.[18]

Co-operation between the probation departments in various states also produces uniformity and efficiency. Such co-operation is now secured to some extent on an informal level by the National Council on Crime and Delinquency. In addition, some specific interstate agreements have been made. In 1937, for example, 25 states entered into interstate compacts for supervision of probationers and parolees from other states, and by 1952 all states had reciprocal agreements of this kind.[19] Also there is an agreement, made in 1917, that the probation departments in the principal cities will supervise probationers moving into their cities from other districts.

SELECTION OF PROBATIONERS.   In almost all jurisdictions adult probation is granted only after the offender has been found guilty. There must be a conviction of a specific offense. However, a few jurisdictions use a pro-

[17] Charles L. Chute, "Ideals and Realities in the Probation Field," National Probation Association Yearbook, 1938, pp. 43–52.

[18] See Robert M. Hill, "State Administration of Adult Probation and Parole," National Probation Association Yearbook, 1942, pp. 243–245.

[19] B. E. Crihfield, "The Interstate Parole and Probation Compact," Federal Probation, 17:3–7, June, 1953.

cedure comparable to that of the juvenile courts, since persons merely *charged* with crime are granted probation. The courts of Rhode Island and Kentucky and the Superior Court of Massachusetts possess the power, with some reservations, to grant probation under such conditions, and in one county in Maine certain persons accused of misdemeanors may be granted probation even before they are arraigned.[20] This "deferred prosecution" procedure is used extensively with juveniles; it has been used by the Federal Courts in Brooklyn since 1936 and is sometimes called the "Brooklyn Plan."[21] The possession of such powers by the court enables the accused person to maintain certain rights which might be forfeited by a conviction and it eliminates expensive trials, but these advantages might be completely offset by the denial of the traditional rights to due process of law.

In about two-thirds of the states, the probation statutes stipulate that before a guilty person may be placed on probation an investigation of his character and of the conditions surrounding his crime should be made and the results submitted to the judge. This investigation is for the purpose of determining the characteristics of the prospective probationer, so that the judge will have factual information on which to base his decision. However, a pre-probation investigation is mandatory in only a few states.[22] And even in these states many judges do not wait for an investigation; instead, they base their decisions on the offender's statement about himself, his personal appearance, the social status of his family, the nature of the offense, or the recommendations of persons outside the probation department. These are likely to be decidedly inadequate as a basis for policies, and it is largely because of this inadequacy that probation has been brought into ill repute. Pre-probation investigations are mandatory in Illinois, yet in the period September 1, 1945, through August 31, 1947, thirteen percent of the probations granted to felons in Cook County were granted without proper continuance of court proceedings so that the investigation could be made.[23] One judge granted 43.9 percent of his probations within one day of the time of application, and the proportion granted by other judges without time for a pre-probation investigation ranged from 3.1 to 38.7 percent. Probation was granted to nineteen defendants who were not, by law, eligible for probation.

20 Harry Elmer Barnes and Negley K. Teeters, *New Horizons in Criminology*, Third Edition (New York: Prentice-Hall, 1959), p. 560.
21 Conrad P. Printzlien, "Deferred Prosecution for Juvenile Offenders," *Federal Probation*, 12:17–22, March, 1948.
22 Will C. Turnbladh, "Probation and the Administration of Justice," *Prison World*, 12:11–12, November–December, 1950.
23 Don T. Blackiston, *The Judge, the Defendant, and Criminal Law Administration* (Unpublished Ph.D. Dissertation, University of Chicago, 1952).

When investigations are made, they are generally made by regular probation officers. Using an analogy with medicine, these investigations are sometimes referred to as "diagnosis," since they provide the factual basis for later individual or group treatment. As Reckless has said, "An adequate pre-sentence investigation not only indicates whether the defendant is probationable; it also gives clues as to the causes of the criminal behavior, the assets and liabilities of the total case, and the need for a constructive probation program."[24] The ideal investigation covers such things as the person's attitude toward the offense, his previous criminal record, his family situation, his neighborhood and other group associations, his educational and work history, his personal habits (particularly in reference to the use of alcohol and drugs), his physical and mental health, and his perspective on life.[25] Such ideal investigations are characteristic of large probation departments in which specialized officers can be assigned to the work, but in smaller departments the investigations are likely to be mere routine interviews with the prospective probationer and his family. Sellin has suggested that specially trained personnel, not probation officers, be employed to conduct the pre-sentence investigations, leaving probation workers time to interact with probationers.[26]

Probation departments characteristically have insufficient funds for the employment of adequate manpower. In this situation adequate investigation of each case is, of course, impossible. Probation investigation often is handicapped, also, by the fact that the investigator frequently is regarded as a detective by the offender and the other persons interviewed. This attitude is not without some justification, for in some cases, especially when the prospective probationer has insisted that he is innocent of the crime for which he has been found guilty, the investigation takes on the characteristics of a retrial. After such an investigation, supervisory work will be extremely difficult, particularly in small departments where investigation and supervision are performed by the same officer. The absence of organized and central records is a further detriment to probation investigation. In some communities official records are not available to probation investigators. Juvenile court files frequently cannot be cited in preparation of reports of adult probation investigations. Educational and social service records usually are scattered throughout the community, although in large cities social service records are now centralized by means of a

[24] Walter C. Reckless, *The Crime Problem*, Second Edition (New York: Appleton-Century-Crofts, 1955), p. 511.

[25] Cf. Helen D. Pigeon, *Probation and Parole in Theory and Practice* (New York: National Probation Association, 1942), pp. 260–269; and Reckless, *op. cit.*, p. 512.

[26] Thorsten Sellin, "Adult Probation and the Conditional Sentence," *Journal of Criminal Law, Criminology and Police Science*, 49:533–556, April, 1959.

social service exchange.[27] The Los Angeles County Probation Department maintains a confidential central registry of all juveniles handled by the law enforcement agencies in the county, but the registry cards are destroyed when the child reaches his eighteenth birthday. Where probation is administered on a statewide basis, records ordinarily are maintained in a central state file. The maintenance of centralized records not only aids in the investigation of individual cases, but it makes statistical comparison of certain types of classes of offenders possible as well. Analysis of the data in such files might indicate needs for special supervisory and treatment techniques among some groups.

Probation is used, as explained previously, primarily as a substitute for discharge without supervision and for imprisonment. The principle that should be used in determining whether probation should be substituted for discharge without supervision is: Does this offender need supervision and assistance in adjusting to community conditions, and will he profit by this assistance and supervision? The principle that should be used in determining whether probation should be substituted for imprisonment is essentially the same, but includes also the danger to the community during the period of readjustment. For both groups these questions can be answered best by intensive study of individual cases supplemented by analysis of the rates of probation violation by offenders in the past. In 1963, California Superior Court judges reversed the recommendations of probation officers in about 3 percent of the cases in which probation was recommended and in about 22 percent of the cases in which it was not recommended.[28]

THE TERMS OF PROBATION. The terms of probation are generally fixed jointly by the legislature, the court, and the probation department or staff. The following are generally included: observance of all laws, good habits, keeping good company, regular reports as required, regular work or school attendance, payment of fines or reparation, abstinence from the use of alcohol and drugs, avoidance of unnecessary debts. Often the probationer may not marry, may not become divorced, or may not change his residence without permission of the probation department. Sometimes the probationer is required to live in a specified place. It may be necessary to require him to live at home, not to live at home, or to live in some philanthropic institution. He may be required to undergo specific medical or psychiatric treatment. In some states these terms must be communicated

[27] Beatrice R. Simcox, "Social Service Exchanges," *Social Work Year Book*, 1949, pp. 494–497.
[28] *Delinquency and Probation in California*, 1963, op. cit., p. 186.

to the probationer in writing in order that there may be no misunderstanding. It has been observed that when the conditions of probation are too stringent the probation officer is prone to overlook violations, thus losing the respect of his probationer.[29]

Payment of restitution, fines, or costs is frequently imposed not as a sentence but as a condition for being placed on probation.[30] Of the persons granted probation by California Superior Courts in 1963, about 60 percent received a fine, an order to pay restitution, or both. Though restitution or reparation is a valuable requirement in many cases, two objections have been made regarding the method by which this is enforced. First, probationers may be required to pay so much that their dependents suffer seriously. In Los Angeles County, the probation department investigates all pertinent claims against the offender and regulates payments according to his ability to pay. Second, this frequently interferes with other work of the probation department and makes it primarily a collecting agency. The average probation officer in California collected about $9,000 in this way in 1956, and this amount was frequently secured in very small sums. Probation officers object to acting as collecting agents, principally on the ground that the assumption of such duties destroys the confidential relationship necessary to constructive case work.[31] Men who have been imprisoned after failing to make restitution payments, thus violating the conditions of their probation, often believe they are being punished not for crime but for failure to pay their debts.

The maximum probationary period is generally fixed by law and is the same as the maximum prison sentence for the offense. Within that limit the court may fix the period of probation and, after fixing it once, may subsequently alter it. In many states the average period of probation for all offenders is less than one year. If treatment or rehabilitation is the actual objective of probation it is logical to have absolutely indeterminate probation, with no fixed maximum. Some individuals can get along satisfactorily in the community as long as they have the supervision and guidance of a probation officer but return to crime if that assistance is withdrawn too soon.

The probation officer has the duty of informing the court if the probationer does not maintain the conditions imposed upon him. The court may then warn the probationer or order execution of the sentence for the original offense, in which case the time served on probation ordinarily is

[29] William S. Meacham, "Conditions of Probation and Parole, Do They Help or Hinder?" *National Probation and Parole Association Yearbook*, 1947, pp. 50–59.

[30] See Stephen Schafer, *Restitution to Victims of Crime* (London: Stevens and Sons, 1960).

[31] See Irving E. Cohen, "Twilight Zones in Probation," *Journal of Criminal Law and Criminology*, 37:291–296, November–December, 1946.

not counted as part of the prison term. In some states if the probationer is arrested for a new crime probation is merely revoked, but in other states he is tried for the new offense. If he is convicted he may again apply for probation. If a prison term is ordered, the sentence which was suspended for purposes of probation may be ignored, or it may be made to run either concurrently or consecutively with the new sentence. If the probationer maintains the conditions imposed upon him, discharge from probation may, depending on the jurisdiction, come automatically at the end of the probationary period, be ordered by the court before or at the end of the period, or be ordered by the probation officer without court action.

SUPERVISION AND GUIDANCE OF PROBATIONERS.    After he has been granted probationary status by the court, the probationer is assigned to a specified probation officer who administers the probation program. In many instances this is the same officer that made the original probation investigation for the court.

*Assignment.*   Three systems of probation assignments are used: by districts; by sex, race, or religion; and by problems. The first method, which is used most frequently, gives to one officer all probationers living in a particular district. The second method makes assignments of male probationers to male officers, female probationers to female officers, and similarly for race and religion.[32] The specialization of probation work by problems is possible only in the larger urban probation departments.

Fifty probationers are now generally given as the recommended number to be assigned to one officer, provided he has a densely populated territory and can give his entire time to supervision and guidance. In practice most probation officers have several times that number of probationers under supervision; in some departments the average case load is as high as four hundred. When the case load is more than about fifty, intensive work with each probationer is impossible. This is in contradiction to the principle of probation, since release without supervision and guidance is mere suspension of sentence. According to probation principles, if offenders do not need supervision and guidance they should not be placed on probation; if they do need supervision and guidance, the number assigned to one officer should be restricted so that his work will be effective.

Effectiveness of supervision and guidance is also limited by the training of the officers to whom the probationer is assigned. As indicated, in some areas officers are unpaid and untrained volunteers, and considerable experience with such officers has resulted in the almost unanimous con-

[32] See Don J. Hager, "Race, Nationality, and Religion—Their Relationship to Appointment Policies and Casework," *National Probation and Parole Association Journal,* 3:129–141, April, 1957.

clusion that paid workers are essential. But even many of the paid probation officers are untrained, inefficient, and ineffective. This is due largely to the fact that few persons have been trained for the work, the importance of skill is not realized, salaries are small, and the positions are sometimes used as rewards for political service. Few trained probation officers are found outside of large cities, and even in these cities many of the officers have had no training. Among 720 California probation officers studied in 1956 (out of a total of 976 working in the state), 9 percent of those employed in counties with populations over 100,000 and 65 percent of those working in smaller counties had less than three years of college.[33] A more recent survey of 2000 probation officers in 405 courts in the United States indicated that 86 percent had bachelor's degrees; in cities of 500,000 or over, 92 percent had college degrees, but in cities with less than 50,000 population only 55 percent were college-trained.[34] In the Netherlands, and in other European countries, probationers are supervised by a combination of voluntary workers and well-trained full-time probation officers, apparently with great success.[35]

*Diagnosis.* Ideally, as we indicated previously, experts would always make the diagnosis before the offender is admitted to probation. This procedure is necessary, first, in order to determine whether he should be placed on probation, and, second, in order to determine the policies that should be used by the supervising officer. Though the method of making such diagnoses has not been standardized and the importance of diagnoses has not been generally realized, it is clear that probation work would be greatly improved if it could be based on precise diagnoses.[36] Until probation has such a basis, it can only be largely kind-hearted assistance.

*Contacts between probation officer and probationer.* Contacts between the probation officer and the probationer are generally made either in the office of the probation officer or the home of the probationer. Home visits are regarded as more effective because they enable the probation officer to come into contact with this most important part of the offender's environment, thus making possible a better understanding of the offender. Also, since the attitudes of the probationer's family and other intimate associates are important in determining his criminality or non-criminality, contacts with these associates are important in any effort to modify the

[33] Special Study Commission on Correctional Facilities and Services, op. cit., p. 123.
[34] Gladys M. Krueger, *Survey of Probation Officers,* 1959 (Washington: Government Printing Office, Children's Bureau Report No. 15, 1960).
[35] N. Muller, *Work of Rehabilitation in the Netherlands* (The Hague: National Bureau voor Reclassering, 1954).
[36] See Gilbert Geis and Fred W. Woodson, "Matching Probation Officer and Delinquent," *National Probation and Parole Association Journal,* 2:58–62, January, 1956.

offender's criminal attitudes. Yet the number of home visits per month and the number of hours per visit often are so small as to be insignificant. The probation officer who visits a probationer once a month for ten minutes cannot be, from the point of view of the frequency, duration, and intensity of contacts, a very important influence. He is in contact with the probationer during one 43,200th part of the month, while many of the companions of the probationer are with him almost constantly during the waking hours.

Most probationers are required by the order of the court to report at regular intervals to the probation officer in his office or some other place selected by him. Sometimes these reports are made once a week, sometimes once a month; at one time in Detroit the probationers who were not working were required to report daily. The procedure in making these reports varies widely. In some places the officer merely checks a card which the probationer hands through a window to him. In slightly less perfunctory systems the officer questions the probationer about his work, companions, recreations, habits, and other things; he gives advice on many topics—economic, family, legal, habits, reading, self-improvement, etc. The probationers are frequently required to bring written reports, such as school reports, reports from employers, receipts for payment toward support of the family or for restitution or reparation. Since "supervision" in such systems is practically nonexistent, it has been suggested that the system not be called "probation" and that, instead, it be called what it is, the suspended sentence:

It would be easy to say that we need more and highly trained probation officers, but so long as probation is so conceived that it can be used as a cover for the kind of clerical and fiscal tasks that probation officers for adults do in Pennsylvania, there is need for more clerks rather than for more professional staff. Instead of urging the extension of probation, we should urge that it be more restrictively used, thereby reserving it for carefully selected offenders, giving it the status it should have in accordance with the official definitions, and thus creating the absolute necessity of employing professionally trained people to administer it. . . . Legislation clearly defining the use of the suspended sentence by the courts could remove from the roster of probationers a considerable percentage of those now there, especially in states where a suspended sentence now can be granted only when a probation order is issued, thus forcing the courts in such states to foist on the probation officers individuals whom they merely wanted to give a scare—or a kindly favor.[37]

[37] Sellin, op. cit., p. 555.

*Treatment.* The word "treatment" here refers to the efforts of the probation officer to guide and assist the probationer. The word is unsatisfactory, for most of the efforts are educational, and we do not ordinarily think of education as "treatment." But the guidance and case work efforts of the probation officer do constitute a part of the general treatment reaction to crime, although they are ordinarily made within the authoritarian frame of reference required by the court. The probationer is both "supervised" (*i.e.*, required to live up to the terms of the probation contract) and guided, assisted, or led toward non-criminality.[38] It is to the latter activities that the word "treatment" is applied. Among probation workers there is a good deal of controversy about whether effective treatment can be executed in the authoritarian setting of probation. One group contends that treatment cannot be forced upon a person and that, consequently, attempts to treat probationers in the authoritarian setting will usually be unsuccessful. Another group holds that the authoritarian setting is valuable in treatment or, at least, that the authoritarian frame of reference and the treatment frame of reference can be dovetailed.[39] The conflict between the punitive and treatment reactions to crime and criminality has not been resolved, even in probation work.

The objective in probation work is to change the attitudes of the probationers. A scientific technique for the modification of attitudes has yet to be stated. Instead of descriptions of techniques we find such statements as "by gaining the confidence and friendship of the young man," "through friendly admonition and encouragement," "by stimulating the probationer's self-respect, ambition, and thrift," and "by relieving emotional tensions." It is necessary to know how confidence is secured, or how ambition is stimulated, or how tensions are reduced, and also to know how those processes produce reformation. Korn and McCorkle have commented:

[38] See Dale G. Hardman, "The Function of the Probation Officer," *Federal Probation,* 24:3–10, September, 1960; and Lewis Diana, "What is Probation?" *Journal of Criminal Law, Criminology and Police Science,* 51:189–208, August, 1960.

[39] See William A. McGrath, "Case Work in the Authoritarian Setting," *National Probation Association Yearbook,* 1937, pp. 176–187; Robert C. Taber, "The Value of Case Work Services to the Probationer," *National Probation Association Yearbook,* 1940, pp. 167–179; Helen D. Pigeon, *op. cit.,* pp. 329–334; Mazie F. Rappaport, "The Possibility of Help for the Prostitute through Functional Case Work in an Authoritarian Setting," in Rosa Wessel, Editor, *A Case Work Approach to Sex Delinquents* (Philadelphia: University of Pennsylvania Press, 1947), pp. 16–18; Ben Meeker, "Probation is Case Work," *Federal Probation,* 12:51–54, June, 1948; Marilyn Blake, "Probation is not Case Work," *Federal Probation,* 12:54–57, June, 1948; Irene Kawin, "Therapeutic Use of Authority," *Federal Probation,* 17:22–26, September, 1953; Glynn B. Smith, *The PICO Project, A Measure of Casework in Corrections* (Sacramento: Department of Corrections, 1959).

Stripped to their essentials, these "instructions" boil down to exhortations to treat, to befriend, and to encourage. In effect, our treatment personnel are often told little more than to *go out there and rehabilitate somehow*—precisely how is not indicated. A military commander who confined his strategic orders to the commands, "Be brave, be careful, and be victorious!" would be laughed out of uniform. Often, however, the technical directions given to correctional workers are scarcely more specific.[40]

In the absence of specific techniques for the modification of attitudes, the general principle which is involved may be recalled. The attitudes of the individual are a product of social interactions. The interactions that are of the greatest importance in determining attitudes are those that are frequent and intimate, as in the family, the play-group, and the neighborhood. The procedure for modifying attitudes consists essentially in changing the person's group relations. For this purpose it is necessary either to remove the probationer from the web of his former relations or insert new elements into that web of relations. While it is easier to remove the probationer from his situation, the modification of the situation is more profitable in the long run.[41]

It is not practical for probation officers to become members of probationers' intimate groups, and law-abiding groups tend to ostracize probationers. Consequently, some probation workers try to transform groups of probationers into law-abiding groups. This feature is included in the Citizenship Training Department of the Boston Juvenile Court. This court requires probationers aged 12 to 17 to participate in this program, five days a week from 3:30 to 6 P.M. for twelve weeks. The program consists of organized recreation, group discussion of problems, and remedial reading.[42] Such group activities can be anti-criminal in emphasis, and they also provide opportunities for the staff to observe the probationers and thus to secure a better understanding of them.[43]

If it be true that behavior is determined largely in local personal groups

[40] Richard R. Korn and Lloyd W. McCorkle, *Criminology and Penology* (New York: Holt, 1959), p. 593.

[41] Cf. P. Deutschberger, "Case Work Failure and the Psychology of Restriction," *Probation*, 24:103–108, March–April, 1946.

[42] Citizen Training Group, *Annual Report* (Boston: Author, 1956). See also Louis G. Maglio, "The Citizenship Training Program of the Boston Juvenile Court," *Juvenile Court Judges Journal*, 7:12–21, December, 1956; and L. Haddock, "It's Boston for Beans, Books, and Better Boys," *Rotarian*, 82:34–36, February, 1952.

[43] Kenneth I. Wollan, "The Use of Group Activity in Probation Work," *National Probation Association Yearbook*, 1938, pp. 240–255; Kenneth I. Wollan, "A New Treatment Program for Juvenile Delinquents," *Journal of Criminal Law and Criminology*, 31: 712–719, March–April, 1941; Kenneth I. Wollan and George E. Gardner, "A Group Clinic Approach to Delinquency," *Mental Hygiene*, 22:567–584, October, 1938; George E. Gardner and Kenneth I. Wollan, "Activity Interview in the Study of Delinquency," *American Journal of Orthopsychiatry*, 11:143–149, January, 1941.

and that a probation officer can accomplish little by his own direct efforts, the policy of probation must be implemented principally by organization of the local community for the readjustment of the delinquent. Efforts of this type have been made in the Chicago Area Projects, where the local community is organized for probation work as well as for other programs for the reduction of delinquency.[44] Probation officers are selected, so far as practicable, from the local community. This selection is based on the belief that such officers will be culturally homogeneous with the community and therefore more effective than officers imported from other groups both in influencing the delinquent who is on probation and also in inducing other residents of the community to participate in programs for the rehabilitation of the probationer. These other residents give information to the probation officer regarding the behavior of the probationer which they would not give under any circumstances to an "alien" probation officer. This illustrates the tendency of the community to identify itself with the probation program. While little objective evidence of the success of the Area Projects in this respect is available, the principle seems to be correct.[45]

Probation officers make many efforts to render material assistance to probationers, in the form of jobs, relief, vocational guidance. Some probation departments maintain regular employment agencies. The New York City Probation Department at one time maintained a vocational guidance bureau. In many states the probation officers, especially in earlier years, administered mothers' pensions or other relief. Such duplication of the work of other community agencies does not appear to be advantageous, and probation departments now generally refer their probationers to these other agencies.[46]

As indicated previously, some judges and some probation officers contend that the achievements of probation departments rest basically on fear of punishment. Fear of imprisonment, and fear of the probation officer because he has the power to recommend imprisonment, is considered the essential factor in rehabilitation. Of course, some fear of the probation officer and of imprisonment is inevitable in the current legal system. But the logic of this argument leads to universal imprisonment of offenders;

[44] See Fred A. Romano, "Organizing a Community for Delinquency Prevention," *National Probation Association Yearbook*, 1940, pp. 1-12.

[45] See Donald R. Cressey, "Social Psychological Foundations for Using Criminals in the Rehabilitation of Criminals," *Journal of Research in Crime and Delinquency*, 2:49-59, July, 1965.

[46] This practice is called the "executive" method of case work. For discussion of this method and of "leadership" and "relationship" case work methods see Pauline V. Young, *Social Treatment in Probation and Delinquency*, Second Edition (New York: McGraw-Hill, 1952), pp. 373-384. See also David Dressler, *Practice and Theory of Probation and Parole* (New York: Columbia University Press, 1959), pp. 151-165.

the logic of probation is that contacts and assimilation in normal groups are most important in modifying behavior; fear places social distance between probationer and probation officer and retards contact with assimilation. However, fear unquestionably has some value in deterring persons from violations of law and the question is whether it cannot be replaced generally by methods which are more effective than fear and, specifically, whether it is not inconsistent with the principles of probation work and does not interfere with the efficiency of probation work.

The psychiatric school of criminology has a conception that the primary value to be attained in "treatment" is insight by the probationer into the reasons for his delinquent behavior. This school argues that a probationer who attains this insight will be unlikely to violate the law in the future. The probation officer who attempts to use this method should be trained in psychiatry and should generally be a psychiatrist or at least a psychiatric social worker. The probation officer with this training can understand the delinquent only by intensive interviews which probe the basic motivations of the delinquent, and these interviews will at the same time reveal the delinquent to himself. A further value of these interviews, according to this school of thought, is that the probationer in the interviews will develop an identification with the probation officer and through this identification will tend to behave as the probation officer behaves. One of the psychiatric problems, thereafter, is to break up this feeling of identification so that the probationer can make independent decisions. Although this school of thought and treatment has an extensive vogue in the United States at the present time, the value of the techniques has not been demonstrated by objective studies and the validity of the theories is open to question. The principal reason for scepticism is that the procedure is based on the mistaken assumption that criminality can be treated in an office or a clinic just as an infectious disease can be.

SUCCESS AND FAILURES ON PROBATION. Probation departments generally report that about 75 percent of their probationers succeed on probation. However, the percentage varies a great deal from department to department. For example, it is reported that in 1958 about 84 percent of the persons placed on federal probation made good while under supervision,[47] while for six counties in Michigan in 1936 only 53.9 percent of the probationers were classed as "successful."[48] The 75 percent figure is a very

[47] *Annual Report of the Director of the Administrative Office of the United States Courts, 1958* (Washington: Government Printing Office, 1959), p. 130.

[48] Lowell J. Carr, *Delinquency Control* (New York: Harper and Brothers, 1950), p. 249.

rough average of the reports of many departments in many different years.[49] Even in this sense it is inadequate in at least three respects. *First,* the number reported to be failures is incomplete because the probation officer is not in sufficiently close contact with his probationers to know how many of them become delinquent, and also because the identification records of police departments are so restricted that they do not adequately supplement the knowledge of the probation officer. Sometimes reports are made of probationers who without the knowledge of the probation officer are arrested or even who serve short terms in institutions while on probation for another offense. During a fifteen-year period, the behavior on probation of 806 boys was studied intensively by the Gluecks, who concluded that 57.9 percent were failures.[50] In a similar study of 390 male criminals placed on probation during a fifteen-year period, 92.4 percent failed.[51] The Gluecks considered as a failure one who either had been arrested, had more than occasionally violated probation conditions, had been committed to an institution for probation violation, or had committed an offense for which arrest was possible, even if it had not occurred. Most probation departments consider as failures only those persons against whom official action (revocation or probation) has been taken. This is illustrated by recent findings regarding the juvenile court in Chicago. Of the white male delinquents placed on probation by the judges of the Cook County, Illinois, Juvenile Court between March 4, 1943, and October 31, 1944, 35.3 percent were classified as "failures"; 92 percent of those classified as failures had committed a delinquent offense while under probationary supervision; 87 percent of these offenses were adult felonies.[52] The 11,638 defendants granted probation by the California Superior Courts in 1956–1958 were followed until December 31, 1963. At that cut-off date, 62 percent had no violations, 7 percent had one violation, 2 percent had two or more violations, and for 29 percent probation had been revoked and not reinstated. The probationers with no violations were considered successes; those whose probation was revoked were considered failures, and those with one or more violations were viewed as neither successes nor

[49] Ralph W. England, Jr., "What is Responsible for Satisfactory Probation and Post-Probation Outcome?" *Journal of Criminal Law and Criminology,* 47:667–676, March–April, 1957.

[50] Sheldon and Eleanor T. Glueck, *Juvenile Delinquents Grow Up* (New York: The Commonwealth Fund, 1940), pp. 153, 161.

[51] Sheldon and Eleanor T. Glueck, *Criminal Careers in Retrospect* (New York: The Commonwealth Fund, 1943), p. 151.

[52] Albert J. Reiss, Jr., "Delinquency as the Failure of Personal and Social Controls," *American Sociological Review,* 16:196–207, April, 1951; Albert J. Reiss, Jr., "The Accuracy, Efficiency, and Validity of a Prediction Instrument," *American Journal of Sociology,* 56:552–561, May, 1951.

failures. One county revoked the probation of about forty percent of its probationers, and the county at the other extreme revoked in nineteen percent of its cases. The highest revocation rates were for persons convicted of forgery and bad checks (46 percent) and automobile theft (41 percent); the lowest revocation rates were for manslaughter (4 percent) and bookmaking (8 percent).[53] These inadequacies in the official records are being corrected in some jurisdictions. The departments which have the reputation of doing the best probation work show the smallest proportion of successes, probably because they have more complete information regarding the behavior of their probationers than do the departments which are doing their work in a less satisfactory manner.[54]

*Second*, the statistics of probation departments are confined to behavior during the period of probation and do not include the behavior subsequent to release from probation. Several studies have been made for the purpose of supplying this information. A study of 200 former probationers in New York, in 1920, showed that 72 percent of those who had been reported as successful during probation remained successful during the subsequent period.[55] A similar study of 400 boy and 100 girl probation cases of the Boston Juvenile Court revealed that, five to seven years after termination of probation, 21 percent of the boys and 12 percent of the girls were failures.[56] Recent studies of federal probationers in Alabama have indicated that during a period of from 5.5 to 11.5 years after successful completion of probation 83.6 percent had not been convicted of any crime, 14.3 percent had been convicted of misdemeanors, and 2.0 percent had been convicted of felonies.[57] In another Federal District, 82.3 percent of 500 probationers were convicted of no crimes in periods from 6 to 12 years after completing probation.[58] These studies seem to indicate that the number of failures is not greatly increased after the end of the probation period.

*Third*, the "success" of probation in individual cases logically should be determined by comparing it with the success of alternative methods of dealing with offenders. Since probation is generally a substitute either for

[53] *Delinquency and Probation in California*, 1963, op. cit., pp. 209–223. See also George A. Davis, "A Study of Adult Probation Violation Rates by Means of the Cohort Approach," *Journal of Criminal Law, Criminology and Police Science*, 55:70–84, March, 1964.
[54] Special Study Commission on Correctional Facilities and Services, op. cit., pp. 91–92, 95, 109.
[55] New York State Probation Commission, *Report* (New York: Author, 1920, p. 31).
[56] Belle Boone Beard, *Juvenile Probation* (New York: American Book, 1936), p. 147.
[57] Morris G. Caldwell, "Review of a New Type of Probation Study Made in Alabama," *Federal Probation*, 15:3–11, June, 1951.
[58] Ralph W. England, Jr., "A Study of Postprobation Recidivism Among 500 Federal Offenders," *Federal Probation*, 19:10–16, September, 1955.

release without supervision or for imprisonment, efforts should be made to compare the subsequent behavior of probationers with the subsequent behavior of those released without supervision and those committed to institutions. Such comparison is extremely difficult, however, since probationers generally are selected from the criminal population as those least likely to become recidivists. It is probably for this reason that no recent comparisons have been made.[59] Conclusions regarding the value of probation are sometimes erroneously based on the number of prison or reformatory inmates who are ex-probationers. Such statistics are inadequate, for they show nothing regarding the number of probationers who do not appear subsequently in institutions.

Almost everyone agrees that probation should be used to some extent. The important question, therefore, is not whether probation in general is a success or failure, but what types of offenders succeed on probation and under what conditions probationers succeed. A few intensive studies contain organized information on this point.[60] These studies agree in the conclusion that the highest rates of violation of probation are found among the probationers who had previous criminal records, previous records of irregular work, low economic status, low occupational level, previous institutional placement, residence in deteriorated or commercial areas, families with records of crime or vice, immoral associates, great mobility in residences, and few or irregular contacts with schools or churches. Reiss, for example, found that among the probationers from the Chicago Juvenile Courts, 44.8 percent of those who resided in areas with the highest delinquency rates violated probation, as compared with 30.7 percent of those who resided in the areas of lowest delinquency rates. Similarly, Glaser and Hangren found that probation was violated by 80 percent of 30 cases whose leisure time was spent predominantly in association with persons describable as "criminogenic," or in opposition to "respectable" moral standards, while it was violated by only 7 percent of 69 offenders whose recreational activities were describable as taking place in groups predominantly oriented toward socially approved patterns of behavior. These studies make specific the general proposition that excessive intimate association

[59] For an example of this kind of comparison, see J. M. Hepbron, "Probation and Penal Treatment in Baltimore," Journal of Criminal Law and Criminology, 19:64–74, May–June, 1928.

[60] Massachusetts Commission on Probation, Report on an Inquiry into the Permanent Results of Probation, Massachusetts Senate Document 431 (Boston: State Printing Office, 1924); E. D. Monachesi, Prediction Factors in Probation (Hanover: Sociological Press, 1932); C. H. Young, Prediction in Probation in the Boys' Court in Chicago (Mss.); Reiss, op. cit.; J. L. Gillin, "Predicting Outcomes of Adult Probation in Wisconsin," American Sociological Review, 15:550–553, August, 1950; Daniel Glaser and Richard F. Hangren, "Predicting the Adjustment of Federal Probationers," National Probation and Parole Association Journal, 4:258–267, July, 1958.

with criminal behavior patterns characterizes second offenders as well as first offenders.

When data on offenders and non-offenders is organized in statistical form, courts have a basis for intelligent selection of offenders to be placed on probation, and probation officers have a fund of information on which to base treatment policies.[61] Prediction studies utilizing such statistical data have been carried somewhat further in regard to parole than in regard to probation, and prediction instruments are used by several parole boards. The statistical information on probation is not adequate at present from the point of view of reliability, classifications, or significance, but these defects can be corrected.

APPRAISAL OF PROBATION. The advocates of probation do not insist that all offenders should be placed on probation, but rather that certain types of offenders will get along better and do less injury to society if they are placed on probation than if they are imprisoned or are dismissed without supervision. The probation policy enables these offenders to remain in the general society, which is the best situation in which to develop character, and at the same time to receive assistance in adapting themselves to the conditions of life, so that they will not be so impotent in struggling against the conditions which produced the delinquency.

Probation, furthermore, has the advantage that the probationer, being at liberty, has a better opportunity to make payments toward the support of his family or toward reparation or restitution. In 1956, 84,100 probationers in California paid, through the probation officers, $2,747,000 toward the support of their families, and $902,000 in reparation and restitution.[62] Also, probation, as now operated, is very much cheaper than imprisonment. In New York, the current cost of imprisonment is eighteen times as high as probation per offender dealt with under each system, and in Massachusetts ten times as much. In 1958, the per capita cost for federal probationers was $156.75 and for federal prisoners $1,593. Probation would cost more if it were properly administered. However, a study in Saginaw county Michigan indicated that reducing case loads and improving the quality of probation services actually reduces the total cost of correctional programs.[63]

Probation officers, while assisting their charges, attempt to modify the family or neighborhood situations that are producing delinquency. Thus,

[61] See John Otto Reinemann, "Research Activities in the Probation Department," *Proceedings of the American Prison Association*, 1946, pp. 39–48.
[62] Special Study Commission on Correctional Facilities and Services, *op. cit.*, p. 117.
[63] Alfred C. Ball, *The Saginaw Probation Demonstration Project* (East Lansing, Michigan: Michigan Crime and Delinquency Council, 1963), pp. 2–3.

by their own efforts, the co-operation of other agencies, and the public opinion which they develop, they are instruments for the prevention of crime. In this way, as well as by producing reformation in the probationers, probation should be regarded as one of the crime reducing agencies in modern society. Moreover, probation not only represents a change in the societal reaction to crime, but it is producing a further change in that reaction.

Certain objections have been raised against probation, of which the most important are the following: (a) probation decreases the average penalty for crime and therefore tends to increase crime; (b) probation replaces the offender in the environment which produced him and is not likely to modify his behavior; (c) probation does not satisfy the desire for revenge and therefore tends to eliminate the incentive for prosecution.

The first objection, as has been shown previously, has little basis in fact. Extensive use of probation does not in itself result in an immense increase of serious crimes. The argument that probation does not alter the environment of the offender is a sound argument and is presented primarily by those who insist that case work must be expanded to include the family, other intimate groups, and larger community if it is to be effective. It is not an argument against probation, but against the specific methods of probationary work. However, a study of California counties indicated that there is no correlation between the percentage of convicted Superior Court defendants placed on probation, and the rate of failure among these probationers.[64] This indicates that probation can be safely used for more cases in most counties, even if the probationers are placed in the environment which produced them.

The last of the objections requires additional comment. Some years ago Professor Kocourek advanced the argument as follows: Support for prosecution must ordinarily be secured from the injured party and this support is given because of the desire for revenge. As probation increases, the number of injured persons who will be willing to go to the trouble of prosecuting offenders will decrease, because they will secure so little satisfaction from it. Though restitution may be made by probationers, this does not serve as a sufficient incentive to the injured party, since civil process is a much more certain means of securing restitution.[65]

First of all, the amount of injury that must be inflicted in order to satisfy this desire for revenge is variable; a few centuries ago nothing short of the death of the offender would satisfy; at present imprisonment will generally satisfy, and there is no reason for doubting that a smaller amount

---

[64] Special Study Commission, op. cit., pp. 93–94.
[65] Albert Kocourek, "An Unconsidered Element in the Probation of First Offenders," Journal of Criminal Law and Criminology, 6:9–17, May–June, 1915.

of suffering will eventually serve just as well. But it is quite fallacious to assume that at present the desire for revenge is the only or most important reason for prosecution. One alternative general motive is to prevent a repetition of the offense. And many injured persons now refrain from prosecution because their reaction to crime is nonpunitive. That is, they feel that imprisonment or other punishment will make a confirmed and hardened criminal of one who might be turned into a law-abiding citizen if treatment rather than punitive efforts were made. These persons probably would be much more willing to prosecute if they thought prosecution would lead to treatment of the offender. Despite the fact that a large proportion of criminal cases involve no particular injured party,[66] if court procedures were speeded up and organized more efficiently and the technicalities reduced, the number of persons, whether motivated by revenge or something else, who would be willing to appear in criminal trials probably would be greatly increased. The desire for restitution also is a general motive, alternative to revenge, for prosecution. Resort to civil courts will not generally serve the purpose of the victim. For, though the judgment of the court may be more certain if the process is civil, most of the offenders are impecunious and the judgment is worthless to the victim. The criminal court, with its combination of probation and restitution, is a more effective means of securing financial compensation for injury than the civil court in a large proportion of cases.

## SUGGESTED READINGS

Bates, Sanford, "The Establishment and Early Years of the Federal Probation System," *Federal Probation*, 14:16–21, June, 1950.

Blake, Marilyn, "Probation is not Case Work," *Federal Probation*, 12:54–57, June, 1948.

Caldwell, M. G., "Review of a New Type of Probation Study Made in Alabama," *Federal Probation*, 15:3–11, June, 1951.

Cosulich, Gilbert, *Adult Probation Laws of the United States.* New York: National Probation Association, 1940.

Cressey, Donald R., "Professional Correctional Work and Professional Work in Correction," *National Probation and Parole Association Journal*, 5:1–15, January, 1959.

Crihfield, B. E., "The Interstate Parole and Probation Compact," *Federal Probation*, 17:3–7, June, 1953.

Davis, George F., "A Study of Adult Probation Violation Rates by Means of the Cohort Approach," *Journal of Criminal Law, Criminology and Police Science*, 55:70–84, March, 1964.

England, Ralph W., Jr., "A Study of Postprobation Recidivism Among

66 See Edwin M. Schur, *Crimes Without Victims* (Englewood Cliffs, New Jersey: Prentice-Hall, 1965).

500 Federal Offenders," *Federal Probation*, 19:10–16, September, 1955.

Geis, Gilbert, and Fred W. Woodson, "Matching Probation Officer and Delinquent," *National Probation and Parole Association Journal*, 2:58–62, January, 1956.

Glaser, Daniel, and Richard F. Hangren, "Predicting the Adjustment of Federal Probationers," *National Probation and Parole Association Journal*, 4:258–267, July, 1958.

Grinnell, Frank W., "The Common Law History of Probation," *Journal of Criminal Law and Criminology*, 32:15–34, May–June, 1941.

Mannheim, Hermann, "Comparative Sentencing Practice," *Law and Contemporary Problems*, 23:557–582, Summer, 1958.

Meeker, Ben, "Probation is Case Work," *Federal Probation*, 12:54–57, June, 1948.

Meyer, Charles H. Z., "A Half Century of Probation and Parole," *Journal of Criminal Law, Criminology and Police Science*, 42:707–728, March–April, 1952.

Ohlin, Lloyd E., Herman Piven, and Donnell M. Pappenfort, "Major Dilemmas of the Social Worker in Probation and Parole," *National Probation and Parole Association Journal*, 2:211–225, July, 1956.

Olney, Warren, III, "The Federal Probation System in 1963: Where We Stand," *Federal Probation*, 27:3–8, September, 1963.

Reiss, Albert J. Jr., "The Accuracy, Efficiency, and Validity of a Prediction Instrument," *American Journal of Sociology*, 56:552–561, May, 1951.

Rumney, Jay, and J. P. Murphy, *Probation and Social Adjustment*. New Brunswick: Rutgers University Press, 1952.

Schafer, Stephen, *Restitution to Victims of Crime*. London: Stevens and Sons, 1960.

Sellin, Thorsten, "Adult Probation and the Conditional Sentence," *Journal of Criminal Law, Criminology and Police Science*, 49:553–556, April, 1959.

Timasheff, N. S., *One Hundred Years of Probation*. New York: Fordham University Press, 1941.

Turnbladh, "Current Status of Probation," in Paul W. Tappan, Editor, *Contemporary Correction*. New York: McGraw-Hill, 1951, pp. 394–396.

Young, Pauline V., *Social Treatment in Probation and Delinquency*, Second Edition, New York: McGraw-Hill, 1952.

# 22. DEVELOPMENT OF TREATMENT METHODS IN AMERICAN PRISONS

WE HAVE CONSIDERED previously the development of imprisonment until it became an established and generally used policy in England about the beginning of the nineteenth century. The present chapter continues this discussion with reference to the development of prisons in the United States, especially after the beginning of the nineteenth century.

EARLY AMERICAN PRISONS. Jails and houses of correction were established in the American colonies soon after settlement. The jail was designed originally for the detention of persons awaiting trial. It soon came to be used as a place of punishment after conviction. As was the case in England, this change accompanied increasing opposition to the use of corporal and capital punishments, and it was thus a modification of the prevailing system for implementing the punitive societal reaction to lawbreaking. Convicted drunkards and vagrants, especially, were confined in these institutions. The house of correction began as an institution for vagrants but before long was not different except in name from many of the jails. The modification in the punitive reaction was made only gradually. For example, the number of persons confined either in jails or workhouses after conviction was small throughout the eighteenth century, and in New York state it was not until 1788 that a general law was passed for the use of jails or workhouses as places of punishment. Previously, commitments to those institutions were made only by a special law in each case.[1]

By present-day standards, the conditions in these jails and houses of correction were horrible. The prisoners spent their time in association, without labor, depending upon charity for their maintenance. There was no attempt to treat the inmates; even religious services were absent. Drunk-

---

[1] P. Klein, *Prison Methods in New York State* (New York: Columbia University Press, 1920), pp. 25–26. See also E. W. Capen, *The Historical Development of the Poor Law of Connecticut* (New York: Columbia University Press, 1905).

enness and vice generally prevailed, as had been customary in England. The following description of the Walnut Street (county) Jail in Philadelphia at the end of the Revolutionary War could be duplicated with regard to many other institutions of the time:

It is represented as a scene of promiscuous and unrestricted intercourse, and universal riot and debauchery. There was no labor, no separation of those accused, but yet untried, nor even of those confined for debt only, from convicts sentenced for the foulest crimes; no separation of color, age or sex, by day or by night; the prisoners lying promiscuously on the floor, most of them without anything like bed or bedding. As soon as the sexes were placed in different wings, which was the first reform made in the prison, of thirty or forty women then confined there, all but four or five immediately left it; it having been a common practice, it is said, for women to cause themselves to be arrested for fictitious debts, that they might share in the orgies of the place. Intoxicating liquors abounded, and indeed were freely sold at a bar kept by one of the officers of the prison. Intercourse between the convicts and persons without was hardly restricted. Prisoners tried and acquitted were still detained till they should pay jail fees to the keeper; and the custom of garnish was established and unquestioned; that is, the custom of stripping every newcomer of his outer clothing, to be sold for liquor, unless redeemed by the payment of a sum of money to be applied to the same object. It need hardly be added, that there was no attempt to give any kind of instruction, and no religious service whatsoever.[2]

The Quakers of Philadelphia made decided efforts to change these conditions. In 1776 Richard Wistar at his own expense provided soup for some of the prisoners in the county jail, when it became known that some of them had died of starvation. Others became interested in his efforts, and in that year the Philadelphia Society for Alleviating Distressed Prisoners was formed. Its activities were stopped by the war. It was revived in 1787 with the name Philadelphia Society for Alleviating the Miseries of Public Prisons. About half of its members were Quakers. It had the primary purpose of relieving the physical suffering of prisoners, but soon attempted, in addition, to modify the punitive reaction, largely by advo-

---

[2] F. C. Gray, *Prison Discipline in America* (London: J. Murray, 1848), pp. 15–16. It has been reported frequently that when the first attempt was made to preach to the prisoners in this Walnut Street jail, the prison authorities remonstrated and opposed it for fear of an outbreak by the prisoners, but finally agreed on condition that the preacher leave all of his valuables outside and that a loaded cannon be placed facing the prisoners, with a man standing ready with a lighted fuse to touch it off. It seems probable that this was merely a device of the keeper of the prison to frighten the preacher rather than the prisoners. J. T. Scharf and T. Westcott, *History of Philadelphia* (Philadelphia: L. H. Everts, 1884), Vol. I, pp. 444–445, note.

cating reduction of the number of capital penalties and substitution of imprisonment in solitary confinement for the death penalty.

THE DEVELOPMENT OF THE STATE PRISON.     During the colonial period no institutions similar to the present state prison were established until, in 1773, Connecticut purchased an old mine near Simsbury and turned it into a prison. This was used by the state as a prison until 1827. The prisoners were fastened during the night by heavy chains attached to their necks at one end and the heavy beams above them at the other; in addition heavy iron bars were fixed to their feet. In 1785 Massachusetts provided that persons sentenced to solitary confinement and hard labor should serve the sentence in Castle Island, a military post in Boston harbor, instead of in the county jails and houses of correction, most of which were insecure. Massachusetts authorized a new state prison in 1803. The movement spread rapidly during the last part of the eighteenth and the first part of the nineteenth centuries. New York erected a state prison in 1796, New Jersey in 1798, Virginia in 1800, Vermont in 1808, Maryland in 1812, New Hampshire in 1812, and Ohio in 1816. The following inscription, placed over the door of the New Jersey state prison, indicates the punitive philosophy which prevailed in such institutions:

Labor, silence, penitence. 1797. That those who are feared for their crimes may learn to fear the laws and be useful. *Hic labor, hoc opus.*

The immediate motive for the erection of state prisons, as contrasted with county or other local prisons, was not humanitarian concern for prisoners' welfare. Instead, the motive was to obtain greater security for persons sentenced to long terms of imprisonment. The number of prisoners with long sentences was increasing because of the development of opposition to the death penalty. Zephaniah Swift stated that Connecticut authorized a state prison because of opposition to the death penalty and because long-term imprisonment was the only available substitute for the death penalty.[3] This motive stands out more clearly in Pennsylvania than in any other state. The constitution of that state in 1776 directed that imprisonment at hard, punitive labor be substituted for capital punishment. Immediately after the war, under the direction of Benjamin Rush, Benjamin Franklin, William Bradford, Caleb Lownes, and others, a plan was prepared, which was made law in 1786 and amended several times during the next decade. By these laws, capital punishment was abolished

[3] *A System of the Laws of the State of Connecticut* (Windham: Byrne, for the author, 1796), Vol. II, p. 295; L. N. Robinson, *Penology in the United States* (Philadelphia: Winston, 1921), p. 69.

for all crimes except murder, corporal punishment was abolished, and fines and imprisonments were the only penalties left. It was directed that imprisonment should be "with hard labor, public and disgracefully imposed." At first this resulted in gang labor on the streets with the prisoners restrained by ball-and-chain, dressed in a distinctive garb, and with heads shaved. They were soon returned to the prison because street labor was unsatisfactory. At this time, the state had no prison of its own and therefore made an arrangement that the state prisoners be kept in the county jails; a part of the expenses of these institutions was paid from state funds. An unsuccessful attempt was made in 1803 to secure an institution exclusively for state prisoners, but it was not until 1818 that the effort succeeded. Of the 130 state prisons with more than 400 inmates operating currently, 40 percent were opened before 1900, 66 percent before 1925.

In addition to this desire to obtain more secure places of confinement for long term prisoners, the hope that these prisoners, because they were confined for long periods, might be able to pay the expenses of the institution by their labor was instrumental in the development of the state prison. Doubtless, also, labor was introduced because imprisonment was not believed to be sufficient punishment in itself.

THE PENITENTIARY. About the time the state became interested in the maintenance of prisons of its own, a new conception of prison discipline appeared, which resulted in calling these institutions penitentiaries. The word "penitentiary" had a significance at that time which it has generally lost at the present, viz., an institution not for retribution but for producing penitence or penitentiary reformation. As indicated earlier, the medieval prisons under the control of the Church had this ideal and the same purpose was reflected in the law of England passed in 1778, authorizing a penitentiary. The purpose of this institution was stated by the law to be:

By sobriety, cleanliness, and medical assistance, by a regular series of labour, by solitary confinement during the intervals of work, and by due religious instruction to preserve and amend the health of the unhappy offenders, to inure them to habits of industry, to guard them from pernicious company, to accustom them to serious reflection and to teach them both the principles and practice of every Christian and moral duty.

This law was framed by Blackstone, Eden, and Howard. Howard stated:

The term penitentiary clearly shows that Parliament had chiefly in view the reformation and amendment of those to be committed to such places of confinement.

This institution was not erected, but the law incorporated the idea that prisoners should be "amended" and "inured" by constructive action, and it undoubtedly influenced the Quakers of Pennsylvania. They developed not only a state prison, but also a new conception of prison discipline which made their institution, and others modeled on it, penitentiaries. These innovators looked upon imprisonment as in itself a sufficiently severe penalty and they insisted that the prisoner should be assisted in his effort to become rehabilitated. This notion, which is indicative of the rise in popularity of a treatment reaction to crime, was in opposition to the opinion of many persons of the time. Judge Walworth, in declaring whipping in prison a proper punishment, in 1826 stated:

That confinement with labor merely had no terrors for the guilty; that the labor which the human body was capable of performing without endangering its health was but little more than many of the virtuous laboring class of the community daily and voluntarily perform, for the support and maintenance of their families; that to produce reformation in the guilty or to restrain the vicious from the perpetration of crime by the terrors of punishment, it was absolutely necessary that the convict should feel his degraded situation . . . ; that the system of discipline adopted by the inspectors under the sanction of the laws was well calculated to have the desired effect of reforming the less vicious offenders and of deterring others from the commission of crime . . . ; that it was, however, through terror of bodily suffering alone that the proper effect upon the mind of the convict was produced.[4]

THE PENNSYLVANIA SYSTEM. The prison leaders in Pennsylvania contended that the association of all types of criminals in prisons was disastrous. They suggested, as had been suggested frequently for several centuries, that prisoners should be kept in solitary confinement. Arrangements for this were made in the Walnut Street Jail, in which the state prisoners were confined. Solitary confinement, it was contended, not only prevented the disastrous association of criminals, but also had the positive virtue of forcing the prisoners to reflect on their crimes and therefore of producing reformation. During a part of the history of the system of solitary confinement the prisoners were not permitted to work at anything, and when they were permitted to work, the work was made subordinate to reflection. It was realized that solitude would be injurious if too long continued, and provision was therefore made for association with the following official visitors: the governor of the state, the members of the state legislature, the judges of all courts, the mayors of Philadelphia, Pittsburgh, and Lancaster,

4 Quoted by Klein, *op. cit.*, p. 206.

the county commissioners and sheriffs, and a committee of the Philadelphia Society for Alleviating the Miseries of Public Prisons. The relation
between the prisoner and these official visitors could not have been very
intimate. The committee of the Society did very well to average four and
a half hours a year per prisoner, and their conversation was confined largely
to theological exhortations. The solitude was not frequently broken, therefore. But it was argued that the effect of this solitude was to cause an appreciation of these good men when they did come.

The Western Penitentiary at Allegheny, Pennsylvania, which opened in
1828, adopted this "separate and silent" system. As in the Walnut Street
Jail, the prisoners were at first kept in idleness. After a few years, however,
they were permitted to work in their cells. But it was in the Eastern State
Penitentiary, whch was opened in Philadelphia in 1829, that the "Pennsylvania System" really developed. As in the other institutions, the prisoners
were to work alone at such occupations as spinning, weaving, and shoe-
making, and were to do maintenance work outside their cells only when
blindfolded. The system was not practical, and it was formally abolished in
1913. However, strict solitude probably never was enforced.

THE AUBURN SYSTEM. On the demand of Governor John Jay for the improvement of the criminal law of New York State, a commission was sent
to Pennsylvania in 1794 to study the new system. After the report of this
commission in 1796 a law was passed in New York, reducing the capital
offenses to two, and substituting imprisonment for the death penalty and
for corporal punishment. Also, the construction of two prisons was authorized. However, Newgate Prison, which opened in 1797, was the only one
erected. The institution was small, and there were no provisions for solitary confinement. Newgate proved to be inadequate and in 1816 another
prison at Auburn was authorized. A part of this institution was to be used
for solitary confinement. By act of 1821, the prisoners in Auburn were
divided into three classes: the first class, composed of the "oldest and
most heinous offenders," were to be kept in solitary confinement continuously; those in the second class to be kept in their cells three days a week,
and the others one day a week. The cells were small and dark and no provision was made for work in the cells. This experiment with strict solitary
confinement proved to be a great failure; of eighty prisoners who had been
in solitary confinement continuously all except two were out of the prison
within two years, as the result of death, insanity, or pardon. A legislative
commission which investigated the policy in 1824 recommended that it be
abandoned at once and this recommendation was adopted. Being now thoroughly opposed to the method of solitary confinement, which had not,

however, been tried under as favorable conditions as in Pennsylvania, the Auburn authorities provided for work by the prisoners in association but in silence during the day and solitary confinement during the night. This has been known as the Auburn system, in contrast with the Pennsylvania system, which was solitary confinement by day and night.

THE CONTROVERSY BETWEEN THE AUBURN AND PENNSYLVANIA SYSTEMS. The literature of criminology during the forty years subsequent to the establishment of the Auburn system is devoted almost entirely to a hot controversy between these two systems. It was carried on largely by two prison reform associations: The Philadelphia Society, mentioned above, which supported the Pennsylvania system, and the Boston Society for the Improvement of Prison Discipline and for the Reformation of Juvenile Offenders, organized in 1815 which supported the Auburn system.[5] Both societies were intensely interested in the reformation of offenders, both were convinced of the merits of their method and the demerits of the other method, and both were entirely unscrupulous in their use of statistics to prove their arguments. When Dickens, after a visit to America wrote his *American Notes*, he included a severe arraignment of the Pennsylvania system which still further increased the antagonism between the two parties in America.

The Pennsylvania system was tried in a number of the states, but was generally abandoned in favor of the Auburn system after a short trial. The principal advantages claimed for the Auburn system were economic; that is, it cost less to construct the congregate type prison and the congregate system made possible more efficient utilization of the labor of prisoners for production of wealth. At the same time, the system of silence was thought to be sufficient for reformation through reflection. European visitors, however, generally secured and carried away an impression that the Pennsylvan system was superior. In 1835, commissioners were sent from England, France, Prussia, and Belgium to examine the American prison systems; they made their visits together and presented practically identical reports to their home governments in favor of the Pennsylvania system. These reports produced a great effect in Europe and most of the European countries adopted the Pennsylvania in a modified form.

The controversy between these two systems, after raging for more than half a century, was diverted by the importation of a new system from Europe and Australia. This system was started in an organized manner in

[5] See Stewart H. Holbrook, *Dreamers of the American Dream* (New York: Doubleday, 1957), pp. 240–244.

the Australian convict camps by Captain Maconochie.[6] His methods were imported into Ireland and England and under the name of the Irish system became known to and were discussed by American leaders shortly before the Civil War. The Irish system consisted of the indeterminate sentence, the mark system as a method of measuring good behavior in prison, and a form of parole. The first institution using these methods was the Elmira Reformatory in New York, created by law in 1869 but not opened until 1876. Emphasis was placed on education, productive labor, the mark system, the indeterminate sentence, and parole, all of which were designed to produce reformation. It is not correct to think of this as the first reformatory, for the penitentiaries three-quarters of a century earlier were designed to produce reformation. But with the establishment of the Elmira system the treatment reaction to crime was more explicitly incorporated into institutional policy. Also, the conflict between the treatment and punitive reactions became institutionalized. It is significant in this connection that the Elmira Reformatory was constructed as a maximum-security penal institution and that efforts at "treatment" were made in this setting. Similarly, corporal punishment was a part of the Elmira routine. Almost all reformatories constructed in the United States since 1875 have been based on the Elmira system, including the conflict between treatment and punishment. This system of organized conflict between the treatment and punitive reactions also spread rather quickly to state prisons, so that it is now difficult to draw a line between state prisons and state reformatories so far as methods are concerned. Some state prisons use more definitely reformatory methods than do some reformatories. Fifty years after Elmira was opened, New York prisoners were begging the sentencing judges to send them to Auburn prison, rather than to Elmira reformatory, because the disciplinary system at Elmira was so severe. A high official at Elmira boasted of this fact, believing that such a state of affairs was a credit to his institution.[7]

JUVENILE REFORMATORIES AND INDUSTRIAL SCHOOLS. The first American institution specifically for juvenile delinquents was opened in New York City in 1825 after more than a generation of discussion. It was under the control of a private society called the New York Association for the Prevention of Pauperism, but the state made annual grants for its maintenance. A similar institution under private control was started in Philadel-

[6] See John V. Barry, "Pioneers in Criminology: XII, Alexander Machonochie (1787–1860)," *Journal of Criminal Law & Criminology*, 47:145–161, July–Aug., 1956, and John V. Barry, *Alexander Maconochie of Norfolk Island* (Melbourne: Oxford University Press, 1958).

[7] Harry Elmer Barnes and Negley K. Teeters, *New Horizons in Criminology* (New York: Prentice-Hall, 1951), pp. 533–534.

phia in 1826. The first institution of this type under state control was started in Massachusetts in 1847. Even this institution received assistance from private funds. Seven institutions had been opened by 1850, thirty-two more by 1875, and sixty-six more by 1900. At present there are about 130 state training schools. Though these institutions started and made their best progress in the early period under private control, the private institutions at present show no clear superiority to the public institutions. Several institutions have changed from private to public management though none has changed from public to private management.

From the first, it was contended that these institutions were not penal institutions or prisons, but schools. The children were to be educated or "treated," not punished. The contention was supported by the courts, especially by the Supreme Court in a decision regarding the institution in Philadelphia in 1828. In certain respects the institutions incorporated non-punitive policies, and many efforts were made to reform the delinquents by methods other than solitary confinement: they had self-government, religious teaching, academic teaching, indeterminate sentence, release on good behavior, which was similar to parole. In the second year of the New York House of Refuge, the president of the board made the following statement, which was quite opposed to the prevailing punitive reaction to law-breaking:

A child may be made quiet and industrious by beating, but it seldom happens, I believe, that kindheartedness, morality, and intelligence are induced by whipping.[8]

Some of these non-punitive policies were only temporary, and in some respects from the time of their origin the rationale of these institutions was punitive.

The earliest institutions for juvenile delinquents were organized under the dominance of the prison idea. . . . In all regards this was true; the establishments were distinctly prison enclosures, the dormitories were blocks of cells, the dining-rooms were chambers of silence, with only the meagerest provision of the crudest table furniture; the earning capacity of those confined was exploited to the highest possible figure, and education in letters was only provided for during such hours as could not be profitably employed in work; and the greatest ambition and strongest claim for popular approval was a low per capita cost of maintenance.[9]

8 B. K. Peirce, *A Half Century with Juvenile Delinquents, or the New York House of Refuge and Its Times* (New York: Appleton-Century-Crofts, 1869), p. 120.
9 F. H. Nibecker, "Education of Juvenile Delinquents," *Annals of the American Academy of Political and Social Science,* 23:483, May, 1904.

It seems probable, therefore, that, with temporary exceptions in regard to certain punitive policies, these institutions were during the first half century of their history primarily prisons, and their principal contribution was the removal of juvenile prisoners from association with adult prisoners. Though it may properly be argued that these institutions have changed very much since that time and therefore are not prisons now, at least, it is clear that the ideal of the prison for adults has changed, also, and that in practice there is more that is penal in some institutions for juvenile delinquents than in some institutions for adult criminals. The punitive reaction to crime was modified first in connection with juvenile offenses, spread to offenses of youths, and then spread to adult offenses. But in no case was the punitive reaction completely replaced. Even today some institutions for juveniles can best be described as congregate prisons.

One of the important developments in juvenile reformatories was the cottage system of architecture, in place of the old cell-block structure. In America the first examples of the cottage system, which was copied from European systems, were a Massachusetts institution for girls and the Ohio School for Boys at Lancaster, established in 1858. This system won general approval and most of the state institutions have adopted a similar plan because of the more homelike surroundings and the greater ease of classification. Such surroundings, however, do not necessarily mean that the conflict between treatment and punitive policies is absent. It was reported that as recently as 1948 whipping and other corporal punishments were used in the Lancaster institution, as well as in nine other juvenile institutions visited by one investigator.[10]

SPECIALIZATION OF PRISONS. As the previous discussion implies, one of the evident trends accompanying the development of treatment methods in American prisons has been toward specialization of prisons. The jail once was the only penal institution. In the past two hundred years various groups of prisoners have been withdrawn from the jail for incarceration in specialized institutions. Vagrants were first withdrawn and placed in houses of correction. This proved to be abortive and the houses of correction have now either been abandoned or become identical with the jail except in name. Then state prisons, with differing names, were established for juvenile delinquents, for insane criminals, for young adults, for women, for Negroes, for defective delinquents, for misdemeanants, for the sick, and for other groups of criminals. Thus, in the development of these specialized institutions, the principles which have been used in the selection of of-

---

[10] Albert Deutsch, "Is This Reform?" *Woman's Home Companion*, March, 1948, pp. 30 ff. See also Albert Deutsch, *Our Rejected Children* (Boston: Little, Brown, 1950).

fenders have included the governing unit, the seriousness of the crime, the age, color, sex, and mental or physical condition of the offenders. The motives for specialization have included the prevention of contamination of one type of offenders by another, and the adaptation of methods of work and of facilities to the characteristics of the special groups of offenders.

Until recent years the principles used in specialization had little, if anything, to do with treatment. Even now the most prevalent principle of specialization is the seriousness of the particular offense of which the prisoner was convicted; the state institutions generally care for felons, the county and municipal institutions for misdemeanants. This kind of differentiation is unsound from both the punitive and treatment point of view, for the particular offense is not a suitable index of character, dangerousness, or needs of the offender. The misdemeanant generally violates a law of the state as well as of the municipality, and the state would therefore be justified in taking charge of the prisoner rather than transferring this work to the local community. Moreover, the number of offenders in the typical county jail is so small that adequate facilities and personnel for segregation of various types of offenders is impractical.

The local prisons of England were taken over by the central government and have been thus operated for more than half a century with improvement in efficiency and great decrease in expense. Several states in America have established state farms for misdemeanants which, to some extent, take the place of county jails. Indiana, for example, established a state farm for misdemeanants in 1915. The law provides that male misdemeanants are to be sent to this state farm unless their sentences are thirty days or less, in which case they may be retained in the county jail or sent to the state farm at the discretion of the judge. The expenses of transportation are paid by the county, the expenses of maintenance by the state. The average population of the state farm in recent years has been about twelve hundred, of the county jails (including only convicted prisoners) about four hundred. This shows that most of the convicted misdemeanants have been removed to the state farm. But state farms, like county jails, are seldom specialized except in respect to the age and sex of inmates. Many misdemeanants, for instance, are chronic alcoholics who make almost continuous rounds of jails, saloons, police stations, and jails again.[11] Special institutions could be established for this group, for they present a problem which is unique and which requires a uniform method of treatment. The remainder of the jail and state farm population resembles the prison population more than the chronic alcoholic population.

[11] See David J. Pittman and C. Wayne Gordon, *Revolving Door: A Study of the Chronic Police Inebriate* (Glencoe: The Free Press, 1958).

Specialization of institutions by sex of inmates is now characteristic of all types of prisons—jails, houses of correction, reformatories, and state prisons. When both sexes are confined in one institution, the two departments are separated almost as completely as though they were different institutions.

Another principle of specialization is by age. The desirability of special institutions for juveniles, if they are to be kept in institutions at all, is beyond question. However, the state reformatory for young adults is not clearly justified. It was established on the theory that it would serve younger, less criminal, and more easily reformable men. But 63 percent of the men committed to the Massachusetts state reformatory at Concord in 1963 were recidivists, as compared to 77 percent of the men sentenced to the Massachusetts state prison at Walpole. Also, there is considerable overlapping in age. In Massachusetts in 1963, 86 percent of the persons sentenced to the Concord reformatory were under twenty-five, and 38 percent of those sentenced to the state prison were under twenty-five.[12] Thus the distinction between the state prison and the state reformatory is not at all clear. It has never been drawn as clearly for women as for men offenders, and at present practically every institution for women offenders might be called a reformatory.

Still another principle of specialization is by the personal characteristics of offenders. The federal government and states with large populations, like California, have been able to establish a series of prisons, graded from "maximum security" to "minimum security" and with quite different rehabilitative programs. Some special institutions have been established for vagrants, some for insane criminals, some for defective delinquents, some for alcoholics, and some for drug addicts. Such arrangements could be considered as specialization on the basis of the kind of punishment considered necessary in each case, but it also is specialization according to the kind of treatment methods deemed advisable for the various categories of offenders. In relatively recent years, "classification" of prisoners has come to include recommendation as to the kind of specialized institution in which an offender should be incarcerated, as well as recommendation for a particular kind of program within the institution. Classification will be discussed in the next chapter.

SOCIAL CONTACTS FOR PRISONERS.  The solitary confinement of the early Pennsylvania system has been generally abandoned in the United States except as punishment for infraction of prison regulations, and it is rapidly

---

[12] Commissioner of Correction, *Statistical Report* (Commonwealth of Massachusetts, Public Document No. 115, December 31, 1963), pp. 26–28, 36.

being abandoned in most of the European countries which adopted it. Even the rule of silence, which was substituted for this, has been abandoned in most institutions. Unquestionably the horrors of prison life have been reduced. Improvements have been made in diet, cleanliness, ventilation, lighting, and methods of discipline. In most institutions the marks of degradation, such as shaving of the head, the lockstep, striped clothing, and the ball-and-chain, have been eliminated. Also, the monotony of prison life has been reduced. Entertainments have been provided, athletics and other recreations developed, libraries and educational classes provided. Also, visiting and correspondence privileges have been introduced, and self-government in a complete or modified form established in many institutions. There are efforts both to promote contacts among the inmates and between the inmates and the outside world. They are based in part on the conviction that open contacts between prisoners are better than secret contacts which prevail in spite of a formal policy of isolation, in part on the conviction that reformation is a process of assimilation of culture of the outside world and that assimilation of culture is promoted by contact with that culture rather than isolation from it. These methods attempt to implement the treatment reaction to crime. While the prison in its general plan is a means of isolating offenders from social life, these logically contradictory methods are introduced in the effort to facilitate the reformation of the inmates by breaking down the isolation to some extent. Barnes has argued that training for a life of freedom can be secured only in an institution in which prisoners have freedom and responsibility.[13]

IMPRISONMENT AS PUNISHMENT.[14]    Almost all changes occurring in prisons prior to the present generation were directed, explicitly or implicitly, by the doctrine that restriction of a criminal's liberty *is*, by itself, punishment and that this punishment is adequate for meeting the societal needs for retribution, deterrence, and reformation.[15] In the early days of their existence, democratic societies were not sure of themselves—they deprived criminals of their freedom and *also* inflicted physical suffering on them. American prisons have abandoned corporal punishments as a regime for supplementing the suffering which "mere imprisonment" is expected to produce. Most prison officials now maintain that men are committed to prisons as punishment rather than *for* punishment.

13 H. E. Barnes, *The Evolution of Penology in Pennsylvania* (Indianapolis: Bobbs-Merrill, 1927), p. 400.

14 This section is adapted from Donald R. Cressey, "Rehabilitation Theory and Reality, I, The Pain of Restriction," *California Youth Authority Quarterly,* 10:3–9, Spring, 1957.

15 See the discussion below, pp. 519–521.

Yet "mere imprisonment" continues to be ordered because it is painful to offenders. It is no coincidence that imprisonment as a system for dealing with criminals arose with the democratic revolutions of the Eighteenth century. Neither is it a coincidence that imprisonment has remained as the principal method for dealing with serious offenders in democratic societies. As democracy developed, so did an appreciation of liberty, and restriction of freedom by imprisonment came to be regarded as a proper system for imposing pain on criminals. It was in this period that our current system of criminal laws, each law calling for a measured amount of loss of freedom and, thus, a measured amount of pain, was initiated.

Of course, "mere imprisonment" has never been consistently defined and has meant many things to many people, as has been true of the concept "liberty." In the Walnut Street Jail it meant only perimeter control, with freedom to commit crime and engage in debauchery within prison walls. At the other extreme, it meant confinement of all prisoners in solitary, as in the Pennsylvania system. Now we adopt, or try to adopt, a middle-of-the-road position, allowing inmates physical mobility within the walls but directing their actions and choices. Nevertheless, incarceration *is* intended as punishment in contemporary American society. It is this fact which helps pose the dilemma for contemporary prison workers, who are admonished to treat criminals, as well as to punish them. Only a generation ago it was common to assume that a system or technique for implementing society's punitive reaction to crime was also a method for "correcting" or "reforming" criminals. Now it is ordinarily assumed (perhaps erroneously) that any *real* correctional method is nonpunitive in nature.

While there is wide variation in opinion as to what a positive "treatment" or "rehabilitative" program *is*, there is wide consensus on what it *is not*: A program which involves purposive infliction of suffering is not a treatment program. Psychotherapy, vocational education, counselling, and library privileges are viewed as "treatment" principally because they are nonpunitive, not because they have been demonstrated to be effective methods of changing criminals into noncriminals. Prison workers, then, are to be nonpunitive in an institution which, by definition, is punitive.

The notion that treatment must be nonpunitive if it is to succeed has led to a popular conception of the prison as something other than a prison. The mental hospital is often used as a model of what the prison should become.[16] This is logical only if it is assumed that criminals are not responsible for their actions and are in need of nonpunitive treatment for the sources of that irresponsibility. Prisons cannot become nonpunitive organizations like mental hospitals, however, because they are used by society for

[16] See the statement by Karpman on page 366 above.

the purpose of inflicting suffering. No hospital for treating *criminality* exists in fact, because in our legal system proof of criminality ("badness") is followed by commitment to a prison, while proof of insanity ("sickness") is followed by commitment to a mental hospital.[17] And the prison remains as a place of punishment because the act of taking away a criminal's liberty is an act performed by the state in a deliberate attempt to produce suffering. The principal difference between committing a criminal to a prison and a psychotic to a mental hospital lies in the fact that we want the prisoner, but not the psychotic, to suffer from the incarceration. Patients in mental hospitals may suffer from confinement behind bars, but the suffering is not deliberately imposed by the state. Patients are not committed to an institution on the assumption that the suffering resulting from the incarceration will have some positive value in their rehabilitation or in deterring others from becoming patients. This, as we have seen, is precisely the assumption behind committing men to prison, and it is this assumption that makes the prison a place of punishment.

Since the prison is a place of punishment, incarceration cannot officially be ordered or viewed solely as an inconvenient but necessary means to the application of nonpunitive treatment methods. The notion that effective treatment for prisoners must be nonpunitive is in fundamental conflict with one of the tasks society assigns to the prison—purposive infliction of pain.

## SUGGESTED READINGS

Barnes, H. E., "The Historical Origin of the Prison System in the United States," *Journal of Criminal Law and Criminology*, 12:42–47, June, 1921.

Barnes, H. E., *The Evolution of Penology in Pennsylvania*. Indianapolis: Bobbs-Merrill, 1927.

Bates, Sanford, "Of Time and Memory—Changing Views of Congress of Correction," *American Journal of Correction*, 19:6–10 ff., November–December, 1957.

Beaumont, Gustave de, and Alexis de Tocqueville, *On the Penitentiary System in the United States and Its Application to France*, translated by Francis Lieber, Philadelphia: Carey, Lea and Blanchard, 1833.

Brockway, Z. R., *Fifty Years of Prison Service*. New York: Charities Publication Committee, 1912.

Cressey, Donald R., "Achievement of an Unstated Organizational Goal: An Observation on Prisons," *Pacific Sociological Review*, 1:43–49, Fall, 1958.

---

[17] See the discussion on pp. 12–13, 166–167, 311–313, above. See also Donald R. Cressey, "The Differential Association Theory and Compulsive Crimes," *Journal of Criminal Law and Criminology*, 45:25–40, May–June, 1954.

Cressey, Donald R., "The Nature and Effectiveness of Correctional Techniques," Law and Contemporary Problems, 23:754–771, Autumn, 1958.

Gray, F. C., Prison Discipline in America. London: J. Murray, 1848.

Grünhut, Max, Penal Reform. Oxford: Oxford University Press, 1948.

Herre, Ralph S., The History of the Auburn Prison from the Beginnings to About 1867. Unpublished Ed.D. Dissertation, Pennsylvania State University, 1950.

Ives, George, A History of Penal Methods. London: Stanley Paul, 1914.

Klein, P., Prison Methods in New York State. New York: Columbia University Press, 1920.

Lewis, O. F., The Development of American Prisons and Prison Customs, 1776–1845. Albany: Prison Association of New York, 1922.

Mattick, Hans (Editor), The Future of Imprisonment in a Free Society. Chicago: St. Leonard's House, 1965. (Published as Volume 2 of Key Issues: A Journal of Controversial Issues in Criminology, 1965.)

McKelway, Blake, American Prisons. Chicago: University of Chicago Press, 1936.

Robinson, L. N., Penology in the United States. Philadelphia: Winston, 1921.

Rose, Gordon, The Struggle for Penal Reform. London: Stevens and Sons, 1961.

Sellin, Thorsten, "Prison Tendencies in Europe," Journal of Criminal Law and Criminology, 21:485–498, February, 1931.

Sellin, Thorsten, "Philadelphia Prisons of the Eighteenth Century," Transactions of the American Philosophical Society, 43:326–330, Part I, 1953.

Teeters, Negley K., They Were in Prison. Philadelphia: Winston, 1937.

Teeters, Negley K., The Cradle of the Penitentiary: The Walnut Street Jail at Philadelphia, 1773–1835. Philadelphia: Pennsylvania Prison Society, 1955.

Wines, E. C., The State of Prisons and Child-Saving Institutions in the Civilized World. Cambridge: J. Wilson and Sons, 1880.

Wines, E. C., Report on Prisons and Reformatories of the United States and Canada. New York State Assembly Document No. 35, 1867.

Wines, E. C., Punishment and Reformation. New York: Crowell, 1895.

# 23. OBJECTIVES AND CONDITIONS OF
#     IMPRISONMENT

THE HISTORY of imprisonment in the United States reveals a trend toward emphasis on treatment and away from punishment. The view which is now formally expressed by most prison leaders is that the prison should make every possible effort to treat prisoners, within the framework of a system of security. It is observed that practically all prisoners return to free society sooner or later and that the use of punitive methods alone does not produce the desired reformation of these prisoners. Consequently it is emphasized that nonpunitive methods should be used to change the prisoners so that they will desist from crime. At the same time, the prison system is organized in such a way that it impedes the efforts at treatment. As a result, treatment programs often are described in official statements of prison policy although they do not exist in fact. Some of the impediments to treatment are due merely to inefficient prison administration, but most of them are rooted in the attitudes which we have described earlier as the punitive reaction to crime. The prevailing conflict between punitive and treatment policies in prisons is a reflection of the more general conflicting societal reactions to crime. The analysis presented in the next two chapters is intended as an interpretation of prison conditions in terms of these general societal conditions.

OBJECTIVES OF IMPRISONMENT. Contemporary society seems to have a variety of objectives in regard to control of crime, and it considers imprisonment the means for attaining each of them. *First*, as is implied by the relatively recent emphasis on reform, rehabilitation, and treatment of criminals, society wants criminals changed, so that they will commit no more crimes. The prison is expected to "reform" or rehabilitate criminals. *Second*, society wants protection from criminals. The prison isolates criminals from general society so that they cannot commit crimes during certain periods of time. *Third*, society wants retribution. The prison is expected to make life unpleasant for people who, by their crimes, have made others' lives unpleasant. *Fourth*, society wants to reduce crime rates. The prison is expected to reduce crime rates not only by reforming criminals but also by deterring the general public from behavior which is punishable by imprisonment. Since the prison has been assigned the task of working toward each of society's goals, the attainment of the goals may be considered the objective of imprisonment.[1]

Within the prison, the attempt to perform the duties necessary for the accomplishment of the various tasks assigned—*reformation, incapacitation, retribution,* and *deterrence*—results in conflict. Especially, the conditions necessary for the performance of the first task, reformation, may be in conflict with the conditions necessary for exacting retribution and for maximum incapacitation and deterrence. When reformation is assumed to be induced by treatment, rather than by purposive infliction of pain, the conditions which led to inmates' crimes are determined, and the inmates are then introduced to the psychological, social, educational, and technical skills which are considered important to their reformation. Efficient performance of this task depends on prison conditions which are conducive to free inquiry and to intimate, helpful, constructive action based on the inmates' needs. The conditions viewed as conducive to reformation through treatment, thus, almost never include the purposive infliction of suffering. Such punitive action is considered to detract from the intimate, confidential, amoral, relationship necessary to obtaining valid information from inmates, and it also is thought to alienate inmates from personnel when the latter attempt to take positive action for inmate reformation.

On the other hand, retribution and deterrence by purposive infliction of suffering always, obviously, necessitates prison conditions which are punitive, even if the suffering merely results from the severe limitations on personal freedom imposed by incarceration. Moreover, restrictions on freedom-within-walls are deliberately imposed. Some prisons whose administrators stress only perimeter control are often referred to by outsiders and by "old-time" prison administrators as "country clubs," and others—those in which inmates engage in petty rackets and debauchery—are viewed as "too lax" or even "corrupt." As a result, rigid systems of punitive control and discipline supplement the punitive conditions brought about by the mere fact of incarceration.

Incapacitation of criminals need not include purposively inflicted suffer-

[1] See Louis N. Robinson, "Contradictory Purposes in Prisons," *Journal of Criminal Law and Criminology,* 37:449–457, March–April, 1947.

ing, any more than the incapacitation of psychotics by confinement in a hospital need include such suffering. But incapacitation of criminals usually does involve the intentional infliction of suffering, particularly when a system of rigid discipline and control is considered essential to incapacitation. However, it is difficult to determine precisely whether punitive discipline and control are considered part of the routine necessary for gaining the incapacitation objective or, instead, conditions necessary for obtaining the deterrence and retributive objectives. Probably they are regarded as necessary for the attainment of all these objectives.

The administrative problems brought about by the fact that prisons are expected both to treat criminals and punish criminals have been attacked in many ways. In some prisons the problems have been resolved by open abandonment of any serious attempt to treat inmates, on the ground that persons who expect criminals to be reformed by treatment are foolish and misguided. The opposite kind of resolution would be open abandonment of all punitive aspects of incarceration. This solution is frequently advocated by persons who consider punishment unnecessary and inhumane, but it is unrealistic.[2] Another system for resolving the conflict is compromise. Here, the punitive conditions are mitigated in favor of treatment conditions, and treatment conditions are modified in favor of the punitive aspects of imprisonment. This really does not resolve the conflict; it merely makes it less intense. Finally, the problems have been resolved by formally maintaining that the prison both treats and punishes, while informally abandoning almost all conditions conducive to effective treatment. Perhaps this is the most common contemporary system for resolving the conflict. As two experienced prison administrators have said:

> There does seem to be one problem that all institutions face; the conflicted orientation of the public. . . . Confronted with these contradictory pressures, correctional personnel frequently must decide which to translate into practice and which to honor in public statements. They are like repertory actors, who must vary their performance according to the expectations of a moody and unpredictable public. By and large, they have attempted to resolve this problem by satisfying the more fundamental demands of security by means of concrete action and the demands for increased liberality by means of public statements.[3]

These alternative kinds of solution for the administrative problems may be observed in the varied use of "classification" in prisons.

[2] See pp. 516–517 above.
[3] Richard R. Korn and Lloyd W. McCorkle, *Criminology and Penology* (New York: Holt, 1959), p. 470. See also Lloyd E. Ohlin, *Sociology and the Field of Corrections* (New York: Russell Sage Foundation, 1956), pp. 15–16.

CLASSIFICATION. The primary condition against which early American prison reformers enveighed was the association of all types of criminals in a conglomerate group. At first, "classification" consisted of mere segregation, for purposes of discipline and administrative control, of prisoners according to such criteria as age, sex, race, and dangerousness. Formally, this kind of definition and practice has been abandoned. As the treatment reaction became popular, differentiation was to be made on the basis of individual needs and probable reformability of inmates, and specific treatment programs were to be directed toward individuals who, as the basis for differentiation implied, could most benefit from them.[4] In the last thirty or forty years "classification" has come to refer to this whole system of differentiation according to inmates' needs and individualized execution of treatment programs consistent with the needs. The term is now used to designate the entire process by which prisons attempt to attain the objective of reformation through individualized treatment. This process is said to consist of four separate but co-ordinated procedures.[5]

First, the prisoner's case history is taken and his personality studied. This is sometimes performed by a staff of professionally trained workers such as psychologists, social workers, sociologists, and psychiatrists. Each of these workers can make contributions which grow out of the background of knowledge of the discipline represented. The contribution of the sociologist is different from that of the social worker, as is the contribution of the psychologist different from that of the psychiatrist. This diagnostic procedure ideally involves "the use of every available technique, such as social investigations; medical, psychiatric, and psychological examinations; and educational, vocational, religious, and recreational studies."[6]

Second, the information regarding the prisoner is presented to a classification committee. This committee decides upon a program of individualized treatment and training based upon the diagnosis. Sometimes the classification committee is made up of only the professionally trained staff, but ordinarily it also includes the warden or superintendent, the deputy warden or wardens, the superintendent of industry, the educational direc-

---

[4] Paradoxically, treatment programs were introduced before diagnosis. Such programs were at first administered on a "shot gun" basis to all criminals or to all criminals of a certain class, such as an age group. Then as it became obvious, in the 1920's, that effective treatment was not possible without knowledge of the persons being treated, diagnostic facilities were set up. See Frank Loveland, "Classification in the Prison System," in Paul W. Tappan, Editor, Contemporary Correction (New York: McGraw-Hill, 1951), pp. 91–106.

[5] American Prison Association, Committee on Classification and Case Work, Handbook on Classification in Correctional Institutions (New York: Author, 1947), p. 2.

[6] Ibid. See also Robert G. Caldwell, "Classification: Key to Effective Institutional Correction," American Journal of Correction, 20:10–ff., March–April, 1958.

tor, and the chaplain. Generally, the warden is chairman of a committee consisting of representatives of all administrative departments. The committee assigns the inmate to a designated type of custody—usually minimum, medium, or maximum—to a certain kind of cell or living quarters, to a job, to health services, to educational classes, to recreations, and to other activities and services. The inmate usually appears before the committee within sixty days after his arrival from court.

The third step is application of the treatment policies. The classification committee has the responsibility of seeing that its recommendations are carried out. The diagnostic analysis of the inmate and his background is utilized not only as a basis for a decision as to how he *should* be treated but also as a basis for his actual treatment.

Finally, the treatment program is kept current with the inmate's changing needs and with new analyses, based on any information not available at the time of the initial classification committee meeting, of the inmate's case. This procedure is known as "reclassification," and it is carried out by the classification committee. Presumably, it guarantees that there will be no "dead end" placements nor "forgotten men" in the prison.[7] The reclassification procedure continues from the time of the first classification until the inmate is released. Consequently the diagnostic report, generally called an "admission summary," the initial classification report, and the reclassification reports presumably comprise a complete pre-institutional and institutional history of the individual.

The classification system and, consequently, the treatment program can, and does, break down at any point in the process. Obviously the entire process depends to a large extent upon the original diagnosis. Yet it is axiomatic that most prisons have insufficient professional (diagnostic) personnel. In the spring of 1954, only 29 full-time psychiatrists were employed to aid in diagnosing and treating all inmates in state prisons and reformatories for adults. Twelve of these men were located in California, seven in New York. Eighteen states had no psychiatric services at all, and only nine had the services of a full-time psychiatrist. Similarly, in 1957 only 67 full-time psychologists were employed to work with about 162,000 inmates in the United States. Schnur calculated that inmates who in 1957 took more than one hour and twenty minutes of service from the whole classification, training, and treatment staff (including institutional parole officers, chaplains, sociologists, social workers, psychologists, psychiatrists, and teachers) in one month were taking more than their fair share.[8]

---

[7] American Prison Association, op. cit., p. 60.
[8] Alfred C. Schnur, "The New Penology: Fact or Fiction?" *Journal of Criminal Law and Criminology*, 49:331–334, November–December, 1958.

PRINCIPLES OF CRIMINOLOGY

Even when diagnostic personnel are present, diagnoses accurate enough for treatment planning might not be made. Inmates often are available for diagnostic interviews only for about two hours in the morning and two hours in the afternoon, the remainder of the time being given over to routine prison activities such as "count," "yard," "bath," "barber," and meals. Accordingly, much of the case history information must be hurriedly collected in the allotted periods, often with the aid of inmate clerks. The diagnostic interviews themselves sometimes are only five to fifteen minutes in duration, and on the basis of them an appraisal is made of the inmate's home life, community life, etiology of his criminality, and his story of the offense. Also on the basis of these brief contacts the interviewer makes a prognosis as to the probabilities for reformation of the offender, classifies him as to personality type, decides whether the inmate was improvable, unimprovable, or somewhere in between, makes a recommendation for a program of treatment and training, and does many other things.

Even if the diagnoses are accurate, the treatment planning for the inmates might not be based on them. In some institutions the classification committee never meets, or meets only rarely, and the decisions regarding program planning are made by one person. In other institutions the classification committee meets regularly, but bases its decisions not on treatment considerations but on custodial and punitive considerations. That is, rather than reading diagnostic reports for evidence of inmates' individual needs for specific kinds of treatment, these committees read them for evidence of the kinds of precautions which must be taken to insure incapacitation and just punishment.[9] Probably, in the average institution in which classification has developed, the classification committee bases its decisions on considerations of custody, convenience, discipline, and treatment, in that order. Thus, it may be decided that a particular inmate must be handled as a maximum security risk, and if, for example, psychiatric services are not available to maximum-risk prisoners, then that decision will mean that psychiatric help will not be available to the inmate in question, no matter what his treatment needs. Stated in another way, it may be observed that for maximum effect on his rehabilitation a prisoner should work on the prison farm, but if he is not considered a minimum-security risk he cannot be assigned to the farm. When a warden who knows that he will lose his job if escapes occur is the chairman of the classification committee, security against escapes takes precedence over everything else. The warden or the deputy warden in charge of custody can, in effect, veto the recommendation of the professional staff or the

<hr>

[9] See H. G. Moeller, "Changing Trends in Classification," *Proceedings of the American Correctional Association*, 1960, pp. 212–219.

deputy warden in charge of care and treatment. In this way many institutions which appear to both treat and punish prisoners have solved the conflict by informally abandoning the treatment program.

Also, classification committees may operate merely as assignment boards, in which case the requirements of the institution rather than the needs of the prisoners determine the program which is recommended. An inmate who needs vocational training may be assigned to kitchen duties because "someone has to do the maintenance work." In some systems, the official who is responsible for custody brings to the classification committee meetings a list of the institutional jobs which are "open," and inmates are only rarely given an assignment not on that list. Many institutions have established industries which require a certain quota of men for operation, and it sometimes appears that the task of the classification committee is that of keeping the industries going, regardless of whether assignment of an inmate to the industry will aid in his rehabilitation. In the autumn, incoming inmates will be assigned to the cannery because "if we don't get someone in the cannery the tomatoes will spoil." Ordinarily when convenience is the criterion used for assignment a compromise is made in regard to the treatment objective. The inmate may be required to devote mornings to labor which everyone recognizes as having no rehabilitative value, but he is given the option of participating in a rehabilitative program during the afternoons. Or he may be assigned to the cannery in the autumn, to the nursery in the summer, and to a rehabilitative program in the winter. Again, he may be given a full-time assignment as a janitor, with the recommendation that he enroll in educational classes in the evenings.

It is at the third step in the process that classification work has most frequently broken down in the past and still, perhaps to a lesser extent, breaks down today. When the classification committee does not include custodial personnel, such as the warden or his deputy, the recommendations of that committee are likely to be ignored. In such instances the classification committee is merely diagnostic and advisory; it is an addition to the institutional program but not an integral part of it. Sometimes detailed reports on inmates' needs for particular kinds of treatment are never read by the personnel who are expected to administer the appropriate programs. Sometimes the recommendations are impractical because the institution does not have the facilities for carrying out the recommendations; sometimes the recommendations are considered to be impractical by custodial personnel because they conflict with custodial and punitive programs.[10] In such a system the assignment to workshops, to cell blocks or to educational grades and treatment programs is made by a correctional

[10] Cf. R. L. Jenkins, "Treatment in an Institution," *American Journal of Orthopsychiatry*, 11:85–91, January, 1941.

officer whose chief criteria for assignment are, again, custody, convenience, and discipline. Even when both professional and custodial personnel are involved in program planning there is no guarantee that the committee's recommendations will be carried out. Treatment recommendations which are not vetoed in the committee might be in conflict with recommendations based on custody and convenience, in which case the latter recommendations are most likely to be acted upon. Also, prisoners may be removed from treatment programs as a form of punishment, or they may be permitted to enroll in educational or vocational programs as a reward for "good behavior" with reference to the punitive aspects of imprisonment. Similarly, participation in treatment programs may be interpreted by individual guards as a form of malingering.

Even the professional staff may be extremely negligent in carrying out its own recommendations for treatment. It is apparent, for example, that staff members who are so occupied with report writing and meetings that they are unable to perform their diagnostic duties also will be too busy to perform their duties as administrators of the recommended programs. The treatment programs then become meaningless and superficial. Powelson and Bendix report, as an illustration of a somewhat similar point, the case of a prison psychiatrist who openly boasted that he could hold fifty "therapy" interviews during a working day. Similarly, in one institution when inmates are selected for group therapy, the custodial officer in charge will give the order that all violators of a certain section of the penal code, who are between the ages of twenty and forty, and who are non-veterans, are to appear for group therapy at a given hour.[11] In 1954, the psychiatrists in only fifteen states could find time to engage in individual therapy, usually on a very limited basis.[12] Even prison educational and medical programs are often inefficiently administered. The existence of such conditions again illustrates one system for informally abandoning prison programs which are conducive to effective treatment while maintaining in the formal organization of the institution the ideology that the prison should both punish and treat.

The final step in the classification process, reclassification, also is a point at which the entire system frequently breaks down. When periodic reclassification is required, the classification committee sometimes merely examines the inmate's record for evidence of infraction of custodial rules, or simply "rubber stamps" his existing program. When reclassification is not required at periodic intervals the inmate is likely to see the classification

---

[11] Cf. Harvey Powelson and Reinhard Bendix, "Psychiatry in Prison," Psychiatry, 14: 73–86, February, 1951.
[12] United Prison Association of Massachusetts, op. cit., p. 6.

committee only at the time of his initial classification and at the time of his pre-parole consideration. If the inmate has a desire for reclassification he usually can apply to the committee, but his request can be denied on the ground that his work record is poor, or on the ground that he has violated custodial rules, or on the ground that it would not be convenient for the institution if his assignment were changed, as well as on the ground that the desired program, in the opinion of the committee, would be useless to the inmate. Frequently it is difficult to determine just which grounds are used for reclassification, just as it is difficult to determine the grounds for the original classification. Probably the order of precedence is, again, custody, convenience, discipline, and treatment. Application by an inmate for reclassification so that he can participate in a specific treatment program might be interpreted as an attempt to avoid punishment. An inmate with an escape record only very rarely is assigned to a program which would necessitate reclassifying him as a minimum security risk, no matter what his needs in respect to treatment. One prisoner who was working as a saw-filer applied for an assignment in vocational drafting, but this application for reclassification was denied by the committee, at the simple request of a custodial officer, "because saw-filers are hard to find."[13] When such practices are present, reclassification certainly does not guarantee that there will be no "dead end" placements nor "forgotten men" in the prison.

The reception center is the most recent development in the field of classification. The principal difference between classification systems which use reception centers and those which do not is that in the former the inmates are sent to specialized *institutions* on the recommendation of professional workers. All inmates in the state are committed to the reception center and, after a period of about sixty days during which the diagnostic studies are made, the reception center staff assigns them to appropriate institutions where classification committees take over. The general notion on which such reception center systems are based is that the two most important objectives of imprisonment are reformation and incapacitation. Those prisoners who are most likely to reform and who are least dangerous or desperate, no matter what their offenses or sentences, are to be housed in minimum security prisons, where the program is largely one of treatment. The inmates who are less likely to respond to treatment and who are somewhat more dangerous are to be kept in secure institutions, where they are subject to the usual classification procedures. But those inmates who do not respond to treatment and who are most desperate and danger-

---

[13] Powelson and Bendix, *op. cit.*

ous are to be confined, for the protection of society, in a bastille-type prison. The latter would be primarily a custodial institution, organized for incapacitation rather than for retribution or deterrence, and it would only to a slight extent endeavor to provide facilities and staff for treatment.

Illinois established such a reception center system in 1933. From the Diagnostic Depot at Joliet an inmate may be sent to Pontiac, which is for young, improvable offenders; to Stateville, which is for older improvable offenders; to Joliet, which is for unimportant offenders; or to Menard, which receives psychotic prisoners. Michigan's system, established in 1937, is similar, except that all prisoners are committed to the Southern Michigan Prison at Jackson, from which about one-third are transferred to one of three other institutions, where there are local classification committees.[14] Pennsylvania and New Jersey use similar procedures. The reception center program has been developed most fully in New York and in California. In the latter state there are two "guidance centers," one in the northern and one in the southern part of the state, each of which sends prisoners to any of the state's five prisons for adults. In addition to diagnosis, the guidance center staff conducts an admission-orientation program, a counseling program, and a group-therapy program. In general, the treatment program is actually initiated at these institutions.

There is evidence that the reception center system is subject to the same conflicts as is the classification system within a single institution. Offenders who are obviously reformable are likely to be sent to minimum-security prison farms not because they need farming in their plan of treatment but because they are "minimum-risk" inmates. For example, in Pennsylvania a young man for whom printing might constitute effective trade training but who is a good custodial risk must be sent to the minimum-security prison, where he cannot learn printing, rather than to the maximum-security institution, where there is a well-equipped print shop.[15] In Illinois, youthful offenders, no matter what their degree of "improvability," are likely to be sent to Pontiac, and older men usually go to Joliet; consequently the system amounts to little more than could be effected by direct assignment by the courts on the basis of age alone. Reporting on conditions prevailing in 1950 in California, Powelson and Bendix, observed that when an inmate moves from the guidance center to San Quentin, after his classification on the basis of his case record and test results, he was classi-

[14] E. R. Akers, "Classification in the State Prison," *Journal of Criminal Law and Criminology*, 34:16–25, May–June, 1943. See also Herman Venter, *The South African Prison System* (African Information Service, Fact Paper No. 68, 1959), pp. 7–8.
[15] Harry Elmer Barnes and Negley K. Teeters, *New Horizons in Criminology* (New York: Prentice-Hall, 1951), p. 639. See also Donald Clemmer, "A Beginning in Social Education in Correctional Institutions," *Federal Probation*, 13:32–55, March, 1949.

fied in accordance with the custodial officers' estimates of him as a security risk:

> Our impression is that Custody has a separate and independent system of classifying prisoners which has little, if anything, to do with the recommendations made by the Guidance Center. Each prisoner, who has been classified in the Center on the basis of his case record and a battery of tests, is now reclassified in accordance with Custody's estimate of the prisoner as a security risk. The three degrees of security risk—minimum, medium, and maximum—are only remotely related to these earlier findings. They also have little to do with any objective standard which might enable one to distinguish between prisoners of different degrees of security risk. The custodial classification seems to be based rather on the conventional middle-class evaluation of different crimes. Crimes involving violence, sexual or other, are rated as maximum security risks, despite the fact that murders and sex offenders have the best parole records. Similarly, former escapees from reform schools never get less than a medium security classification, presumably on the ground that once an escapee, always an escapee. Yet, the individual case might well warrant less severe treatment.
>
> To classify prisoners as Custody does, involves a theory of criminality for which there is no evidence. The theory holds that those who have committed crimes most severely punished in our society are most likely to repeat them and are, therefore, least likely to benefit from the program of the Care and Treatment Division. The facts point to the opposite conclusion. . . . The seriousness of a person's crime or the length of his sentence is not a measure of his chances of rehabilitation. This chance can only be judged on the basis of careful examination of the individual case. The custodial classification, in terms of security risk, is therefore unrelated to the program of correction.[16]

It is clear that under the present system of organization the treatment objective of imprisonment cannot be attained without some degree of conflict with the efforts to achieve the incapacitation, deterrence, and retribution objectives. Classification, which has become synonymous with individualized treatment, requires extensive compromise with "custody," sometimes to a degree which makes classification ineffectual. The nature and extent of the compromise in specific institutions depends upon the attitudes of the personnel involved and, indirectly, on the attitudes toward crime of the social group which employs the personnel, ascribes their duties, and provides them with equipment. Public response limits prison officials' attempts to establishment treatment programs and the success of attempted programs. The existence of an effective treatment program is

---

[16] Powelson and Bendix, *op. cit.*, pp. 76–77. Reprinted by permission of the publisher.

not easily discernible to casual prison visitors and is far more difficult for an administrator to demonstrate than is the readily observable fact of a clean, well-maintained and well-ordered physical plant, equipment, and prison routine. The administrator, then, emphasizes that which is observable and, consequently, rewarding. Also, from the standpoint of prison administrators, one escape or riot could cancel the opportunity to do any treatment work with inmates, since successful treatment is not newsworthy while an escape or riot dramatically focuses public attention on the prison. Consequently, treatment programs must be cautiously attempted only within the framework of custody. Generally, when a society sends to an institution only persons whose behavior is punishable by law, it is to be expected that those persons will be punished while in the institution, even if such punishment interferes with treatment programs.

DISCIPLINE AND CONTROL.[17]   Prison discipline means, conventionally, the regulation or attempt at regulation of the details of prisoners' lives by means of punishment for infraction of rules. In any prison, some minimum of "organization" is necessary in order to provide a division of labor for the staff and for inmates, a schedule of work and meals, a satisfactory relationship with the outside community, and similar arrangements. Employee and inmate work schedules ordinarily must be closely co-ordinated, meals for inmates must be served and eaten at scheduled times, baths and haircuts must be taken at an assigned period rather than at will, and almost all activities involving choice must be rationed. Although different physical plants and budgets alter the degree of precision needed, the perceived necessity for dominating inmates makes essential a degree of scheduling and co-ordinating which is higher than the degree ordinarily experienced in democratic societies.

Nevertheless, probably no topic of conversation is as popular, general, or unsettled among prison workers as discussion of the degree and kind of "organization" which is best for institutional operation and for rehabilitation of inmates. Almost all relations between staff members, between staff and inmates, and even between inmates are colored by the positions which are taken, in conversation and in action, on this subject. These positions are based on a variety of conceptions of the "proper" relationships between security measures and rehabilitation measures. There are many ramifications, however, for such conceptions when generalized are notions about the proper balance between responsibility to the group (organization) on

[17] Parts of this section are adapted from Donald R. Cressey, "Rehabilitation Theory and Reality, II, Organization and Freedom," *California Youth Authority Quarterly*, 10: 40–47, Summer, 1957.

the one hand, and individual freedom on the other. Among prison workers, variation in this respect appears in reference to many aspects of the total program. For example, there are wide differences in evaluations of various "creative activities," such as art, music, hobbycraft, and even school work. One opinion is that such behavior is psychologically therapeutic—it enables the inmate to express himself (minimal restriction) or it enables him to escape momentarily from the formal organization of prison life. From another viewpoint, however, such activities are considered frivolous "wasting time," as a means of escaping work tasks that need to be accomplished, or as opportunities for inmates to "blow off steam" so that they will more readily accept the organization in which they live.

More significantly, contradictory notions about the proper degree of organization are illustrated by alternative positions taken in reference to inmate discipline. Everyone connected with prisons, including inmates, agrees that there must be "discipline" among the inmates and among staff members. There are wide variations, however, in the meanings of the term and, thus, in the opinions about the degree to which "organization" is vital to institutional functioning and to rehabilitation.

The American Prison Association's official statement on discipline is couched in language which identifies, but by no means solves, the problem. "Prison discipline," the committee says, is concerned with "the reasonable regulation of everyday institutional life so that the institution will be an orderly, self-respecting community." The aim of discipline, so far as the individual inmate is concerned, is "self-reliance, self-control, self-respect, self-discipline: not merely the ability to conform to institutional rules and regulations, but the ability and *desire* to conform to accepted standards for individual and community life in free society."[18]

The principal difficulty here is with the word "reasonable." Three basic questions arise: (1) Shall the regulation be reasonable only in the way that the requirement that guards be to work on time and work an eight-hour day is reasonable? (2) Or shall it reasonably attempt to control almost all the details of the prisoner's life by means of punishment for rule infractions? (3) Can "self-reliance," "self-control," and "the desire to conform to accepted standards," actually be induced by either reasonable regulation of the kinds implied in the first two questions, or can it be induced only by non-punitive "treatment"? These are questions on which prison personnel are in disagreement and which many prison workers have not satisfactorily resolved even for themselves.

But prison personnel are not alone in their dilemma about prison "or-

[18] American Prison Association, Committee on the Model State Plan, *Model of Suggested Standards for a State Correctional System* (New York: Author, 1946), p. 61.

ganization" or the desirable degree of restrictive "discipline." In their attempts to arrive at a solution regarding the degree to which inmate actions should be regulated (and, therefore, the degree to which regulation is valuable), prison personnel are participating in an unsettled theoretical controversy about the relationship between personality and the "organization" of social relationships. As Stanton and Schwartz have pointed out, there are social scientists at one extreme who think of the "organization" of social interaction and "personality" as two facets of the same thing.[19] The person is viewed as a product of the kinds of social relationships and values in which he participates; he obtains his satisfactions and, in fact, his essence from participation in the rituals, schedules, customs, rules, and regulations of various sorts which surround him. Moreover, the person (personality) is not separable from the social relationships in which he lives. He behaves according to the rules (which sometimes are contradictory) of the large organization (society) in which he participates; he cannot behave any other way. On the other hand, social scientists at the opposite pole think of the individual as essentially autonomous, and they view his relationships with the rules and regulations of society and other organizations as *submission* rather than participation. "Personality" is an outgrowth of the effect that the "restrictions" necessary to organization have on an individual's expression of his own pristine needs. These social scientists emphasize "individual self-determination" and attempt to make a distinction between the "real" or "natural" part of the person and the "spurious," "artificial," or "consensual" part. The former is viewed as primary, free, and spontaneous; the latter (obtained from the social relationships making up society) is formal, secondary, and restrictive. In discussing prison organization, these men are likely to emphasize rigidity, cruelty, unresponsiveness, and sadism, without recognizing the usefulness of the organization to the broader society or to the inmates.

Certainly the two theories of the relationship between personality and culture are more complex than this simple statement implies, and probably no social scientist maintains one or the other of them explicitly and with no qualifications. But these ideas, in form even more garbled and unqualified than they have been stated here, have made their way into the policies of prisons. They have come into the prison precisely because members of our society subscribe to both of them. The prison is assigned punitive functions because of concern for the criminal's disruption of the ongoing organization which is society. But at the same time the prison

[19] Alfred H. Stanton and Morris S. Schwartz, *The Mental Hospital* (New York: Basic Books, 1954), pp. 37–38.

is asked to reform criminals by means which are consistent with the theory that the prison's rules and regulations are harsh, restrictive, and punitive. While groups external to the prison demand that it perform treatment functions, other groups, or perhaps the same group at a different time, demand that the institution be restrictive and, hence, punitive.

When a prisoner breaks the rules of some prisons, punishment follows as a matter of course. Reports of infractions ordinarily are given to a senior custodial officer or to a subcommittee of the classification committee. A hearing is held and the inmate is allowed to state his case and, if the offense is a serious one, to call witnesses. The guard reporting the infraction also makes a statement to the disciplinary officer or committee. If the inmate is found guilty he is punished. In the earlier days, punishment practically always meant some form of bodily suffering. At present punishment more frequently consists of loss of privileges, such as moving pictures, athletic contests, radio earphones, visiting and correspondence, and educational classes. Also, the "good-time" which has been credited to the inmate for early release frequently is revoked, and solitary confinement is used in serious cases. But such practices as confinement in cramped sweat boxes, exposure to extreme heat or cold, standing on a line or in a circle for hours, spraying with a firehose, and stringing up by the wrists are occasionally used, even today.

This system for administration of discipline corresponds roughly to the general system of policing, arresting, trying, convicting, and punishing criminals. There are two great differences between the contemporary legal system and current prison disciplinary systems. *First,* in prison the inmate is expected to obey not only all laws, but a host of additional rules. Many of these rules and regulations stem from the mere fact that a large number of people must live together within rather narrow quarters, but others are designed to aid the prison attain its punitive objectives. Some rules are very general in nature, such as: "Inmates are expected at all times and in all parts of the institution to conduct themselves in an orderly manner and to respect the rights of others."[20] Much behavior which is routine and customary in free society—such as cutting across a lawn, running if one is late for work, leaving unwanted food on a plate, horseplay, personal untidiness, evading work, and oversleeping—is a violation of prison rules. *Second,* the reaction to a violation of a prison rule is almost never one of treatment, while in the contemporary legal system there are at least formal provisions for treatment in some cases. An inmate who is found guilty by the "court," which is the name inmates usually give to the disciplinary

[20] A rule recommended by the American Prison Association, Committee on the Model State Plan, *op. cit.*, p. 63.

board or officer, is almost always punished, even if the punishment is a mere reprimand. One who has committed a serious infraction of the rules is sent to the "hole," which is the name inmates give to above-ground solitary confinement quarters, although such confinement obviously interferes with treatment activities.

Four principal attitudes or conditions enter into maintenance of the punitive system of discipline: the ideal of reformation by denial of choice, the attitude of dominance, the attitude of retaliation, and the danger of escapes:

(a) The earlier psychology of reformation was based on the assumption that a habit formed by compulsion would be retained after the compulsion was removed. It was felt that since the prisoner had failed to make the proper choices before his entrance into the prison he should be given no opportunity to make choices afterward, but that all of his acts should be imposed upon him from without. Brockway stated this ideal as follows:

In order to train criminals for social life they must have a strict régime and learn quick and accurate self-adjustment to a uniform requirement, habituation to the yoke of established custom. Exactness of observance is of the greatest importance . . . so that the newly formed habit of precision calls up the instinctive impulse to social orderliness quite independent of conscious volition.[21]

It is now generally believed that this theory is incorrect, and policies based on it have already changed to a great extent. However, contemporary conditions of imprisonment are such that lack of rather uniform conformity to rules by inmates may have adverse effects on any prospect for rehabilitation. Compulsion, thus, might be more conducive to rehabilitation than poor discipline which gives inmates an opportunity to exploit other inmates and also to "beat" the system which society has designed to punish them. An inmate who, while in prison, learns that he can use brute strength, lying, cheating, and stealing to get what he wants from other inmates certainly would not be on the road to rehabilitation. Similarly, poor disciplinary control which permits inmates to use fraud and other crimes to obtain goods, services and privileges which the prison and society deny them cannot be conducive to the rehabilitation of men who have been sentenced to prison precisely because they obtained such things in an illegal manner while on the outside. Even if we abandon the idea that habits are formed by compulsion, we need not abandon the notion that criminality should be made unattractive to prisoners. Korn and McCorkle

21 Z. R. Brockway, *Fifty Years of Prison Service* (New York: Charities Publication Committee, 1912), p. 355.

have presented the following statement, which is quite consistent with the theory of differential association:

Whatever the personality disturbances or problems of repeated offenders, it may be agreed that their social adjustment is most often characterized by exploitation of and devious dealings with other people. It therefore becomes the goal of treatment to assist them in abandoning these ways of dealing with people—ways that bring them into the prison. This process of abandoning old ways and learning new ones involves repeated demonstrations of the failure of old ways, and it is indispensible that the treatment situation be one in which these ways are made to fail. In other words, the treatment situation must be one in which the devious are frustrated and exposed and the exploiters defeated in their attempts to exploit.[22]

(b) The crime rate in prison is likely to be high unless inmate activities are carefully policed. Just as saturation of a high-delinquency area in a city with policemen is considered by many persons to be a desirable way to prevent crime, so careful scrutiny and regulation of inmate actions is viewed as a necessary and desirable system for preventing prisoners from attacking each other and stealing from each other. In a general sense, prison officials are hired to dominate convicted criminals. It is not surprising, therefore, that some guards attempt to dominate inmates in a specific sense. A man who is responsible for keeping inmates inside the walls cannot be expected to have the same attitudes toward inmates as a psychologist who has the duty of providing the nonjudgmental, relaxed atmosphere necessary for psychotherapy and counselling. To be effective, personnel who are hired to guard must view inmates as dangerous, scheming, conniving men who are in need of close surveillance and domination. They cannot only watch and wait, in the way traffic policemen sometimes hide behind billboards waiting for violations, for this would grant inmates an opportunity to gamble the advantages of nonconformity against the disadvantages of possible detection and punishment. They must minimize *potential* violations, and one way to do this is to maximize the domination of individual inmates. This means that they must show their authority, and the making and enforcing of rules and the infliction of punishment are methods of showing this authority.[23] The officer also may express this attitude in subtle ways, such as by saying, "Keep your hands at your sides," to prisoners who are not doing so as they walk by, and then saying "That's right,

22 Korn and McCorkle, *op. cit.*, p. 475. See also the discussion below, p. 584–585.
23 F. Tannenbaum, *Wall Shadows* (New York: G. Putnam's Sons, 1922), pp. 19, 25–29.

keep your hands at your sides," to inmates who have not even thought of having their hands anywhere else. Inmates are believed to have come into the prison because they could not or would not respect the rights of others in free society, and domination of their activities is considered corrective of these deficiencies in social relationships.

(c) Prison officers often have an attitude of retaliation toward the prisoners. Restriction of freedom within walls, like the general restriction of freedom stemming from "mere incarceration," is imposed merely because it is painful to the recipient. The pain may or may not be viewed as having a reformative effect; it is desired as retribution and as a deterrent. Individual officers reporting an infraction of the rules often are disappointed or angry if the offender is not punished. This attitude tends to perpetuate the system of punitive discipline, even when there is a "court" which hears cases of alleged infractions. Something like the following takes place. First, the persons on the disciplinary board ordinarily are the superior prison officials, and, consequently, some guards are eager to report infractions since they feel that such reports indicate that they are alert and capable. Next, since offenders "should get what's coming to them," non-punishment of an offender is apt to be interpreted by the reporting guard as a reprimand for overzealousness in reporting offenses, even if that is not the motive of the "court." Finally, the "court" is apt, then, to use punitive rather than non-punitive methods in handling infractions because it feels that employee morale will suffer if there is no punishment.

However, it is not true that officers are free to report all violations to the disciplinary court. On the contrary, inmates know that they can "fire" a guard from a specific post by forcing him to write numerous conduct reports. Court officials who observe that a large number of reports are written on a group of inmates when one guard is on duty, and that a small number is written on the same group when a second guard is on duty, are likely to conclude that the first guard is an agitator who cannot get along with the men. If they fall into the inmates' trap, the guard may be transferred to a wall tower or some other post where contact with inmates is minimal. Even in circumstances in which an officer appears to be overenthusiastic and "ticket happy," however, the court must punish the inmates reported. Failure to do so in a consistent manner would be to turn administration of the prison over to the inmates.[24] This, in a sense, is also what occurs when inmates are permitted to "fire" officers.

(d) The great danger in prisons, which is perhaps the principal source of rigid discipline, is escapes. Security against escape takes precedence over

[24] See Gresham M. Sykes, "The Corruption of Authority and Rehabilitation," *Social Forces*, 34:257–262, March, 1956.

537 : *Objectives and Conditions of Imprisonment*

everything else, and all policies are limited by considerations of the danger of escape. Emphasis on prevention of escapes results from the attempt to attain the objective of incapacitation, but it also results from the attempt to obtain the retaliatory and deterrence objectives. While some prisoners have become so adapted to institutional life that they do not wish to escape, in the appropriate circumstances a large number would even attempt to escape from a prison which is as delightful as some of the newspapers picture the actual prisons. Permitting prisoners to determine their own schedules, rules, and routines is, then, likely to be dangerous, for it allows inmates to join forces. The fundamental reason for opposition to confinement is the fact of confinement, and the most delightful entertainments, recreations, and food will not make such a place desirable to most inmates. Even if the methods used in an institution are primarily those of individualized treatment, many prisoners will attempt to escape, since not all inmates are convinced that they need whatever services the institution has to offer. At the California Institution for Men, a "model" minimum-security institution which is part of the state's reception-center system, about 3 percent of the nine thousand inmates received between 1941 and 1952 escaped.[25] At one private institution, 35 percent of the delinquent boys confined in 1951–1953 ran away; 13 percent of the 489 boys confined in 1953 ran away more than once.[26]

While it would be absurd to contend that the antagonism between prison officials and inmates cannot possibly be eliminated, it appears to be inherent in the prison system in a way that unsanitary conditions or poor food are not. This does not, however, make it impossible to eliminate brutal disciplinary practices which mitigate the effects of treatment programs. But as long as prisons are considered the means for attaining punitive as well as treatment objectives some aspects of the system of rigid discipline must remain.

ADMINISTRATIVE AND CUSTODIAL PERSONNEL. Efficient administration of prisons has been generally lacking. When personnel are selected on the basis of political patronage, it is very difficult to secure efficiency, even in routine matters. A warden who is a political appointee appoints guards and administrative personnel who have shown some evidence of loyalty to the political party he represents. Often the county or state committee of the political party in office submits a list of loyal party workers from which the warden must make his appointments. When the party in power

[25] Kenyon J. Scudder, *Prisoners are People* (New York: Doubleday, 1952), p. 214.
[26] William C. Kvaraceus, *The Community and the Delinquent* (Yonkers: World Book, 1954), pp. 506–509.

changes, the warden changes or, at least, there is a general shake-up of the prison personnel. Over a period of fifty years, the average tenure of 612 wardens was 5.2 years. Only 13 percent held their jobs for ten years or more, and 22 percent were in office one year or less.[27] Although about forty percent of the states provide for civil service appointments, twenty years ago only about one-fourth of all guards in American prisons were carefully selected.[28] Civil service examinations do not necessarily assure appointments on the basis of efficiency, since civil service examinations and requirements may be circumvented by making "temporary" appointments. Also, examinations for a high position, such as warden or deputy warden, may be "rigged," so that a particular person will almost certainly make the best score and, thus, become qualified for the position. Even when examinations are fairly administered they may do little more than eliminate the obviously unfit rather than assure the appointments of the most capable men. One study in a maximum-security prison indicated that the best guards, as judged by rating scales, tended to score only average or below average on the civil service examination. Conversely, many of the guards who were rated as "poor" had received high scores on the examination.[29]

Unqualified men obviously cannot, by reason of sheer indifference or ignorance, perform the duties necessary for prevention of waste and for efficient, businesslike operation of the institution. Moreover, filling institutional positions on the basis of political patronage often means that the personnel will be corrupt as well as inefficient.

Appointment of unqualified personnel often means, also, that the prison cannot attain its reformation objective. It is becoming increasingly apparent that the success of treatment programs depends to a large extent upon the attitudes of the subordinate staff toward prisoner participation in such programs. Guards probably have more opportunities for changing inmates' attitudes than any other class of prison workers, yet they are seldom equipped for this exceedingly difficult task.[30] Many released prisoners report that even under the present system the influence of a guard was the most important factor in their reformation. Studies of inmates

[27] Walter A. Lunden, "Then Tenure and Turnover of State Prison Wardens," American Journal of Correction, 19:14-15, ff., December, 1957.

[28] D. E. Lundberg, "Methods of Selecting Prison Personnel," Journal of Criminal Law and Criminology, 38:14-39, May–June, 1947.

[29] Korn and McCorkle, op. cit., p. 503.

[30] Donald R. Cressey, "Social Psychological Foundations for Using Criminals in the Rehabilitation of Criminals," Journal of Research in Crime and Delinquency, 2:49-59, July 1965; See also Charles W. Slack, "Experimenter-Subject Psychotherapy: A New Method of Introducing Intensive Office Treatment for Unreachable Cases," Mental Hygiene, 44:238-256, April, 1960.

who were leaving the Federal Reformatory at Chillicothe and the Ohio Penitentiary indicated that guards and industrial workers had more impact on the inmates than did the professional treatment specialists.[31] However, 77 percent of the inmates engaged in a special counselling program chose their counsellors as the person who helped them most; 4 percent chose correctional officers. Twenty-one percent of a control group chose correctional officers and 45 percent chose vocational instructors or job supervisors.[32] A prison worker has reported:

When we talk with alumni from the correctional institutions which boast the finest diagnostic and treatment facilities, we find that the persons who exerted the greatest influence on the thinking of these boys were not from professional groups. The man who fired the boiler, the institutional baker, or a certain officer influenced the thinking of many more boys than did the sociologist or psychologist.[33]

It is probable, however, that the number of inmates unfavorably influenced by guards is at least as high as the number favorably influenced.

Generally speaking, the status of custodial officers is undergoing a change. In many states, they are called "correctional officers," rather than "guards," in keeping with their new responsibilities. In some institutions, programs for technical training of guards are being developed. Some authorities believe that such programs are likely to result in a closer integration of the punitive and treatment activities.[34] It takes some time for treatment workers and custodial workers to come to an understanding of each other and to develop co-ordinated programs through systems of compromise.[35] Pre-service and in-service training for guards, no doubt could accomplish a great deal in this respect. But the current in-service

---

[31] These unpublished studies were conducted under the direction of Walter C. Reckless and are summarized by Korn and McCorkle, op. cit., p. 495.

[32] Alvin Rudoff, *The PICO Project, A Measure of Casework in Corrections*, Second Technical Report (Sacramento: Department of Corrections, 1959), pp. 16–17.

[33] Vernon Fox, "The Michigan Counseling Program," *Prison World*, 12:6–9, January–February, 1950. Reprinted by permission of the publisher.

[34] Thorsten Sellin, "Historical Glimpses of Training for Prison Service," *Journal of Criminal Law and Criminology*, 25:594–600, November–December, 1934; Joseph Roucek, "Sociology of the Prison Guard," *Sociology and Social Research*, 20:145–151, November, 1935; Joseph Roucek, "Social Attitudes of the Prison Warden," *Sociology and Social Research*, 21:170–174, November, 1936; and Joseph J. Motivans, "Occupational Socialization and Personality: A Study of the Prison Guard," *Proceedings of the American Correctional Association*, 1963, pp. 186–196.

[35] See George H. Weber, "Conflicts Between Professional and Non-Professional Personnel in Institutional Delinquency Treatment," *Journal of Criminal Law and Criminology*, 48:26–43, June, 1957. See also George H. Weber, "Emotional and Defensive Reactions of Cottage Parents," in Donald R. Cressey (ed.), *The Prison; Studies in Institutional Organization and Change* (New York: Holt, Rinehart and Winston, Inc., 1961), pp. 189–228.

training programs for guards do not ordinarily accomplish the purpose of promoting an appreciation of the attempts to treat inmates, although they do orient the guards to particular jobs.[36]

It must be emphasized, however, that even if institutions secure well-trained personnel, the overload of work and the social structure of the institution generally restrict attempts to develop adequate treatment programs. Occasionally, as in Massachusetts, New Jersey, New York, California, Wisconsin, and the federal prison system, capable leaders have been able to secure appointments on the basis of efficiency and ability, but institutions in these states have not been shown to be outstanding successes as rehabilitation agencies.

Prisons differ significantly from other organizations because their personnel hierarchies are organized down to the lowest level for the administration of the daily activities of men.[37] In a factory, for example, there are hierarchies of management personnel and of the workers. By way of contrast, the guard, who is the lowest-level worker in a prison, is both a worker and a manager. He is managed in a system of regulations and controls from above, but he also manages, in a corresponding system of regulations, the inmates who are in his charge. He is a low-status worker in interaction with administrators, but a higher-status foreman or officer in interaction with inmates. He has no exact counterpart in the business and industrial world. The closest analogy is the overseer of a crew of slaves who are viewed as being "outside" the organization designed to utilize their labor. Even here, however, the analogy is fallacious except as it refers to the guards who serve as foremen of inmate industrial or maintenance crews. Most guards do not "use" inmates productively any more than they, in their roles as guards, are used productively by prison wardens. They manage and are managed in an organization where management is an end, not a means. This fact makes the guard's job an extraordinarily difficult one. Unlike popular stereotypes which picture the guard as either a brutal sadist with a club or as a robot standing on a wall with a rifle, guards are managers of men. They are responsible for keeping convicted criminals quiet and secure and for supervising groups of men who have no loyalty to the prison. Yet they do not have the help of ordinary "incentives" such as wages, promotions, threat of discharge, or even force.

The emphasis upon humanitarianism and treatment in modern prisons has effectively deprived guards of many means of control. At a minimum,

---

[36] Walter C. Reckless, "Training of the Correctional Worker," in Paul W. Tappan, Editor, Contemporary Correction (New York: McGraw-Hill, 1951), pp. 35–50.

[37] See Donald R. Cressey, "Contradictory Directives in Complex Organizations: The Case of the Prison," Administrative Science Quarterly, 4:1–19, June, 1959. See also Donald R. Cressey, "Prison Organizations," in James G. March (ed.) Handbook of Organizations (Chicago: Rand McNally & Company, 1965), pp. 1023–1070.

custodial practices must be "humane." Thus, inmates cannot be kept docile by severe punishments or severe deprivations; neither can a large number be kept in solitary confinement. Guards control prisoners who must be handled humanely and permitted to work together and in other ways consort with each other. Guards maintain discipline, but they must do this by means which do not arouse antagonism, hostility, and uncooperativeness in inmate populations. When treatment is stressed, the guards' job is even more difficult. They must preserve some measure of order and discipline, since this is essential to the prison's custodial goal, but they also must contribute to accomplishment of the treatment goal. Generally speaking, it is believed that for effective treatment guards must relax in custodial and disciplinary matters, to take the personality needs of each inmate into account, and to individualize the handling of inmates accordingly. These practices are viewed either as constituting treatment itself or as a means of assisting (or at least not hindering) the treatment practices of professional personnel such as social workers and psychologists.

The introduction of humanitarianism and treatment in prisons has, therefore, had as one of its effects the introduction of conflicting directives for guards. They are expected to enforce rules and maintain discipline, but at the same time they are to minimize friction among inmates and between inmates and staff. They are to contribute to inmate rehabilitation by relaxing, being nondirective, and showing concern for inmate personality problems, but they also are expected to maintain order, keep inmates busy at maintenance, housekeeping, and production tasks, administer justice, and see that escapes do not occur. These conflicting directives make it almost impossible for the guard to do anything which will be judged to be correct by his superiors. If guards attempt to get strict conformity to institutional rules, they risk being accused of antagonizing inmates. Rules must be enforced, but the enforcement must not be so rigid and arbitrary that the inmates are stimulated to riot or rebel. If they attempt to use common sense and "discretion" in attempting to get conformity to rules, then they risk being accused of not being alert to potential danger or even of corruption. If they enforce discipline and insist on inmate orderliness, they risk undesirable diagnosis as "rigid," "punitive," or "neurotic," for such enforcement theoretically interferes with individualized treatment. But if they relax to a degree that institutional security and organization seems to be threatened, then they risk undesirable diagnosis as lazy or unmotivated.

**THE SUCCESS AND FAILURE OF IMPRISONMENT.** As a means of incapacitation, imprisonment has a relatively high degree of efficiency. Very few crimes against society are committed by prisoners during the period of incarceration. Though cases have been reported of prisoners coining and issuing counterfeit money and of practicing confidence games, these are so few that they are negligible. The crimes of prisoners are committed principally against prison guards and other officers, against prison property, and against other prisoners. Such crimes within prison communities are very frequent. Prison property is seldom safe from theft. Prisoners frequently commit crimes against each other in the form of theft, assault, and murder. Perverted sex practices and the use of narcotic drugs flourish in many prisons and exist to some extent in most prisons. Intramural crimes, as well as extramural crimes, vary in frequency in different prisons and are affected by the prison policies. Probably the strict isolation of the original Pennsylvania system was more effective than any other prison policy in incapacitating prisoners. This does not justify a conclusion that the Pennsylvania system is in general most efficient, for other values must be considered.

The success of the prison in deterring the general public from crime is probably much less than its success in incapacitating criminals. It certainly has some deterrent effect, but it is difficult to compare the deterrent effects of different prison policies or to isolate the effect of any prison policy from the effect of the whole process of arrest and conviction. Perhaps the deterrent effect of imprisonment increases slightly with the horrors of prison life, though this is likely to be off-set by the difficulty of securing convictions if the public feels that the horrors of imprisonment are greater than the horrors of the crimes. Perhaps the fact of incarceration, regardless of conditions within prisons, is the most important factor in deterrence. In New Jersey it has been found that the parole violation rate among reformatory inmates is lower when the average length of stay is under two years than when the average length of stay is from 32 to 35 months.[38]

The success of imprisonment as a means of reformation is very slight, although this, also, is difficult to determine accurately. It actually is not known whether recidivism is decreased by prisons in which individualized treatment methods have developed. The statistics on this point are inadequate, but they indicate that the methods thus far developed have not been attended by very significant changes in recidivism. In 1964, 56.4 percent of the persons committed to federal prisons and reformatories had previous records of commitments to penal or reformatory institutions, and this record is certainly incomplete.[39] In California during 1963, 34 percent of the male felons newly received from court had previously been impris-

[38] Sol Rubin, "Recidivism and Recidivism Statistics," National Probation and Parole Association Journal, 4:233–240, July, 1958.

[39] U.S. Department of Justice, Federal Bureau of Prisons, Statistical Tables, Fiscal Year 1964 (Washington, Bureau of Prisons, 1964), p. 44.

oned, but of the men imprisoned as of December 31st, 1963, 48 percent had served a previous prison term.[40] Of the boys discharged from English reformatories in 1938–1944, about half were reconvicted at least once within five years.[41] Glueck found that 63.7 percent of 510 young men released consecutively from the Massachusetts State Reformatory committed serious offenses either during the parole period or a five-year post-parole period, that an additional 20.8 percent committed minor offenses either in the parole or post-parole period, and that only 15.5 percent had no record of serious or minor offenses subsequent to release.[42] This perhaps exaggerates somewhat the number of serious crimes as ordinarily understood, especially because among the serious post-parole crimes are included "escape or rescue, fugitive from justice, desertion or dishonorable discharge from the army and navy, and serious automobile offenses" and these constitute 23 percent of the serious post-parole crimes. Larceny, burglary, and robbery constitute 80 percent of the offenses for which offenders were committed to the reformatory and only 60 percent of the serious post-parole offenses. Another study also indicates that the crimes ordinarily considered "serious" are decreased by imprisonment and parole. Of 3,424 Pennsylvania parolees who violated parole by committing new crimes in 1946–1956, 2,265 had originally committed robbery, rape, burglary, or homicide; but these crimes were repeated by only 1,626 of the parolees, a decrease of 28.2 percent. Of the 1,626 offenses, 45 percent were committed by men originally convicted of some other crime.[43] Of 311 men released from a Massachusetts reformatory, 56 percent returned to prison —half for new offenses and half for technical parole violations.[44] In the most comprehensive study that has been made on recidivism, Glaser in 1960 studied a sample of 1,015 men drawn by taking every tenth case from a list of adult males released from federal prisons in 1956. He found that thirty-five percent of these men could be classed as "failures," a category which included persons returned to prison for a new offense or as a parole violator, and persons given non-prison sentences for felony-like offenses. The "successes" included 52 percent who had no further criminal record whatsoever and 13 percent who had been convicted for mis-

[40] California Department of Corrections, *California Prisoners, 1961, 1962, 1963* (Sacramento, Department of Corrections, 1964), p. 31 and p. 91.

[41] A. G. Rose, *Five Hundred Borstal Boys* (Oxford: Blackwell, 1954), p. 21.

[42] Sheldon and Eleanor T. Glueck, *Five Hundred Criminal Careers* (New York: Knopf, 1930), pp. 167–169, 182–192.

[43] William L. Jacks, "Why are Parolees Returned to Prison as Parole Violators?" *American Journal of Correction,* 19:22–24, December, 1957.

[44] Ralph Metzner and Gunther Weil, "Predicting Recidivism: Base-Rates for Massachusetts Correctional Institution at Concord," *Journal of Criminal Law, Criminology and Police Science,* 54:307–16, September, 1963.

demeanors or arrested (but not convicted) on felony charges.[45] Table XVII shows the percentage of failures in various offense, age, and confinement categories.[46] The high failure rates should not be regarded as the responsibility of the last institution which dealt with these offenders. No institution, receiving the failures of the rest of society, should be expected to reform a very large proportion of them. Also, the reformatory cannot properly be given the credit for those who do reform after imprisonment.[47] There is a tendency to believe prison is a success if it does not make offenders worse.

Persistence in crime and desistence from crime are affected by other conditions than the institutional policies. In 1933, 300 boys from Chicago who had been in confinement in the Illinois School for Boys during 1925–1930 were located as follow: 187 in prisons and reformatories, eight shot and killed, two electrocuted for murder, one died with a criminal record, 18 on probation, one a fugitive from justice, 12 in hospitals for the mentally defective, four in the army, 18 good citizens with no subsequent criminality, and 47 whereabouts unknown; only 6 percent were known to have a good record after confinement in the institution. On the other hand, of the boys confined in the same institution who came from rural counties about half were reported to be successful subsequently. A more recent follow-up study of persons committed to the state institutions from one Illinois county revealed a larger proportion of "successes." Of 69 boys sent to St. Charles, three were still at the school and two were in the armed forces overseas. Of the remainder, 38 showed no misbehavior, twelve were serious crime problems or vagrancy repeaters, thirteen had been arrested for traffic or minor alcohol offenses, and one was adjudged feeble-minded. Of 38 girls committed, one had died and six were adjudged feeble-minded. Of the remaining 31, only three were failures.[48] Gottfredson has shown that when certain noninstitutional factors known to be associated with parole success are held constant, differences in the recidivism rates of men released from different prisons tend to disappear. In other words, the eight California prisons studied—ranging from maximum- to minimum-security, and with different programs—performed equally well with respect to the success criterion used, considering the kinds of risks assigned to them.[49]

[45] Daniel Glaser, The Effectiveness of a Prison and Parole System (Indianapolis: Bobbs-Merrill, 1964), pp. 19–20.

[46] Ibid., p. 474.

[47] See Donald R. Cressey, "The Nature and Effectiveness of Correctional Techniques," Law and Contemporary Problems, 23:754–771, Autumn, 1958.

[48] Robert E. Coulson, "Evaluation of Experience in Correctional Institutions," Proceedings of the American Prison Association, 1948, pp. 38–46.

[49] Don M. Gottfredson, "The Role of Base Expectancies in the Study of Treatments," unpublished paper read at the meetings of the Western Psychological Association, April, 1959.

## TABLE XVII

PERCENT OF POSTRELEASE FAILURES[a] AMONG 1956 FEDERAL RELEASES
OF VARIOUS AGES, BY PRIOR INVOLVEMENTS IN CRIME

| | Age at Release from Prison | | | | |
| | 18–21 | 22–25 | 26–35 | 36 & Over | All Cases |
|---|---|---|---|---|---|
| **No. of prior sentences for felony-like offenses:** | | | | | |
| None | 44% (78)[b] | 31% (98) | 21% (151) | 11% (96) | 25% (423) |
| One | 52% (31) | 46% (37) | 34% (105) | 25% (48) | 37% (221) |
| Two | 57% (23) | 52% (27) | 45% (64) | 28% (40) | 44% (154) |
| Three or more | 45% (11) | 63% (16) | 48% (86) | 42% (104) | 46% (217) |
| **Age at first arrest:** | | | | | |
| 16 and under | 53% (94) | 43% (68) | 43% (106) | 40% (36) | 46% (304) |
| 17–20 | 37% (49) | 45% (73) | 41% (116) | 28% (78) | 38% (316) |
| 21 and over | — | 24% (37) | 24% (184) | 24% (174) | 24% (395) |
| **Time confined:** | | | | | |
| 18 months or under | 44% (78) | 39% (96) | 27% (202) | 24% (157) | 31% (533) |
| Over 18 months | 52% (65) | 41% (82) | 41% (204) | 31% (131) | 40% (482) |
| All cases | 48% (143) | 40% (178) | 34% (406) | 27% (288) | 35% (1015) |

[a] "Failure" means return to prison for new offense or as parole violator, or any non-prison sentence for a felony-like offense.
[b] Number of cases in parentheses.

Fundamental and relatively inherent difficulties accompany imprisonment, as has been shown. The prison must necessarily have a low degree of efficiency in reformation. Certain leaders have become convinced that imprisonment as a principal method for dealing with criminals should be regarded as undesirable and other methods substituted for it as rapidly as possible. To some extent, we have begun to carry out these recommenda-tions. The general tendency in the last generation has been to substitute probation for imprisonment; in many states at the present time probation is used for more offenders than is imprisonment, although fifty years ago the ratio could not have been more than one to ten. Nevertheless, the idea that dangerous criminals should be imprisoned has become deeply rooted in the last two centuries, and imprisonment will be with us for some time to come. What is needed is rehabilitation theory and practice which explicitly face the fact that in our present society prisons must, by definition, be abnormally restrictive and, thus, punitive.

## SUGGESTED READINGS

Bennett, James V., "Penology and Architecture," *Architectural Record*, 126:215–218, September, 1959.

Coe, Rodney M., and Albert J. Shafter, "Survey of Classification Systems in the United States," *Journal of Criminal Law, Criminology, and Police Science*, 49:316–320, November–December, 1958.

Cressey, Donald R., "Contradictory Directives in Complex Organization: The Case of the Prison," *Administrative Science Quarterly*, 4:1–19, June, 1959.

Cressey, Donald R., Editor, *The Prison: Studies in Institutional Organization and Change*. New York: Holt, Rinehart and Winston, 1961.

Frank, Andrew G., "Goal Ambiguity and Conflicting Standards: An Approach to the Study of Organization," *Human Organization*, 17:8–13, Winter, 1958–1959.

Galtung, Johan, "The Social Functions of a Prison," *Social Problems*, 6:127–140, Fall, 1958.

Gibbons, Don C., *Changing the Lawbreaker*. New York: Prentice-Hall, 1965.

Glaser, Daniel, *The Effectiveness of a Prison and Parole System*. Indianapolis: Bobbs-Merrill, 1964.

Hulin, Charles L., and Brendan A. Maher, "Changes in Attitudes Toward Law Concomitant with Imprisonment," *Journal of Criminal Law, Criminology, and Police Science*, 50:245–248, September–October, 1959.

Martin, John B., *Break Down the Walls*. New York: Ballantine Books, 1954.

Mattick, Hans, "Some Latent Functions of Imprisonment," *Journal of Criminal Law, Criminology and Police Science*, 50:237–244, September, 1959.

Moeller, H. G., "Changing Trends in Classification," *Proceedings of the American Correctional Association*, 1960, pp. 212–219.

Powelson, Harvey, and Reinhard Bendix, "Psychiatry in Prison," *Psychiatry*, 14:73–86, February, 1951.

Powers, Sanger, "The Social Services in a Correctional Institution," *American Journal of Correction*, 19:1–3, ff., March–April, 1957.

Reckless, Walter C., "Training of the Correctional Worker," in Paul W. Tappan, Editor, *Contemporary Correction*. New York: McGraw-Hill, 1951, pp. 35–50.

Robinson, Louis N., "Contradictory Purposes in Prisons," *Journal of Criminal Law and Criminology*, 37:449–457, March–April, 1947.

Schneckloth, Merle R., "Why Do Honest Employees React Dishonestly?" *American Journal of Correction*, 21:6–ff., March–April, 1959.

Scott, Frances Gillespie, "Action Theory and Research in Social Organization," *American Journal of Sociology*, 64:386–395, January, 1959.

Studt, Elliott, and Bernard Russell, *Staff Training for Personnel in Institutions for Juvenile Delinquents*. Children's Bureau Publication No. 364. Washington: Government Printing Office, 1958.

Sykes, Gresham M., "The Corruption of Authority and Rehabilitation," *Social Forces*, 34:257–262, March, 1956.

Sykes, Gresham M., *The Society of Captives: A Study of a Maximum Security Prison*. Princeton: Princeton University Press, 1958.

Tappan, Paul W., "Objectives and Methods in Correction," in Paul W. Tappan, Editor, *Contemporary Correction*. New York: McGraw-Hill, 1951, pp. 3–16.

Weber, George H., "Conflicts Between Professional and Non-Professional Personnel in Institutional Delinquency Treatment," *Journal of Criminal Law, Criminology, and Police Science*, 48:26–43, June, 1957.

Wilson, Joseph G., *Are Prisons Necessary?* Philadelphia: Dorrance, 1950.

# 24. THE PRISON COMMUNITY

As WAS POINTED out in Chapter Sixteen, the policy of individualized treatment developed as a reaction to the eighteenth-century attempts to impose uniform penalties on criminals. Members of the positive school argued that uniform punishments for all criminals could be no more effective than a policy calling for uniform handling of all medical patients, and the alternative eventually proposed was the system of individualized treatment. In the early period under this system, little or no attention was paid to the offender's relations with groups, presumably on the assumption that personality and behavior disorders have little to do with groups and can, consequently, be treated in a clinic just as tuberculosis can be treated in a clinic. Gradually, the treatment methods based on this "clinical principle" have been supplemented by methods based on the "group-relations principle" that criminality is social in nature and, therefore, can be modified in individual cases only if the criminal's relations with social groups are modified.[1] This trend may be observed in correctional work generally, and it also may be observed in the work with prisoners.

GROUP RELATIONS WORK IN PRISONS.    When considered as a general system for handling criminals, comparable to probation, imprisonment cannot operate on the group-relations principle, for prisoners, by definition, must be to a large extent isolated from law-abiding persons. Consequently, the reformative influences of prisons are distinctly limited by the very nature of imprisonment. Osborne stated that a person might as well train for a race by remaining in bed for weeks as train in prison for a return to social life.[2] Even the use of treatment methods based on the clinical principle is severely limited by the punitive conditions of imprisonment, al-

[1] See the discussion above, pp. 378–380.
[2] Thomas M. Osborne, "Introduction" to F. Tannenbaum, Wall Shadows (New York: G. Putnam's Sons, 1922), p. xii.

though not to the extent that use of methods based on the group-relations principle is limited; it is probably for this reason that in prisons clinical methods currently enjoy a much greater popularity than do group-relations methods. But for at least a century some persons have recognized that the offender can most effectively be trained for participation in law-abiding society by providing him with membership in that society, and this acknowledgement of the importance of group relations to reformation has led to many modifications of the conditions of imprisonment. Implicitly, at least, the group-relations principle has become the basis of many contemporary prison practices and policies. In relatively recent years there has been a growing awareness among prison workers of the necessity for promoting informal contacts between prisoners and law-abiding groups and for studying and developing interaction among the prisoners themselves.

*Reduction of prisoner isolation.* Although prisoners continue to be effectively separated from law-abiding groups and from most kinds of social relations in which they will be expected to participate after release, the isolation of inmates has gradually been reduced by "prison reforms" undertaken for humanitarian reasons during the last century. It also has been reduced by systems of individualized treatment which, while not explicitly acknowledging the importance of group associations on criminality and reformation, have promoted social relations with law-abiding groups, just as probation and parole have promoted such relations.

For example, visiting and correspondence privileges are restricted in all prisons, yet the very fact that they exist and are being extended reveals implicit recognition of the importance of reducing the degree of prisoner isolation from law-abiding society.[3] Furthermore, prison administrators always take precautions to see that visitors and correspondents are law-abiding, again implicitly recognizing the effects of group relations upon criminality and reformation. Also, obviously, the general provision in prisons of newspapers, books, magazines, lectures, moving pictures, and extramural athletic events reduces the inmates' isolation. Even classification, which frequently is used as the best example of a treatment method based on the clinical principle, involves recognition of group effects on the criminality or non-criminality of the prisoners. The separation, by means of classification, of first offenders and habitual criminals must be based on the notion that the behavior of individual first offenders will be positively affected by placing them in association with persons having relatively few criminal attitudes or, at least, that the behavior of first offenders should not be adversely affected by forcing them into membership in groups

[3] See Eugene Zemans and Ruth S. Cavan, "Marital Relationships of Prisoners," *Journal of Criminal Law and Criminology*, 49:50–57, May–June, 1958.

composed of experienced criminals. Similarly, educational, vocational, religious, and even individual psychotherapy programs may be interpreted as efforts to reform inmates by providing them with associations representative of the non-criminal world and by modifying their skills in such a way that upon release they will abandon membership in the groups which promoted their criminality.[4] All such privileges and treatment programs are administered, of course, within the framework of prison security, discipline, and punishment.

*Self-government by prisoners.*  The group-relations principle for treatment also has been recognized in programs designed to develop a prison social life somewhat comparable to the social life outside prisons. One basis for such programs is the notion that if prisoners are to be reformed they must be permitted to participate in social situations which are to some extent representative of the kinds of non-criminal social interaction in which they will be expected to participate upon release. Another basis, of course, is the hope that inmate participation programs will simplify administrative problems of discipline and control. One of the earliest specific attempts to promote social interaction among prisoners was the development of self-government systems.

As early as 1793, a modified system of self-government was used in the Walnut Street Jail in Philadelphia. In the institutions for juvenile delinquents in New York and Boston in the first few years of their history the delinquents had a self-governing court and voting participation in the election of some of the officers. In the Massachusetts state prison about 1845 the prisoners were organized into a society for improvement and mutual aid, primarily by discussion of topics of interest to the prisoners; the warden was president of the organization and it was clearly not spontaneous but was imposed upon the prisoners.[5] Brockway organized a system in the Detroit House of Correction in the decade of the sixties which he described as "almost complete self-government."[6] In 1895, William George founded the George Junior Republic at Freeville, New York, with the principle of self-government very prominent. Apparently it is this institution rather than the earlier precedents which has been important in the development of self-government in the last two generations, for one

[4] The alternative assumption is that such acquired skills somehow enable inmates to resist further criminality regardless of their subsequent associations. This assumption will be considered in detail in subsequent chapters. See pp. 605–606, 613–614, 675–680, below.

[5] O. F. Lewis, *The Development of American Prisons and Prison Customs, 1776–1845* (New York: Prison Association of New York, 1922), pp. 169–170.

[6] Z. R. Brockway, *Fifty Years of Prison Service* (New York: Charities Publication Committee, 1912), p. 97.

of the directors of this Republic was Thomas M. Osborne, who became the chief propagandist for self-government.[7]

Despite favorable accounts of the custodial accomplishments of a system of self-government in some institutions, and despite the theoretical value of a system which stimulates participation in groups which hold non-criminality as an ideal, many students of prison systems have grave doubts about it. A recent poll of fifty-two state penitentiary wardens brought replies from forty-four, only seven of whom had inmate councils in their institutions.[8] Similarly, in 1962 only eight of the thirty-two federal prisons had inmate councils.[9] There are two principal objections to inmate councils and other forms of self-government. First, if the council in fact has any power to govern, it tends to be controlled by inmates who manipulate it to their own advantage. Powerful prisoners use the weapons of imprisonment, including solitary confinement and deprivation of privileges, against inmates who do not do their bidding. When this occurs, self-government represents a neglect of duty on the part of officials, for one function of prisons is protection of inmates from outsiders and from each other.[10] The system of inmate government used by Brockway in a Boston House of Correction some years ago resulted in frequent escapes; the officers of the league were arrogant toward the prison officials and lorded it over the inmates, locking up more in solitary confinement than had ever been locked up under the control of the prison officials. The prisoners finally pleaded to have it abolished. After a trial of self-government for about a year the inmates of the New Jersey State Reformatory at Rahway abandoned it by a vote that was practically unanimous; ward politics had developed, cliques were formed, the shrewd prisoners were elected to offices, and prisoners against whom grudges were held were punished. When, shortly after World War II, Oahu Prison in Hawaii moved away from an authoritarian system of administration to a more democratic system, an inmate council was established with unusually broad responsibilities and

7 See T. M. Osborne, *Society and Prisons* (New Haven: Yale University Press, 1916); W. D. Lane, "Democracy for Law Breakers," *New Republic*, 18:173, March 8, 1919; and Frank Tannenbaum, *Osborne of Sing Sing* (Chapel Hill: University of North Carolina Press, 1933).

8 J. E. Baker, "Inmate Self-Government," *Journal of Criminal Law, Criminology and Police Science*, 55:39–47, March, 1964.

9 Daniel Glaser, *The Effectiveness of a Prison and Parole System* (Indianapolis: Bobbs-Merrill, 1964), p. 219.

10 Donald R. Cressey, "Achievement of an Unstated Organizational Goal: An Observation on Prisons," *Pacific Sociological Review*, 1:43–49, Fall, 1958; see also Amitai Etzioni, "Two Approaches to Organizational Analysis: A Critique and a Suggestion," *Administrative Science Quarterly*, 5:257–278, September, 1960.

direct access to the warden on policy matters.[11] At first, this did not disturb the order of the prison, for the old custodially-oriented inmates gained election to a majority of the seats. Gradually, however, the council was taken over by younger inmates who referred to themselves as a "syndicate" and who used the privileges granted as devices for demanding even more privileges; a wave of violence, disorder, and anarchy then took place.[12] A similar sequence took place in the New Jersey State Prison at Trenton.[13]

Second, in response to incidents such as those indicated above, inmate councils have tended to become mere window dressing. They are made up principally of inmates called "Square Johns" or "do rights," and these types of inmates do not have the respect of the real inmate leaders. They take actions which are of little significance to the government of the prison, and all their actions are subject to veto by the warden. A principal function of contemporary inmate councils, for example, is one of communicating inmate preferences in respect to recreational matters—the movies and television programs to be shown, and the radio programs to be received on the head sets provided in the cells. The councils also organize various "safe" activities, such as athletic tournaments and campaigns for blood bank donations.[14]

These experiences with self-government do not necessarily show that it will be impossible to establish successful self-government systems in the future. It should be recalled, however, that the current system of imprisonment is so designed that inmates can have no loyalty to the prison which keeps them confined, and no loyalty to any majority of their fellow prisoners.

*The honor system.* The honor system is similar to self-government only in that it places responsibility upon prisoners and gives them a chance to make choices. Under the honor system, the prison officials grant, as rewards for good behavior and loyalty, privileges which are conditional upon continued good behavior and loyalty. The loyalty is partly to the officials and partly to other inmates. The prisoner who is given privileges or other rewards in return for his promise not to escape or violate prison rules does not want other trusted prisoners to suffer in case he breaks his trust. Further, because the other prisoners want the privileges, they help the officials control the potential violator. It is obvious that most criminals

[11] Richard H. McCleery, "The Governmental Process of Informal Social Control," Chapter 4 in Donald R. Cressey, Editor, *The Prison: Studies in Institutional Organization and Change* (New York: Holt, Rinehart and Winston, 1961), p. 171.

[12] *Ibid.*, pp. 172–181.

[13] Gresham M. Sykes, *The Society of Captives: A Study of a Maximum Security Prison* (Princeton: Princeton University Press, 1958), pp. 119–120.

[14] Glaser, *op. cit.*, pp. 217–219.

cannot be converted into men of honor and transformed into non-criminals simply by saying, "From now on I am going to trust you." Although inmates released from honor camps and minimum-security honor institutions have lower parole violation rates and recidivism rates than do other prisoners, this record might be due merely to the fact that only the men who are considered most likely to reform are permitted to participate in such programs.

Group Therapy. Since World War II, group therapy has become relatively popular in prisons, and it often is considered a system, similar in principle to self-government, for reforming prisoners by giving them experience in social groups. Although there are many forms of group therapy, it usually consists of a program in which small groups of inmates meet regularly and discuss their problems; a therapist guides the discussion but does not restrict it. The American Group Psychotherapy Association surveyed 312 penal and correctional institutions to determine the status of group therapy in these institutions. Of the 109 institutions responding to the questionnaire, 39 replied that group therapy was a part of their program and ten indicated a desire to start such a program.[15]

The current emphasis on group therapy, also called "group psychotherapy" and "group psychoanalysis," grew out of the difficulty of treating mental disease cases individually during World War II. There has been little careful research and experimentation on the subject, but there is an almost unanimous opinion that group therapy is a markedly effective technique for dealing with mental patients.[16] As a system for dealing with mental patients, the chief contribution of group therapy has been elimination or reduction of social isolation and egocentricity,[17] or, stated positively, the assimilation of the isolated or egocentric patient into the clinical group.

The group-relations principle applied to intramural treatment of prisoners ideally goes beyond this program of group integration in the narrow sense and attempts, by means of prison groups, to present inmates with anti-criminal behavior patterns. The aim is not mere reduction of isolation and belligerence among prisoners as they operate in the prison situation, but the provision of positive contacts with groups which will directly or indirectly implant in the prisoner the anti-criminal values of the larger

[15] Lloyd W. McCorkle, "The Present Status of Group Therapy in United States Correctional Institutions," *International Journal of Group Psychotherapy*, 3:79–87, January, 1953.

[16] Marshall B. Clinard, "The Group Approach to Social Reintegration," *American Sociological Review*, 14:257–262, April, 1949.

[17] S. R. Slavson, *An Introduction to Group Therapy*, New York: The Commonwealth Fund, 1943, p. 1; William C. Menninger, *Psychiatry in a Troubled World* (New York: Macmillan, 1948), pp. 316–317.

society.[18] It is probable that group-therapy programs in prisons do not ordinarily have this positive objective but, instead, merely attempt to provide permissive situations which enable inmates both to discuss their problems with each other freely and to "ventilate" their "suppressed hostilities" toward the courts, the police, and the prison. According to the proponents of the clinical principle, but not those of the group-relations principle, this "reforms" inmates by enabling them to rid themselves of certain individual emotional disorders which are considered the causes of their criminality. There is little difference between the aims of such programs and the aims of individual, clinical, psychotherapy.

Group therapy is used extensively at present in the New Jersey prisons and reformatories, where it is called "guided group interaction," and in the California institutions, where it is called "group counseling." Both labels were invented in an attempt to avoid confusion with the use of group therapy as practiced by psychiatrists and to avoid the implication that all inmates are mentally abnormal.[19] The therapists in these programs are primarily prison guards and tradesmen, and they have tried to go beyond mere ventilation and reduction of isolation and have attempted in a more positive way to utilize the group for reformation of offenders. It has been stated, for example, that in guided group interaction "the major emphasis is on the group and its development rather than on an attempt at exhaustive psychoanalysis of individuals in the group."[20] Similarly, cognizance of the group-relations principle seems to be indicated by the following definition and statement of the aims of guided group interaction: "The use of free discussion in a friendly supportive atmosphere to re-educate the delinquent to accept the restrictions of society by finding greater personal satisfaction in conforming to social rules than following delinquent patterns."[21]

[18] Cf. Lloyd W. McCorkle, Albert Elias, and F. Lovell Bixby, The Highfields Story (New York: Holt, 1958), pp. 68–80; and Don C. Gibbons, Changing the Lawbreaker (New York: Prentice-Hall, 1965), pp. 146–147.

[19] Lloyd W. McCorkle, "Group Therapy," in Paul W. Tappan, Editor, Contemporary Correction (New York: McGraw-Hill, 1951), pp. 211–223; Norman Fenton, An Introduction to Group Counseling in State Correctional Service (New York: The American Correctional Association, 1958); Norman Fenton, et. al., Explorations in the Use of Group Counseling in the County Correctional Program (Palo Alto: Pacific Books, 1962); and Guy Houchon, "Introduction au Group Counseling Pénitentiaire," Bulletin De L'Administration Pénitentiaire (Belgium), 17:311–327, December, 1963.

[20] Lloyd W. McCorkle, "Group Therapy in the Treatment of Offenders," Federal Probation, 16:22–27, December, 1952.

[21] Ibid. This statement is a revision of a definition used in earlier publications: "The use of free discussion to re-educate the delinquent to accept the restrictions of society and to find satisfaction in conforming to social norms." F. Lovell Bixby and Lloyd W. McCorkle, "Applying the Principles of Group Therapy in Correctional Institutions," Federal Probation, 14:36–40, March, 1950.

It is not clear how these aims at reformation are specifically accomplished, but guided group interaction and group counseling programs seem to be based, implicitly or explicitly, on four principal assumptions about the processes by which the group sessions contribute to individual reformation. Three of these assumptions are consistent with the individualization principle, only one with the group-relations principle.

First, there seems to be an assumption that free discussion of an inmates' problem and personality characteristics by and with an inmate group and a therapist will both enable him and force him to "face the facts" of his case by "getting beneath the surface."[22] Inmates who have had experiences similar to his will not let him lie, bluff, or provide *ex post facto* justifications for his criminal behavior. Presumably, the inmate eventually will accept his fellow inmates' friendly denunciations of his behavior and rationalizations more readily than he would accept the rejections and denunciations of the same behavior and rationalizations by an outsider.

Second, it apparently is assumed that stimulation to "face the facts" will give the individual "insight" by enabling him to see that his problems are due to such attitudes as "resentment of authority," or "feelings of guilt," or "frustration." Such insight, combined with the opportunity to ventilate, presumably will reform him. This is obviously in keeping with the notion, based on clinical principle, that if a criminal is able to dissipate the "tensions" and "anxieties" arising from his emotional disturbances he will be reformed.[23]

Third, it seems to be assumed that guided group interaction will give the inmate experience in accepting the analyses, opinions, and arguments of others in the inmate group, and that this, in turn, will give him needed practice in accepting the general "restrictions of society."[24] This assumption is consistent with the individualistic, clinical, notion that there is a war between "the individual" and "society." One variety of this idea in criminology is that the individual, because of something *in him,* "breaks through" the restrictions of society and follows criminal patterns. For reformation, the something *in him* must be modified, and this can be done in a clinic.[25] Another variety, possibly the one used in guided group

[22] See J. Douglas Grant and Marguerite Q. Grant, "A Group Dynamics Approach to the Treatment of Nonconformists in the Navy," *Annals of the American Academy of Political and Social Science,* 322:126–136, March, 1959.

[23] See S. R. Slavson, "Group Therapy in Delinquency Prevention," *Journal of Educational Sociology,* 24:45–51, September, 1950; and Justin K. Fuller, "Group Therapy for Parolees," *Prison World,* 14:9–11, July, 1952.

[24] See Joseph Abrahams and Lloyd W. McCorkle, "Group Psychotherapy of Military Offenders," *American Journal of Sociology,* 51:455–464, March, 1946.

[25] See Irving Schulman, "The Dynamics of Certain Reactions of Delinquents to Group Psychotherapy," *International Journal of Group Psychotherapy,* 2:334–343, October, 1952.

interaction, is that the criminal's character make-up is egocentric rather than altruistic—he thinks in terms of "I" rather than "we" and, consequently, follows delinquent patterns. By guided group interaction this individualistic make-up, which is considered as being in opposition to the spirit of "society" and "group living," purportedly is removed by the therapist and the fellow inmates who will not let the individual "get away with" the expression of his egocentric character. But according to the group-relations principle the problem is not one of "individual versus society" but, instead, of one kind of values (criminal) versus another kind of values (anti-criminal).[26] What we attempt to correct in our prisons is not non-conformity or lack of satisfaction in conformity to "social rules" or "restrictions of society," but, instead, conformity and satisfaction in conformity to the norms and values of which we, the law makers, do not approve.[27]

A fourth implicit assumption is consistent with the group-relations principle. It is expected that each participant in the group sessions gains experience in the role of a law-abiding person and that this experience will carry-over to the life outside the session and outside the prison. Here, the reformative effect of the sessions is considered as operating not on the inmate as his criminal behavior and attitudes are analyzed and denounced, but, instead, on the inmate as he does the analyzing and denouncing.[28] As the participant attempts to change the behavior of others he necessarily recognizes that behavior as undesirable. And he must identify with and "take the side" of anti-criminal groups when he condemns law violation and law violators. He becomes a reformer, rather than a reformee, and in denouncing the criminality of others he denounces his own criminality.[29] Possibly, the entire group will become "anti-criminal," thus supporting the

[26] Cf. Charles Gersten, "An Experimental Evaluation of Group Therapy with Juvenile Delinquents," International Journal of Group Psychotherapy, 1:311–318, November, 1951.

[27] Cf. George B. Vold, "Discussion of Guided Group Interaction in Correctional Work by F. Lovell Bixby and Lloyd W. McCorkle," American Sociological Review, 16:460–461, August, 1951; John R. Ellingston, Protecting Our Children from Criminal Careers (New York: Prentice-Hall, 1948), p. 35.

[28] See Donald R. Cressey, "Changing Criminals: The Application of the Theory of Differential Association," American Journal of Sociology, 61:116–120, September, 1955; Rita Volkman and Donald R. Cressey, "Differential Association and the Rehabilitation of Drug Addicts," American Journal of Sociology, 69:129–142, September, 1963; and Donald R. Cressey, "Social Psychological Foundations for Using Criminals in the Rehabilitation of Criminals," Journal of Research in Crime and Delinquency, 2:49–59, July, 1965.

[29] See Gisela Knopka, "The Group Worker's Role in an Institution for Juvenile Delinquents," Federal Probation, 15:15–23, June, 1951; Freed Bales, "Types of Social Structure as Factors in 'Cures' for Alcohol Addiction," Applied Anthropology, 1:1–13, April–June, 1942; and Joseph A. Cook and Gilbert Geis, "Forum Anonymous: The Techniques of Alcoholics Anonymous Applied to Prison Therapy," Journal of Social Therapy, 3:9–13, First Quarter, 1957.

new anti-criminal views of individual participants. Status in the group may be assigned according to the degree of "pro-reform" behavior which is exhibited. If this occurs, there has been a real modification of the social relations of each participant in the group, and the group itself has become an effective medium of change. The personal satisfaction which a participant now obtains from denouncing criminal behavior and values actually is satisfaction in conforming to *anti-criminal* social norms.

It is not certain as yet that guided group interaction, group counseling, and similar group-therapy programs are more efficient than self-government and honor systems in accomplishing transfers of allegiance from criminal to anti-criminal values. Perhaps the major disadvantage of group therapy in this connection is that it rarely deals with "natural groups" in the prison. Consequently, attitudes acquired in the group sessions may receive little support in the general prison community and there may be a minimum of carry-over to situations outside the prison. Wheeler has shown that the private attitudes of prisoners are quite different from the attitudes they express publicly, and that in their private attitudes many inmates are not antagonistic to therapy.[30] Consistently, Garabedian found that recalcitrant "antisocial" inmates join treatment programs when they are sponsored by inmates but are reluctant to participate in those initiated by officials.[31]

THE PRISON COMMUNITY.[32]   Very little is known, even by prisoners and prison workers, of the kinds of social interaction which takes place among prisoners. Prisoners, by definition, are persons who have been forcibly removed from the social relations in which they have been participating and locked in institutions where, we are prone to say, they "serve their time," "pay their debt to society," and, perhaps, "learn their lesson." But they do more than pay, and serve, and learn in the institutions. They *live* in them. For varying periods of time, each prisoner participates in an extraordinarily complex set of social relations, including a wide variety of social contacts, associations, bonds, alliances, compromises, and conflicts between hundreds of prisoners, guards, administrators, teachers, tradesmen, and professional personnel like social workers, psychologists, and physicians.

[30] Stanton Wheeler, "Role Conflict in Correctional Communities," Chapter 6 in Cressey, *The Prison, op. cit.,* pp. 234–240.

[31] Peter G. Garabedian, "Legitimate and Illegitimate Alternatives in the Prison Community," *Sociological Inquiry,* 32:172–184, Spring, 1962.

[32] Parts of this section are adapted from Donald R. Cressey and Witold Krassowski, "Inmate Organization and Anomie in American Prisons and Soviet Labor Camps," *Social Problems,* 5:217–230, Winter, 1957–1958; Donald R. Cressey, "Foreword" to the reissue of Donald Clemmer's *The Prison Community* (New York: Rinehart, 1958), pp. vii–x; Donald R. Cressey, "Introduction" to Donald R. Cressey, Editor, *The Prison: Studies in Institutional Organization and Change* (New York: Holt, Rinehart and Winston, 1961), pp. 1–12; and John Irwin and Donald R. Cressey, "Thieves, Convicts and the Inmate Culture," *Social Problems,* 10:142–155, Fall, 1962.

During the period of participation in this set of social relations, some prisoners apparently become "reformed" or "rehabilitated," while others become "confirmed" or "hardened" criminals. For still others, prison life has no discernible effect on subsequent criminality or noncriminality. In the last fifteen years, social scientists have begun to study inmate participation in prison life in some detail, and they are beginning to establish as fact the idea that whether any particular prisoner becomes "reformed," or becomes "hardened," or remains neutral during his prison experience depends upon the specific nature of his participation in the prison community.[33] These studies have made two principal points. First, the prison community has a distinctive set of values, norms, positions and roles, the elements that make up a "social system." Second, in the course of incarceration, not all inmates come into association wth the same sets of norms and values in the same way; they hold different positions and play different roles in a set of relationships which are so confused, entangled, complicated and subtle that even the participants are unable to see and describe clearly their own involvements.

The social system. A chart of a prison's administrative hierarchy, showing the lines of authority, does not begin to describe how the prison is organized, who is responsible to whom, or who influences whom. It is even difficult to draw a picture of the official parts of the organization in this way, although these are the least complex aspects of the system. In addition, there are unofficial components of institutional structure, and it is these that are most complicated and, usually, unstated. In one sense, in fact, whether specific aspects of organization are "official" or "unofficial" depends on whether or not they are clear and observable. If a prison warden can "do something about" some aspect of the institution—such as issuing an order that a certain practice is to be changed—he is dealing with official organization; if there is something going on, the nature of which he cannot clearly state and which, consequently, he cannot change by order, he is dealing with unofficial organization.[34] Both the official and the unofficial aspects of social organization are important determinants of behavior, including attitudes, opinions, and beliefs. It is likely, however, that unofficial

[33] For bibliographies of the extensive literature in this area, see Gresham M. Sykes and Sheldon L. Messinger, "The Inmate Social System," in Richard A. Cloward, Donald R. Cressey, George H. Grosser, Richard McCleery, Lloyd E. Ohlin, and Gresham M. Sykes and Sheldon L. Messinger, Theoretical Studies in Social Organization of the Prison (New York: Social Science Research Council, 1960), pp. 5–7; Clarence Schrag, "Some Foundations for a Theory of Correction," Chapter 8 in Cressey, The Prison, op. cit., pp. 320–321, 329; and Don C. Gibbons, Changing the Lawbreaker: The Treatment of Delinquents and Criminals (New York: Prentice-Hall, 1965), pp. 197–198.

[34] Cf. Alfred H. Stanton and Morris S. Schwartz, The Mental Hospital (New York: Basic Books, 1954), pp. 10, 31.

arrangements are of most significance to inmates, for most of their time is spent in them. The "good" or "bad" feeling between an inmate and a guard, between two inmates, or between the warden and the chef, the vocabulary of the psychologists and the social workers, and the sense of justice among inmates and guards are all part of the inmate's world, and they have a powerful effect on the form of his adjustment in the institution and on his subsequent criminality. Similarly, while prison officers have some control over most of the inmate's overt behavior, mostly in the form of authority to punish for deviation, their control is negligible compared to control by prisoners themselves. In a system of friendships, mutual obligations, statuses, reciprocal relations, loyalties, intimidation, deception, and violence, inmates learn that conformity to prisoner expectations is just as important to their welfare as is conformity to the formal controls exerted by "outsiders."[35] From the point of view of some powerful prisoners, inmates must be orthodox in their statements and actions. And orthodoxy is more important in prison than in outside life because in outside life a person has freedom of mobility not possible in prisons. Orthodoxy in the ways of behaving of prisoners is promoted by a system of rewards and punishments, the latter emphasizing gossip, laughter, and ridicule, but including, also, corporal punishments and, occasionally, execution.

The informal control may be seen in the persistence of the fundamental principles of prisoner organization, called "the code." An examination of many descriptions of prison life has suggested that the chief tenets of the inmate code can be classified roughly into five major groups.[36] First, there are those maxims that caution: *Don't interfere with inmate interests.* These center on the idea that inmates should serve the least possible time while enjoying the greatest possible number of pleasures and privileges. Included are directives such as *Never rat on a con; Don't be nosey; Don't have a loose lip; Keep off a man's back; Don't put a guy on the spot.* Put positively, *Be loyal to your class, the cons.* A second set of behavioral rules asks inmates to refrain from quarrels or arguments with fellow prisoners: *Don't lose your head; Play it cool; Do your own time; Don't bring heat.* Third, prisoners assert that inmates should not take advantage of one another by means of force, fraud, or chicanery: *Don't exploit inmates.* This injunction sums up several directives: *Don't break your word; Don't steal from cons; Don't sell favors; Don't be a racketeer; Don't welsh on debts. Be right.* Fourth, some rules have as their central theme the maintenance of self: *Don't weaken; Don't whine; Don't cop out (plead guilty).* Stated

---

[35] See George H. Grosser, "The Role of Informal Inmate Groups in Change of Values," *Children*, 5:25–29, February, 1958.
[36] Sykes and Messinger, *op. cit.*, pp. 6–10.

positively: *Be tough; Be a man.* Fifth, prisoners express a variety of maxims that forbid according prestige or respect to the guards or the world for which they stand: *Don't be a sucker; Skim it off the top; Never talk to a screw* (guard); *Have a connection; Be sharp.*

All inmates learn the code by word of mouth and, to varying degrees, prisoners are guided by the code in their relationships both within the prison and in the free community after release. There is no question that the code is frequently violated, just as the formal legal code is violated. But the fact that a code is violated does not mean that is is not prescribed, nor does it mean that it has no important effects on the behavior of persons sharing it. The effects of the code may be seen everywhere in the prison community. Men who violate the code by becoming "finks," "rats," or "stool pigeons," for example, do so secretly not only because secrecy is essential to their "profession" but also because they know they will, at least, lose the support of their fellow inmates if they are discovered. A known informer is ostracized, ridiculed, hissed, scoffed, and generally made to feel miserable. He may be given the "silent treatment," a system in which the ostracism is so complete that other inmates do not even acknowledge the informer's presence, or he may be almost constantly isolated from participation in all but the most rudimentary social life. In extreme cases, informers are attacked, and many prison systems have a special cell block or a special institution for informers.

The code is not necessarily a "code of honor." The prison community does not have a system of democratic justice. One is guilty if he is not above suspicion or if his associates are not above suspicion. An inmate who has been a witness for the state against another criminal usually is treated as an informer or, at least, as an outsider. However, there are exceptional cases, particularly those in which the witness apparently testified against a disloyal crime partner. To be seen speaking to a guard is a social error, and frequent conversations with guards is in most prisons unthinkable, on the part of both the prisoners and the guards.[37] Professional persons who administer the treatment programs are considered hardly different from guards, and inmates are suspicious of men who participate in research projects or group-therapy programs. The code, thus, makes inmates suspicious of all outsiders, and it also makes them suspicious of each other. The inmates as a group must be constantly on guard to prevent individual members from seeking an advantage with the officials by betraying the group.

The code, like other behavior patterns among inmates, arises in part out

---

[37] See Robert Sommer and Humphry Osmond, "Symptoms of Institutional Care," *Social Problems*, 8:254–263, Winter, 1961; and Elmer H. Johnson, "Sociology of Confinement: Assimilation and the Prison 'Rat'," *Journal of Criminal Law, Criminology and Police Science*, 51:528–533, January, 1961; and Harry A. Wilmer, "The Role of the 'Rat' in the Prison," *Federal Probation*, 29:44–49, March, 1965.

of the conditions of deprivation in the prison. However, it also consists in part of a more general *criminal* code, brought into the prison and utilized there by career criminals and other sophisticated criminals, and adopted by prisoners.[38] So far as the prison itself is concerned, it is significant that the code helps inmates avoid some of the conditions of deprivation which the prison is expected to impose on them. Yet it should not be concluded that the code is necessarily as "anti-administration" in emphasis as it appears to be. On the contrary, the code reflects an important alliance between inmate leaders and prison officials.

We observed earlier that humanitarian and treatment considerations have effectively limited the means available to prison administrators for keeping inmates quietly confined, yet these officials continue to be held responsible for the prisoners' orderly confinement.[39] One solution to this problem is to keep inmates unorganized. To this end, there have been persistent efforts to substitute psychological solitary confinement for the physical solitary confinement characterizing the early Pennsylvania institutions. This practice permits inmates to work and to participate in other activities, but it minimizes the danger of escape or riot. Thus, "incentives" such as parole, good-time allowances, and privileges of various sorts, including the privilege of participating in treatment programs, are administered as rewards to inmates who heed the administrators' admonition to "do your own time."[40] Clemmer estimated that in one prison about forty percent of the prisoners were not in any way intimately integrated in groups in which strong social relationships exist, and that another forty percent engaged in some of the superficial practices of group life but were not genuinely affiliated with primary groups.[41] This higher percentage of "ungrouped" inmates seems attributable to the official system of maintaining control by psychological isolation of inmates. It is much easier to control individual prisoners than to control groups of prisoners.

A second kind of solution to the problem is to enlist, unofficially at least, the aid of some of the inmates. When prisoners far outnumber staff members it is extremely difficult, if not impossible, to keep each of them psychologically isolated. But control is facilitated if inmate elites develop and enforce norms and values which promote psychological isolation among the other inmates. The inmate code and culture which put emphasis upon being an astute criminal, upon maintaining social distance from the guards, and upon inmate solidarity, do precisely this. Thus, inmate leaders operate

[38] See Irwin and Cressey, *op. cit.*
[39] See pp. 540–541, above.
[40] See Richard A. Cloward, "Social Control in the Prison," Chapter 2 in Cloward, Cressey, et. al., pp. 41–48.
[41] *The Prison Community, op. cit.*, p. 129.

in such a manner that the important administrative task of maintaining a quiet, secure institution is indirectly supported, rather than subverted. The values and type of organization which inmate elites attempt to maintain are to a large degree systems for exploiting fellow-captives, a condition attended by control and repression of inmates by inmates rather than by administrators.[42] The advice inmates give to each other is the exact counterpart of the officials' admonitions. This includes directives to be rational, not to bring "heat" by antagonizing employees, not to cause trouble by stealing from fellow-inmates and, generally, to "do your own time."[43] In enforcing the code, of course, the inmate elites necessarily violate it. By insisting that inmates "do their own time" an inmate leader shows that he is not doing his own time.

If inmate control of other inmates is valuable to prison administrators, it would be expected that power of various kinds would unofficially, and perhaps unintentionally, be assigned to inmate elites, rather than seized by them. This seems to be the case. Judicious distribution of goods in short supply, including measures of freedom and symbols of power and status, enables administrators to enlist the aid of certain inmates in the task of controlling other inmates. In return for some of the scarce goods, usually called "favors," inmate leaders control the bulk of other inmates. As Cloward has said, "Stability depends upon reciprocal adjustments between formal and inmate systems." McCorkle and Korn studied the prison as a rehabilitative organization and concluded that "Prison officials have generally tended to use the inmate power structure as an aid in prison administration and the maintenance of good order."[44] McCleery has summarized the relationship between administrative organization and inmate organization in the following terms:

The processes by which the formal hierarchy is sustained create the conditions for a parallel hierarchy in the inmate community. Exploitive and authoritarian inmate leaders may be removed to segregation, but others rise to fill their place because their role is necessary in the situation.[45]

Many inmate elites are men who, like the administrators, have a vested interest in maintaining the status quo. A basic tenet in their code is that

[42] Gresham M. Sykes, "Men, Merchants, and Toughs," Social Problems, 4:130–138, October, 1956; and The Society of Captives, op. cit., pp. 76–78.

[43] Daniel Glaser, The Effectiveness of a Prison and Parole System, op. cit., p. 99.

[44] Lloyd E. McCorkle and Richard Korn, "Resocialization within Walls," Annals of the American Academy of Political and Social Science, 293:88–98, May, 1954.

[45] Richard A. McCleery, "Communication Patterns as a Basis for a System of Authority and Power," op. cit., p. 76; see also Gresham M. Sykes, "The Corruption of Authority and Rehabilitation," Social Forces, 34:257–262, March, 1956.

prisoners must stick together and must not use official channels to gain advantages over other inmates, which is exactly what the leaders do. Officials insist that guards must not fraternize with inmates, and inmate elites insist that prisoners must not fraternize with guards; in this way, both officials and elites control the channels of communication, an important source of power.[46] Like administrators, some elites insist that all inmates are equal, but by this they mean that "outside" criteria such as occupation, wealth, or criminal notoriety shall not be used to determine the power, prestige, and special privileges within the institution. Such rules for the behavior of prisoners protect the elites' privileged positions and are necessary to maintenance of organizational status quo; when they exist, few inmates can seriously threaten the power positions of the leaders. If special privileges and power were awarded on the basis of extra-institutional criteria, the result would be chaotic dethroning of inmate elites at frequent intervals and, consequently, destruction of cooperative alliances between elites and administrators. At the same time, the inmate rules operate to keep the bulk of the inmates unorganized.

To take an oversimplified example of administrative-inmate alliances, an inmate might be allowed by a guard to steal a little coffee from the kitchen in return for being cooperative, working hard, discouraging other inmates from violence and, generally, making the guard's job an easy one. This man then has a vested interest in his coffee-stealing privileges and is likely to take a dim view of other inmates who would steal coffee in such manner and measure that the guard and his superiors woud put all coffee under strict control. He then makes the guard's job even easier, for *he* guards the coffee. But he really doesn't guard it—other inmates are prohibited from making inroads on his coffee-stealing privileges by a code which emphasize the importance of doing one's own time, not bringing heat, sticking together against the administration, and not ratting. Both the prison's coffee supply and the inmate's special coffee ration are thus protected by a man who steals from the supply while enforcing a code which, in these circumstances, prohibits others from doing the same. He exploits other inmates by stealing coffee allotted for their use, and he is permitted to do so by a guard who implicitly recognizes that such exploitation keeps the bulk of the inmates unorganized and, thus, under control.

*Differential participation.* One of the amazing things about prisons is that they "work" at all. Any prison is made up of the synchronized actions of hundreds of people, some of whom hate and distrust each other,

---

[46] *Ibid.*, pp. 52–56. See also Richard H. McCleery, "The Governmental Process and Informal Inmate Control," *op. cit.*, pp. 149–188; and Merle R. Schneckloth, "Why Do Honest Employees React Dishonestly?" *American Journal of Correction*, 21:6–ff., March–April, 1959.

love each other, fight each other physically and psychologically, think of each other as stupid or mentally disturbed, "manage" and "control" each other, and vie with each other for favors, prestige, power, and money. Often the personnel involved do not know with whom they are competing or cooperating and are not sure whether they are the managers or the managed. But despite these conditions, the social system which is a prison does not degenerate into a chaotic mess of social relations which have no order and make no sense. Somehow the personnel, including the prisoners, are bound together enough so that most conflicts and misunderstandings are not crucial—the personnel remain "organized" and the prison continues to "work." Viewed in this way, the prison is a microcosm of the larger society which has created it and which maintains it, for this larger society also is a unit which continues to "work" despite numerous individual disagreements, misunderstandings, antagonisms, and conflicts.

An offender entering a prison for the first time is introduced to the culture in which the way a child is introduced to the ways of behaving of his elders. The general process by which a child is taught the behavior patterns of his group is called "socialization," and the somewhat comparable process among inmates has been named "prisonization."[47] However, like a person moving into a new culture, the new inmate, often called a "fish," usually not only has to learn new ways of behaving but also must "unlearn" some of his former behavior patterns. Also unlike the situation in socialization is the fact that inmates are by no means "neutral" toward accepting or rejecting the behavior patterns presented to them, as is the case with very young children. Among incoming inmates there is variation in the degree of resentment toward the police, courts, county jail officials, or others; variation in the extent of remorse; variation in the extent of fear, bravado, or defiance; and variation in other personal characteristics acquired prior to imprisonment. Regardless of these personal characteristics, however, every man who enters a penitentiary undergoes prisonization to some extent, if only because he must undergo the process of being assigned a number, a standard set of clothing, and a standard haircut.[48]

All inmates who are new to a particular prison, even if they have been previously incarcerated, must learn the technical organization of the new community. They learn "the rules," and the many technical details of prison living. In this phase of prisonization, which continues for only a few days or weeks, the inmate is essentially an "outsider." He maintains

[47] Clemmer, The Prison Community, op. cit., p. 298.
[48] See Erving Goffman, "On the Characteristics of Total Institutions: Staff-Inmate Relations," Chapter 1 in Cressey, The Prison, op. cit., pp. 23–48. See also Alfred Hassler, Diary of a Self-Made Convict (Chicago: Henry Regnery, 1954), p. 177.

the bulk of the attitudes and behavior patterns he possessed upon admission to the prison but changes his personal habits to comply with the folkways of the prison.

Gradually, the new inmate is subject to other, more pervasive, influences. He accepts his inferior status and grows accustomed to having his name replaced by a number. He wears clothing which is not significantly different from that worn by the other inmates, and he realizes that, from the guard's point of view, he is an anonymous figure. He comes to know the meanings of prison slang or argot, and no matter how aloof he may hold himself from the other inmates he finds himself using some of that slang. He refers to the guards as "screws," to the warden by the nickname given him by the inmates, to the psychiatrists and social workers as "bug doctors." He begins to recognize the fact that in many respects the prisoners, not the administrators, control the life in the prison. He becomes aware of his "security," realizing that he owes nothing to anyone for such food, entertainment, recreation, education, and living accommodations as are furnished him. He begins to look for a comfortable job where, as he says, "I can do my time without any trouble and get out of here." He no longer expresses a willingness to "do anything" the officials might ask him to do. All inmates are subjected to these "universal factors of prisonization." They are "swallowed up" by the prison.

For many men, prisonization does not cease when there is mere engulfment by the rather routine prison life. The prison community contains other patterns which are learned and accepted by some inmates. These men learn to gamble, to participate in homosexual activities, and to hate and distrust prison officials and, generally, "outsiders." They not only accept the prescribed "prison code," they attempt to enforce it. They not only hear the prison dogma, they begin to spread it. They not only believe that the environment should administer to them, they attempt to control the environment through prison politics and conniving. These and similar changes do not occur in every man, and all of them usually do not occur in any one man. They are, nevertheless, characteristic of the prison community. The men who participate in these aspects of prison life differ from those subjected only to what Clemmer calls the "universal factors of prisonization" largely in attitudes of allegiance to prisoners as a group.

The general effect of prisonization is the introduction, with varying degrees of efficiency, of all inmates to attitudes, codes, norms, and values which are in many ways contradictory to anti-criminal norms. Because it causes prisoners to identify themselves as persons quite different from non-criminals, even contact with the "universal factors" will render difficult any effort at clinical treatment. As Clemmer says:

Even if no other factor of the prison culture touches the personality of an inmate of many years of residence, the influences of these universal factors are sufficient to make a man characteristic of the penal community and probably so disrupt his personality that a happy adjustment in any [outside] community becomes next to impossible. On the other hand, if inmates who are incarcerated for only short periods, such as a year or so, do not become integrated into the culture except in so far as these universal factors of prisonization are concerned, they do not seem to be so characteristic of the penal community and are able when released to take up a new mode of life without much difficulty.[49]

The men who are most efficiently or completely prisonized adopt the ideology characteristic of the prison. Most of those who are integrated to a lesser extent at least, outwardly espouse the same ideology. A series of studies have demonstrated, however, that inmates show a U-shaped pattern of maximum aloofness to the ideology at the beginning and the end of the prison term.[50] Wheeler concluded from his study that at the beginning and end of their terms, most inmates are primarily influenced by reference groups outside the prison—relatives, friends, and employers whom they have just left or whom they are anxious to rejoin.

Despite the fact that all inmates undergo prisonization, much of the inmate behavior ordinarily considered part of the prison culture is not peculiar to the prison at all. One analysis indicates that a distinction must be made between the "convict subculture" which arises within institutions and the "thief subculture" which is carried into prisons by criminals.[51] The prison code is also part of a criminal code, existing outside prisons. Similarly, many inmates come to any given prison with a record of many terms in correctional institutions, and they bring with them a ready-made set of patterns which they apply to the new situation, just as is the case with participants in various outside criminal subcultures. In view of these processes, a clear understanding of inmate conduct cannot be obtained simply by viewing "prison culture" or "inmate culture" as an isolated system springing solely from the conditions of imprisonment.

The core values of thieves operating in the general community correspond closely to the values which prison observers have ascribed to the

[49] Op. cit., p. 300. Reprinted by permission of the publisher.

[50] Stanton H. Wheeler, "Social Organization and Inmate Values in Correctional Communities," Proceedings of the American Correctional Association, 1959, pp. 189–198; Stanton H. Wheeler, "Socialization in Correctional Communities," American Sociological Review, 26:697–712, October, 1961; Peter G. Garabedian "Social Roles and the Process of Socialization in the Prison Community," Social Problems, 11:139–152, Fall, 1963; and Daniel Glaser, op. cit., pp. 95–98. See also Marvin E. Wolfgang, "Quantitative Analysis of Adjustment to the Prison Community," Journal of Criminal Law, Criminology and Police Science, 51:607–618, March, 1961.

[51] Irwin and Cressey, op. cit.

type of inmate called the "right guy" or "real man." Hans Riemer secured a prison commitment for the purpose of studying the prison community and spent about four months in a state prison without the knowledge of any prisoner or administrative officer that he was not a bona fide offender. He found that each man is "classified" informally by the other inmates in much the way he is classified by the official classification board, and he described the two principal types of inmate leaders as follows:

The prison population is largely in control of a small group of men which has two divisions. There are the "politicians," "shots," or whatever they may be called in varying institutions, who hold key positions in the administrative offices of the prison. They wield a power to distribute special privileges, to make possible the circulation of special foods or other supplies. They, in frequent instances, become "racketeers" and use their positions to force money and services from less powerful inmates. These men are seldom trusted by the top level of the prison hierarchy, are frequently hated by the general population because of the exclusiveness and self-seeking behavior characteristic of them. . . . The other section of this controlling power is held by the so-called "right guys." These men are so called because of the consistency of their behavior in accordance with the criminal or prison code. They are men who can always be trusted, who do not abuse lesser inmates, who are invariably loyal to their class—the convicts. They are not wanton trouble-makers, but they are expected to stand up for their rights as convicts, to get what they can from prison officials, to never permit an opportunity to pass from which they might secure anything from a better job to freedom. . . . These men, because of their outright and loyal behavior, are the real leaders of the prison and impose stringent controls upon the definitions of proper behavior from other convicts.[52]

Similarly, Clemmer found that the most important characteristic of prison leaders was "being right," although the leaders also were above average in intelligence, experienced in crime, and city bred.[53]

High status as a "politician," "shot," "merchant," "peddler," or even as a "tough," "hood," or "gorilla" is based principally on conduct within the prison, but status as a "right guy" depends as well upon participation in the "criminal" or "thief" subculture which exists outside prisons. In the thief subculture outside prisons a man who is known as "right" or "solid" is one who can be trusted and relied upon. High status is also awarded to

[52] Hans Riemer, "Socialization in the Prison Community," *Proceedings of the American Prison Association*, 1937, pp. 151–155. Reprinted by permission of the publisher.

[53] Donald Clemmer, "Leadership Phenomena in a Prison Community," *Journal of Criminal Law and Criminology*, 28:851–872, March–April, 1938. See also Clarence Schrag, "Leadership Among Prison Inmates," *American Sociological Review*, 19:37–42, February, 1954.

those who possess skill as thieves, but to be just a successful thief is not enough; there must be solidness as well. A solid guy is respected even if he is unskilled, and no matter how skilled in crime a stool pigeon may be, his status is low.

Despite the fact that adherence to the norms of the thief subculture is an ideal, and the fact that the behavior of the great majority of men arrested or convicted varies sharply from any "criminal code" which might be identified, a proportion of the persons arrested for "real crime" such as burglary, robbery, and larceny have been in close contact with the values of the subculture. Many criminals, while not following the precepts of the subculture religiously, give lip service to its values and evaluate their own behavior and the behavior of their associates in terms relating to adherence to "rightness" and being "solid." It is probable, further, that use of this kind of values is not even peculiarly "criminal," for policemen, prison guards, college professors, students, and almost any other category of persons evaluate behavior in terms of in-group loyalties. Whyte noted the mutual obligations binding corner boys together and concluded that status depends upon the extent to which a boy lives up to his obligations, a form of "solidness."[54] More recently, Miller identified "toughness," "smartness," and "autonomy" among the "focal concerns" of lower class adolescent delinquent boys; these also characterize prisoners who are oriented to the thief subculture.[55] Wheeler found that half of the custody staff and sixty percent of the treatment staff in one prison approved the conduct of a hypothetical inmate who refused to name an inmate with whom he had been engaged in a knife fight.[56]

Imprisonment is one of the recurring problems with which thieves must cope. It is almost certain that a thief will be arrested from time to time, and the subculture provides members with patterns to be used in order to help solve this problem. Norms which apply to the prison situation, and information on how to undergo the prison experience—how to do time "standing on your head"—with the least suffering and in a minimum amount of time are provided. Of course, the subculture itself is both nurtured and diffused in the different jails and prisons of the country.

As Riemer's discussion of "politicians" and "shots" indicates, there also exists in prisons a subculture which is by definition a set of patterns that flourishes in the environment of incarceration. This is the "convict subcul-

---

[54] William Foote Whyte, "Corner Boys: A Study of Clique Behavior," *American Journal of Sociology*, 46:647–663, March, 1941.

[55] Walter B. Miller, "Lower Class Culture as a Generating Milieu of Gang Delinquency," *Journal of Social Issues*, 14:5–19, 1958.

[56] Stanton Wheeler, "Role Conflict in Correctional Communities," Chapter 6 in Cressey, *op. cit.*, p. 235.

ture" which can be found wherever men are confined, whether it be in city jails, state and federal prisons, army stockades, prisoner of war camps, concentration camps, or even mental hospitals. Such organizations are characterized by deprivations and limitations on freedom, and in them available wealth must be competed for by men supposedly on an equal footing. It is in connection with the *maintenance* (but not necessarily with the *origin*) of this subculture that it is appropriate to stress the notion that a minimum of outside status criteria are carried into the situation. Ideally, as we indicated above, all status is to be achieved by means made available in the prison, through the displayed ability to manipulate the environment, win special privileges in a certain manner, and assert influence over others. The central value of the subculture is utilitarianism, and the most manipulative and most utilitarian individuals win the available wealth and such positions of influence as might exist.

It is not correct to conclude, however, that even these behavior patterns are a consequence of the environment of any particular prison. In the first place, such utilitarian and manipulative behavior probably is characteristic of the "hard core" lower class in the United States, and most prisoners come from this class. After discussing the importance of toughness, smartness, excitement and fate in this group, Miller makes the following significant observation:

In lower class culture a close conceptual connection is made between "authority" and "nurturance." To be restrictively or firmly controlled is to be cared for. Thus the overtly negative evaluation of superordinate authority frequently extends as well to nurturance, care, or protection. The desire for personal independence is often expressed in terms such as "I don't need *nobody* to take care of me. I can take care of myself!" Actual patterns of behavior, however, reveal a marked discrepancy between expressed sentiments and what is covertly valued. Many lower class people appear to seek out highly restrictive social environments wherein stringent external controls are maintained over their behavior. Such institutions as the armed forces, the mental hospital, the disciplinary school, the prison or correctional institution, provide environments which incorporate a strict and detailed set of rules defining and limiting behavior, and enforced by an authority system which controls and applies coercive sanctions for deviance from these rules. While under the jurisdiction of such systems, the lower class person generally expresses to his peers continual resentment of the coercive, unjust, and arbitrary exercise of authority. Having been released, or having escaped from these milieux, however, he will often act in such a way as to insure recommitment, or choose recommitment voluntarily after a temporary period of "freedom."[57]

[57] *Op. cit.*, p. 12–13.

In the second place, the "hard core" members of this subculture as it exists in American prisons for adults are likely to be inmates who have a long record of confinement in institutions for juveniles. As indicated below McCleery observed that, in a period of transition, reform-school graduates all but took over inmate society in one prison. These boys called themselves a "syndicate" and engaged in a concentrated campaign of argument and intimidation directed toward capturing the inmate council and the inmate craft shop which had been placed under council management. "The move of the syndicate to take over the craft shop involved elements of simple exploitation, the grasp for a status symbol, and an aspect of economic reform."[58] Persons with long histories of institutionalization, it is important to note, might have had little contact with the thief subculture. The thief subculture does not flourish in institutions for juveniles, and graduates of such institutions have not necessarily had extensive criminal experience on the outside. However, some form of the convict subculture does exist in institutions for juveniles, though not to the extent characterizing prisons for felons. Some of the newcomers to a prison for adults are, in short, persons who have been oriented to the convict subculture, who have found the utilitarian nature of this subculture acceptable, and who have had little contact with the thief subculture. This makes a difference in their behavior.

A final category of inmates are oriented to "legitimate" subcultures. This category includes men who are not members of the thief subculture upon entering prison and who reject both the thief subculture and the convict subculture while in prison. These men present few problems to prison administrators. They make up a large percentage of the population of any prison, but they isolate themselves—or are isolated—from the thief and convict subcultures. Clemmer referred to these men as "ungrouped," and his statistics, reported above, have often been interpreted as meaning that the prison contains many men not oriented to "inmate culture" or "prison culture"—in our terms, not oriented to either the thief subculture or the convict subculture. This is not necessarily the case. There may be sociometric isolates among the thief-oriented prisoners, the convict-oriented prisoners, and the legitimately oriented prisoners. Whether or not men in this category participate in cliques, athletic teams, or religious study and hobby groups, they are oriented to the problem of achieving goals through means which are legitimate outside prisons.

There are great differences in the prison behavior of men oriented to one or the other of the three types of subculture. The hard core member of

[58] McCleery, "The Governmental Process and Informal Social Control," op. cit., p. 179.

the convict subculture finds his reference groups inside the institutions and, as indicated, he seeks status through means available in the prison environment. But it is important for the understanding of inmate conduct to note that the hard core member of the thief subculture seeks status in the broader criminal world of which prison is only a part. His reference groups include people both inside and outside prison, but he is committed to criminal life, not prison life. From his point of view, it is adherence to a widespread criminal code that wins him high status, not adherence to a narrow convict code. Convicts might assign him high status because they admire him as a thief, or because a good thief makes a good convict, but the thief does not play the convicts' game. Similarly, a man oriented to a legitimate subculture is by definition committed to the values of neither thieves nor convicts.

On the other hand, within any given prison, the men oriented to the convict subculture are the inmates that seek positions of power, influence, and sources of information, whether these men are called "shots," "politicians," "merchants," "hoods," "toughs," "gorillas," or something else. A job as secretary to the Captain or Warden, for example, gives an aspiring prisoner information and consequent power, and enables him to influence the assignment or regulation of other inmates. In the same way, a job which allows the incumbent to participate in a racket, such as clerk in the kitchen storeroom where he can steal and sell food, is highly desirable to a man oriented to the convict subculture. With a steady income of cigarettes, ordinarily the prisoners' medium of exchange, he may assert a great deal of influence and purchase those things which are symbols of status among persons oriented to the convict subculture. Even if there is no well-developed medium of exchange, he can barter goods acquired in his position for equally-desirable goods possessed by other convicts. These include information and such things as specially-starched, pressed, and tailored prison clothing, fancy belts, belt buckles or billfolds, special shoes, or any other type of dress which will set him apart and will indicate that he has both the influence to get the goods and the influence necessary to keeping and displaying them despite prison rules which outlaw doing so.

Since prisoners oriented either to a legitimate subculture or to a thief subculture are not seeking high status within any given prison, they do not look for the kinds of positions considered so desirable by the members of the convict subculture. Those oriented to legitimate subcultures take prison as it comes and seek status through channels provided for that purpose by prison administrators—running for election to the inmate council, to the editorship of the institutional newspaper, etc.—and by, generally, conforming to what they think administrators expect of "good prisoners."

Long before the thief has come to prison, his subculture has defined proper prison conduct as behavior rationally calculated to "do time" in the easiest possible way. This means that he wants a prison life containing the best possible combination of a maximum amount of leisure time and a maximum number of privileges. Accordingly, the privileges sought by the thief are different from the privileges sought by the man oriented to prison itself. The thief wants things that will make prison life a little easier— extra food, a maximum amount of recreation time, a good radio, a little peace. One thief serving his third sentence for armed robbery was a dish washer in the officers' dining room. He liked the eating privileges, but he never sold food. Despite his "low status" job, he was highly respected by other thieves, who described him as "right," and "solid." Members of the convict subculture, like the thieves, seek privileges. There is a difference, however, for the convict seeks privileges which he believes will enhance his position in the inmate hierarchy. He also wants to do easy time but, as compared with the thief, desirable privileges are more likely to involve freedom to amplify one's store, such as stealing rights in the kitchen, and freedom of movement around the prison. Obtaining an easy job is managed because it is easy and therefore desirable, but it also is managed for the purpose of displaying the fact that it can be obtained.

In the routine prison setting, the two deviant subcultures exist in a balanced relationship. It is this total setting which has been observed as "inmate culture." There is some conflict because of the great disparity in some of the values of thieves and convicts, but the two subcultures share other values. The thief is committed to keeping his hands off other people's activities, and the convict, being utilitarian, is likely to know that it is better in the long run to avoid conflict with thieves and confine one's exploitations to the "do rights" and to the members of his own subculture. Of course, the thief must deal with the convict from time to time, and when he does so he adjusts to the reality of the fact that he is imprisoned. Choosing to follow prison definitions usually means paying for some service in cigarettes or in a returned service; this is the cost of doing easy time. Some thieves adapt in a more general way to the ways of convicts and assimilate the prisonized person's concern for making out in the institution. On an ideal-type level, however, thieves do not sanction exploitation of other inmates, and they simply ignore the "do rights," who are oriented to legitimate subcultures. Nevertheless, their subculture as it operates in prison has exploitative effects.[59]

Numerous persons have documented the fact that "right guys," many of

[59] See Donald R. Cressey, "Foreword," to Clemmer, op. cit., pp. vii–x.

whom can be identified as leaders of the thieves, not of the convicts, exercise the greatest influence over the total prison population. The influence is the long run kind stemming from the ability to influence notions of what is right and proper, what McCleery calls the formulation and communication of definitions.[60] The thief, after all, has the respect of many inmates who are not themselves thieves. The right guy carries a set of attitudes, values and norms that have a great deal of consistency and clarity. He acts, forms opinions, and evaluates events in the prison according to them, and over a long period of time he in this way determines basic behavior patterns in the institution. In what the thief thinks of as "small matters," however—getting job transfers, enforcing payment of gambling debts, making cell assignments—members of the convict subculture run things.

It is difficult to assess the direct lines of influence the two deviant subcultures have over those inmates who are not members of either subculture when they enter a prison. It is true that if a new inmate does not have definitions to apply to the new prison situation, one or the other of the deviant subcultures is likely to supply them in the prisonization process. On the one hand, the convict subculture is much more apparent than the thief subculture; its roles are readily visible to any new arrival, and its definitions are readily available to one who wants to "get along" and "make it" in a prison. Moreover, the inmate leaders oriented to the convict subculture are anxious to get new followers who will recognize the existing status hierarchy in the prison. Thieves, on the other hand, tend to be snobs. Their status in prison is determined in part by outside criteria, as well as by prison conduct, and it is therefore difficult for a prisoner, acting as a prisoner, to achieve these criteria. At a minimum, the newcomer can fall under the influence of the thief subculture only if he has intimate association over a period of time with some of its members who are able and willing to impart some of its subtle behavior patterns to him.

It seems a worthy hypothesis that thieves, convicts and "do rights" all bring certain values and behavior patterns to prison with them, and that total "inmate culture" represents an adjustment or accommodation of these three systems within the official administrative system of deprivation and control. It is significant in this connection that Wheeler has not found in Norwegian prisons the normative order and cohesive bonds among inmates that characterize many American prisons. He observes that his data suggest "that the current functional interpretations of the inmate system in American institutions are not adequate," and that "general features of Norwegian society are imported into the prison and operate largely to off-

[60] "The Governmental Process and Informal Social Control," *op. cit.*, p. 154.

set any tendencies toward the formation of a solidary inmate group. . . ."[61] Similarly, Ward and Kassebaum noted that the thief subculture was not apparent in a prison for women, probably because the behavioral rules contained in it are directed to features of behavior that are not relevant to women; the inmate code in this prison referred principally to participation in homosexuality.[62]

REFORMATION IN THE PRISON COMMUNITY. Generally, the organization of prison life is conducive to the retention and development of criminal attitudes, rather than to reformation. As a result of the relationships between prisoners and authorities, some long-term inmates become isolated from intimate contacts with anti-criminal behavior patterns and learn that "success" is to be achieved by deception, manipulation, and crime.

The "anti-reform" emphasis in prison culture. Although inmates learn many criminal techniques from each other and often form alliances for the perpetration of crimes after release, retention of criminal attitudes in prison do not result primarily from mere contamination and individual tutelage of one prisoner by another. Instead, they occur in response to participation in a community which has collectively developed traditions favorable to crime and to the repression of any tendency toward reformation. An inmate of the United States Penitentiary at Atlanta made the following statement:

I know that prisons are wrong because it is self-manifest that were society to attempt to devise a process for the development of the criminal personality; were society to attempt to perfect curricula for the dissemination of anti-social attitudes; were society to attempt to create institutions for the mass production of criminals; then no finer nor no more effective agency for the attainment of these aims could have been evolved than the prison.

This is no attempt to rejuvenate the corny old chestnut about older prisoners teaching the younger ones techniques toward the more effectual penetration of strong-boxes and recipes for outwitting the gendarmerie. Such phenomena serve only for the theses of the more junior penologists and viewers-with-alarm in the ranks of the earnestly public-spirited but sadly misinformed committees for the study and improvement of this and that. . . .

It is not the possibility of an non-legitimate vocational training that

[61] Stanton Wheeler, "Inmate Culture in Prisons," mimeographed report of the Laboratory of Social Relations, Harvard University, 1962, pp. 18, 20, 21. See also Thomas Mathiesen, The Defences of the Weak: A Sociological Study of a Norwegian Correctional Institution (London: Tavistock, 1965), pp. 136–142.

[62] David A. Ward and Gene G. Kassebaum, "Homosexuality: A Mode of Adaptation in a Prison for Women," Social Problems, 12:159–177, Fall, 1964.

makes the prison a man-perverting agency of great power and efficiency. It is the doleful fact that some nebulous something happens to a man between the time that he checks into and checks out of a prison; some inculcation of the essence of bitterness and social antagonism, an inculcation that is not merely a veneering process but a deep inoculation. And this "something" spawns a man who is invariably less desirable as a citizen than he was at the time he stood before the bar of justice.[63]

The "nebulous something" which happens to the inmate is his participation in a group which has developed an *esprit de corps*, with crime and violation of official prison rules as the common interest. The net effect of extensive participation in a group with such an *esprit de corps* is likely to be a definition of one's self as an "elite," as one who has few, if any, obligations to "outsiders" who conform to legal norms. This conception of self is both stimulated and reinforced not only by inmates but also by the attitudes of prison officials. The "social distance" between inmates as a class and officials as a class lengthens the social distance between inmates and law-abiding persons generally.[64] Weinberg has described the attitudes of prison officials which are conducive to this increased social distance.[65]

We have already noted, however, that there are variations in the extent to which inmates participate in the anti-reform and essentially pro-criminal *esprit de corps* of a prison. Wheeler has shown that inmate attitudes and loyalties most closely resemble those of inmate elites when the inmate in question occupies a position which makes the elite deviant subcultures most visible to him.[66] Similarly, our earlier discussion of the prison community in terms of the "thief subculture" the "convict subculture" and the "legitimate subculture" has implications for predicting the behavior of prisoners when they are released. Most inmates are under the influence of *both* the thief subculture and the convict subculture. Without realizing it, inmates who have served long prison terms are likely to move toward the middle, toward a compromise or balance between the directives coming from the two sources. A member of the convict subculture may come to see that thieves are the real men with the prestige; a member of the thief subculture or even a "do right" may lose his ability to sustain his status needs by outside criteria. The fact that time has a blending effect on the

[63] Richard Jordan, "Traumatic Trivia," *The Atlantian*, 3:26–27 ff., July–August, 1941. Reprinted by permission of the publisher.

[64] See Donald Rasmussen, "Prisoner Opinions About Parole," *American Sociological Review*, 5:592–594, August, 1940; and Mathiesen, *op. cit.*, pp. 11–16.

[65] S. Kirson Weinberg, "Aspects of the Prison's Social Structure," *American Journal of Sociology*, 47:717–726, March, 1942.

[66] "Role Conflict in Correctional Communities," *op. cit.*, pp. 250–256. See also Jon E. Simpson, Thomas G. Eynon, and Walter C. Reckless, "Institutionalization as Perceived by the Juvenile Offender," *Sociology and Social Research*, 48:13–23, October, 1963.

participants in the two deviant subcultures suggests that the subcultures themselves tend to blend together in some prisons. The thief subculture scarcely exists in some institutions for juveniles. It is probable also that in army stockades and in concentration camps this subculture is almost non-existent. In places of short-term confinement, such as city and county jails, the convict subculture is dominant, for the thief subculture involves status distinctions that are not readily observable in a short period of confinement. At the other extreme, in prisons where only prisoners with long sentences are confined, the distinctions between the two subcultures are likely to be blurred. Probably the two subcultures exist in their purest forms in institutions holding inmates in their twenties, with varying sentences for a variety of criminal offenses. Such institutions, of course, are the "typical" prisons of the United States.

Despite these differences, in any prison the men oriented to legitimate subcultures should have a low recidivism rate, while the highest recidivism rate should be found among participants in the convict subculture. The hard core members of this subculture are being trained in manipulation, duplicity and exploitation, they are not sure they can make it on the outside, and even when they are on the outside they continue to use convicts as a reference group. This sometimes means that there will be a wild spree of crime and dissipation which takes the members of the convict subculture directly back to the prison. Members of the thief subculture, to whom prison life represents a pitfall in outside life, also should have a high recidivism rate. However, the thief sometimes "reforms" and tries to succeed in some life within the law. Such behavior, contrary to popular notions, is quite acceptable to other members of the thief subculture, so long as the new job and position are not "anti-criminal" and do not involve regular, routine, "slave labor." Suckers work, but a man who, like a thief, "skims it off the top" is not a sucker. At any rate, the fact that convicts, to a greater extent than thieves, tend to evaluate things from the perspective of the prison and to look upon discharge as a short vacation from prison life suggests that their recidivism rate should be higher than that of thieves.

No study of the recidivism rates of "thieves," "convicts" and "do rights" has been made. However, a significant analysis has been made of the recidivism rates, and of the tendencies for these rates to increase or decrease with increasing length of prison terms, for each of four inmate types identified by Schrag.[67] This typology classifies inmates of close-custody

[67] Donald L. Garrity, The Effects of Length of Incarceration Upon Parole Adjustment and Estimation of Optimum Sentence: Washington State Correctional Institutions (Unpublished Ph.D. thesis, University of Washington, 1956); and Donald L. Garrity, "The Prison as a Rehabilitation Agency," Chapter 9 in Cressey, The Prison, op. cit., pp. 358–380.

prisons as prosocial, antisocial, pseudosocial and asocial.[68] These types correspond closely to the argot labels used for various types of inmates by prisoners themselves. Thus, prosocial inmates are those who fall within the "Square John," "do right," or "hoosier" configurations; antisocial inmates are the "right guys" and "real men"; pseudosocial prisoners are the "con politicians," "merchants," and "peddlers"; and asocial prisoners are the "outlaws," "hoods," "gorillas," and "ballbusters"; also in the asocial category are disturbed inmates, usually called "dings" or "rapos."[69] Unfortunately, this typology does not clearly make the distinction between the thief subculture and the convict subculture, probably because of the blending process noted above. Schrag's "right guys" (antisocial offenders), thus, might include both men who perceive role requirements in terms of the norms of the convict subculture, and men who perceive those requirements in terms of the norms of the thief subculture. Similarly, neither his "con politician" (pseudosocial offender) nor his "outlaw" (asocial offender) seem to be ideal-type members of the convict subculture. Schrag's "Square Johns" (prosocial offenders) closely resemble the "legitimate subcultures" category.

Garrity found that a group of "Square Johns" had a low parole violation rate and that this rate remained low no matter how much time was served. "Right guys" had a high violation rate that decreased markedly as time in prison increased. In Garrity's words, this was because "continued incarceration [served] to sever his connections with the criminal subculture and thus to increase the probability of successful parole."[70] The rates for the "outlaw" were very high and remained high as time in prison increased. The rates of the "con politician" were low if the sentences were rather short but increased systematically with time served.

Noting that the origins of the thief subculture and the convict subcul-

---

[68] Clarence C. Schrag, *Social Types in a Prison Community* (Unpublished M.A. thesis, University of Washington, 1944); Clarence C. Schrag, "Leadership Among Prison Inmates," op. cit., Clarence S. Schrag, "Some Foundations for a Theory of Correction," Chapter 8 in Cressey, op. cit., pp. 346–356; and Clarence C. Schrag, "A Preliminary Criminal Typology," *Pacific Sociological Review*, 4:11–16, Spring, 1961. See also Glaser, op. cit., pp. 575–583.

[69] The argot terms for types of prisoners vary from institution to institution. The terms used above do not include all the inmate types identified by prisoners. For example, terms such as "wolf," "punk," and "fag" refer to roles in homosexuality. A notation of types in terms of leisure-time pursuits in the prison brings forth a still different set of types, as indicated by Morris G. Caldwell, "Group Dynamics in the Prison Community," *Journal of Criminal Law, Criminology and Police Science*, 46:648–657, January, 1956. See also Terence Morris, Pauline Morris, and Barbara Biely," It's the Prisoners Who Run This Prison," *Prison Service Journal* (England), 1:3–11, January, 1961.

[70] Op. cit., p. 377.

ture are both external to a prison should change our expectations regarding the possible reformative effect of that prison. The recidivism rates of neither thieves, convicts, nor "do rights" are likely to be significantly affected by incarceration in any particular traditional prison. This is not to say, of course, that the *entire system* of imprisonment, in which both the thief subculture and the convict subculture are nurtured, does not contribute significantly to recidivism. In reference to the ordinary custodially-oriented prison the thief says he can do his time "standing on his head," and it appears that he *is* able to do the time "standing on his head"—except for long-termers, imprisonment has little effect on the thief one way or the other. Similarly, the routine of any particular custodial prison is not likely to have significant reformative effects on members of the convict subculture—they return to prison because, in effect, they have found a home there. And the men oriented to legitimate subcultures maintain low recidivism rates even if they never experience imprisonment.

*Prison riots.* Occasionally the relationships between the inmate body, inmate elites, and the officials are dramatized in a prison riot. During a riot, the loyalty of inmates to inmates and to criminals, the exploitation of prisoners by their leaders, the antagonistic attitudes of guards and officials toward inmates, and the alliances between elites and officials all become manifest. Perhaps the greatest significance of the wave of prison riots which swept the United States in 1952–1953 was the awakening of the public to the fact that prison officials have difficult administrative problems. And in a general sense probably the greatest tragedy of the riots was the fact that inmates were publicly viewed as downtrodden prison reformers.[71]

In the spring of 1952, 69 prisoners at the Trenton, New Jersey, State Prison seized four guards as hostages, barricaded themselves in the prison print shop, and stated that they would not surrender until a committee of citizens investigated the conditions of the prison. Within a week, 232 prisoners at the New Jersey Prison Farm in Rahway barricaded themselves in a dormitory with nine hostages and demanded changes in prison conditions; they smashed all the dormitory windows, tore up the plumbing and heating systems, and destroyed their own lockers. A few days later 176 inmates at the Southern Michigan Prison in Jackson seized eleven hostages, barricaded themselves in a cell block, and wrecked whatever was wreckable;

[71] For analyses of riots which take essentially this position, see American Prison Association, Committee on Riots, *Prison Riots and Disturbances* (New York: Author, 1953), *The Prison Journal*, Volume 33, April, 1953 and Volume 34, April, 1954 (both issues are devoted exclusively to analyses of riots); "U.S. Prisons: How Well Do They Protect Us?" *Platform* (published by the Club Bureau of *Newsweek* Magazine), September, 1952; "Why Convicts Riot," *U.S. News and World Report*, December 19, 1952, pp. 19–21.

prisoners in other sections of the prison armed themselves with make-shift weapons, wrecked the dining hall, set fire to the laundry, tore up the chapel, library, and gymnasium, and broke thousands of windows.[72] Within a few months similar riots occurred in Idaho, Illinois, Kentucky, Louisiana, Massachusetts, New Mexico, North Carolina, Ohio, and Utah. In addition, potentially serious disturbances were quelled in one prison in California, one in Oregon, and two in federal institutions.[73]

None of the riots involved attempts at mass escape and each of them seemed to be a semi-planned "strike" or "demonstration" designed to call public attention to the conditions of prison life. The pattern was the same in all prisons: hostages were seized, the prisoners barricaded themselves, all destructible property in reach was destroyed, and demands, followed by "bargaining," with prison officials or political officials of the state were issued. The formal demands were for better food, better medical care, better recreational facilities, segregation of sex offenders, less rigid disciplinary practices, and more liberal parole practices. But some prison officials and some prisoners have stated that the demands and the bargaining process were only "second thoughts" of the prisoners. For example, one analysis attributes riots to those types of inmates who have earlier demonstrated that they can and will "keep the peace" if only officials will grant them special favors, such as key jobs that bestow access to goods in short supply and an opportunity to exploit fellow-inmates. "Most of the leaders of prison disturbances, up to the time they turned their violence against their keepers, had engaged in repeated offenses against other inmates."[74] The elites might have presented themselves as defenders of institutional policies against "bad inmates"; or they might have pointed out that weakening of their alliance with officials will mean trouble, for the "bad inmates" might rebel; or they simply might have stressed that the institution's best interest lies in furthering the personal objectives of the elites, the "good inmates." "Peace," then, depends upon giving some inmates special privileges and allowing them to exploit other inmates. But should these elites become dissatisfied with the officials' concessions, they can withdraw their pretense of support and define themselves as champions of the "mistreated prisoners." This is the usual role of elites during riots.

Another insightful analysis indicates that a prison becomes a "powder

[72] For a description of this riot, see John Bartlow Martin, *Break Down the Walls* (New York: Ballantine Books, 1954).

[73] Frank T. Flynn, "Behind the Prison Riots," *The Social Service Review*, 27:73-86, March, 1953.

[74] Richard R. Korn and Lloyd W. McCorkle, *Criminology and Penology* (New York: Holt, 1959), p. 529. See also their discussion on p. 480.

keg" which can be touched off by some precipitating incident only when
there is a shift in the semi-official government exercised by the inmates.[75]
In the New Jersey State Prison, gradual transfer of power from the rulers
to the ruled had reached the point where job assignments, cell assignments, recreational activities, and the granting of special privileges all were
in the hands of inmate elites. In the middle of the 1940's the officials
attempted to reverse the tendency of the staff to withdraw to the institutional walls, and it was "this turning point in the administration of the
prison which apparently marks the beginning of the tension and unrest
that finally flowered in the insurrections of 1952."[76] It is concluded that
efforts to "tighten up" prisons undermines control by "real men" or "right
guys" (who stress inmate solidarity but also are rewarded with special
privileges because they emphasize the importance of "peace" with officials), and transfers leadership to more aggressive and violent "toughs,"
"gorillas," and "ballbusters," who seem intent on embarrassing the officials
and, generally, giving the guards a hard time, despite the ultimate hope-
lessness of their position. "The stabilizing elements in the prison are reduced in effectiveness, tensions mount, and new, aggressive leadership fans
the fire of discontent."[77]

A third insightful analysis of the riots also attributes them to the
changed social structure of prisons in the twenty years following 1930.[78]
Much of the power wielded informally by "right guys" and other inmate
leaders during the 1930's were removed by "prison reforms" designed to
make prisons more humane and more rehabilitative, but the services which
the leaders provided for the inmates, and the services which the administrators provided the leaders, were not present in the new organization. The
riots, then, were counter-revolutions rather than revolutions, and they took
the form of strikes for return of inmate "rights" which had been lost.
Further, when prison administrators appear to be making little effort to
implement the progressive measures to which they give public allegiance,
a basis for widespread inmate dissatisfaction is provided.[79] Both Ohlin and
McCleery have emphasized that the "old guard" among the officials also

[75] Sykes, The Society of Captives, op. cit., pp. 109–129.

[76] Ibid., p. 123.

[77] Ibid., p. 129. See also Walter B. Jones, Jr., "How We Broke the Montana Prison
Riot," Saturday Evening Post, 231:26–27 ff., June 13, 1959.

[78] Maurice Floch and Frank E. Hartung, "A Social Psychological Analysis of Prison
Riots: An Hypothesis," Journal of Criminal Law and Criminology, 47:51–57, May–
June, 1956.

[79] Lloyd E. Ohlin, Sociology and the Field of Corrections (New York: Russell Sage
Foundation, 1956), p. 24. See also Clarence Schrag, "The Sociology of Prison Riots,"
Proceedings of the American Correctional Association, 1960, pp. 138–145.

indirectly participated in the counterattacks, in an effort to regain power and privileges lost to the reformers.[80]

**ATTEMPTS TO MODIFY THE PRISON CULTURE.** If the prison is to be efficient as an institution for reformation, the *esprit de corps* or public opinion among prisoners must be changed. No amount of individual therapy, vocational education, or coercion will do this. In addition, there is little reason to think that the prisoners themselves will develop self-government or other community organization favorable to reformation. The leaders of the criminal population look upon themselves as enemies of society, and on society as an enemy of prisoners. They are not to be induced in ordinary prison circumstances to shift their attitudes. Similarly, so long as the prison is expected to perform its retributive and deterrence functions, it is doubtful that the prison community can be greatly modified to bridge the chasm separating the social worlds of the "insiders" and the "outsiders."[81] The organization of prisoners is in part a reaction to the repressive aspects of the prison's administrative organization, and it therefore seems to be modifiable only slightly or not at all as long as the administrative organization efficiently performs the duties society assigns to it.

In the United States, the most impressive attempts to change prisoner organization by modifying the administrative organization have been made in minimum-security institutions. One of the earliest attempts was made by Howard B. Gill, some years before study of the prison community became popular, at the Norfolk Prison Colony in Massachusetts.[82] The Norfolk program differed from honor systems and self-government systems in that the staff was made a part of the community. Twenty-five inmates were assigned to each "house officer" or case worker. These officers did not wear uniforms, and their primary duty was to maintain a friendly, co-operative, and sympathetic relationship with the inmates. "Watch officers," whose duties were custodial, were used, but almost all of them remained on, or outside, the wall. They were not considered part of the

[80] *Ibid.*, p. 17. See also Lloyd E. Ohlin, "New Trends in Research in the Organization of Correctional Agencies," *Proceedings of the American Correctional Association,* 1955, pp. 256–266. Richard H. McCleery, *Policy Change in Prison Management* (East Lansing: Michigan State University Governmental Research Bureau, 1957), pp. 28–34. See also David Mechanic, "The Power to Resist Change Among Low-Ranking Personnel," *Personnel Administration,* 26:5–11, July, 1963.

[81] *Cf.* N. A. Polansky, "The Prison as an Autocracy," *Journal of Criminal Law and Criminology,* 33:16–22, May–June, 1942.

[82] See Howard B. Gill, "The Norfolk State Prison Colony of Massachusetts," *Journal of Criminal Law and Criminology,* 22:389–395, September–October, 1937; W. H. Commons, T. Yahkub, E. Powers, and C. R. Doering, *A Report on the Development of Penological Treatment at Norfolk Prison Colony in Massachusetts* (New York: Bureau of Social Hygiene, 1940), Barnes and Teeters, *op. cit.,* pp. 695–698.

community. From the standpoint of conventional prison organization, the case workers became a part of the informal prison social life, while the watch officers represented a modified type of repressive formal organization. The over-all plan, thus, was to give inmates experience in non-criminal social activities and, especially, to modify inmates' attitudes in the direction of non-criminality by placing them in intimate, informal contact with sympathetic men possessing a strong bias against criminality. Today it would be considered a large-scale group-therapy program which handled "natural groups," included all inmates, and operated on principles similar to those used by Alcoholics Anonymous. The Norfolk program was subjected to severe and caustic criticism almost from its beginning, largely because it did not perform the retributive and deterrence functions which the taxpayers demanded. In 1934 Superintendent Gill was discharged and a more conventional type of prison organization was established.

Sykes and Messinger, among others, have suggested that the inmate code and status system arise as responses to the deprivations imposed on prisoners.[83] The implication is that the inmate system of organization would decline in importance if the pains of imprisonment were reduced and that, therefore, the degree of deprivation ought to be reduced if reformation is a goal. Currently, this system for attempting to modify the traditional inmate structure is one of the principal features of prison camps, prison honor farms, institutions for juveniles, and other minimum-security institutions.[84] The Federal Bureau of Prisons maintains a small minimum-security type institution at Seagoville, Texas, and in this institution carefully selected inmates are allowed to participate in a social life which approaches that of a non-penal community. At the California Institution for Men the inmates are given similar opportunities.[85] Officers are responsible for the enforcement of the very relaxed system of discipline, but they also function as friends and counselors. Inmates wear civilian clothing and there is a definite endeavor to keep "prison tradition" at a minimum. The relatively relaxed discipline of such institutions, as well as the effort to understand rather than blame the inmates, probably means that there is a relatively weak "anti-reform" organization among the inmates. However, it

[83] *Op. cit.*

[84] See Oscar Grusky, "Some Factors Promoting Cooperative Behavior Among Inmate Leaders," *American Journal of Correction,* 21:8–9 ff., March, 1959; Oscar Grusky, "Organizational Goals and the Behavior of Informal Leaders," *American Journal of Sociology,* 65:59–67, July, 1959; Howard W. Polsky, *Cottage Six* (New York: Russell Sage Foundation, 1962); and Mayer N. Zald, "The Correctional Institution for Juvenile Offenders: An Analysis of Organizational 'Character'," *Social Problems,* 8:57–67, Summer, 1960.

[85] For a description of the development of the program at this institution, see Kenyon J. Scudder, *Prisoners are People* (New York: Doubleday, 1952).

is possible that such institutions merely select a disproportionate number of inmates oriented to legitimate values, and do not select many prisoners who bring with them to the prison an orientation to either the thief subculture or the convict subculture. As we indicated earlier, it is not at all certain that the inmate code, and the behavior based on it, arises solely because of the deprivations of prison life. To some degree, the values of inmates are carried into the prison from the outside. Accordingly, reducing the pains of imprisonment will not alone result in modification of the values of the prisoners. As Wheeler has said:

While little is known about the relationship between roles played inside and outside the prison, there is a strong suggestion that the visible inmates are those who have had most experience in exploitative and manipulative roles prior to imprisonment—those most schooled in techniques of aggression and deceit. The combination of greater motivation and more well-developed skills among the more criminalistic inmates suggests the difficulties facing administrative attempts to decrease their visibility and power.[86]

McCleery's reports on changes in Oahu prison indicate that the orientation of inmates can to some degree be shifted by opening new channels of communication between staff and inmates.[87] By means of these channels, Oahu staff members presented their behavior patterns to inmates, and at the same time the "anti-reform" and "anti-administration" behavior patterns ordinarily circulating among prisoners were choked off. Because it is almost literally true among inmates that "knowledge is power," a shift in the distribution of knowledge about appropriate ways of behaving in the prison changed the distribution of power. This kind of program for changing communication patterns and, thus, definitions of what behavior is appropriate, is involved when minimum-security institutions are put into operation. While merely reducing the pains of imprisonment does not change the patterns of behavior brought in from the outside, changing the system of communication should produce some of the desired effects. This kind of program has not been fully explored by prison managers, however. To a degree, it has been used at Highfields, a New Jersey institution housing twenty boys, where the entire program is oriented toward piercing the boys' strong defenses against rehabilitation.[88]

Korn and McCorkle have outlined a program which they believe would

[86] "Role Conflict in Correctional Communities," op. cit., p. 257.

[87] See his "The Governmental Process and Informal Social Control," op. cit.; "Communication Patterns as Bases of Systems of Authority," op. cit.; and Policy Change in Prison Management, op. cit.

[88] McCorkle, Elias, and Bixby, op. cit. See also H. Ashley Weeks, Youthful Offenders at Highfields (Ann Arbor: University of Michigan Press, 1958).

minimize the opportunities for deception, manipulation, exploitation, and dishonesty among inmates in maximum-security prisons and would, therefore, be rehabilitative.[89] An ideal-type rehabilitation program for nondisturbed "adaptive" prisoners would begin and end in a struggle for control. An inmate who early in the program asked, in effect, "Can I dominate you?" would learn that he cannot deceive the officials involved. If he then proceeded to overt rebellion and asked "Can anybody stop me?" he would find the answer to be "Yes," and he would be placed in segregation. Any heroic suffering ("You can't break me") and despair ("Doesn't anybody give a damn?") in which he engaged would be countered by extreme caution and rigor in avoiding brutality. He would be given all institutional privileges except contact with other inmates, and clues to proper modes of conduct would not be given by officials. When self-doubt begins to emerge and the inmate begins to recognize that "This is getting me nowhere," his accessibility to treatment is considered to be at a high point. He then should be released from segregation suddenly and unexpectedly, so that he will return to the prison population asking himself "Can I make it?" The emergence of conflict with inmates who have not gone through similar experiences is to be taken as "the one indispensable symptom of change." If the inmate has become alienated from the core values of the inmate social system, then the system has become a great asset to change, rather than its greatest obstacle. The inmate elites would become a source of derogation or threat, rather than a source of security and status. Finally, when the inmate had negotiated the hazards and temptations of the probationary period he would be transferred to a minimum-custody institution reserved entirely for inmates in this last stage of rehabilitation.

This proposed program is more than a restatement of the old notion that the prisoner's "will" must be broken, although it supports the position of prison authorities whose primary concern is with rigid and secure control of the institution. To a large extent, the program is designed to offset the lack of adequately-trained and experienced officers who can exert positive influence on prisoners and still not be corrupted by them.[90] It recognizes that the ordinary prison situation permits inmates to maintain essentially the same kind of deviant attitudes they possessed when they arrived, and it attempts to take individual inmates out of this situation.

Nevertheless, it appears that at the base of the program is the doubtful assumption that mere negative action—the presentation of painful evidence that deviant behavior is undesirable—is sufficient for reformation. For

[89] Op. cit., pp. 540–552.
[90] Lloyd E. Ohlin, "New Trends in Research in the Organization of Correctional Agencies," op. cit., p. 261.

generations, the whole system of imprisonment has been based on this same assumption that criminals who are made to see the error of their ways will somehow become reformed. Consistently, for generations it has been assumed that the whole system of imprisonment need not involve systematic, positive, constructive help for criminals, and the whole system of imprisonment has not been a notable success at reformation.

If the words "criminal" and "prison" are substituted for Korn and Mc-Corkle's "prisoner" and "segregation" the case becomes clear. We commit criminals to prison in order to demonstrate to them that we can stop their criminal exploits, at least temporarily. Over the years, hundreds of criminals' autobiographies have testified to the fact that criminals have been engaged in heroic suffering and despair; yet these actions have not significantly mitigated the deprivations of the prison. Also, for years it has been maintained that criminals must be alienated from their criminal companions by means of imprisonment, but imprisonment has not necessarily done so.

It is possible that the prison frequently fails to reform because it does not give criminals positive help along the paths law-abiding groups would have them go. If reformation is to be achieved, relations in the pro-criminal culture must be discouraged, but relations in the culture of law-abiding groups also must be provided.[91] If this be true, it follows that Korn and McCorkle's system for segregating nonconformists within the prison also would frequently fail. On the other hand, if the prison's failure to reform the prisoner is due simply to the fact that it has not made the results of criminality unpleasant enough to the criminal, or to the fact that the prison in operation actually provides criminals with pro-criminal behavior patterns, then the reform program should have some success.

In a less than perfect society where confinement is used as a means of deterence and reform, it is possible that the prison is a "success" if only it does not make the offender worse. However, it does not seem overly optimistic to suppose that the prison can do more than simply stand still.[92]

## SUGGESTED READINGS

Anastassios, D. Mylonas, and Walter C. Reckless, "Prisoners' Attitudes toward The Law and Legal Institutions, *Journal of Criminal Law, Criminology and Police Science,* 54:479–484, November, 1963.

Cantine, Holley, and Dachine Rainer, Editors, *Prison Etiquette.* New York: Retort Press, 1950.

[91] See the discussion below, pp. 675–680.
[92] Sykes, "Men, Merchants, and Toughs," *op. cit.*

Clemmer, Donald, *The Prison Community*. Boston: Christopher, 1940. Reissued by Rinehart, 1958.

Cloward, Richard A., Donald R. Cressey, George H. Grosser, Richard McCleery, Lloyd E. Ohlin, and Gresham M. Sykes and Sheldon L. Messinger, *Theoretical Studies in Social Organization of the Prison*. New York: Russell Sage Foundation, 1960.

Cressey, Donald R., Editor, *The Prison: Studies in Institutional Organization and Change*. New York: Holt, Rinehart, and Winston, 1961.

Cressey, Donald R., "Prison Organizations," Chapter 24 in James G. March, Editor, *Handbook of Organizations*, New York: Rand McNally, 1965, pp. 1023–1070.

Cressey, Donald R., "Social Psychological Foundations for Using Criminals in the Rehabilitation of Criminals," *Journal of Research in Crime and Delinquency*, 2:49–59, July, 1965.

Eaton, Joseph W., *Stone Walls Do Not a Prison Make*. Springfield, Ill.: C. C. Thomas, 1962.

Garabedian, Peter G., "Social Roles and Processes of Socialization in the Prison Community," *Social Problems*, 11:139–152, Fall, 1963.

Gibbons, Don C., *Changing the Lawbreaker: The Treatment of Delinquents and Criminals*. New York: Prentice-Hall, 1965.

Glaser, Daniel, *The Effectiveness of a Prison and Parole System*. Indianapolis: Bobbs-Merrill, 1964.

Goffman, Erving, *Asylums: Essays on the Social Situation of Mental Patients and Other Inmates*. New York: Doubleday, 1961.

Grusky, Oscar, "Organizational Goals and the Behavior of Informal Leaders," *American Journal of Sociology*, 65:59–67, July, 1959.

Hassler, Alfred, *Diary of a Self-Made Convict*. Chicago: Henry Regnery, 1954.

Hayner, Norman S., and Ellis Ash, "The Prisoner Community as a Social Group," *American Sociological Review*, 4:362–369, June, 1939.

Hulin, Charles L., and Brendan A. Maher, "Changes in Attitudes Toward Law Concomitant with Imprisonment," *Journal of Criminal Law, Criminology and Police Science*, 50:245–248, September, 1959.

Irwin, John, and Donald R. Cressey, "Thieves, Convicts and the Inmate Culture," *Social Problems*, 10:142–155, Fall, 1962.

James, John, "The Application of the Small Group Concept to the Study of the Prison Community," *British Journal of Delinquency*, 5:269–280, April, 1955.

Johnson, Elmer A., "Sociology of Confinement: Assimilation and the Prison 'Rat,'" *Journal of Criminal Law, Criminology and Police Science*, 51:528–533, January, 1961.

Kassebaum, Gene G., David A. Ward, and Daniel M. Wilner, "Some Correlates of Staff Ideology in the Prison," *Journal of Research in Crime and Delinquency*, 1:96–109, July, 1964.

Mathiesen, Thomas, *The Defences of the Weak: A Sociological Study of a Norwegian Correctional Institution*. London: Tavistock, 1965.

McCleery, Richard, *Policy Change in Prison Management*. East Lansing, Michigan University Governmental Research Bureau, 1957.

McCorkle, Lloyd E., and Richard Korn, "Resocialization Within Walls," *Annals of the American Academy of Political and Social Science*, 293:88–98, May, 1954.

Morris, Terence, and Pauline Morris, *Pentonville: A Sociological Study of an English Prison*. London: Routledge and Kegan Paul, 1963.

Perrow, Charles, "The Analysis of Goals in Complex Organizations," *American Sociological Review*, 26:854–866, December, 1961.

Polsky, Howard W., *Cottage Six*. New York: Russell Sage Foundation, 1962.

Schrag, Clarence, "Leadership Among Prison Inmates," *American Sociological Review*, 19:37–42, February, 1954.

Schrag, Clarence, "A Preliminary Criminal Typology," *Pacific Sociological Review*, 4:11–16, Spring, 1961.

Seeman, Melvin, "Alienation and Social Learning in a Reformatory," *American Journal of Sociology*, 69:270–284, November, 1963.

Sykes, Gresham M., "Men, Merchants and Toughs: A Study of Reactions to Imprisonment," *Social Problems*, 4:130–138, October, 1956.

Sykes, Gresham M., *The Society of Captives: A Study of a Maximum Security Prison*. Princeton: Princeton University Press, 1958.

Vinter, Robert D., "Analysis of Treatment Organizations," *Social Work*, 8:3–15, July, 1963.

Volkman, Rita, and Donald R. Cressey, "Differential Association and the Rehabilitation of Drug Addicts," *American Journal of Sociology*, 69:129–142, September, 1963.

Ward, David A., and Gene G. Kassebaum, *Women's Prison: Sex and Social Structure*. Chicago: Aldine, 1965.

Zalba, Serapio, *Women Prisoners and Their Families*. Sacramento: Department of Social Welfare and Department of Corrections, 1964.

Zald, Mayer N., "Organizational Control Structure in Five Correctional Institutions," *American Journal of Sociology*, 68:335–345, November, 1962.

# 25. PRISON LABOR

As EARLY as the sixteenth century, several European countries established prison labor systems which were thought to be both punitive and profitable, just as the earlier galley labor had been so considered. Hence, the notion that work should be provided for prisoners is almost as old as the prison system itself. When institutions became places of punishment, rather than places of detention for persons awaiting trial, systems for occupying the time of prisoners also arose. This tendency was to some extent offset by the theory on which the early Pennsylvania prisons were based, namely that labor interfered with the meditation considered essential for penitence. Idleness as a prison régime is no longer defended on any ground and, on the contrary, the value of prison labor to inmates and to society is stressed. Despite this emphasis, idleness in prisons has become increasingly prevalent during the last fifty years.

LABOR AS PUNISHMENT.  When labor was introduced into prison it was regarded primarily as a means of punishment, although the possibilities for profits were not overlooked.[1] In some places, primarily in England, prison labor was almost exclusively punitive, consisting of such methods as the "shot drill"—carrying a cannon ball back and forth in a long hall—or treadmills or cranks. Sometimes treadmills and cranks were attached to pumps or other instruments so that the work was productive, but more frequently they were merely attached to a meter which measured the number of units of work performed. A certain number of units had to be performed for each meal, and additional units were assigned to unruly inmates. The laws required that the labor should be "hard and servile" or "publicly and disgracefully imposed." Although the idea that labor should be provided primarily for punishment was soon superseded by concern for

[1] George Rusche and Otto Kirchheimer, *Punishment and Social Structure* (New York: Columbia University Press, 1939), pp. 41–52.

utilization of labor in the production of wealth, the punitive element in labor is still retained in many institutions. Currently, the weight of opinion is that prison labor must be "useful" and must train inmates for post-release vocations, but the idea that monotonous, hard, unpleasant work is necessary, if the prison is to perform its retributive and deterrence functions, also is popular. Also, systems of monotonous or punitive work, like systems of monotonous discipline and punishment generally, are still justified on the ground that they develop habits of industry, obedience, perseverence, and conformity and, hence, have a reformative or rehabilitative effect. Similarly, the fact that routine prison labor often is defended on the ground that it keeps inmates "out of mischief" is evidence that it is, to some extent, considered part of the prison's program of incapacitation. Prison labor systems, then, are expected to accomplish the same goals—retribution, deterrence, incapacitation, and reformation—as is imprisonment itself. Since labor which is punitive can hardly be reformative, the administration of prison labor programs is subject to the same conflicts as is prison administration generally.

PRODUCTIVE LABOR.    In addition to being both punitive and rehabilitative, prison labor is expected to be profitable to the state. Concern for profits was important in the development of imprisonment as a replacement for corporal punishment and the death penalty, and this concern has remained. While in recent years restrictive legislation has seriously curtailed the amount of wealth which can be produced with convict labor, prisoners are expected, at least, to "pay their way" by producing goods or performing services which will reduce the number of tax dollars necessary for support of the prison. Even in institutions whose programs are primarily those of treatment, inmates are considered as "owing" the state a proportion of their time. As a method for production of wealth, prison labor may be either public or private with reference to three items: the maintenance and discipline of the prisoners, the control of the employment, and the control and sale of the products. As may be seen in Table XVIII, the lease system gives a private individual or firm control over all three of these. The contract system gives a private individual control over the employment and the sale of the products, while the public retains control over the maintenance and discipline. The piece-price system gives a private individual control over the sale of the products, but not over the employment or the maintenance and discipline. The public retains control over all three of these in the public account, state use, and public works and ways systems.

The three public systems differ from each other in the extent of the

## TABLE XVIII

PRISON LABOR SYSTEMS

| System | Maintenance & Discipline of Prisoners | Control of Employment | Control of Sale of Products | Market Area |
|---|---|---|---|---|
| Lease | Private | Private | Private | Open |
| Contract | Public | Private | Private | Open |
| Piece Price | Public | Public | Private | Open |
| Public Account | Public | Public | Public | Open |
| State Use | Public | Public | Public | State Agencies |
| Public Works and Ways | Public | Public | Public | State Agencies |

market. In the public account system the market is entirely unrestricted. In the state use system the market is restricted to the public institutions in the state in which the goods are produced. In the public works and ways system the market is restricted to the state, and in addition to the "sale" of public buildings or roads. The last system, therefore, is merely a specialized form of the state use system.

*Development of labor systems.* The first system of convict labor in America was the public works and ways system. After several temporary experiments with this system during the seventeenth and eighteenth centuries, before the great development of prisons, it was practically abandoned until late in the nineteenth century. It was not until about 1880, when the advent of the bicycle helped create a demand for good roads, that the system flourished. The demand was further increased after the invention of the automobile. The "chain gangs" employed by southern states and counties are examples of this system. Some states now make extensive use of the public works and ways system by maintaining forestry camps where prisoners are employed in fire-fighting, insect control, and clearance work. Many states also use convict labor almost exclusively in prison construction.

The public account system was used generally in the early state prisons from about 1800 to 1825. Prison officials were responsible for the labor of the prisoners and the sale of the products; sometimes they were given commissions on the sales. The system failed because inadequate equipment, capital, transportation facilities, and demand for prison-made goods made it impossible to keep the prisoners steadily employed. Also, the introduction of machinery in outside industries resulted in production of goods at prices so low that the prisons, which depended on hand labor, could not compete. After the failure of the system in this early period it was resumed in the decade of the 1880's as a substitute for contract labor and has been utilized to some extent since that time. Perhaps the best current example of this system is supplied by the state prison at Stillwater, Minnesota, where farm machinery and binder twine are produced for sale to Minnesota farmers.

The next system in order of appearance was the contract system, which was authorized as early as 1798 in Massachusetts and was actually used there in 1807. However, the system did not begin to flourish until about 1820. Up to this time is was difficult to use prison labor to advantage, and there was no market for prison products. The merchant-capitalist appeared, and he found that he could use cheap prison labor profitably and could enable the institution to make a profit on it. Thus he supplied the production and marketing organizations which had been lacking in the public account system.[2] The contract system flourished until about 1880, when it was attacked by the rising labor organizations. Auburn prison utilized this system, and the fact that the prison paid for itself was an important stimulus to the diffusion of the "Auburn system" to other states and nations. The number of prisoners employed in contract systems steadily declined after 1880, and by 1940 no inmates were employed in them.

A fourth system was the piece-price system, which was similar to the contract system except that the state directed the labor of the convicts, turning over the finished product to a contractor at a specified price per piece. This system was used in the prisons of Pennsylvania in the beginning of the nineteenth century and in New Jersey from 1798 to 1838 in connection with the public account system. Except for a few such temporary trials it had its greatest development in the decade of the eighties and nineties, when the agitation against the contract system broke out. Although contractors paid for labor on the basis of output, rather than according to the number of hours worked, the piece-price system was merely a subterfuge—really the contract system under a different name and in a somewhat preferable form. This system also steadily declined during the twentieth century; less than one percent of the prisoners in the United States are now employed in it, and their work consists primarily of clerical jobs, such as addressing envelopes.

The lease system, which also is similar to the contract system, was authorized in Massachusetts in 1798, and in Kentucky and a few other states in about 1825. The lease system had its greatest development in the South after the Civil War, where convicts were leased to private parties who used their labor in lumber camps, turpentine camps, or other camps,

---

[2] J. R. Common, *History of Labour in the United States* (New York: Macmillan, 1918), Volume I, pp. 153–155.

but it is related to the indenture system used in the colonies, generally as a substitute for fines. This system is still authorized by law and used somewhat in the county prisons of several Southern states. In South Africa, modified forms of the lease system are used extensively. In one form, farmers' associations construct buildings for the accommodation of prisoners and personnel and then turn them over to the Department of Prisons, which puts its own officers in control. Native male recidivists are assigned to these "labor outposts" and the farmers' associations pay fixed daily rates for their labor. In another form, prisoners with short sentences give their permission to be assigned to individual farmers, who pay them a small wage and provide food, clothing, housing, and medical care. Over 40,000 prisoners with terms under four months voluntarily used this program in 1952.[3] In six European countries, prisoners nearing the end of their term are permitted to work for private parties under conditions closely approximating those of complete freedom.[4]

The state use system came into prominence in the decade of the 1880's when the contract system began to decline. By 1899, the system had been authorized by twenty-four states, and at present in about half the states it is mandatory that state agencies and institutions purchase prison-made products, such as furniture, inmate clothing, and printed materials, if they are available. However, in practice evasions are frequent, and prisons sometimes have difficulty of disposing of goods which compete with commercially–produced products, occasionally because the prison products are inferior. The antagonism of trade unions and manufacturers has been aroused by this system, just as it was aroused by the contract and lease systems. If a prison makes furniture for state agencies, privately manufactured furniture cannot be sold to these same agencies. Of the prisoners who are now employed, about ninety percent are in the state use system or the public works system.

*Trends in labor systems.* The previous survey shows a distinct tendency to substitute public systems of prison labor for private systems. In 1885, only 26 percent of the inmates of state prisons who were engaged in productive labor were employed in public systems, in 1905, 47 percent; in 1914, 64 percent; in 1923, 81 percent; and in 1940, more than 99 percent.[5]

---

[3] Herman Venter, *The South African Prison System* (Pretoria: South African Information Service, Fact Paper No. 68, 1959), pp. 9–10.

[4] Ralph W. England, *Prison Labour* (New York: United Nations Department of Economic and Social Affairs, 1955), pp. 12–13.

[5] Richard F. Jones, "Prison Labor in the United States, 1940," *Monthly Labor Review*, 43:478–606, September, 1941. This is the most recent publication giving official statistics for the United States, and all the 1940 statistics in this chapter are taken from it.

This trend toward public systems culminated in the Hawes-Cooper Law of 1934 which authorized the states to regulate the sale within their boundaries of commodities made in the prisons of other states. As early as 1801 a New York law required prison-made goods to be stamped "State Prison."[6] By 1940, every state had enacted laws which prohibited or restricted the sale in the open market of goods made in prisons. These state laws were supplemented by the Ashurst-Sumners Laws, enacted by Congress in 1935, which prohibited the shipment of prison-made goods into any state whose laws forbade the sale on the open market of goods made in prisons and which required that prison-made goods be labeled as such. By federal law in 1940, most goods made in state prisons were completely barred from interstate commerce, thus restricting prisons to public systems.[7]

A second trend is increased idleness in prisons. The proportion of prisoners engaged in productive labor decreased steadily from 1885 to 1940 but increased slightly in the war years.[8] In 1885, 75 percent of the inmates of state and federal prisons were engaged in productive labor, in 1940, only 44 percent. Glaser reports that currently less than a fourth of the inmates in state and federal prisons are employed in prison industries, which ordinarily do not include prison housekeeping and feeding tasks, and the work of maintaining prison plants.[9] Moreover, the number now engaged in productive labor is padded by over-assignment and probably at least two-thirds of the prisoners are in fact idle on an average day. While the assignments of prisoners to educational activities, to treatment programs, and to institutional maintenance have increased, they have not increased sufficiently to compensate for the reduction in productive employment. In 1951, 21 percent of federal prisoners were unemployed; 29 percent were employed in industries or agriculture, 22 percent in maintenance, 7 percent in construction and conservation, and 21 percent in other activities.[10] Similarly, there has been a reduction in the value of goods produced. The average value of commodities produced per productively-employed prisoner decreased from $1,470 in 1923 to $680 in 1940. This trend is explained in part by the over-assignment to the workshops in prisons and the padding of the productive-labor forces, and in part by the relatively low values placed

---

[6] O. F. Lewis, *The Development of American Prisons and Prison Customs, 1776–1845* (Albany: Prison Association of New York, 1922), p. 48.

[7] See Frank Flynn, "The Federal Government and the Prison-Labor Problem in the States," *The Social Service Review*, 24:19–40, 213–236, March and June, 1950.

[8] For an account of war work in prisons, see Harry Elmer Barnes, *Report on the Progress of the State Prison War Program Under the Government Division of the War Production Board* (Washington: War Production Board, 1944).

[9] Daniel Glaser, *The Effectiveness of a Prison and Parole System* (Indianapolis: Bobbs-Merrill, 1964), p. 226.

[10] England, *op. cit.*, p. 96.

by prison authorities on the commodities sold to other state agencies. In general, the drive for productivity under private systems has not been apparent under public systems in many of the penal institutions.

*Comparative values of the systems.* The systems of prison labor should be appraised by the study of the effects they produce, especially with reference to the immediate welfare of the prisoners, financial returns to the state, competition with free labor, and training and rehabilitation.

The immediate welfare of the prisoners was at the zero point in the lease system, with its private control of the maintenance and discipline of prisoners. Long hours of drudgery, frequent and cruel punishments, poor food, and unsanitary conditions almost always prevailed in lease camps. In one of the lease camps of Alabama, for instance, in the month of June, 1916, there were 280 cases of punishment recorded among 103 convicts. Most of the punishments were whippings; one prisoner received 105 lashes. The contract system was almost as demanding as the lease system. The control was nominally in the hands of the prison authorities, but in many places the prison authorities were merely agents of the contractors. An illustration of some of the worst features of the contract system, which might be found duplicated in many other places, came from the state penitentiary of Maryland for 1909. The records show for that year 3,067 punishments, of which 736 were cases of "cuffing up" (hands stretched up above the head and fastened in iron cuffs, and the weight either lifted off the heels or entirely off the feet). Almost invariably these punishments were recorded as due to "failure to get to work," or "indifferent to work." The prisoners were punished because their work did not satisfy the private contractor. Little difference can be found among the several public systems in their effects on the immediate welfare of the prisoners. The public works and ways system ordinarily has the advantage of being outdoor work, away from the hated walls, and the disadvantage of inadequate facilities for bathing, medical care, recreation, and other necessities.

Of all the systems, the lease system was the most profitable to the state. There was almost no cost to the state and a relatively large return. The contract system, also, usually yielded a big profit. Some prisons have made profits under each of the public systems. Even local institutions with a fluctuating personnel, such as houses of correction, have made a profit. There are also many examples of losses under each of the systems. The equipment has frequently been so poor, the methods of management so inefficient, the initial appropriation so inadequate, that no method could yield profits. The state prison of Minnesota has made a spectacular showing with the public account system. The state use system, theoretically, has the advantage of an assured market, especially if the institutions of the state are compelled by law to purchase their supplies from the penal institutions. The state use system, therefore, stands a better chance of avoiding disastrous losses than does the public account system. In practice, however, the prisons under the state use system have a larger proportion of their inmates idle than did prisons under private systems, due primarily to the relatively recent opposition of private labor and private industry to any competition from prison labor.

From early times, both employers and employees have objected to prison labor on the ground that it is unfair competition. It is not only the trade unions that object. The association of vehicle and implement manufacturers and dealers tried to prevent, and then ruined the development of the manufacture of binder twine and farm machinery in the state prison of Minnesota.[11] A garment manufacturing association reported that it had spent $200,000 in an advertising campaign to combat the competition of prison-made goods. Both employers and employees have tried to restrict competition by requesting legislation requiring that prison goods be stamped "prison made," that prison industries be diversified, that the use of power machinery in prison industries be prohibited, that there be restrictions on interstate marketing of prison-made goods and on exportation of prison-made goods, that the hours of labor of prisoners be reduced, and that prison-made goods be sold at a price not less than the market price. Any system of prison labor competes with outside labor and industry. If a prison makes brooms and sells them exclusively to state institutions, so much work is taken from free industries which previously supplied the brooms. If convicts make roads, so much work is taken from outside contractors and laborers, though it is true that some of the work might not have been done at the same time under private management. In this general sense, the amount of competition is very small. Less than one-tenth of 1 percent of America's productive laborers are in prisons, and many of the prisoners would not be efficiently employed if they were not in prison.[12] However, prison goods have a practical monopoly in certain fields and are in effective competition in several fields. The state use system is less injurious to free industries than any other system, but restricting prisons to state use system has by no means satisfied outside industries. Cotton manufacturers, for instance, are in favor of a state use system but object strenuously if prison labor is used to produce cotton goods for state use; furniture manufacturers are in favor of state use, but object to prison labor

[11] U.S. Department of Commerce, Bureau of Corporations, *Report on Farm-machinery Trade Associations* (Washington: Government Printing Office, 1915), pp. 107–110.

[12] See Richard A. McGee, "Saving Prison Waste," *Annals of the American Academy of Political and Social Science*, 293:59–69, May, 1954.

in the manufacture of furniture for state purposes. And so on for other industries. Probably no other system has resulted in such strenuous efforts to keep the prisoners out of particular industries as has the state use system.

TRAINING AND REHABILITATION.   In recent times, as the treatment reaction to crime has developed, labor has frequently been considered as part of the prison treatment program. Ordinarily, the assumption is that non-punitive labor of almost any kind will instill in inmates habits of industry, so that in the post-release period they will work at socially acceptable occupations and will not commit crimes.[13] Although a part of the treatment reaction, this conception of reformation is very similar to conceptions regarding the reformative effect of punitive labor, or of punishment of any kind. Another popular assumption is that through prison labor inmates learn skills which enable them, in the post-release period, to support themselves and their families by legitimate means so that they "do not have to turn to crime." Both assumptions, in turn, are based on the notion that economic need and attitudes toward work, not attitudes toward legal norms, produce crime. The assumption regarding the "habit-forming" values of prison labor was stated as follows by the Director of the U.S. Bureau of Prisons in 1937:

The great necessity in prison is work. If I had to manage a prison upon condition that I make my choice of one thing, and only one, as an aid to discipline, as an agency for reform, for its therapeutic value, I would un-hesitatingly choose work—just plain, honest-to-goodness work. Of course, I wouldn't like to have to concentrate so on a choice and it would be un-wise to be so restricted. Physical examinations, medical treatments, bodily repairs, educational opportunities, spiritual guidance, psychiatry, psychol-ogy, are necessary and helpful. But the habit of work is what men most need.[14]

An alternative statement regarding the indirect rehabilitative value of prison labor may be made as follows: Work in prison affects reformation

[13] See Ralph D. Edwards, "Correctional Industries and Inmate Training," *Proceedings of the American Correctional Association*, 1963, pp. 197–200.

[14] Quoted by The American Prison Association, *Manual of Suggested Standards for a State Correctional System* (New York: Author, 1946), p. 40. Reprinted by per-mission of the publishers. For the view that prison labor is important for the skills it provides, see Charles V. Jenkinson, "How Can Prison Industries Contribute to the Preparation of Inmates for Release?" *Proceedings of the American Prison Association*, 1948, pp. 159–168 and Walter M. Wallack, "Some Suggestions for Basic Reforms in Prison Industries for Improved Production and Vocational Training," *Proceedings of the American Prison Association*, 1947, pp. 153–160.

largely to the extent that it is conducive to changes in associations upon discharge from prison, but it also contributes to the morale of inmates so that they are psychologically better equipped for making such changes in associations. Many prisoners learn skills which can be used after discharge. But the possession of these skills does not, by itself, produce reformation. Instead, it is at least probable that possession of the skills affects the social mobility of the discharged inmate and that as he moves from the status of an unskilled worker or of an unemployed person to the status of a skilled worker his associations and, consequently, his attitudes toward legal norms also change. Rather than return to the social situation which produced his criminality in the first place, the discharged inmate who has been trained in a useful occupation conceivably will move into a new social situation, perhaps one not conducive to criminality. Also, the work provided in prisons is indirectly important to reformation under the current prison practices, because absence of work means idleness, not participation in programs aimed more directly at rehabilitation. Since idleness in prisons undoubtedly contributes to the incidence of "prison stupor," because it is conducive to low prisoner morale, and because it affects the incidence of prison riots, it may be concluded that idleness seldom equips inmates for shifts in loyalties from criminal groups to law-abiding groups. Until the treatment reaction, and programs based on it, becomes much more extensive than it is at present, prisons will necessarily have to provide work programs which contribute to the psychological well-being of inmates who are merely "doing time." Perhaps it is for this reason that prisoners in Scandinavian countries and in Mexico possess the right to work.[15] Prison labor, then, can contribute to rehabilitation by providing inmates with skills which, in turn, might affect their associations and, consequently, their attitudes toward criminality. It also can contribute to rehabilitation, in a rather negative sense, by keeping inmates occupied so that they leave the prison in good psychological and physical condition.[16]

Both the "inmate-welfare" point of view and the "acquisition-of-skills" point of view must be considered in evaluating the contributions of the various systems of productive labor to rehabilitation. Some people have limited their attention to the first of these and have maintained that because a large proportion of the prisoners are unskilled workers, often engaged in outdoor work, prior to imprisonment, they should be employed in outdoor and relatively unskilled work during imprisonment. The conclu-

[15] England, op. cit., p. 2.
[16] Cf. Allan L. Robbins, "Relation of Industries to Rehabilitation and Prison Administration," *Proceedings of the American Prison Association,* 1953, pp. 61–66.

sion does not necessarily follow; the fact of criminality may indicate that for increasing the probability of reformation just the opposite training should be given.

The importance of continuation after release of the work learned in prison is sometimes minimized, also. It is asserted that the prisoner does not wish to tell where he learned the trade, he wishes to throw off everything that reminds him of his prison career, and, in practice, he seldom learns a trade sufficiently well to pursue it efficiently after his release. The argument is pertinent, but, nevertheless, if other things are equal it seems preferable for a prisoner to learn a trade that he can pursue after release rather than one he cannot possibly pursue, since a change in vocation might indirectly produce changes in attitudes toward crime. In order that prisoners may have the work best fitted to them and most interesting to them and that can be pursued after release it is necessary that the prison industries be diversified. The state use system has a decided advantage over all of the other systems in this respect. Glaser interviewed 140 men four months after they had been released from federal prisons to the supervision of the United States Probation Offices in Chicago, Detroit, Cleveland, and St. Louis.[17] Of these men, 24 had not yet found any post-release employment, and two had had no work assignment in prison, due to hospitalization. Of the 114 men who had worked in prison and who had post-release jobs, 33 reported that some job he had held for a week or longer after having been released from prison was related in some way to a job he had had in prison. The 114 men had held a total of 184 post-release jobs; 47, or about a quarter of these jobs, were related to prison work experience. Among the 47, twenty-four (51 percent) were considered by the men to be related to relatively unskilled prison work, such as construction labor or unskilled kitchen or dining room work; 31 percent of the 47 references (15 cases) were to relatively skilled work in the prison, such as machinist, electrician, printer, cook, and baker assignments. The remaining 18 percent (8 cases) of the 47 references were to white-collar assignments in the prison, predominantly clerical jobs. However, of the 47 men who said their post-release jobs were related to their prison jobs, 25 (52 percent) reported that they had had preprison experience with the job they held in prison. From these data and from responses to a question about the usefulness of the prison work to the 47 jobs, Glaser concluded that "in about one-tenth of inmate post-release jobs there are benefits from new learning acquired in prison work, in about three or four percent of these jobs there are benefits from the preservation of old skills through

17 Glaser, op. cit., p. 250–251.

practice in prison, and in about five or six percent of the post-release jobs the prison provided useful physical or psychological conditioning."[18]

WAGE PAYMENTS TO PRISONERS. Payment of wages to prisoners is not a new device. As early as 1700 Massachusetts provided that inmates of the houses of correction should receive eight pence out of every shilling they made, under a system in which masters or relatives furnished tools and materials. In the county prisons of Pennsylvania in 1790, in the state prison of New York in 1796, of New Jersey in 1798, Massachusetts in 1800, and Maryland in 1811, the wardens were instructed by the laws of the state to put the prisoners at hard labor and give them wages as an incentive to work. It was expected that the sale of the products would produce a profit for the institution from which the wages could be paid, and that the prisoners would pay for their maintenance out of the wages. But no profits were secured, no wages could be paid, and the prisoners had to be maintained at the expense of the state. For a time prisoners were held until they paid for their maintenance, but the prisons soon became congested and the system was modified. After this general failure of the wage system in prisons, it disappeared almost entirely for half a century. But in 1853 the Eastern Penitentiary of Pennsylvania began to pay small wages to prisoners. Other states gradually adopted the same policy. In 1957, thirty-three states paid wages to prisoners, with wages ranging from 4 cents to $1.30 per day.[19] The Federal Prison Industries, a governmental corporation which operates as the industrial division of the Bureau of Prisons, pays inmates at the rate of 12, 18, 24, or 30 cents per hour, according to the grade of work performed. In 1964, the average wage paid per month for those employed in manufacturing was about $40.[20]

Among the states, wages depend on a variety of things other than the efficiency of the inmate; e.g., good conduct, the number of children in the prisoner's family, and especially the profits of the institution. The institution may fail to make a profit because of conditions over which the prisoner has no control, such as inadequate working capital, poor location of prison, poor choice of industries, poor salesmanship, or poor organization of the work. If prisoners are to be paid at all, they should be paid even when idle, if their idleness is due to no fault of their own. This principle is currently used in twenty states and the District of Columbia, where ninety to one hundred percent of the inmates earn money in prison.[21] These

18 *Ibid.*, p. 252.
19 *Ibid.*, p. 235.
20 Bureau of Prisons, *Annual Report, 1964*, p. 4.
21 Glaser, *op. cit.*, p. 235.

include states with above-average per-capita revenue, such as Massachusetts and New York, as well as some of the lower-income states, such as Kentucky and South Carolina. Six states permit no inmate earnings in prison, and in five states no more than ten percent of the inmates earn money.

The Chief of the Section on Social Defense in the United Nations has argued that labor is a right of prisoners under the "Universal Declaration of Human Rights" adopted by the United Nations. He states, further, that prison labor is not treatment, that prisoners should receive the same pay as free men if they do the same work, and that prison labor should be a part of labor in general.[22]

The argument is raised, however, that the prisoner has no right to a wage because he has forfeited his right to the products of his labor. The Attorney General of Texas in 1913 held that a law authorizing the payment of wages to prisoners was unconstitutional on the ground that when an offender is convicted he loses not only his freedom but also his right to the products of his labor, and that the sentence makes him both a prisoner and a slave. The state constitutions, with two exceptions, provide that slavery is illegal except for conviction of crime. This, however, does not mean that the prisoner must necessarily be a slave.

ADMINISTRATIVE PROBLEMS. Three general problems confront the administrative officers and professional workers of a prison with reference to the employment of prisoners, even after the system of labor is settled. One of the problems is the assignment of prisoners to their tasks in the prison industry and to institutional maintenance tasks such as cleaning, cooking, and clerical work. With the development of classification committees a few prisons have developed personnel programs which compare favorably with personnel programs in private industry.[23] The various kinds of jobs are analyzed and each prisoner is studied on entrance to determine the kind of labor he is equipped to do. The prisoner's preferences and needs are noted and, in the ideal system, he is given the occupation he wishes if it is possible to do so in view of his capacities and the institutional opportunities. However, in practice the needs of the institution almost always are given priority over the needs or desires of the inmate. As was pointed out in Chapter Twenty-three, the criteria used for assignment of inmates to specific tasks probably are custody, convenience, discipline, and treatment, in that order.

[22] Manuel Lopez-Rey, "Some Considerations on the Character and Organization of Prison Labor," Journal of Criminal Law and Criminology, 49:10–28, May, 1958.
[23] See, for example, George W. Tilden, "Missouri Department of Corrections Occupational Evaluation and Utilization Program," Proceedings of the American Correctional Association, 1964, pp. 200–204.

A second problem is keeping the prison industries efficient enough to be competitive with outside industries, in face of the low educational levels and poor skills of the inmates who must be employed. So that work can be provided for inmates, prisons use obsolete hand operations.[24] Further, most inmates have little skill, little work experience, poor work habits, and little academic training. They are not able to operate the modern automated equipment that characterizes efficient industrial organizations. In 1952, Correctional Industries at the Michigan State Prison picked sweet corn and green beans by hand, using 150 to 180 inmates; today they use complex mechanical pickers and only two inmate operators.[25] Most inmates cannot qualify as operators of the machines. If prison industries are to compete with private industries, inmates must first be trained in the most basic manual work skills, taught to read operator's manuals, trained to write reports, and instructed in such basic mechanical skills as the use of a ruler or a wrench. Thus, in the modern age the vocational training given in prison schools is almost as essential to employment in the prison as it is to employment outside prison. Even the training function of prison industries is handicapped because hand labor must be used in jobs which have been mechanized in outside industries, and because the prison labor force used in either hand tasks or mechanized tasks has a lower level of skill than does the labor force available to private industry.[26]

Organization of working time poses a third general administrative problem. If prison industry is to be efficient and profitable, interference with work must be reduced to a minimum. At the same time, the reduction in work interference must be consistent with the performance of other necessary activities. It is extremely difficult to organize an efficient prison industry or maintenance system, because men are frequently called from work for interviews, visits, band practice, work in other shops, sick call, discipline, or other routine prison activities. Certain custodial practices also are conducive to inefficiency in inmate work. For example, time must be taken for counts, the inmates must be in their cells at 4:00 P.M. or 4:30 P.M., when the guard is changed, and for security reasons inmates usually must bathe, visit the barber, and patronize the commissary during working hours. It frequently happens that when one prisoner is called from work, a process in which eight or ten other prisoners are engaged is interrupted. Many of

24 See Ralph W. England, Jr., "New Departures in Prison Labor," *The Prison Journal*, 41:21–26, Spring, 1961.
25 Paul Chase, "Correlation of Vocational Education and Correctional Industries," *Proceedings of the American Correctional Association*, 1963, pp. 222–225.
26 Ross V. Randolph, "Automation in Industries," *Proceedings of the American Correctional Association*, 1964, pp. 194–200.

the interruptions of this kind, of course, could be prevented by a well-planned organization of prison activities.

A more fundamental aspect of this problem involves a question of the priority of prison work over more direct treatment programs. Although the increasing idleness in prisons in recent years has been rightfully viewed with alarm, revival of the industrial prison might not, by itself, produce the rehabilitative effects which are demanded of our prisons. Instead, the treatment reaction to crime seems to imply a reduction in the amount of prison labor, so that time can be devoted to more efficient treatment programs. Gill was arguing on this ground for a reduction of prison labor thirty years ago:

The industrial prison has not proven a success penologically. In the early days hard work was the panacea for all ills—especially crime. In these days of social work, scientific medicine and psychiatry, we have come to realize that the cause and cure of crime are by no means merely economic. Practically everyone admits that most men leave prison worse than they enter. This is not the fault of the industries, but it is a strong indication that the present emphasis on industries does not produce the desired results penologically.[27]

In spite of this argument, however, most classification committees and prison administrators still operate as if work were the most important non-punitive activity in the institution, regardless of whether or not the work is of any value to the inmates. In some institutions this is apparent from the fact that the prison labor system is practically the only "treatment" facility available. And in other institutions the assumption is that industries which are profitable to the institution must be manned, even if the value of the work to the inmates cannot be rationalized at all. The treatment reaction to crime is not yet so extensive that a prison administrator can choose to assign inmates to specific rehabilitation programs at the cost of closing down an industry such as a cannery. If there is a choice, the industrial activity must almost always be given preference over the treatment program. Similarly, the notion that free laborers could be hired to perform the prison maintenance tasks, thereby releasing inmates for treatment, would find few supporters today, even though most persons readily accept such a policy as it pertains to inmates of mental hospitals who also are being treated. While closing down industries and freeing inmates from maintenance tasks would be expensive, the expense might be offset in the long run by the development of treatment techniques and programs which

[27] Howard B. Gill, "The Future of Prison Employment," *Proceedings of the American Prison Association*, 1935, pp. 179–185. Reprinted by permission of the publisher.

would reduce recidivism. Even if prisons became almost exclusively institutions for treatment, however, some kind of work activity probably would be provided, just as work activities are provided as a means of "passing the time" in mental hospitals. It cannot be argued that prison labor has no rehabilitative effects, but it is doubtful that labor is the most important activity which is, or could be, provided for the reformation of prisoners.

## SUGGESTED READINGS

Ash, Wesley O., and Walter L. Barkdull, "California's Trade and Advisory Councils," *American Journal of Correction,* 23:10–14, June, 1961.

Barnes, H. E., "Economics of American Penology, State of Pennsylvania," *Journal of Political Economy,* 29:617–642, October, 1921.

Cable, G. W., "The Convict Lease System in the Southern States," *Proceedings of the National Conference of Charities and Correction,* 1883, pp. 265–301.

Curran, J. W., "Trends in Prison Labor," *Proceedings of the American Prison Association,* 1946, pp. 181–184.

Edwards, Ralph D., "Correctional Industries and Inmate Training," *Proceedings of the American Correctional Association,* 1963, pp. 197–200.

England, Ralph W., Jr., "New Departures in Prison Labor," *The Prison Journal,* 41:21–26, Spring, 1961.

England, Ralph W., *Prison Labour.* New York: United Nations Department of Economic and Social Affairs, 1955.

Flynn, Frank, "The Federal Government and the Prison-Labor Problem in the States," *The Social Service Review,* 24:19–40, 213–236, March and June, 1950.

Flynn, Frank, "Employment and Labor," in Paul W. Tappan, Editor, *Contemporary Correction.* New York: McGraw-Hill, 1951.

Gill, Howard B., "The Prison Labor Problem," *Annals of the American Academy of Political and Social Science,* 157:83–101, September, 1931.

Gill, Howard B., "The Future of Prison Employment," *Proceedings of the American Prison Association,* 1935, pp. 178–185.

Grant, J. A., "Interstate Traffic in Convict-Made Goods," *Journal of Criminal Law and Criminology,* 28:854–860, March–April, 1938.

Hiller, E. T., "Development of the Systems of Control of Convict Labor in the United States," *Journal of Criminal Law and Criminology,* 5:241–269, July–August, 1914.

Jones, R. F., "Prison Labor in the United States, 1940," *Monthly Labor Review,* 43:478–606, September, 1941.

Lopez-Rey, Manuel, "Some Considerations on the Character and Organization of Prison Labor," *Journal of Criminal Law, Criminology, and Police Science,* 49:10–28, May–June, 1958.

McKelway, Blake, "The Prison Labor Problem, 1875–1900," *Journal of Criminal Law and Criminology*, 25:254–270, July–August, 1934.

Mohler, Henry C., "Convict Labor Policies," *Journal of Criminal Law and Criminology*, 15:530–597, January–February, 1925.

Proctor, Carroll R., "Prison Industries Apprenticeship Training," *Proceedings of the American Correctional Association*, 1963, pp. 225–235.

Robinson, L. N., *Should Prisoners Work?* Philadelphia: Winston, 1931.

Rusche, George and Otto Kirchheimer, *Punishment and Social Structure.* New York: Columbia University Press, 1939.

Rydeen, H. L., "The Apprenticeship Program in Penal Institutions," *Proceedings of the American Correctional Association*, 1963, pp. 200–208.

Sigler, Maurice H., and John D. Yeomans, "The Incentive Pay Plans of Louisiana and California," *American Journal of Correction*, 19:2–3, ff., May–June, 1957.

Steiner, Jesse F., and Roy M. Brown, *The North Carolina Chain Gang.* Chapel Hill: University of North Carolina Press, 1927.

Whitin, E. S., "The Prisoner: Public Servant," *Survey*, 51:69–71, October 15, 1923.

# 26. EDUCATION IN PRISONS

EDUCATION, as popularly understood, means the process or product of formal training in schools or classrooms. In a broader sense, education includes all of the life experiences which shape a person's attitudes and behavior. Education in prison has been viewed in both ways. On one hand, prison education was once taken to mean little more than the academic school programs which were offered to inmates. This conception of education still persists in some prisons. On the other hand, all intentional efforts to direct inmates away from crime by means of non-academic, as well as academic, measures are now usually considered as prison education. From this point of view, "education" of prisoners is almost synonymous with "treatment" of prisoners. This broad conception of prison education may be observed in the New York State Correctional Law:

The objective of prison education in its broadest sense should be the socialization of the inmates through varied impressional and expressional activities, with emphasis on individual inmate needs. The objective of this program shall be the return of these inmates to society with a more wholesome attitude toward living, with a desire to conduct themselves as good citizens and with the skill and knowledge which wll give them a reasonable chance to maintain themselves and their dependents through honest labor. To this end, each prisoner shall be given a program of education which, on the basis of available data, seems most likely to further the process of socialization and rehabilitation. The time daily devoted to such education shall be such as required for meeting the above objectives.[1]

In this broad sense, the problem of prison education is essentially a problem in reformation. This involves a conversion, a transference of alle-

[1] New York Correctional Law, Chapter 864, Section 136, quoted by Price Chenault, "Education," In Paul W. Tappan, Editor, Contemporary Correction (New York: McGraw-Hill, 1951), pp. 224–237. See also California Department of Corrections, Manual of Procedures in Education, Vocational Training and Recreation (Sacramento: Author, 1948), Part I, p. 2.

giance from one group to another, so that the person is not receptive to criminal behavior patterns, and a redirection of those specific interests and attitudes conducive to contacts with criminal behavior patterns. Little specific knowledge has been acquired regarding the exact techniques for producing the required identification of self with law-abiding groups. But it is essential that prisoners be immersed in the ideals, sentiments, and traditions of law-abiding society. This means not merely an intellectual comprehension of these traditions, but emotional involvement with them. Probably the best way to accomplish this would be by providing inmates with frequent and intimate contacts with people who have the traditions; this is limited by considerations of custody and punishment. An alternative is to provide the contacts, meager and ineffective as they must be in the prison community, by means of educational facilities. Reading and writing can assist in producing the contacts, but contacts also can be provided by means of moving pictures, library facilities, lectures, classroom instruction in academic subjects, group discussions, religious exercises, certain recreations and entertainments, and even individual psychotherapy. Participation in such activities, like participation in vocational training, gives the offender an opportunity, after his release, to change his social position and, conceivably, to associate with persons having strong anti-criminal biases.

**THE DEVELOPMENT OF PRISON EDUCATIONAL POLICIES.** The church has been interested in the religious instruction of prisoners since the origin of imprisonment. During the medieval and early modern periods preachers and priests visited the prisons more or less regularly and conversed with prisoners in congregate or separate meetings. Some of the early houses of correction had resident chaplains who, in addition to holding regular religious services, attempted to teach the elementary subjects, especially to the children confined in these institutions. The first recorded instance of regular visitation of prisoners in America was by the Quakers of Philadelphia just prior to the Revolutionary War. These laymen, as the preachers after this time, distributed Bibles and theological tracts and conversed with the prisoners in the cells. Prior to 1845, few prisons had regular resident chaplains and these were poorly paid and were, in general, inefficient.

The development of secular educational work in prisons resulted directly from the effort to teach prisoners to read the Bible and the tracts. This effort to introduce secular education met with some resistance. The warden of Auburn prison in 1824 successfully opposed an attempt to teach the younger convicts to read and write. His opposition was based on the "increased danger to society of the educated convict." It was regarded as especially dangerous to teach convicts to write, for, it was asserted, this could easily result in forgery. The same fear was expressed in England about this time.[2]

The first organized educational work in America started in the New York House of Refuge. Provision was made there for two hours a day for each child; one hour of this consisted of learning to read the New Testament, the other of lectures and talks by the superintendent. The following year, the school period was increased to four hours a day, and the work consisted of the three R's, geography, and bookkeeping. At about the same time, an effort was made in Auburn prison to determine what proportion of the prisoners were unable to read and write. As a result of this investigation, in 1826, the chaplain organized the prisoners into small groups to learn to read and write; with the assistance of theological students, 31 such classes were formed within the next few years and 160 prisoners were attending them.[3]

In practically all institutions for adults up to the middle of the nineteenth century, prisoners were not permitted to meet in groups and the school work was done at night. As late as 1845, few institutions taught even the three R's, and these few gave a very small amount of time to formal educational work, though systematic efforts were made about the middle of the century to introduce this elementary educational work into all penal and reformatory institutions. Lewis describes the typical prison school at that time as consisting of

the chaplain standing in the semi-dark corridor, before the cell-door, with a dingy lantern hanging to the grated bars, and teaching to the wretched convict in the darkness beyond the grated door the rudiments of reading or of numbers.[4]

The first legal recognition of academic education as desirable in penal or reformatory institutions was in 1847 when the legislature of New York state provided for the appointment of two teachers for each of the state prisons to give instruction in English for not less than an hour and a half a day. Within a comparatively short time, many of the prisons in other states made similar provisions. In most places, the educational work continued to be confined to the evening, and no congregate groups were permitted. This continued in some institutions to the present century.

2 O. F. Lewis, *The Development of American Prisons and Prison Customs, 1776–1845* (Albany: Prison Association of New York, 1922), p. 95; Sidney and Beatrice Webb, *English Prisons under Local Government* (London: Longmans, 1922), p. 157.
3 P. Klein, *Prison Methods in New York State* (New York: Columbia University Press, 1920), pp. 308 and 311.
4 Lewis, *op. cit.*, p. 341.

The greatest stimulation to the development of prison schools and other educational activities in prisons came with the increasing popularity of the treatment reaction to crime after the Civil War. The non-punitive, constructive measures advocated for use in the attempt to reform or treat inmates were largely educational. A growing faith in the importance of academic education to all citizens in a democracy and to the "good life" also permeated prison and reformatory systems. The logic was something like this: If the good citizens are the educated citizens, then the education of bad citizens (prisoners) should make them good. The Elmira Reformatory, which opened in 1876, had a "school of letters" as well as a trade school. Elmira's first warden, Brockway, describe the changes in his own attitudes toward reformation during the last half of the nineteenth century, and this description may be taken as an illustration of the changes in public opinion taking place at the time. He stated that he had at first placed his dependence on regular labor with the expectation that it would form habits that would persist after release; then he was converted in a religious meeting and for a time had great faith in the power of religion to modify the behavior of the prisoners; by 1885, he had developed a greatly enhanced estimation of the reformative value of rational education.[5] By rational education, he meant education in its broadest sense, including vocational education, lectures, certain entertainments, group discussions, and the teaching of ethics, as well as the ordinary academic course.

THE PRISON SCHOOL. The year 1930 has been selected by some American criminologists as the date of an upward trend in correctional education, and efforts prior to that date are appraised as scarcely deserving of mention. While some very encouraging developments have occurred during the last 35 years in a few institutions, the total system of correctional education in the United States shows no distinct break in 1930 or in any other year.[6] At the beginning of the second World War, no more than one-fifth of the state prisons and reformatories had good school systems and approximately the same proportion had no school systems at all. According to a survey in 1941, about one-fourth of the population in 44 state prisons and less than half the population in 17 state reformatories were in school; about 10 percent of the state prison population and 20 percent of the state reformatory population were in school full-time.

[5] Z. R. Brockway, *Fifty Years of Prison Service* (New York: Charities Publications Committee, 1912), p. 279.
[6] United States Attorney General, *Survey of Release Procedures* (Washington: Government Printing Office), Volume V, Part I, Chapter 10; Part II, Chapter 7; United States Office of Education, *Biennial Survey of Education in the United States* (Washington: Government Printing Office, 1938–1940), Volume II, Chapter 5.

In most of the state prisons which provide academic training, the work is confined to the first three, five, or eight grades, and the time spent in the classroom is generally no more than five or ten hours per week. The primary objective in such schools is to teach the use of the tool subjects— reading, writing, and arithmetic. In view of the fact that from 10 to 30 percent of the admissions to correctional institutions throughout the country are functionally illiterate, these are important subjects.[7] Other popular subjects include bookkeeping, drawing, stenography, and civics. Comparatively few institutions give courses in any of the social sciences other than civics, although several advisory commissions which have made surveys of education in correctional institutions have recommended that much more emphasis should be placed on the social studies and especially on those social studies which deal with contemporary life, namely, sociology, economics, and political science. These recommendations have been made on the principle that for purposes of readjustment inmates should understand the social world in which they live and especially should understand and appreciate the traditions of law-abiding society. Seventy percent of 54 inmates questioned in one reformatory stated that an ideal rehabilitation program for them would be based on "the teaching, explanation, and discussion of the fundamental principles for living as a responsible citizen in society."[8]

A few institutions for adults have developed school programs which compare favorably with the school programs of many cities. In California, the prison schools are actually a part of the school system of the city in which the prison is located, and both the administration of the school and the instruction are under the direction of the State Board of Education. The students and equipment are provided by the prison, the teachers and program by the school district. Regular courses from the first grade through high school are given by teachers certified by the board. The content, methods, and procedures employed in the ordinary public schools are followed, and certificates and diplomas are granted by the regular school district rather than by the prison. In addition to the courses leading to a diploma, a wide variety of the general cultural and technical subjects usually included in adult education programs, such as French Literature, Social Living, and Accounting, are offered. New York State and the Federal Bureau of Prisons also have excellent, well-organized, school systems. Institutions for juvenile delinquents have the most adequate schools, while formal education in jails and workhouses is almost entirely lacking.

[7] See p. 204 above.
[8] John F. Sinnott, *The Searchers* (Green Bay: Wisconsin State Reformatory, 1959. Mimeographed), p. 2.

Among the changes in curricula during the last generation, the most significant is the emphasis on what has come to be called "social education." In the narrow sense, social education refers to the classroom attempts to help inmates straighten out emotional difficulties to understand family, home, and work problems, to respect law and order, and to maintain proper relationships with community facilities and agencies.[9] The term "social education," rather than merely "education," apparently is used to emphasize that the prison school curriculum now has direct rehabilitative objectives and is not merely aimed at providing skills in tool subjects and offering interesting ways for inmates to pass the time. But in a broader sense "social education" refers to all efforts to transfer inmate allegiances to law-abiding groups and to induce them to adopt attitudes which are in accord with those of law-abiding members of society, whether or not these efforts are made in the classroom.[10] As Chenault says:

A successful social education program is likely to be spearheaded by the school under the direction of individuals who are well trained in the social sciences. It will be effective only to the degree, however, that all the services and facilities of the institution participate.[11]

Thus, "social education" has come to mean the entire institutional rehabilitative program, in so far as that program is directed toward changing inmate attitudes. The Department of Corrections in the District of Columbia has developed a series of nine courses designed to orient the inmates in social relationships,[12] and many other prison systems have worked social education courses into their school curriculum, often as "admissions-orientation" or "pre-release" courses.[13]

A common practice in the state prisons is to employ one civilian teacher or superintendent, and inmate assistants. Most of the inmate teachers are

[9] Chenault, op. cit.

[10] W. M. Wallack, G. M. Kendall, and H. L. Briggs, Education Within Prison Walls (New York: Columbia University Press, 1939), p. 24; U. Samuel Vucevich, "Teaching Social Adjustment Concepts to Incarcerated Offenders Utilizing Principles of Group Dynamics," Proceedings of the American Correctional Association, 1963, pp. 115–124.

[11] Chenault, op. cit. Reprinted by permission of the publishers. See also C. A. Ullman, "The Educational Process in a Social Environment," American Journal of Orthopsychiatry, 13:89–107, June, 1943.

[12] Donald Clemmer, "A Beginning in Social Education in Correctional Institutions," Federal Probation, 13:32–35, March, 1949.

[13] See Edwin I. Friedman, "Institutional Life—A Program of Social Education," Prison World, 11:14–17, July, 1949; Byron E. Ballard, "Atlanta's Exploration of the Potentialities of Social Education," Prison World, 11:12–13, 33–34, September, 1949; and Martin R. Haskell and H. Ashley Weeks, "Role Training as Preparation for Release from a Correctional Institution," Journal of Criminal Law, Criminology and Police Science, 50:441–447, January, 1960.

poorly equipped for the work, although it was once reported that Oklahoma had such success with inmate teachers that it preferred them to civilian teachers.[14] The inmate teachers interviewed by Glaser, however, reported pressure from inmates to give good grades, to allow cheating, and to let class discussions wander for indefinite periods to sports, crime, or other topics irrelevant to the assigned study topic. The inmate teachers who balked at such practices were subject to reprisals, while those that complied were the recipients of reciprocal favors.[15] In general, it is distinctly preferable to have teachers who represent ordinary society, who have had sufficient experience with delinquents and criminals to be able to understand them and to present the school work in ways that appeal to them. Accordingly, in some prisons and in most reformatories and institutions for juvenile delinquents the teaching force is composed entirely of civilians. Two or three reformatories have used female teachers. As we have seen, in some institutions the prison school is a branch of the regular public school, with types of teachers, curricula, and procedures almost identical with those of the public school. Some institutions give standardized educational tests and assign the prisoners to school work according to their abilities as thus measured. By repeating the tests at regular intervals, the students' progress can be measured. When education is considered in its broadest sense, assignments to various activities are made on a clinical basis—in accordance with the individualization principle, inmates' needs and problems are diagnosed and individual assignments are made on the basis of these diagnoses.

CORRESPONDENCE COURSES.   In most institutions, inmates are permitted to enroll in correspondence courses and to do the necessary studying in their cells during the evening hours. This method of instruction is defended on many grounds: it permits individualization; it appeals to prisoners because of the contact with society outside the prisons; often the courses and methods of teaching are superior to those in prison classes; and it is inexpensive to the state. In a few prisons, correspondence course training has been made an integral part of the educational program, and students are given assistance and counsel in regard to correspondence courses by members of the educational staff. In most institutions, however, the inmates are merely given the opportunity to enroll in correspondence courses; the selection of the course, the rate at which the work is completed, and the decision as to whether the course should be dropped are left entirely to

[14] Leonard Logan, "An Experiment in Prison Education," *Federal Probation*, 1:31–34, March, 1942.
[15] Daniel Glaser, *The Effectiveness of a Prison and Parole System* (Indianapolis: Bobbs-Merrill, 1964), pp. 268–269.

the enrollee. What this system produces is extensive cheating. Glaser found that inmates kept a file of completed lessons for correspondence courses, peddled carbon copies of completed lessons, and had more educated inmates not taking a course complete the papers in exchange for commissary goods or other favors. Such practices are not unknown in colleges and universities. The inmates also cheated simply by getting correspondence school records falsified by the inmate clerks who worked in the school. In one prison, one-third of 220 correspondence school courses were "completed" within a week.[16] The greatest development of the correspondence method has occurred in California and Wisconsin, with the cooperation of the extension divisions of the state universities of those states, and in the federal prisons.[17] Also, intramural correspondence courses with inmate teachers were developed in California and Illinois. In this kind of system, the prison school sets up its own correspondence courses for inmates who are unable to enroll in the regular school program either because of conflicts with other prison activities or because the desired courses are not offered. In 1937, more than 400 prisoners were enrolled in these intramural correspondence courses in Joliet, Illinois, but the program has now been abandoned.

VOCATIONAL EDUCATION.   The best prison vocational training programs are those in which trade training is correlated with related academic subjects and in which an attempt actually to teach vocational skills is made. Only a small number of prisons have such vocational programs. In the vast majority of institutions "vocational training" is merely the maintenance, industrial, or agricultural work to which inmates are assigned. Prison industries were once defended on the ground that they were profitable to the state; now the same industries are often defended, also, on the ground that they provide "vocational education." It is possible to assign inmates to routine prison work—such as painting, baking, barbering, electrical and mechanical repairing, and tailoring—which will furnish the basis for training. But in most institutions participation in such prison work hardly deserves the name "vocational education." Even in institutions where inmates are assigned to certain work activities on the basis of their needs, the training has not been developed in proportion to the development of techniques for classification and assignment. Also, as was discussed in Chapter Twenty-three, the classification committee's recommendations

[16] Op. cit., pp. 269–270.
[17] See Boyd B. Rakestraw, "University of California Extension Division Assists San Quentin's Program," Proceedings of the American Prison Association, 1941, pp. 317–332.

often are ignored, or assignments are made on the basis of considerations other than the value of training. An inmate is likely to be assigned to painting because he is a painter, not because he needs training in painting.

The Walkill Prison in New York, the California Department of Corrections, and the Jackson Prison in Michigan have developed outstanding vocational programs. In the latter institution, unskilled prisoners with six months or less to serve are offered short technical courses in such subjects as machine-shop practice, welding, pattern making, drafting, and sign painting. Also, courses related to the technical training—shop theory, shop mathematics, blueprint reading, etc.— are given.[18] In California, vocational training is a part of the prison school system and is, therefore, administered and taught by civilian educators certified by the State Board of Education.[19] In New York, vocational counselors visit each maximum-security prison seeking men qualified for transfer to Walkill, where more than 20 different trade courses are offered.[20]

The vocational training in reformatories for young adults is not much better, on the whole, than in state prisons. The greatest difficulty is that the inmates either stay in the institution for too short a time to acquire a trade, or else shift from one trade to another. The institutions for juvenile delinquents have attempted to give trade training, but they are handicapped by the fact that most of the inmates are young and remain in the institution for only a short time. Even if they develop vocational skill, they cannot acquire positions when they are released. Jails and workhouses characteristically give no vocational training.

Perhaps the most serious current problem regarding vocational education in prisons is that of determining the amount of emphasis which should be placed on vocational education in the correctional program. Until quite recently it was felt that vocational training was the most essential kind of education and almost all rehabilitative efforts in the prison were vocational. The current emphasis treatment—called social education—has superseded the earlier emphasis on vocational training. We no longer are satisfied if the prison produces competent bricklayers; we want it to produce honest bricklayers. After a careful survey of fifteen state reformatories almost half a century ago, Nadler concluded that the industrial training in those institutions was not successful and that it would be preferable to devote the

18 E. R. Akers, "A Prison Trade School—Students and Training," *Journal of Criminal Law and Criminology*, 35:311–323, January–February, 1945.

19 See H. G. Martin, "Vocational Guidance in a Prison System," *American Psychologist*, 1:542–543, November, 1946.

20 Walter M. Wallack, "Vocational Education in Correctional Institutions," *National Society for the Study of Education Yearbook*, 1943, pp. 334–351.

time to changing inmates' attitudes.[21] While vocational education procedures have been greatly improved in recent years, the notion that prisoners' major difficulties can be resolved by vocational training has declined in popularity. It now appears that vocational education is important to rehabilitation not because of the skills it provides but, instead, because it affects the inmate's conception of himself and influences his post-release associations.

THE PRISON LIBRARY.  The state prison of Kentucky had a small library as early as 1802, but most of the prisons made no effort to establish libraries until about 1840. They depended entirely on Bibles and tracts that were distributed by preachers. Lewis describes the situation as it existed in 1845 as follows:

Only the better organized prisons maintained libraries. Connecticut had small library; each prisoner was furnished also with a weekly temperance paper, and a religious paper. Massachusetts had a library of several hundred volumes, initiated by a donation of $50 "sent by a mother of a life prisoner to her son, to furnish him with proper reading." The prisoners in the Massachusetts prison made frequent donations for the library out of their earnings. The State appropriated, in the early forties, $100 annually for the increase and greater variety of books. Books were distributed at intervals of several weeks in prisons possessing libraries, at the discretion of the warden and chaplain.[22]

It is probable that practically all of the books in these libraries were theological and were intended to compel prisoners to contemplate the eternal sufferings to which they would be subjected if they did not repent. As late as 1853, the moral instructor in the Eastern Penitentiary of Pennsylvania complained because books that were not "of a strictly religious kind" were being placed in the library, resulting in an "alarming decrease in the call for religious books."[23] The chaplain of the women's prison in Sing Sing made public charges against the matron because of her interference with the religious education of the prisoners, charging her, among other things, with supplying the prisoners with such morally destructive literature as Dickens' Nicholas Nickleby.[24]

At present almost all correctional institutions except some of the jails and workhouses have libraries. But even today the funds for purchase of

[21] F. F. Nadler, "The American State Reformatory," University of California Publications in Education, Volume V, No. 3, 1920, p. 420.

[22] Lewis, op. cit., p. 341–342.

[23] H. E. Barnes, "The Progress of American Penology," Journal of Criminal Law and Criminology, 13:206–207, July–August, 1922.

[24] Klein, op. cit., p. 309.

books are seldom more than nominal and most libraries consist of gifts of unwanted books from other libraries. The American Prison Association made the following statement about prison libraries in 1946:

While the number of fairly good libraries is steadily growing, many prison and reformatory libraries in America today, filled with dog-eared discards from a thousand attics, need a house-cleaning more than anything else. Dull books that nobody *would* read, fine-type books that nobody *could* read, out-of-date books that nobody *should* read—all these should be sent remorselessly to the scrap heap.[25]

If the library is to play an important part in the formation of new attitudes, the books must be carefully selected for the institutional library and for the individual prisoner. The number of institutions with library staffs equipped to render such services is close to zero. In 1945, thirty libraries reported that they had purchased no new books during the year.[26]

The open-shelf system in which inmates are permitted to go to the library to select books has been adopted in most of the federal prisons and in a number of state institutions. But in many institutions, inmates still must order books from a printed catalog of titles which is passed among the cells. Of 115 state prisons and reformatories responding to a questionnaire sent out in 1940, 54 reported the use of this system for distributing books.[27] In the same number of institutions the library had no special quarters. Half of the institutions did not include library expense in the regular budget. In some institutions the librarian is an untrained inmate.

HINDRANCES TO EDUCATIONAL WORK. Among the hindrances to educational work in prisons are the attitudes of the prisoners and the informal organization of the prison. Some of the attitudes are developed outside the institution, but many of them are produced by the prison régime and by the conception that the prisons are primarily places of punishment. The wall and bars needed to prevent escapes keep this aspect of the prison continually before the attention of the inmates. Prisoners conventionally react by a hostile attitude toward the institution and all its activities. The school, recreational, religious, and other activities constantly struggle against this attitude and generally with little success. Educational ad-

25 American Prison Association, *Manual of Suggested Standards for a State Correctional System* (New York: Author, 1946), p. 45. Reprinted by permission of the publishers.

26 Benjamin Frank, "Summary of Second Annual Statistical Survey of Prison Libraries," *Proceedings of the American Prison Association, 1945*, pp. 147–150; Edwin I. Friedman, "Penal Institution Libraries in the United States," *Proceedings of the American Prison Association, 1949*, pp. 168–176.

27 S. H. Souter, Jr., "Results of the Prison Library Survey," *Proceedings of the American Prison Association, 1941*, pp. 322–327.

ministrators, like the warden and guards, are considered "outsiders" by the inmates. Prisoners who participate in educational activities are looked down upon and, in some prisons, suspected of being stool pigeons.

A second hindrance to educational work is inadequate equipment and organization. Libraries are often housed in the visiting room, chaplain's office, or a storage room. Money is not available for expensive vocational educational materials or instructors. In certain places no room is provided for school except the mess-hall. In some institutions children's school desks are used for adult prisoners. The textbooks are frequently those used in the public schools for children. Some years ago, according to reports, a class of prisoners was engaged in copying from the blackboard a sentence which read, "How swiftly and pleasantly the hours fly by." Conditions which are similar to those existing in 1931 still prevail in some institutions:

History taught from texts that were published before the World War, and reading from primers published as far back as 1868; 75 men of all ages crammed into the only classroom in the prison, seated on backless benches without desks, taught under the district school method by an earnest but untrained chaplain, and searched by guards on entering and leaving the classroom; sixty reformatory inmates in a single room, taught by an untrained inmate under twenty years of age, with a sleepy, stupid-looking guard on a high stool in the front of the classroom to keep order; guards conducting classes with hickory clubs lying on their desks; guard-teachers, after a hard day's work in the school, "swinging the club" over their erstwhile pupils in the cell houses and mess hall; a $130-a-month guard in charge of the education work in a 3,000-man penitentiary; men studying in the prison of one of the wealthiest states in the country by the light of fifteen-watt bulbs; rules forbidding prisoners attending school to have writing material of any kind in their cells; educational "systems" which consist of allowing prisoners, without guidance, to purchase correspondence courses far beyond their ability and to follow them without assistance; schools that are nothing but dumping grounds for the industries, places of temporary sojourn for men who have not yet been assigned to work, or convenient roosting places for yard gangs that are called on occasionally to unload cars of coal and other supplies; libraries in which there are not more than a dozen up-to-date books possessing educational value; and so on almost endlessly.[28]

A third hindrance to educational work is the productive industry and maintenance activities of the institution. This involves a difficult problem

[28] A. H. MacCormick, *Education of Adult Prisoners* (New York: National Society of Penal Information, 1931), pp. 42–43. Reprinted by permission of the author.

in the comparative importance of labor and of educational activities.[29] School authorities generally insist that the work should not interfere with the school; the warden, interested in the financial status and the smooth operation of the institution, insists that the school should not interfere with prison labor. In general, educational activities are organized so that they interfere as little as possible with productive labor. One experienced warden, however, has stated that he would discharge either the director of education or the supervisor of industries, or both, if they were unable or unwilling to correlate the programs of education and industries.[30] While this attitude may seem harsh, the implication is that if these two programs cannot be coordinated the purpose of a modern correctional institution is defeated.[31] The general point is that the criminal needs a fundamental modification of attitudes unless he is to be retained in the institution all his life. Even if labor has some value for this purpose, many other methods also must be used, and these methods are usually included in the educational system.

RESULTS OF PRISON EDUCATION. While most existing educational programs, like most existing work programs, probably are of very slight value for the purpose of modification of attitudes, many prison administrators and many prisoners have expressed the belief that well-organized prison schools are an excellent reformative influence. Few attempts have been made to measure this influence and most of these attempts have not been reliable. An elaborate statistical study was made in the Wisconsin State Prison, which has an educational system that is decidedly above the average of state prisons. The general conclusion was that, when other things are held constant, men who do not attend the prison school violate parole in significantly larger numbers than do men who attend the school. However, educational training for less than six months appears to have no effect on recidivism.[32] Less detailed studies were made on the post-release behavior of Joliet prisoners who had taken intramural correspondence courses in the institution, with the conclusion that their behavior was slightly

[29] See Ralph D. Edwards, "Correctional Industries and Inmate Training," _Proceedings of the American Correctional Association_, 1963, pp. 197–200.

[30] John C. Burke, "How Can Proper Correlation Between Prison Industries and Prison Education be Attained?" _Proceedings of the American Prison Association_, 1948, pp. 174–178.

[31] Cf. Frank T. Flynn, "Employment and Labor," in Paul W. Tappan, Editor, _Contemporary Correction_ (New York: McGraw-Hill, 1951), pp. 238–253; A. C. Schnur, "Prisoner Education, Prison Industry, and the Correctional Process," _Proceedings of the American Prison Association_, 1951, pp. 25–32.

[32] Alfred C. Schnur, "The Educational Treatment of Prisoners and Recidivism," _American Journal of Sociology_, 54:142–147, September, 1948.

superior to the behavior of the control group.[33] Akers found that of 170 men given trade training, 42 percent secured jobs for which they had been trained and only one was returned as a parole violator. In a control group of 133 untrained inmates, nine were returned as parole violators.[34] More recently, Glaser found that of 114 men who had been released from prison four months earlier and who had found post-release employment, 95 (83 percent) had been involved in some sort of educational activity in prison. These 95 men had held 156 post-release jobs. Of the 95 men, 26 (27 percent) reported that their prison education had helped them in 31 of their 156 jobs. The men said that elementary-school education was helpful in 9 of the 32 jobs, high-school education in 3, white-collar training such as bookkeeping in another 9, personality improvement courses in 5, and mechanical trade courses in the remaining 5.[35] Glaser's more general data on the relationship between prison education and recidivism indicate, contrary to the Wisconsin findings, that 39 percent of 361 men enrolled in prison education were "failures" (returned to prison or received a non-prison sentence for a felony-like offense within four years), while 33 percent of 654 men who never enrolled in prison school programs were failures.[36]

## SUGGESTED READINGS

Chenault, Price, *Diagnostic and Remedial Teaching in Correctional Institutions.* Albany: New York State Department of Correction, 1945.

Chenault, Price, "Education," in Paul W. Tappan, Editor, *Contemporary Correction.* New York: McGraw-Hill, 1951, pp. 224–237.

Clemmer, Donald, "A Beginning in Social Education in Correctional Institutions," *Federal Probation,* 13:32–35, March, 1949.

Eckenrode, C. J., "The Correctional Library Comes of Age," *Proceedings of the American Correctional Association,* 1964, pp. 205–212.

Fenton, N., "Adult Education in the California Prison System," *California Journal of Secondary Education,* 26:179–183, March, 1951.

Friedman, Edwin I., "Institutional Life—A Program of Social Education, *Prison World,* 11:14–17, July, 1949.

Goodsell, James Nelson, "The Penal Press: Voice of the Prisoner," *Federal Probation,* 23:53–57, June, 1959.

Haskell, Martin R., and H. Ashley Weeks, "Role Training as Preparation

---

[33]Anonymous, *Education in Prison and Success on Parole* (Joliet: Stateville Correspondence School Monograph No. 1, 1941).

[34] *Op. cit.*

[35] Glaser, op. cit., pp. 271–272.

[36] *Ibid.,* p. 276.

for Release from a Correctional Institution," *Journal of Criminal Law, Criminology and Police Science,* 50:441–447, January, 1960.

Hobhouse, S., and A. F. Brockway, *English Prisons Today, Being the Report of the Prison System Enquiry Committee.* London: Longmans, 1922.

Ingram, Christine P., *Education in Training Schools for Delinquent Youth.* Washington: U.S. Office of Education Bulletin, No. 5, 1945.

Kendall, Glenn M., *The Organization and Teaching of Social and Economic Studies in Correctional Institutions.* New York: Columbia University Press, 1939.

Kendall, Glenn M., "General and Social Education in Correctional Treatment," *Proceedings of the American Prison Association,* 1946, pp. 105–117.

MacCormick, A. H., *Education of Adult Prisoners.* New York: National Society of Penal Information, 1931.

Marshall, Bertha, "Librarian Goes to San Quentin," *California Library Bulletin,* 11:101–102, March, 1950.

Outten, Ernest R., "What are We Doing—What Should We Do?" *American Journal of Correction,* 18:4–5, ff., May–June, 1956.

Schnur, Alfred C., "Prisoner Education, Prison Industry and the Correctional Process," *Proceedings of the American Prison Association,* 1951, pp. 25–32.

Souter, S. H., Jr., "Results of Prison Library Survey," *Proceedings of the American Prison Association,* 1941, pp. 322–327.

Wallack, Walter M., "Vocational Education in Correctional Institutions," *National Society for the Study of Education Yearbook.* 1943, pp. 334–351.

Wallack, Walter M.; Glenn M. Kendall; and Howard L. Briggs, *Education Within Prison Walls.* New York: Columbia University Press, 1939.

Weaver, LeRoy, and Owens, C. D., "Social Education Program at Elmira Reformatory," *Journal of Correctional Education,* 2:81–93, 1950.

Woughter, C. C., "Vocational Education and the Prisoner," *Industrial Arts and Vocational Education,* 40:279–281, September, 1951.

# 27. RELEASE FROM PRISON

THE EXITS from prison are more numerous than the entrances into prison. Entrance into prison on sentence must always be by way of the court, generally in accordance with conditions fixed by the legislature. But one may be released from prison by completion of the full term imposed by the court, or before the end of the full term by an executive who grants a pardon or commutation, or an administrative board that grants a parole or a release on good time. That is, acting by authority of the constitution or statutes, the legislature, the court, an executive, or an administrative board may determine the time of release of a prisoner. Table XIX shows the methods of release for felons in 1963, as reported by the Federal Bureau of Prisons.[1]

PARDON AND RELATED CONCEPTS. The modification of penalties by the executive may take the form of pardon, commutation, or amnesty. A pardon is an act of mercy or clemency, ordinarily by an executive, by which a criminal is excused from a penalty which has been imposed upon him. It has been held in many decisions that the pardon wipes away guilt and makes the person who committed the crime as innocent as though he had not committed it. Pardon may be either conditional or absolute. The conditional pardon is one in which the guilt is wiped away on condition that the offender perform certain acts or refrain from certain acts specified by the pardoning power, such as leaving the country or abstaining from intoxicating liquors. If a person who has received a conditional pardon fails to perform the required acts, the pardon becomes void and he may be returned to prison for the remainder of his original term.

Commutation of sentence is a reduction of the penalty by executive order. A sentence is frequently commuted so that it expires at once. Commutation differs from conditional pardon in that it does not wipe away

---

[1] Federal Bureau of Prisons, "Prisoners in State and Federal Institutions, 1963," *National Prisoner Statistics*, No. 36, December, 1964, p. 20.

## TABLE XIX

TYPE OF DISCHARGE FROM STATE AND FEDERAL INSTITUTIONS, 1963

| Type of Discharge | All Institutions | | Federal Institutions | | State Institutions | |
|---|---|---|---|---|---|---|
| | Number | Percent | Number | Percent | Number | Percent |
| Parole | 59,061 | 45.7 | 5,127 | 28.6 | 53,934 | 48.5 |
| Conditional Pardon | 85 | .1 | — | .0 | 85 | .1 |
| Other Conditional Release | 7,320 | 5.7 | 3,747 | 20.9 | 3,573 | 3.2 |
| Expiration of Sentence | 34,906 | 27.0 | 6,307 | 35.2 | 28,599 | 25.7 |
| Commutation | 3,650 | 2.8 | — | .0 | 3,650 | 3.3 |
| Pardon | 28 | .0 | — | .0 | 28 | .0 |
| Death, Except Execution | 747 | .6 | 55 | .3 | 692 | .6 |
| Execution | 21 | .0 | — | .0 | 21 | .0 |
| Other Discharges* | 23,350 | 18.1 | 2,698 | 15.0 | 20,652 | 18.6 |
| Total Discharges | 129,168 | 100.0 | 17,934 | 100.0 | 111,234 | 100.0 |

* Includes escapes, court orders, and authorized temporary absences.

guilt in the eyes of the law, and consequently does not restore civil rights as does a pardon. Ohio governors tend to commute to life imprisonment about 38 percent of the death sentences imposed by juries and courts.[2] Amnesty is a pardon applied to a group of criminals, and is illustrated by the act of the President of the United States in 1945 of restoring civil rights to all federal ex-prisoners who had served honorably in the armed forces for one year or more. In February, 1953, Britain granted amnesty to 14,260 wartime deserters from the armed forces. A reprieve or respite is a temporary postponement of the execution of a sentence, generally for the purpose of further investigation of the guilt of the prisoner. It is used in connection with the death penalty rather than with sentences of imprisonment.

In the Anglo-American legal system, the power of an executive to grant pardons was derived from the time when the power of the Crown was almost absolute.[3] In the American colonies the pardoning power was generally vested in the royal governor, acting either alone or with the

[2] Ohio Legislative Service Commission, *Capital Punishment*, Staff Research Report No. 46 (Columbus, Author, 1961), p. 46.
[3] Lewis Mayers, *The American Legal System*, Revised Edition (New York: Harper and Row, 1964), p. 138.

governor's council. After the Revolution, because of the fear of executives, the pardoning power was at first retained by the legislative assemblies, but it soon passed to the governors, generally as an expression of the doctrine of separation of powers. Recently the responsibility of the governor has been limited by the development of pardon boards.

In 21 states, the governor shares the power to pardon with a board or council, and has no more power than any other member of the board in eight of these states. In 27 states, the governor has the sole and complete power to pardon except in impeachment cases. In seventeen of these states in which the governor has final authority, a pardon board or other assistants are appointed for advisory purposes. An advisory pardon board in practice may have complete control of the pardons because in those cases the governor always adopts the recommendations of the board. On the other hand the recommendation of an advisory pardon board in some states is seldom accepted. In South Carolina, the governor is required to report to the legislature his reasons if he rejects the recommendation of the board. In 31 states, the governor or board of pardons is required to report each case to the legislature at the next regular session. It is customary for the pardon board to request a recommendation from the sentencing judge and the prosecuting attorney.

The President of the United States is authorized to grant pardons to those who violate federal laws, except in cases of impeachment. Out of 1,208 applications for federal pardons acted upon in 1940, 532 were thrown out by adverse reports of the attorney; of the 417 on which favorable reports were made, pardons or commutations were granted to 313, or 75 percent. Of the 313 pardons granted, 235 were merely restoration of civil rights, 31 were commutations, 40 were remittances of fines, and only 6 were remission of guilt as usually understood. In 1950–1963, no pardons or conditional pardons, and only 50 commutations, were granted to federal prisoners.

Mayors are given authority, with restrictions, in a few states to grant pardons to those who violate municipal ordinances. This power has been greatly abused in a few cities.

In the earlier period, many prisoners were pardoned to make room for newcomers;[4] in 1813, pardons were granted to 134 prisoners in the state prison at Greenwich Village, New York, and 198 new prisoners were admitted; it was necessary to pardon the others in order to admit the new prisoners. The following are some of the recorded reasons for granting par-

[4] O. F. Lewis, The Development of American Prisons and Prison Customs, 1776–1845 (Albany: Prison Association of New York, 1922).

## TABLE XX

PERCENT OF THOSE DISCHARGED FROM STATE PRISONS WHO WERE PARDONED
IN SPECIFIC STATES, BY DECADES

| Decade | New Jersey | New Hampshire | Pennsyl-vania* | Missouri | Michigan† |
|--------|-----------|---------------|----------------|----------|-----------|
| 1800–09 | 14.3 | — | — | — | — |
| 1810–19 | 25.5 | 9.2 | — | — | — |
| 1820–29 | 25.7 | 20.1 | 21.4 | — | — |
| 1830–39 | 38.1 | 50.8 | 19.0 | 78.6‡ | — |
| 1840–49 | 22.4 | 43.4 | 21.1 | 25.2 | 24.6 |
| 1850–59 | 40.9 | 41.2 | 13.4 | 40.3 | 23.3 |
| 1860–69 | 31.0 | 37.7 | 16.2 | 50.0 | 10.0 |
| 1870–79 | 10.0 | 24.0 | 8.4 | 11.1 | 5.9 |
| 1880–89 | 10.5 | 13.9 | 2.9 | 6.2 | 4.5 |
| 1890–99 | 5.2 | 10.5 | 3.7 | 5.9 | 3.9 |
| 1900–09 | 0.6 | 7.6 | 3.1 | 3.8 | 3.5 |
| 1910–19 | 0.2 | 2.8§ | — | 0.9 | 0.1⟮ |

\* Decades are 1826–1835, etc., the last ending in 1915.
† Decades are 1841–1850, etc.
‡ For the years 1836–1839 only.
§ For the years 1910–1912 only.
⟮ For the years 1910–1916 only.

dons: the offender has been adequately punished, the ends of justice have been met sufficiently, the age (either very young or very old) of the offender, sickness of the offender, injury of the prisoner, dependents need his help, relatives or others are able to care for him, the crime was committed under the influence of liquor, has rendered service in convicting others, meritorious service in prisons (such as saving the life of a prison official or helping extinguish a fire), or serving his country in the war.

The use of pardons began to decrease steadily about a century ago, and currently pardons are seldom used. In 1905–1909, 3.0 percent of those released from federal prisons were released by pardon. This percentage decreased to 0.009 percent by 1940, and since then there have been no releases by pardon. The same decrease is found in many states. Table XX shows this decrease in a few states for which statistics are available over a long period. These states are not representative of the entire United States for they are, with one exception, Northern states, and the pardon rate is at present about eight times as high in the Southern states as in the Northern. The trend has been equally pronounced, however, in the Southern states in recent years.

The general rule of pardons is that the more serious the crime and the more severe the sentence, the more probable is release by pardon.[5] Wines and Dwight presented statistics of releases from the state prison of Massachusetts from 1828 to 1866 which were in accordance with this principle.[6] Of male felony prisoners released from state and federal prisons and reformatories in 1940, the last year for which data are available, pardons were granted to 5.9 percent of those on sentences of ten years or more, to 2.5 percent of those on sentences of five to nine years, and to 0.8 percent of those on sentences of less than five years. Of the same releases, 3.9 percent were by pardon for those on murder charges, 3.3 for those on robbery charges, 2.5 percent for those on burglary charges, and 1.9 percent for those on auto theft charges. The social status of the criminal also affects the decision to pardon. Negroes are pardoned less frequently than white persons, especially in Southern states, and gentlemen thieves more frequently than thieves of the lower socio-economic class. Also, in areas where parole is used frequently, pardons are used infrequently. Wolfgang examined recommendations for commutation of sentence, by judges and district attorneys, in the cases of 368 prisoners who had been convicted of murder. The opinion of the judge differed significantly from that of the district attorney in two-thirds of the cases, a situation arising principally because the attorneys supported the pardon board's decision in significantly more cases than did the judges. In only seven percent of the cases did the board grant commutation when the judge and the attorney both recommended that it not be granted.[7]

Value of the pardoning power. Pardons are regarded as justifiable because of errors of justice which call for some method of review of the evidence. These errors of justice are of two types. The first is the conviction in which doubt regarding guilt arises. The second is the conviction in which doubt regarding the justice of the penalty arises. In Massachusetts prior to 1871, life imprisonment was the only legal penalty for burglary. When less severe penalties were authorized in that year, many of those who had been sentenced previously applied for pardons. In Illinois, the minimum sentence for robbery with a gun was raised from one year to ten years and subsequently reduced again to one year. Many prisoners who had been sentenced with a minimum term of ten years during this interim

[5] This rule was stated by Henry Cabot Lodge, "Naval Courts-Martial and the Pardoning Power," Atlantic Monthly, 50:43–50, July, 1882.

[6] E. C. Wines and T. W. Dwight, Report on the Prisons and Reformatories of the United States and Canada, New York State Assembly Document No. 5, 1867, Volume II, pp. 297–298.

[7] Marvin E. Wolfgang, "Murder, the Pardon Board, and Recommendations by Judges and District Attorneys," Journal of Criminal Law, Criminology and Police Science, 50: 338–346, November–December, 1959.

applied for pardons. Because of these and similar changes in legislation or decisions of courts or because of changes in the spirit of the times, some method of modifying the actions of the courts should be available. If prison sentences were completely indeterminate, few pardons would be needed, for the occasions for pardons are found principally in connection with penalties which are regarded as unjustified.

Aside from the pardons mentioned above, many pardons are granted in some states after the period of imprisonment has ended and for the sole purpose of restoring the civil rights of the offenders. The automatic restoration of civil rights at the time of release from prison, or at least at the time of release from parole, would probably be a much better social policy.

GOOD-TIME LAWS.    As early as 1817, a good-time law was passed in New York State, which provided that first-term prisoners on sentences of five years or less could abridge their sentences by one-fourth for good behavior. Apparently the law was not used. The method was soon adopted in several other places; Connecticut passed a law of this kind in 1821 relating to inmates of workhouses; Tennessee passed a good time law in 1833 and Ohio in 1856; Maconochie put it into general use in 1842 in the convict colonies in Australia; and Marsangy advocated this method in France in 1846. In spite of the earlier precedents in the United States, the method did not become generally known until just after the Civil War when the news regarding the famous Irish system spread.[8] By 1868, 24 states had made provision for reduction of prison terms by good behavior, and at present all states save California have good-time laws.

The general principle of the good time laws is that a prison board is authorized to release the prisoner in less time than the sentence imposed by the court, if, in their opinion, the prisoner maintains good conduct in prison. Generally, for every month of satisfactory conduct, a certain number of days is deducted from the inmate's sentence. A usual procedure is to deduct one month from the first year of satisfactory conduct, two months for the second year, and so on, up to six months for the sixth and each succeeding year. A three-year sentence, thus, can be reduced to two years and six months by good behavior; a ten-year sentence can be reduced to six years and three months. In addition to this "statutory good time," as it is called by inmates, prisoners in some states may earn "merit good time" for extraordinary behavior and "industrial good time" for participation in the prison industries. Merit good-time and industrial good-time laws usually operate to reduce the period of time to be served before

[8] E. C. Wines, "Commutation Laws in the United States," *Report of the Prison Association of New York*, 1868, pp. 154–170.

an inmate is entitled to have his case reviewed by the parole board, rather than to reduce the actual sentence. A prison board is the administrative authority and can determine whether or not the prisoner has earned the reduction in time, but the legislature makes the schedule of reductions in time. Granting "time off for good behavior" differs, in this respect, from commutation of sentence by executive order, in which the sentence is shortened by an authority outside the prison because the inmate's behavior has been good, or for other reasons.

Good-time laws represent an attempt to mitigate the severity of sentences, to get good work from the prisoners, to assist in reformation, and, above all, to solve the problem of prison discipline. The two principal objections to good-time laws are that they tend to become mechanical and that they place emphasis on routine conformity to prison rules, rather than on reformation.[9] Usually a clerk automatically grants the maximum amount of good time to each convict unless good time has been deducted by the disciplinary "court." Prisoners then come to view good-time as a right. The usual practice is to credit the new inmate with the maximum amount of good time permitted by law and then to deduct a certain number of days from that time whenever the disciplinary court finds him guilty of serious infraction of the prison rules. Good time may be deducted from the amount of time imposed in a definite sentence, or it may be applied to either the minimum or the maximum period of an indefinite sentence, according to the laws of the state.

THE INDETERMINATE SENTENCE.  The release time of a prisoner may be determined by the legislature, which fixes a definite sentence for the offense, by the court, which receives authority from the legislature to fix definite penalties within the limits set by the legislature, or by an administrative board, which receives from the legislature authority to fix definite penalties within the limits set by the legislature or by the court. When the time of release is determined by an administrative board and the court merely imposes minimum and maximum limits of the penalty, the sentence is known as an indeterminate sentence. Strictly speaking, the sentence is not indeterminate if the limits are fixed by the court or by the legislature, and it should be called indefinite rather than indeterminate. No state has sentences that are completely indeterminate and the general practice is to call these indefinite sentences indeterminate.

The administrative board which fixes the penalties is called a parole board, but there is no necessary connection between parole and the inde-

[9] G. I. Giardini, "Good Time—Placebo of Correction," *American Journal of Correction*, 20:3–5 ff., April, 1958.

terminate sentence. "Indeterminate sentence" refers to the fact that the exact period of custody is not fixed before the custody begins, while the term "parole" refers to the fact that a portion of the period of custody may be spent outside the institution. Either may be used independently of the other. The federal government and some states have parole systems but no indeterminate sentences; it would be possible to have indeterminate sentences with complete and final release without supervision. Parole is the status of the prisoner after release from the walls of the institution, while still under the special guardianship of the state. It may be granted either to the prisoner on a definite sentence, though this is usually restricted to the period of freedom granted by the good-time allowance,[10] or the prisoner on an indeterminate sentence. A person on an indeterminate sentence may be released either conditionally on parole or unconditionally and completely without parole. The two methods, though distinct in principle, are generally combined in practice and must be combined for the greatest efficiency of either system.

*History of the indeterminate sentence.* As early as the Inquisition, the indeterminate sentence was used, for criminals were sometimes sentenced to prison "for such time as seems expedient to the Church." In some of the early workhouses in the first part of the eighteenth century, commitment might be for an indeterminate period, especially for minors. In 1769, the colony of Connecticut provided that all rogues, vagabonds, sturdy beggars, and other lewd, idle, dissolute, profane, and disorderly persons without settlement in the colony might be confined in the workhouse at hard labor "until released by order of law." The indeterminate sentence has been used in the institutions for juvenile delinquents since their origin, the maximum period of confinement being the minority of the delinquent.

These developments of the indeterminate sentence in the workhouses and houses of refuge did not, however, carry to the public an implication that it should be extended to the state prisons. Occasional arguments to that effect were presented, to be sure, from the time Dr. Benjamin Rush urged it in 1787 to the Civil War. But the system really became known to the United States shortly after the Civil War. Wines and Dwight in a report to the state legislature of New York in 1867 urged that sentences should be indeterminate for certain types of offenders. An indeterminate

---

[10] In the federal system and in Wisconsin an inmate who has served one-third of his time is eligible for release on parole, but if he is denied parole or if he waives parole he may be "conditionally released" for a period of time equal to the good-time allowance. During this period he is handled "as if on parole." See George C. Killinger, "Parole and Other Release Procedures," in Paul W. Tappan, Editor, *Contemporary Correction* (New York: McGraw-Hill, 1951, pp. 361–379).

sentence law, known as the "Three Years' Law," was passed in Michigan in 1869, but it was soon declared unconstitutional. Indeterminate sentences were an essential part of the program of Elmira Reformatory, which was authorized in 1869. Probably the most important influence in America in forming a favorable opinion regarding this sytem was a paper by Brockway on "The Ideal Prison System" before the National Prison Association in 1870, in which he stated the essential reasons for the indeterminate sentence as clearly as they have ever been stated.

It was not until 1889 that a general indeterminate sentence law was secured, this being in New York State. The law gave the court authority to sentence a convicted person to an indefinite term of imprisonment, within the limits fixed by law for the offense. This law was not mandatory and during the twelve years after its passage it was applied in only 115 cases out of about 13,000 in which it might have been used. In 1901, a law was passed in New York State, requiring the court to impose an indeterminate sentence on first offenders, within a minimum of not less than one year and a maximum as fixed for each crime by the laws of the state. Indeterminate sentence laws had been enacted in five states by 1900. The number increased to thirty-one by 1915. At present, all but ten states and the federal government have indeterminate sentence laws.

The use of the indeterminate sentence increased until about 1925, decreased until about 1940, and now is on the increase. Of commitments to federal and state prisons and reformatories in 1910, 37 percent were on indeterminate sentences; in 1926, 55 percent; in 1940, 40 percent; in 1946, 45 percent; and in 1950, 46 percent.

*Restrictions on the indeterminate sentence.* Not all prisoners in the states that have adopted this system are held on indeterminate sentences. The method is often applied only to restricted classes of offenders and the restrictions vary from state to state. It generally does not apply at all to misdemeanors or to the most serious felonies. In various states kidnapers, rapists, murderers, defaulting notaries public, bank or homestead officials who misuse the funds of depositors, and persons guilty of arson, crimes against nature, and treason are excluded from the provisions of the law. It is sometimes restricted to those below a specified age or above a specified age. The treatment reaction to crime is, thus, selective. Such restrictions are based either on the assumption that certain legal categories of offenders should be punished rather than treated or on the assumption that certain categories of offenders are not amenable to treatment. However, in recent years the general tendency has been to extend the indeterminate sentence system to all offenders.

*The minimum and maximum limits.* Originally, the legislature fixed a definite penalty for each offense. As the treatment reaction to crime has arisen, the trend has been for the legislature to transfer to other agencies the authority to fix definite sentences within limits set by the legislature for each offense or class of offenses. It transferred this authority first to the court and then to the parole board.[11] When the court was given authority to fix limits within the limits set by the legislature, some judges who were opposed to indeterminate sentences made the minimum almost identical with the maximum, giving sentences such as: two years and nine months to two years and ten months; thirty to thirty-one years; one hundred and fifty to one hundred and sixty years. The legislature tried at first to correct these abuses by providing that the minimum set by the court must be not more than one-half, or some other specified fraction, of the maximum. More frequently, the legislatures have deprived the courts of the authority to fix any limits within those set by the legislature and have given authority to the parole boards to fix the sentence within these limits.[12] In that case, the court has authority merely to impose the minimum and maximum sentences provided in the law.[13]

The question arises, Why should either the court or the legislature fix the limits? Why should not the sentences be completely indeterminate and the parole board have complete and unlimited authority to determine the time of release? The sentences of 39 percent of the prisoners committed to state prisons and reformatories in 1960 were definite. Of the indeterminate sentences, 17 percent had no minimum limit and 13 percent either had a maximum of 20 years or more or had a maximum of life.[14] The problem of the minimum limit is somewhat different from the problem of the maximum limit.

[11] See Mayers, *op. cit.*, pp. 125–130.

[12] A reversal of this trend has occurred in Illinois. This state experimented for a few years with a rather ideal indeterminate sentence law of one year to life for many offenses, the exact time of release to be determined by the parole board. But in 1943 the law was amended and it again became the duty of the judges to fix the minimum and maximum terms of imprisonment within the limits set by the legislature. Illinois judges then imposed such short spreads in years between the minimum and the maximum that in the majority of cases the parole board had practically no authority to determine the length of sentence. For example, of the Cook County inmates released from Illinois penal institutions on parole and expiration of sentence in 1941, 84 percent were paroled; in 1948, under the amended law, only 25 percent were paroled. Nat Cosnow, "Viewing the Crime Statistics, Chicago and Cook County, 1948," *Criminal Justice*, No. 77, January, 1950, pp. 10–19. See also George W. Schwaner, Jr., "The Illinois Sentence and Parole Act, 1943 Amendments," *Criminal Justice*, No. 77, January, 1950, pp. 27–28; and Don T. Blackiston, "The Inadequacies of the Sentence and Parole Act of 1943," *Criminal Justice*, No. 77, January, 1950.

[13] See Paul T. Tappan, "Sentencing Under the Model Penal Code," *Law and Contemporary Problems*, 23:528–543, Summer, 1958.

[14] Federal Bureau of Prisons, "Characteristics of State Prisoners, 1960," *National Prisoner Statistics* (Washington, Federal Bureau of Prisons, 1961), p. 42, 49.

The principal argument for the minimum limit is that it is needed as a check in case the parole board should become sentimental or corrupt. Generally, this argument is part of the punitive reaction to crime. In some states, a large proportion of the prisoners on indeterminate sentences are released as soon as the minimum sentence is served. This is taken as proof that many prisoners would not be punished at all unless the legislature or the court imposed a minimum penalty. As a matter of fact, the few states in which the minimum limit has been removed have witnessed no wholesale prison deliveries.[15] An administrative board given the authority to determine whether a prisoner should be held one year or five years, can be trusted to decide whether the prisoner should be held six months or ten months. It is probable that the very existence of the minimum sentence serves as a convenient time of release of all offenders against whom no bad behavior in prison has been recorded. If no minimum were provided, a decision on the merits of each case would be necessary.

The absolute maximum penalty probably results in more injury to society than does the minimum. Often it is perfectly clear to prison authorities that certain offenders have not reacted favorably to the rehabilitative efforts and that they will repeat their offenses as soon as released. Nevertheless, the law requires that authorities release them when the maximum period of imprisonment has been served.[16] The legal maximum is an expression of the fear that the administrative board will make mistakes and keep confined for life some prisoners who would be perfectly safe in society. But such mistakes are less likely to be made when a decision is reached by a board that is intimately acquainted, as a result of long study, with the particular prisoner, than when a decision is reached by the legislature which is not acquainted with the individual at all and attempts to prescribe limits for the entire class, or by the court which has a superficial knowledge of a particular offender.

It is quite possible that juries will not convict offenders if they may be held in prison for life for comparatively trivial offenses. This argument is supported by the experience with capital punishment and with the "habitual criminal acts." If the sentences were absolutely indeterminate, the judge and jury would not know whether a particular offender would be held for one year or for life; they would know only that the administrative board would hold the offender as long as necessary for the protection of society. However, the administrative board must be able to do much more

[15] Cf. Norman S. Hayner, "Sentencing by an Administrative Board," Law and Contemporary Problems, 23:477–494, Summer, 1958.
[16] See John B. Waite, The Prevention of Repeated Crime (Ann Arbor: University of Michigan Press, 1943), p. 58.

efficient work than at present before it can be trusted with authority of this nature. One study indicates that there is a wide discrepancy between statutes and popular judgement as to how severe punishment should be for selected offenses.[17] Efficient boards could take such discrepancies into account.

*Determining the time of release.* The American Parole Association stated in 1933 that fitness for limited freedom should be the principle used in determining the release time of particular offenders:

Has the institution accomplished all that it can for him; is the offender's state of mind and attitude toward his own difficulties and problems such that further residence will be harmful or beneficial; does a suitable environment await him on the outside; can the beneficial effect already accomplished be retained if he is held longer to allow a more suitable environment to be developed?[18]

While parole boards generally attempt to use this principle, they often must depart from it. Sometimes the departure is a matter of convenience. For several years in New York over 95 percent of the inmates of state prisons were released as soon as they had completed the minimum term. Moreover, this procedure was defended and there is no final proof that it is not as good a method as any. Several studies of successes on parole indicate that the prisoners who remain longer violate parole more often than those who remain a shorter time in prison. This may result either from the imposition of longer terms upon prisoners who are least fit for life in society or from the decrease in fitness for life in society with the length of the period of isolation from society.

Parole boards also must depart from the principle when it would be politically or administratively disadvantageous to release an offender, even if he is rehabilitated. This is especially the case when the board is dealing with men who have committed notorious crimes—release of one man, even if he is rehabilitated, might result in such severe attacks on the board and on the indeterminate sentence system that the opportunity to use the principle in other cases is lost. A man must be sacrificed for the system. Similarly, if the public reacts to crime punitively and insists on long terms for certain types of offenders, the parole board may not insist on short terms. The policies and actions of parole boards are sometimes carefully watched by police, district attorneys, newspapers, crime commis-

[17] Arnold M. Rose and Arthur E. Prell, "Does the Punishment Fit the Crime? A Study in Social Valuation," *American Journal of Sociology*, 61:247-259, November, 1955.
[18] *Journal of Criminal Law and Criminology*, 24:791, November–December, 1933.

sions, and other agencies which believe that long periods of imprisonment should prevail. These interests must be balanced against the interests of groups which clamor for the idea that the board should release men whenever the board believes they are ready to be released.

In some institutions the principle of fitness for release has been used, but actual fitness for release has been determined by a marking or credit system, designed to measure the behavior of the prisoner while in the institution. These systems differ considerably from one institution to another, but the essential points are as follows: (a) Release is granted only to those who have secured a specified number of credits, just as graduation from an educational institution is dependent upon securing a specified number of units or hours of credit. (b) Credits are secured by good conduct and lost by bad conduct. The prisoner generally secures a uniform credit per day or per month unless reports have been made against him for bad conduct, negligence, or laziness. (c) The prisoner is promoted to a higher grade when he has secured a specified number of credits. He has additional privileges in that grade and is able to earn credits at a more rapid rate than in the lower grade. He is not eligible for release until he reaches the highest grade. (d) A bonus in addition to the regular credits may be granted for especially meritorious acts, and an additional demerit may be given for especially bad conduct. In one of the New York institutions, three thousand credits, which were equivalent to good conduct for six months, were given for catching a runaway inmate. (e) In some institutions these credits are stated merely as credits, in others as units of time, in others as dollars. An experiment in using real money was tried in Westchester County, New York, and the prisoner was released when he had earned a specified amount of money. (f) An individual is awarded extra credits if his work group or living group displays good conduct. Extra credits were given in Westchester County Penitentiary to the inmates of a corridor for good behavior in the corridor during a week. The group as a whole must maintain good conduct in order to earn this extra credit and this makes the group self-disciplining.

The credit system is a doubtful method of measuring good conduct. If the inmate "stays out of sight" he wins his credits. The system places too much power in the hands of inmates and guards. Powerful inmates can insure that other men will lose credits. A guard might report a specific act as disobedience, causing a loss of ten credits, or disrespect, causing a loss of one hundred credits, or insubordination, causing a loss of two hundred credits. When inmates secure release automatically when they have earned the required number of credits, they look upon such release as a right.

No matter what the system for measuring good conduct, it is doubtful that fitness for release can be determined by good conduct in the institution. Three types of prisoners behave well in prisons: those who attempt to secure an early release by good behavior in order to return more quickly to crime, those who reach their highest level under the careful control of others, and those who really profit from the institutional program. The good behavior of the last group alone indicates fitness for release. On the other hand, some prisoners who behave badly under the surveillance of prison guards get along satisfactorily in the general community. The United States Board of Parole specifically states that men are not eligible for parole if they have not "observed substantially the rules of the institution."[19]

In a number of institutions, a "progressive merit system" has been tried. By this method, the liberty of the prisoner is increased gradually, as an experiment or test, before he is released entirely from the institution. For example, prisoners might be placed outside the walls of the institution, on their honor, for six months before they are released. During this time they do road work, farm work, construction work, and other tasks. In the Illinois State Prison at Joliet several years ago, the prisoners passed through the following stages: confinement in the prison with little personal responsibility, increased opportunity, positions of trust in the prison, life in cottages outside the walls but under the supervision of prison officials, work on the prison farm without guards, and parole. Some institutions now maintain special quarters, custody programs, and treatment programs for men about to be released,[20] and "half-way houses" have been established in the community for men who have been released.

It seems evident that everything that has demonstrable significance should be taken into account in determining the time of release of a particular prisoner, and that this information should be organized and tested. In the following chapter a description of the methods of prediction of behavior on parole, in relation to this organized and tested information, will be presented.

*The length of the indeterminate sentence.* It is frequently asserted that indeterminate sentences result in a decrease in the average period of imprisonment and therefore tend to increase crime. The evidence, on the contrary, indicates that the average sentences have increased under the indeterminate sentence system. This does not necessarily mean that crime

[19] *Rules of the United States Board of Parole* (Washington: Board of Parole, 1955), p. 16.
[20] For description of one program of this kind see William MacDermott and Victor Ruderman, "A Pre-release Unit," *Journal of Correctional Education*, 3:5-7, 1951.

PRINCIPLES OF CRIMINOLOGY

rates are reduced by the system, for it is conceivable that the longer prison terms actually contribute to recidivism. An analysis of state and federal prisoner statistics for 1948 revealed that on the whole penalties in indeterminate sentence states are considerably more severe than in definite sentence states. When sentences are short, the average time served under definite sentences is about the same as the average time served under the maximum indeterminate sentence, but when the sentences are for ten years or more the average time served on definite sentences is considerably greater than the average time served on maximum indeterminate sentences. However, in the definite sentence states 68 percent of the prisoners were sentenced to less than five years, as compared to only 28 percent in the indeterminate states (referring only to the maximum in the latter states).[21] Clearly, therefore, the average length of time served by all prisoners sentenced under an indeterminate sentence law is considerably greater than the average served by prisoners sentenced under a definite sentence system.

The same thing is shown in Table XXI, which is a comparison of the average time served by prisoners in Joliet prison, Illinois, in the last five years under the definite system (1890 to 1894) with two years under the indeterminate system (1932 to 1933) for certain types of offenses and offenders.[22] Similar evidence has been published regarding at least six other states. The average time served in the New Jersey State Prison increased from 31 months in 1860, to 51 months in 1920 for robbery, from 23 to 30 for burglary, from 15 to 29 for assault, and from 18 to 20 for larceny.[23]

These statistics need to be interpreted. They do not mean that every prisoner serves a longer term of imprisonment under the indeterminate sentence system than he would have under a definite sentence, i.e., that the parole board is universally more severe than the court. Rather they mean that the parole board makes more discriminations among offenders than the courts do. It also should be noted that probation has developed since the indeterminate sentence system started. A large proportion of offenders who a generation ago would have been held in prison for short terms are now placed on probation, and only those judged to be most dangerous are imprisoned. When these differences are taken into account, it is reasonable to conclude that it makes practically no difference in the

[21] Sol Rubin, "Long Prison Terms and the Form of the Sentence," National Probation and Parole Association Journal, 2:337–351, October, 1956. Sol Rubin, "The Indeterminate Sentence—Success or Failure?" Focus, 28:47–52, March, 1949.

[22] See, for similar comparison of 1890–1894 and 1916–1920, Illinois Department of Public Welfare, The Illinois Parole Law (Springfield: Author, 1920), p. 8.

[23] Emil Frankel, "One Hundred Years of Prison Sentencing in New Jersey," Proceedings of the American Prison Association, 1936, pp. 22–23.

## TABLE XXI

COMPARISON OF THE AVERAGE TIME SERVED UNDER THE DETERMINATE
AND INDETERMINATE SENTENCE SYSTEMS, ILLINOIS

| Type of Offense or Offender | Determinate Sentence 1890–1894 | | Indeterminate Sentence 1932–1933 | |
|---|---|---|---|---|
| | Number Discharged | Average Time Served; Years | Number Discharged | Average Time Served; Years |
| Burglary | 1483 | 1.64 | 263 | 2.55 |
| Larceny | 776 | 1.36 | 307 | 2.35 |
| Robbery | 286 | 1.77 | 349 | 5.39 |
| Second term | 392 | 2.08 | 204 | 5.04 |
| Third or more terms | 131 | 2.56 | 90 | 5.20 |

length of time served in an institution whether the offender is sentenced on a definite or an indeterminate term.

It is possible that suffering on the part of prisoners is increased by indeterminate sentences. Some prisoners would prefer a long term fixed in advance to a short term accompanied by a period of worry and anxiety while they await a decision or "setting" by the parole board. Using a semi-free interviewing technique based on some 100 standard questions, Farber found that the following five things are significantly related to the degree of suffering of prisoners: indefiniteness of knowledge as to time of release, feeling of injustice of sentence, feeling of injustice of length of time served, lack of hope of getting a break, and apparent unfriendliness on the outside.[24] The following statement by an ex-prisoner illustrates the effect of the first three of these.

I was sentenced to San Quentin on an indefinite term. The prisoner there has no notion during the entire year regarding the term the parole board will set for him to do. At the end of that year the parole board fixes his maximum, and may later reduce it. That first year is a perfect hell for the prisoner. He keeps asking others who were convicted of a similar offense about the details of their crimes and of their maximum sentences. One man committed the same crime I did and he received a sentence of nine years but he had a long previous record and he was armed. Another man who was a first offender and was not armed got four years. I was a first offender and was armed. Consequently I figured that I will get between four and nine years. But I keep thinking and worry-

24 M. F. Farber, "Suffering and Time Perspectives of the Prisoner," *University of Iowa Studies in Child Welfare*, 20:153–227, 1944.

ing about it, for every year in prison makes a big difference. My worry interferes with my work, and I get sent to the "hole" for inefficiency in work. That looks bad on my record and I wonder whether it will increase my maximum sentence. This worry drives a person mad. As soon as the sentence is fixed the prisoner can settle down to serve his time, and it is a great relief to have it settled.

The prisoner must be released by some agency unless he is to be held for life. No one can now determine in advance how long the prisoner should be held, and there is little possibility of developing a scientific prediction instrument for doing so. The method can be more scientific if the length of imprisonment is determined by observation of the prisoner during the time of his incarceration, in connection with his previous record and situation, and the technique can improve with experience. When the sentence is definite the criminal is given a right to feel that when he has finished that term he has paid the penalty and balanced the account. This is a dangerous doctrine for the criminal or others to hold. There is no such account. When the criminal is on an indeterminate sentence he knows that his release will depend on his efforts to reform and might make a decided attempt in that direction. His desire for an early release might make him more favorably inclined toward efforts to produce reformation for himself and others in the institution. Release should therefore be under the control of an administrative board.

HABITUAL-CRIMINAL LAWS. For more than a century laws have made provision for increasing the severity of penalties for offenders who have earlier criminal records. Massachusetts enacted an habitual-criminal law in 1817, and before 1900 similar laws were passed by nine other states. Thirty-four states have passed habitual criminal laws since 1900. One of these states repealed its law in 1933 and two other states changed their mandatory life-imprisonment penalty to a permissive life-imprisonment penalty for repeated offenders. At present, five states make a life sentence mandatory on conviction of a third felony and ten states on conviction of a fourth felony.[25]

These habitual criminal laws of the mandatory type developed after World War I as a result of pressure of various crime commissions. They had the purpose of depriving courts and parole boards of the authority to fix penalties in these cases. The legislative assembly made the pronounce-

[25] Paul W. Tappan, "Habitual Offender Laws in the United States, Federal Probation, 13.28–31, March, 1949. See also N. S. Timasheff, "The Treatment of Persistent Offenders Outside the United States," Journal of Criminal Law and Criminology, 30: 455–469, November–December, 1939.

ment that no one who had the specified number of previous convictions should be granted freedom by any authority other than a governor.

Those who advocated these habitual-criminal laws believed they would practically eliminate serious crimes. At present their effects cannot be determined accurately. Within a short time after the laws were enacted, claims were made that crimes had decreased decidedly. No statistical evidence of this decrease can be secured. On the other hand, these laws did increase the proportion of charges which were reduced to minor offenses. In the year 1927, 28.6 percent of the charges under the fourth offender act in New York were reduced to misdemeanors, while only 16.1 percent of all felony charges were thus reduced. Furthermore, it is possible that the professional criminals for whom this law was designed were not much affected by it, and that the occasional criminals were the principal victims of the law. Tappan found that habitual criminal laws are regarded with disfavor in the states where they operate, "on grounds of their excessive severity, their encroachment upon the powers of the judiciary, their interference with diagnostic and clinical goals in failing to individualize treatment according to the particular requirements of the offender, and their encouragement to nullification wherefrom a loss in the deterrent efficacy of the law results."[26]

## SUGGESTED READINGS

Barnett, J. D., "The Grounds of Pardon," *Journal of Criminal Law and Criminology*, 17:490–530, January–February, 1927.

Cozart, Reed, "Clemency Under the Federal System," *Federal Probation*, 23:3–6, September, 1959.

Crosswhite, Robert G., and Maurice A. Breslin, Jr., "Bridging the Gap From Confinement to Freedom," *Federal Probation*, 23:46–52, June, 1959.

Frankel, E., "One Hundred Years of Prison Sentencing in New Jersey," *Proceedings of the American Prison Association*, 1936, pp. 22–23.

Glaser, Daniel, *The Effectiveness of a Prison and Parole System*. Indianapolis: Bobbs-Merrill Co., Inc., 1964.

Goodrich, J. P., "The Use and Abuse of the Power to Pardon," *Journal of Criminal Law and Criminology*, 11:334–342, November, 1920.

Hayner, Norman S., "Sentencing by an Administrative Board," *Law and Contemporary Problems*, 23:477–494, Summer, 1958.

Humbert, W. H., *The Pardoning Power of the President*. Washington: American Council on Public Affairs, 1941.

Killinger, George C., "Parole and Other Release Procedures," in Paul W.

[26] *Ibid.*

Tappan, Editor, *Contemporary Correction*. New York: McGraw-Hill, 1951, pp. 361–379.

Lindsey, E., "A Historical Sketch of the Indeterminate Sentence and Parole System," *Journal of Criminal Law and Criminology*, 16:9–16, May–June, 1925.

Morris, Norval, *The Habitual Criminal*. Cambridge: Harvard University Press, 1951.

Rose, Arnold, and Arthur E. Prell, "Does the Punishment fit the Crime? A Study in Social Valuation," *American Journal of Sociology*, 61:247–259, November, 1955.

Rubin, Sol, "The Indeterminate Sentence—Success or Failure?" *Focus*, 28:47–52, March, 1949.

Tappan, Paul W., "Habitual Offender Laws in the United States," *Federal Probation*, 13:28–31, March, 1949.

Tappan, Paul W., "Sentencing Under the Model Penal Code," *Law and Contemporary Problems*, 23:528–543, Summer, 1958.

Waite, John B., *The Prevention of Repeated Crime*. Ann Arbor: University of Michigan Press, 1943.

# 28. PAROLE

PAROLE IS the act of releasing or the status of being released from a penal or reformatory institution in which one has served a part of his maximum sentence, on condition of maintaining good behavior and remaining in the custody and under the guidance of the institution or some other agency approved by the state until a final discharge is granted. The term "parole" is used in analogous manner with reference to institutions for insane and feeble-minded persons. A conditional pardon is similar to parole in that both are liberation from an institution on conditions, with restoration of the original penalty if the conditions of liberation are violated. They differ in that conditional pardon carries with it the remission of guilt, and parole does not; parole refers to imprisonment only, while conditional pardon may refer to other penalties also; and they generally differ in administrative details, such as the age of guidance and supervision, which is generally greater in parole than in the conditional pardon.

Parole is related to but should be distinguished from probation. Like probation, it represents a break with the classical theory of the criminal law, since an attempt is made to select individual offenders who are expected to change their attitudes and habits while residing in the free community. Also, parole ideally includes treatment in the form of guidance and assistance to the offender, just as probation ideally includes such guidance and assistance. Thus both systems attempt to implement the treatment reaction to crime and criminality. On the other hand, the influence of the punitive reaction to crime is more clearly present in parole than in probation; parole is less "purely" treatment than is probation. Parole is granted by an administrative board or an executive, and it is always preceded by serving part of a sentence in a prison or in a similar institution, while no formal penalty is imposed in probation or, if imposed, is not executed. Probationers are considered as undergoing treatment while under the threat of punishment, should they violate the conditions of their probation, but probation is granted by the courts as a substitute for punishment as well as for mere suspension of sentence. Parolees are considered as "in custody" and undergoing both punishment and treatment while under the threat of more severe punishment—return to the institutions from which they have been released.[1] Without the threat of return to prison, release from prison before the maximum term was served would merely represent the workings of the indeterminate sentence, not parole. Since parole is expected to both punish and treat, the conflicts between punishment and treatment which are found in prisons are also found in parole.

HISTORY OF PAROLE.    Parole is a combination and extension of penal practices that had existed for some time, although the notion of giving treatment, in the form of guidance and assistance, is relatively new. The first trace of parole was the system of indenturing prisoners. By this means prisoners were removed from institutions and placed under the supervision of masters or employers and could be returned to the institution if they did not behave properly. Later, the supervision was centralized by appointment of state visiting agents with the special function of protecting the juvenile wards of the institutions against imposition. Several other systems for handling prisoners were combined with the indenture system before a parole system for adults was formed. One of these was after-care of discharged convicts. As early as 1776 philanthropic societies attempted to help ex-prisoners adjust to social life. Such societies worked most energetically in the 1840's and 1850's.[2] Later the state made efforts in the same direction. In 1845 Massachusetts appointed a state agent for discharged convicts, and this agent used public funds to assist ex-prisoners to secure employment, tools, clothing, and transportation to places of employment. Other states appointed similar agents, and these agents began to ask for continuing the custody over the ex-prisoners. For example, the New York agent for discharged convicts pointed out in his reports that his work could be greatly improved if the state retained custody over prisoners for some time after their release; he suggested that good-time allowances should be used merely to determine the time of release from the institutions, but not from custody.

As early as 1820 the English convict colonies developed a primitive parole system, with little supervision or guidance after release, under the

[1] Cf. J. P. Shalloo, "Legal and Social Concepts of Parole," *Federal Probation*, 11:37–41, April, 1947.
[2] For a history of such societies, see H. H. Hart, "Prisoners' Aid Societies," *Proceedings of the National Prison Association*, 1889, pp. 270–287.

name of ticket-of-leave. This was later made a part of the Irish system and in that form became known to American penologists. When members of the Massachusetts Prison Board made a plea for a parole system in 1865 they called it "the English ticket-of-leave system." The English Prevention of Crimes Act of 1871 also helped create a demand for a parole system in the United States. That act provided for surveillance by the police for a period of seven years after release from prison of all except those on their first terms. The Massachusetts Prison Board called attention to this act repeatedly and urged the adoption of a similar law.

Parole in its developed form was first adopted by New York State in the 1869 law which authorized the Elmira Reformatory. It was hailed at the time as a great invention, and Brockway believed that he was the inventor. But it is evident that the system had existed for over fifty years in European countries and, as indicated, in its essential features had a long history in the United States. The parole method was first extended to state prisons by Ohio in 1884, and by 1898 it had been adopted in twenty-five states. Although parole and the indeterminate sentence are now generally combined in practice, in 1898 only five states had indeterminate sentence laws. By 1922, parole laws had been passed by forty-five states, and since 1922 by all the other states, the last being Mississippi, which enacted a parole law in 1944. Many states make extensive use and others little use of it. In 13 states, more than 75 percent of the releases from state prisons and reformatories in 1963 were by parole, while in 6 states less than 25 percent of the releases were by parole; in one state, New Hampshire, 96.6 percent of the discharges were by parole.[3] Parole is used most extensively in the New England and Middle Atlantic states, and in a few states scattered among the North Central, Pacific, and Mountain regions. A few states have authorized parole for inmates of institutions for misdemeanants. This, however, is generally a farce in most states and amounts to little more than "floating."

THE PAROLE BOARD.   The parole board has the duty of determining when a prisoner shall be released on parole. Parole boards are of three principal types, with various combinations of these types: first, a special parole board limited to one institution, which is sometimes composed of institutional staff members, and at other times merely includes the warden of the institution as one member of the board; second, a general state parole board which is located in the state department of correction and which has authority to release from any state institution; third, a general state

[3] U.S. Department of Justice, Bureau of Prisons, "Prisoners in State and Federal Institutions, 1963," *National Prisoners Statistics,* No. 36, December, 1964, pp. 30–32.

parole board which is located outside of the department of correction and has authority to release from any state institution.[4] The general state board system, of either the second or third type, is now used in 29 United States jurisdictions. Parole boards of the first type are generally dominated by the prison staff. In some states this means that the classification committee which directs and supervises the treatment of the prisoners also determines when they shall be released. In this way, the prison rehabilitation pro- grams can be closely co-ordinated with parole selection and supervision. But in other states domination of the parole board by the prison staff means that the board grants parole as a reward for good conduct in the prison, rather than as a correctional device, that the board seeks to main- tain prison discipline by means of threats in regard to chances for parole, or that the board may be willing to grant paroles indiscriminately when the prison is overcrowded. At the other extreme is the parole board which is entirely independent of the department of correction. In some states, this type of parole board, like governor's advisory boards, is concerned less with the progress of the prisoner than with the possible reactions of the public toward parole. However, California's Adult Authority is an excellent example of a competent board of this type. Until recently, the Adult Authority had independent control over the length of the prison term, treatment while in prison, length of time on parole, and supervision of parolees.

The trend during the last three decades has been toward centralization of parole authority and toward removal of the parole board from the de- partment of correction. While this has been supported by the prison staff in many cases on the ground that it relieves them of a troublesome respon- sibility which interferes with their efficiency in the institutional work, it has been criticized by others on the ground that the prison staff knows better than any other agency when a prisoner should be released. This criticism has been negated in states such as California, where the Adult Authority maintains institutional parole officers who are in close contact with inmates, the custodial personnel, and the paroling authority; preparation for parole begins as soon as the criminal enters the institution.[5]

Parole boards currently include members from all walks of life. For example, the Mississippi board in 1960 included a contractor, a business- man, a farmer, and a clerk; the Florida board included a newspaperman,

<hr/>

[4] In seventeen states the sole power to grant parole is vested in the governor, acting independently or assisted by an advisor or an advisory board. George K. Killinger, "Parole and Other Release Procedures," in Paul W. Tappan, Editor, Contemporary Correction (New York: McGraw-Hill, 1951), pp. 361–379.
[5] See Walter A. Gordon, "Parole in Relation to the Classification Process," Focus, 27:129–132 ff., September, 1948.

an attorney, and a man with experience in both business and probation; the Washington board had persons with training and experience in sociology, in government, in law, in the ministry, and in juvenile rehabilitation.[6] When various court, probation, parole, police, and institutional staff members, and prison inmates, were asked to select the best occupational training for an ideal parole board, there was little consensus.[7] While all the respondents favored training in law, sociology, and psychiatry, there was a tendency for each respondent to select a representative of his own occupation.

**ELIGIBILITY FOR PAROLE.**   Almost all contemporary penologists agree that if a prisoner is to be released at all he should be released on parole. All released prisoners, it is held, could benefit from the guidance of parole officers, and society could also benefit if all offenders were kept under close surveillance during the period of adjustment immediately following incarceration. Even the prisoners who are released by pardon after proof of innocence could benefit from the assistance which parole officers could provide. Many criminals are opposed to this policy and some of them, when the time between eligibility for parole and final discharge is not too great, waive the parole hearing. This opposition is based on a feeling that parole unduly extends the period of control by the state. One thoughtful and sincere criminal made the following statement:

The criminal does not feel that he has been treated unjustly if he is forced to pay the penalty for his crime, but when he gets out of prison he wants to regard it as finished. Parole means that the state still regards him with suspicion, keeps snooping around, and is unwilling to give him a fair chance to get along as an ordinary individual. Consequently it has a bad effect psychologically upon the prisoner who is paroled.

Many laymen are also opposed to the policy of paroling all prisoners, but this opposition, unlike that of criminals, is based on the belief that parole is a form of leniency. In 24 states, the opposition is reflected in statutes which exclude certain types of criminals from parole. These are generally the prisoners convicted of the more serious crimes, such as murder, rape, or any offense for which life imprisonment is imposed. Often these offenders are in great need for the guidance and supervision which is afforded

---

[6] Washington State Legislative Council and the Washington State Board of Prison Terms and Paroles, *Parole Board Structure: A Report on the Structure of Boards in the United States* (Olympia: Author, 1960).

[7] Joseph W. Rogers and Norman S. Hayner, "The Ideal Parole Board: Views From the Correctional World and the Society of Captives," *Proceedings of the American Correctional Association*, 1963, pp. 287–300.

in efficient parole work. If they are dangerous they need the supervision which parole affords; if they are not dangerous they at least need the guidance and help which parole officers can give, especially when they have been isolated from free society for long periods of time. The mistaken notion that parole is a form of leniency should have been corrected before this time by comparison of time served by those released on indeterminate sentences and those released on expiration of a definite sentence.

For those persons eligible under the statutes, two specific prerequisites of parole are frequently made. One is that the prisoner have no "detainer" against him. This requirement is made partly out of courtesy to the jurisdiction in which the prisoner is wanted for a former crime, and partly because success on parole is unlikely if the prisoner goes immediately into another trial or another prison.[8] The second specific requirement is a guarantee of employment. Four objections have been made to this requirement. First, many of the positions which are guaranteed are fictitious. Second, many prisoners who have reached the point where they are best prepared to go out are detained in prison because no jobs are available. Third, the paroled man is exploited because the employer must be notified of the prison record. Fourth, parole officers spend much time in locating positions which the offenders should find for themselves.

Everyone agrees that the prisoner should have employment into which he can go immediately after release. However, a California study has shown that releasing men who have no employment does not necessarily increase recidivism.[9] Yet in May, 1959, New York institutions held 1,700 men who could not be paroled only because approved jobs could not be found, and in Montana, 10 percent of the prison population was being held because no suitable jobs were available.[10] Much of the work of securing employment is, in fact, done by friends and relatives of the prisoner, and in the future most of this may be done by public employment offices.[11] Of 497 inmates re-

---

[8] For discussion of the detainer problem, see Carroll C. Hinks, "The Need for Comity in Criminal Administration," *Federal Probation*, 9.3–7, July, 1945; James V. Bennett, "The Correctional Administrator Views Detainers," *Federal Probation*, 9:8–10, July, 1945; VanBuren Perry, "Effect of Detainers on Sentencing Policies," *Federal Probation*, 9:11–12, July, 1945; Garrett Heyns, "The Detainer in a State Correctional System," *Federal Probation*, 9:13–16, July, 1945; Sanford Bates, "The Detained Prisoner and His Adjustment," *Federal Probation*, 9:16–18, July, 1945.

[9] Ernest Riemer and Martin Warren, *Special Intensive Parole Unit, Phase II, Thirty-Man Caseload Study* (Sacramento: Department of Corrections, 1958), p. i.

[10] Albert Morris, "What's New in the Employment of Ex-Prisoners?" *Correctional Research* (United Prison Association of Massachusetts), Bulletin No. 9, November, 1959.

[11] See Charles E. Odell, "Job Adjustment for Probationers and Parolees," *Federal Probation*, 15:12–15, June, 1951; and William L. Jacks, "Release on Parole to Plans with and without Employment," *American Journal of Correction*, 24:12 ff., December, 1962.

leased on parole in 1949 from Elmira Reformatory to communities in New York State, 74 percent obtained jobs by their own efforts or those of their families, 5 percent through friends or other persons, and 21 percent through parole officers.[12]

There is variation among the states in the amount of help given prisoners who are seeking employment, so as to become eligible for parole. Similarly, five states give no money to men released on parole and the others ordinarily pay from $5 to $30. Vermont pays $1 for each month served in prison, up to $100.[13] These funds are in addition to any funds the prisoner might have saved from his paid work in the prison. Ten states have loan funds from which parolees can borrow, and most provide clothing and transportation home. Parolees sometimes cannot afford to buy the expensive tools required for a skilled job such as carpenter or mechanic.

CONDITIONS OF PAROLE.   Parole is "conditional liberation," that is, liberation on condition that the prisoner live in accordance with specified rules. The conditions are sometimes fixed by law, sometimes by the parole board, and sometimes by other agencies. These conditions may include: leading a law-abiding life, abstaining from intoxicating liquors and drugs, keeping free from bad associates, spending evenings at home, refraining from gambling, supporting legal dependents, remaining in a specified territory, not changing residence or employment without permission (sometimes merely without reporting the change), attending church at least once each Sunday, not marrying without permission, not becoming dependent on charity, making reparation or restitution for the crime, and making written or personal reports as required.[14] Mabel Elliott has pointed out the absurdity of attempting to impose on parolees standards of conduct not imposed on law-abiding persons.[15] Unrealistic rules and conditions usually are mitigated informally by parole officers, who count as "parole violation" only the more serious violations of rules.

ORGANIZATION OF SUPERVISION.   The board that has authority to grant paroles generally has supervision over the parolees, but sometimes the parole supervision is under the direction of an independent board. On the

[12] Jean Long, "Job Placements for Overtime Inmates," *National Probation and Parole Association Yearbook*, 1952, pp. 53–61.

[13] Daniel Glaser, Eugene S. Zemans, and Charles W. Dean, *Money Against Crime: A Survey of Economic Assistance to Released Prisoners* (Chicago: John Howard Association, 1961), pp. 3–4.

[14] See Nat R. Arluke, "A Summary of Parole Rules," *National Probation and Parole Association Journal*, 2:6–13, January, 1956.

[15] Mabel A. Elliott, "The von Hentig-Bates Parole Controversy," *Journal of Criminal Law and Criminology*, 34:96–99, July–August, 1943.

principle that imprisonment and parole should constitute a continuous series of efforts to prepare for a life of complete freedom, there is a theoretical superiority in a parole system in which the board that controls the institution also determines the time of release and supervises the parolees from that institution. This has the disadvantage of duplication of efforts in supervision, for an officer from each of the institutions of the state must work in the same territory. Therefore, in the interest of economy, parole supervision which is more than nominal is generally organized on a territorial rather than an institutional basis.

Parole supervision is little more than nominal in most states, for very few have a sufficient number of officers to make adequate supervision possible. As in probation, caseloads sometimes run as high as two or three hundred per officer. In California, the usual load in recent years has been ninety parolees. An experimental program showed that when the caseloads were reduced to fifteen and parolees were accorded intensive supervision during the first ninety days after release, and then transferred to the regular ninety-man caseloads for regular supervision, only slight reductions in parole violation rates occurred. It also was found that men whose parole release dates were advanced three months violated parole slightly less frequently than did men whose release dates were not advanced.[16] A follow-up study indicated that "intensive supervision"—defined as a caseload of thirty with frequent controls during the first six months—did not produce rates significantly lower than the rates of men in ninety-man caseloads; about 55 percent of each group violated parole in the first year.[17] In Pennsylvania, the caseload is about 60, but a recent study indicated that even with this number, adequate supervision is difficult—only 34 percent of work time was spent in contact with parolees.[18]

It has generally been found that supervision by philanthropic agencies is inadequate, though the co-operation of these societies is unquestionably beneficial.[19] Probation officers are used in some places for purposes of supervision. In the federal system the officer has supervision both of probationers and parolees. Early experiences with supervision by the police and other officers of the law were generally unfavorable.

[16] Ernest Riemer and Martin Warren, "Special Intensive Parole Unit: Relationship Between Violation Rate and Initially Small Caseload," National Probation and Parole Association Journal, 3:1–8, July, 1957.

[17] Ernest Riemer and Martin Warren, Special Intensive Parole Unit, Phase II, Thirty-Man Caseload Study, op. cit., pp. 13–16.

[18] William L. Jacks, A Time Study of Parole Agents (Harrisburg: Pennsylvania Board of Parole, 1961), pp. 4–5.

[19] See Albert G. Fraser, "The Function and Program of a Prisoner's Aid Society," Federal Probation, 8:25–29, July, 1944.

PRINCIPLES AND METHODS OF SUPERVISION.  At least three different views of supervision, differentially emphasizing punishment and treatment, are found among lay and professional parole workers.[20] One conception, which is rapidly disappearing, is based on the assumption that parole is a system of leniency which permits the early release of many dangerous criminals who should continue to suffer punishment. Consequently, in parole work based on this view, emphasis is placed on supervision rather than guidance, and "supervision" is taken to mean zealous "police work," "parole officer" to mean "police officer." It is assumed that most parolees have not reformed and that they will commit new crimes if given the opportunity. The parole officers are charged, then, with the duty of keeping parolees under close surveillance and coercing the offender into conformity by means of punishment and threats of punishment.

A second conception is based on the assumption that reformation is a matter of individual self-determination to "make good" in free society. The essential notion is that reformation is practically complete at the time of release, and that the function of the parole officer is to watch the parolee to determine whether he is maintaining the conditions fixed for his parole. A supervisory system based on this view may be characterized as "watchful waiting." The emphasis is upon supervision rather than guidance, but "supervision" is considered as "inspection." In parole work based on this view, the behavior of the parole officer is similar to a competent traffic patrolman's behavior: he is indifferent toward persons in his care who obey the law, but he is more skillful than the average person in detecting violations. Coupled with the idea that society must be protected by a careful watch over the parolee is a belief that the parolee must be protected from society. Parole officers using this system are likely to give direct help and assistance in locating jobs or solving other problems, to lecture, and to use both praise and blame. They believe that frequent contacts will destroy the parolee's initiative or confidence in himself.

Another conception is based on the belief that essential work of promoting adjustment has to be done after release from an institution, and that this requires assitance, not to prevent the parolee from exercising his own initiative, but to assist him in exercising it correctly, so that crimes will not be repeated. While it is not assumed that all parolees are dangerous criminals, it is recognized that "reformation" in the form of self-resolution to "make good" is not always sufficient to prevent recidivism. Parole is viewed as a system for improving the welfare of the parolee (often called a

---

[20] Cf. Lloyd E. Ohlin, Herman Piven, and Donnell M. Pappenfort, "Major Dilemmas of the Social Worker in Probation and Parole," *National Probation and Parole Association Journal*, 2:211–225, July, 1956.

"client") by helping him in his individual adjustment, within the limits of his capacity. Guidance, rather than surveillance, is emphasized, on the ground that we already have police to act as surveillants and detectives. In parole work based on this conception, parole officers are essentially social workers.

In practice, of course, it is difficult to separate supervision and guidance or treatment, and even in parole systems emphasizing guidance the parole officer must do some policing.[21] Also, from the parolee's viewpoint almost any contacts, whether called "guidance" or "supervision," are regarded as "snooping." Parole officers, like prison officials, are charged with maintaining a delicate balance between punishment and treatment. That balance seems to be most effectively maintained in supervisory systems where the dominant view is that parolees must be given friendly assistance within the framework of the punitive restrictions on freedom imposed as conditions of their parole, thus protecting society.

In order that the parole officer may be of real assistance to the person on parole it is necessary that he should have in advance an intimate acquaintance with the personality and background of the offender. This information must be secured before the proper method for dealing with the offender can be determined. In the most efficient systems, the information secured through the original investigation for the institutional classification committee (the "diagnosis"), and the data on the institutional career of the offender are accessible to the parole officer. In addition, an efficient parole officer must have an intimate knowledge of the family and other personal groups into which the individual will go, so that he can attempt to prepare these groups for the parolee's return before parole begins. If he is to have lasting reformative effect the parole officer must enter into intimate association with those under his supervision and teach them anticriminal behavior patterns. This part of parole work has been performed most successfully with juvenile delinquents.

Even when he is part of an ideal parole system in which parole agents have time for such personal contacts, however, it is important that the officer assist the parolee in securing friends and contacts of his own, for the period of parole must end sooner or later. A study of 50 prisoners in the District of Columbia revealed that the men had four main areas of concern about their release on parole: community acceptance, employment, family relationships, and relationships with police and parole officers[22] The important thing is to make the parolee feel that he is part of society. While

---

[21] Cf. Donald R. Cressey, "Professional Correctional Work and Professional Work in Correction," *National Probation and Parole Association Journal*, 5:1–15, January, 1959.
[22] Reuben S. Horlick, "Inmate Perception of Obstacles to Readjustment in the Community," *Proceedings of the American Correctional Association*, 1961, pp. 200–205.

in the institution he has been able to establish only rather remote contacts with law-abiding society, and when he is released on parole he is likely to feel that he is ostracized. The following statement from a prisoner's letter reveals the feelings of being set apart from law-abiding groups:

We are the anonymous ones who move amongst you with wary eyes. We are among you but not of you; constantly on guard, lest by an incautious word or gesture we may betray ourselves to you, and thereby lose our anonymity—and your respect. You may find us in your factories, in your garages, on your farms, and, sometimes in your offices and places of business. We live next door, work at the next lathe, sit next to you in the movies. In short—we are your neighbors. Yet we are a group of men set apart, divided by our experiences from those around us. We are the parolees from your prisons; still doing time, still paying our debt to society. Although we walk the streets to all outward appearances free men, we wear invisible numbers. . . .[23]

Supervision in the form of close surveillance is likely to contribute to this attitude, and mere inspection of the parolee's activities will do little to reduce it. In order to reduce the feeling of isolation, and in order that the parolee will not in fact be isolated, positive, constructive, action must be taken. Contacts with groups which possess a bias against criminality must be developed.[24] The larger the number of intimate associations that can be formed between the parolee and law-abiding groups, the more likely he is to become and remain a law-abiding person. To this end, the federal system, and some states, have opened "half-way houses" where parolees can live while they attempt to re-enter the community.

VIOLATION OF PAROLE. The law usually states that any violation of the conditions imposed upon the person on parole constitutes a violation of parole, and that for a violation of parole the person is to be returned to the institution. In practice the supervising parole agent generally uses discretion and permits some technical violations without formally pronouncing them violations of parole. Also, many violations are not observed by the parole officer. When a formal declaration of violation of parole is made, a warrant for the arrest of the parolee is issued and served if he can be located.

When a parole violator is arrested, a court trial is not necessary in order to return him to prison, and the decision of the supervising authority usu-

[23] Quoted in James V. Bennett, "Wise Men Have Enough to Do . . . ," *Federal Probation*, 14:25–29, June, 1950.
[24] Rita Volkman and Donald R. Cressey, "Differential Association and the Rehabilitation of Drug Addicts," *American Journal of Sociology*, 69:129–142, September, 1963.

ally is final.[25] However, if he has violated his parole by committing a new crime he may be tried and sentenced for that crime. In many states the violator may be returned to the prison with no hearing at all, although this practice has been held as denial of due process of law.[26] Since persons on parole are still being punished, in violation hearings the usual rights to counsel and to other court procedures designed for protection of accused persons are not available. If the parole violator is returned to prison he may be required to serve the remainder of his unexpired term if he was on a definite sentence, or the remainder of the maximum term if he was on an indeterminate sentence. He may lose the good time he had earned prior to his parole or he may be denied the privilege of earning good time after his return to prison, thus lengthening his prison term. He may lose his right to another parole or it may be stipulated that he will not be allowed to apply for a new parole until a certain period of time has lapsed. In some states the length of time to be served in prison after parole violation is determined by statute, in other states by the supervising authority, and in others by the parole board which has control of releases.

In a few states, the prisoner may be returned to the prison without a violation of parole. This may occur in several ways. He may desire to return because he cannot find work outside, or because he wishes to complete a course in trade training. He may be returned by action of the supervisor because the supervisor believes the parolee needs additional training or needs medical care or for other reasons which do not involve a formal violation of the conditions of parole. An appreciable number of returns of this nature is reported in states where the program of training within the institutions is somewhat closely integrated with the parole program.

DISCHARGE FROM PAROLE. A person may not be kept on parole beyond the end of his maximum sentence to prison. In some states, he cannot be discharged from parole before the end of that maximum period; in others he can be discharged when he has served a shorter period specified by law or by the regulations of the parole board; in others the parole board has complete authority to determine, within the limits of the maximum sentence, how long parole should continue. Vold reported that in Minnesota the period of parole extended to the maximum limit in only 25 percent of the state prison cases. Glueck reported that paroles from the Massachusetts Reformatory extended approximately half the possible length.

[25] Carter H. White, "Legal Aspects of Parole," Journal of Criminal Law and Criminolgoy, 32:600–623, March–April, 1942.
[26] See Henry Weihofen, "Revoking Probation, Parole and Pardon Without a Hearing," Journal of Criminal Law and Criminology, 32:531–539, January–February, 1942.

Violations of parole are concentrated in the early periods of parole, but the evidence as to the extent of this concentration is not consistent. Of all persons who violated paroles in Washington in 1956–1958, 51 percent had been on parole less than six months, 65 percent for less than a year.[27] Among federal parolees who violated parole in 1949, 57 percent violated during the first six months of parole, 82 percent during the first year, and 96 percent during the first two years.[28] Of 308 returned parole violators interviewed by Glaser, 17 percent had committed the act for which they were returned to prison within a month of their release, and 6 percent during their first week out of prison.[29] Hakeem found that the violation occurred early in the parole period if the paroled burglar had a previous criminal record, came from a large city, returned to a large city, had an irregular work record, was unemployed at the time of arrest, and had few or no family connections, and that the violation occurred late in the parole period if the circumstances were reversed.[30]

Civil rights, which are lost in most states on conviction of certain types of crimes, are restored in some states automatically when parole is granted; in others they are restored only when one is discharged from parole; and in others they are restored, if at all, only by a pardon by the governor.[31] In California, the parole board is authorized to restore civil rights to persons on parole at such time and to such a degree as they see fit, except that they cannot restore the right to be an elector, hold public office, or act as trustee.

The deprivation of civil rights was originally devised as a punitive system for placing social distance between the offender and law-abiding citizens.[32] As the treatment reaction to crime has become more popular, however, it has become apparent that if the prisoner is to be released to the community at all he should be made to feel, as much as possible, that he is a member of that community.[33] For the protection of social and political institutions, prisoners probably should not be permitted to vote, hold office, or exercise some of the other rights. But for the maximum degree of refor-

[27] *Twelfth Biennial Report of the Board of Prison Terms and Paroles* (Seattle: Author, 1958), p. 24.

[28] George C. Killinger, "The Federal Government's Parole Program," *Federal Probation*, 14:26–64, June, 1950.

[29] Daniel Glaser, *The Effectiveness of a Prison and Parole System* (Indianapolis: Bobbs-Merrill, 1964), p. 81.

[30] Michael Hakeem, "Parole Prediction Variables and the Time Factors in Violations by Burglars," *Journal of Criminal Law and Criminology*, 31:157–165, September–October, 1944.

[31] See Paul W. Tappan, "Loss and Restoration of Civil Rights of Offenders," *National Probation and Parole Association Yearbook*, 1952, pp. 86–104.

[32] See pp. 319–321, above.

[33] James M. Reinhardt, "The Discharged Prisoner and the Community," *Federal Probation*, 21:47–51, June, 1957.

mation and hence, protection of society, his rights probably should be automatically restored as soon as he is placed in the outside community, at the beginning of the parole period. Criminals are returned to the community so that the law-abiding group may assimilate them. Assimilation is not promoted by this device for maintaining social distance.

SUCCESS OR FAILURE ON PAROLE. The annual reports of parole departments customarily state the parole violation rate as the ratio between paroles granted during a year and paroles violated during the same year. The parole violation rates, calculated by this method, in the several states tend to cluster around 25 percent, with a range of 10 to 40 percent. Even these percentages include only the violations known to the parole officers and, in general, are restricted to the relatively serious violations for which paroles are revoked. In many states the parole force is not sufficient in numbers or activities to have reliable or complete information regarding the conduct of the parolees. Consequently, considerable scepticism regarding the stated violation rates has developed. In the states in which parole supervision is most efficient, the percentages of success are generally lower than in the states where supervision is superficial.

Also, questions have been raised as to the adequacy of the usual method of measuring parole violations, since most prisoners remain on parole for many years.[34] The proportion of parolees released in a specified year who subsequently violate parole sometime during the parole period generally is higher than the ratio of paroles violated to paroles granted in a certain year. Glueck made an analysis of the careers of 500 young-adult male offenders paroled from the Massachusetts Reformatory and reported that 55.3 percent of these offenders violated paroles, as recorded by the parole department of the State, and 5.3 percent more violated paroles by new crimes committed during the parole period which were not known to the parole department but which were discovered by Glueck in independent investigations. Thus he concluded that the parole violation rate was 60.6 percent, while the state department was reporting a parole violation rate of about 25 percent.[35] A similar study of the behavior of 256 of the women during a five-year period while they were on parole showed that 55 percent were violators.[36] Studies of the parole violations of other groups have indicated rates lower than those found by the Gluecks. For example, of 6,807 male

[34] Harry Willback, "Measuring Parole Violation," Journal of Criminal Law and Criminology, 27:357–373, September–October, 1936; Milton G. Rector, "Factors in Measuring Recidivism as Presented in Annual Reports," National Probation and Parole Association Journal, 4:218–232, July, 1958.

[35] Sheldon and Eleanor T. Glueck, Five Hundred Criminal Careers (Cambridge: Harvard University Press, 1930), p. 169.

[36] Sheldon and Eleanor T. Glueck, Five Hundred Delinquent Women (New York: Knopf, 1934), pp. 209, 387.

offenders paroled in California in 1962, 51 percent had been declared violators by 1963.[37] A study of 1,409 men who were paroled from Pennsylvania prisons during the years 1926–1933 revealed that 44.2 percent were violators; 32 percent of the paroled first offenders and 45 percent of the paroled recidivists violated parole.[38] Forty-four percent of the men paroled from the Illinois State Penitentiary between 1926 and 1943 have been violators.[39] Of 1015 men released from federal prisons in 1956, 35 percent were classed as "failures" by 1960.[40] Precise comparisons of reports are not possible because the definitions of "violation" and "failure" are not the same in all studies.

The parole violation rate, however it may be computed, refers only to the period of parole and does not include the career of the offender after he is released from parole. From early decades studies have been made of the subsequent careers of ex-prisoners, beyond the period of parole. One of the first studies of this nature was made in 1888 by Brockway regarding former inmates of Elmira Reformatory. He concluded that 78.6 percent of those released during the preceding decade were leading law-abiding lives and were self-supporting at the time of the investigation.[41] The most intensive studies of this type in recent years have been made by Sheldon and Eleanor Glueck and refer to 500 young-adult male offenders over a fifteen-year period, and 1,000 juvenile delinquents over a ten-year period.[42] They report regarding the 500 young-adult male offenders that 79 percent committed new crimes during the first five-year period after parole, 68 percent during the second five-year period, and 68 percent during the third five-year period. Stern reports, however, that in 1947 only 11.8 percent of 1,409 persons paroled from Pennsylvania prisons in 1926–1933 had committed new crimes following the expiration of their parole.[43] Three and one-half years after release from a Borstal institution, 45 percent of a group of 720 boys had no further record of crime.[44]

[37] California Department of Corrections, *California Prisoners, 1961, 1962 and 1963; Summary Statistics of Felon Prisoners and Parolees* (Sacramento, Department of Corrections, 1964), p. 128.

[38] Leon T. Stern, "Popular or Scientific Evaluation of Probation and Parole," *National Probation and Parole Association Yearbook,* 1948, pp. 55–70.

[39] Hans W. Mattick, *Parole to the Army* (Chicago: Cook County Jail, 1958. Mimeographed), p. II.

[40] Glaser, op. cit., pp. 19–20. See Table XVII, p. 545, above.

[41] Z. R. Brockway, *Fifty Years of Prison Service* (New York: Charities Publication Committee, 1912), p. 297.

[42] *Five Hundred Criminal Careers,* op. cit.; *Later Criminal Careers* (New York: The Commonwealth Fund, 1937); *Criminal Careers in Retrospect* (New York: The Commonwealth Fund, 1943); *One Thousand Juvenile Delinquents* (Cambridge: Harvard University Press, 1934); *Juvenile Delinquents Grow Up* (New York: The Commonwealth Fund), 1940.

[43] Op. cit.

[44] Hermann Mannheim and Leslie T. Wilkins, *Prediction Methods in Relation to Borstal Training* (London: Her Majesty's Stationery Office, 1955), pp. 53, 65.

One study has compared the subsequent careers of a group of prisoners released on parole with the subsequent careers of a group released unconditionally without parole.[45] Of the 345 men released from the Minnesota State Reformatory between July 1, 1944, and June 30, 1945, 110 were released on expiration of sentence, 183 on parole, and 52 on other kinds of release. Five years later, 30 percent of the men released on expiration of sentence and 21.4 percent of those releasd on parole had been convicted, sentenced, returned to custody, or had paroles revoked for felonies. In addition, 7.3 percent of those released on expiration of sentence and 4.9 percent of those released on parole had been fingerprinted for felonies, but there was no record of conviction. Among those released on expiration of sentence, 6.4 percent had been convicted and sentenced for misdemeanors, as compared to 4.9 percent of the parolees. Statistics from certain other states also indicate that those released on parole are returned for new crimes less frequently than those released at the termination of their sentences. These differences, however, may not be due to the treatment given while on parole; the inmates least likely to commit new crimes probably are selected for parole, while the inmates most likely to commit new crimes remain in prison until the end of the maximum sentence.

CONDITIONS AFFECTING SUCCESS OR FAILURE ON PAROLE.   During the last generation many statistical studies have been made of the factors associated with success or failure on parole.[46] The criterion of failure used in most of these studies is a violation of parole by behavior which is noticed by the parole authorities and which leads to the issuance of a parole violation warrant. Such warrants ordinarily are requested and issued only when the parole agent is reasonably certain that the parolee cannot make an adequate social adjustment, or when a new crime is committed. Consequently, parole violation warrants as a measure of outcome tend to over-estimate the actual adjustment achieved by parolees.[47] Information regarding many of the "factors" or conditions which are said to affect success or failure—such as

[45] Stanley B. Zuckerman, Alfred J. Barron, and Horace B. Whittier, "A Follow-up Study of Minnesota State Reformatory Inmates," Journal of Criminal Law, Criminology, and Police Science, 43:622–636, January–February, 1953.

[46] Bibliographies of such studies are given by Robert M. Allen, "A Review of Parole Prediction Literature," Journal of Criminal Law and Criminology, 32:548–554, January–February, 1942; Michael Hakeem, "Prediction of Criminality," Federal Probation, 9:31–38, July, 1945; Lloyd E. Ohlin and Otis Dudley Duncan, "The Efficiency of Prediction in Criminology," American Journal of Sociology, 54:441–452, March, 1949; Karl F. Schuessler, "Parole Prediction: Its History and Status," Journal of Criminal Law and Criminology, 45:425–431, November–December, 1954; Mannheim and Wilkins, op. cit.

[47] Lloyd E. Ohlin, Selection for Parole (New York: Russell Sage Foundation, 1951), pp. 43–45.

"home status" and "previous work record"—are customarily taken from unverified statements made by the inmates. Others, such as "social type," "type of offense," and "personality rating," are taken from official prison documents or from classification committee reports.

These statistical studies are consistent in their conclusions in certain respects and inconsistent in other respects. They show considerable consistency in the conclusions that failures decrease as the age of first delinquency increases, and increase as the number of previous arrests, the irregularity of previous work habits, the frequency of institutional punishments, and the size of the community in which the offender resided increase. Generally, older offenders succeed on parole more often than do the younger offenders, foreign-born more often than native-born of native parents, white offenders more often than Negroes, sex offenders and murderers more often than those engaged in crimes against property.

The several studies either show no consistent relation or a very slight relation between failure on parole and such characteristics as height and weight, intelligence, religious preference, occupational classification, and work habits in the institution. On the other hand, the studies which are pertinent to this point show a close association between success on parole and post-release behavior such as regular work habits, frequent church attendance, and constructive use of leisure time, as well as between parole success and such conditions as close family ties and residence in low-delinquency areas.

PREDICTION OF SUCCESS ON PAROLE. The information regarding the conditions of success or failure on parole of those who have been paroled in earlier years has been organized into "experience tables" and used to predict probable success or failure on parole and the probable violation rates for specific groups of parole applicants.[48] For example, in one of the earlier prediction studies Burgess[49] found that parolees who had more than fifteen "unfavorable" factors (e.g., poor work record previous criminal career, institutional punishments, and residence in a deteriorated neighborhood), violated parole in 98.5 percent of the cases, while those who had less than five unfavorable factors violated parole in only 24.0 percent of the cases. On the basis of this experience in the past he predicted that a person who had more than fifteen unfavorable factors was almost certain to violate parole, and that a person who had less than five unfavorable factors had three

[48] For an exceptionally clear description of how experience tables are constructed and used in parole, see Ohlin, *Selection for Parole, op. cit.*

[49] A. A. Bruce, E. W. Burgess, and A. J. Harno, *The Workings of the Indeterminate-Sentence Law and the Parole System in Illinois* (Springfield: The State of Illinois), 1928.

chances out of four of success on parole.[50] The reliability of the original data, the methods of classification, and the statistical methods of organizing the information are being improved by further studies.[51] The improvement of prediction techniques has been strongly stimulated by the State of Illinois. Since 1933, this state has employed actuarial sociologists to conduct research on parole prediction and to assist the parole board by preparing a prediction of the success or failure of each person who comes before the board. This gives the board organized information, which may or may not be used as the basis of decision by the board.

While the prediction technique has customarily been considered as a device for selecting for parole those prisoners who are most likely to succeed, it is potentially more useful as a device for directing the supervision and guidance of prisoners who are placed on parole. That is, men who are "poor risks" could be given close parole supervision and careful guidance, and men who are "good risks" could be given a minimum of supervision and guidance.[52] In an experimental study, California placed good parole risks under minimal supervision and found that they did as well as they were predicted to do under regular supervision.[53]

Three principal criticisms have been made of this prediction technique as a method of selecting persons for parole. The first is that it does not provide a standard for selecting parolees. Should the parole board grant parole to those who have fifty chances out of a hundred or only to those who have seventy-five or ninety chances out of a hundred? The prediction technique, if adequately developed, may be able to give information regarding the chances of success but it cannot provide a standard. Moreover, the question recurs: Should prisoners who have little chance of success on parole be held to the end of the maximum sentence and then released without supervision or should they be released on parole anyhow? It is clear that the prediction technique cannot provide the standards, but prediction studies may assist the parole board in defining the standards. Goodman has devised a system whereby an estimate of the "social costs" of paroling and not-paroling the

[50] See Michael Hakeem, "Glueck Method of Parole Prediction Applied to 1861 Cases of Burglars," Journal of Criminal Law and Criminology, 36:87–97, July–August, 1945; Michael Hakeem, "The Validity of the Burgess Method of Parole Prediction," American Journal of Sociology, 53:376–386, March, 1948.

[51] See Leslie T. Wilkins and P. Macnaughton-Smith, "New Prediction and Classification Methods in Criminology," Journal of Research in Crime and Delinquency, 1:19–32, January, 1964.

[52] See J. Douglas Grant, "It's Time to Start Counting," Crime and Delinquency, 8:259–264, July, 1962.

[53] Joan Havel, Special Intensive Parole Unit, Phase IV, The High Base Expectancy Study (Sacramento: Department of Corrections Research Report No. 10, 1963), and The Parole Outcome Study (Ibid., Report No. 13, 1965).

various kinds of inmates would be included in the prediction information submitted to the parole board.[54]

The second criticism is that this technique largely neglects the fact that every prisoner reaches a point where he is a better risk on parole than at any other time.[55] The prediction technique is concerned principally with events and characteristics which preceded the period of imprisonment, only to a slight extent with behavior while in prison, and not at all with the changing attitudes of the prisoner while in prison.[56] In 1936, Laune attempted to take these attitudes into account and to base predictions on them,[57] but a later check on the parolees whose success or failure was predicted by Laune indicates that, in general, prediction by use of objective factors would have been more efficient than the prediction based on inmate attitudes.[58] This does not mean, however, that prediction systems using objective factors are necessarily more valuable than the systems using attitudinal factors when the aim is the efficient *selection* of parolees.

A third criticism is that prediction methods do not predict. The predictive efficiency of an experience table can be measured by comparing (a) the number of errors in prediction occurring when the table is used with (b) the number of errors that would have occurred had the prediction been based on the crudest method available—prediction from total violation rates alone.[59] For example, it might be found, after the parole results are in, that an actuary using an experience table had predicted incorrectly in, say, 30 percent of the cases. On the other hand, it might be observed that 40 percent of the parolees under consideration actually violated their parole, so that the best possible prediction for each individual case, on the basis of this total violation rate alone, would have been "non-violation."

[54] Leo A. Goodman, "Generalizing the Problem of Prediction," *American Sociological Review*, 17:609–612, Otcober, 1952; Leo A. Goodman, "The Use and Validity of a Prediction Instrument. I. A Reformulation of the Use of a Prediction Instrument," *American Journal of Sociology*, 58:503–512, March, 1953. See also Otis Dudley Duncan, Lloyd E. Ohlin, Albert J. Reiss, Jr., and Howard R. Stanton, "Formal Devices for Making Selection Decisions," *American Journal of Sociology*, 58:573–584, May, 1953.

[55] Cf. Norman S. Hayner, "Why Do Parole Boards Lag in the Use of Prediction Scores?" *Pacific Sociological Review*, 1:73–76, Fall, 1958; and Jerome K. Skolnick, "Toward a Developmental Theory of Parole," *American Sociological Review*, 25:542–549, August, 1960.

[56] See Ralph W. England, "Some Dangers in Parole Prediction," *Crime and Delinquency*, 8:265–269, July, 1962.

[57] F. F. Laune, *Predicting Criminality: Forecasting Behavior on Parole*, North western University Studies in the Social Sciences, No. 1 (Evanston: Northwestern University Press, 1936); F. F. Laune, "The Application of Attitude Tests in the Field of Parole Prediction," *American Sociological Review*, 1:781–796, October, 1936.

[58] Lloyd E. Ohlin and Richard A. Lawrence, "A Comparison of Alternative Methods of Parole Prediction," *American Sociological Review*, 17:268–274, June, 1952.

[59] Ohlin and Duncan, *op. cit.*

But if he had predicted "non-violation" for all the parolees, on the basis of the total violation rate, the actuary would have been incorrect in 40 percent of the cases. By using the experience table, then, he reduces the percentage of error from 40 to 30, an improvement of 25 percent. Ohlin and Duncan report that all of the 26 major experience tables which have been used in research studies provide some reduction in the error of prediction for the original samples; the percentage reduction of error in the various studies ranged from 43 percent down to only 3 percent, with an average of about 12 percent. Hence, it may be concluded that the experience tables do have some predictive efficiency.

However, the predictive ability of the tables generally fails to stand up in follow-up samples to which the tables are applied for the purpose of validation. Both Huff and Sanders determined the factors which were associated with success on parole of federal prisoners and applied these factors to a second group of federal prisoners, and reached the conclusion that these factors had little significance for the second group.[60] Gillin determined the factors which were associated with failure of prisoners released from correctional institutions of Wisconsin in 1933–1934, applied them to prisoners released from the same institutions in 1932–1933 and in 1935, and found that few of the factors were significant for all three groups. He found, also, that the factors which were used by Burgess in Illinois and by Glueck in Massachusetts were not significantly associated with success or failure of parolees in Wisconsin, and that the factors which were associated with failure of parolees from the state prison of Wisconsin were not associated significantly with failure of parolees from the state reformatory of Wisconsin.[61] In the Gluecks' study of 500 young-adult male offenders over a fifteen-year period, the factors which were selected as most highly associated with failure in the first five-year period did not apply to the second five-year period, and an almost completely new set of factors were adopted; neither the first nor the second set of factors applied satisfactorily to the third five-year period and a third set of factors was therefore adopted. When the entire fifteen-year period is considered, if one extreme class with only six cases is excluded because of the small number, the group with the most favorable prognosis had four chances out of ten to reform completely, while the group with the worst prognosis had three chances out

[60] R. L. Huff, "Is Parole Prediction a Science?" *Journal of Criminal Law and Criminology*, 27:207–218, July–August, 1936; Barkev S. Sanders, "Testing Parole Prediction," *Proceedings of the American Prison Association*, 1935, pp. 222–233; Attorney General's *Survey of Release Procedures*, op. cit., pp. 545–659.

[61] John L. Gillin, "Prediction of Parole Success in Wisconsin," *Journal of Criminal Law and Criminology*, 34:237–239, November–December, 1943; John L. Gillin, "Parole Prediction in Wisconsin," *Sociology and Social Research*, 34:407–414, July–August, 1950.

of ten to reform completely. The method of flipping a coin would be almost as accurate as this prediction technique. Ohlin and Duncan found that when existing experience tables are applied to new samples of parolees some of them do not significantly decrease the amount of error which would have been present had prediction been based simply on knowledge of the total violation rates alone, and others even *increase* the amount of error.[62]

The general failure of the prediction instruments to predict for new samples may be attributed to four principal kinds of error which occur in practice.[63] *First*, there are many errors which result from lack of association between the "factors" and the actual outcome on parole. The predictive techniques, at best, rest on the assumption that some categories of individuals will get involved and other categories or individuals will not get involved in the unknown causal systems which lead to parole violation.[64] Intensive analysis of the cause of parole violation probably would reduce the incidence of this type of error. *Second*, errors arise because of sampling fluctuations; that is, the characteristics of the new sample may differ from those of the first sample in such a way that the predictive efficiency of the instrument is reduced. *Third*, errors occur because of the unreliability of the information used to establish the "factors" and of the "factors" themselves. Although the extent of the unreliability of prison records has not been determined, research workers agree that these sources of information are usually unreliable. This source of error can be corrected by basing prediction on data collected for the specific purpose of making predictions. Scientific prediction can hardly be based on data collected by prisons for non-scientific purposes. The unreliability of the "factors" is due to lack of rigorous definition and to lack of knowledge of the cause of parole violation. *Fourth*, errors correlated with time frequently occur. The prediction tables are based on the assumption that parole conditions remain constant over the years. Actually, many conditions which affect violation rates but which do not affect the factors used in prediction occur from time to time. Among these are the effectiveness of the treatment measures used in the prison, the policy of the parole board, the employment possibilities for parolees (unemployment is usually cause for revocation of parole), the efficiency of the parole agent, the efficiency of law-enforcement officers, the policy of the supervising agent in regard to what constitutes "violation," and the attitude of the community toward parole. This type of error con-

[62] *Op. cit.*

[63] *Cf.* Lloyd E. Ohlin, "The Routinization of Correctional Change," *Journal of Criminal Law and Criminology*, 45:400–411, November–December, 1954.

[64] See Robert M. Martinson, Gene G. Kassebaum, and David A. Ward, "A Critique of Research in Parole," *Federal Probation*, 28:34–38, September, 1964.

stitutes perhaps the most serious obstacle to efficient parole prediction. Ohlin has developed a technique for routine adjustment of the prediction instrument so that it will take account of such changes in parole conditions.[65]

However, the "condition" which probably has the most effect on violation and non-violation is the behavior of the persons with whom the parolee interacts, and this social interaction is not precisely taken into account in most prediction systems. Glaser recently attempted to do this by deriving his prediction factors from the differential association theory.[66] He found that such factors are more efficient predictors than are case study personality ratings.[67] Some of the prediction systems in criminology attempt to predict behavior on parole and even throughout life from traits and circumstances in infancy and early childhood. While certain behaviors appear fixed in infancy and remain relatively inflexible throughout life, behavior like crime and serious infractions of parole regulations appear to depend much more completely upon a process of continuing social interaction. If this be correct, the criminal behavior of a person can be accurately predicted only if the behavior of the persons with whom he will come in contact is known.

APPRAISAL OF PAROLE. The antagonism toward parole is probably greater than toward any other policy for control of crime. This is surprising, for there is no well-known student of penology who is not wholeheartedly in favor of the principle of parole, and who does not insist that parole in practice is better than any available alternative in practice. These students insist, first, that parole should be evaluated not as an abstract principle but in comparison with the only available alternative, which is the determination in court at the time of the trial of the definite date of release, and the complete release at that time without subsequent supervision. They insist, second, that those who are released on parole serve at least as long inside prison walls for a specific type of crime as do those sentenced on definite terms, and in addition remain under supervision and guidance outside the prison for periods which generally range from one to three years, and that parole therefore is not leniency but on the contrary is more severe and is a better method of protecting society against crime than the alternative method. They insist, third, that persons released from prison on parole do not commit more crimes than persons released at the expiration of sen-

[65] Selection for Parole, op. cit., pp. 62–64, 119–121.
[66] Daniel Glaser, "A Reconsideration of Some Parole Prediction Factors," American Sociological Review, 19:335–341, June, 1954.
[67] Daniel Glaser, "The Efficacy of Alternative Approaches to Parole Prediction," American Sociological Review, 20:283–287, June, 1955.

tences without supervision, for the same offenses. J. Edgar Hoover has claimed that at least 30 percent of the "mad dogs" listed by the Bureau of Investigation "had been paroled by lenient or foolish parole boards." Since "mad dogs" are defined as confirmed criminals, who have therefore probably been in prison previously, it means that 70 percent had been released at the expiration of sentences without supervision. From this one might conclude that those released at the expiration of the sentence without parole are more than twice as likely to get into the list of most dangerous criminals as those released on parole.

In spite of this clear-cut justification for parole in comparison with its alternative, the parole system as currently administered can be greatly improved. Improvements can be made at all three principal points in the parole process: the competence of the personnel on parole boards, the adequacy and reliability of the information on which parole boards base their decisions, and the quality of supervision and guidance of those on parole. At each of these three points—the parole board, the case investigators, and the parole supervisors—training is required. However, at present the facilities for training persons for these three occupations are very inadequate, largely because no significant body of knowledge which can be directly applied in such training has been developed. Consequently, our knowledge must be increased before training for these occupations can be professionalized. Generally, the best training is to be obtained in departments of sociology and schools of social work. A few universities have recently developed vocational programs in which staff members train the students in the use of practical skills which have been acquired by persons in the parole field.

## SUGGESTED READINGS

Briggs, Peter F., and Robert D. Wirt, "Prediction," Chapter 6 in Herbert C. Quay, Editor, *Juvenile Delinquency: Research and Theory*. New York: Van Nostrand, 1965, pp. 170–208.

Bruce, A. A.; E. W. Burgess; and A. J. Harno, *The Workings of the Indeterminate Sentence Law and the Parole System in Illinois*. Springfield: State of Illinois, 1928.

Cressey, Donald R., "Professional Correctional Work and Professional Work in Correction," *National Probation and Parole Association Journal*, 5:1–15, January, 1959.

Dressler, David, *Probation and Parole*. New York: Columbia University Press, 1951.

Glaser, Daniel, "A Reconsideration of Some Parole Prediction Factors," *American Sociological Review*, 19:335–341, June, 1954.

Glaser, Daniel, *The Effectiveness of a Prison and Parole System*. Indianapolis: Bobbs-Merrill, 1964.

Goodman, Leo A., "Generalizing the Problem of Prediction," *American Sociological Review*, 17:609–612, October, 1952.

Hakeem, Michael, "Glueck Method of Parole Prediction Applied to 1,861 Cases of Burglars," *Journal of Criminal Law and Criminology*, 36:87–97, July, 1945.

Hakeem, Michael, "The Validity of the Burgess Method of Parole Prediction," *American Journal of Sociology*, 53:376–386, March, 1948.

Johnson, Elmer H., "The Parole Supervisor in the Role of Stranger," *Journal of Criminal Law, Criminology, and Police Science*, 50:38–43, May–June, 1959.

Kirby, Bernard C., "Parole Prediction Using Multiple Correlation," *American Journal of Sociology*, 59:539–550, May, 1954.

Mannheim, Hermann, and Leslie T. Wilkins, *Prediction Methods in Relation to Borstal Training*. London: Her Majesty's Stationery Office, 1955.

Martin, John P., *Offenders as Employees*. London: Macmillan, 1962.

Martinson, Robert M., Gene G. Kassebaum, and David A. Ward, "A Critique of Research in Parole," *Federal Probation*, 28:34–38, September, 1964.

McSally, Bernard F., "Finding Jobs for Released Offenders," *Federal Probation*, 24:12–27, June, 1960.

Meyer, Charles H. Z., "A Half-Century of Federal Probation and Parole," *Journal of Criminal Law, Criminology, and Police Science*, 42:707–728, March–April, 1952.

Moran, F. A., "The Origins of Parole," *National Probation Yearbook*, 1945, pp. 71–98.

National Parole Institutes, *The Sentencing and Parole Process*. New York: National Council on Crime and Delinquency, 1964.

Odell, Charles E., "Job Adjustment for Probationers and Parolees," *Federal Probation*, 15:12–15, June, 1951.

Ohlin, Lloyd E., *Selection for Parole*. New York: Russell Sage Foundation, 1951.

Ohlin, Lloyd E., and Otis Dudley Duncan, "The Efficiency of Prediction in Criminology," *American Journal of Sociology*, 54:441–452, March, 1949.

Ohlin, Lloyd E., and Richard A. Lawrence, "A Comparison of Alternative Methods of Parole Prediction," *American Sociological Review*, 17:268–274, June, 1952.

Ohlin, Lloyd E., Herman Piven, and Donnell M. Pappenfort, "Major Dilemmas of the Social Worker in Probation and Parole, *National Probation and Parole Association Journal*, 2:211–225, July, 1956.

Panton, James H., "Use of the MMPI as an Index to Successful Parole,"

*Journal of Criminal Law, Criminology and Police Science*, 53:484–488, December, 1963.

Rogers, Joseph W., and Norman S. Hayner, "The Ideal Parole Board: Views from the Correctional World and the Society of Captives, *Proceedings of the American Correctional Association*, 1963.

Schuessler, Karl F., "Parole Prediction: Its History and Status," *Journal of Criminal Law, Criminology, and Police Science*, 45:425–431, November–December, 1954.

Shalloo, J. P., "Legal and Social Concepts of Parole," *Federal Probation*, 11:37–41, April, 1947.

Skolnick, Jerome K., "Toward a Developmental Theory of Parole," *American Sociological Review*, 25:542–549, August, 1960

Wilkins, Leslie T., and P. Macnaughton-Smith, "New Prediction and Classification Methods in Criminology," *Journal of Research in Crime and Delinquency*, 1:19–32, January, 1964.

# 29. PREVENTION OF CRIME AND DELINQUENCY

Two GENERAL systems for reducing the frequency of crimes have been tried. One method aims at reducing the amount of repeated crime, the other at forestalling commission of first crimes. The name "crime prevention" has been given to both systems, but it is becoming common practice to consider the effort to prevent recidivism as the method of *reformation*, the effort to forestall first crimes as the method of *prevention*. This terminology is slightly inaccurate, for the policies of execution and of permanent segregation of certain offenders are aimed at reduction of repeated crime, yet they can hardly be considered methods of reformation. Furthermore, a single program or policy, such as imprisonment, may be aimed at both reformation and prevention. When the punitive reaction to crime was most popular, the usual assumption was that severe punishment both reforms those who are punished and deters or "prevents" other from committing first crimes. Even today, legislative commissions appointed to make suggestions for programs to reduce crime rates generally confine their recommendations to measures designed to increase severity of punishment. However, as we have seen, this policy is being supplemented, and to some extent replaced, by policies based on the treatment reaction to crime. Consistent with this trend, "reformation" and "prevention" are coming to refer exclusively to positive, non-punitive efforts to rehabilitate criminals and to forestall criminality.

Though punishment is one method of building up anti-criminal attitudes in the general public, it is not the most efficient method for preventing crime. The development of habits and attitudes by education, by the spreading of traditions, by the contacts and interactions between those who appreciate the values and those who do not is probably a more efficient method. As we find out more about crime causation, we shall have a better basis for the determination of specific policies for this purpose. These policies, if carried out consistently, may be expected to protect society from crime in three ways: *First*, they would secure a relatively permanent segregation of persons who, because of gross lack of appreciation of conventional values or social situations, or some other condition, constitute the greatest menace to the group. Segregation will probably not reform these offenders but it will protect the group by incapacitating them and by indicating societal disapproval of deviance from legal norms. Apparently no other policy can be used in the present state of techniques of control for a considerable number of offenders. *Second*, these policies would restore to society without alienating them a large proportion of those who have not definitely broken away from the general anti-criminal culture of organized society. *Third*, these policies would define the type of personality and the social situations from which crimes are most likely to issue, and would make it possible to deal with such persons in advance of crime and to attack and eliminate those social situations. Thus protection against crime would be secured by modifying those who could be modified by available techniques, segregating those who could not be so modified, and correcting or segregating in advance of crime those who were proved to be most likely to commit crime, and attacking and eliminating the social situations which were most conducive to crime. Such policies would be as much evidence that the organized society disapproved of crime as would punishment, and it is this disapprobation, rather than punishment of individual criminals, which tends to deter the large majority of the population from crime.

RECIDIVISM. A large proportion of the offenders under the care of any agency are recidivists. Of the offenders committed to federal prisons and reformatories in 1958, 67 percent had been committed previously to such institutions, and 32 percent had been committed three or more times. Fifty-one percent of the men and 37 percent of the women committed to Wisconsin prisons in 1956–1957 had at least one prior felony conviction.[1] In some states the percentage known to be recidivists is even higher. About 77 percent of the offenders admitted to the prison reformatories of Massachusetts in 1963 had been in correctional institutions previously.[2] Of the persons whose fingerprints were reported to the Federal Bureau of Investigation in 1954, 63.8 percent had prior records on file. Christie found that of all males born in Norway in 1933, 1035 (5.08%) had become registered offenders by January 1, 1958. Twenty-two percent of the 1035 were recidivists, and four percent had repeated their offenses three or more times. Of the men who had committed their first offenses at ages 14–17 and who, thus, had from 7½ to 9½ years in which to become recidivists, 36 percent had repeated.[3]

[1] John W. Mannering, "Significant Characteristics of Recidivists," *National Probation and Parole Association Journal*, 4:211–217, July, 1958.

[2] Massachusetts Department of Correction, *Statistical Report for the Year Ending December 31, 1963* (Boston: Author, 1964), p. 36.

[3] Nils Christie, *Unge Norske Lovovertredere* (Young Norwegian Lawbreakers) (Oslo: University of Oslo Press, 1960), pp. 51, 55.

This high rate of recidivism is extremely important, for it means that a large proportion of the crimes committed can be attributed to repeaters. A large part of the work of the police, the courts, and the penal and reformatory institutions must be devoted to recidivists. Moreover, the recidivists must be given more than their share of the time and efforts of the agency personnel. They provide more than their share of the failures on probation and parole, and more than their share of the disciplinary problems in the institutions. Massive walls and other devices to prevent escapes are needed principally for recidivists.

The persistence of criminals in their crimes may be explained either in terms of the characteristics and conditions of the offenders or in terms of the inadequacy of agencies of reformation. The first involves a social psychology of the recidivist, the second an analysis of the techniques of reformation.

SOCIAL PSYCHOLOGY OF RECIDIVISM.    One of the findings of the prediction studies is that, with some exceptions, the personal characteristics and social situations which are associated with criminality in the first place are also associated with persistence in crime. Persons who live in areas having low crime rates, who are reared in non-delinquent homes, and who have a comfortable scale of living are least likely to return to crime after any method of treatment. They, like persons with minor physical ailments, probably "cure" themselves. Repeaters frequently were reared in deteriorated areas, in homes where destitution, vice, and criminality were usual, in isolation from the constructive, law-abiding agencies of the community. Recent studies of delinquents indicated that recidivists, as compared to nonrecidivists, are older, have older mothers, are better educated, have fewer known delinquencies, are more intelligent, and are less likely to have a father with a criminal record.[4] Negroes have a higher rate of recidivism than whites, and boys have a higher rate of recidivism than girls, and urban dwellers have a higher rate than rural dwellers. Various explanations have been suggested for this persistence in crime in such situations.

One of the explanations of recidivism is habit formation; persistence in crime is merely persistence of habits. Some of the habits were formed prior to the official treatment, others during the course of the treatment. Drug addiction and drunkenness are illustrations of offenses which persist after official treatment as the result of habit formation. It is doubtful, however, whether the term "habit formation" is an adequate explanation of the per-

[4] Dugald S. Arbuckle and Lawrence Litwack, "A Study of Recidivism Among Juvenile Delinquents," *Federal Probation*, 24:45–48, December, 1960; and Jerome Laulicht, "Problems of Statistical Research and Its Correlates," *Journal of Criminal Law, Criminology and Police Science*, 54:163–174, June, 1963.

sistence even of drug addiction or drunkenness. This concept implies physiological mechanisms and leaves the social conditions in obscurity. Both the recidivism of any individual and the high rate of recidivism in some groups are much more complex than is ordinarily conceived when explained in terms of habit formation.

Isolation from law-abiding society has been suggested as another explanation of recidivism. Ordinarily the offender acquires no facility in the manners of law-abiding groups and he has little opportunity to come in contact with them after or during his period of official treatment. Upon discharge by an agency, the offender is rather necessarily confined in his group membership by his occupational skill, his table manners, his methods of conversation, his manners in recreation and in wearing clothes, and other characteristics. By these manners, skills, and other traits he is confined to certain social groups, and for that reason he must remain in the situations in which his criminality developed. If he gets out of these groups, he will do so slowly. Furthermore, if the offender lived previously in a law-abiding group he is likely to be ostracized, while if he lived previously in a criminal group he may acquire status by his contact with the agencies for control of crime. This isolation from law-abiding groups occurs more frequently after imprisonment than after other methods of correction but exists to some extent in connection with every method. The following is an illustration of this effect:

After I got out of the Chicago Parental School I couldn't, to save my soul, get used to the freedom and ease of the outside schoolroom. I felt out of place among the boys on the outside. I kind of felt strange and inferior about having come out of such a place. People distrusted me; I couldn't convince my folks that I wanted to go straight, attend high school and finally go to college. Everybody expected me to steal again. I had extreme trouble in finding something to talk about to my fellow students. I felt ashamed and then didn't know anything that was going on to talk about. Conversation had not been permitted in the Chicago Parental School except out in the yard. In the cottage and school you were compelled to keep absolute silence. I hardly ever had a heart to heart conversation with anyone while I was there. The Chicago Parental School kind of made a clam out of me and put a sort of inferiority and shameful feeling in me. I have never since been able to rid myself wholly of the feeling. I kind of felt unpopular with everybody, that people were afraid of me and distrusted me.[5]

[5] Clifford R. Shaw, *Delinquency Areas* (Chicago: University of Chicago Press, 1929), p. 41. Reprinted by permission of the publishers. The boy who wrote this statement was later committed to two other juvenile reformatories and then to the state prison on a sentence of twenty-three years.

Another explanation of the persistence of the criminal is found in the criminality and near-criminality in the general society. Just as a person would secure no satisfaction from smoking in church because a church is not a suitable situation for smoking, an offender can feel comfortable in committing crimes only in a situation where that behavior has become customary. Shaw has shown that the urban areas with high rates of crime and delinquency are also areas with high rates of recidivism in crime and delinquency. Mack found that among the delinquents residing in 1946–1958 on the street with the highest crime rate in the Scottish city studied, 29 percent had become adult criminals by 1964; the comparable figure for all Scottish delinquents is less than 5 percent.[6] Patterns of dishonesty, however, are prevalent outside of these deteriorated areas. Advertisements of toothpaste, cigarettes, and hundreds of other commodities are notoriously fraudulent in their claims and suggestions. The bribery of purchasing agents by business concerns is almost universal in many trades. Sharp practices have become customary in many lines of business. Ruthlessness in making money has become an important part of the business code. Trade unions have become involved in racketeering. Political graft and corruption are widespread. Evasion of taxes is commonplace. Thus, lying, cheating, fraud, exploitation, violation of trust, and graft are prevalent in the general society. The offender who remains reformed must be superior to the society in which he lives.[7] Certainly the reformation of the offender would be very much easier if the general society contained fewer persons of criminal and near-criminal types.

Again, the criminal, by reason of his crime and the methods of dealing with his crime, forms associations, loyalties, and attitudes which tend to persist. The offender who manifests a desire to reform is called "yellow," "rat," "square," or "stool-pigeon" by his associates. He may then be ostracized from delinquent groups, but is not on that account accepted by law-abiding society. Or violence and threats of violence may be used to keep him a criminal. Opportunities for crime are placed in his way. One offender while on parole stated that he had at least forty opportunities for crime suggested to him in a month but not a single opportunity for legitimate work. Probably more important than any of these is his feeling of obligation to assist those who have assisted him in the past. Jack Black described his difficulties when he attempted to desist from crime thus:

[6] John Mack, "Full-time Miscreants, Delinquent Neighbourhoods, and Criminal Networks," British Journal of Sociology, 15:38–53, March, 1964.

[7] Cf. David Matza and Gresham M. Sykes, "Juvenile Delinquency and Subterranean Values," American Sociological Review, 26:712–719, October, 1961. See also David Matza, Delinquency and Drift (New York: Wiley, 1964).

The more strictly a criminal adheres to the underworld code, the greater will be his handicap if, and when, he decides to mend his ways. This adherence makes him friends and he is proud of it; but these very friends help to anchor him in that life. . . . Many former associates had a right to expect and demand help from me, and of course they did demand it. In the fifteen years that I have been playing Society's game, I have many times had one foot in a jail as the result of trying to reconcile the underworld and upperworld codes. I have been asked to send pistols and explosives and narcotics into jails by men who had a right to demand them because they had done favors for me in the past. . . . Many ex-prisoners who try to go straight become involved with the law in an effort to discharge their obligations. The underworld is always reaching out to them, and the more help they are in a position to give, the greater the demands upon them will be.[8]

Finally, persistence in criminal behavior has been explained as due to personality traits, most frequently as due to pathological traits of personality, such as mental defectiveness, emotional instability, mental conflicts, egocentrism, and psychosis.[9] The Gluecks' explanation of persistence in crime beyond the age of forty is almost entirely in terms of mental deviations which are not corrected by the natural maturation of the individual.[10] In contrast with this, Thompson reports that of 1,380 repeaters in the clinic of the Court of General Sessions in 1935, the mental defectives, psychotics, and psychopathic personalities were 8.8 percent of all repeaters and were approximately the same proportion in all clinic cases; the defectives practically disappear from among the repeaters after the age of 30, and the psychopathic personalities appear among the repeaters above the age of 45 in the same proportion as in the repeaters below that age.[11] Personality characteristics, whether pathological or not, tend to persist in spite of the treatment currently given in any of the correctional processes. Since the situation subsequent to the treatment remains essentially the same as

[8] Jack Black, "A Burglar Looks at Laws and Codes," *Harper's,* 160:308–310, February, 1930. Reprinted by permission of the publishers. See also Jerome J. Rozycki, *Early Recidivism Among First Offenders* (Washington: The Catholic University of America), 1948; and John Irwin and Donald R. Cressey, "Thieves, Convicts and the Inmate Culture," *Social Problems,* 10:142–155, Fall, 1962.

[9] See D. Northrup, "Facing Facts About Recidivism," *Probation,* 20:109–111, September, 1942.

[10] See p. 272, above.

[11] Charles B. Thompson, "A Psychiatric Study of Recidivists," *American Journal of Psychiatry,* 94:591–604, November, 1937. See also Hulsey Cason and M. J. Pescor, "A Statistical Study of 500 Psychopathic Prisoners," *Public Health Reports,* 61:557–574, April 19, 1946; Hulsey Cason and M. J. Pescor, "A Comparative Study of Recidivists and Non-recidivists among Psychopathic Federal Offenders," *Journal of Criminal Law and Criminology,* 37:236–238, September–October, 1946.

prior to the treatment, and the personality traits remain the same, the old behavior must persist.

REFORMATION. The second general type of explanation of recidivism is stated in terms of the inadequacy of the methods of reformation. If the offender were reformed by the first agency with which he came in contact, the crime rate would be greatly reduced. As our previous discussion has indicated, every major policy (e.g., corporal punishment, fines, imprisonment, probation, and parole) has resulted in a large proportion of failures. Such failures may be due to the inefficiency of the theories of reformation which are used, or they may be due to the inability to apply the theories when adequate facilities and personnel are not available. In the following review, we shall be concerned with the theories of reformation and the technical policies based on such theories, rather than with personnel and facilities.

*Mechanical methods of reformation.* Until the present century, almost all reformative efforts were mass methods designed to modify the criminal in some mechanical manner. In the light of contemporary psychological and sociological knowledge, these methods of reformation are obsolete. However, they maintain a certain popularity among laymen.

The classical theory was that reformation could be accomplished by inflicting a sufficient amount of pain upon the offender. This was a strictly hedonistic theory, and it is still held by considerable numbers in the general public. It has generally been discarded by psychologists and sociologists. Pain undoubtedly has some value in the control of behavior, but the value is more or less completely balanced by the antagonism, isolation, and group loyalties which it produces. Furthermore, the infliction of punishment upon the offender does not change the situation which produced the criminality. In some cases there is not much more justification for punishing a criminal than for punishing a person with tuberculosis or smallpox.

A second method designed to produce reformation was meditation, generally enforced by isolation from all or almost all other persons. The theory was that crime was due to a failure to think, and that meditation would develop remorse and repentance. Early in the nineteenth century Mease made a clear-cut statement of this method of producing reformation. He maintained that repentance was produced by:

(1) A tiresome state of mind from idle seclusion; (2) self-condemnation arising from deep, long-continued and poignant reflections upon a guilty life. All our endeavors, therefore, ought to be directed to the production of

that state of mind, which will cause a convict to concentrate his thoughts upon his forlorn condition, to abstract himself from the world, and to think of nothing except the suffering and the privations he endures, the result of his crimes. Such a state of mind is totally incompatible with the least mechanical operation, but is only to be brought about, if ever, by complete mental and bodily isolation.[12]

Some prisoners have testified that during the period of solitude they were compelled to think over their careers and that this did result in decisions to desist from crime. In general, however, this procedure does not seem to be effective. Hobhouse and Brockway accumulated considerable documentary evidence that isolation results in deterioration and degradation.[13] Saleilles maintained that "The constant thought of remorse and, still more, of shame, becomes the greatest hindrance to individual regeneration."[14]

A third method, used in earlier and in later times, was moralizing. By tracts, sermons, and personal exhortations, in the name of God, mother, and country, appeals were made to the offenders. These exhortations generally produce antagonism in prisoners. Exhortation is an extremely important method of social control when it is used by members of a group upon other members of the same group. It is seldom effective when used by one group upon another group.

A fourth method is by inducing the offender to sign a pledge or make resolutions in some other form. This method is based upon the assumption that reformation can be accomplished merely by inducing the offender to "make up his mind" to reform. The fallacy of this assumption is abundantly illustrated every New Year's Day. Reformation involves a complex of social relationships which is not altered by resolutions. Furthermore, when the individual breaks his resolution, as is almost certain to be the case if the attempt at reformation involves nothing more than the resolution, the psychological effect is likely to be injurious.

A fifth method of reformation is mechanical habituation, produced by various compulsory methods. The constant surveillance of the offender, which was made possible by Bentham's panopticon type of prisons, was justified by him as resulting in the formation of good habits.

[12] James Mease, *Observations on the Penitentiary System and Penal Code of Pennsylvania* (Philadelphia, 1828), p. 73. Quoted by F. C. Gray, *Prison Discipline in America* (London: J. Murray, 1848), p. 30.

[13] S. Hobhouse and A. F. Brockway, *English Prisons Today, Being the Report of the Prison System Enquiry Committee* (London: Longmans, Green, 1922), pp. 476–589.

[14] R. Saleilles, *The Individualization of Punishment* (Boston: Little, Brown, 1911), p. 195.

If you prevent men from doing mischief, almost anything will suffice as a motive to induce them to do good. The pain of being idle is a never failing impulse. Restrain it from operating in a wrong direction; the gentlest means will be sufficient to turn it into a direction that is good.

To render a man totally unable to do mischief, you have only to keep him constantly in sight, after depriving him of such offensive instruments as would render him dangerous to you. Place a man by himself, in an iron cage, for example, and keep him every hour and every minute of his life in sight, and it is evident you can prevent him from doing mischief, whether by making his escape to prey again upon society, or by exerting his powers to any pernicious effect where you have him confined.

To place criminals then under perpetual inspection is the object, the all-powerful object, which it is required to accomplish. If this can be done, without loading society with exorbitant expense, the problem respecting a better disposal of criminals than killing them is already resolved.[15]

The panopticon prison was constructed in circular form with a central guard tower, from which one guard could look into all the cells and thus keep all the prisoners under constant surveillance. When this prison architecture was used in the Joilet prison it was found that the construction which enabled the guard to watch all of the prisoners also enabled any prisoner to watch the guard and therefore any prisoner could do whatever mischief he pleased while the guard's back was turned. In addition, the constant surveillance produced antagonisms in the prisoners. Hard work in prison was another device from which results were expected. The following statement was made by the superintendent of a boys' reformatory:

Every boy should have something to do every waking hour. What this effort is, is not important. . . . It may be drudgery, but it is part of the price he must pay for better things. That every day has its work, and every hour of every day its task must be well understood by the young malefactor, and the habit of doing what comes to his lot must become a fixed habit. In time a spirit of pride in doing well even the uninviting task will become a stimulus to greater skill.[16]

Brockway seemed to have the same mechanical psychology during a part of his career, though he did not state it in this crude form. Some mental

[15] Jeremy Bentham, "On Houses of Safe-Custody and Industry," *Philanthropist*, 1:229, 1811.
[16] H. W. Charles, "The Problem of the Reform School," *Proceedings of the Child Conference for Research and Welfare,* 1910, p. 88.

defectives, perhaps, can be trained in that way, and the habits once formed remain fixed. But habits shift very quickly in ordinary individuals as soon as the situation changes. Unless interest in labor is developed, the habit of mechanical exertion will be quite unavailing to produce continuance of hard work after release, let alone a law-abiding character.

These methods are examples of the efforts to produce reformation in the past. Although they have "carried over" to the present, they reveal the necessity of understanding the principles of human behavior better than they were understood in the last century.

*The clinical method of reformation.* Strictly speaking, adherence to the policy of individualized treatment for delinquents and criminals does not imply the use of any specific technique or theory of reformation. Rather, commitment to this policy means only that those conditions considered as causing the individual to behave criminally will be considered in the attempt to reform him. Attention is focused on the criminal rather than on the crime. Generally, an attempt is made to diagnose the cause of criminality and to base the technique of reformation upon the diagnosis. An analogy with the *method* of diagnosis, prescription, and therapy for medical patients is apparent.[17]

The clinical method of reformation has extended this analogy, and it has become similar to clinical medicine in theory and content as well as in procedures. Criminality is considered as a defect or disorder, or as a "symptom" of a defect or disorder, which can be treated on an individual basis without reference to the offender's groups, just as biological disorders can be treated on an individual basis. An extreme position in this regard is that criminality actually is a biological disorder, treatable by modification of the physiology or anatomy of the individual through lobotomy, castration, interference with glandular functioning, or something else.[18] However, the much more popular view is that criminality is an individual psychological disorder which may or may not have a strictly biological basis. According to this view, the essential difference between clinical medicine and the proper system for treatment of criminals lies in the nature of the disorder being treated—clinical medicine deals with organic disorders, clinical treatment for criminals with psychological disorders, with "mental disease." The clinical method of reformation is, thus, based upon an individualistic, psychiatric theory of criminality.

The essence of the popular individualistic theory is that criminality is an

[17] See the discussion above, pp. 375–378.
[18] See Edward E. Mayer, "Prefrontal Lobotomy and the Courts," *Journal of Criminal Law and Criminology*, 38:576–583, March–April, 1948.

expression of emotional disorders or conflicts in the make-up of the individual. The criminal may be considered as a person who is unable to canalize or sublimate his "primitive," antisocial impulses or tendencies; or he may be considered as expressing symbolically in criminal behavior some unconscious wish or urge created by an early traumatic emotional experience; or he may be considered as possessing some other kind of defective personality component. In any event, the implication for treatment is that the internal emotional maladjustment must be eradicated before the external, behavorial maladjustment (criminality) will be corrected.[19]

The specific techniques for reformation of criminals, then, make no attempt to modify the offender's group relations in any direct way. Rather, the techniques used for treating criminals are the same as the techniques used for treatment of emotionally maladjusted non-criminals. The many clinical techniques for administering therapy to emotionally disturbed persons cannot be reviewed here.[20] Generally, the emotional disorders which are considered as criminality-producing are now usually recognized as the product of social conditions, but the treatment is aimed at modification and correction of the criminal's purported emotional maladjustments rather than at modification of the social conditions. For example, rejection by parents might be considered as the source of the emotional disorder which produced a child's delinquency, yet the therapy might be directed exclusively at the emotional disorder, rather than at the social relationships in the family. The parental rejection is considered as having produced a defect in the individual's personality, a defect which will continue to direct and determine his overt behavior until such time as it is modified by treatment.

One clinical system or technique for modification of criminality through modification of emotional maladjustments or disorders can be broken down into five steps or stages. While this analysis greatly oversimplifies the procedures used in clinical therapy, it illustrates basic operations performed. *First*, in discussions with a therapist the criminal is urged to talk freely about his criminality and the conditions which he thinks are responsible for it. *Second*, the therapist identifies a character defect. This defect may

[19] See Don C. Gibbons, *Changing the Lawbreaker* (New York: Prentice-Hall, 1965), pp. 143–157.

[20] Hakeem has pointed out that over fifty definitions of psychotherapy were necessary to accommodate the variety of viewpoints expressed in one professional conference, and that one textbook lists twenty-six different types and schools of thought of individual therapy. Michael Hakeem, "The Psychiatric Approach to Juvenile Delinquency," in Joseph Roucek, Editor, *Juvenile Delinquency* (New York: Philosophical Library, 1958).

be labeled "feelings of guilt," "resentment of authority," or any of a host of other terms. *Third*, this interpretation of the interview materials is communicated to the criminal, giving him "insight" into the "basic motivation" for his criminal behavior. *Fourth*, the criminal is urged to recall his life experiences in an attempt to discover the original source of the emotional defect. *Fifth*, the subject's awareness of the source of the emotional disorder may alone "cure" that disorder, and "cure" of the disorder, in turn, "cures" the criminality. However, in some cases merely "raising unconscious emotional circuits to the surface of consciousness so that they are observed by the individuals in whom they occur"[21] will not be sufficient for eradication of the emotional defects produced by these traumatic experiences, and further guidance and counseling may be necessary.

This system may be seen in the following description, by a psychiatrist, of psychotherapy and "intensive treatment" for prisoners:

The purpose of this discipline is the uncovering of unconscious material which has been expressed in the form of disordered behavior, of disabling subjective symptoms, or demonstrable derangements of function. This material is uncovered in order to bring it to the awareness of the person suffering from the disability, and for the purpose of helping him to alter favorably his behavior patterns; of effecting as deeply-ranging a change as is possible and is necessary, of the disposition and expression of his impulses. . . . To put it differently, the aim of this therapy would be to assist a person toward the goal of socially-acceptable behavior, through his understanding of the unconscious purposes served by his former unacceptable behavior.[22]

*The group-relations method of reformation.* Recent sociological and psychological discoveries about the nature of personality have provided an alternative theory upon which to base diagnosis and treatment of criminals. The personality is viewed as "situation determined" rather than "trait determined"; the behavior of an individual is said to be the product of his group relationships, rather than of the presence of specific individual traits or characteristics. The traits which an individual exhibits are the properties of groups, not of the individual alone. John Dewey in 1922, and Dorwin Cartwright in 1951, expressed this viewpoint as follows:

[21] Justin K. Fuller, "Group Therapy for Parolees," *Prison World*, 14:9–11, July, 1952.

[22] David Sherbon, "Definition of 'Intensive Treatment,'" in Harold B. Bradley and Jack D. Williams, *Intensive Treatment Program: Second Annual Report* (Sacramento: Department of Corrections, 1958), pp. 23–24.

To change the "working character" or will of another, we have to alter objective conditions which enter into his habits. Our own schemes of judgment, of assigning blame and praise, of awarding punishment and honor are part of these conditions. . . . We cannot change habit directly: that notion is magic. But we can change it indirectly by modifying conditions, by an intelligent selecting and weighing of the objects which engage attention and which influence the fulfillment of desires.[23]

The behavior, attitudes, beliefs and values of the individual are all firmly grounded in the groups to which he belongs. How aggressive or co-operative a person is, how much self-respect or self-confidence he has, how energetic and productive his work is, what he aspires to, what he believes to be true and good, whom he loves or hates, and what beliefs and prejudices he holds—all these characteristics are highly determined by the individual's group membership. In a real sense, they are properties of groups and of the relationships between people. Whether they change or resist change will, therefore, be greatly influenced by the nature of these groups. Attempts to change them must be concerned with the dynamics of groups.[24]

In criminology, the differential association theory is consistent with this conception of the nature of individual behavior. Also, as was pointed out in Chapter Sixteen, the general implication of the differential association theory for reformation of criminals is that relations in the culture of law-abiding groups must be promoted, and relations in pro-criminal culture must be discouraged. Negatively, this means that criminality cannot be modified to any significant extent in a clinic, for clinical methods do not deal with group relations.

Although correctional programs are including more and more provisions for contact with anti-criminal culture, a specific set of techniques for promoting reformation by this method has not been worked out. Instead, the contacts provided have been promoted in a rather haphazard fashion, often with no explicit acknowledgement of the group-relations theory of criminality and reformation. Perhaps a general statement of some principles of reformation consistent with the group-relations theory of behavior in general and the differential association theory in particular will provide a basis for explicit attempts to utilize the group-relations principle in correctional programs. Research and experimentation may eventually produce precise, detailed rules of action for correctional workers interested in achieving

[23] John Dewey, Human Nature and Conduct (New York: Henry Holt, 1922), pp. 19–20. Reprinted by permission of the publishers.

[24] Dorwin Cartwright, "Achieving Change in People: Some Applications of Group Dynamics Theory," Human Relations, 4:381–392, 1951. Reprinted by permission of the publishers.

change in criminals, but current knowledge of the techniques of reformation is very scanty. The following statement, adapted from a more general statement by Dorwin Cartwright,[25] should be regarded as tentative, as directing attention to areas where research and experimentation should prove fruitful:

(a) Criminals who are to be reformed and the persons who are to exert influence or change must have a strong sense of belonging to the same group. The two general processes in reformation are the *alienation* of the criminal from groups which support values conducive to criminality and, concurrently, the *assimilation* of the criminal into groups supporting values conducive to law-abiding behavior. The latter process can be accomplished only when the social distance between the criminals and the reformers is small enough to permit a genuine "we" feeling. Consequently, the reformers and the reformees should be similar in social status and ethnic backgrounds; ideally, they would be similar in all respects except attitudes toward law-violation. Neither the view that all criminals are "outsiders" nor the view that correctional workers are "hoosiers" or "cops" is conducive to reformation. However, these two views currently prevail, and it is probably for that reason that non-professional persons, such as the family of a girl with whom the criminal is in love, often exert more influence than do the correctional workers themselves.

(b) The more attractive the group to the criminal, the greater is the influence that the group can exert on the criminal. The group must be so constituted that the criminal desires and can achieve status in it. He must be given recognition for anti-criminal and non-criminal behavior. In psychiatric terminology, the group must fill his "unmet needs," "provide an opportunity for ego-expansion," etc. Not all persons are attracted to the same groups, and it can be safely asserted that few criminals are attracted to groups in which they are made the object of ridicule, hate, sermons, or tear-jerking sympathy. A judge in New York sent a criminal who had shown remarkable organizing ability in the field of crime to oversee the reclamation of large tracts of abandoned farm land. The criminal acquired status in the community by this method, and his opinion of the behavior that was appropriate to the status no longer included crime. He came to think of himself as a useful member of society. Similarly, the provision of material services by the group may serve to attract criminals to a net-work of anti-criminal personal relations. The correctional worker must appeal to criminals with as much skill as the salesman uses in appealing to customers, and he must produce an effect that will be much more permanent

[25] *Ibid.*

than that produced by salesmen. This appeal must be based on study of the offender's background and past experiences. For example, a delinquent who thinks that Boy Scouts are "sissies" is not likely to join the Scouts. But if he should join, the group probably will change him only very slowly, for he will resist entering into intimate personal relationships with the other boys.

(c) The more relevant the basis of attraction of the group to the reformation of criminals, the greater will be the influence that the group can exert on the criminal's attitudes and values. This means that groups organized largely for the purpose of occupying the criminal's time—such as hobby and recreational groups—will not have the influence of a group organized for the explicit purpose of changing criminals. If the basis of attraction of the group is some tangential interest which the criminal might have (e.g., an interest in music), the criminal's values regarding criminality are likely to remain unchanged, while his values regarding the tangential interest are changed. He might become a criminal educated in music, rather than a non-criminal. A group in which "Criminal A" and some non-criminals join together to change "Criminal B" probably is most effective in changing "Criminal A." This system is sometimes rather inadvertently used in institutions for delinquents, where one of the older children is appointed as "monitor" or "Big Brother" for each newcomer. The newcomer takes his troubles to the monitor, and, more significantly, the monitor, even when not consulted, tries to direct and protect the newcomer. The monitor probably benefits more than does his charge. The system also is effective in Alcoholics Anonymous and in Synanon, a self-help organization for drug addicts.[26] It has been tried, in modified form, in the California Institution for Men, at Chino.[27]

(d) The greater the prestige of a group member in the eyes of those who are to be reformed, the greater the influence he can exert. The prestige assigned to a group member may spring from the member's social position outside the group, or it may spring from some attribute or trait which the member seems to possess. In assigning prestige, reformees may use criteria different from those used by other reformers.

(e) Strong resistance will be encountered when the efforts to change individual criminals or the criminal members of a group would, if success-

[26] Rita Volkman and Donald R. Cressey, "Differential Association and the Rehabilitation of Drug Addicts," *American Journal of Sociology* 69:129–142, September, 1963; and Donald R. Cressey, "Social Psychological Foundations for Using Criminals in the Rehabilitation of Criminals," *Journal of Research in Crime and Delinquency*, 2:49–59, July, 1965.
[27] Dennie L. Briggs, "Convicted Felons as Social Therapists," *Corrective Psychology and Journal of Social Therapy*, 9:122–127, 3rd Quarter, 1963.

ful, have the result of making them deviate from the norms of the group.[28] The group must be, first of all, a strongly anti-criminal group, so that deviation from group norms will be deviation in the direction of criminality. If the reformers are in such a minority—in numbers, influence, or prestige—that exhibition of essentially "anti-reform" attitudes is the real basis of group cohesion, any reformation of individuals will be extremely unlikely. The offender who understands both the psychological and social mechanisms involved in criminal conduct and the reasons for the prohibitions against that conduct probably will accept anti-criminal values more readily than an offender who does not. Sometimes an understanding of the situation can be secured only if the offender's rationalizations, by which he justifies and defends himself, are broken down. Such an understanding can be promoted only by persons who themselves have some understanding of the psychology and sociology of crime.

(f) The source of pressure on the criminal whose change is sought must lie within the group. The group must not rely upon the criminal to change himself. So far as the processes are concerned, there is no essential difference between abandoning crime and backsliding in church. The person who changes has transferred his loyalties from one group to another. The change is sometimes rapid, sometimes gradual. Often the reformee does not repent and resolve to do right. Instead, his behavior is modified by the changes in group relations. Perhaps the most effective group for reformation of criminals would be one in which status is achieved by exhibition of "pro-reform" attitudes. That is, those persons who show the most marked tendency toward anti-criminal values, attitudes, and behavior would become leaders. Criminality is learned in intimate, personal groups, and non-criminality and anti-criminality are learned in similar groups.

This last principle has been demonstrated in a highly significant experiment with hospitalized drug addicts. When the experiment began, the hospital wards contained an essentially "anti-reform" culture, and the ward leaders were the older, more experienced addicts. The social organization on the wards was described as follows:

Pro-social attitudes, such as a desire for psychotherapy or real cooperation with hospital authorities, were frowned upon. Patients who held these beliefs were "squares" or "chickens" and were ostracized by the dominant antisocial group on the ward. On the regular wards, it was found that the bulk of the patients' free time was spent in "breaking up jack pots" (group discussion of past addiction or plans for future use of the drug), group

[28] Cf. Harold H. Kelley and Edmund H. Volkart, "The Resistance to Change of Group-Anchored Attitudes," *American Sociological Review*, 17:453–465, August, 1952.

expressions of hatred and contempt for authority (hospital and community), and how to do "easy time" (devices for seducing authority so as to get easy or pleasant jobs in the hospital).[29]

In connection with a group-therapy program this anti-reform culture was changed, so that prestige was assigned by ward members to persons exhibiting signs of abandoning the use of drugs, rather than to persons exhibiting anti-reform attitudes:

Continuous observation of the Treatment Ward revealed a significant change in the subculture developed on this ward. On the Treatment Ward, a premium was placed by the patients "on getting better," as evidenced by realistic relations with other patients on the ward and with authority figures. Group discussions of drugs for their own sake were discouraged. The leaders that evolved were people who could demonstrate by their relations to others that they had utilized and benefited from "treatment." All the patients on this ward were in a [therapy] group. The group was used to explore the personal problems and interpersonal experiences on the ward. . . . [The treatment] ward developed a pro-social therapeutic climate that fostered psychotherapy. This was not true of the other wards of the hospital.[30]

This experiment has great significance for a theory of reformation, since almost all of the participants were reformees. The culture observed among the addicts was not unlike that existing in many prisons, making the task of reformation exceedingly difficult. When the reformees are probationers or released prisoners, the reformer has the advantage of being able to direct the reformee to an anti-criminal group or to draw him into group relations which are already anti-criminal. Under such circumstances, achievement of reformation should be much easier than it is under conditions in which the subculture itself must be changed.[31]

*Professional services and reformation.* The courts and correctional agencies are adding professionally trained persons to the staff to assist in the diagnosis and treatment of offenders. This work is relatively recent in origin, and the proportion of time and energy given to diagnosis is much

[29] James J. Thorpe and Barnard Smith, "Phases in Group Development in the Treatment of Drug Addicts," *International Journal of Group Psychotherapy*, 3:66–78, January, 1953. Reprinted by permission of the publishers. See also LaMar T. Empey and Jerome Rabow, "The Provo Experiment in Delinquency Rehabilitation," *American Sociological Review*, 26:679–695, October, 1961.

[30] *Ibid.* Reprinted by permission of the publishers. See also Willis H. McCann and Albert A. Almada, "Round-table Psychotherapy: A Technique in Group Psychotherapy," *Journal of Consulting Psychology*, 14:421–435, December, 1950.

[31] See Gibbons, *op. cit.*, pp. 163–174.

greater than that given to treatment. Professional training for the specific work of diagnosing and treating criminals and delinquents is nowhere adequate.[32]

The social worker acquires in a training school a theory of interviewing and experience in interviewing. Moreover, he has had some practice in the collection, verification, and application of social data. But the social worker is seldom trained specifically in the field of crime and delinquency, and has no specific knowledge of the processes which lead to delinquency. In recent years, social work has become psychiatrically oriented, and therefore the social worker is usually individualistic in his approach. His clinical theory of reformation makes it difficult for him to work with agencies that are concerned with the immediate welfare of society rather than with the welfare of the criminal.[33]

The psychologist is generally trained to give intelligence, aptitude, interest, and personality tests, and to conduct interviews. Almost anyone can be trained in a very short time to give these tests and interviews in a routine manner. The contribution of the psychologist, in comparison with those who may acquire the ability to give the tests and interviews routinely, is to be found in the background of knowledge regarding psychology, by reason of which he can make interpretations of test and interview results and of incidents which occur during the interviewing and testing processes. The psychologist, like the social worker, generally has had no acquaintance with the field of criminology prior to employment in correctional work.

The psychiatrist has generally been trained in a medical school; during most of his training he has been compelled to confine his efforts to the study of the organism and has given relatively little attention to behavior problems. In so far as he gets specialized courses in behavior problems, he becomes acquainted with the major psychoses. He has practically no opportunity to become acquainted with the body of knowledge in criminology or with criminals in person. Psychiatrists have shown a tendency, which is now on the wane, to interpret all crime as due to psychopathology.

The sociologist is the only member of the professional group who ordinarily has an academic training in criminology and penology, for academic work in this field is confined almost entirely to departments of sociology. On the other hand, he has had no training in clinical methods; he has

[32] Evan Louis Sanchez, *An Analysis of California Correctional Workers' Academic Training and Needs* (Sacramento: California Probation, Parole and Correctional Association, 1959).

[33] See Donald R. Cressey, "Professional Correctional Work and Professional Work in Correction," *National Probation and Parole Association Journal*, 5:1–15, January, 1959.

been concerned with research work and general interpretations of crime rather than with the diagnosis and treatment of the individual offender. At the same time he has a background knowledge of society, of groups, and of culture which is indispensable for an understanding of individual offenders.[34]

Experience in correctional work indicates that almost anyone can secure the case histories and give the tests in a large proportion of the cases, and that disagreements occur principally in the interpretations of certain types of cases and in theories of reformation. Consequently, until our knowledge of criminality and reformation becomes more valid, correctional agencies should have at least the four types of professionally trained persons to participate in diagnoses and in treatment programs.

CRIME PREVENTION. The methods of reformation, like the methods of punishment, have not been notably successful in reducing crime rates. They have failed most frequently in reforming offenders who have been reared in the situations where crime flourishes most. Thus they have been least effective in dealing with the offenders who come from the most potent crime-breeding situations, from which a considerable proportion of all the criminals who are dealt with by official methods do come. Moreover, a very small proportion of those who commit crimes receive official treatment for those crimes. Perhaps 10 percent of the serious crimes result in arrests, and certainly a much smaller percentage result in official action. This is especially true of fraud, bribery, and similar white-collar crimes which flourish in the business world and the political world, and which almost never result in arrest, although they do great injury to property and to institutions in modern society.

The implication of these facts is that the policy of prevention must be emphasized if the crime rate is to be reduced significantly. Punishment and methods of treatment are, at best, methods of defense against criminals or of rescuing animals. It is futile to take individual after individual out of the situations which produce criminals and permit the situations to remain as they were. A case of delinquency or crime is more than a physiological act of an individual. It involves a whole network of social relations. If we deal with this set of social relations we shall be working to prevent crime.[35] It has become a commonplace in medicine that pre-

[34] Saul D. Alinsky, "A Sociological Technique in Clinical Criminology," *Proceedings of the American Prison Association*, 1934, pp. 167–178. See also Marshall B. Clinard, "The Group Approach to Social Reintegration," *American Sociological Review*, 14:257–262, April, 1949.

[35] Cf. Marshall B. Clinard, "Prevention of Crime," *Journal of Correctional Work* (India), 7:1–12, 1960.

vention is better than cure. The same superiority exists in the field of crime.

The superiority of prevention may be illustrated in the problem of school discipline. Two generations ago corporal punishment was used with great frequency in the schools and disorder was generally prevalent in spite of the punishment. Orderly behavior did not develop by increasing the severity and frequency of punishment or by "treating" unruly students. Rather the improvement in the behavior of school children came as the result of improvement in the teachers and the curricula, and in the gradual development of a tradition of orderly behavior, together with liberality in the criteria of good behavior. The school system was adjusted to the needs of the children much better than it had been previously. It is probable that analogous changes must be made in the social organization before great reductions can be made in crime rates.

Most criminals in their earlier stages are probably much like the person who is dishonest in reporting his personal property to the assessor. This man would be willing to make an honest report if others made honest reports. Each individual is driven to dishonesty by the fact that dishonesty is prevalent. In that sense most criminals probably do not need to be reformed, at least in their earlier stages of criminality. Instead, the prevalence of dishonesty needs to be modified and individual crime prevented.

*General programs of prevention.* Many general programs of crime prevention have been outlined. Bentham in the last part of the eighteenth century made a comprehensive outline of the "indirect methods" (that is, methods other than punishment) which might be used to prevent crime. He included such things as taking away the physical power of injury, diverting the course of dangerous desires, decreasing susceptibility to temptations, general education, a code of morals similar to a code of laws, and other things.[36]

Ferri, a member of the Italian school, in the last part of the nineteenth century paid considerable attention to the prevention of crime. He had a doctrine of criminal saturation, namely, that a group has the crimes it deserves in view of the type of people and the conditions of the group, and that as long as the type of people and the conditions remain constant, crime will remain constant regardless of methods of punishment. Consequently, he insisted that penal substitutes, or methods of modifying the conditions and traits of people, should be used. He outlined a long list of these, including free trade, reduction in consumption of alcohol,

[36] Jeremy Bentham, "Principles of Penal Law," in John Bowring, Editor, *The Works of Jeremy Bentham* (Edinburgh, W. Tait, 1843).

metal (instead of paper) money, street lights, reduction in hours of labor, lower interest on public securities, local political autonomy, and many other things.[37]

Other elaborate programs for the prevention of crime have been developed and these programs have included practically every reform that has been suggested by anyone. The programs tend to be somewhat utopian, principally because the knowledge of crime causation has not been sufficiently precise to isolate the conditions and traits which need attention in programs of prevention. Policies for the prevention of crime are based, implicitly or explicitly, on theories of the causes of crime. Those who believe that crime is due to innate defects advocate a policy of sterilization. Those who believe that it is due to acquired personal defects advocate agencies for education or psychiatric clinics. Those who believe that it is due to the immediate personal groups advocate reorganization of the family and of the neighborhood. Those who believe that it is due to the more general culture advocate a more general social reorganization. Almost everything in the universe is found to be associated in some direct or indirect manner with criminality. These multiple factors have not been reduced to a clear-cut system, with immediate and remote relationships established. No universals have been discovered; until they are discovered, programs of prevention as well as programs of punishment and programs of treatment must operate on the trial-and-error principle. No one can show in advance that crime will be significantly reduced if a particular program of prevention is adopted. At present the greatest need in crime prevention is irrefutable facts about crime causation and sound means for transforming that knowledge into a program of action.[38] Until such information is secured, the general public is opposed to modifications of the status quo, which will in almost all cases increase taxes. The general public is opposed to crime, to be sure, but it is opposed also to high taxes and individual financial sacrifice and apparently would prefer to make emotional gestures in regard to crime rather than risk capital on an unproven crime prevention program. If reliable information on which to base programs of prevention were available, the public could probably be educated and induced to carry out programs based on such information. However, in view of the fact that persons administering crime prevention programs have vested interests in maintaining only vague procedures for

---

[37] E. Ferri, Criminal Sociology, translated by J. I. Kelly and John Lisle (Boston: Little, Brown, 1917), pp. 209–287.

[38] Cf. Virgil W. Peterson, "Facts and Fantasies in Crime Prevention," Journal of Criminal Law and Criminology, 38:466–474, January–February, 1948.

measuring the effectiveness of the programs, such reliable information is not likely to be forthcoming.[39]

*Local community organization.* The policy implied in the earlier chapters of this book is that control of delinquency lies principally in the personal groups within the local community. It was shown that delinquency is explained principally by an excess of delinquent associations over anti-delinquent associations; in such associations, intimacy and the prestige of the source of a pattern are the principal characteristics of associations which result in behavior concordant with that pattern. Moreover, it was shown that the factor in these local and personal groups which had the greatest significance was the definition of behavior as desirable or undesirable; even in the more extremely deplorable family and neighborhood situations girls are less delinquent than boys and this is due to the fact that delinquency is defined as more dangerous and undesirable for girls than for boys.

The closest approximation to a general formula for the control of crime and delinquency that can be made at present is that crime and delinquency must be defined as undesirable by the personal groups in which a person participates. The correlate of this is that lawful behavior must be defined as desirable by such groups. The personal groups in question may be the family, school and neighborhood groups, work or recreational groups, religious groups, or others.

Policies for prevention of delinquency and crime, therefore, should be directed primarily at these personal groups. In this sense, control of delinquency and crime lies within the local community. This means, first, that the local community must be the active agency in reducing its own delinquency. The personal groups can be modified through the efforts of local organizations such as the school, the church, the police, welfare agencies, and civic groups. Second, modifications of the general institutional structure are important in reducing crime and delinquency rates to the degree that they affect local community organization.

Experiments in the control of delinquency along the lines suggested in the preceding paragraph have been developed in Chicago under the guidance of the sociologists in the Institute for Juvenile Research. The principle involved in these "Chicago Area Projects" is that the persons who reside in an area of high delinquency are induced to form an organization for the purpose of reducing their own delinquency rates. The "natural leaders" in these areas direct the organizations, with some suggestions from outsiders and with financial aid from agencies outside the area. The groups

[39] Donald R. Cressey, "The Nature and Effectiveness of Correctional Techniques," *Law and Contemporary Problems*, 23:754–771, Autumn, 1958.

which are most important in the lives of the residents of an area become the agencies through which operations are conducted.[40]

These Area Projects have been in operation for about thirty years, and twelve neighborhood units are now operating in high-delinquency areas. The approach has remained the same over the years, although the community committees now attempt both to assist in the rehabilitation of parolees and to prevent delinquency and crime. Undoubtedly, the community units are as important in modifying the attitudes and behavior of the adult participants as they are in directly changing the activities of children and youth.[41] Adults who band together to prevent delinquency in their community rather automatically modify their own attitudes. An "anti-delinquency" group is formed, and status in the group is achieved by expressions of anti-delinquent behavior. This subtle modification of adults' attitudes of indifference to delinquency is itself delinquency prevention, for a new set of social influences for the child is created. The child begins to live in an anti-delinquency setting where he, also, gains status by non-delinquent or anti-delinquent, in contrast to pro-delinquent, activities. Even probationers, parolees, and ex-criminals may work to improve the community and to keep others out of delinquency, thus reforming themselves.[42] In addition, the attempts to deal directly with the behavior of children and youth probably are most effective when the cultural differences between the adults and the children are at a minimum, as is the case in the Area Project communities. The Area Projects have been criticized for using "untrained" workers and "bad" people as leaders, yet the use of such natural leaders is one of the program's greatest assets.[43]

Up to date, little objective evidence has been presented as to the effect the projects have had on the delinquency rates of the subject areas. Some persons connected with the program believe that significant reductions in delinquency rates have resulted, while others connected with the program are sceptical as to the results. Delinquency rates have shown a greater de-

[40] E. W. Burgess, J. D. Lohman, and Clifford R. Shaw, "The Chicago Area Project," *National Probation Association Yearbook*, 1937, pp. 8–28; Fred A. Romano, "Organizing a Community for Delinquency Prevention," *National Probation Association Yearbook*, 1940, pp. 1–12; Clifford R. Shaw and Jesse A. Jacobs, "The Chicago Area Project," *Proceedings of the American Prison Association*, 1939, pp. 40–53; Clifford R. Shaw and Henry D. McKay, *Juvenile Delinquency and Urban Areas* (Chicago: University of Chicago Press, 1942), pp. 442–446.

[41] See Solomon Kobrin, "The Chicago Area Project—A 25-Year Assessment," *Annals of the American Academy of Political and Social Science*, 322:19–29, March, 1959.

[42] Cressey, "Social Psychological Foundations for Using Criminals in the Rehabilitation of Criminals," *op. cit.*

[43] Cf. E. M. Haydon, "Re-education and Delinquency," *Journal of Social Issues*, 1:23–32, Winter, 1945.

crease in project areas than in nearby areas, but this difference may be due merely to a difference in delinquency reporting in the two kinds of areas. In project areas, delinquencies might be more frequently handled informally. Perhaps the best that can be said in appraisal of the Area Projects is that they are consistent with an important theory of criminal behavior and with the ideals of democracy. Communities which have been indifferent to high delinquency rates are gradually being converted to a set of values which, like the values of most middle-class communities, place a premium on non-delinquency. The establishment of such an anti-delinquency public opinion obviously is very difficult in areas with highly mobile populations.[44]

*Organized recreation.* One of the features of the Chicago Area Projects, as well as of many other programs for the control of delinquency, has been emphasis on organized recreation. This emphasis is essentially negative, in the sense that it implies that juveniles who are engaged in conventional recreation activities will not, at the same time, engage in delinquency. It is a method of occupying the leisure time of children; as such, it does not change attitudes or tendencies regarding behavior. In Chicago many small parks and playgrounds were established early in this century and for a time seemed to have definite value in reducing delinquency. Before long the politicians secured control, park funds were looted by grafters, and positions in the system were filled by ward heelers. In some cases these places became sources of infection for delinquency.

Youth centers, recreational groups, and boys' clubs have been established by social settlements, churches, police departments, and other organizations as a means of occupying the leisure time of the boys. Some of these clubs have reading rooms, swimming pools, vocational work, and many games.[45] Claims have been made that delinquency rates have been greatly reduced in certain neighborhoods by these clubs. Thirty years ago, Healy made the following statement regarding the South End of Boston, and its essence has been repeated in annual reports of community agencies ever since:

This is a district in which there has been no marked change of population and in which police attitudes toward delinquency have not altered. In this district three main settlement houses have built up a preventive program, school people have co-operated and churches of several denomina-

---

[44] See Albert Morris, *Criminology* (New York: Longmans, Green, 1935), pp. 188–190.

[45] For descriptions of youth centers, see Heman G. Stark, *Teen Centers* (Sacramento: California Youth Authority, 1945); and Louise D. Yuill, "Teen Centers and the Adult Community," *Sociology and Social Research*, 32:519–526, September–October, 1947.

tions have entered into the spirit of the project by organizing boys' clubs and scout groups. The probation officer of long experience in this district states that the former tendency toward delinquent gang formation is practically overcome. Many of the more difficult cases which we ourselves were accustomed to study came from this part of the city, but we have noted a great decrease of these cases. Ten years ago this probation officer carried in this district a case load regularly of about eighty to ninety offenders, many of them serious. The number has gradually gone down until at the present time he has only twenty-two and asserts that none of them is what he would call a serious offender. Another proof of the value of this preventive program is shown by the fact that while there has been a special effort to draw in the younger potential delinquents, it was possible to hold their interest for years in a constructive program. Many of them now twenty-two or twenty-three years old continue their club activities. The spirit has spread so that there is an overwhelming number of applicants at the various centers.[46]

On the other hand, some years ago a study of the Boys' Club of New York City found that boys who were members of the club had a larger number of delinquencies than boys in the same neighborhood who were not members; that boys who belonged to the club for four years had more delinquencies than those who belonged for one year; that they had more delinquencies while members of the club than prior to or subsequent to that membership.[47] While it is true that this club attracted boys of the underprivileged classes more than other boys and was therefore likely to have boys with more delinquencies, it does not seem possible to explain these findings except by the proposition that the club was directly or indirectly promoting delinquency, probably through the association of boys who were inclined to delinquency. It does not necessarily follow that all clubs must have the same effects. Many of them are successful in their attempt to provide their members with an excess of definitions unfavorable to delinquency.[48]

*Case work with near-delinquents.* Certain children have been called potential delinquents or predelinquents. These terms, from the etymological point of view, are misleading, for every child is a potential delinquent, every child in earlier years is a predelinquent, and every able-bodied person who has passed the earlier years of childhood commits delinquencies more

---

[46] William Healy, "Prevention of Delinquency," *Journal of Criminal Law and Criminology,* 24:74–77, May–June, 1933.

[47] Frederic M. Thrasher, "The Boy's Club and Juvenile Delinquency," *American Journal of Sociology,* 42:66–80, July, 1936.

[48] See Roscoe C. Brown, Jr., and Dan W. Dodson, "The Effectiveness of a Boys' Club in Reducing Delinquency," *Annals of the American Academy of Political and Social Science,* 322:47–52, March, 1959.

or less frequently. The term is used, however, to refer to the children who are believed to be extraordinarily likely to become confirmed delinquents. These predelinquents have not been definitely identified, but are believed by certain psychiatrists and social workers to be the children who manifest emotional problems such as enuresis, temper tantrums, sullenness, timidity, and in later years, difficulties in school and with companions. It is believed that if these problems can be corrected in early childhood by appropriate procedures, the child will develop into a more wholesome and less delinquent adult.

Two principal agencies have developed in the attempt to turn these near-delinquents away from their trend toward delinquency, namely, child guidance clinics and visiting teachers. The Commonwealth Fund started child guidance clinics in several cities, as demonstrations of what might be accomplished.[49] These clinics were maintained in many communities after support was withdrawn from outside, and many others have been started. Some of the clinics have been operated by the public schools, some by public welfare departments, some by private welfare agencies, some by state hospitals, and some by independent agencies organized for this purpose. The clinic staff usually is made up of psychiatrists, psychologists, and psychiatric social workers. Only rarely is a sociologist included, in spite of the fact that sociologists have a knowledge of group relations which could be profitably utilized.[50] Problem children are referred to the clinic by parents who are anxious about their children, by kindergartens and schools, by welfare societies and by other agencies and persons. Some of them are referred because they have been delinquent, some because they have deviations in their personal characteristics, and some because of disturbing behavior which is not in violation of the law, such as temper tantrums, enuresis, or bashfulness. These children are sometimes divided into behavior problems and personality problems.

The St. Paul "Community Service" project may be used as an illustration of the work of child guidance clinics. The project was in operation between January, 1937, and July, 1943. Schools, police, the juvenile court, churches, health agencies, and social welfare agencies were instructed as to the kinds of behavior considered symptomatic of delinquency, and these organizations were encouraged to refer children to the clinic. The following kinds of behavior were considered symptomatic of delinquency:[51]

[49] On the guidance clinic in general, see George S. Stevenson and Geddes Smith, *Child Guidance Clinics* (New York: The Commonwealth Fund, 1934).
[50] Louis Wirth, "Clinical Sociology," *American Journal of Sociology*, 27:49–66, July, 1931.
[51] Sybil A. Stone, Elsa Castendyck, and Harold B. Hanson, *Children in the Community*, Children's Bureau Publication No. 317 (Washington: Government Printing Office, 1946), pp. 47–48.

Bashfulness
Boastfulness
Boisterousness
Bossiness
Bullying
Cheating
Cruelty
Crying
Daydreaming
Deceit
Defiance
Dependence
Destructiveness
Disobedience
Drinking
Eating disturbances
Effeminate behavior
(of boys)
Enuresis
Fabrications
Failure to perform as-
signed tasks
Fighting
Finicalness
Gambling

Gate-crashing
Hitching rides
Ill-mannered behavior
Impudence
Inattentiveness
Indolence
Lack of orderliness
Masturbation
Nailbiting
Negativism
Obscenity
Overactivity
Over-masculine be-
havior (of girls)
Profanity
Quarreling
Roughness
Selfishness
Sex perversion
Sex play
Sexual activity
Shifting activities
Show-off behavior
Silliness
Sleep disturbances

Smoking
Speech disturbances
Stealing
Stubbornness
Sullenness
Tardiness
Tattling
Teasing
Temper displays
Thumbsucking
Tics
Timidity
Truancy from home
Truancy from school
Uncleanliness
Uncouth personality
Underactivity
Undesirable companions
Undesirable recreation
Unsportsmanship
Untidiness
Violation of street-trade
regulations
Violation of traffic regu-
lations

A total of 1,466 children were referred to the clinic, and of this number 727 were considered as possessing undesirable personality traits or as exhibiting definite behavior problems. These 727 children were given five types of service, including psychiatric treatment, psychological testing and counseling, case work, group work, and tutoring in school projects. Emotional disturbances were considered of major importance in 432 cases, 53 of which were treated with "deep therapy." The staff estimated the effect of therapy in the 432 cases, judging that 18 percent had made "major improvement," 65 percent "partial improvement," and 17 percent "no improvement."[52]

The studies of child guidance clinics generally indicate that from a fourth to a third of the children treated continue to be problems, and that approximately a third manifest no further difficulties. One study showed no significant difference in the outcome of a group of children receiving psy-

[52] *Ibid.*, pp. 70–72.

chiatric treatment in a clinic and a group not receiving such treatment.[53] Another study indicated that 47 percent of a group treated in a psychiatric clinic thirty years earlier had been arrested, as compared with 16 percent of a control group; sixty percent of the persons referred to the clinic for delinquency had arrests, as compared to 20 percent of those referred for neuroses or learning problems.[54] Modification of an "undesirable personality trait" undoubtedly is valuable to the individual and to society, but such modification does not necessarily mean that the individual in question will refrain from law violation.

In general, the child guidance clinic seems to be only slightly more successful in dealing with its problems than do the institutions for delinquents and criminals. Doubtless this failure is due to the fact that the problem is not confined to the organism of the child, but involves wider social relationships in the family, the neighborhood, the institutions, and the general culture. However, the child guidance clinic is at a great disadvantage, both in preventing delinquency and in aiding emotionally disturbed children, for it cannot initiate treatment. It must wait for cases to be referred to it. Accordingly, the delinquents seen in clinics are not likely to be drawn from all segments of the population, and in fact, they might not be serving the delinquents who are most in need of their services.[55]

Somewhat related to the child guidance clinic is the visiting teacher movement.[56] The visiting teacher, who is the extension agent of the school in problem cases, first appeared in New York, Boston, and Hartford, about 1906, as the result of pressure from persons outside of the school system. In 1955, visiting teacher services were available in about 265 cities.

The visiting teacher receives reports from the regular school teacher regarding attendance, scholarship, misbehavior in school, and other difficulties. On the basis of these reports the visting teacher makes an investigation of the home and neighborhood with the purpose of tracing the difficulty to its source, and attempts control on the basis of this information. The justification for visiting teachers lies in the fact that about 88

[53] LaMay Adamson and H. Warren Dunham, "Clinical Treatment of Male Delinquents: A Case Study in Effort and Result," *American Sociological Review*, 21:312–320, June, 1956.
[54] Lee N. Robins and Patricia O'Neal, "Mortality, Mobility, and Crime: Problem Children Thirty Years Later," *American Sociological Review*, 23:162–171, April, 1958.
[55] Helen L. Witmer and Edith Tufts, *The Effectiveness of Delinquency Prevention Programs* (Washington: U.S. Children's Bureau, 1954), p. 40. See also Ralph Schwitzgebel, "A New Approach to Understanding Delinquency," *Federal Probation*, 24:31–35, March, 1960.
[56] See Harry J. Baker, "The Visiting Teacher Program and Delinquency Prevention," *Federal Probation*, 11:3034, January, 1947; and Katherine M. Cook, *The Place of Visiting Teacher Services in the School Program*, Office of Education Bulletin No. 6 (Washington: Government Printing Office, 1945).

percent of the time of the child during the first eight years of school is spent outside of the school building. The school that is organized for delinquency prevention during this time can have a tremendous effect on its pupils.[57]

A ten-year experiment in delinquency and crime prevention by methods which can best be described as case work revealed that the professional workers' efforts were not highly successful.[58] In the late 1930's, 650 boys under twelve years of age were selected for the project from a list of about 1,900 names submitted by teachers, social agencies, police officers, and probation officers. Some of these boys were believed destined to become delinquent and others were not. The 650 boys were paired on the basis of about one hundred factors such as age, religion, intelligence, educational performance, personality, neighborhood, and social adjustment. The information regarding these factors had been obtained from social work agencies, schools, interviews with parents, and physical and psychological examinations of the boys. On the basis of these factors, prognostications as to probable delinquency also were made. One set of the matched pairs was randomly selected as the "treatment group," while their "diagnostic twins" became the "control group." The members of the treatment group were given help in educational problems, were given special counseling, guidance, and health services, were taken on camping trips, etc. The control group members were given none of these services. After two or three years, 65 of the boys in the treatment group were dropped because they presented no special problems and were definitely nondelinquent; this left 260 boys in the treatment group. At the end of the experimental period, in 1945, 76 or 23.4 percent of the 325 treatment group members had appeared in court for serious offenses and 90 or 27.7 percent has committed either serious or minor offenses. Among the 325 control group members, the proportions were slightly less in each instance: 67 or 20.6 percent had

[57] For discussion of the role of the school in delinquency prevention, see William C. Kvaraceus, *Juvenile Delinquency and the School* (Yonkers: World, 1947); and Edwin Powers, "The School's Responsibility for the Early Detection of Delinquency-Prone Children," *Harvard Educational Review*, 19:80–86, March, 1949; U.S. Senate Subcommittee to Investigate Juvenile Delinquency, *Education and Juvenile Delinquency, Interim Report*, 84th Congress (Washington: Government Printing Office, 1956); and Myles W. Rodehaver, William R. Axtell, and Richard E. Gross, *The Sociology of the School* (New York: Crowell, 1957).

[58] Edwin Powers, "An Experiment in Prevention of Delinquency," *Annals of the American Academy of Political and Social Science*, 261:77–88, January, 1949; Edwin Powers and Helen L. Witmer, *An Experiment in the Prevention of Delinquency—The Cambridge-Somerville Youth Study* (New York: Columbia University Press, 1951). See also William McCord and Joan McCord, *Origins of Crime: A New Evaluation of the Cambridge-Somerville Youth Study* (New York: Columbia University Press, 1959); and Jackson Toby, "Early Identification and Intensive Treatment of Predelinquents: A Negative View," *Social Work*, 6:3–13, July, 1961.

court appearances for serious offenses and 85 or 26.1 percent had committed either serious or minor offenses. At the time of the original diagnosis, delinquent careers were predicted for 70 boys in the treatment group and for 68 in the control group; 23 (32.9 percent) of the members of this treatment subgroup became delinquent, and 27 (39.7 percent) of the control subgroup became delinquent. Similarly, "probable delinquency" was predicted for 163 members of the treatment group and for 165 members of the control group; 14.1 percent of the treatment subgroup became delinquent, as compared to 13.3 percent of the control subgroup. These differences are hardly significant, indicating that the "treatment" had little effect; they also cast doubt upon the feasibility of identifying "predelinquents" accurately. There was evidence, however, that the control group members who became delinquent were more persistent offenders than the treatment group members who became delinquent.

*Group work with near-delinquents.* One of the significant developments in social work during the last two decades is group work. The development is to some extent based on the desirability of extending case work beyond the person and his family to groups of approximately the same age as the delinquent or near-delinquent who is being treated. Group work with delinquents and near-delinquents may be regarded as falling into two types, both of which were used in the St. Paul Community Service project. First, an individual is induced to become a member of a group, as a means of satisfying his needs as a person. The group may be a ball team, a hiking club, an art-crafts class, or it may be concerned with some other activity. While in this group, the person is given particular attention to aid him in adjusting to the group and to overcome tendencies considered to be conducive to delinquency. This type of group work is individualistic, concentrating on the problems of particular individuals; it is based on the same general philosophy and theory as individual case work.[59] One study revealed that group work agencies using this approach are not even "identified closely with the underprivileged and insecure elements in our population, nor with the age groups among which delinquency is most prevalent."[60]

A second type of group work consists in re-directing the activities of a group of persons, all or nearly all of whom are delinquents or near-delinquent. One of the early applications of this procedure was made by Keltner in St. Louis under the sponsorship of the YMCA. In a deteriorated section of St. Louis, which had been the headquarters of a notorious adult gang, Keltner attempted to redirect the boys' gangs so that they would be assets

---

[59] S. R. Slavson, *Creative Group Education* (New York: Association Press, 1937).
[60] Ellery F. Reed, "How Effective are Group Work Agencies in Preventing Delinquency?" *Focus*, 28:170–176, November, 1959.

to the community. After a period of fifteen years, forty of these gangs, now turned into boys' clubs, were carrying on their activities in this section, with an average membership of about 25 members. Keltner stated that the members were seldom in difficulties with the police, that the older members assisted in developing similar groups for their younger brothers, and that the businessmen of the district wholeheartedly co-operated with the movement.[61]

In a recent program conducted in Central Harlem, trained workers were assigned to five street gangs and these workers attempted by informal methods to influence the activities of the gang. At the end of its third year, the program was judged successful.[62] Somewhat similar policies have been used in many other places, with varying degrees of success.[63] The essential characteristics of this policy, as differentiated from other policies, is that some person attempts to enter into friendly participation with delinquent gang members and change them into law-abiding citizens, not as separate individuals, but as a group.[64]

*Co-ordinating councils.* Traditionally, case-work agencies, group-work agencies, child-guidance clinics, and character-building organizations have worked separately and independently toward achievement of the common goal, delinquency prevention. During the last generation, this tradition has broken down in many communities, and the work of the various agencies and organizations, both public and private, has been integrated by means of local "co-ordinating councils." Like the Chicago Area Projects, these councils are based on the theory that local community resources must be mobilized if the community needs are to be met. Unlike the Area Projects, however, a co-ordinating council is a formal co-ordination of the agencies which deal with behavior problems or prevention of behavior problems, rather than a co-ordination of the residents of the community. The co-ordinating council usually is composed of representatives of the

[61] Harold S. Keltner, "Crime Prevention Program of the YMCA, St. Louis," in Sheldon and Eleanor Glueck, Editors, *Preventing Crime* (New York: McGraw-Hill, 1936), Chapter 24.

[62] Paul L. Crawford, Daniel I. Malamud, and James R. Dumpson, *Working with Teen-age Gangs* (New York: Welfare Council of New York City, 1950); James R. Dumpson, "An Approach to Anti-Social Street Gangs," *Federal Probation*, 13:22–29, December, 1949.

[63] See Walter B. Miller, "The Impact of a Community Group Work Program on Delinquent Corner Groups," *Social Service Review*, 31:390–406, December, 1957; Walter B. Miller, "Preventive Work with Street-Corner Groups: Boston Delinquency Project," *Annals of the American Academy of Political and Social Science*, 322:97–106, March, 1959; and John M. Gandy, "Preventive Work with Street-Corner Groups," *Ibid.*, pp. 107–116.

[64] See David M. Austin, "Goals for Gang Workers," *Social Work*, 2:43–50, October, 1957; and David J. Bordua, *Sociological Theories and Their Implications for Juvenile Delinquency* (Washington: U.S. Children's Bureau, 1960).

juvenile court, probation department, the police department and sheriff's department, schools, churches, social welfare agencies, character building organizations such as the YMCA and Boy Scouts, and civic organizations such as parent-teacher's associations and women's clubs. However, there are wide variations in the specific types of organization.[65] The council has the function of forming policies and promoting and carrying out the policies. It acts as a counseling body rather than as an agency. It attempts to advise, through a case study committee, regarding policies in individual cases, to determine, through a research committee, the community needs and resources, to build up and co-ordinate constructive community agencies, to promote public understanding of the problems which welfare agencies face, and to eliminate community influences which lead to crime and delinquency. Usually, the assumption is that crime is a composite problem, caused by multiple factors or by personality defects.

Many of these councils have been short-lived, finding little result from the co-ordinating efforts, perhaps because little was accomplished by the various agencies and organizations when not co-ordinated. Probably the major defect of the council plan is the failure to recognize the importance of participation by the persons who are to receive the services which the council co-ordinates. The Chicago Area Projects, in fact, developed as a reaction to this system of "foreigners" bringing a program into a local area. Some doubts have been raised regarding the claims of the co-ordinating councils which have been reported to be most successful. But there probably is a residue of substantial achievement from the co-ordination of agencies which are independently working effectively.

*Institutional reorganization.* Many persons have advocated widespread modifications of the general institutional structure and have done so from the point of view of prevention of crime and delinquency. Taft has suggested that only partial and temporary reduction in crime rates can be expected from the methods currently employed in the attempt to prevent crime and delinquency: repression, clinical treatment, special school classes for deviates, visiting teachers, character education, education of parents, case work and group work with parents and children, domestic relations courts, foster homes, club and camp programs, neighborhood reorganization, etc.[66] According to Taft, none of these cuts the "deeper roots" of crime. After acknowledging the tremendous difficulties and opposition

[65] See John F. Hall, "The Administration and Supervision of Community Councils," *National Probation Association Yearbook,* 1936, pp. 70–71.
[66] Donald R. Taft, *Criminology: A Cultural Interpretation* (New York: Macmillan, 1950), pp. 664–666.

which institutional modification would entail, he makes the following statement regarding the characteristics of a "crimeless society":

Since social change implies maladjustment, a crimeless society had best be static. To avoid culture conflict it should be internally homogeneous. On the economic side, a crimeless society must avoid excessive competition and greed for material gain and must be planned rather than chaotic. This would be essential to avoid such sources of maladjustment as relative failure, city slums, struggle for speculative gains, monopolistic advantages, and various types of exploitation.

A crimeless society might have to reverse the trend toward impersonal relationships and restore the personalized culture of the past. It might need to restrict human freedom. It might resort to a return to religious superstitions as agencies of social control. Though different in some respects, such a crimeless society would seem more nearly to approximate primitive or peasant society, than does modern society. . . .

A crimeless society should also be largely free from preferential group loyalties which we have found to be at once so cherished and so productive of strife and crime. A society so homogeneous as we have indicated might perhaps accept and enforce a puritanical morality, otherwise it would seem to need a "new morality" permitting considerable freedom of sex and other personal behavior.

Perhaps the most basic change needed in the interest of crime prevention would be the incorporation in our culture of a genuinely scientific point of view which sees criminals as products. Such a society would not hold the individual criminal responsible, though it would continue to hold him in every way accountable for his behavior.

The reader may decide for himself, first which of the changes needed to prevent crime he desires, and second whether the criminogenic conditions he would hate to sacrifice are or are not more desirable than crime prevention. A program of cultural change solely in the interest of crime prevention would be based upon the, perhaps false, assumption that a crimeless society is the one great good. It is not the task of the criminologist to determine what is the major social good.[67]

Saul Alinsky has similarly suggested that crime and delinquency must in the last analysis, be prevented through institutional reorganization, and he has initiated a program to achieve that reorganization. His program, variously known as the "Back of the Yards Project," the "Industrial Areas Foundation," and the "People's Organization," is not aimed directly at control of delinquency and crime. Instead, it attempts to eradicate "un-

[67] Ibid., pp. 666–667. Reprinted by permission of the publisher. See also pp. 756–757 of the third edition of this book (1956).

employment, undernourished, disease, deterioration, demoralization, and other aspects of social disorganization." The implication is that as these conditions are altered, crime and delinquency rates will decrease:

It is very clear that if any intelligent attack is to be made upon the problem of youth or the causes of crime the community council will have to concern itself with the basic issues of unemployment, diseases, and housing, as well as all other causes of crime. This the conventional community council cannot do. It is not equipped to attack basic social issues, and its very character is such that it never was meant to do that kind of job. The community council organized to prevent crime will tell you that its function is in the field of crime purely and it has no place in such controversial fields as conflict between labor and capital, private *vs.* government housing, public health, and other fundamental issues. Intellectually and logically members of such council will admit that one cannot hope to attack the causes of crime unless one gets into all the related fields, yet in actual practice they will vigorously abstain from entering any controversial field. . . . You don't, you dare not, come to a people who are unemployed, who don't know where their next meal is coming from, whose children and themselves are in the gutter of despair—and offer them not food, not jobs, not security, but supervised recreation, handicraft classes and character building! Yet *that is what is done!* Instead of a little bread and butter we come to them with plenty of bats and balls![68]

As an alternative to the conventional community council, Alinsky advocates the formation of local community "people's organizations," made up of the citizens of the community. In this sense, the program is similar to the Chicago Area Projects. It differs from the Area Projects, however, in at least three significant respects. First, the membership is wider; each local organization, such as a church, a union, an industry, a club, is represented. Second, the primary purpose is the development of groups composed of persons who are interested in their own welfare and are organized for political action to improve their welfare. Third, the ultimate aim is the development of a nation-wide federation of people's organizations, involving millions of people; through such a federation powerful political influence could be exerted.[69]

While general institutional reorganization may be desirable, its relation

[68] Saul D. Alinsky, *Reveille for Radicals* (Chicago: University of Chicago Press, 1946), pp. 81–82. Reprinted by permission of the publishers. See also Saul D. Alinsky, "Community Analysis and Organization," *American Journal of Sociology,* 46:797–808, May, 1941.

[69] Saul D. Alinsky, "Heads I Win and Tails You Lose," *National Probation Association Yearbook,* 1946, pp. 40–50.

to the control of delinquency is highly speculative at present. Those who are interested in the control of delinquency can find more justification for approaching their problem in the local community than in the general institutional structure. The local community, to be sure, is not completely autonomous; it is affected in many ways by the general culture. This effect is produced most obviously in great national disasters, such as wars and inflations, and also by the mobility and stability of the population which are related to the institutional structure. However, within a given institutional structure, wide variations are found from one community to another, and these variations in delinquency rates seem to be related to the local rather than the national conditions.

## SUGGESTED READINGS

Adamson, LaMay, and H. Warren Dunham, "Clinical Treatment of Male Delinquents: A Case Study in Effort and Result," *American Sociological Review*, 21:312–320, June, 1956.

Alinsky, Saul D., "Community Analysis and Organization," *American Journal of Sociology*, 46:797–808, May, 1941.

Bales, Freed, "Types of Social Structures as Factors in 'Cures' for Alcohol Addiction," *Applied Anthropology*, 1:1–13, April–June, 1942.

Bordua, David J., *Sociological Theories and their Implications for Juvenile Delinquency*. Washington: U.S. Children's Bureau, 1960.

Cartwright, Dorwin, "Achieving Change in People: Some Applications of Group Dynamics Theory," *Human Relations*, 4:381–392, 1951.

Crawford, P. L., D. I. Malamud, and J. R. Dumpson, *Working with Teen-age Gangs*. New York: Welfare Council of New York City, 1950.

Cressey, Donald R., "Changing Criminals: The Application of the Theory of Differential Association," *American Journal of Sociology*, 61:116–120, September, 1955.

Cressey, Donald R., "The Nature and Effectiveness of Correctional Techniques," *Law and Contemporary Problems*, 23:754–771, Autumn, 1958.

Dumpson, James R., "An Approach to Anti-Social Street Gangs," *Federal Probation*, 13:22–29, December, 1949.

Empey, LaMar, T., and Jerome Rabow, "The Provo Experiment in Delinquency Rehabilitation," *American Sociological Review*, 26:679–695, October, 1961.

Gibbons, Don C., *Changing the Lawbreaker*. New York: Prentice-Hall, 1965.

Kelley, Harold H., and Edmund H. Volkart, "The Resistance to Change of Group-Anchored Attitudes," *American Sociological Review*, 17:453–465, August, 1952.

Lunden, Walter A., "The Theory of Crime Prevention," *British Journal of Criminology*, 2:213–228, January, 1962.

Mannering, John W., "Significant Characteristics of Recidivists," *National Probation and Parole Association Journal*, 4:211–217, July, 1958.

Mattick, Hans W., and Nathan S. Caplan, *The Chicago Youth Development Project*. Ann Arbor, Michigan: Institute for Social Research, 1964.

Peterson, Virgil W., "Facts and Fantasies in Crime Prevention," *Journal of Criminal Law and Criminology*, 38:466–474, January–February, 1948.

Powers, Edwin, "An Experiment in Prevention of Delinquency," *Annals of the American Academy of Political and Social Science*, 261:77–88, January, 1949.

Powers, Edwin, and Helen L. Witmer, *An Experiment in the Prevention of Delinquency—The Cambridge-Somerville Youth Study*. New York: Columbia University Press, 1951.

Shibutani, Tamotsu, "The Sentimental Basis of Group Solidarity," *Sociological Inquiry*, Spring, 1964, pp. 144–155.

Sorrentino, Anthony, "The Chicago Area Project After 25 Years," *Federal Probation*, 23:40–45, June, 1959.

Toby, Jackson, "Early Identification and Intensive Treatment of Pre-delinquents: A Negative View," *Social Work*, 6:3–13, July, 1961.

Volkman, Rita and Donald R. Cressey, "Differential Association and the Rehabilitation of Drug Addicts," *American Journal of Sociology*, 69: 129–142, September, 1963.

Waite, John B., *The Prevention of Repeated Crime*. Ann Arbor: University of Michigan Press, 1943.

Wattenberg, W. W., "Juvenile Repeaters from Two Viewpoints," *American Sociological Review*, 18:631–635, December, 1953.

Witmer, Helen L., and Edith Tufts, *The Effectiveness of Delinquency Prevention Programs*. U.S. Children's Bureau Publication No. 350. Washington: Government Printing Office, 1954.

Yablonsky, Lewis, "The Anticriminal Society: Synanon," *Federal Probation*, 26:50–57, September, 1962.

# INDEX OF NAMES

# INDEX OF SUBJECTS